PYLA-*KOUTSOPETRIA* I
ARCHAEOLOGICAL SURVEY
OF AN ANCIENT COASTAL TOWN

AMERICAN SCHOOLS OF ORIENTAL RESEARCH
ARCHEOLOGICAL REPORTS

Kevin M. McGeough, Editor

Number 21

Pyla-*Koutsopetria* I:
Archaeological Survey of an Ancient Coastal Town

PYLA-*KOUTSOPETRIA* I

ARCHAEOLOGICAL SURVEY
OF AN ANCIENT COASTAL TOWN

By

WILLIAM CARAHER,
R. SCOTT MOORE,
and DAVID K. PETTEGREW

with contributions by

MARIA ANDRIOTI, P. NICK KARDULIAS, DIMITRI NAKASSIS,

AND BRANDON R. OLSON

AMERICAN SCHOOLS OF ORIENTAL RESEARCH • BOSTON, MA

Pyla-*Koutsopetria* I:
Archaeological Survey of an Ancient Coastal Town

by
William Caraher, R. Scott Moore, and David K. Pettegrew

The American Schools of Oriental Research © 2014

ISBN 978-0-89757-069-5

Library of Congress Cataloging-in-Publication Data

Caraher, William R. (William Rodney), 1972-
  Pyla-Koutsopetria I : archaeological survey of an ancient coastal town / by William Caraher,
      R. Scott Moore, and David K. Pettegrew ; with contributions by Maria Andrioti, P. Nick
      Kardulias, Dimitri Nakassis, and Brandon Olson.
    pages cm. -- (Archaeological reports ; volume 21)
  Includes bibliographical references and index.
  ISBN 978-0-89757-069-5 (alkaline paper)
  1. Pyla-Kokkinokremos Site (Cyprus) 2. Archaeological surveying--Cyprus. 3. Excavations
      (Archaeology)--Cyprus. 4. Bronze age--Cyprus. 5. Cyprus--Antiquities. I. Moore, R.
      Scott (Robert Scott), 1965- II. Pettegrew, David K. III. Title.
  DS54.95.P94C37 2014
  939'.37--dc23
                        2014034947

Printed in the United States of America on acid-free paper.

Contents

List of Illustrations

List of Tables

Chapter 1

Introduction

by William Caraher, R. Scott Moore, and David K. Pettegrew

Some 10 km east of the modern port city of Larnaca lies a series of three abrupt and eroded plateaus, known locally as Vigla, Mavrospilios, and Kokkinokremos, that stand within the British controlled Sovereign Base Area (SBA) and Dhekelia Cantonment (figs. 1.1–1.2). These plateaus have visually dominated the coastline for at least 200,000 years and form part of an extensive Pleistocene marine terrace that runs northward and eastward to Pyla village and the Kokkinochoria. On these ridges and on the plain of Pyla-*Koutsopetria* below are the physical remains of a series of settlements dating between the Bronze Age and the Modern period.

The archaeological remains of these past habitations are largely invisible to the casual observer. Situated inside the British Dhekelia Firing Ranges, which continue in active use for military exercises, signs warn tourists to keep out, and police on patrol ensure that they do. Any beachgoer who should happen to cross the coastal road and enter the cultivated plain of Koutsopetria ("lame stones") (fig. 1.3), would unknowingly tread on numerous Late Roman remains in the fields, such as fragments of roof tiles, storage amphorae, table ware, ancient glass, and occasional marble fragments. Tourists who should drive their ATVs up to the prominent height of Vigla, whose name recalls a local "outpost" or "watchtower," would likely

miss the faint line of massive ancient fortification walls encompassing the ridge that testify to the military utility of the area in the Hellenistic period. Without the training to see archaeological remains, the visitor would overlook the low to moderate density of the significant Late Bronze Age settlement on the heart-shaped hill of Kokkinokremos ("red cliff") or the Iron Age pottery scattered in low densities across the shapeless plateaus of Kazama and Mavrospilios ("black cave") (fig. 1.4). The traveler along the coastal road would be surprised to learn that the flat fields just above sea level were once an ancient embayment that offered safe harbor for coasting vessels (fig. 1.5; Section 2.4). The use of this stretch of coastline for farming and military exercises hides the complex range of human activities — including religion, agricultural production, military fortification, commerce, and settlement — that occurred in the region before the present age.

Our work with the Pyla-*Koutsopetria* Archaeological Project (henceforth PKAP) between 2003 and 2011 sought to make visible the dynamic past of this landscape through various methods of regional survey. As we will outline below and unpack in the course of this book, our work in the Pyla micro-region documented how the coastal communities in this area connected with their neighbors, engaged in local and

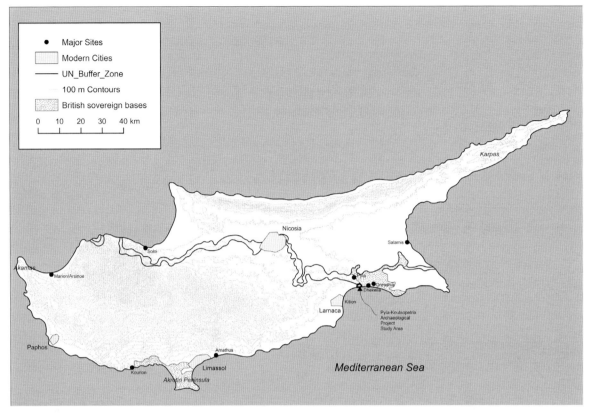

FIG. 1.1   *Map of Cyprus.*

regional resources, forged economic relationships, worshipped, and defined their culture. Surface remains, invisible to the outsider and casual visitor, speak directly to questions of connectivity, town and territory, regionalism, and religion.

1.1.   HISTORY OF WORK
IN THE MICRO-REGION

Archaeological work at the coastal sites of the Pyla region began in the second half of the nineteenth century. During the 1870s, both R. Hamilton Lang and Luigi Palma di Cesnola conducted "excavations" in the area. Lang's digging likely took place a few kilometers inland from the coastal site and revealed the remains of a long-lived and apparently wealthy Iron Age sanctuary. We can perhaps associate Lang's work with the remains of the site called Pyla-*Stavros* (Masson 1966; Lang 1905), which produced artifacts now stored in Vienna, the Louvre, the British Museum, and the Metropolitan Museum of Art. Contemporary with Lang's excavations, his friend, Cesnola, noted the remains of

a relatively well-preserved Venetian fortification in the region and excavated tombs on the coastal road to Ormidhia that passed through the plain of Koutsopetria (Hadjicosti 2001). The finds from these tombs, however, are unknown, and the brief published description reveals little detail (Cesnola 1877). Early twentieth-century work at the coastal site by F. Couchoud produced an outstanding Cypro-Archaic head of the god Bes with a Phoenician inscription (Hermary 1984; Counts 2008). The exact findspot of this important statue is unknown, but it likely derived from the remains of an Iron Age sanctuary on the southern edge of the coastal plateau (Section 5.3.2.3).

While the earliest work focused on Iron Age occupations, later work concentrated on the Late Bronze Age site on the hill of Kokkinokremos (fig. 1.6; Brown 2012, for a recent survey). The initial exploration by Dikaios in the 1950s, in conjunction with work at the sites of Koukouphoukthia and Steno, demonstrated significant habitation in the Late Bronze Age (Dikaios 1971). Later excavations on the eastern lobe by Karageorghis and

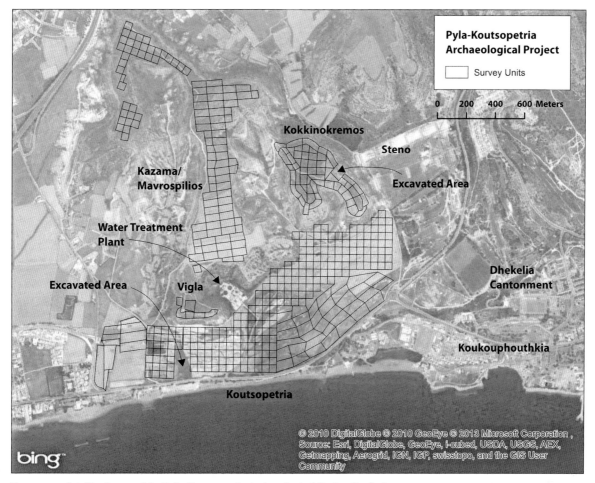

FIG. 1.2   *Satellite Image of the Pyla-Koutsopetria Archaeological Project Study Area.*

Demas revealed a substantial, if short-lived, settlement with a "casemate style" fortification system (Karageorghis and Demas 1984). Karageorghis and Demas were also the first to identify the infilled embayment at the base of Kokkinokremos (Section 2.4) and argue for its economic impact on local settlement. The location, arrangement, chronology, and function of Kokkinokremos has defied simple comparisons with other major Late Cypriot sites on the island, leading scholars to regard it as an outlier to traditional typologies of settlement.

In the rest of the study area, chance finds occurred sporadically over the course of the twentieth century. Activity by treasure hunters with metal detectors produced an impressive assemblage of lead sling bullets, many inscribed (Nicolaou 1977, 1979, 1980). The exact find spot of these objects remains obscure, but the discovery of significant Hellenistic fortification walls at Vigla

makes that acropolis a likely candidate (Caraher et al. 2014; Chapter 6). The installation of an electrical pylon on the coastal plain at the base of Vigla uncovered a limestone separation vessel or settling basin with an inscription to Apollo Karaiates dating to the Cypro-Classical or Hellenistic periods (Mitford 1961: 116; Hadjisavvas 1992: 75–76, 83; Section 5.3.2.3). The installation of pipes for a sewage treatment plant below the coastal cliffs revealed ancient walls and occasional graves, and unsystematic walks across the plain identified substantial architectural and ceramic remains. Collectively, such finds made the micro-region familiar to the archaeological community, even if the prominence of the post-Iron Age material was not generally conspicuous in earlier publications.

The most recent archaeological investigation prior to PKAP was the small-scale excavation in 1993 and 1999 of an Early Christian basilica and

FIG. 1.3   *View to Vigla looking across Koutsopetria.*

FIG. 1.4   *View to Kokkinokremos from the southwest.*

associated annex building on the Koutsopetria plain (Hadjisavvas 1993: 70–72; 2000: 693) (fig. 1.7). The excavations revealed an apse with preserved *opus sectile* floors and a vaulted, two-story annex room that was lavishly decorated with wall-paintings, marble revetment, carved marble column capitals, and gypsum floors. Material from the excavations dated the construction of this build-

ing to the sixth century AD and its abandonment a century later. The excavated area is now covered and enclosed behind a fence.

In 2003, after conversations with John Leonard and discussions with various officials in the Department of Antiquities, R. Scott Moore identified the coastal site of Koutsopetria as a candidate for further investigation. Moore, an expert

FIG. 1.5   *View to west from Kokkinokremos showing the former harbor area.*

Intensive survey officially began in 2004 when we launched a high-resolution distributional survey of the coastal zone of Pyla, an enterprise completed in 2008 — although limited ridge survey and experimental survey occurred also in 2010. In five short seasons between 2004 and 2008, we sampled systematically 100 hectares (hereafter, ha) of the coastal zone of Pyla, recorded hundreds of cut blocks and *in situ* architectural features, and documented hundreds of thousands of artifacts on the surface. The processing, analysis, study, digitization, and data entry of 15,000 artifacts occurred intermittently between 2004 and 2011 at the Larnaca District Archaeological Museum. This volume showcases the finds and the findings of these nine years of fieldwork and study (for preliminary reports of our survey in *RDAC*, see Caraher et al. 2005 and 2007).

in Late Roman pottery on Cyprus, enlisted two landscape archaeologists and Late Antique historians, David Pettegrew and William Caraher, to design an intensive survey to document the material on the coastal plain. Work at the site would occur in collaboration with Dr. Maria Hadjicosti, who, during our time working on Cyprus, served as Curator of Ancient Monuments, Director of the Cyprus Museum, and Director of the Department of Antiquities. She generously provided us with permission to work at the site and explained that much of the land had been in her family prior to independence and the establishment of the SBA. Her personal experiences in the region expanded and enriched our understanding of the archaeological remains and the place of these fields in the lived, contemporary landscape.

The first unofficial season of PKAP took place in summer 2003 when the three directors wandered and extensively surveyed the coastal micro-region just inside the British base and began to formulate a strategy for the systematic documentation of what was clearly a significant ancient micro-region. The immense quantity and broad distribution of well-preserved Hellenistic, Roman, and Late Roman material on the surface led us to conclude that intensive pedestrian survey was the obvious choice to record the function and chronology of this stretch of coastline.

This monograph marks our first book-length report on work in the region. In 2007 and 2008, as we were completing our intensive survey, we introduced a new program of investigation that included aerial photography (2007), geophysical prospecting (2007–2010 and 2012), and trial excavations (2008, 2009, and 2012). This next phase of research has continued to this day (Caraher et al. 2014), and we are now preparing, with Dr. Hadjicosti, a second volume presenting the results of geophysical survey and excavation at Vigla and Koutsopetria between 1993 and the present.

1.2.   DEBATES IN MEDITERRANEAN STUDIES

During our fieldwork, five scholarly discussions in Mediterranean studies informed our research in the micro-region: methodological intensification in landscape archaeology; town, territory, and state formation; regionalism and comparative analysis; religious landscapes; and connectivity and trade. These interrelated discussions not only prompted our initial interest in working at the rural Late

FIG. 1.6   *Aerial photo of Kokkinokremos (area of earlier excavation visible right of center). Photo taken June 11, 2007, courtesy of 84 Sqd. RAF Akrotiri.*

FIG. 1.7   *The excavated site of Pyla-*Koutsopetria *(enclosed within fence), view from Vigla.*

Antique coastal site of Koutsopetria, but also informed our formulation of cogent research questions and framed our public dissemination of the results through conference papers and articles (see, for example, the various publications of Caraher, Moore, and Pettegrew in 2005, 2007, 2008, 2010, and 2013). These themes will be implicit throughout the volume and drive the synthetic conclusions proposed in the final chapter.

The primary methodological context for our study was a debate among landscape archaeologists about the value of intensification in survey archaeology (Theme 1). The introduction of more intensive methods in survey archaeology in Greece and the Aegean, especially, has had the effect of increasing the "resolution" of the surface by improving our ability to see patterns of past cultural activity. Critics of intensification have noted the concomitant loss of efficiency and total coverage and bemoaned the loss of the full regional picture and our increasing inability to speak to large-scale debates (Blanton 2001; Stanish 2003). Defenders of intensification have claimed that it is impossible to return to the days of putting dots on the map, since intensification is fundamental to both documenting material remains accurately and understanding the complexities of artifact distributions. Archaeologists employing high-resolution collection strategies, for example, have detected "hidden landscapes" of different periods missed by more extensive approaches to documenting the countryside (Bintliff, Howard, and Snodgrass 1999; Davis 2004).

Our experience working with the Eastern Korinthia Archaeological Survey in Greece and the Sydney Cyprus Survey Project in Cyprus helped us appreciate the value of methodological intensification. We had come to accept that high-resolution methods, most especially "siteless survey" or artifact-level distributional approaches, were the most accurate way of recording and interpreting past human patterns in the landscape (Caraher, Nakassis, and Pettegrew 2006). Mapping the distribution of artifacts across the space of small survey units provided a means, through databases and GIS analysis, of deconstructing the archaeological landscape by taking surface remains down to their most basic ingredient, the artifact (Pettegrew

2007). High-resolution methods of artifact analysis and typology like the chronotype system offered a way to parse all periods chronologically (Section 2.3.2) and to evaluate the connections between the Pyla littoral and other micro-regions in the eastern Mediterranean.

Our previous positive experiences with high-resolution distributional survey methods led us to devise an approach for Koutsopetria that would produce a robust assemblage without overwhelming our ceramicists, analysts, and museum space. As we shall outline more fully in the next chapter, we selected grid units of 1,600 m² which were significantly smaller than typical siteless or non-site surveys (3,000–10,000 m²), but larger than the smallest units (25–100 m²) used in intensive gridded collection of smaller sites (on the use of similar methods for investigating large sites, see Lolos, Gourley, and Stewart 2007). We collected artifacts from the landscape using the chronotype system, which requires that each walker collect all unique parts (rim, base, handle, and sherds) of each type of artifact present in their swath (Meyer and Gregory 2003; Gregory 2004; Moore 2008). We also devised a series of experiments, discussed in Chapter 3, to assess the quality of our sample and sampling methods.

The resulting assemblage, we will argue in this volume, represented consistently the typological, chronological, and functional range of material in each survey unit while eliminating, as much as possible, the collection of redundant data. In practice, our limited sampling of artifacts prevented the survey team from being overwhelmed by the number of artifacts. At the same time, the small unit size and relatively intensive collection of the material visible in each unit created an overall assemblage that captured both changes across the micro-region and a robust sample of the artifact types and periods that less intensive regimes might have overlooked. This, in turn, provided a sound foundation for addressing scholarly discussions about town and countryside, regionalism, religious landscapes, and inter-regional connectivity.

The centerpiece of our book is the careful study of the distribution of material across our survey area and micro-region, which includes the three prominent ancient sites of Kokkinokremos, Vigla, and Koutsopetria. From the start, we recognized the artifact as the basic unit of analysis and this prompted our detailed approach to sampling the surface, the development of an extensive catalogue, and the substantial dataset. At the same time, the distribution of artifacts across the study area and the variations in surface conditions and topography prompted us to divide the survey area into a series of zones. These zones are fundamentally arbitrary, as they do not represent any single set of variables, but are a heuristic concession to the need to describe our study area in text. As we will note below (1.3), the survey assemblage and the zones are certainly not the only way of discussing the distribution of material across the micro-region.

As landscape archaeologists and historians of Late Antiquity, we were initially interested in how the abundant remains of fifth- to seventh-century date at the site of Koutsopetria could contribute to the long-standing debate about the city in Late Antiquity and the relationship between town and territory (Theme 2). The now-infilled embayment at Koutsopetria was located only 10 km east of Kition, far enough to give the micro-region some autonomy, but not so far as to develop entirely on its own. Our initial assessment of the low-lying coastal areas suggested occupation covering 40 ha, an area not as extensive as Cypriot cities, but clearly exceeding the size and complexity of small villages. Rautman and Manning have shown that even the small village at Kalavasos-*Kopetra* and smaller coastal church at Maroni-*Petrera* evidenced economic integration and complex material culture (Manning et al. 2002; Rautman 2003); we thought the larger site at Koutsopetria could inform our knowledge of Kition in Late Antiquity. As our fieldwork developed and expanded to incorporate earlier sites, such as Vigla and Kokkinokremos, we saw the PKAP micro-region as an important piece in understanding Kition, state formation, and the history of Larnaca Bay from the Bronze Age to Late Antiquity.

Our interest in regionalism (Theme 3) stemmed from our comparative experience working with regional survey data and ceramic remains in the Corinthia and Kythera in Greece, as well as the foothills of the Troodos Mountain range. In a spate of recent scholarship, regionalism has become the key to understanding the ancient world and its transformation (Horden and Purcell 2000; Wickham 2005). A wide range of published or partially published sites and regional surveys offered many useful points of comparison in site size and amenities, diachronic change, and especially patterns of artifact classes like imported and local pottery. Small sites such as Kalavasos-*Kopetra* and Maroni-*Petrera* in the Kalavasos region, and Panayia-*Ematousa* in the immediate hinterland of ancient Kition, produced particularly suitable comparanda for the assemblages collected at Koutsopetria. Moreover, regional work on the nearby Malloura Valley (Toumazou, Kardulias, and Counts 2012) and, farther west, in the Troodos region (Given et al. 2001; Given and Knapp 2003), has offered a regional level context for the post-Iron Age remains from the Pyla littoral. These studies have made one thing abundantly clear: the size, extent, and complexity of the artifact assemblage in the micro-region represent a distinct phenomenon not comparable to artifact assemblages produced at single-period sites. The character of Bronze Age Kokkinokremos, Hellenistic Vigla, and Hellenistic–Late Roman Koutsopetria as a mid-size coastal settlement highlights an important component in the network of ancient Mediterranean connectivity (Horden and Purcell 2000).

Another area of interest was the changing religious landscape evident at Koutsopetria (Theme 4). As outlined above, the micro-region had previously produced several religious finds of major significance, such as the Hellenistic dedication to Apollo Karaiates and an Iron Age head of the god Bes with Phoenician inscription. These collectively pointed to sanctuaries associated with the sites. Excavations at Koutsopetria in the early 1990s similarly exposed parts of an early Christian basilica and annex room that evidently had some ritual purpose in connection with the church. We saw in these fragmented glimpses of religious landscapes the opportunity to explore the concepts of connectivity, city and country, and regionalism beyond simply ecology, economy, and trade.

The final intellectual discussion to which we directed our research was connectivity (Theme 5), a concept that Horden and Purcell have popularized through their massive volume, *The Corrupting Sea* (2000). Connectivity, as Horden and Purcell have described it, highlights the Mediterranean Sea as a conduit for human contact that is not only economically beneficial for scattered local populations, but also necessary for survival (Horden and Purcell 2000; for further discussion of connectivity, see Shaw 2001; Harris 2005; LaBianca and Scham 2006; Knapp 2008; Pettegrew 2013). The uncertainties of weather, soils, and crop yields from year to year demand good relationships with other places both along the coast and inland, as each "micro-region" possesses its own fragile "micro-ecology" consisting of resources in timbered mountain zones, rolling hills, pasture land, marshes, lowland plateau, and alluvial plains. The relationship between different regions ensured that surpluses of one fulfilled the deficit of another in terms of daily economic practice and as social insurance in times of severe need. The general state of connection in the Mediterranean is a fixture, as pre-modern caboteurs, for example, traveled constantly along the Cypriot coastline trading in small embayments and anchorages, and major harbors (Leonard 2005). Yet, the network of interconnected regions constantly shifted, and connectivity intensified in certain places and periods (see Morris 2005 for the temporal development of connection).

Horden and Purcell's arguments have received substantial critique and response (Shaw 2001; Harris 2005), but the vision of constant, albeit constantly shifting, connectivity resonates particularly well for the Roman world and the island of Cyprus (Knapp 2008). The dynamic nature of the Roman and Late Antique economy, with the broad distribution of currency, resources, markets, and specialization, made its economy deeply interconnected. The location of Cyprus at a crossroads of eastern Mediterranean trade throughout antiquity, but most especially in its evident prosperity in the Roman and Late Roman periods, has made the island a particularly important context for considering questions of Roman imperial control and economy. Bowersock, for example, has outlined the cultural and religious internationalism of Cyprus in the networks of the eastern Mediterranean in Late Antiquity (Bowersock 2000). John Leonard has exhaustively documented the relationship of

Roman and Late Roman towns, settlements, and harbors (2005) via the Cypriot coastline. Rautman and others have highlighted the distribution of wealth outside of urban administrative centers and the great variation in the articulation of Roman culture across the island, including small villages and villas (Rautman 2000, 2003; cf. Caraher, Moore, and Pettegrew 2008).

The abundant and diverse material of Late Bronze Age to Modern date at Koutsopetria presented us with the opportunity to study the changing realignments of connection of this micro-region to local, regional, and trans-Mediterranean networks. Our initial work in the area focused on the Late Antique period, the era of most intensive connection, but we soon documented evidence for numerous dramatic shifts in connection: the location of the harbor and the roads, the social and religious predilections of the populations who passed through and settled the area, and the political and economic environment. The location of settlement reflected different modes of interaction with the world via the sea and over the land. In this context, the artifacts recovered from the sites of the micro-region, especially the pottery, represent the dynamic intersections of local, regional, and global networks and produced the cultural identities of the inhabitants.

1.3.   PLAN OF THE WORK

The volume aims to move the reader from the methods of our survey (Ch. 2) to an evaluation of the data (Ch. 3) and finds (Ch. 4), patterns and meanings of artifact distributions (Ch. 5) and features (Ch. 6), and, finally, historical conclusions (Ch. 7).

The two chapters that follow this introduction survey our method and the kind of data resulting from it. Chapter 2 (Intensive Survey, by Caraher, Nakassis, and Pettegrew) contextualizes our survey (2003–2008 and 2010) in respect to the methodological literature in survey archaeology, outlines our phases in investigation of the landscape, justifies our selection of methods in light of a broader debate about intensification, and considers the geological and geomorphological study of the micro-region. The third chapter ("Survey Data and

Experiments in Sampling") presents the results of a series of resurvey experiments (2004, 2006, and 2010) designed to test the core assumptions of our sampling strategy. These experiments, while basic and descriptive, present data that support the integrity of the counting and collecting (chronotype) system. Our sample of survey units did not always collect the full range of types present, but it has accurately represented the periods and functions present on the surface.

With our methods contextualized in terms of the scholarly literature and the physical micro-region, the three subsequent chapters (Chs. 4–6) deal in detail with the artifacts and their distributions. The theme of connectivity is a thread that links these chapters, in the discussion of our finds, their relationship of the assemblage to other published assemblages, and the ancient harbor as an orienting point for local settlement. The Catalogue (Chapter 4) locates the various artifacts in local, regional, and Mediterranean-wide context. This includes a full catalogue of all ceramic wares by R. Scott Moore and Brandon R. Olson and studies of the terracotta figurines by Maria Andrioti, inscribed lead sling bullets by Brandon R. Olson, and the lithic artifacts by P. Nick Kardulias. Chapter 5 places the artifacts in their spatial context and analyzes both the total distribution of material across the zones of the survey area and the chronological distribution of material. The sixth chapter ("Features in the Landscape") discusses the numerous features in the landscape, such as the decorative gypsum, marble fragments, structural limestone, and brick on the coastal plain of Koutsopetria and the Hellenistic fortification wall on Vigla.

The concluding chapter ("Historical Conclusions") attempts to make the connections between the sites of the Pyla district and the history of the broader region and island more explicit. It brings in a wider array of scholarship related to contexts outlined above (Section 1.2): the place of the micro-region within broader regional patterns of activity, the role of the state in the organization of settlement, the development of the local religious landscapes, and connectivity. Any effort to write a history of even a small micro-region will almost certainly be incomplete, but we are confident that our continued work here will expand,

enrich, and deepen our understanding of the region of Kition and support the level of intensity with which we pursued our initial documentation.

The chapters in this work include extensive discussions of methodology and equally expansive descriptions of the evidence produced by our methods. Our broad synthetic chapters (Chs. 5–7) can be read independently of our earlier chapters, but the reader must keep in mind that our methods (Chs. 2–3) and our chronological and typological schemes (Ch. 4) have directly shaped our analysis and conclusions. The reader who wants only an archaeological or historical overview of the micro-region (Chs. 5 and 7) will benefit from our brief restatement of our basic methodological positions and arguments in those chapters. We have sought to keep this redundancy to a minimum, but have taken the position that it is better to reinforce the tie between methods and results than to leave this relationship unstated.

In one respect, this volume continues the tradition of formal archaeological work at the sites of the area begun in the 1950s (Dikaios 1971) and continued in subsequent decades (Karageorghis and Demas 1984; Hadjisavvas 1993: 70–72; 2000: 693). In another respect, it marks a whole new chapter in presenting the history of the micro-region of Koutsopetria in terms of the surface remains. Yet, since PKAP is an ongoing project with continuing programs of fieldwork and study, it is a necessarily incomplete chapter. To conclude this section, we can note several specific components of our unfinished research that inform our specific presentation of data in this volume and will refine our knowledge of the area in the future.

First, we hope that our analysis of artifact distributions in terms of assemblages and zones will itself form the first of many presentations of the data. We ourselves hope to refine our picture of the patterns of surface remains through more detailed intra-zone analysis of the artifacts in terms of chronology and function, and through programs of geophysical survey and excavation. We appreciate that scholars better versed in statistics might find untapped significance in our data as well as problems with our interpretations based on rather simple quantitative analyses. To encourage the critical re-examination of our data, we have released both the data collected from the field and our finds data through the Open Context interface (Caraher, Moore, and Pettegrew 2013). By making our data freely available, we hope that scholars will continue to consider its patterns in new and more sophisticated ways, and link it to similar datasets from across both Cyprus and the Mediterranean more broadly.

A second incomplete aspect of our research is the study of geomorphology and geology of the micro-region. In 2005, Prof. Jay Noller, in collaboration with the Cyprus Geological Survey, took a series of core samples from the embayment. While we had hoped that the results of the coring would be available for this publication along with a more detailed treatment of the geomorphology of the area, the data and results were not ready for inclusion at the time we finished this volume. Consequently, in Section 2.4, we have summarized the preliminary geomorphological work in 2005 (Caraher et al. 2005), as well as an unpublished report on the geological cores (Noller and Zomeni 2006). We remain optimistic that the final analysis of the geomorphology of the area and publication of the cores will support our overall conclusions based on the preliminary observations.

A third component of ongoing work is our program of geophysical survey at the sites of the region. Beginning in 2007 and continuing in subsequent seasons, we conducted a campaign of geophysical prospecting at Vigla, Koutsopetria, and Kokkinokremos (Section 2.2.3) that included electrical resistivity (in collaboration with Michael Brown, and Mr. John Hunt of Limassol) and ground penetrating radar (under the supervision of Dr. Beverly Chirulli of Indiana University of Pennsylvania). Regrettably, the results of this fieldwork are mostly unprocessed and not publishable in their current form, although the electrical resistivity work on Kokkinokremos has appeared in Brown's recent dissertation from the University of Edinburgh (2012). Since our geophysical survey work is not complete, we hope that a more extensive application of non-invasive techniques will refine our knowledge of the sub-surface architecture in the future.

A final ongoing component of our work is excavation. In 2008, the Department of Antiquities kindly granted us permission to ground truth the results of our geophysical survey and to assist in the publication of Dr. Maria Hadjicosti's excavations at the basilica site in the Koutsopetria plain. Our initial plan was to publish the results of excavation at this site alongside the results of our survey. The increasing length and complexity of such a volume, along with delays in the study of the results of excavations, led us to move forward in publishing the results of our survey separately from excavations. Nonetheless, the excavations have greatly informed our analysis of both artifacts (Ch. 4) and features (Ch. 6). The interested reader may learn more about our excavations at Vigla through two preliminary reports (Olson et al. 2013; Caraher et al. 2014).

Finally, the reader should know that we drafted the text for this volume in 2009–2011, and the bibliography reflects the state of the field up to that point. We made some effort to update our references in subsequent revisions of the initial draft, but certain chapters of the volume, such as Chs. 2 and 3, mark our reflections on our work at the completion of our survey, well before the printing of this book.

This volume marks the first monograph detailing the micro-region of Pyla from a systematic documentation of the surface remains. We are currently preparing another volume that will present the results of more intensive sub-surface prospecting in the micro-region, including a discussion of extensive geophysical survey work (2007–Present), trial excavations at Vigla and Koutsopetria in 2008, 2009, and 2012, and Dr. Hadjicosti's excavations at Koutsopetria in the 1990s. This current work establishes the context of survey for understanding subsequent, more intensive investigations in the area.

1.4. ACKNOWLEDGEMENTS

Our work over the last decade has benefitted from the support of numerous individuals, institutions, and agencies, and the participation of many volunteers. We thank former Directors of the Cyprus Department of Antiquities, Dr. Maria Hadjicosti, Dr. Pavlos Flourentzos, and Dr. Sophocles Hadjisavvas, for their generous permission to work

Fig. 1.8   *2004 Field Team.*

Fig. 1.9   *2005 Field Team.*

in the area. Dr. Hadjicosti's knowledge of the area proved invaluable throughout the different stages of our work. We thank Dr. Tom Davis, Vathoulla Moustoukki, and the staff at the Larnaca District Archaeological Museum for facilitating our work at every step of the way. We also greatly appreciate the support, encouragement, and conversation of Drs. Michael Toumazou, Derek Counts, and P. Nick Kardulias, along with the other project members of the Athienou Archaeological Project. Derek Counts, Timothy Hampton, Brandon Olson, and several anonymous reviewers kindly commented on this work at different stages between initial submission of the proposal and final publication; their suggestions have significantly improved the quality of the volume.

Our work would not have been practically possible without consistent financial assistance. A number of agencies generously provided us with grants that funded each season of fieldwork: the American Schools of Oriental Research, the Institute of Aegean Prehistory, the Kress Foundation, the Mediterranean Archaeological Trust, and the Pennsylvania State System of Higher Education Faculty Professional Development Council. Our own institutions consistently offered financial assistance year after year: Indiana University of Pennsylvania (College of Humanities and Social Sciences and Dean Yaw Asamoah, IUP's Department of History, the IUP University Senate, and Dr. Mark Staszkiewicz, IUP Provost and Vice President for Academic Affairs), Messiah College (Office of Faculty Development, the School of Humanities and Dean Powers, Department of History, and the Grants Office), and the University of North Dakota (Office of Instructional Development, University of North Dakota Office of Research and Compliance, and the University of North Dakota Department of History). We also thank individual sponsors whose support was critical, especially in our first years of the project: Fred and Nancy Caraher, the late Elizabeth Reynolds, and Robert and Joyce Moore.

Finally, this project would not have been possible without the participation of numerous volunteers — undergraduates, graduate students, and faculty from across the United States, Canada, Australia, the United Kingdom, and Cyprus — who expended their resources, energy, and summer vacations to walk across fields, survey the ground for artifacts, excavate trenches, and catalogue the finds. Their collective work and diligence made the past inhabitants of the micro-region gradually visible before our eyes.

2003 Team

Cantelas, Frank	Moore, R. Scott
Caraher, William	Pettegrew, David

2004 Team

Caraher, William	Noller, Jay
Eckerd, Kevin	Pettegrew, David
Fortnam, Sara	Willis, Brian
Horowitz, Mara	
Moore, R. Scott	

2005 Team

Bechtel, Luke	Lepinski, Sarah
Caraher, Susan	Moore, R. Scott
Caraher, William	Noller, Jay
Fisher, Greg	Patrow, Joe
Fronda, Mike	Pettegrew, David
Gill, Erin	Pettegrew, Kate
Haines, Jordan	Shumar, Alesha
Hastings, Allison	Willis, Brian

2006 Team

Caraher, William	Olson, Brandon R.
Fisher, Greg	Papademetriou, Olympia
Gleditsch, Kathy	
Glessner, Carrie	Pettegrew, David
Moore, R. Scott	Pettegrew, Kate
Noller, Jay	Trenbreath, Jean

FIG. 1.10   *2006 Field Team.*

FIG. 1.11   *2007 Field Team.*

FIG. 1.12 *2008 Field Team.*

2007 Team

Brown, Michael	Moore, R. Scott
Caraher, Susan	Nakassis, Dimitri
Caraher, William	Olson, Brandon R.
Crowley, Jon	Patrow, Joe
Dalton, Mat	Pettegrew, David
Fisher, Greg	Pettegrew, Kate
Iverson, Mara	Pearce, Brice
Lepinski, Sarah	Powell, Slade
McLaughlin, Megan	Terry, David

2008 Team

Andrioti, Maria	Kochinski, Joe
Brown, Michael	Moore, R. Scott
Caraher, Susan	Nakassis, Dimitri
Caraher, William	Olson, Brandon R.
Crowley, Jon	Pettegrew, David
Dalton, Mat	Pettegrew, Kate
Deforest, Dallas	Pflager, Julie
Freas, Jessie	Richards, Dan
Gust, Chris	Weber, Bret
Horowitz, Mara	Wise, Nick
Howell, Jennifer	

2009 Team

Babcock, Caitlin	Little, Dalton
Brown, Michael	Lovelace, Alex
Caraher, Susan	Moore, R. Scott
Caraher, William	Nakassis, Dimitri
Costello, Sarah	Olson, Brandon R.
Crowley, Jon	Pettegrew, David
Deforest, Dallas	Ragsdale, Ian
Federer, Paul	Ragsdale, Randi
Henesy, Matt	Savaria, Becky
Hey, Kyle	Schmuck, Nick
Hogan, Melissa	Skotnicki, Rachel
Horowitz, Mara	Stander, Ryan
Karatjas, Nick	Weller, Courtney
Lepinski, Sarah	

2010 Team

Bachert, Zane	Gill, Amanda
Beltowski, Chester	Hartline, Andrew
Caraher, William	Henry, Andrew
Crowley, Jon	Hogan, Melissa
Deforest, Dallas	Horowitz, Mara
Fortnam, Sarah	Jagnarain, Matthew

FIG. 1.13 *2009 Field Team.*

FIG. 1.14 *2010 Field Team.*

Lepinski, Sarah	Pettegrew, David	*2011 Team*
Mace, Luke	Pirone, Ashleigh	
Moore, R. Scott	Savaria, Becky	Caraher, William
Nakassis, Dimitri	Weaver, Valerie	Crowley, Jon
Olson, Brandon R.		Moore, R. Scott

Deforest, Dallas	
Olson, Brandon R.	
Pettegrew, David	

Chapter 2

Intensive Survey

by William Caraher, Dimitri Nakassis, and David K. Pettegrew

Our goal in this chapter is to lay out the theoretical and methodological frameworks and the specific procedures that guided our survey of the Koutsopetria micro-region. Our principal methodological thesis is that intensification yields higher-resolution data that open up new possibilities for patterning and interpreting past land use. This chapter, which details the methods of pedestrian survey, should be read in conjunction with subsequent discussions of experiments (Chapter 3), distributional analysis (Chapter 5), and features (Chapter 6), as well as the results of geophysical survey and excavation currently being prepared for a second volume.

In the following sections, we detail the approaches we initially adopted for documenting and analyzing surface scatters and the development of these methods between 2004 and 2008. We outline the guiding principles and frameworks of high-resolution survey that drove our methodology (2.1), the specific procedures adopted in different phases of pedestrian survey (2.2), and the qualitative and quantitative nature of the distributional data (2.3). We also include in the final section (2.4) a discussion of the geological and geomorphological survey carried out in the earliest years of our survey, since it marks a form of methodological intensification that relates to the interpretation of artifact patterns. Collectively, these sections present the methodological contexts for understanding and interpreting the results that follow in subsequent chapters.

2.1. HIGH-RESOLUTION SURVEY

To judge from trends in scholarly literature, Mediterranean archaeological survey has become increasingly intensive in recent decades. Second-wave survey projects of the 1970s and 1980s introduced a more rigorous and systematic method for documenting surface assemblages (Cherry 1994; Galaty 2005), while recent projects have adopted even more intensive approaches — which we refer to as "high-resolution survey" — to address problems of recognition and to gain more information from artifact scatters. Archaeologists are today describing and analyzing human territories with greater precision and care than ever before through more intensive surface collection and robust sampling systems, artifact counting and distribution analysis, application of varied digital technologies, assessments of geomorphology, geophysical prospecting, experiments in survey method, and excavation, among others (for reviews of these trends, see Cherry 2002, 2004; Galaty 2005; Fish and Kowalewski 2009). The result of this shift is that researchers are able to parse complex and artifact-rich landscapes, but at the cost of time, resources, and spatial coverage. The question that has divided landscape archaeologists in recent years is whether the benefits of intensification (more information) justify the cost (less area examined). We adopted procedures for the investigation of the sites of the Pyla region in awareness of these trends and as stakeholders in the debate over intensification.

2.1.1. Survey Intensification, High-Resolution Approaches, and Micro-Regional Frameworks

There are manifold reasons that landscape archaeologists have adopted higher-resolution survey approaches and a focus on micro-regions. We highlight below five explanations that account for the trends: adaptation to Mediterranean landscapes, improved understanding of the relationship between sample and surface artifact populations, control over the cultural and natural processes creating archaeological landscapes, a new scholarly interest in the micro-region, and the application of survey methods to large sites like urban centers.

One of the most important reasons (1) for the recent increase in intensification is the realization that higher-resolution methods more accurately document the abundant material remains of Mediterranean landscapes. In the late 1970s, when survey was still relatively new in the Mediterranean, archaeologists noted that the "extensive methods" they were using (20–50 m walker spacing) were failing to record smaller sites in the landscape. The adoption of more intensive walker spacing (10–20 m) accounted for, in some estimates, 20 to 50 times the number of sites (Cherry 1983; Bintliff and Snodgrass 1985). Scholars also observed that their approaches to documenting the landscape, namely, recording high-density artifact scatters or "sites," frequently missed individual artifacts and lower-density scatters (Bintliff and Snodgrass 1988). Some surveyors began to record the presence of "off-site" scatters in addition to sites (Gallant 1986; Mee and Forbes 1997), and others abandoned site-based approaches altogether to assess the distribution of artifacts across the landscape. The recognition that *how* one looks at the surface tremendously affects what one finds led to more intensive strat-

egies of fieldwalking and recording, resulting in more robust samples of the landscape. The intensification in landscape methods in recent years, including the use of smaller survey units to map the distribution of artifacts, marks a culmination of earlier efforts to account for the abundance of cultural material in Mediterranean landscapes (Caraher, Nakassis, and Pettegrew 2006).

A better understanding of the differences between a survey sample and the actual population of artifacts present on the surface and in subsurface deposits has encouraged more intensive collection of surface material and environmental data (2). Landscape archaeologists, for example, have commonly adopted experiments in recent years to measure the effects of factors that distort the sample of the surface, such as vegetation patterns, the amount of "background noise" (rocks, plants, and leaves on the surface that confuse and strain the eye), or the biases of collection strategies. High-resolution survey projects have also valued basic environmental "context" data, such as measurements of visibility and geomorphological studies, that assess how the landscape developed and affected cultural debris (Jameson et al. 1994: 228–46; James et al. 1997; Zangger et al. 1997; Tartaron et al. 2006). Many projects have adopted more intensive collection strategies to improve the sample of artifacts, such as, for example, "hoovering" or "vacuuming" techniques, which exhaustively gather all artifacts from a small area of space by collection on hands and knees (Chapter 3). All of these mark efforts to assess surface patterns more accurately and control for the contexts that distort the samples.

In a related vein, archaeologists have become very interested in understanding and controlling for the complex processes that produced and transformed artifact patterns over time (3). Surveyors, for example, have become deeply aware that archaeological "sites" documented in the landscape are hardly straightforward equivalents of ancient settlements (Dunnel 1992; Pettegrew 2001). Scholars now recognize that artifact scatters and architecture are, rather, aggregate clusters of human activity formed and changed over time through depositional human behaviors, such as habitation, discard, and abandonment, and transformational processes that include human activity, animal movement, rainfall, erosion, and earthquakes (Schiffer 1976, 1985, 1986; LaMotta and Schiffer 1999; Winther-Jacobsen 2010a, 2010b). Even the debris across the landscape today is not consistently discrete and well-bounded, but fluctuates between very low and very high densities.

In response, archaeologists have intensified their methods to understand and measure the processual nature of assemblages. The adoption of geomorphological assessments, as noted above, has given archaeologists the tools for understanding post-depositional processes affecting artifact scatters. Higher-resolution collection of artifacts has allowed archaeologists to discern ephemeral habitation depleted by behaviors of abandonment or taphonomy (Bintliff, Howard, and Snodgrass 1999) and more accurately record the histories of individual sites (Bintliff, Howard, and Snodgrass 2007). The application of digital tools such as databases and GIS platforms has allowed scholars to parse artifact distributions of different ages with relative ease. In other cases, surveyors have employed geophysical survey and excavation to understand how surface scatters relate to buried sites. New technologies and procedures have established a varied toolset for deconstructing, analyzing, and interpreting archaeological sites.

High resolution surveyors have justified their approach with the recognition that the smaller region, or micro-region, forms an appropriate level for documenting human activity in the landscape (4). If survey projects in the 1960s–80s highlighted large regions as the proper arena for explaining settlement patterns and the relationship of town and countryside, more recent scholarship has accentuated the micro-regional niches that formed the basis of small worlds (Acheson 1997). As we outlined in the introduction, the most popular argument for the value of micro-regions has come from Horden and Purcell's *The Corrupting Sea* (2000). Their vision of the Mediterranean as a fluid network of thousands of unique micro-regions, each consisting of varied ecological niches, is uniquely suited to the spatial framework of high-resolution regional survey, which studies habitation, production, exchange, and environment in terms of smaller territories.

Finally (5), landscape archaeologists have intensified methods in order to document the most complex archaeological sites of the ancient world, the large urban sites that have left substantial surface remains. "Large-site," or "urban survey," is the name given to the systematic investigation of extensive sites, such as *polis* centers, palace complexes, villages, and other significant secondary settlements, that cover areas ranging from 5 to 100+ ha (Bintliff and Snodgrass 1988a; Alcock 1991; Cavanagh, Shipley and Crouwel 2002: 50–54; Rautman 2003: 22; Tartaron 2003: 41–42; Lolos, Gourley, and Stewart 2007; Johnson and Millett 2012). The investigation of large sites is common to world archaeology generally, but in the Mediterranean it has developed into its own unique subfield of regional studies (see, recently, Lolos, Gourley, and Stewart 2007. For investigations of large sites in other areas of the Mediterranean, see Perkins and Walker 1990; Hurtado 2000; Mušič, Slapšak, and Perko 2000; Tringham 2003; Poulter 2004). A Mediterranean environment replete with extensive urban centers, palace complexes, towns, villages, and villas demands archaeological study of the larger settlements along with the smallest. Moreover, survey has provided an effective counter to more intensive approaches such as excavation. Large-site survey has consequently emerged as a component of landscape archaeology bound to the interpretation and definition of surface scatters, usually without excavation (exceptions in Cyprus include Rautman 2003; Webb and Frankel 2004). The study of the high densities of artifacts across the largest sites of the Mediterranean has demanded high-resolution, yet efficient approaches to discern general patterns.

The collective result of all these developments in understanding Mediterranean landscapes has been a more focused examination of territory than ever before. In Greece, for example, pioneering first- and second-wave Greek survey projects in Kea, Laconia, Boeotia, Messenia, and Methana surveyed 10 to 70 km² of the territory. The EKAS project, in contrast, examined only 4.4 km² over the course of three field seasons. A comparison of recent projects in Cyprus with older projects, such as the Canadian Palaipaphos Survey and the Kalavasos Valley project, reveals similar differences in scale. High-resolution survey archaeology is producing dramatically more information about landscapes, but is covering much less territory.

Because a micro-regional framework and higher-resolution data have come at the cost of the amount of area covered, intensification has evoked increasing reaction and critique. As we outlined in the introduction, some archaeologists have accused high-resolution surveyors of "Mediterranean myopia," a myopic focus on micro-regions through increasing methodological rigor at the expense of the big-picture questions (Blanton 2001; Cherry 2003; Kowalewski 2008). By intensifying method or focusing on smaller regions, some have said, surveyors can no longer effectively answer broad questions about demographic cycles and flows, the relationship between town and countryside, and regional patterns and hierarchies of settlement (Stanish 2003). Other scholars, however, have advocated high-resolution, artifact-level methods for producing survey data at the scale and resolution necessary to reveal the dynamic character of the productive micro-region and to establish empirical signatures for different kinds of past human behaviors (Caraher, Nakassis, and Pettegrew 2006; Tartaron 2008; Winther-Jacobsen 2010b).

We believe that the discrete nature of Mediterranean micro-regions and their abundant material landscapes justify high-resolution approaches. This is not the place for a detailed defense of modern Mediterranean survey, but we would simply point out that the methods employed by any research project are always, whether implicitly or explicitly, a product of research questions shaped by local histories of fieldwork. One must not judge the intensification of survey methods in the Mediterranean by standards developed and utilized in other parts of the world, but according to the trajectories of our particular discourse about landscape. This volume, which marks our own contribution to this debate, aims to show the difference that higher-resolution approaches make in documenting an extensive "large site," which consists of multiple distinct occupations—Kokkinokremos, Vigla, and Koutsopetria—with different chronological phases and spatial focal points.

2.1.2. Distributional Survey in Greece and Cyprus

Our immediate inspiration for applying high-resolution survey approaches in the Pyla region was our previous experience in two projects in Greece and Cyprus. Bill Caraher, Dimitri Nakassis, and David Pettegrew had supervisory roles in the Eastern Korinthia Archaeological Survey (EKAS), in the Corinthia, Greece, between 1999 and 2003, and R. Scott Moore participated as a ceramicist in the Sydney Cyprus Survey Project (SCSP). The two projects shared similar distributional approaches, chronotype collection procedures, and even some of the same archaeologists and geomorphologists. Our work with these projects strongly influenced the specific procedures we applied in PKAP.

As we were formulating our methods for the survey of Koutsopetria in 2003, we had just begun to seriously reflect on the survey methods employed in EKAS, the data resulting from the methods, and the interpretive potential and problems of the material. Our feeling at the time was that high-resolution methods had prevented the project from covering a significant amount of territory but had simultaneously opened up a whole range of possibilities for patterning and interpreting the landscape. Before our first season in Cyprus, our queries of the EKAS data revealed fascinating new insights on the "signatures" of rural habitation, the definition of archaeological sites, the effects of visibility on artifact density, poorly surviving historic periods (e.g., Ottoman), the differential visibility of successive periods (e.g., Early vs. Late Roman), and trade and economic connectivity. Our work with these projects also encouraged reflection on the nature and value of the chronotype system, which SCSP and EKAS employed to classify finds and collect pottery. This made us sensitive to the close relationship between archaeological method, survey data, and historical interpretations in drafting pictures of past landscapes. The first fruits of our reflection appeared in Caraher et al. 2005; Caraher, Nakassis, and Pettegrew 2006; Tartaron et al. 2006; Pettegrew 2007; Moore 2008.

The EKAS project was itself part of a larger extended family of high-resolution survey projects that included the Nikopolis Survey and the Australian *Paliochora*-Kythera Archaeological Survey in Greece, and the Sydney Cyprus Survey Project and the Troodos Archaeological Environmental Survey Project in Cyprus (for discussions of the methods of these projects, see Given et al. 1999; Coroneos et al. 2002; Given and Knapp 2003; Tartaron 2003; Gregory 2004; Caraher, Nakassis, and Pettegrew 2006; Tartaron et al. 2006). Besides sharing some personnel, staff, and organizers, these projects had in common their adoption of a range of higher-resolution methods, including artifact-level survey, gridded collection of "sites," experimental archaeology, geomorphological study, and geophysical survey, among others. These forms of intensification did not exclude more traditional extensive and intensive approaches to studying landscapes (see Tartaron 2003), but together they comprised a high-resolution approach to studying territories that resulted in smaller areas covered.

The specific procedures adopted for the study of Koutsopetria were consequently products of a specific methodological approach to survey that had developed to address particular problems in archaeological landscapes.

2.2.   PEDESTRIAN SURVEY (2003–2008, 2010)

We knew from the beginning that the site of Koutsopetria was substantial and would warrant intensive sampling and artifact collection. As the project developed between 2003 and 2005, we developed a method to map the distribution of cultural material with a resolution high enough to assess chronological and functional diversity at the site, but not so great that we would never finish our work, overburden our ceramicists and storage facilities, or produce redundant data. We recognized the value of different techniques in sampling the landscape and considered which collection strategy would best represent the complexities of the archaeological record.

Our principal means of sampling the landscape was to lay out "tracts" or "survey units" of consistent size, which we then "fieldwalked" at systematic 10 m intervals, counting artifacts for each transect and collecting pottery and tiles in standardized ways (figs. 2.1–2.2). These sorts of "pedestrian survey" techniques parallel intensive methods practiced in most regional survey projects. In the following sections, we discuss the different phases of our survey that correspond to our investigation of four distinct "zones" of differing artifact density, topography, and method; chapter 5 will consider in detail the distributional character of these zones.

2.2.1.   *Reconnaissance Survey and Planning (2003)*

Our initial assessment of the site of Koutsopetria took the form of a reconnaissance survey over a three-day period in 2003 that was designed to assess efficiently the broad patterns of cultural material across the coastal plain and surrounding ridges and define the borders of the site. The three project directors walked

FIG. 2.1   *Fieldwalking in Zone 1.*

FIG. 2.2   *Fieldwalking on Vigla.*

transects at intervals of 10 to 30 m (closer spacing when cultural material became denser), jotted brief notes about artifact densities (low, medium, and high) and features, and took GPS points at places that seemed significant. We noted, recorded, photographed, and occasionally collected a few diagnostic artifacts from each area. Much to our surprise, this informal walk across the plain demonstrated that artifacts extended in moderate to high densities half a kilometer parallel to the coast and inland to the north for some 300 m, an area of 18 ha (180,000 m²). Aware that 18 ha was only a minimum estimate of site size, we recognized Koutsopetria as a substantial coastal settlement significantly larger than other published Roman and Late Antique villages documented on Cyprus. We realized that we needed to develop methods for the following seasons that would allow us to survey the entire area at a level of intensity sufficient for establishing control over the chronological and functional resolution of the artifact distributions.

In selecting our method of survey, we took into account two methodological traditions of Mediterranean survey. First, as noted earlier, our own positive experiences with EKAS and SCSP encouraged our adoption of a *distributional survey* approach that would focus on the artifact as the basic unit of analysis and record the number of artifacts across the landscape according to survey unit or "tracts" ranging in size from 2,000 to 10,000 m² (Caraher, Nakassis, and Pettegrew 2006). Second, we considered that many Mediterranean projects have made use of *gridded systematic surveys* of "sites" which control for the collection of artifacts through small spatial grid units (Redman and Watson 1970 provide the most well-known justification for this form of surface investigation). In the eastern Mediterranean, researchers have adopted gridded survey to refine the spatial, functional, and chronological character of sites discovered in regional survey (for examples, see Wright et al. 1990; Davis et al. 1997: 405–6, 428–30, 459–65, 467–69; Harrison 1998; Stone and Kampke 1998; Broodbank 1999; Given et al. 2001: 427; Manning et al. 2002: 7–16; Given and Meyer 2003: 35; Rautman 2003: 22–25; Tartaron et al. 2006).

In Greece and Cyprus, where we have worked, archaeologists have studied rural sites by employing small grid squares, often no larger than 10 m on a side, together with total collection of artifacts to produce higher resolution data and more robust assemblages (examples include Cherry et al. 1988; Wright et al. 1990: 606–7, 611–612, 619; Whitelaw 1991; Davis et al. 1997: 459–65).

These two traditions, one born in the recording of entire landscapes and the other developed out of the high-resolution investigation of small sites, have spawned a variety of approaches in the Mediterranean. As Table 2.1 indicates, surveyors of major settlements have typically used larger survey units or non-gridded "tracts" as a way of efficiently assessing their sites. However, this general trend is not absolute, for recent urban surveys have sometimes employed smaller units at larger sites (Lolos, Gourley, and Stewart 2007; Whitelaw 2012). In the intellectual climate outlined in this chapter, we may see even more intensive paradigms applied to large urban contexts, but there are certainly diminishing returns for intensification. As we will suggest in the next chapter, the key is determining the appropriate intensity to produce the desired results.

Aware of this broader literature about gridded collection and distributional approaches, we adopted a 40 × 40 m grid across the Koutsopetria plain as the most efficient way of sampling space

Table 2.1   Large sites surveyed in the eastern Mediterranean (ranked by size).

Archaeological Project	Site Name	Site Size (m²)	Unit Size (m²)	Ratio of Site Size to Unit Size	Number of Units Sampled	% of Unit Sampled	% of Site Sampled	% of Surface of Site Examined
Bradford-Cambridge Boeotia Project	Thespiai (town)	1,000,000+	50 × 60 (3,000)	333:1	598	ca. 33%	100%	33%
Nemea Valley Archaeological Project	Phlius (town)	1200000	(10,000-3,000)	400:1 to 120:1	484	100%	100%	100%
Pyla-*Koutsopetria* Archaeological Project	Koutsopetria (town)	300,000+	40 × 40 (1,600)	188:1	185	20%	31%	6%
Pylos Regional Archaeological Project	Palace of Nestor	300,000 to 200,000	20 × 20 (400)	750:1 to 500:1	484	100%	100%	100%
Maroni Valley Archaeological Survey Project	Maroni-*Petrera* (village)	100,000 to 50,000	50 × 50 (2,500)	40:1 to 20:1		ca. 8-16%		
Kalavasos-*Kopetra* Project	Kalavasos-*Kopetra* (village)	60000	20 × 20 (400)	150 : 1	77	100%	50%	50%
N. Keos	Kephala (Neolithic site)	22000	10 × 10 (100)	220:1	215	13%	100%	13%
N. Keos	Paoura (Neolithic site)	< 12,500	25 × 25 (625)	20:1	271	1%	100%	1%

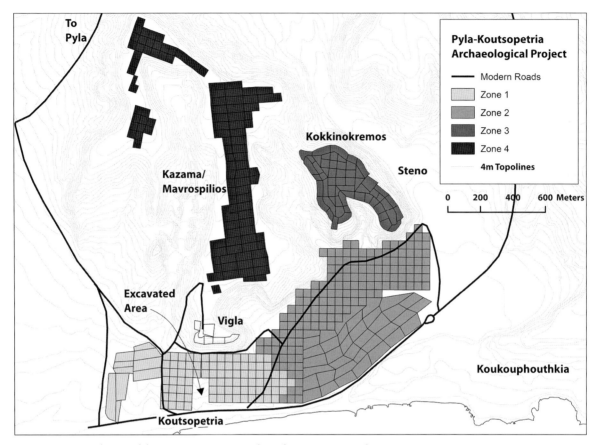

FIG. 2.3　*Map of zones of the PKAP survey area with modern toponyms and sites.*

at an *order of magnitude* smaller than the archaeological phenomenon that we intended to study
(Van de Velde 2001: 25–26; this method stands in
epistemological contrast to full coverage surveys
that assume no prior knowledge of the archaeological phenomenon under investigation and
therefore seek to collect all visible data within a
survey unit in order to produce a "complete" dataset: see Fish and Kowalewski 1990). We put forth
our approach as a compromise between highest-
resolution gridded survey procedures (e.g., 5 ×
5 m units) and less intensive transect walking of
normal pedestrian survey (2,000–10,000 m²). We
believed that the resolution would be sufficient
to understanding the patterns of functional and
chronological data of the ancient settlement site,
while avoiding the problems of collecting data
that would not contribute to our understanding
of the micro-region (Chapter 3). In the end, the
survey grid at Koutsopetria provided total coverage of the coastal plain from the north–south

road to Pyla to the area below Kokkinokremos,
and generated fine archaeological resolution for
mapping artifact densities across the site. Since the
ratio of the area of Late Roman Koutsopetria to
the size of grid squares (188:1) was consistent with,
if not slightly better than, the ratio of site size to
unit size for other large-site survey projects in the
Mediterranean (Table 2.1), we felt justified that our
approach to sampling Koutsopetria was appropriate in respect to the size of the settlement.

2.2.2.　Gridded Survey of Zones 1 and 2: The Coastal Plain below Koutsopetria (2004–2005)

Our procedure for surveying survey units on the
coastal plain was as follows. In 2004, we laid out a
40 × 40 m grid in the area east and west of the early
Christian site excavated by Dr. Maria Hadjicosti
(fig. 2.3). We recorded a 10 ha area of exceptionally
high artifact density, which we quickly discerned
as the center of a Late Roman coastal site. As our

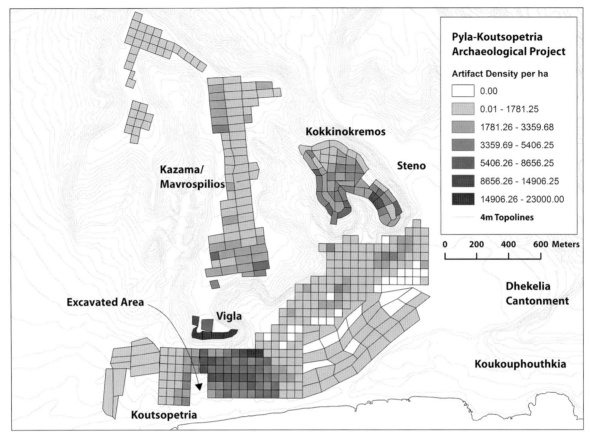

FIG. 2.4   *Total Artifact Density.*

procedure was to continue the grid of 40 × 40 m units until they no longer produced substantial scatters of artifacts, we extended our grid along the southern base of the coastal ridge for over a kilometer. Doing this identified a second zone of moderate to high artifact density constituted by relatively isolated high-density areas along the base of the Mavrospilios and Kokkinokremos ridgeline. Both of these areas, which we later designated Zones 1 and 2, produced high "site-level" artifact densities.

At the western and southeastern parts of the coastal plain, we discontinued our grid squares and used larger non-grid survey units. In the west, reconnaissance survey in 2003 and gridded survey in 2004 and 2005 had shown that artifact densities trailed off beyond 200 m of the excavated site of Koutsopetria (fig. 2.4), which justified a different approach. Pragmatic reasons also encouraged the change. This part of the survey area consisted of fields irrigated and cultivated on a day-to-day

basis. As we did not have time to set up and carefully walk measured grid units, we surveyed these freshly harvested fields as they became available. We consequently employed survey units that were larger than the gridded units on the plain, although we made use of the same counting and collection methods adopted elsewhere.

In the southeastern part of the plain, our reconnaissance survey of 2003 had recorded an even more dramatic decline in density across a broad area of sandy soil just above sea level. The absence of artifacts here supported the conclusions of a geological study of the area indicating that the southern section of the coastal plain was once an ancient embayment, which had infilled only in recent times (Section 2.4). In this area, we used larger survey units (ave. 5,000 m²; total area 16.2 ha) because we were certain we would not find much in the way of surface material and any material that we did find was unlikely to be related to local subsurface remains.

Despite the variation in size of survey units, we employed a consistent set of survey procedures throughout the plain (fig. 2.5). Fieldwalkers spaced at 10 m intervals walked transects across each unit, counting all artifacts and collecting artifacts according to the chronotype system (Section 2.3.2). Intensive methods followed those that were developed for the Eastern Korinthia Archaeological Survey (cf. Tartaron et al. 2006). Ten-meter spacing with two-meter-wide coverage produced in ideal conditions a 20% sample of the surface of a grid square of 1,600 m², although poor visibility reduced that examined sample to about 12% on average (Chapter 5) and surveyors underestimated the true quantity of artifacts on the surface (Chapter 3). We did monitor "walker efficiency," that is, the ability of a fieldwalker to recognize artifacts, but we discovered no great variation in the abilities of individual walkers (see Chapter 3 for the minor differences between experienced and inexperienced walkers). Fieldwalkers recorded features such as cut stone blocks, column fragments, and walls, as well as information that would help to locate the unit in space or contribute to the later interpretation of artifact patterns: location and toponym, evidence of current land use (e.g., olives, wheat, or barren), vegetation cover (e.g., weeds, trees, and phrygana), vegetation height in relation to the fieldwalker (e.g., ankle high, knee high, and waist high), condition of the soil, surface clast composition, and surface visibility (recorded at 10% intervals). These data sets provided the environmental context for assessing artifact densities across the whole of the survey region.

The survey of the coastal plain via grid squares and larger units for lower-density areas suggested evidence for two distinct "zones" of activity. We defined Zone 1 as the high-density area surrounding the basilica excavated by Dr. Hadjicosti. The 100 units in this zone, which represent an area of 19.8 ha, include 90 grid squares, each 1,600 m² in area, and 10 larger units along the western border that average 5,356 m². The southern border of the zone was the modern coastal road, the northern border the abrupt ridge of Koutsopetria, the western border the modern road to Pyla, and the eastern border the area of declining artifact densities. This abrupt reduction in the quantity of

artifacts relates in part to the ancient embayment mentioned above, and in part to local disruptions associated with the installation of the treatment plant (fig. 2.6).

Zone 2 extended for over a kilometer along the base of the ridges of Mavrospilios and Kokkinokremos (fig. 2.7). The southern border was, like Zone 1, the coastal road linking Dhekelia and Larnaca; on the south, the zone captures the coastal area of the now in-filled embayment. Defining the eastern border were the Dhekelia Firing Ranges and a golf course. The northern border was the coastal ridgeline of Mavrospilios and Kokkinokremos that includes the steep valleys punctuating the southern slopes. The 192 units of Zone 2 represent an area of 42.6 ha and include 156 grid squares (1,600 m²) and 36 larger units in the south (4,766 m²).

The 2004 and 2005 surveys adopted identical methods to sample 246 grid squares (Units 1–252) over a total area of 39.4 ha and to delimit a site with two zones of moderate to high densities. The use of slightly larger survey units over an area of 23 ha highlights the "trailing off" of densities to both the southeast and west. Gridded survey demonstrated that this was a far more extensive scatter than we had estimated from the 2003 reconnaissance survey; more extensive, in fact, than many large sites investigated through gridded collection (cf. Table 2.1). The survey of the coastal plain required two seasons, followed by a study season in 2006.

2.2.3. Zone 3: Kokkinokremos (2007)

In 2007, we corresponded with Michael Brown, then a doctoral student at the University of Edinburgh, to plan a geophysical survey on the ridge of Kokkinokremos for his dissertation study on the Late Bronze Age in Cyprus. In the following season, we partnered with him and Dr. Hadjicosti to initiate a program of research in the area that would involve geophysical work at Kokkinokremos and Koutsopetria as well as an intensive pedestrian survey of the broad plateau that comprises the site of Kokkinokremos. The goals of this pedestrian survey were 1) to produce a density map of the surface remains to assess better the size and intra-site functional organization of the Bronze Age

Unit Number: _____   **Recorder** _____

Date (mm/dd/yy): _____   Start Time _____
                                  End Time _____

Area / Toponym: _____

Location & Description (Relate to other units & local topography: dimensions, distance and bearing to nearest landmarks, land use, etc…)

[blank box]

Survey Procedure

Walker Spacing [ ]   Bearing (in degrees) [ ]   Direction of walker array:
FROM: [ ]   TO: [ ]

Walker Initials	Sherds #	Tiles #	Lithics #	Other #	Walker Initials	Sherds #	Tiles #	Lithics #	Other #
1	[ ]	[ ]	[ ]	[ ]	9	[ ]	[ ]	[ ]	[ ]
2	[ ]	[ ]	[ ]	[ ]	10	[ ]	[ ]	[ ]	[ ]
3	[ ]	[ ]	[ ]	[ ]	11	[ ]	[ ]	[ ]	[ ]
4	[ ]	[ ]	[ ]	[ ]	12	[ ]	[ ]	[ ]	[ ]
5	[ ]	[ ]	[ ]	[ ]	13	[ ]	[ ]	[ ]	[ ]
6	[ ]	[ ]	[ ]	[ ]	14	[ ]	[ ]	[ ]	[ ]
7	[ ]	[ ]	[ ]	[ ]	15	[ ]	[ ]	[ ]	[ ]
8	[ ]	[ ]	[ ]	[ ]	16	[ ]	[ ]	[ ]	[ ]
					TOTAL	[ ]	[ ]	[ ]	[ ]

Standard [ ]   Unsurveyed [ ]   Resurveyed [ ]

Number of Bags [ ]   Photography (circle): Digital, B&W, Color

General Comments about Unit (identify "other"; nature of field procedures)

[blank box]

1

FIG. 2.5A   *Survey Unit form, front.*

Vegetation & Land Use (check all that apply)

Evergreens ☐   Deciduous ☐   Scrub / Phrygana ☐   Maquis ☐

Grass / Weeds ☐   Barren ☐   Other ☐

Olives ☐   Vineyard ☐   Citrus ☐   Apricot ☐   Almonds ☐   Other Orchard/Grove ☐

Vegetation, Small-Leafed ☐   Veg., Broad-Leafed ☐   Greens ☐

Grain ☐   Grain Stubble ☐   Kalamboki ☐   Other ☐

Dominant vegetation height   none | <=ankle | <=knee | <= waist | <=head | >head

Percent Visible   (walked area, 0-100, by 10s) [＿＿＿＿＿＿＿＿＿]

Comments on Vegetation & Land Use:

[   ]

Field Conditions

Plowed? ☐   Unplowed? ☐

Soil Loose? ☐   Soil Compacted? ☐

Background Disturbance: None ☐   Light ☐   Moderate ☐   Heavy ☐

Sherd Crusting (check one)   None ☐   Light ☐   Heavy ☐

Surface Clast   Boulder ☐   Cobble ☐   Coarse Gravel ☐   Fine Gravel ☐   Sand ☐
Size (check one)   (>300mm)   (300-75mm)   (75-19mm)   (19-5mm)   (<5mm)

Comments on Field Conditions:

[   ]

Features

[   ]

Fig. 2.5B   *Survey Unit form, back.*

FIG. 2.6   *Survey of Zone 1 (Koutsopetria), view from Vigla.*

settlement site, 2) to produce a record of artifacts to compare with the geophysical information, and 3) to produce density data for a prehistoric site to compare to the Late Roman site of Koutsopetria and the Hellenistic site of Vigla. The results of the regional survey of the Kokkinokremos ridge (later defined as Zone 3) we will discuss in Chapter 5. The results of the geophysical survey appeared in Brown's completed dissertation (Brown 2012).

While a grid of 40 × 40 m was appropriate for the topographically featureless and consistently cultivated coastal plain, the more topographically complex height of Kokkinokremos required procedural adjustments to take into account the shape of the hill and the limits of cultivation (fig. 2.8). A regular grid would have produced units across Zone 3 that included parts of the flat top of the hill and its sloping sides. This was problematic for two reasons. First, taphonomic processes affecting different areas of Kokkinokremos were variable,

with a recent history of extensive plowing and cultivation on the plateau in contrast to uncultivated slopes overgrown with phrygana and weeds. Second, the perimeter wall noted by past researchers ran along the modern break in slope, with the Late Bronze Age settlement within the wall and the slopes outside and below. A regular grid would inevitably have left some units overlapping slope and plateau, combining different cultural and environmental patterns within the same units.

We surveyed Zone 3 using units that approximated the area of the grid squares on the Koutsopetria plain (1,600 m²) while isolating changes in slope and surface conditions owing to cultivation. We generally kept units between 1,000 and 2,000 m², with an average unit size of 1,804 m²; the 58 survey units covered an area of 10.5 ha.

Survey methods were identical to those at Koutsopetria despite the irregular shape of the units. These units included the level plowed top

Fig. 2.7   *Survey of Zone 2 (harbor area), view from Kokkinokremos.*

Fig. 2.8   *Survey of Slopes of Zone 3 (Kokkinokremos).*

FIG. 2.9   *Survey of Zone 4, with Vigla visible in the distance.*

of the plateau and those slopes gentle enough for fieldwalkers to survey safely. We laid out units by using hand-held compasses and laser rangefinders, and then used a GPS Trimble unit to record the corners of units. Rather steep cliffs marked the limits to our survey in this zone. As in the survey of the plain below, we noted and photographed, but did not always collect, larger and heavier items such as stone basins, stone vessels, and ground-stone fragments.

2.2.4.   Zone 4: The Broader Micro-Region (2006–2008)

Following the surveys of Zones 1–3, we conducted additional intensive survey of the coastal plateaus north of Koutsopetria and west of Kokkinokremos. We began with an efficient and informal walk across the region in 2006, with the goal of assessing terrain, cultural material present, and thresholds of artifact densities. Procedures were identical to the reconnaissance survey across the Koutsopetria plain in 2003. Our cursory examination of the ridges revealed that although there were scattered ceramic artifacts (broken pottery

and tile) inland north of the coast, they did not appear to be continuous and constituted a threshold of density well below those of the Late Roman harbor site of Koutsopetria. There appeared to be no high-density areas north of the coastal site of Koutsopetria and Vigla, but this initial observation turned out to be misleading, as we later discovered a significant concentration of material of Cypro-Archaic to Hellenistic date just above the water plant and some localized concentrations elsewhere on the ridge.

In 2007 and 2008, we conducted tract-level distributional survey across these plateaus to place the exceedingly high artifact densities of the sites of Vigla, Koutsopetria, and Kokkinokremos within their broader archaeological context (fig. 2.9). Zone 4, as we later defined it, extended over 25.5 ha and 109 units. Rather than using a digital theodolite to lay out units precisely, our survey of this area employed hand-held GPS units and laser rangefinders. Unlike the regular grid used to survey the Koutsopetria plain, we expanded the survey unit size to accommodate the irregular shapes of the fields and cover terrain more efficiently. The units were usually 80 × 40 in size

FIG. 2.10   *View of the ridges in the survey area, from Kokkinokremos (photo by Brandon Olson).*

(3,200 m²), which we walked along the 80 m axis and recorded artifact densities at the 40 m point; we collected artifacts according to the chronotype sampling system using the 80 × 40 m unit (rather than the 40 m point). For units in the far northern part of the Kazama ridge, we reverted to 40 × 40 grid squares owing to local topography. The ridge throughout this area became quite narrow and it was difficult to arrange larger units consistently within the boundaries of the fields. With a larger average unit size for the entire zone of 2,344 m², we were able to survey the ridge more efficiently and quickly.

We later defined this entire area of ridgeline north of Vigla, Koutsopetria, and Kokkinokremos as Zone 4. The limit to Zone 4 to the south is the line of a *taphros*, or ditch, cut into the bedrock at the northern border of the height of Vigla. The presence of beehives filled with swarms of hostile, stinging bees and areas of dense overgrowth, however, prevented us from surveying as far south as the *taphros* itself. Steep, overgrown cliffs mark the northern and western boundaries of the zone. The

fields in this zone were generally under cultivation and either fallow or filled with grain stubble.

The survey of Zone 4 produced some areas of moderate to high density, especially north of Vigla along the southern edge of the coastal plateau. These units have high visibility, low vegetation, and had recently been plowed. They produced a higher overall density (1,741 artifacts per ha) and a lower average visibility (51%) than the average for the entire zone (1,220 artifacts per ha). As these moderate- to high-density units were nearer to the ancient sites, it is logical to associate them with the broader cultural landscape of occupation to the south.

2.2.5.   Vigla and the Ridge Survey (2006–2007, 2010)

The coastal site of Koutsopetria is bordered by a line of ridges that run along its northern edge and separate the site on the plain from the sites on the plateau (fig. 2.10). This line extends from the prominent rocky hilltop known as *Laksha tou*

Papa, northwest of Koutsopetria, to Mavrospilios in the east below the site of Kokkinokremos (although the ridges actually continue eastward beyond the survey area). As Lolos, Gourley, and Stewart have discussed (2007), Mediterranean surveyors have not often considered the value of ridge survey as an integral component of interpreting sites. The survey of the sides of ridges can potentially identify unique kinds of information, such as well-preserved pottery eroding out of slopes, or features (tombs, cut stone blocks, or walls) that survive better in uncultivated zones (fig. 2.10).

We had two main objectives in surveying the slopes. We were especially interested in whether there were tombs on the ridges associated with the settlements of Koutsopetria, Kokkinokremos, and Vigla. And we wanted to determine the relationship between high-density artifact scatters noted in the coastal plain at Koutsopetria and those on the ridges above and beyond. This was especially important for the eastern end of the site of Koutsopetria where the moderate to high artifact densities were unexpected (Zone 2), and we believed an inspection of the ridges would help to determine the relationship between areas on the plain and the higher-density areas on the top of the plateau. In the end, our survey of the ridges produced some interesting finds and helped to define the extent of activity on "marginal" parts of the survey area and the influence of erosion and other local depositional processes on the nature of the assemblage on the plain below.

We surveyed ridges in two ways. For two ridge segments, we followed the same procedures adopted elsewhere in walking 10 m intervals and collecting chronotype samples. As noted above, we systematically surveyed the ridge below Kokkinokremos (2007) in this manner. We also used the same procedures to survey the height of Vigla and its surrounding slope. We walked the unit on the top of the plateau (501) as a typical grid square and surveyed five units to the south and west (1400–1404) as larger irregular units that followed the contours of the slope and avoided the steep cliffs farther downslope. We kept the size of the units (ave. 1,983 m²) on the slopes below Vigla relatively close to units from the plain (1,600 m²). Artifact densities were especially high in these units.

Apart from the areas below Vigla and Kokkinokremos, however, our survey of ridges in 2006, 2007, and 2010 followed a different procedure because we were unable to carry out typical intensive survey owing to the steepness of the slopes and the density of vegetation. For most of the steep slopes that separated the coastal plain from the flat-topped ridgeline, we carried out a survey that was intensive but non-systematic and assessed artifacts in a qualitative manner. In practice, this meant that two to five fieldwalkers spaced at 10–20 m intervals walked along the slopes from west to east in accordance with the contours of the slope, navigating their way around thick vegetation, obstacles, and cliffs. Instead of counting artifacts, surveyors recorded observations about artifact densities (low, medium, or high) and collected artifacts that were exceptional (e.g., figurines) or highly diagnostic (rims, bases, handles, and decorated sherds). We documented all features by recording location (with GPS unit), measuring dimensions, taking digital photographs, and making basic descriptions. This feature information was integrated into the GIS digital structure of the survey region.

The survey of the ridge slopes resulted in a remarkable amount of qualitative data. We observed additional kinds of artifacts such as figurines (Chapters 4 and 5). In most of the ridgeline from Vigla east, we noted numerous pits, quarry cuttings, several walls, and tombs that relate to broader activities in the land. In one place, in particular, the ridge survey proved significant to our overall research. On the western end of the ridge, immediately below Vigla, our reconnaissance survey in 2006 documented cut stairs and a substantial wall along the ridge. Heavy rains and erosion prior to the 2007 season revealed that the wall was a fortification of ancient date. Low-altitude aerial photographs and excavations later helped us establish the chronology of this site, and we detail the results in a separate chapter devoted entirely to the fortifications (Chapter 6). The study of the finds from the excavation of this wall is currently being completed and prepared for a second volume.

2.2.6. *Resurvey (2006, 2007, 2010)*

The final form of pedestrian survey we carried out was *resurvey*. There are many reasons to resurvey the landscape, but the most important is that ground conditions change from year to year, revealing different artifacts and densities (Ammerman 1995). Given that pedestrian survey typically produces only a small sample of what lies beneath the surface, it is generally good practice to implement programs of resurvey as part of a project design.

As one example of the importance of resurvey for PKAP, well-preserved artifacts (such as carved marble basins, limestone settling basins, and enormous roof tiles) were revealed in 2006 by deep plowing in a previously uncultivated patch of coastal plain (fig. 2.11). This reexamination also revealed substantial new building materials and monumental architecture that allowed us to make reasonable estimations of subsurface architecture. As Volume 2 will detail, such knowledge factored

directly into our placement of geophysical transects on the Koutsopetria plain.

An even more important form of resurvey was the series of experimental units surveyed in 2004, 2006, and 2010. These experimental units proved essential for assessing the reliability of our method, so much that we have elected to discuss them separately in the next chapter.

2.3. DISTRIBUTIONAL DATA: COUNTING AND CHRONOTYPES

The previous section outlined how we organized the landscape to ensure that we consistently covered the various topographical areas of the Pyla micro-region. The goal in this section is to present our strategies for quantifying and collecting surface scatters and discuss why we chose them. Such sampling strategies are close to the core of all intensive survey because the manner in which one records artifacts in the landscape determines the kinds of archaeological and historical conclusions

FIG. 2.11 *Area of deep plowing at Koutsopetria.*

that one draws about past land use and settlement. We recorded the distribution of artifacts through total count (2.3.1) and chronotype collection (2.3.2).

2.3.1   Total Counts and Densities

Selecting a system for documenting artifact distributions is difficult because surface scatters represent complex aggregates of different processes, periods, and types that vary across space. The most common standard for documenting the material landscape is to map the distribution of "sites" across a landscape, that is, areas of exceptionally high artifact density or material. However, the "site" is a slippery concept that is ontologically problematic and methodologically difficult to define and delimit in the field (Dunnel 1992). Sites defined in the field may in fact be high-density artifact scatters resulting from overlapping layers of pottery of different periods (e.g., Hellenistic and Late Roman), in which case the concept does not retain its value when each of the periods is measured individually and separately (Caraher, Nakassis, and Pettegrew 2006).

On the other hand, some regional survey projects in the Mediterranean aim to record the *distribution of artifacts* (rather than sites) across the landscape, reflecting a belief that the quantity of artifacts presents a metric valuable for parsing the landscapes into different chronological and functional layers (Winther-Jacobsen 2010b). Distributional surveys typically count the total number of artifacts found in survey units or tracts. Since the 1970s, archaeologists have used tally counters to record the quantity of different kinds of artifacts within each fieldwalker's "swath:" potsherds, especially, but also tiles, stone artifacts, glass, and miscellaneous other objects. In some cases, these counts highlight low and high-density spots in the landscape that reflect real geological or cultural processes in the past such as occupation. In other cases, high-density scatters are the products of a complex mixture of processes that include aggregate settlement over long periods of time, high-intensity use in a single period, particular episodes of land use that produced large quantities of material, post-abandonment behaviors, and geological and geomorphological conditions.

Assigning cultural significance and categories to places of high or low artifact density involves assessing the chronological and functional character of the artifact scatters.

PKAP fieldwalkers sampled the *total density* of artifacts in the area in a manner consistent with the procedures employed by those within its survey family, including the Eastern Korinthia Archaeological Survey and the Sydney Cyprus Survey Project. As noted earlier, fieldwalkers spaced at 10 m intervals walked transects across each unit counting with tally counters all pottery, tile, lithics, and other types of artifacts one meter to the right and left of the fieldwalkers' transect (cf. Tartaron et al. 2006 for review of this procedure.; note that "lithic artifacts" refer to chipped stone flint and chert; "other artifacts" denote all artifacts that are not pottery, tile, or lithics, and include materials such as glass, mortar, gypsum, marble revetment, cut stone, andesite, limestone bowls, metal, coins, and slag). Ten-meter spacing with two-meter-wide coverage produced a maximum surface sample of 20% for each survey unit as well as sub-unit data (four samples of a maximum of 5%) as each fieldwalker covered exactly the same percentage of the surface of the unit. The "total count" of artifacts for each survey unit was used to generate its "total density" (=total count divided by area). The variation of these densities over the landscape provides a coarse approximation of the areas of least and most intensive human activity through time.

2.3.2.   Chronotype Collection

To assess the function and chronology of habitation and land use in any landscape, we analyzed a sample of the artifacts counted. The most commonly used system for sampling artifacts from sites and landscapes is *grab sampling*, which entails picking up all visible "diagnostic" artifacts, which are typically feature sherds such as rims, bases, and handles, or decorated body sherds. The advantage of the grab sample system is that it greatly reduces the number of artifacts collected and assigns some chronological and functional value to a site from a few identifiable artifacts. Its disadvantage, however, is that it requires fieldwalkers to determine which artifacts appear to be "diagnostic," which may result in the neglect of sherds that are more generic or less distinctive in appearance. The uncritical collection of large quantities of any particular artifact class can lead to misinterpretations of the landscape since it potentially gives one period or artifact type more prominence than another. As we have argued elsewhere, surveyors must develop a better appreciation of the inherent biases of grab samples (Caraher, Nakassis, and Pettegrew 2006; Tartaron et al. 2006). For example, Classical-Hellenistic black-glazed body sherds and Late Roman combed ware body sherds are highly visible in the landscape, while the body sherds of Early Roman utilitarian vessels are not (Pettegrew 2007). Without accounting for the differential visibility of artifacts, sampling strategies dependent on grab samples are likely to misrepresent the differences in quantity of artifacts of different periods and functions. Grab samples also favor features sherds and these typically represent less than 10% of the ceramic material visible on the surface (Chapter 3) and leave on the ground 90% of artifacts, many of which provide important functional and chronological clues to interpreting past human activities.

Some archaeologists have favored more robust and systematic sampling strategies that provide better assessments of the chronological and functional character of surface assemblages, highlight biases in recognition of artifacts, and reveal "hidden landscapes" poorly represented in regional survey (Bintliff, Howard, and Snodgrass 1999; Caraher, Nakassis, and Pettegrew 2006; Pettegrew 2007). The best way to avoid the problems of differential visibility noted above is to intensify the sample of artifacts through *total collection*, i.e., collecting all artifacts visible at a site or, in the case of distributional survey, in a survey swath. Total collection establishes a very robust sample of artifacts, which can add new information about a site (Winther-Jacobsen 2010b. See Chapter 3). However, it is practically impossible to implement this method over a large area or where artifact densities are high, since it yields enormous amounts of material that easily overwhelm ceramic specialists and the storage facilities, often without providing much new information (Section 3.3). Moreover, it

is a mistake to conclude that total collection constitutes some kind of representative sample of all the material present, since the material visible on the surface forms only a fraction of the plowzone, let alone the full array of sub-surface assemblages or the original systemic assemblage (see Winther-Jacobsen 2010b). Our own experiments in total collection question whether the new information gained from total collection is worth the increased investment of resources of time, energy, and storage at a site as large as Koutsopetria (Chapter 3).

In contrast to both grab sampling and total collection, a number of surveys in the eastern Mediterranean have adopted variations of the *chronotype system*, which seeks to strike a balance between an efficient and representative sample. Timothy Gregory, a ceramicist, and Nathan Meyer, a data analyst, developed the system as part of the Sydney Cyprus Survey Project in an effort to produce more data for less analysis (Meyer 2003: 14–16; Meyer and Gregory 2003: 48–52; Gregory 2004). From its initial use in the SCSP project (Given et al. 1999), it was then refined for use in the Australian *Paliochora*-Kythera Archaeological Survey (Coroneos et al. 2002: 139–40), the Troodos Archaeological and Environmental Survey Project (Given et al. 2001), and the Eastern Korinthia Archaeological Survey (Tartaron et al. 2006). As an experimental system designed to deal with theoretical and practical problems in investigating surface scatters, its potentials and problems have been the subject of a range of recent discussions (Caraher, Nakassis, and Pettegrew 2006; Pettegrew 2007; Moore 2008; Winther-Jacobsen 2010b).

In the chronotype system, every artifact type (i.e., chronotype) fits into a chronological and descriptive hierarchy based on specific physical typological characteristics. Chronotypes range from the very precise (e.g., "African Red Slip Form 99 - rim sherd," or "Micaceous Water Jar - body sherd") to the very imprecise (e.g., "Medium-Coarse body sherd - Post-Prehistoric," or "Ancient Millstone"), but chronotypes are always assigned to a period, however narrow or broad. As a sampling strategy, the system compromises between less-systematic and lower-intensity grab sampling and the logistically problematic and higher-intensity total collection. In principle, each fieldwalker should collect a maximum of one rim, base, handle, and body sherd of each chronotype in his or her transect. If a walker has already collected a combed-ware body sherd and an ARS Form 50 rim, for example, she would not collect additional examples of combed-ware and ARS Form 50 rims found in the tract, but would count them as part of the total count and only collect additional examples of grooved body sherds of different thickness, color, and fabric. If four fieldwalkers walking at 10 m intervals in a 40 × 40 m square were to collect the unique objects visible in their swaths, each unit should produce as many as 16 examples of a single chronotype, corresponding to 4 rims, 4 bases, 4 handles, and 4 bodysherds of the same kind of pottery. A different color of the same chronotype, however, would warrant collecting an additional example, which means that the number of examples could theoretically be higher (see discussion of batches in 2.3.3 below).

Scholars have criticized the chronotype system for reasons that include both problems of quantification and implementation (see discussion in Caraher, Nakassis, and Pettegrew 2006; Tartaron et al. 2006; Pettegrew 2007; Moore 2008). In respect to the former, critics have noted that the system's elimination of duplicates prevents true quantification of total numbers of artifact types. The system allegedly produces qualitative rather than quantitative data, or simple indication of presence or absence of material. With no power to account for the frequency of types or periods, it is consequently not useful for relative representation of types and periods in the landscape.

We have argued elsewhere that the system does in fact allow one to quantify (Pettegrew 2007), but the quantification is a measure of the sample, i.e., the diversity of artifact types sampled, which provides a rough approximation of the relative quantities of types of artifacts visible. The system cannot shed light, of course, on the total quantity of artifacts of chronotypes *seen* in the swath but not collected because they are redundant. There is no way of knowing, for example, how many examples of Late Roman spirally grooved amphora body sherds were counted but not collected in a transect. Since the maximum total number of spirally grooved body sherds *collected* is in theory

limited to the number of transects (but see below for the tendency to duplicate), the system is biased against particularly common types of artifacts that produce redundant sherds (Tartaron et al. 2006; Pettegrew 2007).

The second serious criticism concerns the implementation of the chronotype system during survey. Critics have suggested that fieldwalkers cannot confidently differentiate similarity and dissimilarity in the attributes (color, fabric, thickness, and surface treatment) that distinguish one chronotype from another, with the result that they systematically under-collect chronotypes. Moreover, when pottery is encountered in the field, dirt from the field further hinders chronotype identification during survey. In fact, studies have shown that fieldwalkers tend to "over-collect" chronotypes by collecting more artifacts than the chronotype system requires (Tartaron et al. 2006). Volunteers, who are instructed to collect when there is a question of duplication, end up gathering artifacts that they recognize as different in the field but that our ceramic analysts batch together into single chronotype categories. For this reason, certain broadly-defined chronotypes, such as "Medium-Coarse Ware, Ancient," are very overrepresented for survey units. The system aims to eliminate redundant sherds, but in practice our surveyors still end up collecting more sherds than they should according to the logic of the system.

In our view, the advantages of the chronotype collection strategy outweigh its limitations, and make it preferable to the alternatives of total collection and grab sampling in artifact-rich environments. In contrast to the former, the use of the chronotype collection strategy in PKAP produced an assemblage that was only 44% of the total number of artifacts counted. This technique produced a record of the types of artifacts present in a unit while leaving over half of the material on the ground *in situ*. Moreover, the system is more systematic than grab samples, which ask fieldwalkers to determine whether sherds are diagnostic in the field and produce grosser, less systematic, and less robust samples. Indeed, inattention to the biases of grab sampling has often led archaeologists to misinterpret change in the landscape (Pettegrew 2007; Winther-Jacobsen 2010b). In chronotype collection, a more complete assemblage of rims, bases, sherds, and handles foregrounds the influence of particular type-fossils in shaping our perception of time and function in the landscape. And this level of "source criticism" ultimately makes our interpretations of change in occupation more circumspect and accurate (for "source criticism" of surface assemblages, see Rutter 1983; Alcock 1993: 49–53; Millett 1985, 1991, 2000a, 2000b; Caraher, Nakassis, and Pettegrew 2006: 21–26; Pettegrew 2007: 749–51).

We do not believe the chronotype system to be a methodological silver bullet that provides the perfect solution for any survey, but we do regard it as a sampling method that maximizes the production of interpretable data, limits the impact of survey on the archaeological landscape, and reduces cost in time and logistics. To verify the validity of the system, the PKAP project conducted a series of analyses and experiments that we will discuss in the next chapter.

2.3.3. Principles of Description and Analysis

In our survey, grid-squares and survey units represent the spatial unit that forms the basis for our sampling of the surface of the ground and the assemblage. As distributional and non-site surveys over the past three decades have recognized, the basic unit of analysis is not the archaeological site itself but the individual artifacts distributed in units across a micro-region. A distributional approach begins with the chronological and functional values of the total collection of artifacts to construct meaningful understandings of past activities in the landscape (Caraher, Nakassis, and Pettegrew 2006; Winther-Jacobsen 2010b). Our approach is to parse the archaeological landscape into its atomic units — the individual artifacts — and then reconstruct these units into broader historical patterns. By employing relational databases, GIS, and a particular sampling strategy (cf. Chapters 3 and 5), the finely-parsed landscape of artifacts marks the evidence for dynamic shifts in culture, economy, and society.

We feel this form of analysis contributes in an efficient way to realistic evaluations of the patterns and meaning of artifacts within their surface context. A distributional artifact-based approach gives archaeologists a tool to make inferences about the relationship between artifacts observed on the surface of the ground (the sample) and artifacts *actually present* on the surface (total population) — and even the empirical correlates to specific ancient behaviors, as Winther-Jacobsen has recently proposed (2010b). In distributional survey, archaeologists use basic quantification to describe, summarize, and interpret data collected from the landscape. We have highlighted three variables important to our quantification and statistical description of the landscapes in the Pyla region: density, diversity, and visibility.

Density

Total density is a measure of the aggregate quantity of artifacts left over time and visible on the surface today. We have computed artifact density per hectare (10,000 m²) in order to make the figures more accessible. Our estimates of overall artifact density are based on counts produced by fieldwalkers in each unit, which represent, at maximum, a 20% sample of the surface of each unit. In optimal conditions, the total number of artifacts counted corresponds to the number of artifacts actually on the surface of the survey unit, although in reality, as Chapter 3 will show, the pedestrian procedure produces only a sample of artifacts visible according to our fieldwalking procedure. Within the limits of this sample, total artifact density nevertheless represents a coarse index for assessing past activities. Since we subjected the entire region to the same pedestrian procedure, the areas of high density define the culmination of various formation processes over time.

Diversity

Total density allows for the assessment of site formation processes over time, but it is an inherently coarse method for measuring land use in the landscape. The first step toward parsing the overall density patterns across the landscape involves identifying the various chronological and functional components of the scatter. Typological, chronological, and functional variations in the assemblage of artifacts collected from units are important indicators of the intensity and character of ancient activity in an area. Even when the total density of a unit is relatively low, a diverse assemblage might still point to vestigial patterns of particular kinds of land use. High artifact densities and low diversity, moreover, may suggest short but relatively intense occupation of areas. Diversity marks an independent category for drawing meaning from artifact assemblages.

Our basis for measuring diversity derives not from the total artifacts counted by the fieldwalkers, but from the sample of *collected artifacts*. This includes the individual chronotypes representing unique artifact types. As noted above, the chronotype system assigns every artifact to a category that combines aspects of chronology, function, extant part, and basic description of the fabric. Fieldwalkers collected unique artifacts (chronotypes), which ceramicists read for basic properties of material, fabric, color, size, weight, vessel part, decoration, and period. The databases combined with the spatial relationships stored in the project's GIS allowed us to produce patterns in the landscape according to typological, functional, and chronological values.

The chronotype system provided the project with a useful set of heuristic tools to pull apart aggregate artifact densities and determine the relationship between artifact scatters and past human activities. The chronotype system does not offer a single solution to the challenges of unpacking the complex patterns produced by intensive pedestrian survey, and we do not recommend it as the only or best method for sampling every landscape encountered in the Mediterranean basin. Nonetheless, the system does seem particularly well-suited to landscapes characterized by high artifact densities, since it produces a robust sample in an efficient manner.

If the count of chronotypes forms an important index of diversity in a unit, the *batch* marks a related but slightly different assessment. A "batch" denotes a group of similar pottery from a survey unit that shares the same chronotype, fabric, color, and vessel part to one another. A single batch, for example, could consist of four buff Late Roman 1 amphora handles. Red handles of the same shape

and chronotype would be separated into their own batch, as would buff rims from the same amphora chronotype. Because batches are created and subdivided according to color and extant part, they form a more sensitive index of the diversity of material present in each unit than grouping artifacts by chronotypes alone. It is possible for there to be several batches of sherds identified as the same chronotype, such as "Late Roman 1 Amphora," with each one representing a different color, fabric, or extant part of the same basic ware. Since the chronotype system is at least partially hierarchical, these different batches could theoretically represent chronological and functional categories that fall outside of existing typologies. Returning again to our example of Late Roman 1 Amphora, different colors and fabrics likely represent different places of production and may indicate different contents and functions. Some Late Roman 1 amphorae could be imported vessels to the island and others may mark commodities prepared for trans-shipment from the settlement.

Visibility

The final feature that is important to our description of the surface record is the "visibility" of the surface recorded for each unit (Section 2.2.2, and fig. 2.5). Visibility is an important environmental factor that influences our ability to record the number of artifacts present. Total densities are less meaningful without understanding whether the surface of the ground was *actually* visible to the fieldwalker and how this and related factors influenced the ability to count and recover archaeological objects from the surface. Visibility encompasses a range of environmental factors in each unit, ranging from the height and nature of vegetation, to the amount of confusion generated by non-ceramic artifacts in the soil matrix, and the time of day and direction walked. We have focused on visibility over other factors, because we have found that the percentage of the surface visible represents the most influential factor in our ability to recover cultural material from the field.

Chapter 5 will frequently discuss visibility as a factor that influences our knowledge of diversity and density across the landscape. Generally,

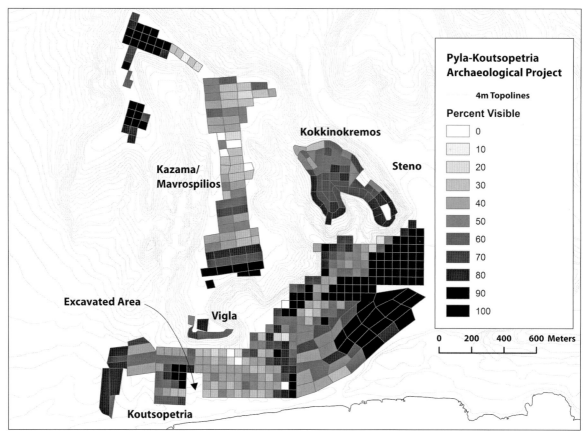

FIG. 2.12 *Map showing visibility in the survey area.*

the surface visibility across the micro-region was both relatively high (ave. 64%) and consistent (fig. 2.12). Most of our survey area was subject to cereal cultivation—56% of units were covered with low grain stubble and 10% of units were covered with grain—which limited average visibility levels, respectively, to 63% (fields with grain stubble) and 60% (grain) (fig. 2.13). Most units (65%) also had some grass and weeds, and those units had average visibility of 63% (fig. 2.14). A small percentage of units (15%) with low scrubs had lower average visibility of 55% (fig. 2.15). In only a handful of units did walkers note pine trees, deciduous trees, maquis, apricots, *kalamboki* (maize), or small-leaf vegetation. No olives or vines were noted in the area.

A statistical correlation between visibility and density was strongest when surface conditions were limited and densities were high. There was a strong linear correlation ($r^2=0.922$) between density and visibility, for example, in units on the Koutsopetria plain with low surface visibility

(20–50%) and high artifact densities (ave. 7,900 artifacts/ha). In these cases, a small increase in visibility correlated closely with an increase in density. However, outside this high-density artifact zone, visibility and density correlated rather poorly ($r^2=0.548$). It is significant to note, then, that artifact recovery rates did not consistently increase as visibility improved.

2.4.　GEOLOGICAL AND GEOMORPHOLOGICAL SURVEY

Our previous work with the Eastern Korinthia Archaeological Survey project had trained us to value assessments of the natural and anthropogenic transformations of the landscape. In that survey, geomorphology was integrated into the fabric of the project (Tartaron et al. 2006). Team leaders joined up with geomorphology interns to lay out survey units that followed the natural breaks, the geomorphic boundaries, in the countryside. In

Fig. 2.13 *Grain stubble and grain in the survey area.*

Fig. 2.14 *Weeds in the survey area.*

FIG. 2.15   *Low scrub and shrubs in the survey area.*

continuous consultation with geomorphologists during the course of survey, archaeologists learned to recognize the evidence for the processes that made and remade the landscape over time.

Enriched by this experience, we made it a point from the start to collect geological, environmental, and geomorphological data to interpret the settlement of Koutsopetria. We gathered a range of data, such as visibility and land use, that related directly to the interpretation of individual units of the survey territory (Section 2.2.2, fig. 2.5 above). We also consulted Dr. Jay Noller, a geomorphologist and soil scientist, for feedback and assessments about the movement of soils in the area. Our reconnaissance survey in 2003, for example, documented a tremendous drop in artifact densities at the eastern end of Zone 1, which seemed to confirm the hypothesis of earlier scholars (Karageorghis and Demas 1984; Leonard 2005) that the low-lying sandy zone had once been an

embayment and natural harbor. Involving soil scientists was integral to our research design and key to our assessment of the history of the area.

Consultation with Dr. Jay Noller from 2004 to 2006 contributed directly to our work in a number of concrete ways. Most immediately, Noller provided advice, feedback, and assessments. Our survey, for instance, documented a 200-m-wide gap in artifact densities at Koutsopetria between Zones 1 and 2, immediately south of the Mavrospilios and Kokkinokremos ridges, and in soils of different composition. Although we suspected that this discontinuity in archaeological materials was associated with the construction of the water treatment facility east of Vigla, Noller's observations helped us to understand the specific lines of disturbance in the landscape. (We later learned that the construction of the water facility plant involved large-scale excavations for its foundations and routing pipes through the easternmost

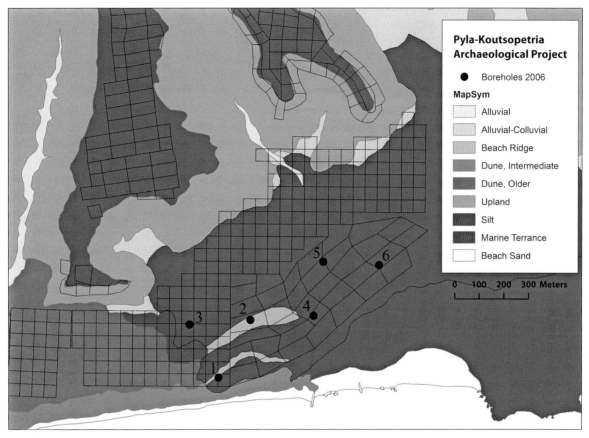

FIG. 2.16 *Geological map of the Pyla-*Koutsopetria *region showing the location of bore holes.*

section of the high-density areas associated with Koutsopetria proper.) Noller also showed us parts of the landscape, such as fields near Mavrospilios and Kokkinokremos, where artifacts probably washed in through several ancient riverbeds.

A more significant outcome of this consultation and collaboration was the production of a map of the region in terms of the soils of the surface (fig. 2.16) and subsequent coring samples. On several occasions in 2004, Noller visited the sites of the region, recording notes about geomorphology and preparing a geological map of the area based on library research and discussions with other geologists. This initial assessment provided clear justification for viewing the low-lying area as a potential ancient harbor site. Noller's study also demonstrated the uniqueness of this embayment in Cypriot coastal geography and called for a more intensive examination. In 2005, in collaboration with the Cyprus Geological Survey Department, drilling operations were conducted in the area of

the suspected embayment. The following sections summarize the results of the initial geological survey (2004–2005) and a preliminary report of the drilling operations (Noller and Zomeni 2006).

2.4.1. Geological and Archaeological Survey of the Embayment in the Koutsopetria Region (2004–2005)

During the course of a geomorphological survey of the entire Cypriot coastline, Noller and colleagues at the Cyprus Geological Survey Department (GSD) identified the lowland south of Kokkinokremos as having the definitive characteristics of a prehistoric to historic harbor, with lacustrine and alluvial Holocene silts extending for some 500–700 m inland, interrupted only by a Holocene alluvial fan at the mouth of a drainage west of the Kokkinokremos ridge. Their investigations identified a definitive paleocoastline in this lowland, recognized as a low curvilinear ridge of

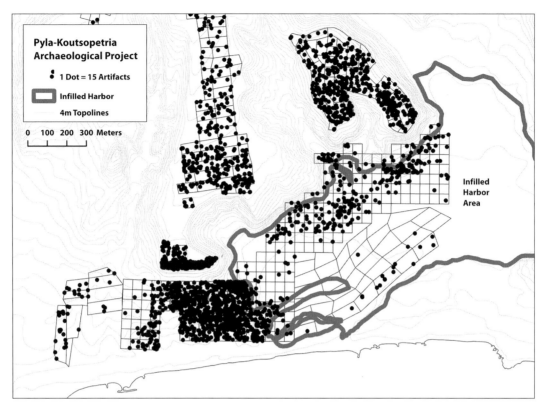

FIG. 2.17   *Distribution map of the area of the embayment, showing total density.*

shelly sand deposits 150 m inland from the current beach and running parallel with the coastal road. This low ridge enclosed a bay of 42.5 ha in surface area and protected it from waves.

Southeast of the embayment, Noller documented an east–west trending Pleistocene marine terrace dating older than 80,000 years BP that would have provided further internal shelter from the prevailing southerly winds. The southern exposure of this ridge, called Koukouphoukthia, is the location of a Late Bronze Age cemetery and settlement (Catling 1963: 168). The entrance to the embayment fell between this Pleistocene marine terrace and the extension where the remains of the Venetian fortification are visible.

Our surface survey of this embayment produced only a low-density scatter of water-worn artifacts. Of the 192 survey units incorporated within the embayment, 89 produced fewer than 10 artifacts, and 25 produced no artifacts at all (fig. 2.17). Densities were largely insubstantial, except close to the modern roads in the southwestern corner of the infilled embayment. For the entire

area, the mean density of 752 artifacts/ha is markedly lower than density of 2,960 artifacts/ha for the survey in general. Most of the artifacts date specifically to the seventeenth century or later (fig. 2.20; compare figs. 2.18 and 2.19), a pattern consistent with the dates suggested by the core samples (below) and the remains of the Venetian fortification. Artifacts of Late Roman date along the western and northern edge of Zone 2 may be explained by smearing through plowing. Early Modern artifacts in the area of the estuary proper suggest a *terminus ante quem* for the final infilling of the bay in the Medieval and post-Medieval periods.

To the north of the embayment, we documented a distinct change in soil color during our intensive survey in 2005, running roughly parallel to the coastal ridge. This color change marked the division between terrigenous (alluvial and colluvial) sediments and marine sediments. It also corresponded to a transition point in artifact scatters. Very few artifacts derive from the area of marine sediments, suggesting that this

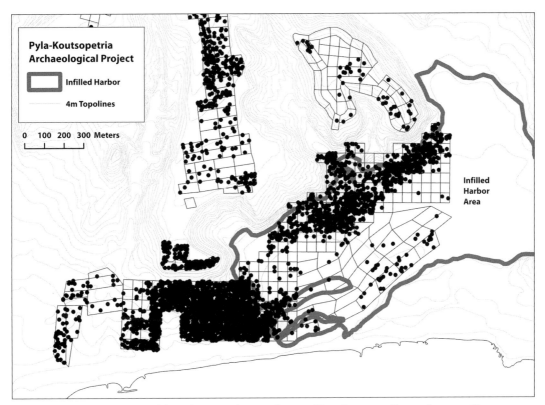

FIG. 2.18 *Distribution map of the embayment showing density of Late Roman artifacts. 1 dot = 1 artifact.*

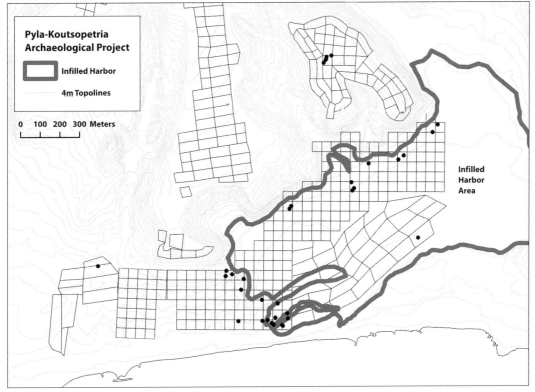

FIG. 2.19 *Distribution map of the embayment showing density of Medieval artifacts. 1 dot = 1 artifact.*

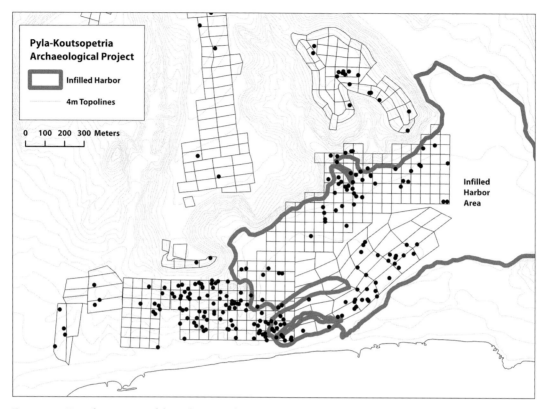

Fig. 2.20   *Distribution map of the embayment showing density of Modern artifacts. 1 dot = 1 artifact.*

area remained unavailable for use during the Late Roman period (fig. 2.18). A low to moderate density of Late Roman artifacts, however, began immediately where the surrounding terrigenous sediments started. These were deposited along the former coastline of Late Antique date now situated several hundred meters inland from the present beach.

2.4.2.   The Core Samples (2005)

More definitive evidence about the nature, depth, and age of the sediments on the plain came from a series of core samples in 2005 and 2006. In collaboration with the Cyprus Geological Survey, Noller and a team of researchers extracted cores from Koutsopetria by using air-rotary technology mounted on a truck. The soil samples were taken from the low-lying sandy fill between the Kokkinokremos ridge to the north and the low sea-side ridge of Koukoufouthkia to the south. The goal of extracting cores was to verify the existence of the ancient embayment, determine its depth, and ascertain the chronology for infilling.

2.4.2.1. The Boreholes

The half dozen boreholes were placed over a narrow band of coastal plain parallel to the coastal road (fig. 2.16), running 700 m across the entire length of Zone 2 and 30–400 m north of the current coastline. Drilled to varying depths between 5 and 27 m (ave. depth 17 m), the deepest samples came from boreholes 4 and 5 that penetrated 24–27 m below surface. Boreholes 1, 4, and 5 were designed to extract materials from the mouth of the estuary, borehole 2 to capture finer-grained sediments, and borehole 3 to sample sediments in the context of the archaeological site of Koutsopetria immediately to the west.

2.4.2.2. Preliminary Results

At the time of the fieldwork, the teams noted fine-grained marine sediments such as shelly, pebbly sand and silty sand, shelly silt, sandstone, and clay, as well as fossils like algae, sea glass, and shell. The cores demonstrated that in some locations of the coastal plain (boreholes 4 and 5), such sediments penetrate well over 20 m below surface before bedrock appears. The dominance of sandy sediments in the sample made extraction particularly difficult and has delayed full publication, but the marine character of the sediments and the depth of the cores generally confirm an interpretation of the area as an ancient estuary.

As we await the final analysis of the core samples extracted in 2005 and 2006, our conclusions about the geological history of the estuary are necessarily tentative. Yet the results of the archaeological survey support the conclusions reached by Noller and Zomeni in their preliminary analysis (2006: 1):

> The core evidence shows that the lowland was indeed a bay for all known occupations of the area — from Late Bronze Age until sometime after the Venetian Period… Nowhere else in Cyprus do we know of such a large, enclosed bay.

Even as the geological team noted no cultural material in their core samples, our surface survey has yielded very few artifacts, and most are recent. When exactly the sediments from the Pyla area watershed began to fill in the embayment and raise the land surface to within a meter of modern sea level is unknown, but it must have occurred sometime after the Medieval era. Throughout the pre-modern age, the estuary apparently offered a natural harbor for a full range of human activities.

2.5. CONCLUSIONS

The new breed of distributional survey presents an opportunity for archaeologists to explore the relationship between their methods of assessment, terms of definitions, and archaeological interpretations and historical conclusions. High-resolution surveys represent significant investments of time and energy; consequently they offer a fruitful opportunity for exploring the meaning and patterns of distributions of cultural material. The advent of more intensive survey procedures, experiments, and artifact recording systems now allow archaeologists to move beyond maps of site locations and measures of total artifact density to analyze the patterns of artifact distributions in the landscape over time. Parsing landscapes and sites not only produces more meaningful occupational biographies and diachronic histories but also finer assessments of intra-site functional variation.

Chapter 3

Survey Data and Experiments in Sampling

by David K. Pettegrew

Having explained how and why we chose our methods for sampling artifacts from the landscape, our aim in this chapter is to reflect on how well these methods recorded the quantities and types of artifacts actually present on the surface. How do our total counts of artifacts approximate the total population of artifacts in the landscape, and how accurately does our collected assemblage approximate real chronological and functional variation? Our answers to these questions undergird the picture of settlement and land use that we will trace in the rest of the volume.

To assess the relative strength and weakness of our sampling strategies, we designed experiments in 2004, 2006, and 2010 on the plain of Koutsopetria to measure its two defining aspects: the overall quantity of artifacts and the kinds of material visible in the landscape. We refer to the former (overall quantity of artifacts) as the *total density* of material and have computed it from the total count of artifacts in each survey unit. We refer to the latter (the kinds of material) as *chronotypes* or *batches* (groups) of chronotypes, and have derived it from the collection of artifacts from the surface.

In the different experiments, we compared the results of our normal method of fieldwalking, which sampled 20% of the surface of a unit for total density and chronotypes, to the results of a more intensive examination of the surface. In the first set of experiments, conducted in 2004 and 2006 (Section 3.1), our more intensive method involved "hoovering" a 5% sample of the unit to determine 1) the total density of artifacts and 2) temporal and functional data of chronotypes present. In the second set of experiments, carried out in 2010 (3.2), we hoovered a 6.25% sample of the unit to ascertain 1) the total density of artifacts and 2) fabric, vessel part, and artifact class (pottery, tile, lithics, and other) of the artifacts present.

Altogether, the experiments of 2004, 2006, and 2010 support the view, outlined in the previous chapter, that our counting and collection strategies marked an efficient approach to documenting artifacts in the landscape. The experiments also address a range of specific critiques of the chronotype system (Section 2.3.2), namely, problems of representation and quantification of surface assemblages, and the practicalities of implementing chronotype collection. The 2010 experiments, moreover, were designed to assess the questions of surveyor experience and dusting on sherds in the area of the coastal plain.

In the final part of this chapter (3.3), we discuss the results of the experiments collectively to evaluate the relative completeness of our record of the landscape in terms of total density and chronotypes or batches. These experiments provide significant insight into the quality of our data and inform the substantive discussion of distribution

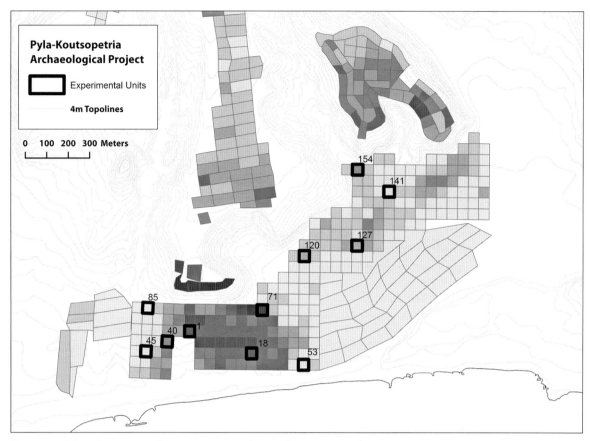

FIG. 3.1   *Map of survey area showing experimental units of 2004, 2006, and 2010.*

patterns in Chapter 5, while also contributing to a growing body of literature that adopts archaeological experiments to calibrate the results and interpretations of intensive pedestrian survey (For recent work in experimental survey, cf. Schon 2000, 2002; Gibson 2001: 428–29; Meyer and Schon 2003: 52–56; Tartaron et al. 2006; Banning 2006, 2011).

3.1.   THE 2004 AND 2006 EXPERIMENTS: PEDESTRIAN SURVEY (20%) VS. HOOVERING (5%)

During the 2004 and 2006 survey seasons, we resurveyed 21 grid units on the Koutsopetria plain using more intensive techniques than the 20% sample obtained during the initial gridded survey in 2004 and 2005 (fig. 3.1). Specifically, we were interested in comparing the data produced by 1) our original gridded pedestrian survey, where fieldwalkers spaced at 10 m intervals counted and collected a maximum of 20% of the surface of the

unit (the 20% sample was always an ideal that was usually reduced through surface vegetation: Section 2.3.3), with 2) a more intensive hoovering of all artifacts from a focused 5% sample of the survey unit (resurvey). In 2004, our experiments consisted of collecting and counting *all artifacts* from a 5% sample (*Hoovering Circles*) of 10 survey units that we had surveyed with pedestrian methods earlier in the same field season. In 2006, we used the same method to examine an additional 11 units for total density, but we *did not collect* artifacts; experimental units in 2006 resurveyed survey units walked in 2004 and 2005.

Thus, between the 2004 and 2006 seasons, we intensively hoovered 21 survey units, which comprised 8.6% of the total number (n=245) of units on the Koutsopetria plain. Ten of these 21 units (2004) produced samples of total density and chronotypes that we compared directly with the total density and chronotypes of pedestrian survey during the same year; 11 of the 21 units (2006) produced total density figures that we compared with the total density figures from pedestrian survey during the previous year. It is also noteworthy that the 2004 experiments resurveyed units with the same set of environmental and surface conditions, while the 2006 experiments resurveyed units after a new plowing. Since the hoovering circles in 2004 had a radius of 5 m and a diameter of 10 m, they overlapped to varying degrees the transects of the previous pedestrian survey spaced every 10 m. To some extent, then, the experimental sample missed objects previously collected by fieldwalkers and underrepresented the count and diversity of the surface assemblage. Thus, the differences between experimental and pedestrian samples may be even greater than we outline below.

The focus of this assessment was to compare the quantity and quality of data produced from our standard fieldwalking techniques to a more intensive but smaller experimental unit, yet the experiments also introduced and compared the additional variables of visibility and field conditions. In both years, hoovering neutralized variation in surface visibility by sweeping the entire surface. Because the 2006 experiments examined units surveyed in previous years, we can assess the degree to which different surface conditions including plowing and visibility levels influenced densities.

In each year, we numbered the experimental circles by assigning a decimal place after the number of the unit in which the circle was located (e.g., Unit 18.1, 71.1). Each hoovering circle had a radius of 5.1 m (80 m²), which represented a 5% sample of the area of each unit (1,600 m²). The teams of surveyors "hoovered" the circles to collect all artifacts visible on the surface. As we noted in the previous chapter, "hoovering" underscores the method of sampling: hands-and-knees searching for artifacts. Surveyors gathered together all artifacts present and marked their progress with ropes attached to central points. Teams took as long as was necessary to remove all material from inside the circles, and the time spent varied from thirty minutes to four hours, depending upon the amount of material in the unit.

In the 2004 and 2006 seasons, we hoovered the circles by gathering all material and counting the number of individual fragments of pottery, tile, lithic, and other artifact types. In the 2004 experiments, besides counting artifacts, we also collected all pottery sherds and lithics. We sorted and recorded hundreds of tiles on site because they had a volume too great to remove from the field; the pottery and other small artifacts we took to the museum for analysis and accession in the project database (artifacts from the experiments are identified by the decimal point and number 1 after the unit: 18.1, 40.1, 45.1, 53.1, 71.1, 85.1, 120.1, 127.1, 141.1, and 154.1).

In both years, we selected units for experimental survey according to two criteria. First, we sought to resurvey units with a wide range of densities, and consequently selected units that roughly corresponded to the quartile breaks in overall artifact densities for the survey area as a whole up to that time. We were especially concerned with sampling from the lowest-density units because our analysis of data from the Eastern Korinthia Archaeological Survey suggested that our sampling strategy produced the most distorted picture of the artifacts on the surface in such units, and that higher-intensity survey could yield a more diverse assemblage (Caraher, Nakassis, and Pettegrew 2006). Second, we sought to sample units distributed across the entire gridded area of the site (see fig. 3.1). Since our gridded survey was still ongoing in 2005, the placement of our experimental units in 2004 obviously reflected the survey grid to that point, with an emphasis on the area surrounding the excavated early Christian buildings at Koutsopetria. To compensate for this bias, we placed some of our 2006 experimental units in areas of the site documented in 2005. Although these 21 units were not spaced at equal intervals, we did resurvey units from each part of the coastal plain, including areas associated with significant features, such as the well-built, stepped, check dam (Unit 154) and the remains of the so-called Venetian castle (Unit 53).

The 2004 and 2006 units produced total density data comparable to the total densities assessed through our standard gridded survey methods, and the 2004 units produced comparable functional and chronological data in a more complete sample of chronotypes. These results allow us to reflect on the two kinds of density data generated by our pedestrian method: a) variations in the total density of artifacts throughout the survey area, and b) the chronological and functional character of the assemblages. We have the ability to determine how a more intensive but focused sample of the landscape (5% sample via total collection) produced data differently than our original sample of 20% of the same units via pedestrian survey.

3.1.1.   Artifact Counts of Pedestrian Survey vs. Hoovering Circles

We have tabulated the results of the experiments related to total artifact density in Table 3.1, which compares 1) the total count and density from 20% pedestrian survey, and 2) the total count and density from 5% hoovering circles. To compare the different percentages of the two samples (5% vs. 20%), we have converted the counts based on samples into putative density figures for 100% of the unit and then corrected for differences in visibility (*estimated totals*). The Putative Total Density represents an estimation of total density if the 5% or 20% sample were extended across the 40 × 40 m unit with 100% visibility. For example, to determine the Putative Total Density of a 5% hoovering circle of a unit with 50% visibility, we would multiply the circle total count × 20 (i.e., a 5% sample = 1/20 of the area of the unit) × 2 (i.e., 50% visibility indicates only half the area of the unit was visible). Or, as another example, to compute the Putative Total Density for a 20% pedestrian survey with 100% visibility, we would multiply the total count

Table 3.1   Total counts and densities of ceramic artifacts compared between pedestrian survey and hoovering.

Grid Unit	Density Rank	Pedestrian Total (20%)	Hoovering Total (5%)	Visibility Original	Pedestrian Estimated Total	Visibility Resurvey	Hoovering Estimated Total	Factor Difference in Estimate
34	Very Low	3	18	60%	25	100%	360	14.4
85*	Very Low	3	13	40%	38	40%	650	17.3
102	Very Low	6	32	50%	60	90%	711	11.9
151	Very Low	1	8	80%	6	90%	178	28.4
169	Very Low	2	4	80%	13	90%	89	7.1
173	Very Low	8	14	70%	57	100%	280	4.9
226	Very Low	1	0	90%	6	100%	0	0.0
45*	Low	17	70	60%	142	60%	2333	16.5
53*	Low	20	18	80%	125	80%	450	3.6
141*	Low	13	37	40%	163	40%	1850	11.4
191	Low	14	11	100%	70	100%	220	3.1
40*	Moderate	117	435	100%	585	100%	8700	14.9
66	Moderate	96	63	20%	2400	100%	1260	0.5
120*	Moderate	65	86	90%	361	90%	1911	5.3
127*	Moderate	88	203	40%	1100	40%	10150	9.2
18*	High	437	736	60%	3642	60%	24533	6.7
61	High	243	1,274	30%	4050	100%	25480	6.3
63	High	218	477	40%	2725	100%	9540	3.5
71*	High	537	1,096	70%	3836	70%	31314	8.2
154*	High	160	236	90%	889	90%	5244	5.9
187	High	105	31	100%	525	100%	620	1.2

× 5 (i.e., a 20% sample = 1/5 of the unit) × 1 (i.e., 100% visibility indicates the entire surface of the unit was examined). Calibrating for differences in sample area and visibility provides a systematic, if approximate, correction for the percentage of the surface sampled by the different methods. The figures show the *factor difference* (final column) between the putative total densities based on our 5% experimental circles and 20% pedestrian survey.

It is important to state at the outset our recognition of the complexity of intra-unit density variation and the relationship of artifact density to surface visibility. Archaeologists have suggested more sophisticated adjustments for surface visibility, for example, including the observation that the relationship between visibility and artifact density is not fully linear (for discussion, cf. Schon 2000, 2002). Moreover, density can vary tremendously across a 40 × 40 m unit — as we will outline below — which challenges an estimation of putative density based on only a 5% sample. Nonetheless, the comparison consistently highlights the differences between sampling techniques and thereby provides a means of reflecting on the particular procedures we adopted for the survey as a whole.

The most obvious conclusion to draw from the comparison is that the more intensive scrutiny of the surface in the hoovering circles produced significantly higher artifact densities than standard pedestrian fieldwalking methods. In 17 of the 21 units, the 5% hoovering circles produced more artifacts than the 20% sample of the surface produced through our standard survey. More dramatic is the factor increase between the density of artifacts in *Putative Total Density (Pedestrian)* and *Putative Total Density (Hoovering)*, which ranges from .5 to 28 and averages ca. 8.6. With only two exceptions, scrutinizing the surface using more intensive techniques produced at least three times the density levels (and usually many times more) than less intensive techniques that covered a greater percentage of the unit. Put another way, the pedestrian putative total density was on average 25.4% of the hoovering putative total density.

The numbers also show another pattern between the different survey units. The factor difference between our pedestrian survey and

hoovering circles tends to decrease as overall density increases. For example, in the seven units measured as "very low" density in the course of pedestrian survey, hoovering produced an artifact density on average 12 times higher than pedestrian survey. That average factor difference decreases to 8.6 in units with "low" density rank, 7.5 in units with moderate density, and 5.3 in units with high density. Hence, although total density nearly always increased in a more intensive (hoovering) but smaller (5%) sample of surface, the increase was most dramatic in units with the lowest density ranking.

It is important to highlight that the different environmental contexts between 2004 and 2006 did not change the overall results of dramatic factor increase in density with hoovering. The experiments in 2004 occurred with the same visibility and field conditions, while the 2006 experiments resurveyed fields after fresh plowing and with different visibilities. In both years, hoovering dramatically increased the putative total density, with the 2004 experimental units showing an average factor difference increase of 9.9 in total density, and the 2006 experiments showing 7.4. That there was a greater difference in densities produced by pedestrian 20% vs. hoovering 5% methods *during* the same year (2004) of survey than between successive years (2004 and 2006) proves that the total density increase was not simply a result of changed field conditions between years.

The consistent pattern, then, is that more intensive approaches greatly increase putative total artifact density even when significantly less ground is covered. This pattern is consistent enough to rule out the possibility that small hoovering circles simply sampled a different part of the survey unit than pedestrian survey and reflect sub-unit variation in density. Indeed, our 2010 experiments (Section 3.2) were designed in part to rule out this possibility. The more obvious explanation for the general pattern is that pedestrian surveyors walking across units miss a large proportion of visible artifacts because of the pace of walking and the distance between standing position and the surface. Whether the additional quantity of pottery counted through more intensive and time-consuming methods like the total collection circles is ultimately worth the investment of time and energy (cf. Section 3.3) depends upon a closer analysis of the chronological and functional attributes of the finds.

3.1.2. The Nature of Data in Pedestrian Survey vs. Hoovering Circles

We analyzed the artifacts collected from the 10 total collection circles in 2004 in the same way as artifacts from standard survey units. The experiment, then, allows us to compare how two different sampling systems represent the attributes of artifacts in a survey unit: the pedestrian systematic collection of a *selective representation of chronotypes* from four 10 m intervals (20%) across the entire unit and the more intensive *total collection of artifacts* in a smaller sample of the unit (5%).

We have argued elsewhere that chronotype collection strategies are as effective for determining the chronology of a unit as more intensive regimes that tend to produce redundant chronological data (Caraher, Nakassis, and Pettegrew 2006; Moore 2008).

If more intensive hoovering of 5% of the units produced a greater quantity of pottery than a sample of chronotypes from 20% pedestrian survey, hoovering also produced slightly higher resolution in the attributes of the fabric classes of the artifacts (Table 3.2). Hoovering produced significantly more material from each fabric group (See the final two rows showing "Average Pedestrian" and "Average Hoovering") but also changed the relative proportions of coarse, fine, and kitchen ware. Coarse ware sherds comprised on average 80% of the overall pottery of pedestrian units, but 88% in hoovered

Table 3.2 Comparison of relative percentages of fabric groups between pedestrian (20%) sample and hoovering (5%).

UNIT	COARSE	%	FINE	%	COOKING	%	TOTAL	%
85	2	100%	0	0%	0	0%	2	100%
85.1	13	100%	0	0%	0	0%	13	100%
45	12	80%	1	7%	2	13%	15	100%
45.1	28	80%	3	9%	4	11%	35	100%
53	3	43%	3	43%	1	14%	7	100%
53.1	7	88%	1	13%	0	0%	8	100%
141	9	82%	2	18%	0	0%	11	100%
141.1	31	86%	1	3%	4	11%	36	100%
40	37	80%	3	7%	6	13%	46	100%
40.1	260	85%	12	4%	35	11%	307	100%
120	43	98%	1	2%	0	0%	44	100%
120.1	75	91%	3	4%	4	5%	82	100%
127	52	91%	4	7%	1	2%	57	100%
127.1	173	91%	7	4%	10	5%	190	100%
18	88	66%	13	10%	32	24%	133	100%
18.1	224	91%	6	2%	17	7%	247	100%
71	53	61%	12	14%	22	25%	87	100%
71.1	485	73%	49	7%	133	20%	667	100%
154	96	98%	0	0%	2	2%	98	100%
154.1	224	98%	4	2%	1	0%	229	100%
Average Pedestrian	39.5	80%	3.9	11%	6.6	9%	50	100%
Average Hoovering	152	88%	8.6	5%	20.8	7%	181.4	100%

units. Fine ware sherds, which comprised 11% of the pottery of pedestrian units, formed only 5% of hoovered units, and kitchen ware dropped less markedly from 9% to 7% between pedestrian and hoovered units. In short, our normal survey procedure recorded high levels of amphora, coarse, and medium-coarse sherds, but it overrepresented fine and kitchen ware sherds at the expense of coarse wares. The probable reason for this is that since the chronotype sampling method discourages collecting duplicate sherds of the same type, our fieldwalkers collected fewer of the most abundant artifacts in the landscape, coarse-ware body sherds. Total collection, on the other hand, allowed us to see more of the redundancy.

There is also an evident correlation between the overall density of the unit and the improvement in resolution of fabric groups. In the lowest-density unit (85), hoovering did not alter the general picture of fabric groups: the number of coarse ware sherds increased with more intensive collection, but fine ware and kitchen ware sherds did not. In the three low-density units (45, 53, and 141), hoovering produced consistently more examples of coarse ware, but did not consistently increase the sample of fine and kitchen ware: sometimes more fine ware or kitchen ware sherds were noted through hoovering, but in other cases, fieldwalkers collected fewer. In moderate and high-density units (40, 120, 127, 18, 71, 154), in contrast, the number of coarse ware, fine ware, and kitchen ware sherds generally increased with hoovering, but coarse wares usually assumed a greater relative percentage of the total at the expense of fine and kitchen ware (cf. the percentage figures in the final row of Table 3.2 comparing the average of pedestrian vs. hoovering). Thus, hoovering 5% of survey units produced more total artifacts than pedestrian methods, but these additional sherds were mostly coarse in fabric, and fine and kitchen ware sherds did not increase in lower-density units.

In respect to the parts of ceramic vessels, hoovering did not greatly affect the relative proportions (Table 3.3). Although hoovering produced on average more examples of each vessel part than a 20% pedestrian sample, and especially increased the number of rims and body sherds, hoovering made very little overall difference in the overall propor-

tions of vessel parts (cf. the individual rows of the table and the final "average" row). Rim sherds tended to increase in relative proportion with hoovering, but bases, handles, and sherds sometimes increased and sometimes decreased; the average of these percentages shows that body sherds increased slightly in their relative percentage, and rims, bases, and handles decreased slightly. Considering the overall density thresholds of these units highlights no consistently significant patterns.

As for chronological properties, more intensive hoovering did not contribute to a better understanding of the presence or absence of periods in the survey units (Table 3.4). For the 10 units resurveyed in 2004, the 20% pedestrian chronotype collection produced an assemblage representing on average 5.4 total periods per unit, whereas 5% total collection circles showed a meager increase to an average of 5.9 periods per unit. This shows that total collection circles produced a slightly more chronologically refined assemblage, but it is notable that half of the units (n=5) produced the same number of chronological periods as the normal collection. In some cases, the additional periods represented in total collection had very broad chronological ranges such as "Post-Prehistoric" or "Ancient" that contributed little to refining the dating of artifacts in the unit. Nor did the narrow periods appear more frequently in total collection units than in pedestrian survey units. A couple of units (45 and 85) showed no change at all in resolution, and other units either declined (n=3), improved (n=1), or simply changed (n=4). For example, in some units (18, 120, 127, 141, 154), total collection revealed Cypro-Archaic, Cypro-Classical to Hellenistic, Hellenistic, Early Roman, Roman, Medieval-Modern, and Modern pottery not noted in pedestrian survey. In other units (18, 40, 53, 71, 120, 127, 141), total collection through hoovering circles missed examples of Bronze Age, Cypro-Geometric to Archaic, Cypro-Archaic to Hellenistic, Cypro-Classical, Hellenistic, Early Roman, Late Medieval, Ottoman, Medieval-Modern, and Modern noted through our standard pedestrian chronotype collections. Evidently, neither of the two main variables in this experiment — intensity of scrutiny (walking vs. hoovering) and the extent of sampling (20% vs.

Table 3.3   Comparison of extant part (RBHS) between pedestrian 20% sample and hoovering 5%.

Unit	Rim	%	Base	%	Handle	%	Sherd	%	Total	%
85	0	0.0%	0	0.0%	0	0.0%	2	100.0%	2	100.0%
85.1	0	0.0%	0	0.0%	0	0.0%	13	100.0%	13	100.0%
45	1	3.0%	1	3.0%	0	0.0%	31	93.9%	33	100.0%
45.1	3	8.3%	1	2.8%	1	2.8%	31	86.1%	36	100.0%
53	2	15.4%	0	0.0%	0	0.0%	11	84.6%	13	100.0%
53.1	0	0.0%	0	0.0%	0	0.0%	15	100.0%	15	100.0%
141	0	0.0%	1	8.3%	0	0.0%	11	91.7%	12	100.0%
141.1	2	5.6%	0	0.0%	4	11.1%	30	83.3%	36	100.0%
40	2	1.4%	2	1.4%	7	5.0%	129	92.1%	140	100.0%
40.1	11	3.7%	2	0.7%	21	7.0%	265	88.6%	299	100.0%
120	1	2.1%	0	0.0%	7	14.9%	39	83.0%	47	100.0%
120.1	2	2.3%	1	1.2%	6	7.0%	77	89.5%	86	100.0%
127	4	6.0%	0	0.0%	8	11.9%	55	82.1%	67	100.0%
127.1	5	2.6%	4	2.1%	9	4.6%	176	90.7%	194	100.0%
18	10	2.0%	3	0.6%	18	3.6%	473	93.8%	504	100.0%
18.1	12	4.7%	2	0.8%	17	6.6%	226	87.9%	257	100.0%
71	8	2.2%	8	2.2%	9	2.4%	345	93.2%	370	100.0%
71.1	22	3.2%	5	0.7%	13	1.9%	643	94.1%	683	100.0%
154	6	6.7%	0	0.0%	14	15.6%	70	77.8%	90	100.0%
154.1	6	2.6%	3	1.3%	3	1.3%	219	94.8%	231	100.0%
Average Pedestrian	3.4	3.9%	1.5	1.6%	6.3	5.3%	116.6	89.2%	127.8	100.0%
Average Hoovering	6.3	3.3%	1.8	0.9%	7.4	4.2%	169.5	91.5%	185	100.0%

5% of the surface area) — consistently produced a more chronologically diverse assemblage.

For the sake of comparison, we have shown in the same table the chronological patterns for the "diagnostic artifacts" from 5% hoovering and 20% pedestrian chronotype samples. (By the term "diagnostic," we mean feature sherds and artifacts with surface treatment that are typically used to attribute chronological value to artifact scatters. See Section 2.3.2.) Interestingly, the "diagnostic artifacts" in most units produced very similar chronological information as total collection or chronotype samples, but also eliminated four kinds of chronological information. First, examining

only diagnostic sherds usually eliminated artifacts associated with only broad periods such as "Ancient," "Ancient Historic," "Late Helladic–Modern Present," and "Post-Prehistoric." Second, examining the diagnostic sherds eliminated in half of the units (40, 53, 71, 127, and 154) certain periods such as the Medieval–Modern and Modern periods, which were identified by plain body sherd of particular fabric and hardness. Third, one unit (85) was of sufficiently low density that chronological resolution disappeared entirely when body sherds were excluded. Fourth, examining only diagnostic sherds reduced knowledge of the relative quantities of particular periods. In short, the collection

Table 3.4 Comparison of chronological resolution for four different samples of the landscape.

Unit	Pedestrian 20% (Chronotypes)	Pedestrian 20% (Diagnostics)	Hoovering 5% (Total Collection)	Hoovering 5% (Diagnostics)
85	Ancient Historic, Late Roman		Ancient Historic, Late Roman	
45	Ancient Historic, Roman, Late Roman	Roman, Late Roman	Ancient Historic, Roman, Late Roman	Ancient Historic, Roman, Late Roman
53	Ancient Historic, Bronze Age, Late Roman, Ottoman/Venetian, Medieval–Modern, Modern	Bronze Age, Late Roman, Ottoman/Venetian, Medieval–Modern, Modern	Ancient Historic, Late Roman, Medieval–Modern	Ancient Historic, Late Roman
141	Ancient Historic, Bronze Age, Late Roman, Modern	Bronze Age, Late Roman, Modern	Post-Prehistoric, Ancient Historic, Roman, Late Roman, Modern	Post-Prehistoric, Ancient Historic, Roman, Late Roman, Modern
40	Post-Prehistoric, Ancient Historic, Archaic–Hellenistic, Classical, Roman, Late Roman, Present Modern	Post-Prehistoric, Ancient Historic, Archaic–Hellenistic, Classical, Roman, Late Roman	Late Helladic–Modern Present, Post-Prehistoric, Ancient Historic, Roman, Late Roman	Post-Prehistoric, Ancient Historic, Roman, Late Roman
120	Ancient, Ancient Historic, Geometric–Archaic, Late Roman	Ancient Historic, Geometric–Archaic, Late Roman	Post-Prehistoric, Ancient Historic, Archaic, Roman, Late Roman	Archaic, Roman, Late Roman
127	Ancient Historic, Classical–Hellenistic, Roman, Late Roman	Ancient Historic, Classical–Hellenistic, Roman, Late Roman	Ancient Historic, Roman, Early Roman, Late Roman, Medieval–Modern, Modern	Ancient Historic, Roman, Early Roman, Late Roman
18	Ancient Historic, Roman, Early Roman, Late Roman, Roman–Modern, Medieval–Modern, Modern	Ancient Historic, Roman, Early Roman, Late Roman, Roman–Modern, Medieval–Modern, Modern	Ancient, Post-Prehistoric, Ancient Historic, Hellenistic, Roman, Late Roman	Post-Prehistoric, Ancient Historic, Hellenistic, Roman, Late Roman
71	Ancient Historic, Classical, Hellenistic, Roman, Early Roman, Late Roman, Late Medieval	Ancient Historic, Classical, Hellenistic, Roman, Early Roman, Late Roman, Late Medieval	Late Helladic–Modern Present, Post-Prehistoric, Ancient Historic, Hellenistic, Roman, Early Roman, Late Roman, Medieval–Modern, Modern	Post-Prehistoric, Ancient Historic, Hellenistic, Roman, Early Roman, Late Roman
154	Ancient Historic, Roman, Late Roman, Modern	Ancient Historic, Roman, Late Roman	Ancient, Post-Prehistoric, Ancient Historic, Classical-Hellenistic, Roman, Late Roman, Modern	Ancient Historic, Classical-Hellenistic, Roman, Late Roman

strategies generated similar estimates of chronology in the landscape, but significant information was lost when only the diagnostics were considered. In the fifth chapter, we will return to these points through sections on differential visibility (Section 5.1.4) and aoristic analysis (Section 5.1.5); that discussion will show how even chronologically coarse data contributes to a more nuanced interpretation of the landscape.

The 5% hoovering and 20% pedestrian survey contributed slightly different assessments of functional and typological diversity in the landscape. Higher-intensity survey methods produced more varied assemblages. On average, pedestrian chronotype collections produced 11.9 chronotypes per unit and 2.1 chronotypes per chronological period, and hoovering circles produced 15.6 chronotypes per unit for 2.5 chronotypes per period. For the densest and most diverse period at Koutsopetria, the Late Roman period, hoovering led to substantial increase in the number of chronotypes: standard survey unit collection produced 49 chronotypes, whereas hoovering circles produced 69 chronotypes. Two units in particular, 40 and 71, registered significant gains in the number of Late Roman chronotypes present, and Unit 71 recorded a greater number of Roman artifacts.

In one other respect, hoovering circles produced higher-resolution results. In the case of non-ceramic artifacts such as metal, glass, and stone, examining the ground more intensively revealed numerous additional artifacts. Overall, hoovering produced twice (n=10) the glass count of pedestrian survey (n=5), three times the metal count (6 vs. 2), and 14 times the count of marble, gypsum, and stone. This is a point we will consider in more detail in the context of our discussion of the 2010 experiments.

The results of the 2004 experiments are vital to understanding the assemblage produced by standard chronotype sampling. We have shown that traditional diagnostic grab samples produce the lowest resolution results from our survey sample by missing both chronologically and functionally diagnostic artifacts. Hoovering at 5%, in contrast, produces results that showed little consistent improvement in either chronological or functional resolution over the 20% chronotype sample.

Chronotype sampling offers a useful balance that captured the right amount of information in a relatively efficient manner.

3.2. THE 2010 EXPERIMENTS: PEDESTRIAN RESURVEY AND HOOVERING SUB-UNITS

In 2010, we designed an additional experiment to refine the results of our previous ones. Although we had compared pedestrian survey to hoovering, the 5% circles and 20% pedestrian survey marked very different percentages of the unit examined as well as areas of the unit that did not overlap in consistent ways. We questioned whether the differences in area covered within the unit contributed as much to the results of our experiments as the differences in sampling methods. Aware of the substantial fluctuations in density possible within a 40 × 40 m unit, we sought in our 2010 experiment to hoover a greater percentage (25%) of the 40 × 40 m unit through larger sub-units (10 × 10 m = 100 m² = 6.25% of the unit). Our aim then, was firstly to compare the densities and kinds of artifacts documented through 20% pedestrian survey sample with the *total population* of artifacts visible on the ground. Our second goal was to assess the degree of intra-unit variation in artifact density through the different methods of hoovering and pedestrian survey.

Due to the significant investment in time and manpower needed to do this experiment, we decided to only resurvey a single unit, which we laid in the highest-density area immediately northeast of the excavated apse of the early Christian basilica. We placed this resurvey unit to overlap exactly with Survey Unit #1, a grid square of 40 × 40 m surveyed in 2004 northeast of the enclosed excavated part of Koutsopetria. We divided the unit into sixteen 10 × 10 m sub-units, each marking 6.25% of the overall unit area (1,600 m²), an area slightly greater than that encompassed by the 5% circles of the previous experiments. Each grid square in Unit [1] was given the prefix of G followed by a number between 1 and 16 (as shown in fig. 3.2).

There were two phases to the experiment. In the first phase, four fieldwalkers aligned in four transects (T1–T4) walked across the unit from

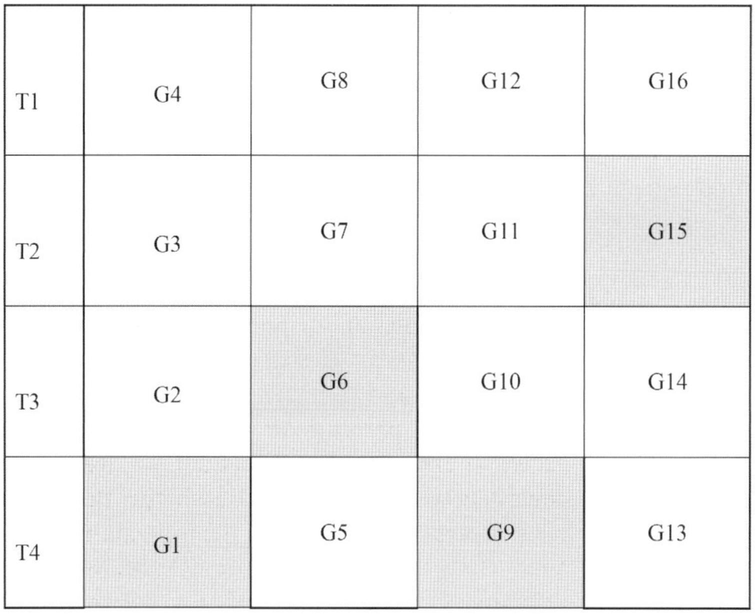

T1	G4	G8	G12	G16
T2	G3	G7	G11	G15
T3	G2	G6	G10	G14
T4	G1	G5	G9	G13

FIG. 3.2   *The grid squares and survey transects of the 2010 experiments. Lightly shaded cells are sub-units selected for hoovering.*

west to east recording *all* artifacts visible in their 2-m wide swath, giving a 20% count of artifacts for every 10 m of space across a 40 m transect (fig. 3.2). The fieldwalkers *did not collect* the artifacts observed in their swaths according to the chronotype system, as they would in normal fieldwalking procedures. Rather, they *counted* sub-tract artifact totals every 10 m, thereby providing densities for each of the sub-units (G1–G16) and allowing an assessment of the fluctuating quantities of pottery, tile, and lithic artifacts across the survey unit.

In this phase, we repeated this procedure three different times (Tables 3.5 and 3.6). The first time a group of untrained students walked the units. We

decided to have students walk the units again the following day after a light rain had washed off some of the dust from the sherds. Finally, a group of experienced fieldwalkers walked the unit and counted artifacts on the same day after the light rain. The variables in these three episodes of pedestrian survey were experience (significant experience vs. no training) and the amount of sherd crusting or dust, two points of critique of the chronotype system (Section 2.3.2). Otherwise, environmental factors were constant (100% visibility, freshly plowed, loose soil, occasional low weeds, and surface clast of cobble and coarse gravel), as were other environmental factors such as temperature and time of day.

In the second phase of our 2010 experiments, we selected four 10 × 10 m sub-units for hoovering based on the sub-unit densities observed by the experienced fieldwalkers. As with past experiments, we selected sub-units to cover the range of density variation, with representatives from the lowest density quartile (G15), highest density quartile (G9), and two middle quartiles (G1 and G6). Our procedure for hoovering was for a team of 5 volunteers to walk very slowly in adjacent passes across each selected square, gathering together in a corner of the unit all the artifacts present. The initial pass typically missed numerous artifacts so additional passes were necessary to vacuum the

Table 3.5   Three estimates of total count, with variables being experience vs. inexperience among walkers, and dry vs. wet conditions.

UNIT	POTTERY	TILE	OTHER	TOTAL
Inexperienced Walkers in Dry Conditions	522	414	6	942
Inexperienced Walkers in Wet Conditions	684	369	3	1,056
Experienced Walkers in Wet Conditions	468	460	12	940

Table 3.6 Estimates of counts per 10 m grid square by inexperienced walkers (1),inexperienced walkers after rain (2), and experienced walkers after rain (3).

POTTERY COUNT						
T1	1	16	15	19	32	82
	2	50	32	56	60	198
	3	29	22	36	41	128
T2	1	90	28	28	27	173
	2	54	27	35	39	155
	3	17	14	12	14	57
T3	1	18	31	19	29	97
	2	29	28	35	27	119
	3	32	32	45	37	146
T4	1	27	34	48	61	170
	2	19	30	70	93	212
	3	20	26	46	45	137

TILE COUNT						
T1	1	11	6	9	8	34
	2	14	6	10	13	43
	3	19	15	15	11	60
T2	1	70	22	13	11	116
	2	20	20	14	28	82
	3	8	32	26	27	93
T3	1	11	44	19	27	101
	2	23	45	34	20	122
	3	35	28	40	31	134
T4	1	36	52	23	52	163
	2	11	25	48	38	122
	3	38	41	51	43	173

OTHER COUNT						
T1	1	0	0	0	2	2
	2	0	1	0	1	2
	3	0	0	0	0	0
T2	1	0	0	0	0	0
	2	0	0	0	1	1
	3	4	3	2	0	9
T3	1	1	0	1	0	2
	2	0	0	0	0	0
	3	1	0	0	0	1
T4	1	0	1	1	0	2
	2	0	0	0	0	0
	3	2	0	0	0	2

TOTAL COUNT						
T1	1	27	21	28	42	118
	2	64	39	66	74	243
	3	48	37	51	52	188
T2	1	160	50	41	38	289
	2	74	47	49	68	238
	3	29	49	40	41	159
T3	1	30	75	39	56	200
	2	52	73	69	47	241
	3	68	60	85	68	281
T4	1	63	87	72	113	335
	2	30	55	118	131	334
	3	60	67	97	88	312

Table 3.7 Difference between lowest and highest fieldwalker count according to sub-unit.

POTTERY COUNT					
T1	34	17	37	28	116
T2	73	14	23	25	116
T3	14	3	26	10	49
T4	8	8	24	48	75

TILE COUNT					
T1	8	9	6	5	26
T2	62	12	13	17	34
T3	24	17	21	11	33
T4	27	27	28	14	51

OTHER COUNT					
T1	0	1	0	2	2
T2	4	3	2	1	9
T3	1	0	1	0	2
T4	2	1	1	0	2

TOTAL COUNT					
T1	37	18	38	34	125
T2	131	3	9	30	140
T3	38	15	46	21	81
T4	33	32	46	43	22

surface completely; surveyors took to their hands and knees in the final passes to ensure that they did not miss anything. Each total collection sub-unit was 10 × 10 m, representing 1/16 (6.25%) of the 1,600 m² survey unit; with four sub-units, we hoovered 25% of the survey unit. In contrast to the few minutes it took to walk across a sub-unit, it took an hour to hoover a low-density sub-unit and two hours to hoover a high-density sub-unit.

Shortage of time prevented us from taking all artifacts back to the Larnaca District Museum for analysis into specific chronotypes. However, we were able to collect some general kinds of information in the field: material class (pottery, tile, lithic, other), vessel part (rim, base, handle, body sherd), and fabric group (fine / semi-fine, coarse / medium-coarse, and kitchen). As discussed in sections 3.2.3 and 3.2.4 below, our quantification of these categories provides interesting insights about our pedestrian chronotype sampling strategy.

3.2.1. *Resurvey, Environment, and Experience*

The results of the first phase of the survey (the three pedestrian survey exercises) are shown in the tables below. In one respect, none of the variables tested in this phase of the experiment changed the assessment of total density for artifact classes in the unit in any significant way (Table 3.5). The total counts for three different survey transects across the unit varied only between 940 and 1056 total artifacts — a pattern that is easily explained by certain fieldwalkers looking more closely than others, or a slightly different path taken in the transect. While walkers in each survey episode were spaced at 10 m intervals, a walker who veered even a meter to the left or right might see different artifacts within the transect. Only two overall differences require more explanation. First, the proportion of pottery to tile appears to be more equal for experienced fieldwalkers (ca. 1:1) than inexperienced (1.3:1 and 1.9:1), and, second, experienced walkers counted significantly more "other" artifacts than inexperienced walkers. We will consider the reasons for these patterns later in the section.

Changes in overall density may even out over the course of a 40 × 40 m unit (Table 3.5), but there is great variety in the counts of the individual 10 × 10 m sub-units (Tables 3.6 and 3.7). In some transects (e.g., T3 Pottery; T1 Tile), one can see comparable counts across all sub-units, no matter the level of experience or the condition of rain. In other transects (e.g., T4 Pottery), the counts are clearly different but still follow the general pattern of artifacts increasing from west to east. For others, however, there is tremendous intra-unit variation that defies explanation. In considering the differences between the lowest and highest estimates for the sub-units (Table 3.7), the count of "other" artifacts varies least of all (average difference 1.2 artifacts), while tile count varies (18.8 artifacts on average) less than pottery (24.5 artifacts on average) and overall count (35.9).

Isolating individual variables like rainfall (1 vs. 2) helps to explain this variation in count. Table 3.8 shows the positive or negative difference in count of different artifact classes *after* rain cleaned dust from pottery. Overall, rain appears to have improved artifact recognition, evident in the higher total counts (942 → 1,146 = +22%). This increase, though, was the result of averaging negatives and positives (compare individual cells of Table 3.8). More units showed an increase in the amount of pottery than a decrease after the rain: 10 of 16 sub-units (63%) show increase, six of 16 (33%) show decrease, and the overall pottery counts increased by 22% after rainfall. Tile, however, was less frequently identified after rain: 63% of the sub-units (10 of 16) show increase of tile count after rain fall, but the overall decrease was greater than increase (see final column of Table 3.8). Wet conditions, then, generally allowed walkers to identify more artifacts as pottery, fewer artifacts as tile. The general increase in the pottery after the rain probably occurred in part at the expense of tile, but is also quite likely that wet conditions eliminated false positives like flat stones covered in dust that had the appearance of tile.

The other variable tested in the first phase, experience, also goes some way to explaining a few of the differences noted at the start of this section. Overall, the general pattern is comparable between experienced and inexperienced walkers (cf. Tables 3.5 and 3.6: cp. rows [2] and [3]). Experienced (3) and inexperienced walkers (2) identified different sub-units as lowest and highest-density after rain-

Table 3.8   Difference in counts by inexperienced walkers between dry and wet conditions.

POTTERY					
T1	34	17	37	28	116
T2	-36		7	12	-18
T3	11	-3	16	-2	22
T4	-8	-4	22	32	42

TILE					
T1	3	0	1	5	9
T2	-50	2	1	17	-34
T3	12	1	15	-7	21
T4	-25	-27	25	-14	-41

OTHER					
T1	0	1	0		0
T2	0	0	0	1	1
T3		0		0	-2
T4	0			0	-2

TOTAL					
T1	37	18	38	32	125
T2	-86	-3	8	30	-51
T3	22	-2	30	-9	41
T4	-33	-32	46	18	

fall, but artifact counts were comparable for the entire 40 × 40 m square: students counted 1,056 artifacts (2) and experienced walkers counted 940 artifacts (3). Experienced walkers, however, counted less pottery and more tile than inexperienced walkers, suggesting that inexperienced students could not consistently recognize artifacts as tile and used "pottery" as their default category, and experienced walkers could distinguish tile more easily from pottery.

A more significant difference with broader repercussions was the different abilities to identify "other" kinds of artifacts. This category includes all artifacts besides pottery and tile, such as marble revetment, gypsum, shell, glass, and ground stone. Experienced walkers (3) noted 2–4 times the number of "other" artifacts than inexperienced fieldwalkers (2) (see "Other Count" in Table 3.6). Moreover, an experienced walker counted four lithic artifacts (chipped stone and ground stone) in G3 and G7 that an inexperienced walker missed entirely. Most of the artifacts of the "other" category are not very diagnostic, but their discovery certainly contributes to the functional assessment of the unit. As we will discuss later (3.3), there may be value in introducing more intensive collection for the specific purpose of improving resolution on these kinds of non-ceramic objects.

In sum, sub-unit variation within the 10 × 10 m sub-unit squares was significant, especially for pottery and total artifact count, but some of this variation appears to have washed out in the total

count for the entire 40 × 40 m unit. Inexperienced fieldwalkers identified more pottery after rainfall and fewer tiles, or, alternatively, misidentified fewer stones as tile. Experience made the most difference in identification of "other" objects and tiles, evident in a more equivalent ratio of pottery to tile. We will discuss the implications of these experiments after we consider the results of the second phase of the 2010 experiments.

3.2.2.   Pedestrian Survey vs. Hoovering: Total Counts and Artifact Classes

In the second phase of the experiments, we selected four 10 × 10 m sub-units for complete hoovering. Unlike the 2004 and 2006 experiments, which compared hoovering of a 5% circle with the 20% pedestrian survey of the 40 × 40 m unit as a whole, our 2010 experiments sampled the same spaces, the 10 × 10 m sub-units, within a period of a few days, using two different sampling methods (hoovering and pedestrian survey). This phase of the experiment, therefore, allows us to directly compare our normal sampling method of pedestrian survey with a more exhaustive documentation of the surface in respect to total density and counts of artifact classes.

A comparison of total count for squares hoovered and surveyed in a normal way shows that hoovering produced 2.1 to 3.9 times (average 3) the density of pedestrian survey (Table 3.9). Put another way, the putative count of experienced fieldwalkers in the pedestrian survey (i.e., adjusted from the 20% sample to 100% coverage) marked only 25–50% (average 36%) of the number of artifacts *actually* on the surface. Using the average figure, we estimate that the 940 artifacts counted by experienced fieldwalkers in Transect 3 as a 20% sample of the unit represent *not* simply 4,700 artifacts (the number factored by 5), but 13,202 artifacts *actually* on the ground (the number factored by 5 and by 3). This conclusion is consistent with the results of the experiments of 2004 and 2006 (Section 3.1.1), although the former experiments showed even greater differences between pedestrian and hoovering methods.

Our 2010 experiments also showed, in agreement with the previous experiments, that hoovering made some difference for understanding the overall character of the assemblage. Although we did not identify chronotypes in 2010, our division of artifacts into broad general classes (pottery, tile, lithics, other) highlights some dif-

ferences. The number of pottery sherds increased on average by a factor of 3.4 with hoovering, and tile increased on average by a factor of 2.8. This makes sense in light of the fact that some kinds of pottery (see below) fragment into smaller pieces, which hands-and-knees hoovering detects better than pedestrian survey.

Hoovering made the greatest difference in revealing non-ceramic artifacts in the unit. Hoovering revealed, for G1, 7 pieces of ancient glass, 1 lithic artifact, and 4 shells; for G6, 4 lithic artifacts, 1 gypsum slab, and 1 shell; for G9, numerous gypsum fragments (n=139), 2 bricks, 8 slabs, 1 stone vessel, 17 shell, 2 lithic, 1 glass shard, 2 marble revetment, and 1 ceramic tessera or gaming piece; for G15, 1 marble revetment, 2 gypsum fragments, 2 shells, 4 slabs, and 1 glass fragment. Although time intensive, this information is extremely useful in completing our picture of types of artifacts in the survey unit and suggests significantly more functional variability within a 40 × 40 m survey

Table 3.9   Comparison of total counts between pedestrian survey and hoovering.

CLASS	METHOD	G1	G6	G9	G15
Pottery	Pedestrian (20%)	20	32	46	14
	Pedestrian (100%)	100	160	230	70
	Hoovering (100%)	445	461	716	227
	Factor Difference	4.5	2.9	3.1	3.2
Tile	Pedestrian (20%)	38	28	51	27
	Pedestrian (100%)	190	140	255	135
	Hoovering (100%)	344	716	768	197
	Factor Difference	1.8	5.1	3.0	1.5
Other	Pedestrian (20%)	2	0	0	0
	Pedestrian (100%)	10	0	0	0
	Hoovering (100%)	12	6	30	8
	Factor Difference	1.2	6.0	30.0	8.0
Total	Pedestrian (20%)	60	60	97	41
	Pedestrian (100%)	300	300	485	205
	Hoovering (100%)	801	1183	1514	432
	Factor Difference	2.7	3.9	3.1	2.1

Table 3.10   Fabric classes of hoovered artifacts from 2010 survey of Unit 1.

FABRIC	G1	%	G6	%	G9	%	G15	%	AVERAGE
Coarse	387	87%	393	85%	624	87%	182	80%	85%
Fine	34	8%	60	13%	81	11%	35	15.5%	12%
Cooking	24	5%	8	2%	16	2%	10	4.5%	3%
Total	445	100%	461	100%	716	100%	227	100%	

unit. Most of this information is chronologically coarse, but gypsum slabs, marble revetment, lithic artifacts, a tessera, and glass do add resolution to our picture of the landscape.

3.2.3.   Hoovering: Total Counts and Artifact Classes

In addition to counting artifact classes in our 2010 experiments, we also collected additional kinds of information about the visible pottery. We did not have the time to subject the collected artifacts to chronotype analysis, but we did collect information about fabric and vessel part. In contrast with the 2004 experiments, in which we examined only 5% of the total grid square, our total collection in 2010 extended over four 10 × 10 m sub-units that collectively constituted 25% of the grid square. This data provides unique information about the number and kinds of artifacts *actually* on the surface of Koutsopetria.

For the sake of this analysis, we sorted all pottery from each hoovered sub-unit into three broad fabric groups: semi-fine and fine ware (decorated or not), kitchen ware, and medium-coarse and coarse wares (including amphora sherds). The results (Table 3.10) indicate that fine ware constitutes on average about 12% of the number of potsherds in the 10 × 10 m grid squares, kitchen ware on average 3% of the number of potsherds, and coarse wares consistently 85% of the overall assemblage. For a predominantly Roman–Late Roman assemblage with some earlier survivors, it is no surprise that the great majority of the sherds in the ground of Unit 1 were coarse and a tiny percentage kitchen ware, but it is interesting that fine ware was so important (12%) among the assemblage. This may

Table 3.11   Fabric classes of chronotype artifacts from 2004 survey of Unit 1.

FABRIC	QUANTITY	%	WEIGHT	%
Coarse	23	79%	726	80%
Fine	4	14%	114	13%
Cooking	2	7%	65	7%
Total	29	100%	905	100%

suggest the significance of table ware for the Late Roman habitation at Koutsopetria.

A comparison of these figures with the chronotype artifacts from the 2004 pedestrian survey of the entire Unit 1 is informative (Table 3.11). Coarse ware also constituted the majority of artifacts sampled as chronotypes, as we would expect, but the percentage of coarse ware (79–80%) was less than the percentage range of coarse wares (80–87%) for the hoovered sub-units of 2010. Fine and kitchen ware from the 2004 survey represented, respectively, 13% and 7%, of the overall assemblage of pottery, figures slightly higher than the average for those fabric groups in the 2010 hoovered units (12% and 3%). As we concluded in an earlier section regarding 2004 experiments (3.1.2), the reason for these differences must be that the chronotype system eliminated redundant sherds, which reduced the overall quantity of rather common coarse wares. Hoovering highlights the redundancy filtered out by the chronotype system.

We also counted the vessel parts of all hoovered artifacts in the pottery category according to the standard categories of rims, bases, handles, shoulders or necks, and body sherds (Table 3.12). The comparison shows that, on average, rims repre-

Table 3.12 Comparison of relative percentages of extant parts between 2010 resurvey (hoovering 100%) and 2004 survey (pedestrian 20% sample).

Part	2004 Survey	G1	%	G6	%	G9	%	G15	%	Ave. 2010
Rim	6 (21%)	22	5%	15	3%	21	3%	16	7%	4.5%
Base	0	5	1%	9	2%	9	1%	5	2%	2%
Handle	5 (17%)	10	2%	21	5%	17	2%	12	5%	3.5%
Neck	0	1	0.2%	1	0.2%	5	1%	7	3%	1%
Sherd	18 (62%)	407	92%	415	90%	664	93%	187	83%	89%
Total	29 (100%)	445	100%	461	100%	716	100%	227	100%	

sented only 5% of the total surface assemblage, bases 2%, handles 4%, neck and shoulders 1%, and body sherds 89%. Comparison with the 2004 chronotype data highlights informative differences (see second column of Table 3.12). Pedestrian survey failed to detect bases and necks / shoulders, the scarcest group documented through hoovering in 2010. More interestingly, rims, handles, and body sherds assumed more even proportions in the 2004 pedestrian survey than in the hoovering collection of 2010. Although body sherds constituted the majority of material in 2004 (62%), the relative percentages of rims and handles were five times greater in the 2004 pedestrian survey. This, again, is a result of the chronotype system, which samples the full assemblage but leaves redundant sherds on the ground. Here we have evidence that surveyors actually eliminated numerous redundant body sherds during survey to the relative favor of rims and handles.

Tabulating the same data to break down fabric group by vessel part interestingly shows that different fabric classes produce different relative percentages of vessel parts (Tables 3.13–15). Fine ware sherds are mainly body sherds (74% of fine wares) and rims (20%), kitchen ware mainly body sherds (85% of kitchen wares) and handles (7%), and coarse ware mainly body sherds (93%). Coarse ware body sherds make up 80% of the total number of sherds counted for all four sub-units, fine ware rims make up only 2% of the total pottery assemblage, and kitchen ware rims form only .1% of the total pottery assemblage. In our 2004 original survey using the chronotype system and sampling

20% of the unit, in contrast, we collected for fine ware two body sherds (50%), one handle (25%), and one rim (25%); for kitchen ware two rims; and for the 23 fragments of coarse ware mainly body sherds (70%) and a selection of rims (13%) and handles (17%). The best explanation for this pattern is that walkers reduced the overall number of body sherds in each category by not collecting duplicate examples of similar chronotypes.

In this phase of experiments, we also collected information to assess the percentage of body sherds that had either surface treatments and decorations, such as grooving, combing, and ridging (in the case of coarse wares), or slip and glazing (in the case of fine wares). In regional surveys, the presence of these surface treatments provides most of the chronological information for dating body sherds and contributes to the collection of these artifacts in a grab sample. In our experiments, the 71 fragments of fine ware with slip or glaze represented only 4% of the total number of potsherds counted (n=1854). Coarse sherds with spiral grooving, combing, or wheel ridging represented only 13% of the total number of coarse body sherds and 10% of the total number of sherds. Such "diagnostic body sherds," which are so visible in the landscape, comprise only a small percentage of the pottery as a whole.

3.3. DISCUSSION

The results of our experiments in 2004, 2006, and 2010 allow us to draw several conclusions about our survey methods and the nature of our data. The first and clearest is that hoovering produces

Table 3.13   Relative percentages of extant parts according to Fine Ware in 2004 survey unit (chronotype) and 2010 grid squares (hoovering).

Unit	R	B	H	S/N	S	Total
Unit 1 (2004)	1 (25%)	0	1 (25%)	0	2 (50%)	4
G1	18	1	1	0	14	34
G6	3	4	0	0	53	60
G9	13	3	0	2	63	81
G15	7	1	2	0	25	35
Total	41	9	3	2	155	210
Percentage of Total	20%	4%	1%	1%	74%	100%

Table 3.14   Relative percentages of extant parts according to Cooking Ware in 2004 survey unit (chronotype) and 2010 grid squares (hoovering).

Unit	R	B	H	S/N	S	Total
1 (2004)	2 (100%)	0	0	0	0	2
G1	0	0	1	1	22	24
G6	2	1	0	0	5	8
G9	0	0	1	0	15	16
G15	0	0	2	1	7	10
Total	2	1	4	2	49	58
Percentage of Total	3%	2%	7%	3%	85%	100%

Table 3.15   Relative percentages of extant parts according to Coarse Ware in 2004 survey unit (chronotype) and 2010 grid squares (hoovering).

Unit	R	B	H	S/N	S	Total
1 (2004)	3 (13%)	0	4 (17%)	0	16 (70%)	23
G1	4	4	8	0	371	387
G6	10	4	21	1	357	393
G9	8	6	16	3	591	624
G15	9	4	8	6	155	182
Total	31	18	53	10	1474	1586
Percentage of Total	2%	1%	3%	1%	93%	100%

dramatically higher artifact densities than do standard pedestrian survey methods, even when hoovering samples a smaller part of the unit (5%) than pedestrian survey (20%). The 2004 and 2006 experiments indicate that the factor increase in density between hoovering and pedestrian methods was usually more than three, with an average of 8.6; our 2010 experiments in the high-density Unit 1 showed that hoovering produced on average 3 times the putative total density of pedestrian survey. On average, the results of the 2004 and 2010 experiments showed that our normal method of pedestrian survey produced putative total counts about 27% of the number of artifacts counted through hoovering. Considering that our count in the pedestrian survey marked only a 20% sample of the surface of the unit, we can conclude that our total count represents, in a best-case scenario, 5.4% of the number of artifacts *actually* on the surface of the unit. And considering our chronotype collection strategy, which collected on average 33% of the artifacts counted, we can also conclude that in best-case scenarios (100% visibility), our collected sample represents less than 2% of the artifacts actually on the surface of the unit. The 2004 and 2006 experiments showed, furthermore, that our pedestrian method underrepresented total density most significantly (by factors of 12) in the lowest-density units. Hoovering allowed us to see the landscape at a completely different resolution.

Our experiments in Unit 1 in 2010 also showed how intra-unit density can vary significantly within a 40 × 40 m unit. On the one hand, as our total collection of 10 × 10 m units showed, this was a product of real density variation within the unit in overall artifact count, artifacts of particular fabric groups, and even particular vessel parts. On the other hand, our measure of that density through 20% pedestrian survey was inconsistent between episodes of resurvey. The count of pottery and overall artifacts varied most greatly between episodes of resurvey, while tile showed modest differences and non-ceramic artifacts showed minor changes. The field conditions after rain improved artifact recognition overall by 22%, an increase consisting mainly of more potsherds, as the count of tile and other artifacts declined after rain. Experience in fieldwalking also accounted for some difference in

the more equal proportion of pottery to tile — experienced walkers simply counted more tiles — and in the significantly greater recognition of non-ceramic artifacts such as lithics, marble revetment, glass, and gypsum (experienced walkers noted 2–4 times more). Despite the importance of these variables (rainfall and experience), two conclusions stand out: 1) the overall picture of density for the entire 40 × 40 m unit changed little between the 2010 episodes of resurvey, and 2) the assessment of density through pedestrian survey was itself only a small sample (ca. 33% for 2010) of what was actually on the ground. In general, these experiments remind us that the total densities produced through traditional fieldwalking may not consistently represent the *actual* total densities on the surface of the ground.

Our experiments documented the effectiveness of our chronotype sampling method especially in the comparison of our chronotype sample from a 20% pedestrian survey with a more exhaustive procedure of collecting everything through hoovering. Both experiments showed that our pedestrian sample under-represented the actual percentages of amphora, coarse, and medium-coarse sherds to the benefit of fine and kitchen wares. Moreover, our pedestrian sample under-represented the actual percentages of body sherds and, consequently, overrepresented the percentages of rims, bases, and handles. Our chronotype sampling strategy effectively discouraged collecting duplicate sherds of the same chronotype.

More intensive collection strategies such as hoovering also increased the resolution of our assemblages in terms of fabric and vessel part. In all units, hoovering produced more examples of the most common kind of artifact, the medium-coarse and coarse body sherd, which also tends to be the least diagnostic. In the lower-density units, however, hoovering produced more of these artifacts, usually without producing information about other kinds of artifacts. Indeed, in the case of some of the 5% circles in low-density units in 2004, hoovering actually reduced information about fabric group, vessel part, or chronology. In moderate and high-density units, on the other hand, hoovering did often produce many additional examples of fine and kitchen ware, rims, bases, and handles, but their relative percentages tended to decline in terms of the overall number of sherds. Even still, it is clear that a five-fold increase in rims and handles through hoovering (Section 3.2.3) can greatly increase the resolution of chronotype diversity in the units even if does not consistently improve chronological resolution (see below).

Our hoovering experiments, moreover, showed that pottery across the coastal plain of the Late Roman site tends to follow general patterns. For fabric groups, coarse ware is always dominant (2004: ave. 88%; 2010: ave. 85%), while fine ware forms a small percentage (2004: ave. 5%, 2010: ave. 12%) and kitchen ware an even smaller percentage (2004: ave. 7%, 2010: ave. 3%). In vessel part, body sherds dominate (on average 89% in 2004, 92% in 2010), and rims (2004: 5%, 2010: 3%), handles (2004: 4%, 2010: 4%), bases (2004: 2%, 2010: 1%), and necks and shoulders form relatively small percentages on average. Body sherds made up a substantial majority of coarse wares in 2010 (93%), a significant percentage (85%) of kitchen wares, and a less impressive majority (74%) of fine wares; coarse wares tend to be thicker, large vessels that simply produced more body sherds. For fine wares noted in 2010, rims were more common (20%), and handles were an important vessel part for kitchen wares. Overall, coarse ware body sherds constituted 80% of all the pottery in Unit 1, and fine ware rims and kitchen ware rims formed only 2% and .1%, respectively, of the total pottery assemblage. The vast majority of additional artifacts produced through hoovering marked redundant information in respect to chronology and function.

Despite the seemingly significant difference between the assemblage produced by hoovering and standard survey, our knowledge of chronology changed remarkably little from one sampling system to another. Hoovering most consistently added additional examples of the coarsest chronological information — "Ancient Historic" or "Late Bronze Age–Medieval" body sherds — that are mainly of use in aoristic analysis (Section 5.1.5). If hoovering sometimes did bring to light previously unidentified narrow periods, it also simultaneously led to other narrow periods previously identified in the pedestrian survey being overlooked.

At the same time, hoovering was very useful in increasing the typological resolution of units,

showing more types of artifacts. Hoovering produced more chronotypes on average than pedestrian survey, and certain periods (Late Roman) gained many more chronotypes through scouring the ground. Hoovering also documented greater quantities of rims, bases, and handles of pottery, and non-ceramic objects like glass, metal, marble, gypsum, and stone tools. Surveyors using pedestrian methods collected those "other" artifacts less consistently.

Total collection through hoovering was a valuable means of improving resolution by vastly increasing the amounts of pottery sampled, but came at the cost of a substantial increase in time and labor. Experienced fieldwalkers in 2004 and 2005 required only 2–30 minutes (ave. 8 minutes) to pedestrian walk across a 40 × 40 m unit. In contrast, five individuals hoovering 10 × 10 m sub-units of Unit 1 in 2010 took 1–2 hours (ave. 1.5 hours), while total collection in 2004 and 2006 through hoovering 5% circles required between thirty minutes and four hours. If we use the total time (6 hours) required to hoover 25% of Unit 1, we estimate that 5 individuals could have hoovered 100% of Unit 1 in about 24 working hours (about 3 field days). To put this difference another way, total collection at 100% of a 40 × 40 m unit would have required 72 times the amount of time required for pedestrian survey of 20% of the same space.

Besides issues related to time and the enormous quantity of pottery that a team would produce for a high-density survey area, it is important to restate that total collection did not consistently improve the chronological or functional resolution of the assemblage in a way that would justify the cost. In consequence of this, we believe that the standard 20% sample using the chronotype collection has provided a means of gathering data from the soil matrix at maximum efficiency. We are not recommending the chronotype system as the only workable sampling system, but in artifact-rich environments such as large sites, we do recommend it as a system capable of producing good data that minimizes inefficiency and does not burden storage facilities. The advantages of a chronotype sample over a grab sample of "diagnostic artifacts" will be discussed further in Chapter 5.

Chapter 4

Catalogue of Finds

by R. Scott Moore and Brandon R. Olson
with contributions by Maria Andrioti and P. Nick Kardulias

Pottery discovered during a field survey often provides a visible record of the human activity in the area, and the different occupation sites reflect the importance of the area to the larger region. While it is standard practice for excavations to include a formal ceramic catalogue in their final publications, survey projects have been more flexible in their approach, ranging from not including a catalogue (Bevan and Conolly 2013), to a sampling of ceramics (Knapp and Givens 2003), to a more traditional catalogue (Sørensen and Rupp 1993). As part of PKAP's commitment to distributional, artifact-level analysis we present an extensive catalogue of artifacts from the survey area. Unlike an excavation catalogue that can provide independent comparanda for datable artifact types, the following survey catalogue relies on established typologies to classify the ceramic evidence and should, consequently, be used with care.

Artifacts were selected for inclusion in the catalogue as they came out of the field and underwent preliminary identification, and prior to more sophisticated and extensive analysis of the landscape that took place during subsequent study seasons. Artifacts suitable for cataloguing were set aside in separate crates, photographed, and labeled, whereas the remaining artifacts were returned to the bags associated with their respective collection units. As archaeological storage is a common problem for projects across the eastern Mediterranean,

it is important to note that at some point after our preliminary analysis and recording of the survey finds, the bags of non-catalogued artifacts vanished in the densely packed storerooms of the museum, leaving us only with those artifacts set aside for cataloguing. As one can see from the following catalogue, this setback did not substantively affect our analysis, but it did mean that it was not possible to augment the catalogue in response to subsequent in-depth distributional analysis.

This chapter follows a standard format of fine wares, kitchen wares, medium-coarse wares, coarse wares, amphora, roof tiles, lamps, and figurines. Within each ware category, the ceramics are arranged chronologically from oldest to the most recent. For each type, there is a description of the ware followed by the number of sherds collected, and the entries for the catalogued sherds. Variants are provided under the main heading numerically. Each catalogue entry includes extant part, followed by its dimensions, description (Munsell color, decoration, inclusions, and shape), and illustration or photo number if available. Each catalogue entry is accompanied by a unique catalogue number that is a combination of the survey unit and the batch number assigned during analysis. The unit designation is the first part of the catalogue number and is separated from the batch number by a period. So, for example, an artifact designated 141.23 is from batch 23 and was collected in unit 141. The ceramic fabric colors are drawn from the standard Munsell soil color chart (Munsell Soil Color Charts 2000), while the inclusion descriptions and sizes, as well as the descriptions of shapes are based on the work of the Corinth Excavations (Sanders et al. 2008). All measurements provided below are in meters, except in the sections devoted to sling bullets (4.11) and lithic artifacts (4.12) where centimeters are used.

Abbreviations Used:
Diam. = Diameter
PH = Preserved Height
PL = Preserved Length
PW = Preserved Width
Th. = Thickness

4.1. FINE WARES

The class of ceramics that tends to attract the most attention from archaeologists is fine wares (Sørensen and Rupp 1993), a ceramic category consisting of a well-prepared fabric worked and manufactured into certain shapes. As such, fine wares are the most decorative forms and typically were used for the consumption of food and drink. They are typically of higher quality than other pottery classes, such as amphora or kitchen ware. For a ceramicist there are several advantages to analyzing fine wares. Since there is a limited number of vessel types that were manufactured at specific production centers that remained in existence for several centuries, the ceramic type lends itself to typological analysis. Furthermore, fine wares were traded widely throughout the Mediterranean, on both a local and global scale, meaning that the more popular industries are ubiquitous throughout the eastern Mediterranean. As a result of the increased scholarly attention, fine ware typologies and chronologies are far more refined than those devised for coarse, kitchen, and utility wares. Fine wares comprise an important pottery category at Koutsopetria, accounting for 837 sherds or 5.15% of all sherds, but as we have argued in Chapter 3 and will argue in Chapter 5, fine wares exert a much greater influence over our understanding of the landscape.

4.1.1. Fine Wares, Iron Age

There were only a few sherds collected that predate the Cypro-Classical Period. The paucity of such sherds is typical of many of the recent large-area survey projects on Cyprus (Clarke and Todd 1993; Sørensen and Rupp 1993: 190; Fejfer 1995; Given and Knapp 2003). The typologies created by the Swedish Cyprus Expedition in the 1940s remain the basis for the modern typologies used for classification of ceramics from these periods (Gjerstad 1948). Unfortunately, there are several drawbacks to these publications, such as the fact that they are difficult to use, not well-illustrated, and based almost exclusively on material recovered from tombs or sanctuaries. In the years since the Swedish Cyprus Expedition, there has been little progress in developing or refining the typologies based on excavated material, or studying the distribution of individual wares on the island (Sørensen and Rupp 1993: 37). As a result, the study of pottery from the Cypro-Geometric and Cypro-Archaic periods has not advanced as much as for other periods, such as the Roman and Late Roman. For survey projects, these issues make the study of these periods and the creation of chronologies for the survey area especially difficult.

The following category of fine ware contains sherds that can only be dated very broadly to the Iron Age (Cypro-Archaic to Cypro-Classical). These sherds lack the decoration, distinctive fabric, or shape that would permit a more precise identification. As a result, projects do not typically include this broad category in their publications. We relied on Sørensen's descriptions of the painted and plain wares from Panayia Ematousa and Palaipaphos for fabric descriptions and general shapes (Sørensen 1993b, 1996, and 2006). Such sherds range in color from a light gray to a yellowish-red fabric with red, black, and white inclusions. Many have a partial painted band or design. The majority of the sherds in this category are most likely White Painted Ware, but because of their fragmentary state and the fact that they share similar characteristics with other wares, the material has been added to a more inclusive category so as to avoid misidentification. For example, sherd 1403.61 (below) is similar in fabric to Sørensen's White Painted Ware fabric

B (Sørensen 1993b: 38), but its banding design is closer in appearance to Bichrome B-86 (Sørensen 1993b: 51, no. B-86).

31 finds
21 body sherds
4 rims
4 bases
2 handles

1013.30. Rim. Diam. = uncertain, PH = 0.013, PW = 0.021, Th. = 0.007. Fine, yellowish-red fabric (5YR 5/8) with yellow slip (10YR 8/6), and frequent medium black inclusions with rare fine micaceous inclusions. The upper surface is painted a very dark gray (10YR 3/1) with a reserved band in the center of the rim. Lower surface is painted black with a reserved band towards the outer edge of the rim. Downturned rim of large bowl.

1402.6. Base. Diam. = 0.080, PH = 0.031, PL = 0.049, Th. = 0.009 (wall), Th. = 0.015 (base). Medium-coarse, light red fabric (2.5YR 7/8) with a very pale brown slip (10YR 8/2), and a few, medium to large white and red inclusions, and small mica inclusions. Thick band of black paint on exterior surface of base. Thick torus ring.

1403.61. Body sherd. PH = 0.028, PW = 0.034, Th. = 0.006. Fine, light olive gray fabric (5Y 6/2) on interior and reddish yellow exterior (7.5YR 7/6) with rare, medium to large red inclusions. Black painted lines (7.5YR 2.5/1) suggest the top of two chevrons with peaks pointing towards the top of the vessel.

4.1.2. Fine Wares, Cypro-Geometric and Cypro-Archaic

The fine ware groups from the Cypro-Geometric and Cypro-Archaic periods manufactured on the island include White Painted Ware, Black on Red Ware, Bichrome Ware, Bichrome Red Ware, Red Slip Ware, and Black Slip Ware. While the painted wares can be easy to identify, the later Cypro-Archaic sherds are mostly undecorated and are harder to identify and date with certainty. In addition to locally produced ceramics, excavations on

the island have uncovered foreign imports from Phoenicia and other eastern Mediterranean locales (eastern Greece and the Aegean; Sørensen 2006b: 161, 180). For Koutsopetria, the best comparanda for these periods comes from material excavated from Panayia Ematousa and Kition, which are adjacent to the PKAP survey area (Jehasse 1981; Marquié 2004, 2005; Sørensen and Winther-Jacobsen 2006). (See Section 5.3.2 for distributional analysis.)

Cypro-Geometric and Cypro-Archaic fine wares are not well-represented in the PKAP survey assemblage, as only 12 sherds dating to these periods, or 1.4% by quantity of all fine wares, were identified. The pieces, consisting of small body sherds with painted geometric designs, were confined to a limited number of locations (see Chapter 5). The three identifiable wares from these periods include White Painted, Black on Red, and Bichrome, while no examples of other common wares of the period present at other Cypriot sites were found.

This Cypro-Geometric and Cypro-Archaic breakdown is comparable to Panayia Ematousa, although not all of the wares present at that site were found at Koutsopetria. An examination of the wares present at other sites, moreover, does not provide a standard ceramic signature for different types of sites from the period (sanctuary, tomb, or settlement), which would have allowed us to understand better our ceramic assemblage in this period (Sørensen 2006b: 161).

While fine wares from these periods are not well-represented at Koutsopetria, a few observations can be made. First, the kinds of wares typically found in tombs, like Bichrome and Black Slip (Sørensen 2006b: 161–62), are not present at Koutsopetria. The majority collected are small body sherds which do not provide information concerning the specific types of shapes present at Koutsopetria. Those that do allow for an identification of shape seem to be from small open vessels, such as cups and bowls. Finally, there were no imported wares collected from these periods. All these factors, the small number of finds, the abraded condition of the sherds, and the apparent absence of imported material suggest that the area did not sustain an active settlement during the Cypro-Geometric through Cypro-Archaic periods.

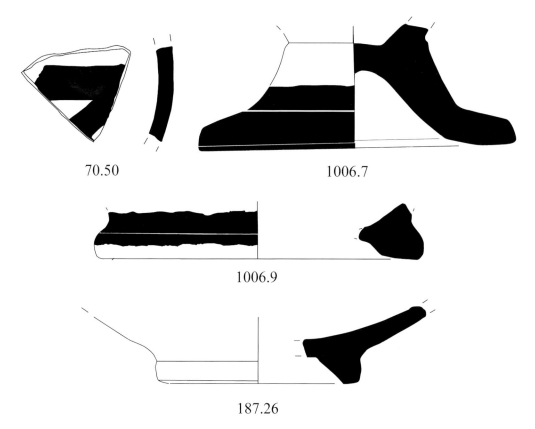

70.50   1006.7

1006.9

187.26

Fig. 4.1   *White Painted Ware and Archaic Fineware sherds.*

4.1.2.1. White Painted Ware

The fabric is generally brown in color with small black stones and decorated with a brown or black paint on a lighter fabric. The decoration is typically applied to the neck, shoulder, or handles in bands or a recurring pattern (Sørensen 2006b: 162–70). The standard typology for this ware was developed by the Swedish Cyprus Expedition and remains mostly unchanged (Gjerstad 1948: 48–60). The lack of diagnostic rims and the small size of the body sherds prevented us from dividing the ware into shape categories as Sørensen did for Panayia Ematousa (Sørensen 2006b: 162–70).

9 finds
6 body sherds
2 bases
1 handle

70.50. Body sherd (fig. 4.1). PH = 0.022, PW = 0.030, Th. = 0.005. Coarse, light reddish-brown fabric (5YR 6/4) with a few, medium-sized black spherical stones and a painted linear design (5YR 5/6) on a pale yellow slip (2.5 Y 8/3). See Sørensen 1993: 47, no. B58.

122.17. Body Sherd. PW = 0.016. Fine-grained, pink fabric (5 YR 7/4) with mica inclusions, and black paint with small inclusions of white lime.

1006.7. Base (fig. 4.1). Diam. = 0.090. Coarse, light red fabric (2.5YR 7/6) with rare, medium red inclusions and a solid black painted line on bottom half of a wide, flat stem base. See Sørensen 1993b: 40, no. B-9.

1006.9. Base (fig. 4.1, reproduced at 1:2). Diam. = 0.050, PH = 0.029, PL = 0.069, Th. = 0.027 (ring). Coarse, light reddish-brown fabric (2.5Y 7/4) with frequent, medium to very large black inclusions. False ring foot with black paint on exterior surface. See Sørensen 1993b: 47, no. B-51.

4.1.2.2. Black on Red Ware

The fabric for Black on Red Ware can range from fine to coarse with small red, black, and/or white inclusions. The slip, while usually red, can run from light red to yellowish red. The shapes both open and closed are typically decorated with banding around the neck or on the shoulder (Gjerstad 1948: 68–73; Sørensen 2006: 173–78).

1 find
1 rim

[501.1].198. Rim. Diam. = 0.140. Medium-coarse, reddish yellow fabric (5YR 6/6) with pink slip (7.5YR 8/3) and a very dark gray paint (7.5YR 3/1) applied on exterior. Fabric contains common, medium to large white and red inclusions, and some mica. Rim of open bowl.

4.1.2.3. Bichrome Ware

The fabric for Bichrome Ware ranges from a pale brown to a reddish or reddish-brown color, and has small white, black, and red inclusions. It is typically decorated with black or red lines, and concentric circles in a black or red paint (Gjerstad 1948: 73–76; Sørensen 2006b: 170–73).

1 find
1 body sherd

[501.1].40. Body sherd (fig. 4.26). PL = 0.093, PW = 0.058, Th. = 0.014. Medium-coarse, very yellow-brown fabric (10YR 8/3) with rare medium black inclusions. Red-painted floral design (2.5YR 5/8). See Sørensen 2006b: 173, no. 68, 1993: 52, no. B-96.

4.1.2.4. Cypro-Archaic

This category of fine ware contains examples that can only be dated broadly to the Cypro-Archaic period due to their fabric and style of decoration. The decoration, fabric, shape, and physical condition of these sherds are not distinctive enough to allow for a more precise identification, and unfortunately, there is little published comparanda available. As a result, we relied on fabric and shape descriptions provided by the Swedish Cyprus Expedition (Gjerstad 1948) and published material from Panayia Ematousa and Palaipaphos (Sørensen 1993b and 2006).

4 finds
2 body sherds
1 base
1 rim

187.26. Base (fig. 4.1). Diam. = 0.030, PH = 0.019, PL = 0.034, PW = 0.030. Fine, light reddish-brown fabric (5YR 6/4) with some sherd encrusting. Reddish-gray slip (5YR 5/2) with black paint (GLEY2 4/2) on sides and on base. False ring foot.

1402.18. Body sherd (fig. 4.26). PL = 0.043, PW = 0.051, Th. = 0.006–0.009. Coarse, light red fabric (10R 7/6) with rare, medium white and black inclusions and small mica. Row of teardrops painted in red (10R 3/4–4/8) over a lighter reddish yellow slip (7.5YR 7/6). Sherd is from the shoulder of a closed vessel.

4.1.3. Fine Wares, Cypro-Classical through Early Roman

In the Cypro-Classical and Hellenistic Periods, the number of fine wares at Koutsopetria increases with the majority of the sherds belonging to two wares, Black Glaze and Colour-Coated Wares. In examining the Black Glaze, it is difficult to distinguish between Attic and Atticizing due to the fragmentary nature of the sherds, but it does appear that the majority are Atticizing in style rather than Attic in origin. Only a few of the fine wares are Attic Black Glaze, 6 sherds, or 0.7% by quantity of the total fine ware collection. (See Section 5.3.2.3 for distributional analysis.) The most common ceramic ware dating to the third and second centuries BC is Hellenistic Colour-Coated Ware, which accounts for 54 sherds, or 45.7% of the total quantity of Cypro-Classical and Hellenistic fine wares. This signals a shift from importing fine wares (Black Glaze) to a reliance on locally produced Hellenistic Colour-Coated Wares that most likely were produced at an interior site, perhaps in the Mesaoria Plain (Lund 1993: 184). (See Section 5.3.3 for distributional analysis.)

Such a trend continues in the late Hellenistic and Early Roman Periods as the numbers of fine wares and imports decrease. The common imported western wares of this period, such as the sigillatas, are present at Koutsopetria in very small numbers only, as 1 sherd of Arretine, 36 sherds of Eastern Sigillata A, and 1 sherd of Eastern Sigillata B were discovered. While it is interesting that Cypriot Sigillata, a probable Cypriot product, is present in small numbers (only 21 sherds or less than 1% of all fine ware sherds by quantity), the decline in imported wares (ESA, ESB, and Arretine) indicates either a decline in activity at the site or a decline in trade reaching the area. The decline in Cypriot Sigillata appears to reinforce the idea that Koutsopetria experienced some economic contraction or functional change from the first century BC to the third century AD, or that connections with the western half of the island (other suggested production sites for Cypriot Sigillata) were more tenuous.

4.1.3.1. *Attic and Hellenistic Black Glaze*

One of the more common fine wares of the Cypro-Classical to Hellenistic periods in the eastern Mediterranean included a lustrous black gloss fine ware, generally referred to as black glaze despite the inaccuracy of the term (Lund 2006: 182). The standard typologies for Attic Black Glaze were developed by Sparkes and Talcott, and Rotroff from material excavated from the Athenian Agora (Sparkes and Talcott 1970; Rotroff 1997), while Jehasse and Salles provide important comparanda for Cypriot sites (Salles 1983; Jehasse 1998). This ware was widely traded in the eastern Aegean and numerous examples have been found at various sites on Cyprus (Salamis: see Jehasse 1978, 1981; Kition: Jehasse 1981; Palaipaphos: Maier 1986: 160–64; Lund 1993: 80–82; Nea Paphos: Mlynarczyk 1990: 74–75, 102, 109; Hayes 1991: 5; Kourion: Connelly 1983; Kition-Bamboula: Salles 1983; Panayia Ematousa: Lund 2006: 186–89). In examining the Black Glaze sherds from Koutsopetria, it is difficult to distinguish between traditional Attic and Atticizing wares because of the abraded nature of the sherds, but based on the few surviving diagnostic sherds and the appearance of the

fabric, it does appear that the majority represent Atticizing forms from the late Cypro-Classical and early Hellenistic periods, which date from the fifth through third centuries BC. The Koutsopetria assemblage presents a fabric that is typically reddish or orangish in color with a thick, dark black or grayish black gloss. The fabric and slip suggest a coastal Levantine place of manufacture. The identifiable vessels include primarily cups and bowls with very few dishes and plates. At the nearby sites of Kition and Panayia Ematousa, these black gloss wares were typically imported into the region during the fifth and fourth centuries, and it appears that the Koutsopetria material most likely followed this model (Lund 2006: 184).

37 finds
17 body sherds
13 rims
4 bases
3 handles

10.11. Base (fig. 4.2). Diam. = 0.025. Fine, pale yellow fabric (2.5Y 8/3) with rare, sub-rounded stones. Red and black slip (10R 5/6 to 10R 2.5/2) on exterior. Flat disc base. See Lund 1993: 82, no. C-10.

48.29. Rim. Diam. = 0.340. Light, reddish-brown fine fabric (5YR 6/4) with rare, fine mica and shiny black glaze that shows erosion in some places. Tapering rim from a bowl with a convex, flaring body.

183.26. Rim (fig. 4.2). Diam. = 0.058. Fine-grained, light pink fabric (7.5YR 7/4) with a fine, shiny black slip. Slightly in-turned, tapered rim of flat, low bowl. See Lund 2006: 187, no. 8.

[501.1].137. Base. PH = 0.031, PW = 0.048. Fine, light red fabric (10R 7/8) containing no visible inclusions and with a dark red slip (10R 5/6). Base of a cup or bowl with a flaring torus ring.

[501.1].140. Handle (fig. 4.26). PH = 0.070, Th. = 0.010 (min.), Th. = 0.018 (max.). Fine, reddish yellow fabric (5YR 7/6) with rare, micaceous inclusions and black slip. Oval handle with diagonal loop.

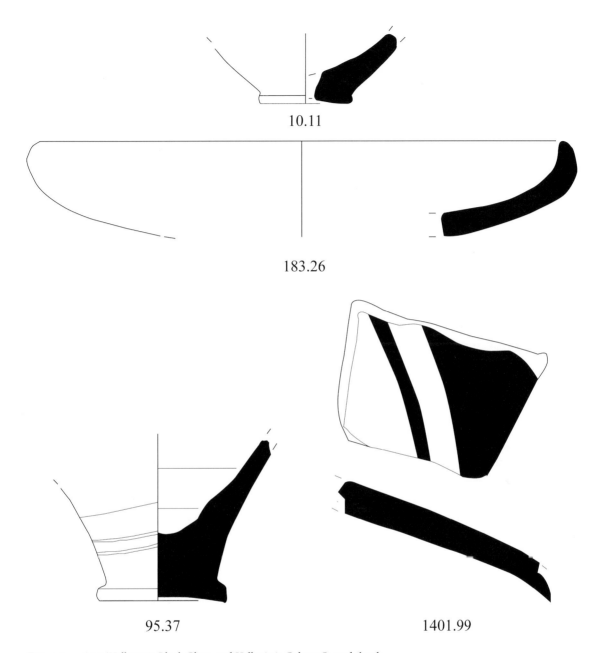

10.11

183.26

95.37   1401.99

FIG. 4.2   *Attic/Hellenistic Black Glaze and Hellenistic Colour-Coated sherds.*

4.1.3.2. Hellenistic Colour-Coated

In the third and second centuries BC, Hellenistic Colour-Coated ware represents the most common ceramic industry from Koutsopetria, comprising 28.5% by quantity, 187 sherds, of the total quantity of Cypro-Classical and early Hellenistic fine wares. This shift signals a change in preference from imported fine wares to a reliance on a locally produced industry (Lund 1993: 184). For Colour-Coated wares the initial typology was based on the excavations at the TE I well at Evriti (Maier and von Wartburg 1986: 161). In recent years, this typology has been refined by Hayes' work at the House of Dionysos in Paphos (Hayes 1991: 26–31), while Lund's analysis of the Cypro-Classical to Hellenistic fine wares from Panayia Ematousa provides additional refinements and regional comparanda (Lund 1993: 190–202). Interestingly, the excavations at nearby Kition-Bamboula produced a contemporary assemblage fairly distinct from the ceramics recovered at Panayia Ematousa and Koutsopetria (Lund 1993: 183; Salles 1995: 397–414). The differing assemblages from Kition-Bamboula and Panayia Ematousa prompted Lund to theorize that the inhabitants of Panayia Ematousa relied more on interior sites to supply fine ware pottery (Lund 1993: 183). The ceramic similarities between Panayia Ematousa and Koutsopetria, as well as the proximity, suggest that Koutsopetria probably also relied more on connections with the interior than with Kition in the Cypro-Classical and Early Hellenistic periods.

In order to prevent Hellenistic Colour-Coated ware from becoming a proverbial ceramic catch-all for any and all red-slipped ceramic forms, both imported and local, dating from the beginning of the Hellenistic period to the introduction of Eastern Sigillata (see below) in the middle of the second century, there has been a concerted effort to begin to identify specific ceramic groups assigned to the ware. Recent excavations at Kedesh, in northern Israel, have prompted Berlin, Herbert, and Stone to propose refinements to the Hellenistic Colour-Coated category (Berlin, Herbert, and Stone 2014). In excavating a Persian-period administration building repurposed at various stages during the Hellenistic period, they identified two clear Hellenistic horizons and what appears to be a third "sketchy" occupation (Herbert and Berlin 2003: 18–21; Berlin, Herbert, and Stone forthcoming). Based on a careful analysis of the historical record, stamped Rhodian amphora handles, coins, and the nature of the stratified deposits, Herbert and Berlin provide the following Hellenistic occupational chronology: Ptolemaic (beginning during the reign of Ptolemy II Philadelphus [ca. 283–246] and certainly by Zenon's first visit to the site around 259 to Ptolemy V's defeat at Battle of Kedesh in 199), Seleucid (199 to 144 or 143, following the defeat of Demetrius I Soter by Jonathan Maccabeus), and Post Demetrius (144 or 143 to the third quarter of the second century).

Archaeologists recovered four distinct fine ware industries within the Hellenistic levels, Coastal Fine South, Coastal Fine North, Black-Slipped Predecessor, and ESA. At two locales, archaeologists identified a semi-fine, red, poorly slipped pottery assemblage consisting of small saucers and bowls used as construction fill for floors dated to the Ptolemaic occupation. Petrographic analysis suggests a production zone in the coastal plain around the Carmel Mountains. Dubbed Coastal Fine South ware, the industry represents the common ceramic table ware utilized by Ptolemaic officials stationed at Kedesh in the third century. Within the Seleucid-period abandonment levels, another red slipped table ware assemblage was discovered. Also consisting of small saucers and bowls, the ware is fine with cleaner fabric and a better-adhering slip than the earlier Coastal Fine South assemblage. Despite its improved quality, Berlin, Herbert, and Stone characterize the ware as an early to middle of the second century variant of the Coastal Fine South and suggest that because the quality of the two differs, the later variant may have been produced around Tyre, an area with superior clay beds. Also within the abandonment levels, archaeologists discovered an assemblage of saucers and small bowls very similar to ESA with a clean fabric and vessels covered wholly or partially with a lustrous red-orange slip. In addition to similarities in fabric and slip, petrographic analysis yielded a mineralogical profile identical to that of ESA, while NAA analysis of similar vessels from Gezer fell within same chemical group as ESA. Berlin, Herbert, and Stone, however, call the industry Coastal Fine North and do not lump it in with the Hellenistic Colour-Coated industry or the traditional ESA repertoire for the following reasons: most vessel forms are middle Hellenistic and not indicative of the standard ESA repertoire, most vessels are covered by a slip applied with a brush and not dipped like ESA, most vessels are only partially slipped unlike ESA vessels which are completely covered in a slip.

Since this suggested modification by Berlin, Herbert, and Stone was not available during our analyses, we relied on Lund for forms and dating, and Hayes for fabric groups. The majority of the examples collected during the survey consist of Colour-Coated examples dating from the third through first centuries BC. The sherds have a semilustrous slip that varies in color from dark gray to reddish brown to red, and lack the thick gloss of the Attic Black Glaze discussed above (Hayes 1991: 23–31; Papuci-Wladyka 1995: 47–54, 246–47; Elaigne 2000). These wares were manufactured locally at several sites on Cyprus, and while they were not typically exported, are found throughout the island (Hayes 1984: 92; 1991: 26; Maier and Wartburg 1986: 161–64; Burkhalter 1987: 356; Lund 1993: 84–85). While only about half of the PKAP material is body fragments, the rims and bases were, in most cases, too damaged and fragmentary to securely identify individual forms.

54 finds
28 body sherds
9 rims
11 bases
6 handles

95.37. Base (fig. 4.2). Diam. = 0.040, PH = 0.040, PW = 0.054. Fine, light red fabric (2.5YR 6/6) with a slip that ranges from dark to light (2.5YR 3/1 and 10YR 8/2) with rare, rounded spherical black stones. False ring foot.

[501.1].145. Handle. PH = 0.021, PL = 0.041, PW = 0.039, Th. = 0.010. Fine, light red fabric (10R 7/8) with very rare, micaceous inclusions. Vertical strap handle of cup.

[501.1].146. Base. Diam. = 0.053, PH = 0.020. Fine, buff-pink fabric (5YR 7/6 to 10R 7/8) with dusky red slip (10R 3/4) with rare, medium white and gray inclusions. False ring base.

1013.26. Base. PL = 0.045, Th. = 0.008. Very fine, reddish yellow fabric (7.5YR 7/6) with partially preserved light red slip (2.5YR 6/8) and rare, fine inclusions. False ring foot of a dish or plate.

1401.99. Body sherd (fig. 4.2). PL = 0.065, PW = 0.036, Th. = 0.008. Medium-coarse, reddish-brown fabric (2.5YR 4/4) with a light brown surface (7.5YR 6/4) with rare, fine to small dark inclusions. Surface is decorated with a very dark brown paint (7.5YR 2.5/3).

4.1.3.3. Hellenistic Colour-Coated, Imported

The imported Colour-Coated Wares are similar to the Cypriot manufactured ones in shape, but differ in fabric. At Koutsopetria, there was one sherd that was similar in shape to the imported Colour-Coated Ware identified as Ware A by Hayes at Paphos. This ware, whose origin is unknown but believed by Hayes to be the southeast Aegean, is characterized by a brownish fabric with a red slip (Hayes 1991: 23–24).

1 find
1 rim

71.37. Rim (fig. 4.3). Diam. = 0.160, PH = 0.018, PL = 0.026. Medium-grained, light red fabric (2.5YR 6/6) with rare, white inclusions and a red slip (2.5YR 4/6) on interior and exterior. Very thin in-turned rim of a bowl. See Hayes 1991: 24, no. 5171; and fig. 13, no. 5.

4.1.3.4. Eastern Sigillata A (ESA) and Eastern Sigillata B (ESB)

By the middle of the second century BC and well into the Roman Period, the standard fine wares found throughout the eastern Mediterranean, red-slipped sigillatas, are present at Koutsopetria, but only in very small quantities, consisting of 38 sherds representing ESA and to a lesser extent ESB and Arretine forms. The lacuna is significant, as ESA in particular literally dominated the eastern Mediterranean for three centuries. Archaeologists have excavated, and more importantly published, substantial quantities of the ware from major Near Eastern sites including Antioch (Waagé 1948: 18–28, 32–38), Samaria (Kenyon 1957: 281–357), Tel Anafa (Slane 1997: 269–74, 283–346), Gindaros (Kramer 2004: 181–201), Hama (Christensen and Johansen 1971: 55–204), Athens (Hayes 2008: 13–30), and Tarsus (Goldman 1950: 172–76, 179–83), while the ware has been found in significant quantities at a number of Cypriot sites, most prevalently at Paphos (Hayes 1991: 32–36), Geronisos (Connelly 2002; 2005; 2009; Młynarczyk 2009), Panayia-Ematousa (Lund 2006: 205–15), and Amathous (Burkhalter 1987).

The ESA ceramic industry is the earliest and most prevalent form of the Eastern Terra Sigillata repertoire and, as such, has received the most scholarly attention. The ware is characterized by a series of standardized vessel shapes comprising mostly hemispherical bowls, cups, and plates. The fabric is fine with few inclusions varying in color from very pale brown to pink, while all forms are covered entirely with a red to reddish-orange slip. ESA was the standard fine ware in the Near East from the middle of the Hellenistic through early Roman periods. ESB, on the other hand, was manufactured from the late first century BC to the middle of the second century AD. ESB is ubiquitous throughout the eastern Aegean, but found in smaller quantities at eastern Mediterranean sites (Lund 1993: 96). It was manufactured in western Turkey, perhaps Tralles (Williams 1992: 18–19) and produced in two series, 1 and 2 (Hayes 1991). The fabric is characterized by an orange, orangish-red, or brownish-red color with silver mica and an orange or brown slip that has a waxy feel (Williams 1992: 19).

Despite well over a century of continued study, archaeologists have yet to identify definitively the geographic origins of ESA. Gunneweg, Perlman, and Yellin, using neutron activation analysis, argue that ESA is chemically indistinguishable from sample clay collected near Enkomi, suggesting an eastern Cypriot origin (Gunneweg, Perlman, and Yellin 1983: 1–14). Subsequent studies, however, have cast doubt on their interpretation. In separate publications Slane, also using neutron activation analysis (Slane et al. 1994) and the spatial distribution of the earliest and latest ESA forms (Slane 1997), promotes a north Syrian origin. More recently Lund, Malfitana, and Poblome suggest that *rhosica vasa* was in fact ESA and produced in Rhosos, modern Arsuz on the eastern coast of Cilicia (Lund, Malfitana, and Poblome 2008). They note that Arsuz possessed the requisite resources, including a harbor and significant quantities of clay, water, and fuel, to support the industry. Recent fieldwork in the area by the Mopsos Survey also appears to provide evidence in support an Arsuz origin (Olson and Killebrew 2011).

Shortly after the development of ESA in the east, the concept of a well-fired red slipped fine ware spread west, as evidenced by the development of Eastern Terra Sigillata B (ESB) in southwestern Anatolia, Çandarli ware (ESC), Cypriot Sigillata (ESD), and what scholars collectively refer to as Terra Sigillata in the west at, among other locales, Gaul and Arezzo. The Terra Sigillata and Eastern Terra Sigillata variants ultimately inspired subsequent red slipped industries in the east such as Cypriot Red Slip (CRS) and African Red Slip (ARS).

At Koutsopetria, there were only 36 ESA sherds discovered. When compared to other Cypriot projects, Panayia Ematousa (335 sherds or 23.4% of all fine wares), CPSP (169 sherds), and the numerous sherds from the House of Dionysos at Paphos, the low number of ESA sherds is surprising (Hayes 1991: 32–36; Lund 1993: 90; 2006: 205). While ESB has been found on Cyprus, at Amathous, Paphos, and Kourion for example, it is typically not found in large numbers, and thus the single ESB sherd at Koutsopetria is not unusual (Lund 1993: 96).

Eastern Sigillata A

36 finds
28 body sherds
4 rims
4 bases

ESA Atlante Form 4

70.48. Rim (fig. 4.3, reproduced at 1:2). Diam. = 0.190, PH = 0.020, PL = 0.039. Dark red slip (10R 4/8) over reddish yellow (7.5YR 6/6) fine fabric. Rare, small inclusions with occasional mica. See Hayes 1991: fig. 17, no. 2.

188.44. Rim. Diam. = 0.031. Fine, very pale brown fabric (10YR 8/4) with few inclusions and a red slip (2.5YR 4/8 to 6/8).

Eastern Sigillata B

1 find
1 body sherd

207.12. Body sherd. Diam. = 0.045. A fine-grained pink fabric (7.5YR 8/4) with lime inclusions, some large, and a red slip (2.5YR 5/8). Sherd has lightly incised lines on exterior.

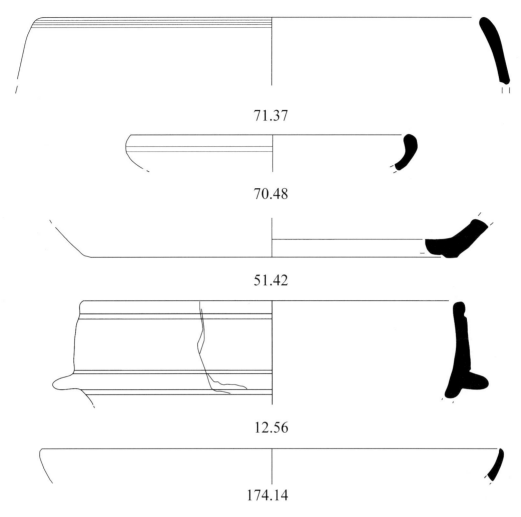

71.37

70.48

51.42

12.56

174.14

FIG. 4.3   *Imported Hellenistic Colour-Coated, ESA, CS, and Unclassified Hellenistic to Early Roman Red Ware sherds.*

4.1.3.5. Cypriot Sigillata (CS)

Cypriot Sigillata, first identified as such by Hayes, is a red-slipped fine ware industry consisting of a wide array of open and closed vessels dating from the last decade of the second century BC to shortly after the middle of the second century AD, a period in which, according to Hayes, a rapid decline in the ware occurred (Hayes 1967, 1991). The fabric can range from a light pink to a reddish brown with a purplish tint and at times includes small lime inclusions. The slip, reddish-brown to brown, is usually a darker color than the fabric and is often unevenly applied to the vessel and discolored due to uneven firing (Williams 1992: 2). The ware's earliest phase included two varieties, one gray and one red, both of which

are chemically indistinguishable. Initially identified as the predecessor of subsequent red-slipped CS by Slane, Meyza has shown that the short-lived gray variant is contemporary with the red group, and in fact shares a number of common vessel forms (Slane 1997: 366–67; Meyza 2002). Consisting of typical Hellenistic period forms through the first half of the first century BC, CS incorporated a series of distinct forms within half a century. The ware became tremendously popular and, as evidenced by first-century BC levels at Nea Paphos, Geronisos, and Panayia-Ematousa, replaced ESA as the dominant fine ware in Cyprus (Hayes 1991: 38; Młynarczyk 2005, 2010; Lund 2006: 217). Following the Augustan period, the ware supplanted ESA in Palestine and Egypt (Hayes 2008: 54).

Without the identification of CS kilns, scholars continue to postulate a place of manufacture, though most agree that it was a Cypriot product. Some researchers have, however, looked to Asia Minor as a possible place of manufacture (Gunneweg, Perlman, Yellin 1983: 14–15). Hayes proposes a western Cypriot origin, possibly near Soli, while Lund, noting that contemporary red ware kilns in western Asia Minor at Pergamon, Ephesus, and Sagalassos are situated on the peripheries of their respective cities, suggests that CS was produced in the periphery of Nea Paphos (Hayes 1967: 74; 1991: 27; Lund 2002: 188–89; 2006: 218). Interestingly, archaeological investigations at Anemurium, a mere 65 km from Cyprus, have yielded assemblages of the local red ware industries of western Asia Minor. The ubiquity of CS at Anemurium led Williams to also suggest a Cypriot origin. Furthermore, Młynarczyk, based on excavation at Geronisos and the identification of a potential progenitor, generally attributes the ware to the Ayios Georghios and Peyia regions of southwestern Cyprus. The popularity of CS and its replacement of ESA in the second half of the first century BC in Cyprus, compared to the transition from ESA to CS in Palestine and Egypt more than a generation later, clearly supports a Cypriot origin.

With Meyza proving that the early gray ware variant was contemporary with the traditional red group, the question regarding the origins of CS remained open. Recent excavations at Geronisos, however, have shed light on the issue. The short-lived Hellenistic occupation of the site, dated securely by ceramic and numismatic evidence from 80/70 BC to 40/30 BC, is represented by three fine ware assemblages, ESA, CS, and what Młynarczyk first identifies as "Pink Powdery Ware" (PPW) and later as "Pseudo-Sigillata" (Młynarczyk 2005; 2010). PPW vessels include a hard body displaying a "pinkish tinge" with a distinct powdery feel. The poorly preserved red slip is thin and has a matte sheen, while the fabric is identical to the Local Fabric B from terra cotta lamps (Młynarczyk 2005: 138; 2010: 355). The repertoire includes a vast array of both open and closed forms ranging in size from small juglets to large jugs and table amphorae. Młynarczyk considers the ware local to southwestern Cyprus because of its ubiquity, large assemblage of closed forms, and presence of four varieties (standard PPW, unslipped PPW, painted PPW, and PPW/CS transitional). Because the better fired PPW variety includes forms found in the CS repertoire and macroscopic similarities in fabric, the author argues that PPW and CS shared a common clay source and PPW was the progenitor of CS (Młynarczyk 2005: 149; 2010: 362).

Despite its popularity and its local manufacture, there were only 21 CS sherds found at Koutsopetria, and the only identifiable forms, based on Hayes' typology, were Cypriot Sigillata P9 and P12 (Hayes 1991). Compared to other Cypriot projects, such as Panayia Ematousa (133 sherds) and CPSP (297 sherds), the scarcity of CS sherds at Koutsopetria is striking (Lund 1993: 99–101; Lund 2006: 217–18). In light of the low ESA numbers discussed earlier, however, the low number of CS sherds is not unexpected and speaks either to a lack of imports (or at least those from western Cyprus), or to a decline in the importance of Koutsopetria in this period.

21 finds (all forms)
15 body sherds
5 bases
1 rim

Cypriot Sigillata Form P12

1 find
1 rim

51.42. Base (fig. 4.3, reproduced 1:2). Diam. = 0.010, PW = 0.025, PH = 0.016. Fine grained light red fabric (10R 6/6) with a thick light red slip (2.5YR 6/6) and some lime particles and rare, rounded spherical black stones. See Lund 1993: 103, no. C-193; Hayes 1991: fig. 18, no. 12.

4.1.3.6. Italian Sigillata

Typically manufactured at various sites throughout Italy (such as Arezzo, Pisa, Padana, Puteoli), the ware was also manufactured at sites in Germany and Gaul (Lund 1993: 97). This ware is characterized by a finely levigated fabric with a thick, lustrous slip.

1 find
1 rim

12.56. Rim (fig. 4.3). Diam. = 0.050. Fine light red fabric (2.5YR 7/6) with rare, rounded black stones. Thick, lustrous red slip (10R 4/8) with molded figure on outer edge above a flanged edge. See Lund 1993: 99, no. C-152.

4.1.3.7. Unclassified Hellenistic to Early Roman Red Ware

This category of fine ware contains examples that can only be dated broadly to the Hellenistic–Early Roman period due to their fabric and style of decoration. The decoration, fabric, and shape of these sherds are not distinctive enough to allow for a more precise identification. They are characterized by a red to reddish-brown fabric with a thin red or brown slip that is well-worn and often missing. The walls are thin and the fabric is well-levigated. These fine wares are most likely produced on the island, and are probably regionally manufactured.

40 finds
24 body sherds
7 rims
6 bases
3 handles

174.14. Rim (fig. 4.3, reproduced 1:3). Diam. = 0.190, PH = 0.027, PL = 0.023. Fine-grained, very pale brown (10YR 8/4) fabric with no visible inclusions and a red slip (2.5YR 4/8) preserved on interior. Tapered rim of a convex bowl. See Lund 1991: 87, no. C-42.

4.1.4. Fine Wares, Roman and Late Roman

By the Late Roman period the general trend of the Hellenistic and Early Roman period of relying on locally produced ceramics changes as the number of fine ware examples at Koutsopetria increases to 477. The variety of industries, as well as the number of imported wares, increases significantly. For the Late Roman Period, as expected, the three main red slip wares, Cypriot Red Slip, African Red Slip, and Phocaean Red Slip dominate the Roman and Late Roman fine wares, accounting for 70.8% of these sherds, with other categories such as Egyptian Red Slip (>1%) and various imitation wares (2%) accounting for lower percentages. The most distinctive feature at Koutsopetria in the Late Roman period, especially when compared to other sites on the island, is the frequency of African Red Slip, which accounts for 83 sherds, or 17.4% by quantity, of the Roman and Late Roman fine wares. In part, this could be due to the highly diagnostic fabric of African Red Slip that makes it easy to identify even from body sherds, but it is still appreciably higher than Phocaean Red Slip Ware, another easily identifiable ware roughly contemporary with African Red Slip, which accounts for only 52 sherds, or 10.9% by quantity. As expected, it is lower than locally produced Cypriot Red Slip, which accounts for 203 sherds, or 42.5% by quantity of the Roman and Late Roman fine wares. The frequency of African Red Slip at Koutsopetria is also high when compared to other sites on the island. At Panayia Ematousa, African Red Slip accounts for only 2% of the diagnostic Late Roman fine wares; Phocaean Ware and Cypriot Red Slip form the greater proportion of wares (Lund 2006: 183). At Kopetra and Maroni, Cypriot Red Slip dominates, followed by Phocaean Red Slip and African Red Slip (Manning 2002: 49–50; Rautman 2003: 163–66). Large urban centers like Kourion produced low numbers of Phocaean Ware and African Red Slip and seem to have better parallels with the variety of Late Roman material at Koutsopetria rather than the site of Panayia Ematousa, which is also in the immediate neighborhood of Kition (Hayes 2008: 435–76). For example, Panayia-Ematousa has a limited number of CRS forms (1, K1/1, 2, 9, and 11), while Koutsopetria has a greater variety (1, 2, 7, 8, 9, 10, 11), the primary difference being the larger CRS basin forms (7 and 10).

The majority of the Late Roman fine wares at Koutsopetria date to the sixth and seventh centuries, with the most commonly encountered forms being African Red Slip 105, Cypriot Red Slip 9, and Phocaean Ware 10. In the post Late Roman period (Medieval to Modern Periods), the number of fine wares drops to 57 sherds, or 6.8% by quantity of the total fine wares, and suggests a sudden and abrupt decline in activity at Koutsopetria (see Section

4.3.7). This rapid decline in the late seventh century at sites around Cyprus is often equated with the beginning of the Arab raids on the island and the destruction of coastal sites. (See Section 5.4.4 for distributional analysis).

4.1.4.1. African Red Slip (ARS)

The nomenclature of the ceramic industry known today as African Red Slip is as convoluted as those of the earlier eastern sigillatas. Although there were attestations to the ware, identified as "false sigillata" to differentiate the group from western sigillatas, prior to his publication of Hellenistic and Roman pottery from the Athenian Agora, Waagé was the first to name the industry (Waagé 1948: 43). Under the broad heading of "Late Roman," Waagé identified four distinguishable wares that he dubbed A, B, C, and D from finds in Athens, a characterization he later expounded upon when he published the Roman ceramics from Antioch (Waagé 1933: 293–308; 1948: 43–58). Late Roman A, B, and C represented what he identified as Egyptian imports to Athens, while Late Roman D (LRD) included all red ware local products and imitations (Waagé 1933: 293). Late Roman A (LRA) vessels consist of a very fine pure red fabric and are covered with a thin red porous slip. In most cases the exterior, and at times the interior, of the vessel are completely slipped. The fabric of Late Roman B (LRB) ware is brick-like in consistency and is browner than LRA. Late Roman C (LRC) consists of a thin well-fired fabric that ranges in color from brown to red and contains small yellow inclusions. In noting the similarities on LRA and LRB in his Antioch publication, Waagé rejects his previous theory supporting an Egyptian origin of the wares and proposes a broader North African origin (Waagé 1948: 45). In his analysis of the ceramics from the Athenian Agora, Robinson also saw similarities between Waagé's LRA and LRB and decided to combine the variants into a single industry he calls "Roman Red Ware" (Robinson 1959: 60 and fn. 9). It was not until 1972 that Hayes, in adopting the term first used by Kenyon in her excavations at Sabratha, proposed the now current African Red Slip (ARS). He proposed ARS in order to stress the continuity between LRA and LRB as North

African products and to differentiate the two from LRC and LRD, eastern products (Hayes 1972: 13; 2008: 68). This discussion of ARS focused on the changes in nomenclature from an eastern perspective. Scholars working in the west developed yet another set of names such as Terra Sigillata Chiara and Terra Sigillata Africana (for a discussion of the western perspective see Carandini 1981; Hayes 2008: 67–68).

Dating from the second through seventh centuries AD, ARS became the most popular red slipped ware of the late Roman period as the industry was traded throughout the eastern and western Mediterranean. Since the publications of Waagé and Robinson, who argued that ARS originated somewhere in northern Africa, the identification of kilns in modern Tunisia and a number of astute observations made by Hayes appear to make certain that both the standard variants of ARS (Waagé's LRA and LRB) were produced in Tunisia (Hayes 1972: 296–99; 1980: 517–19). In addition to the kilns, Hayes argues that because sites in northern Tunisia have ARS vessels that are strikingly consistent in fabric and form, the earliest ARS forms, the largest concentration and diversity of closed vessels, and many local variant forms, it is difficult to suggest an alternative production region.

The ARS repertoire includes an array of open and closed vessels that Hayes divides into 200 individual forms, some of which have numerous sub forms (Hayes 1972, 1980). Building on and indeed updating Waagé's initial characterization of the ware, Hayes notes that ARS vessels present an orange-red to brick-red coarse body with a granular appearance (Hayes 1972: 13). The fabric often includes inclusions such as lime — which frequently erupts during the firing process leaving distinct voids in the body and slip — quartz, small black particles, and on occasion traces of silver mica. Most forms are covered with a matte red to reddish-orange slip. Other forms of decoration include incised lines, rouletting, and, between the fourth and sixth centuries, stamped decorations (Hayes 1972: 217–81; 1980: 512–14).

While the number of ARS sherds discovered at Koutsopetria is relatively high, the variety in forms is not, with only nine forms present (61, 67,

93B, 99A, 103, 104, 105, 106, and 107). The majority of the identifiable rims are from the sixth and seventh centuries AD. The size of the total ARS sherd collection at PKAP (83) is smaller than the ARS assemblages at Anemurium (150) and Kopetra (143) in number of sherds (Williams 1992: 38; Rautman 2003: 164). Both sites have a wider variety of forms (Anemurium 15 and Kopetra 10) than the nine present at Koutsopetria. Of these nine, only forms 61 and 103 (which is an uncommon form) are not present at Kopetra, and only form 103 is not present at Anemurium. It is interesting to note that the only later form present at other sites near our location (Panayia Ematousa and Kopetra) and not present at Koutsopetria is ARS 109 (Williams 1992: 38; Rautman 2003: 188). ARS form 109 is a common find and is often found with ARS form 105, the most frequently collected ARS rim at PKAP (Hayes 1972: 172). The characteristics of the ARS collection at PKAP, a large corpus of a limited number of forms dating to the sixth and seventh centuries AD, would suggest that in this period Koutsopetria had fairly significant growth in both its trade and wealth.

83 finds (all forms)
31 body sherds
31 rims
21 bases

ARS 61

African Red Slip Form 61 is a large shallow dish with an inturned rim that is triangular in appearance and decorated with a stamp and groove on the floor. It is a common find in the Mediterranean and dates to the fourth and fifth centuries AD (Hayes 1972: 100–107).

1 find
1 rim

68.21. Rim (fig. 4.4, reproduced 1:3). Diam. = 0.340, PH= 0.038, PL= 0.108. Medium-coarse red fabric (2.5YR 4/6) with red slip (2.5YR 5/8) wearing only slightly on lip. The slip is not present on exterior except for one line and there are some pitting scars. Fabric includes frequent, small to medium black

and white inclusions, frequent sparkling. Groove on inside below lip, also one on body 0.014 m below lip on inside. See Hayes 1972: 103, fig. 17, no. 61.33.

ARS 67

African Red Slip Form 67 is a large bowl with a hooked or rolled rim and is usually decorated with a stamp and grooves. It is a common find in the Mediterranean and dates to the fourth and fifth centuries AD (Hayes 1972: 112–16).

1 find
1 rim

62.36. Rim (fig. 4.4, reproduced 1:3). Diam. = 0.240, PH = 0.048, PL = 0.087. Medium to fine-grained, light brown fabric (7.5YR 6/4) with slip not preserved. Inclusions include abundant very small mica, and common very small black and white inclusions. Two-part flaring curved rim, thickened to exterior with rounded lip, but flattened top surface. See Hayes 1972: 114, fig. 19, no. 67.5.

ARS 93B

African Red Slip Form 93 is a large bowl that has a flat rim and high foot. It is a common find and dates to the late fifth to early sixth century AD. Hayes identifies two main types, and our one example is a type B, which has a shorter rolled rim and dates to the sixth century (Hayes 1972: 145–48).

1 find
1 rim

23.18. Rim (fig. 4.4, reproduced 1:2). Diam. = 0.210, PH = 0.017, Th. = 0.008 (rim), Th. = 0.005 (body). Medium-coarse red fabric (2.5YR 5/8) with thick, light red glossy slip (2.5YR 6/8) wearing slightly, and frequent fine mica and small to large white, red, and dark inclusions and some encrustations. Rim is turned outward and thickened with rounded lip. See Hayes 1972: 146, fig. 27, no. 93.21.

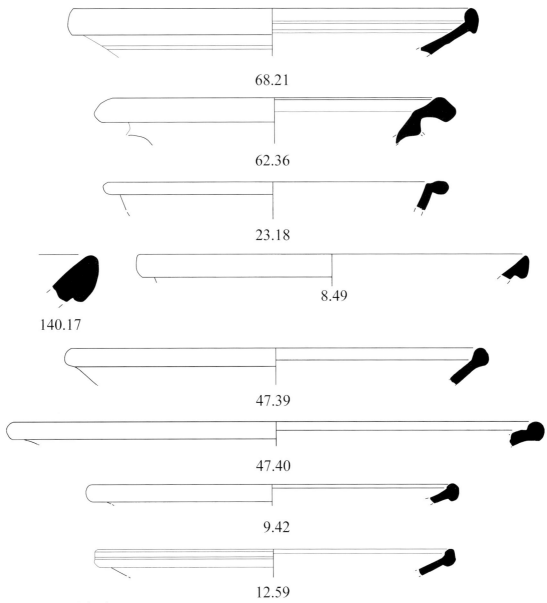

68.21

62.36

23.18

140.17

8.49

47.39

47.40

9.42

12.59

FIG. 4.4   *ARS sherds.*

ARS 99A

African Red Slip Form 99 is a hemispherical bowl with a rolled rim and is usually decorated with a stamp on the floor. It is broken into three subcategories (A, B, and C) and the only find at Koutsopetria is from subcategory A. This subcategory is differentiated from the other two by its larger diameter and thicker rim. It is a common find in the Mediterranean and dates to the sixth century AD (Hayes 1972: 152–55).

1 find
1 rim

140.17. Rim (fig. 4.4). Diam. = uncertain, PL = 0.020, Th. = 0.010. Fine fabric is light red (10R 6/8 or 2.5YR 5/6) with no noticeable inclusions. Bowl with thin rim and tapered lip. See Williams 1992: 41–42, no. 236.

ARS 103B

African Red Slip Form 103 is a large bowl or basin with a hooked rim and decorated with a stamp encircled by a groove. It is broken into two subcategories (A and B) and the one find at Koutsopetria is from subcategory B that has a low foot instead of the high foot of subcategory A. It is a relatively uncommon find and dates to the sixth century AD (Hayes 1972: 157–60).

1 find
1 rim

8.49. Rim (fig. 4.4, reproduced 1:2). Diam. = 0.210, PH = 0.013, PL = 0.028. Medium to medium-coarse red fabric (2.5YR 4/8) with thick glossy red slip (2.5YR 4/8–5/8). Rare, sparkling and small, white inclusions. Rolled rim with tapered lip. See Hayes 1972: 158, fig. 29, no. 103.6.

ARS 104

African Red Slip Form 104 is a large plate or bowl that has a knobbed rim and is decorated with a stamped decoration in the floor surrounded by grooves and one groove under the rim on the interior and one on the exterior. It is a common find in the eastern Mediterranean and dates to between the sixth and seventh centuries AD. Hayes breaks the form into three subcategories (A is a plate which dates from 530–580 AD, B is a plate which dates from 570–600 AD with a few later variants, and C is a bowl which dates from 550–625 AD; Hayes 1972: 160–66).

3 finds
3 rims

ARS 104B

47.39. Rim (fig. 4.4, reproduced at 1:3). Diam. = 0.350, PH = 0.030, PL = 0.049. Coarse, gritty red fabric (2.5YR 4/6 to 2.5YR 5/6) with slip worn off and pitted. Fabric contains common but very small mica inclusions, and common, very small to small black, red, and white inclusions. Knobbed rim with rounded lip. See Hayes 1972: 162, fig. 30, no. 104B.16.

ARS 104C

47.40. Rim (fig. 4.4, reproduced at 1:2). Diam. = 0.260, PH = 0.016, PL = 0.037. Medium-coarse, reddish-yellow fabric (5YR 6/6), pitted with an orange-red slip with common, small (to very small) red and black inclusions, and common sparkling. Rounded, small knobbed rim with no groove. See Hayes: 1972, 162, fig. 30, 104C.23.

ARS 105

African Red Slip form 105 is a large undecorated plate with a rounded foot and a knobbed rim. It is a common find in the eastern Mediterranean and is dated to between the end of the sixth century and the end of the seventh century AD (Hayes 1972: 166–69).

16 finds
16 rims

1.30. Rim. Diam. = 0.240, PH = 0.031, PL = 0.040. Medium grained red fabric (2.5YR 4/8) with frequent, small to large white inclusions, rare black inclusions, frequent sparkling inclusions, and no preserved slip. See Hayes 1972: 168, fig. 32, no. 105.8.

9.42. Rim (fig. 4.4, reproduced at 1:3). Diam. = 0.260, PH = 0.018, PL = 0.042. Medium-grained light red fabric (2.5YR 6/8) with few lime, mica, and quartz inclusions, and no visible slip. Late form. See Williams 1992: 52, no. 299.

12.59. Rim (fig. 4.4, reproduced at 1:3). Diam. = 0.270, PH = 0.025, PL = 0.052. Medium-grained, light red fabric (2.5YR 6/8) with frequent, medium lime and quartz inclusions. Very little of red slip preserved on rim that has single incised line. See Hayes 1972: 164, fig. 31, no. 105-17.

18.61. Rim. Diam. = 0.280, PH = 0.032, PL = 0.071. Medium-grained red fabric (2.5YR 5/8) with darker core and a thick red slip (2.5YR 4/8) preserved on rim and interior. Frequent, sparkling inclusions, medium-large white inclusions, and rare black inclusions. See Hayes 1972: 168, fig. 32, no. 105.9.

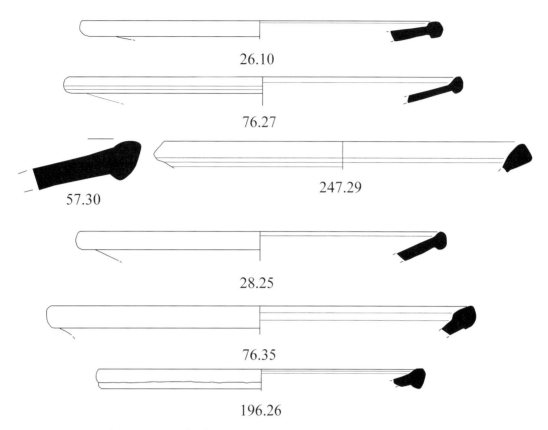

26.10

76.27

57.30   247.29

28.25

76.35

196.26

Fig. 4.5   *ARS and Imitation ARS sherds.*

26.10. Rim (fig. 4.5, reproduced at 1:3). Diam. = 0.310, PH = 0.021, PL = 0.066. Fine light red fabric (2.5YR 6/6) with rare, very large lime inclusions, and a light red slip (2.5YR 6/8) on interior and exterior.

76.27. Rim (fig. 4.5, reproduced at 1:3). Diam. = 0.480, PH = 0.027, PL = 0.047. Coarse red slip (2.5YR 4/8) thinly applied with light encrustation on red core (2.5YR 5/8) and medium, frequent inclusions, some sparkling, and some lime. Slip eroding on exterior and interior (to lesser extent), only slightly rounded on lip. Convex rim on exterior, hooked on underside. See Hayes 1972: 168, fig. 32, no. 105-19.

ARS 106

African Red Slip form 106 is a large plate with a rolled rim. It is an uncommon find in the eastern Mediterranean and is dated to the first half of the seventh century AD (Hayes 1972: 169–71).

1 find
1 rim

57.30. Rim (fig. 4.5). Diam. = uncertain, PH = 0.026, PL = 0.036. Medium-coarse, fabric (5YR 4/6) with a poor, red slip (5YR 4/6 to 5YR 5/6) and numerous very small mica, and small, white and black inclusions. Lip is rounded with a faint groove on exterior, 0.005 m below lip. See Williams 1992: 43, no. 247.

ARS 107

African Red Slip form 107 is a large bowl with a flat rim and a knobbed foot. It is a common find in the eastern Mediterranean and is dated to the first half of the sixth century AD (Hayes 1972: 171).

1 find
1 rim

23.18. Rim. Diam. = 0.210, PH = 0.017, PL = 0.066. Medium-coarse, red fabric (2.5YR 5/8) with thick light red glossy slip (2.5YR 6/8) that is wearing slightly, frequent fine mica and small to large white, red, and dark inclusions.

4.1.4.2. African Red Slip Imitation (Also known as Imitation Late B ware and Egyptian C ware)

Imitation African Red Slip is characterized by a coarse orangish fabric with lime inclusions, dark grits and mica with a thin slip that is often not preserved. Its most distinctive feature is the sandpaper feel to the fabric and its presence at various sites around the Mediterranean attests to the popularity of the African Red Slip forms (Williams 1992: 51–52). While its manufacturing centers are not known, it is found at numerous sites throughout the Mediterranean and has also been classified as Imitation Late B and Egyptian C ware (Hayes 1972: 399–401).

Despite the ware's wide-spread discoveries, Koutsopetria appears to be one of the few areas in Cyprus with ARS imitation wares, as its presence was not recorded at sites in the immediate area, such as Kopetra, Panayia Ematousa, or Athienou, nor by projects in other regions, such as SCSP or CPSP (Lund 1993; Keswani, et al: 2003; Rautman 2003; Lund 2006; Moore and Gregory 2012). Its presence is most often noted at Anatolian sites, such as Anemurium (Williams 1992: 51–52) and Aphrodisias (Hudson 2008: 343), and, like the relatively large quantity of African Red Slip sherds discovered during the survey, seems to indicate that Koutsopetria's regional trading connections are to the east.

22 finds (all forms)
13 rims
6 bases
3 body sherds

ARS 104–106 Imitation

1 find
1 rim

247.29. Rim (fig. 4.5, reproduced at 1:2). Diam. = 0.250, PH = 0.016, PL = 0.050. Medium to coarse, light red fabric (2.5YR 5/8) with lime inclusions and no visible slip.

ARS 104 Imitation

1 find
1 rim

70. 35. Rim. Diam. = 0.350, PH = 0.041, PL = 0.061. Medium to coarse reddish yellow fabric (5YR 7/6) with frequent, medium to large inclusions of lime, mica and quartz. Slight incised line on interior of rim.

ARS 105 Imitation

8 finds
8 rims

8.50. Rim. Diam. = 0.240. PH = 0.014, PL = 0.054. Medium-grained, light red fabric (2.5YR 7/8) with a light red slip (2.5YR 6/8) preserved on interior below rim. Common, very small to medium, black and white inclusions, a few larger inclusions, and common, sparkling inclusions.

28.25. Rim (fig. 4.5, reproduced at 1:3). Diam. = 0.260, PH = 0.027, PL = 0.051. Medium to coarse grained, light red fabric (2.5YR 6/8) with no traces of slip. See Hudson 2008: 343, no. 5.3.

76.35. Rim (fig. 4.5, reproduced at 1:3). Diam. = uncertain, PH = 0.025, PL = 0.037. Very coarse, light red fabric (2.5YR 4/8) with well-worn red slip (2.5YR 5/8) and abundant, small to medium inclusions, some glittering, some black.

196.26. Rim (fig. 4.5, reproduced at 1:3). Diam. = 0.250, PW = .028, PL = .049, Th. = .011. Medium grained, light red fabric (10R 6/8) with some lime and quartz and no visible slip. Incised line on outside of rim. See Williams 1992: 52, no. 299.

4.1.4.3. Cypriot Red Slip (CRS)

In his publication of the ceramic assemblage from Antioch, Waagé slightly modified his Late Roman typology. Having identified a distinct ware with a brown fabric and a red-brown to purple body, Waagé renamed his Late Roman D ware from Athens "Local (Athenian) Late Roman Pottery" and reassigned the LRD label to this newly identified industry (Waagé 1948: 52 and fn. 14). He also identified a fifth Late Roman ware, Late Roman E (LRE), with a similar fabric color as LRD, but a body with a metallic sheen (Waagé 1948: 52). Following Waagé, Hayes combined LRD and LRE into a single ware, identified a series of fairly standardized forms, and renamed the industry Cypriot Red Slip (CRS) (Hayes 1972: 371). While this has remained the standard nomenclature for the ware, an increasing number of scholars have argued for a modification, such as so-called Cypriot Red Slip or Cypriot Red Slip Derivatives, or even a reversion back to Late Roman D (Firat 2000; Kenkel 2007; Armstrong 2009). Since archaeology projects on Cyprus refer to the ware as CRS, we have elected to do so as well.

The analyses of CRS sherds from excavated sites throughout Cyprus and the Levant has led to a well-established chronology demonstrating that the ware was first produced at the end of the fourth century and continued throughout the seventh century. As with CS, the identification of CRS kilns on Cyprus has eluded scholars, but because of the ubiquity of the ware and diversity of forms found in Cyprus, most scholars have supported a western Cypriot origin (See for example Hayes 1972, 1980, 2008; Gomez et al. 1996, 2002; Lund 2006). Recent survey work by the Pisidia Survey Project in southern Turkey, however, has located seven production centers that were manufacturing sites for all of the standard CRS forms (Jackson, et al. 2012: 89–90). Support for CRS production in Anatolia is further supported by chemical analyses of CRS sherds from Sagalassos, Perge, and Hierapolis that indicate a probable Anatolian origin (Poblome et al. 2001: 119–26). While it is now clear that CRS was manufactured in Anatolia, this does not rule out production sites in other regions, such as western Cyprus. In fact, the large number of large basin sherds, including a unique folded over rim discovered at Polis and Paphos, would seem to indicate the strong possibility of a kiln site in the region (Rowe 2006).

The earliest and latest phases are poorly attested outside of Cyprus, but CRS was a common export from the middle of the fifth through early seventh centuries (Hayes 1972: 385; Meyza 2007). Despite the nearly two-century gap between the end of the production of CS in the second century and the appearance of CRS in the late fourth century, similarities in fabric have led some to interpret the wares as a single, western Cypriot ceramic tradition (Hayes 1972: 371; 2008: 89; Gomez et al. 2002). Using neutron activation analysis of both Roman and Late Roman fine ware sherds and clay samples collected throughout Cyprus, Gomez et al. argue that similarities in CRS and CS fabric are representative of a specific clay source from western Cyprus (Gomez et al. 2002: 32). Meyza, however, argues that CRS fabric is not as homogeneous as initially thought. In conducting a proportional analysis of CRS in relation to other contemporary fine wares from four different phases (Phase I: 350–440 AD, Phase II: 440–540, Phase III: 540–580, and Phase IV: 580–670) in sites throughout the eastern and western Mediterranean, Meyza contends that the resulting spatial distribution suggests multiple CRS production areas in both Cyprus and Palestine (Meyza 2007: 101 and 103).

While Hayes' dating for the standard forms has been modified, it has not been significantly altered in the last forty years. Recent attempts, however, have been made to shift the dates for many of the forms. Meyza's work in Paphos has led him to suggest the lowering of the date for initial production for some of the more popular forms (Meyza 2007). Rowe, also working in Paphos, has suggested a more radical redating of Hayes' chronology that would also lower the initial production of early CRS forms, such as CRS1, to the mid-to-late third century AD (Rowe 2006: 299). On the other hand, Armstrong argues for pushing the end date of certain CRS forms, such as CRS 9 and Well Form, into the eighth and ninth centuries AD (Armstrong 2009: 174–78).

The standard typologies of CRS are Hayes' 1972 and 1980 works, in which he identifies twelve forms, though Meyza's reassessments added a number of vessel shapes to the repertoire and renamed others (Hayes 1972, 1980; Meyza 2000 and 2007). Our initial analyses of our CRS forms, which began in 2005, were based on Hayes' 1972/1980 typology. The ware includes a number of shallow dishes and basins. Like CS, there are few impurities present in CRS, primarily lime inclusions that often erupted during the firing process. The body color varies and includes hues of yellow, orange, brown, red, deep maroon, and purple (Hayes 1972: 371). With the exception of the earliest forms that present a slip with a metallic luster, most subsequent vessels were covered with a matte red to reddish-orange slip. Most forms were decorated with an irregularly aligned rouletting, grooves, or stamps (Hayes 1972: 372; Meyza 2007: 82–84).

There are several observations that can be made about the CRS forms that are present and absent at Koutsopetria. The CRS forms identified are fairly standard with all common forms present. The CRS forms not present (CRS 3, 4, 5, and 6) are rarer at sites on Cyprus, and thus their absence at Koutsopetria is not surprising (Meyza 2007). The one CRS form that would be expected to be present and is not, is the fairly common late form, CRS Well Form. This form, which dates from the late fifth to seventh centuries, is typically present at most large Late Roman sites on Cyprus, such as Kopetra, Kourion, and Paphos (Rautman 2003: 183; Meyza 2007: 79–80), but not at smaller sites near Koutsopetria, such as Panayia Ematousa or Athienou (Lund 2006; Moore and Gregory 2012). Given the size of the Late Roman site at Koutsopetria and the large number of other sixth and seventh century AD fine wares present, however, its absence is unusual. With the recent discovery of CRS kilns near Gebiz, Turkey (Jackson et al. 2012), which is only 256 km northwest of the Akamas peninsula, and the relatively larger numbers of CRS sherds present in the western half of Cyprus, the apparent trading route to Cyprus for CRS forms produced in Asia Minor would be to Cypriot coastal sites in the north and west, such as Polis, Paphos, and Soli. From these points they would be distributed across the island through local trading connections, or south and then east (counter-clockwise) around Cyprus by coasting traders.

203 finds (all forms)
80 body sherds
79 rims
40 bases
4 handles

CRS 1 (Waagé 928)

Cypriot Red Slip Form 1 is an undecorated dish with a thickened rim that is rounded on the exterior. It is a relatively uncommon find in the Mediterranean that Hayes dates to the late fourth and fifth centuries AD, while Rowe proposes pushing its initial production back to around 350 AD (Hayes 1972: 372–73; Williams 1992: 29–30; Lund 1993: 113–14; 2003: 228; Rautman 2003: 164–65; Rowe 2006: 107–10; Meyza 2007: 44–45). Meyza proposes dividing this form into three subdivisions (1A, 1B, and 1C) based on the size of the bowl and variations in rim (Meyza 2000: fig. 9, 2007: 44–48). A reexamination of our catalogued pieces shows that Meyza's form H1B was the most common CRS1 form at PKAP, which is consistent with it being the most common of the three Meyza CRS1 sub-forms (Meyza 2007: 46).

11 finds
10 rims
1 base

19.10. Rim (fig. 4.6, reproduced at 1:3). Diam. = 0.240, PH = 0.042, PL = 0.053. Medium-grained, red to light red fabric (10R 5/6) with few lime inclusions. Slip is blackened on rim with red slip (10R 5/8) on interior and exterior. Slight incised line on interior of rim. See Meyza 2007: Pl. 1, no. H1A.

126.23. Rim (fig. 4.6, reproduced at 1:3). Diam. = 0.340, Th. (body) = 0.011, Th. (rim) = 0.015. Fine-grained, light red fabric (2.5YR 7/8) with few inclusions and red slip (10R 5/8) on interior. Heavy and thick rim with line on interior. See Meyza 2007: Pl. 1, no. H1B.4.

56.53. Rim (fig. 4.6, reproduced at 1:2). Diam. = 0.240, PH = 0.025, PL = 0.061. Medium to fine-grained, light reddish-brown fabric (2.5YR 6/4) with rare, large lime inclusions and a mottled red

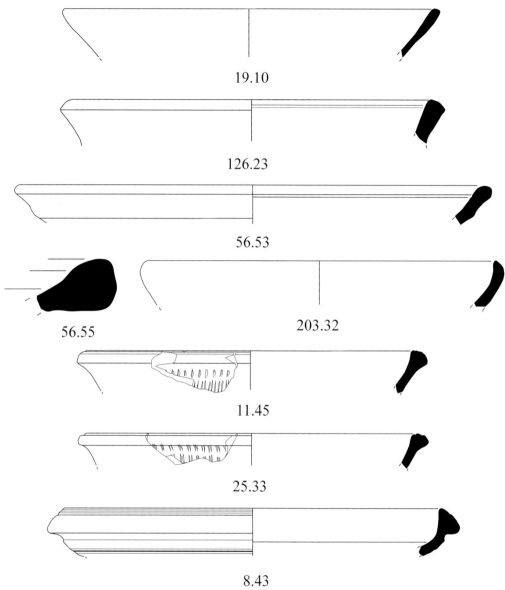

19.10

126.23

56.53

56.55   203.32

11.45

25.33

8.43

FIG. 4.6   *CRS sherds.*

slip (2.5YR 4/8) on interior and exterior of rim. See Meyza 2007: Pl. 1, no. H1B.6.

56.55. Rim (fig. 4.6). Diam. = 0.340, PH = 0.021, PL = 0.031. Medium-grained, red fabric (10R 5/8) with a few lime inclusions, and a light red slip on interior. Incised line on top of rim. See Hayes 1972: 374, fig. 80, no. CRS1.2; Rautman 2003: 181, no. 1.

203.32. Rim (fig. 4.6). Diam. = 0.210, PH = 0.026, PL = 0.031. Medium to fine-grained, red fabric (2.5YR 5/6) with a glossy red slip (2.5YR 5/8–4/8)

that is browner and redder in appearance than the fabric. Fabric contains numerous very small, micaceous inclusions, and small, occasional limestone inclusions. Rim hooks inward with a tapered lip. See Williams 1992: 30, no. 157.

CRS 2

Cypriot Red Slip Form 2 is a dish characterized by a knobbed rim with grooves and rouletting on the exterior. This form is an imitation of African Red Slip Form 84. It is a common find in the

Mediterranean and Hayes dates it to between the fifth and sixth centuries AD, while Meyza modifies the chronology slightly and dates it from the beginning of the fifth century to the middle or third quarter of the sixth century (Hayes 1972: 373–76; Williams 1992: 30–31; Lund 1993: 114–15; 2003: 228–29; Rautman 2003: 164–65; Meyza 2007: 51–53).

6 finds
6 rims

11.45. Rim (fig. 4.6, reproduced at 1:3). Diam. = 0.30. Fine-grained light red fabric (10R 6/8) with rare inclusions of lime and a poorly-preserved slip. Deep bowl with steep wall and a slightly inturned rim. See Lund 1993: 114, no. C-302.

25.33. Rim (fig. 4.6, reproduced at 1:3). Diam. = 0.240, PH = 0.023, PL = 0.075. Medium-grained light reddish-brown (5YR 6/4) fabric with rare, large lime inclusions and reddish-brown slip (2.5YR 4/4) on interior and exterior. Possibly overfired. Rouletting on exterior wall of bowl beginning under the rim, and the rim is incised with a double groove. See Williams 1992: 30, no. 160.

[40.1] 52. Rim. Diam. = indeterminate, PH = 0.013, PL = 0.019. Medium fine-grained, very pale brown fabric (10YR 8/2) with common, sparkling small inclusions. Light brown slip (7.5YR 6/3) is worn and there are two rows of rouletting beginning at 0.006 and 0.013 below top of rounded lip. Transitional form similar to Williams 1992: 30, no. 158.

CRS 7

Cypriot Red Slip Form 7 is a thick-walled basin with rouletting and groove marks. It is a common find in the Mediterranean and Hayes dates this form to the late sixth/early seventh century AD, while Meyza proposes a date of 450 AD to the late sixth/early seventh century AD (Hayes 1972: 377–79; Williams 1992: 36; Meyza 2007: 58).

1 find
1 rim

8.43. Rim (fig. 4.6, reproduced at 1:3). Diam. = greater than 0.240, PH = 0.042, PL = 0.046. Fine to medium-grained, light brown fabric (7.5YR 6/4–6/6) with red slip (2.5YR 5/8). Uneven surface; poorly made. Two grooves on exterior of large everted rim. See Rautman 2003: 181, no. 12.

CRS 8 (Rodziewicz D3, D4, and D5)

Cypriot Red Slip Form 8 is a dish or bowl with a flat rim and decorated with rouletting on the exterior. It is an uncommon find and Hayes dates it to the sixth century DA, while Meyza proposes a date of the fifth century to the second half of the seventh century AD (Hayes 1972: 379; Rodziewicz 1976: 46–47; Williams 1992: 34; Lund 1993: 114; Rowe 2006: 116–17; Meyza 2007: 60).

2 finds
2 rims

232.31. Rim (fig. 4.7, reproduced at 1:2). Diam. = 0.160, PH = 0.010, PL = 0.030. Medium-grained, light red fabric (2.5YR 6/6) with a poor slip. Fabric contains common, sparkling inclusions, and rare, medium black and white inclusions. Rim is broken in two and is downturned.

CRS 9 (Meyza K2, K3, K4 and K5)

Cypriot Red Slip Ware Form 9 is a large dish with a flat base that has a groove encircling it and a thickened vertical rim that curves inward. It is decorated with rouletting underneath the rim and a wavy line on the rim. It is a common find in the Mediterranean and dates from the middle of the sixth century to the end of the seventh century. Hayes divided the form into three sub-forms (CRS 9A, 9B, and 9C) based on their rim decoration and style of base (Hayes 1972: 379–82). Meyza proposes a reclassification of Hayes' forms 9 and 10 into new forms K2 (shallow platters), K3 (Hayes 9A and 9B), K4 (Hayes 9C deep versions and Hayes 10.1–2), and K5 (Hayes 10.3) (Meyza 2007: 61–62).

37 finds (all forms)
35 rims
2 bases

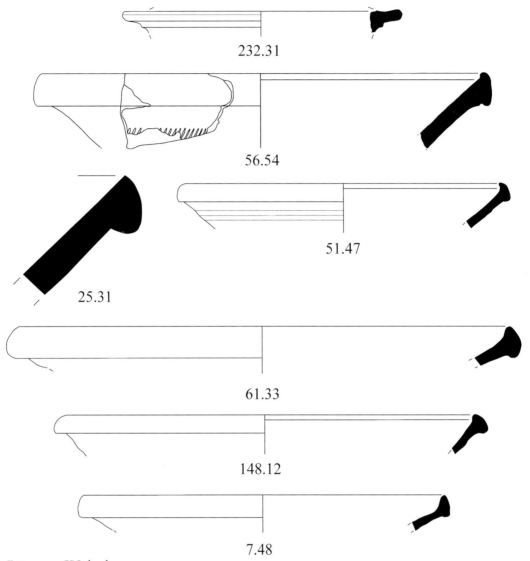

FIG. 4.7   *CRS sherds.*

56.54. Rim. Diam. = 0.20, PH = 0.044, PL = 0.059. Fine-grained, red to light red fabric (10 R 6/6) with rare lime inclusions and red slip (10 R 5/8). Vessel has a slightly inturned rim and rouletting half the way down the side. Form is a transitional phase between Meyza K1 and Meyza K3 (K1/K3). See Meyza 2007: 65, and Pl. 8, K1/3 no. 1. (Fig. 4.7, reproduced at 1:2)

CRS 9A (Meyza K3)

Cypriot Red Slip Ware Form 9A is distinguished by its lack of a grooved rim and low ledge foot and Hayes dates it from 550–600 AD, while Meyza's

K3 form is dated between 530/540 and 670–680 (Hayes 1972: 379–82; Meyza 2007: 64).

25.31. Rim (fig. 4.7). Diam. = 0.250, PH = 0.036, PL = 0.031. Medium-grained, red to light red fabric (2.5YR 6/8) with few lime and mica inclusions. See Hayes 1972: 378, fig. 81, no. 9.1; Rautman 2003: 181, no. 16.

51.47. Rim (fig. 4.7, reproduced at 1:3). Diam. = 0.240, PH = 0.030, PL = 0.066. Medium grained, red fabric (2.5YR 4/8) with occasional, small to medium white inclusions and a discoloration in slip (red to yellowish-red) with wearing on rim.

Plain knob rim, hooking inward toward lip and on the interior the lip is sharply demarcated from body. Convex rounded lip and low uneven ridges on exterior. See Williams 1992: 31, no. 169; Rautman 2003: 181, no. 20.

61.33. Rim (fig. 4.7, reproduced at 1:2). Diam. = 0.30, PH = 0.027, PL = 0.038. Fine-grained, red fabric (10R 5/6) with some small lime and sparkling inclusions and an inconsistent red slip (2.5YR 4/8 to 2.5YR 5/6). Encrusted lightly on core in a few places. See Meyza 2007: Pl. 9, K3 no. 2.

148.12. Rim (fig. 4.7, reproduced at 1:2). Diam. = 0.220, PH = 0.023, PL = 0.039. Fine-grained, light reddish-brown fabric (2.5YR 7/3) with a few, very large lime inclusions and a light red slip (2.5YR 6/6). Rim has a slight groove under rim. See Meyza 2007: Pl. 9, K3.1.

CRS 9B (Meyza K3)

Cypriot Red Slip Ware Form 9B is distinguished by its lack of a grooved rim and its flat base with a shallow groove. Hayes dates it from 550–600 AD, while Meyza's K3 form is dated between 530/540 and 670–680 (Hayes 1972: 379–82; Meyza 2007: 64).

7.48. Rim (fig. 4.7, reproduced at 1:3). Diam. = 0.210, PH = 0.034, PL = 0.053. Medium to fine-grained, pink fabric (5YR 7/4) with traces of red slip on exterior. See Hayes 1972: 380, fig. 82, no. 9.11.

12.55. Rim (fig. 4.8, reproduced at 1:3). Diam. = 0.20, PH = 0.048, PL = 0.059. Medium to fine-grained, light red fabric (2.5YR 6/6) with rare lime inclusions and red slip (2.5YR 4/8) on exterior. See Hayes 1972: 380, fig. 82, no. 9.12.

CRS 9C (Meyza K4)

Cypriot Red Slip Ware Form 9C is distinguished by its rim with two grooves and its flat base with a shallow groove. Hayes dates it from 550–600 AD, while Meyza's K3 form is dated between the middle of the 6th century and the end of the 7th century AD (Hayes 1972: 379–82; Meyza 2007: 69).

4.35. Rim (fig. 4.8, reproduced at 1:3). Diam. = 0.340, PH = 0.027, PL = 0.074, Th. (rim) = .008, Th. (body) = .007. Medium to fine-grained, light red fabric (2.5YR 6/6) with rare, lime inclusions and a mottled red slip (2.5YR 4/8) on interior and exterior. Inturned rim with two incised lines. See Williams 1992: 32, no. 174.

28.26. Rim (fig. 4.8, reproduced at 1:3). Diam. = 0.33. Fine-grained, light red fabric (10R 6/6) with rare inclusions and a red slip (2.5YR 5/6) on interior and exterior. Inturned rim with two incised lines on rim, and two incised lines immediately below rim on exterior. Rouletting on wall. See Meyza 2007: Pl. 9, K4A.

CRS 10 (Meyza K4 and K5)

Cypriot Red Slip Ware Form 10 is a basin and a deeper version of CRS 9C with a grooved rim and irregular rouletting underneath the rim. It dates to the seventh century AD (Hayes 1972: 382–83).

1 find
1 rim

181.21. Rim (fig. 4.8, reproduced at 1:3). Diam. = 0.225. Fine-grained reddish yellow fabric (5YR 7/6) with some large inclusions and red slip (2.5YR 5/8). Triangular rim with rouletting under rim on body with two grooves / incisions on rim. See Rautman 2003: 183, no. 27.

CRS Saucer

Cypriot Red Slip Saucers are similar to the CRS 9 and CRS 10, but much smaller in diameter, and date to the late sixth and seventh centuries AD (Williams 1992: 33).

1 find
1 rim

65.35. Rim (fig. 4.8, reproduced at 1:2). Diam. = uncertain, PH = 0.041, PL = 0.041. Medium to fine-grained, light red fabric (2.5YR 7/6) with few lime inclusions and a red slip (2.5YR 5/8) on inte-

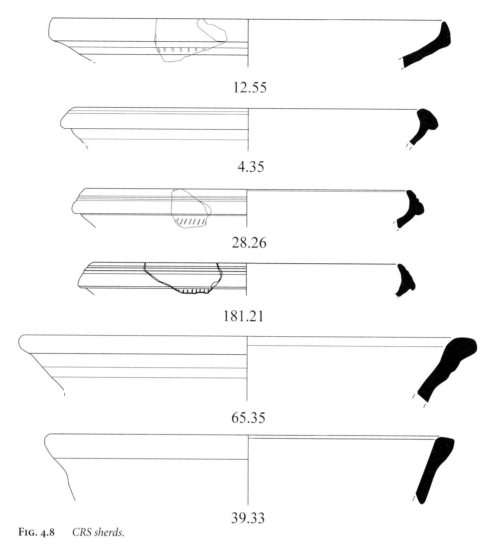

12.55

4.35

28.26

181.21

65.35

39.33

FIG. 4.8   *CRS sherds.*

rior and exterior. Vessel with rounded flaring rim. See Williams 1992: 33, no. 182.

CRS 11

Cypriot Red Slip Ware Form 11 is a deep basin with two thick horizontal handles. The exterior of the walls are irregularly ridged and the basin is covered with a thin slip that is often only on the interior and around the rim on the exterior. Meyza has proposed a refinement to the form and subdivides the ware into H11A, H11B, H11C, and H11D based on rim thicknesses (Meyza 2007: 73–75). It is a common find in the Mediterranean and Hayes dates to the sixth and seventh centuries AD, while Meyza proposes a date of the middle fifth to sev-

enth centuries AD, and Rowe suggests a starting date of the first half of the fifth century AD (Hayes 1972: 383; Rowe 2006: 132; Meyza 2007: 72).

10 finds
8 rims
1 handle
1 body sherd

39.33. Rim with handle nub (fig. 4.8, reproduced at 1:3). Diam. = 0.290, PH = 0.054, PL = 0.082. Medium-grained, pink fabric (5YR 7/4) with few, large lime inclusions and traces of a light red slip (10R 6/6) on interior. See Williams 1992: 36, no. 204; Meyza 2007: Pl. 10, H11B.

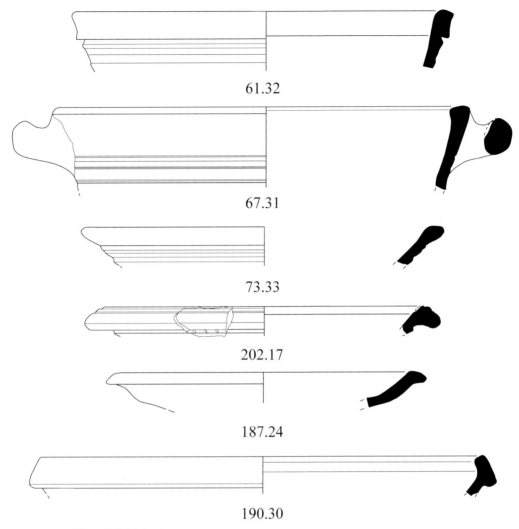

FIG. 4.9 *CRS and PHW sherds.*

61.32. Rim (fig. 4.9, reproduced at 1:3). Diam. = 0.320, PH = 0.048, PL = 0.069. Medium to fine-grained, light red fabric (2.5YR 7/6) with few, large lime inclusions and a red slip (2.5YR 4/8) on interior. Folded rim with a deep incision below edge of rim. See Rowe 2004: 54, no. 49.6.

67.31. Rim with handle preserved (fig. 4.9, reproduced at 1:3). Diam. = 0.240, PH = 0.071, PL = 0.074. Medium-grained yellowish-red fabric (5YR 5/6) with thin red slip (2.5YR 4/6 to 4/8) surviving on interior. There are ridges on exterior and some encrustations. Fabric has common, very small mica and rare, small to medium lime inclusions. Vessel has flaring walls with a slightly thickened rim, and the lip of the rim is squared to slightly rounded with a ridged exterior surface below handle. See Williams 1992: 36, no. 203.

73.33. Rim (fig. 4.9, reproduced at 1:3). Diam. = 0.310, PH = 0.033, PL = 0.067. Medium-grained yellowish-red fabric (5YR 5/6) with rare, small lime inclusions, and sparkly inclusions. A red and reddish-brown slip (2.5YR 5/6 to 4/6) is applied inconsistently in horizontal bands, only surviving on interior. Vessel has flaring walls and three broad ridges/grooves (.004) on exterior below rim.

202.17. Rim with horizontal handle (fig. 4.9, reproduced at 1:3). Diam. = 0.280, PH = 0.028, PL =

0.045. Medium-grained, light red fabric (10R 6/6) with few, medium lime inclusions, and a poorly preserved red slip on interior and exterior. Handle has some molding and an incised line on rim. See Williams 1992: 36, no. 205.

546.50. Rim. Diam. = 0.330, PH = 0.041, PL = 0.057. Medium-grained, reddish yellow fabric (7.5YR 7/6) with frequent, very small sparkling inclusions and a worn red slip (2.5 YR 7/6) on interior. See Rautman 2003: 183, no. 29.

4.1.4.4. Cypriot Red Slip Imitation

Imitation Cypriot Red Slip Ware is similar in form to CRS but is manufactured in a different, coarser fabric. The most frequently imitated shapes are CRS 2, 4, 7, and CRS Well Form (Williams 1992: 50), though locally-produced Roman Red Slips often imitate CRS forms quite closely (Meyza 2007: 104). Due to the lack of certainty surrounding the place (or places) of manufacture for CRS, it has been suggested that the designation CRS, or Late Roman D, might be better characterized as an umbrella designation for a group of wares (Poblome and Firat 2011: 50). If this understanding of the ware is more accurate, then the logical question is whether the two sherds we identified as Imitation CRS are better identified as variations than as imitations. Imitation Cypriot Red Slip is a rare find on Cyprus, most likely due to the ready availability of Cypriot Red Slip.

Cypriot Red Slip 9 Imitation

2 finds
2 rims

31.27. Rim. Diam. = 0.30, PH = 0.030, PL = 0.046, Th. = 0.007. Medium-coarse, light brown fabric (7.5YR 6/4) that is a very pale brown (10YR 7/4–6/4) on the exterior with frequent fine mica, fine to large dark grit, and medium to very large white lime inclusions. Rim is outward thickened with a tapered lip, but is flattened on top. See Meyza 2007: Pl. 20, no. K3B/4A.

4.1.4.5. Phocaean Red Slip (PHW)

Returning again to Waagé's four-tiered typology of Late Roman red slipped wares, he identified a group with a thin hard-baked body ranging in color from reddish brown to red, which he called Late Roman C (LRC) ware. The vessels were covered with a red slip and the fabric included small yellow inclusions (Waagé 1933: 298–304; 1948: 51–52). Without good evidence pointing to a specific geographic place of origin, Hayes adopted Waagé's nomenclature in his *magnum opus* on Late Roman ceramics (Hayes 1972: 323). In the late 1960s, however, through the discovery of wasters and other evidence of ceramic manufacture, as well as a subsequent chemical analysis, Mayet and Picon ultimately proved that LRC was produced in Phocaea in western Asia Minor (Mayet and Picon 1986). The discovery prompted Hayes to rename the industry Phocaean Red Slip (PHW) in his supplement to *Late Roman Pottery* (Hayes 1980: 525).

The production run for PHW was very similar to that of CRS, late fourth through early seventh centuries. The ware was a common export between the fifth and early seventh centuries, and outside of the environs of the ARS production zones in Tunisia and areas producing and heavily importing CRS, namely Cyprus and coastal Palestine, PHW was the Late Roman fine ware *par excellence* in the eastern Mediterranean (Hayes 1972: 368–69; 2008: 85). In identifying similar fabrics in the latest phases of Çandarli Ware (ESC) and the earliest phases of PHW (both products of western Asia Minor), noting identical forms found in both industries, and a production site at Grynion that produced transitional forms, most agree that PHW was a later successor of ESC (Hayes 1972: 369; 2008: 83–84; Williams 1992: 46).

Hayes' PHW typology includes a number of shallow dishes comprising ten separate forms (Hayes 1972: 323–70). PHW vessels present a fine-grained red fabric with small lime inclusions and rarely gold mica specks. The body is well-fired and varies in color from brownish red, to purple, and maroon. Although the exterior of the vessel is covered in a thin red slip, in many instances rims are discolored during the firing process; sepia, black, and creamy white discoloring is common, while in cases of excessive heat, flaking can occur (Hayes 1972: 324). Common decorations include rouletting, especially on forms from the fifth and early sixth century, grooves, and a plethora of stamp motifs.

52 finds (all forms)
52 rims

PHW 2

Phocaean Red Slip Form 2 is a shallow dish with a flaring rim and a low foot. It is a very common find in the Mediterranean and dates to the fifth century (Hayes 1972: 327–29; Williams 1992: 47).

1 find
1 rim

187.24. Rim (fig. 4.9, reproduced at 1:2). Diam. = 0.20, PH = 0.022, PL = 0.036. Fine-grained, reddish yellow fabric (5YR 6/6) that is encrusted on cores with a red slip (2.5YR 4/8) that is worn and eroding. Rim is everted and outturned, with a rounded lip. See Hayes 1972: 328, fig. 66, no. 2.4.

PHW 3

Phocaean Red Slip Form 3 is a dish or bowl with a flanged rim and a low foot. It is a very common find in the Mediterranean and dates to the fifth through eighth centuries AD. It is divided into 8 subcategories (A, B, C, D, E, F, G, and H) based on differences in the rim (Hayes 1972: 329–38).

21 finds (all variations)
21 rims

190.30. Rim (fig. 4.9, reproduced at 1:2). Diam. = 0.240, PH = 0.022, PL = 0.042. Fine-grained, red fabric (10R 4/6) with rare, small lime inclusions and a red slip (10R 4/8) on body and lip, and very dark gray (7.5YR 3/1) on the interior of the rim. The slip on the exterior of the rim appears to be black and is applied inconsistently. The rim has a rounded lip and is not concave as is usual for this form.

PHW 3C

Phocaean Red Slip Form 3C is characterized by a flanged rim and occasional rouletting on the outside and dates to the end of the fifth century AD. This sub-form is characterized by a flat or slightly convex rim and a flat or slightly concave face (Hayes 1972: 329–37).

9.38. Rim (fig. 4.10, reproduced at 1:2). Diam. = 0.240, PH = 0.019, PL = 0.055. Medium-grained, red fabric (10R 5/6) with a few lime inclusions, and a red slip blackened on exterior of the rim. See Hayes 1972: 332, fig. 68, no. 3C.10; Heath and Tekkök 2006–2009: Phocaean Red-Slip no. 19.

12.60. Rim (fig. 4.10, reproduced at 1:2). Diam. = 0.240, PH = 0.019, PL = 0.035. Medium-grained, red fabric (2.5YR 5/8) with frequent lime inclusions, and a red slip on the exterior. See Lund 1993: 48, no. C-269.

94.29. Rim (fig. 4.10, reproduced at 1:2). Diam. = uncertain, PH = 0.020, PL = 0.035, Th. (rim) = 0.006, Th. (body) = 0.005. Medium-grained, yellowish-red fabric (5YR 4/6) that is poorly fired with a discolored gray exterior and a discolored dark gray slip (10YR 4/1 to 7.5YR 4/4) on the exterior. Fabric contains rare, sparkly inclusions.

203.31. Rim (fig. 4.10, reproduced at 1:2). Diam. = 0.240, PH = 0.019, PL = 0.051. Medium-grained, red fabric (2.5YR 4/8) with an uneven red slip (2.5YR 5/8). Core is encrusted and contains some mica, and rare, small limestone inclusions. Rim is offset from body by groove below flange.

246.28. Rim. Diam. = 0.240, PH = 0.021, PL = 0.049. Medium-grained, light red fabric (2.5YR 6/8) with frequent, lime inclusions, and a poorly preserved slip on exterior that has a slightly blackened appearance.

PHW 3E

Phocaean Red Slip Form 3E is a development of Phocaean Red Slip Form 3C. It is characterized by a lower hanging flanged rim and occasional

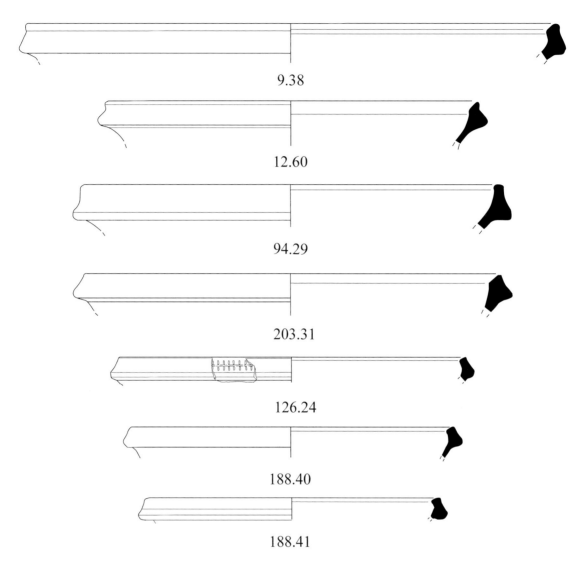

9.38

12.60

94.29

203.31

126.24

188.40

188.41

FIG. 4.10   *PHW sherds.*

rouletting on the outside and dates to the end of the fifth and early sixth century AD (Hayes 1972: 329–37).

70.5. Rim. Diam. = 0.200, PH = 0.019, PL = 0.055. Medium-grained, light red fabric (2.5YR 6/8) with a few quartz and lime inclusions and traces of a poorly preserved red slip on interior.

126.24. Rim (fig. 4.10, reproduced at 1:3). Diam. = 0.300. Medium-grained, light red fabric (2.5YR 6/6) with some lime inclusions. Rouletting on outside of rim. See Hayes 1972: 332, fig. 68, no. 3E.16.

188.40. Rim (fig. 4.10, reproduced at 1:3). Diam. = 0.250, PH = 0.024, PL = 0.019. Fine-grained, light red fabric (10R 7/8) with a few inclusions, and a red slip. Crenellated rim with bulging lower section.

188.41. Rim (fig. 4.10, reproduced at 1:3). Diam. = 0.180, PH = 0.018, PL = 0.037. Medium-grained, light red fabric (10R 6/8) with a few lime inclusions and a poorly preserved red slip on interior. Crenellated rim. See Heath and Tekkök 2006–2009: Phocaean Red-Slip no. 20.

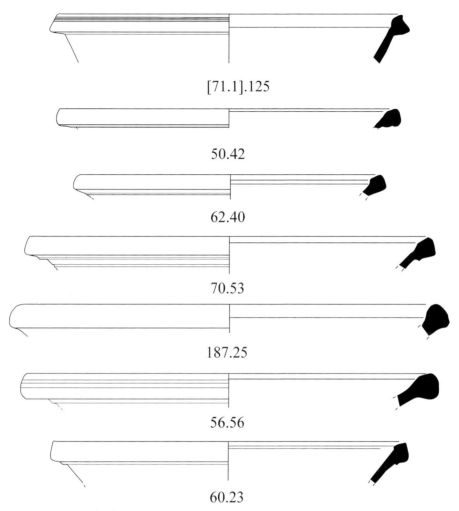

[71.1].125

50.42

62.40

70.53

187.25

56.56

60.23

FIG. 4.11 *PHW sherds.*

PHW 3E/F

Phocaean Red Slip Form 3 E/F is designation we used for a rim that shares the basic shape of Form 3E, but has a lower rim that projects further (Hayes 1972: 331).

1 find
1 rim

[71.1].125. Rim (fig. 4.11, reproduced at 1:3). Diam. = 0.250, PH = 0.032, PL = 0.049. Medium-grained, red fabric (2.5YR 4/8) with a red slip (10R4/8 to 2.5YR 4/8), which is a discolored yellow-red on lip. Common, very small to small white inclusions, and a few mica flakes. Concave on exterior. Flanged

rim, which is thickened on exterior and offset from body with a rounded lip. Compare PHW 3E (Hayes 1972: 332, fig. 68, no. 3E.15) and PHW 3F (Hayes 1972: 334, fig. 69, no. 3F.25).

PHW 10

Phocaean Red Slip Ware Form 10 is a dish or bowl with a knobbed rim that is rounded on the outside and dates to between the late sixth and middle seventh century AD. It is broken down into three subcategories (A, B, and C) based on differences in the rim (Hayes 1972: 343–46).

29 finds (all variations)
29 rims

50.42. Rim (fig. 4.11, reproduced at 1:3). Diam. = 0.240, PH = 0.021, PL = 0.046. Medium-coarse, light red fabric (2.5YR 6/6) with frequent lime inclusions.

62.40. Rim (fig. 4.11, reproduced at 1:3). Diam. = 0.250, PH = 0.018, PL = 0.069. Medium-grained, red fabric (2.5YR 4/8) with a red slip (2.5YR 5/8 to 4/8). Inclusions are frequent, very small to small mica and lime. Rim is very square and off-set from body at exterior.

70.53. Rim (fig. 4.11, reproduced at 1:3). Diam. = 0.240, PH = 0.025, PL = 0.040. Medium to fine-grained, light red fabric (10R 7/8) with rare, medium lime inclusions and red slip (10R 5/6) on exterior. Vessel with everted rim.

187.25. Rim (fig. 4.11, reproduced at 1:2). Diam. = 0.210, PH = 0.016, PL = 0.052. Medium-grained, light reddish-brown fabric (2.5YR 7/4) with a slip of varied color that is pitted. Occasional, small white and black inclusions. Rim is square and slightly rounded at corners with light grooves on exterior face of rim. See Hayes 1972: 344, fig. 71, no. 10.2.

PHW 10A

Phocaean Red Slip Ware Form 10A is characterized by a heavy knobbed rim and dates to the late sixth and early seventh centuries AD (Hayes 1972: 343–46).

56.56. Rim (fig. 4.11, reproduced at 1:2). Diam. = 0.250, PH = 0.021, PL = 0.064. Medium-grained, light red fabric (2.5YR 7/8) with several, medium lime and quartz inclusions and a red slip (2.5YR 4/8) with white discoloration on rim. See Hayes 1972: 344, fig. 71, no. 10A.1.

60.23. Rim (fig. 4.11, reproduced at 1:3). Diam. = uncertain, PH = 0.036, PL = 0.064. Medium-coarse, gritty, red fabric (2.5YR 4/6) and red slip (2.5YR 4/8) with common, very small mica, and small lime inclusions. Slip is a discolored dark color at lip. Rim has a squared to slightly rounded lip, and the everted rim is offset from the body. See Hayes 1972: 344, fig. 71, no. 10A.4.

62.41. Rim (fig. 4.12, reproduced at 1:3). Diam. = 0.290, PH = 0.024, PL = 0.078. Medium-grained, pinkish-white fabric (7.5YR 8/2) with a red slip (2.5YR 5/8), a few, medium lime inclusions, and a few very small white inclusions. See Rautman 2003: 56–57, no. 57.

71.42. Rim (fig. 4.12, reproduced at 1:3). Diam. = 0.300, PH = 0.026, PL = 0.085. Strong brown fabric (7.5YR 5/6) with a red slip (2.5YR 5/8) weakly applied and pocketed with encrustation on breaks and discolored on lip. Common, fine white inclusions. Knobbed rim has a slightly rounded lip.

71.45. Rim (fig. 4.12, reproduced at 1:3). Diam. = 0.240, PH = 0.026, PL = 0.040; Fine to medium-grained, dark yellowish brown fabric (10YR 4/6) with a red slip (2.5YR 4/8 to 7.5YR 5/4) that is discolored brown on lip due to firing. Slip contains frequent, small white inclusions and lime inclusions. Exterior groove separates rim from body, which is flanged.

73.32. Rim (fig. 4.12, reproduced at 1:3). Diam. = 0.200, PH = 0.017, PL = 0.049. Medium to fine-grained, light red fabric (10R 6/8) with a few, medium lime inclusions and a red slip (10R 5/8) on interior and exterior with some white discoloration on rim. See Rautman 2003: 186, no. 55.

76.33. Rim (fig. 4.12, reproduced at 1:3). Diam. = 0.280, PH = 0.017, PL = 0.032. Medium-grained, light red fabric (10R 6/6) with rare, lime inclusions and traces of a red slip (10R 5/8) on interior.

508.9. Rim. Diam. = 0.260, PH = 0.022, PL = 0.047. Medium-grained, light red fabric (2.5YR 6/6) with rare, lime inclusions and a red slip (10R 5/8) on interior and exterior. See Rautman 2003: 187, no. 61; Hayes 1972: 342, fig. 71, no. 10A.2.

PHW 10B

Phocaean Red Slip Ware Form 10B is characterized by an elongated rim that is rounded on the top and dates to the late sixth and early seventh centuries AD (Hayes 1972: 343–46).

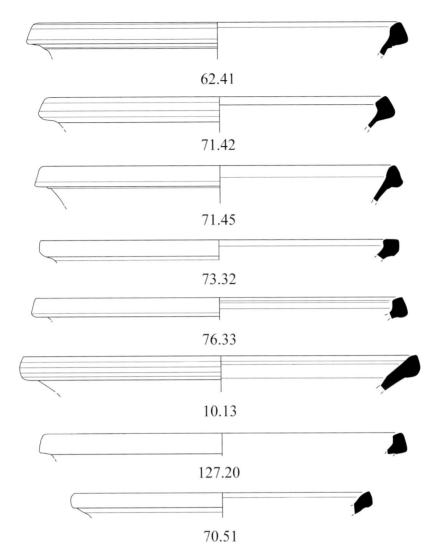

62.41

71.42

71.45

73.32

76.33

10.13

127.20

70.51

FIG. 4.12 *PHW sherds.*

10.13. Rim (fig. 4.12, reproduced at 1:2). Diam. = 0.220, PH = 0.019, PL = 0.060. Medium-grained, red fabric (10R 5/6) with a few, large lime inclusions and a red slip (10R 4/8) slip on interior and exterior.

127.20. Rim (fig. 4.12, reproduced at 1:3). Diam. = 0.300, PH = 0.020, PL = 0.039. Medium to fine-grained, red fabric (2.5 YR 5/8) that is a discolored buff color on the exterior lip with frequent, small to large white inclusions, and abundant sparkling inclusions, Everted rim with squared lip. See Hayes 1972: 344, fig. 71, no. 10B.4.

PHW 10C

Phocaean Red Slip Ware Form 10C is characterized by an elongated rim that is flattened on the top and dates to the early and middle seventh century AD (Hayes 1972: 343–46).

70.51. Rim (fig. 4.12, reproduced at 1:3). Diam. = 0.230, PH = 0.018, PL = 0.084. Medium-grained, pale red fabric (10R 7/4) with red slip (10R 4/8) on interior and exterior. The slip on the exterior of the rim is blackened.

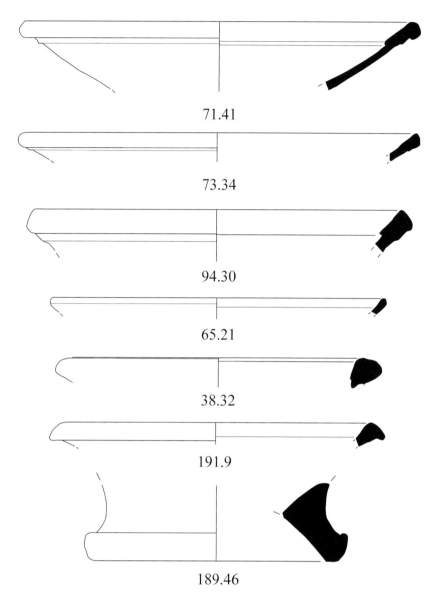

71.41

73.34

94.30

65.21

38.32

191.9

189.46

FIG. 4.13   *PHW, Unclassified Roman Fine Ware, Unclassified Late Roman Fine Ware, and Cypriot Sgraffito Ware sherds.*

71.41. Rim (fig. 4.13, reproduced at 1:2). Diam. = 0.200, PH = 0.046, PL = 0.076. Medium-grained, light red fabric (2.5YR 6/8) with frequent mica, lime, and quartz inclusions and a red slip on exterior. See Hayes 1972: 344, fig. 71, no. 10C.14.

73.34. Rim (fig. 4.13, reproduced at 1:3). Diam. = 0.280, PH = 0.020, PL = 0.046. Medium-coarse, red fabric (10R 4/8) with rare, small to medium inclusions and a red slip (2.5YR 4/8) that is patchy with some parts eroding on interior. Groove demarcates rim. See Williams 1992: 49, no. 280.

94.30. Rim (fig. 4.13, reproduced at 1:2). Diam. = 0.220, PH = 0.023, PL = 0.023. Medium-grained, red fabric (2.5YR 6/8) with few, large lime inclusions and no evidence for a red slip. See Lund 2006: 225, no. 262.

4.1.4.6. Egyptian Red Slip

Egyptian Red Slip Ware is an uncommon find on the island and this holds true for Koutsopetria, where only four sherds were found (Hayes 1972; Rautman 2003: 166; Lund 1993: 138–39; Manning

2002: 42). This ware, which was manufactured in Egypt and dates from the fourth to seventh centuries AD, was an imitation and competitor to African Red Slip. Hayes breaks the ware into three subcategories (A, B, and C). The four finds at Koutsopetria correspond to Form A and are characterized by a pinkish fabric with a darker slip that is thinly applied and rims that are typically discolored. The fabric contains gold mica, black, red, and quartz inclusions. This ware is common in Egypt, but is only found at a few sites outside of Egypt, including Cyrenaica, the Negev, and Cyprus. All are seventh century AD forms (Hayes 1972: 387–401).

4 finds
3 body sherds
1 base

24.24. Base. Diam. = 0.130, PL = 0.028, PH = 0.018. Medium-grained, red fabric (10R 4/8) with red slip (10R 5/8) that is preserved best on the interior, with a few, small to medium dark grit and fine mica. Slip is pockmarked from inclusions. Ring foot with flaring ring.

4.1.4.7. Unclassified Roman Fine Ware

This category of fine ware contains sherds that can only be dated broadly to the Roman period due to their fabric and style of decoration. The decoration, fabric, and shape of these sherds are not distinctive enough to allow for a more precise identification. They are characterized by a red to reddish-brown fabric with a thin red or brown slip that is well-worn and often missing. These fine wares were produced on the island and were probably regionally manufactured.

43 finds
27 body sherds
11 bases
4 rims
1 handle

65.21. Rim (fig. 4.13, reproduced at 1:3). Diam. = 0.250, PH = 0.012, PL = 0.031. Coarse, red (10R 4/8) to yellowish red fabric (5YR 4/6) with several very large lime inclusions, and no visible slip. Bowl or deep plate.

4.1.4.8. Unclassified Late Roman Fine Ware

This category of fine ware contains sherds that can only be dated broadly to the Late Roman period due to their fabric and style of decoration. The decoration, fabric, and shape of these sherds are not distinctive enough to allow for a more precise identification. They are characterized by a range of fabric colors, ranging from yellow and orange to red and brown. They are coated with a red or brown slip that is usually poorly preserved.

5 finds
2 rims
2 body sherds
1 base

38.32. Rim (fig. 4.13, reproduced at 1:3). Diam. = 0.240, PH = 0.029, PL = 0.077. Medium-grained, pale yellow fabric (2.5Y 7/3) with light brown core (7.5YR 6/4) and some encrustation. Common, sparkling, rare small-medium black and red inclusions. Everted form with thickened, knobbed rim, and rounded lip.

191.9. Rim (fig. 4.13, reproduced at 1:3). Diam. = 0.240, PH = 0.020, PL = 0.042. Fine-grained, yellowish-red fabric (5YR 6/6) with no preserved slip. The exterior is a discolored very pale brown (10 YR 7/4) with frequent, sparkling inclusions and a few, very small red and white inclusions. Rim is very abraded.

4.1.5. Fine Wares, Medieval through Modern

Work on Medieval Cypriot fine wares is based on the early work of du Plat Taylor and Megaw in the 1930s (du Plat Taylor 1933: 24–25; du Plat Taylor and Megaw 1937: 1–13). These early typologies remained relatively unchanged until the 1990s when scholars began refining these studies using excavation data to identify important production centers such as Lemba and Lapithos (Papanikola-Bakirtzis 1993: 115–30). While work on Medieval Cypriot ceramics has increased in recent years, it has lagged behind other fine wares due to the fact that excavations have tended not to study or publish their Medieval finds, and the fragmentary nature of survey artifacts prevents precise identifications (Moore and Gregory 2012: 208). (See Sections 5.4.5 and 5.4.6 for distributional analysis.)

The Medieval and later fine ware assemblage at PKAP is limited in both number of sherds and in variety of wares. There is a fairly lengthy break between the disappearance of fine wares in the late seventh and early eighth centuries and their reappearance in the twelfth century. While there are very few fine wares produced locally in this period, imported fine wares are present on Cyprus, particularly at Paphos (von Wartburg 2003). These wares, such as Glazed White Ware I (also known as Talbot Rice's Group A4 White Inscribed Ware and Constantinopolitan Whitewares), Plain Glazed Ware (also known as Talbot Rice's Group B and Hayes' Coarse Glazed Ware I–II), and Plain Glazed Ware in a White Fabric (also known as White Painted Ware and Glazed White Ware II–V), are not present at Koutsopetria (Vroom 2005: 62–65, 74–77).

Starting in the twelfth century, fine wares reappear at Koutsopetria in locally produced and imported fabrics. Despite their reappearance, the number of fine wares from all periods between the Late Roman and Modern periods remains low, only 31 sherds or less than 0.2% of all fine wares.

4.1.5.1. Cypriot Sgraffito Ware
(Polychrome Brown and Green Sgraffito Ware
from Cyprus, Brown and Green Sgraffito A and B)

Cypriot Sgraffito Ware is a fine ware manufactured in Cyprus at Lemba, Enkomi, and Lapithos, and is characterized by a red or buff fabric with a green, brown, and white glaze and a Sgraffito design incised in the base (Papanikola-Bakirtzis 1993; Vroom 2005: 120–21). The most common shape is a carinated bowl with a ring foot that dates to between the thirteenth and fifteenth centuries AD (Gregory 1993: 163–67). At Koutsopetria, due to the fragmentary nature of our survey artifacts, we relied on the basic typology for subcategories created by Taylor and Megaw (Taylor and Megaw 1937: 1–13).

10 finds (all forms)
5 body sherds
1 rim
4 bases

189.46. Base (fig. 4.13). PH = 0.020, PL = 0.037. Fine-grained, reddish yellow fabric (5YR 6/6) with a very pale brown slip (10YR 7/4). Flaring ring foot.

4.1.5.2. Cypriot Green and Brown Glazed Group IV

This group is characterized by a reddish or pinkish fabric with a brown glazed interior and unglazed exterior. It has a Sgraffito design on the interior and dates to the thirteenth and fourteenth centuries AD (Gregory 2003: 287).

1 find
1 base

222.8. Base. PH = 0.016, PL = 0.062. Fine-grained, pink fabric (7.5YR 7/4) with yellow-green glaze (5Y 5/3–Gley 1 7/10Y) preserved on interior and with frequent, fine mica, and rare lime, and fine to medium inclusions. Concave ring foot.

4.1.5.3. Cypriot Green and Brown Glazed Group V

This ware is characterized by a white slip over reddish fabric with a high foot. It has a brown and green glaze and a Sgraffito design, and dates to the fourteenth century AD (Gregory 2003: 287).

2 finds
1 base
1 rim

54.4. Rim (fig. 4.14, reproduced at 1:2). Diam. = 0.210, PH = 0.038, PL = 0.045. Medium-grained, reddish yellow fabric (7.5YR 7/6) with few, mica and lime inclusions. Flaring, outturned rim of a bowl.

161.8. Base. Diam. = 0.043, PH = 0.014, PL = 0.044, Th. = 0.011. Fine-grained, reddish yellow fabric (5YR 7/6) with rare lime inclusions.

4.1.5.4. Cypriot Green and Brown Glazed Group VI

This form is characterized by a white slip with a yellowish glaze and green abstract lines in a soft fine pinkish-buff clay. It dates to the fourteenth century AD (Megaw and Taylor 1937; Gregory 2003 287).

1 find
1 base

222.8. Base. Diam. = uncertain, PL = 0.062, PH = 0.016. Fine-grained, pink fabric (7.5YR 7/4–7/6) with an olive glaze (5Y 5/3–Gley 1 7/10Y) preserved on interior, with frequent, fine mica and rare lime, and fine to medium inclusions. Ring foot.

4.1.5.5. Cypriot Green Painted Group IX

This form is characterized by a white slip with a yellowish glaze and green abstract lines. It dates to the sixteenth and seventeenth centuries AD (Megaw and Taylor 1937; Gregory 1993: 159; 2003: 287).

3 finds
2 body sherds
1 base

208.18. Ring foot (fig. 4.26) PH = 0.014, PW = 0.037, PL = 0.04. Fine-grained, yellow fabric (5Y 7/6) with rare, white spherical rounded stones. See Keswani et al. 2003: 209, no. 5021.51.1.

4.1.5.6. Incised Ware

This ware was manufactured in the Aegean in the twelfth and thirteenth centuries AD and is characterized by a red fabric covered with a white slip. The background of the design was created by removing the white slip (Gregory 1993: 163).

1 find
1 body sherd

82.6. Body sherd (fig. 4.26). PH = 0.050, PW = 0.031, Th. = 0.009. Medium-coarse, red fabric (2.5YR 5/6–2.5YR 5/8) with frequent, fine white and mica inclusions. Wavy finishing lines on interior and exterior.

4.1.5.7. Slip Painted Ware from Didymoteicho

This ware, which dates to the mid-nineteenth and mid-twentieth centuries, was manufactured in Didymoteicho in Thrace and is found at sites throughout the eastern Mediterranean. It is also known as Drip-painted Bowls, Monochrome Glazed Slip Painted Ware, and Hayes' Ware P1 (Hayes 1992: 344). Its most common shape is an open vessel, such as a plate with a hooked rim. It is characterized by an orange fabric that is decorated with a white slip that is allowed to drip down the sides and then covered with a green or yellow glaze (Vroom 2005: 186–87).

14 finds
7 body sherds
7 rims

53.7. Body sherd. PL = 0.028, PW = 0.029, Th. = 0.007. Medium-coarse, reddish yellow fabric (7.5YR 7/6) with a light red core (2.5YR 6/8) that has a few, fine dark and white inclusions, and a few, fine mica inclusions. Bluish-gray glazed exterior surface (Gley 2 5/10B) with a light greenish-gray glazed band (Gley 1 7/5G).

539.13. Rim (fig. 4.14, reproduced at 1:2) Diam. = 0.140, PL = 0.036, Th. = 0.008. Fine-grained, red fabric (2.5YR 4/6) with few, rounded spherical black stones, and a yellow glaze (2.5Y 8/6) on interior that is dripped on exterior of rim. Exterior has reddish-brown slip. Flaring rim. See François and Vallauri 2001: 540, no. 8; Vroom 2005: 186, no. 3.1, 3.2, and 3.3.

1065.15. Rim. Diam. = 0.170, PL = 0.042, PW = 0.039, Th. (rim) = 0.008, Th. (body) = 0.005. Medium-coarse, strong brown fabric (7.5YR 5/6) with rare, small black and gray inclusions. Yellow (5Y 7/8) and yellowish brown glaze (10YR 5/6) on the interior which is very consistently pocketed on inside of rim. Exterior is undecorated, but has low ridges below rim. Shallow dish.

4.1.5.8. Proto-Maiolica Ware

Proto-Maiolica was manufactured in Southern Italy at Apulia. It is found at sites throughout the Mediterranean and dates to the thirteenth and fourteenth centuries AD (Vroom 2005: 126–27). It is characterized by a buff or pale brown fabric that has small inclusions, a white slip, and a tin glaze with blue or green decorations (Gregory 1993: 162).

1 find
1 body sherd

176.17. Body sherd. White fabric (10YR 8/1) with a blue and white glazed exterior, and a white glazed interior. Body sherd is composed of two pieces that join together.

4.2. KITCHEN WARES

While many projects define cooking ware as any vessel that was designed to be exposed to heat (Riley 1979: 97–98), at PKAP we adopted a broader definition that includes any vessel used in the preparation of food. These vessels include bowls, jugs, cooking pots, casseroles, frying pans, and lids. The quantity of kitchen ware that PKAP fieldwalkers collected during the survey was relatively small, accounting for only 6.49% of the total collected sherds. The low percentage of kitchen wares collected during the PKAP survey compares favorably to other survey projects on Cyprus, for example the kitchen wares collected during the Akamas project accounted for 12% of their total ceramic collection (Lund 2002a: 44). The majority of the PKAP kitchen ware sherds are small and not well-preserved due to their thin walls, which are brittle because of their exposure to heat. These factors make specific identification difficult and in fact, a sizeable portion of these sherds could only be dated to broad chronological periods, such as Ancient-Medieval or Ancient-Historic. This is further compounded by the fact that the overwhelming majority of the kitchen ware ceramics are body sherds, with very few rims discovered.

While at larger Cypriot cities, such as Paphos, high-quality cooking wares were imported from Italy, Egypt, and the Aegean (Hayes 1991: 78),

smaller sites on the island relied on locally or regionally produced kitchen wares. For example, 95% of the kitchen wares discovered by the Akamas project were locally made (Lund 2002a: 43). As a result, the study of kitchen wares on Cyprus tends to rely heavily on excavated material from secure contexts, and even then, it often proves of limited value as comparanda for other archaeological projects due to the fact that most kitchen wares were not exported far from their production centers (Lund 2002a 43–58; Ikäheimo 2005: 509). While recent work with petrography holds out the promise of sourcing kitchen ware ceramics, it is still in its earliest stages and will take time for a database of ceramics to be constructed (Gabrieli and Merryweather 2002: 33–41).

One exception to the limited circulation of kitchen ware, at least for Cypriot kitchen wares, is the large Late Roman kitchen ware production site at Dhiorios. This production site did not start large-scale production until the latter half of the seventh century AD (as Koutsopetria begins its rapid decline) and as result, only a few Dhiorios products were discovered in the PKAP survey area, with only five sherds tentatively identified as Dhiorios vessel fragments. This is supported by the lack of imported 8th–9th-centuries micaceous cooking wares from Asia Minor that are found at other sites on the island (Hayes 1980a: 378, figs. 9.2, 11–13; 2003: 452).

Kitchen wares that date to the Iron Age are scarce in the PKAP collection, accounting for only 2 sherds. This low number can be explained somewhat by the fact that the kitchen fabrics from this period are difficult to distinguish from contemporary coarse wares (Winther-Jacobsen 2006a: 231) and some of the Iron Age kitchen ware sherds are probably contained in the coarse ware category.

In the Roman and Late Roman periods, the number of cooking ware sherds at PKAP increases dramatically, accounting for 610 fragments, or 57.8% of all cooking ware sherds. The Roman period saw an increase in the popularity of Cypriot cooking wares at other archaeological sites in the eastern Mediterranean, indicating that some kitchen wares were more widely exported from the island. The Cypriot cooking wares that seem to have been most frequently exported in the eastern Mediterranean are the Dhiorios vessels (sometimes referred to in the literature as a Cypriot type), which are characterized by a thickened rim, rounded shoulders with narrow ridging, vertical strap handles, and thin, brittle walls. This ware, which dates to the Late Roman and early Byzantine periods (sixth–eighth centuries AD), has been found at numerous sites such as Caesarea, Yassi Ada, Anemurium, and Kelia (Magness 1992: 133; Williams 1992: 68–70).

It is interesting to note that while there were both fine ware and coarse ware sherds that date to the periods between the Late Roman and Modern periods, albeit not very many, there were no kitchen wares. While it is possible that some of these sherds may have been classified as coarse ware, the kitchen wares of the thirteenth to eighteenth centuries AD had only a limited number of standardized shapes, and imported cooking wares of this period are also easily recognizable (Gabrieli 2007: 402).

Finding useful comparanda for the PKAP assemblage was difficult. While the publication of the nearby site of Panayia Ematousa provides a nice range of Hellenistic cooking wares (Winther-Jacobsen 2006a: 231–43), and the catalogues of Kopetra and Anemurium provide a range of Roman cooking wares, the lack of distinctive rim profiles discovered at Koutsopetria prevented their use in identifying our cooking wares (Rautman 2003: 175–76; Williams 1992: 61–75), resulting in our broad categories. Attempts at fabric differentiation for identifying locally produced wares also proved difficult, as noted by Hayes and Rautman (Hayes 1991: 81; Rautman 2003: 176).

4.2.1. Kitchen Wares, Iron Age to Cypro-Classical

Kitchen wares from the pre-Hellenistic periods are hard to identify due to their thick walls, which makes their body sherds indistinguishable from pre-Hellenistic coarse wares (Winther-Jacobsen 2006a: 231). As a result, the low number of pre-Hellenistic kitchen wares are likely underrepresented in the assemblage. The sherds in these categories are characterized by walls that are slightly thinner than coarse wares, but thicker than Hellenistic

and Roman kitchen wares. The fabric tends to be a lighter color, ranging from a light green or pale yellow to a light orange. The fabric is friable and contains many inclusions, usually red or white stones. At Panayia Ematousa, only two small sub-categories were securely identified as pre-Hellenistic (Winther-Jacobsen 2006a: 231).

4.2.1.1. Kitchen Wares, Iron Age

7 finds
3 handles
2 rims
2 bases

184.1. Handle. PH = 0.037, PW = 0.025, Th. = 0.014-0.011. Fine-grained, very pale brown fabric (10YR 8/4–2.5Y 8/4) with few, fine, dark inclusions and heavily encrusted. Oval handle that joins vertically to the vessel at the rim.

1402.10. Rim. Diam. = uncertain, PH = 0.029, PL = 0.072, Th. = 0.007 (ring), Th. = 0.005 (wall). Fine-grained, light red fabric (2.5YR 6/6) with reddish yellow slip (7.5YR 7/6) and rare, medium white and red inclusions. Interior and exterior of rim painted in red-black paint. Outward thickened rim.

4.2.2. Kitchen Wares, Cypro-Classical to Hellenistic

This small category of sherds contains a small handle that shared attributes from both the Cypro-Classical and Hellenistic periods, though it most likely is an early Hellenistic vessel.

1 find
1 handle

15.32. Handle. PL = 0.055, PW = 0.014. Fine-grained, reddish yellow fabric (7.5YR 7/6) with a light red core (2.5YR 6/6), and rare, small red inclusions. Small, round handle.

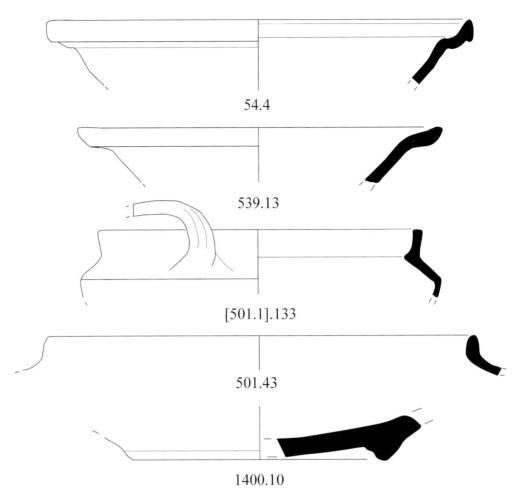

54.4

539.13

[501.1].133

501.43

1400.10

FIG. 4.14 *Cypriot Green and Brown Glazed, Slip Painted Ware from Didymoteicho, Hellenistic Kitchen Ware, and Hellenistic to Early Roman Kitchen Ware sherds.*

4.2.3. Kitchen Wares, Hellenistic to Late Roman

The Hellenistic to Late Roman Kitchen Wares are more easily identified than their earlier counterparts, which can be mistakenly assigned to coarse wares. Starting in the Hellenistic period and running through the Roman period, kitchen wares became more distinct from coarse wares as their walls became thinner and the fabric changed. Comparanda from Paphos (Hayes 1991; Gabrieli and Merryweather 2002; Rowe 2004), Panayia Ematousa (Winther-Jacobsen 2006a), Kopetra (Rautman 2003), and Dhiorios (Catling 1972) provided a basis for the basic identification of our kitchen wares.

4.2.3.1. Hellenistic

With the arrival of the Hellenistic Age, a series of changes occurred that assist in the differentiation of kitchen wares, such as distinctive rims and specific body shapes. For example, Hellenistic casseroles have sides that taper inwards (Winther-Jacobsen 2003a: 231–32). At PKAP, this category is characterized by a buff, orange, or reddish fabric with small, red and black inclusions. Unfortunately, the fragmentary nature of the kitchen ware assemblage probably resulted in the identification of a large portion of PKAP's Hellenistic kitchen wares as Hellenistic–Early Roman kitchen ware chronotype. In fact, the largest category of the Hellenistic kitchenware sherds were handles.

11 finds
6 handles
2 bases
2 rims
1 body sherd

[501.1].133. Rim (fig. 4.14, reproduced at 1:2). PH = 0.046, PL = 0.068, Th. = 0.005 (rim and body), Th. = 0.013 (handle). Cooking fabric, orange with gray core (2.5YR 4/6–4/8–5YR 4/4). Heavy encrustation and rare, small to medium inclusions. Vertical, round loop handle. Similar to Hayes 1991: 97, no. 14 with different handle.

501.43. Rim (fig. 4.14, reproduced at 1:2). Diam. = uncertain, PH = 0.023, PW = 0.044, Th. = 0.005. Coarse, friable red fabric (10R 5/8) with abundant, inclusions of many types including mica, and red and gray stones. Everted rim. See Winther-Jacobsen 2006a: 236, no. 27.

4.2.3.2. Hellenistic to Early Roman

This category shares attributes from both the Hellenistic and Early Roman periods, and the sherds lack unique identifying features that would permit them from being more precisely assigned to either the Hellenistic or Early Roman kitchen ware categories. This is reflected in the low number of rims assigned to this chronotype. These sherds have a fabric that ranges from a dark red (2.5YR 4/6) to dark gray (2.5YR 4/1) and is characterized by numerous inclusions, and the occasional presence of mica.

71 finds
29 body sherds
25 handles
8 bases
7 rims
1 lid
1 toe

1400.10. Base (fig. 4.14). Diam. = 0.008, PH = 0.010, PL = 0.055, PW = 0.042, Th. = 0.005. Coarse, red fabric (2.5YR 4/6) with abundant, large buff and black inclusions, and fine micaceous inclusions. A weak red exterior (2.5YR 5/2). Flattened base.

1400.49. Lid (fig. 4.15). PH = 0.020, PL = 0.045, PW = 0.038, Th. = 0.006. Thin, friable fabric that has a dark reddish-gray core (2.5YR 4/1) with a red exterior (2.5YR 5/6) that has common, large inclusions of brown, white, and gray stones, and fine to large mica inclusions.

4.2.3.3. Early Roman

As with the Hellenistic kitchen wares, the fragmentary nature of the kitchen ware assemblage probably resulted in the identification of a large portion of PKAP's Early Roman kitchen wares as the broader Hellenistic–Early Roman kitchen ware chronotype. This ware is characterized by a reddish-brown fabric, ranging from a light red (2.5YR 6/8) to a yellowish-red (5YR 4/6), with numerous inclusions including mica.

23 finds
13 handles
5 rims
4 body sherds
1 base

204.17. Rim. Diam. = 0.090, PH = 0.014, PL = 0.038. Medium-grained, red fabric (2.5YR 5/8) with lime inclusions. Slightly thickened vertical rim with handle.

204.25. Rim Diam. = 0.022. Medium-grained, light red fabric (2.5YR 6/8) with a few lime inclusions. See Williams 1992: 63, no. 366.

4.2.3.4. Roman

This chronotype is the largest kitchen ware category at PKAP. During the Roman period, kitchen wares become more standardized with fewer fabric variations. For example, starting in the fourth century at Paphos, kitchen ware sherds are a medium-coarse fabric that is reddish brown to dark brown in color with white, red, and brown inclusions (Rowe 2006: 174–75). At PKAP, our Roman kitchen wares are characterized by a dark fabric, ranging from red (10R 4/6) to a light brownish-gray fabric (10 YR 6/2) with numerous inclusions.

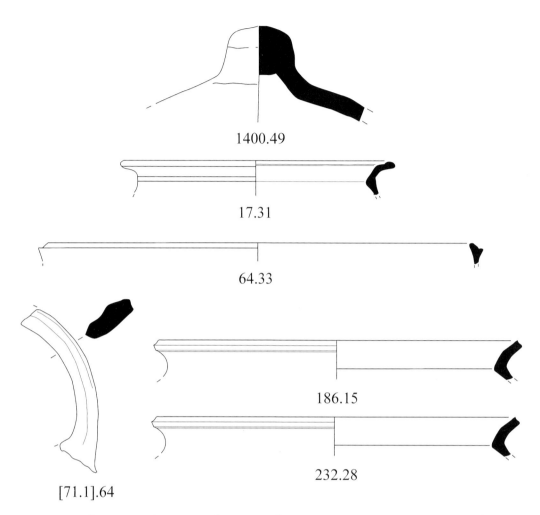

1400.49

17.31

64.33

186.15

232.28

[71.1].64

FIG. 4.15   *Hellenistic to Early Roman Kitchen Ware and Roman Kitchen Ware sherds.*

474 finds
335 body sherds
58 handles
54 rims
13 bases
11 neck/shoulders
2 lids
1 toe

17.31. Rim (fig. 4.15, reproduced at 1:2). Diam. = 0.10, PH = 0.019, PL = 0.039, Th. = 0.003. Medium-coarse, red fabric (10R 4/6) with few, sub-rounded lime inclusions. Nearly horizontal rim with rolled edge. See Winther-Jacobsen 2006a: 240, no. 46.

64.33. Rim (fig. 4.15, reproduced at 1:3). Diam. = uncertain, PL = 0.043, Th. = 0.011 (rim), Th. =

0.005 (body). Thin, friable red fabric (2.5YR 4/8) with a red exterior (10R 5/6). Triangular rim with crenelated lip turning inward toward interior of vessel. Open vessel. See Winther-Jacobsen 2006a: 236, no. 18.

[71.1].64. Handle (fig. 4.15, reproduced at 1:2). PL = 0.028, PW = 0.011. Coarse, light brownish-gray fabric (10YR 6/2) with a red core (10R 5/6) that contains a few, rounded, spherical white and black stones. Vertical handle. Shares similarities with Winther-Jacobsen 2006a: 239, nos. 35 and 36.

186.15. Rim (fig. 4.15, reproduced at 1:2). Diam. = 0.090, PH = 0.02, PL = 0.033. Coarse, red fabric (2.5YR 5/8) with sherd encrustation. Fabric has frequent, medium rounded spherical white and black stones. Outturned rim. Similar to Winther-Jacobsen 2006a: 239, no. 41.

232.28. Rim (fig. 4.15, reproduced at 1:2). Diam. = 0.260, PH = 0.015, PL = 0.032. Coarse, red fabric (10R 5/8) with rare, small black spherical rounded-stones. Horizontal rim with upturned edge.

501.62 Rim. Diam. = 0.210, PH = 0.035, PL = 0.038. Coarse, red fabric (2.5YR 5/8) with few, medium white and black rounded spherical, and rub-rounded tabular stones. Two grooves on top of rim. Squared rim. See Lund 1996: 142, no. 23.

4.2.3.5. Late Roman

This ware is characterized by a dark fabric, ranging from red (10R 4/6) to a light brownish-gray fabric (10 YR 6/2), with numerous inclusions including mica. The most distinctive feature in this period is the ribbed exterior, which, as Hayes notes, does not appear on Cypriot wares until the later Roman period (Hayes 1991: 124).

112 finds
77 body sherds
24 rims
7 handles
3 bases
1 lid

4.37. Rim. Diam. = 0.120, PH = 0.016, PL = 0.047. Medium to coarse-grained, light red fabric (2.5YR 6/6) with frequent, medium to large inclusions of lime and mica. Almost horizontal folded rim. See Williams 1992: no. 388.

70.42. Rim. Diam. = uncertain, PH = 0.025, PL = 0.034. Thin, friable red fabric (2.5YR 5/8) with numerous sparkling, very small, dark and white inclusions with occasional, medium white and dark inclusions. The interior is a lighter red (2.5YR 4/8). Flanged rim.

76.28. Handle. Diam. = 0.270, PH = 0.029, PL = 0.034. Medium-grained, red fabric (10R 4/8) with a few lime inclusions and wheel ridging on body.

4.2.3.6. Late Roman Frying Pan

This ware, which typically dates from the second century BC to the second century AD, is characterized by a small casserole body that has a handle that is folded double. The ware is very common in the western half of Cyprus, but is very rare in the eastern half of the island. There is a later version (seventh century AD) from Dhiorios that is smaller with a handle that is similar in appearance, but is made from two strips of clay, not one strip folded over (Lund 2002a: 45). The one example found at PKAP appears to be the Late Antique variant.

1 find
1 handle

9.43. Handle (fig. 4.16). PL = 0.048, PW = 0.020. Coarse gray exterior (5Y 5/1) and gray interior (5Y 6/1) with a brown core (7.5YR 5/3) that has frequent, medium rounded spherical white and black stones, quartz, and some voids. See Catling 1972: fig. 20, no. P119; Lund 2002a: fig. 7.

4.2.3.7. Dhiorios

In 1958, a rescue excavation at the ancient site of Mersineri, two miles west of Dhiorios, in north-western Cyprus discovered a pottery factory dating to the seventh and eighth centuries AD. This production site manufactured four basic styles of cooking ware that are characterized by a thin, wheel-ridged body whose fabric ranged in color from red to black, and contained a grit temper. The most common design was a cooking pot that was a closed vessel with sloping shoulders, a wheel-ridged body, and two ridged, vertical strap handles. The next most frequent find was a deep casserole with two horizontal loop handles. The third design was a small frying pan with a double handle made of two clay strips. The least numerous find was a category of lids for casseroles (Catling 1972: 1–82). At PKAP, we have three examples of a Dhiorios cooking pot, one example of a Dhiorios casserole dish, and one example of a frying pan (see Kitchen Ware, Late Roman Frying Pan above).

4 finds
4 rims

18.37. Rim (fig. 4.16, reproduced at 1:2). Diam. = 0.014, PH = 0.029, PL = 0.035. Coarse-grained, friable fabric that has a reddish yellow interior (5YR 6/6) with a yellowish-red core (5YR 5/6) and a very dark gray slip (10YR 3/1) on exterior with frequent, small to medium white and dark inclusions. Inturned rim with a tapered lip, and a light groove on exterior that defines the junction of rim and neck. See Winther-Jacobsen 2006a: 241, no. 48.

71.39. Rim. Diam. = 0.240, PH = 0.021, PL = 0.053. Medium-grained, light red fabric (2.5YR 6/6) with rare, lime inclusions and a buff slip. Horizontal rim has two broad grooves on top. Possible casserole. See Catling 1972: 39, no. P402, and 33, no. P242.

74.36. Rim. Diam. = 0.125, PH = 0.022, PL = 0.043. Medium-grained, light red fabric (10R 6/8) with a gray core and ridging on body below rim. Inturned folded rim. See Catling 1972: 47, no. P433; Williams 1992: 69, no. 399.

4.2.4.   Kitchen Wares, Post-Ancient

This broad class of kitchen wares includes all post-Medieval kitchen ware sherds, of which there were very few, and all dated to the Modern era. The four sherds in this category are characterized by a hard, almost fine fabric with a few inclusions, and are covered with a glaze on the interior. All are small containers used for storage in the refrigerator or food service on a table, and typically held food items such as yogurt and olives. These sherds were a fairly common find in the SCSP survey (61 sherds) and were identified as a Contemporary Yogurt Pot (Gregory 1993: 289). These containers can still be seen in modern Cypriot grocery stores in the deli section.

4 finds
4 body sherds

55.8. Base. PH = 0.062, PW = 0.032, Th. = 0.009. Hard semi-fine, yellowish-red fabric (5YR 4/6) that has a reddish yellow surface (5YR 7/6) and common, fine mica inclusions. Interior is covered with a thick yellow glaze (5Y 8/6). Base of Modern yogurt pot.

4.3.   MEDIUM-COARSE WARES

As is typical with most projects in the Mediterranean, the bulk of the sherds that the PKAP fieldwalkers collected were coarse wares and body sherds (see Chapter 3). This class of wares has received the least amount of scholarly attention, and studies focusing on coarse wares have only recently emerged in press (Degest 2001; Gabrieli et al. 2007). The lack of distinctive shapes and decorations have made the creation of typologies difficult, and projects have developed different systems for classifying coarse wares based on the coarseness of fabric or usage (Winther-Jacobsen 2006b: 244). Recent attempts at scientific analyses, such as X-Ray Fluorescence, hold the possible promise of more precision in classification (Gerber 2005: 725).

The PKAP coarse wares are similar to the coarse wares at Panayia Ematousa in general appearance, with a chalky fabric that ranges in color from a pale yellow or brown to a reddish yellow or light pink (Winther-Jacobsen 2006b: 244). The fabric contains numerous colored inclusions (usually red, black, and white), ranging in size from small grits to large stones. The lack of diagnostic sherds limited the classification of most coarse ware sherds to large chronological periods. While Winther-Jacobsen has recently suggested dividing coarse wares into three categories (light utility, heavy utility, and transport), we followed the model of SCSP and divided our coarse wares into two categories (medium-coarse and coarse) based on wall thickness (Winther-Jacobsen 2010b). Due to the lack of distinctive forms, the sherds were divided into chronological divisions based on their fabrics.

4.3.1.   Medium-Coarse Wares, Iron Age

This category of coarse wares is characterized by a yellowish-red or red fabric with possible red, black, or gray inclusions of varying size.

176 finds

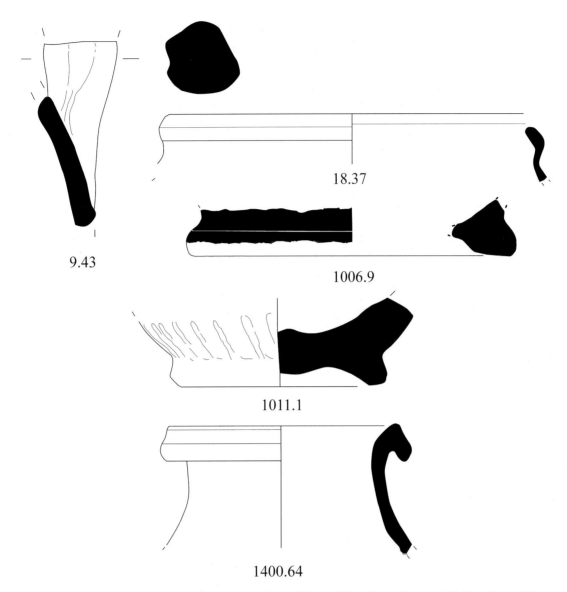

9.43

18.37

1006.9

1011.1

1400.64

FIG. 4.16 *Late Roman Frying Pan, Dhiorios, White Painted Coarse Ware, Cypro-Geometric Medium Coarse Wares, and Hellenistic to Roman Medium Coarse Ware sherds.*

124 body sherds
22 handles
17 rims
12 bases
1 toe

[501.1].129. Rim. Diam. = uncertain, PH = 0.023, PL = 0.049, Th. = 0.007 (wall), Th. = 0.020 (rim). Semi-fine, pink fabric (2.5YR 8/3) with a red slip (10R 5/6) and rare, medium inclusions of white, red, and gray stones. Downturned rim of large bowl or basin

1010.28. Rim. Diam. = 0.36, PH = 0.028, PL = 0.042, PW = 0.029 (rim), Th. = 0.012 (lip), Th. = 0.017 (body). Coarse, porous brown fabric (7.5YR 5/3) with a very pale brown surface (10YR 8/2) that has frequent, medium to large red and black inclusions. Downturned rim of large open vessel.

1402.9. Rim. Diam. = uncertain, PH = 0.029, PL = 0.096, Th. = 0.010 (tip), Th. = 0.007 (body). Medium-coarse, red (2.5YR 5/8) and pinkish-white fabric (7.5YR 8/2) with a pale yellow surface (5Y 8/2) that has rare inclusions. Horizontal rim has a slight downturn and rounded lip that tapers to the outside with a ridge beneath the lip that demarcates rim from body.

4.3.2.   White Painted

The fabric was generally a brownish color with numerous small black stones, and decorated with a brown or black paint on a lighter fabric. The decoration is typically applied to the neck, shoulder, or handles in bands or a recurring pattern.

1 find
1 base

1006.9. Base (fig. 4.16, reproduced at 1:2). Diam. = 0.200, PH = 0.029, PL = 0.069, Th. = 0.027 (ring). Coarse, light red fabric (2.5YR 6/6) with frequent, medium to very large black inclusions, and black paint on a pale yellow exterior surface (2.5Y 7/4). False ring foot.

4.3.3.   Medium-Coarse Wares, Cypro-Geometric

This ware is characterized by a light colored fabric (10YR 7/4–5YR 7/4) with small black inclusions and occasional mica.

5 finds
2 bases
2 body sherds
1 rim

74.27. Handle. Diam. = 0.081, PW = 0.045, Th. = 0.023. Very pale brown to light yellowish brown fabric (10YR 7/4–6/4) with frequent, fine to medium large grit, and rare fine mica. Vertical spined handle with very low, smoothed spine.

1011.1. Base (fig. 4.16). Diam. = 0.07, PH = 0.022, PW = 0.036, Th. = 0.011 (wall). Medium-coarse pink fabric (5YR 7/4) with frequent, medium dark inclusions. Black painted with radiating grooves from base up. Base is slightly flared.

4.3.4.   Medium-Coarse Wares, Cypro-Classical to Hellenistic

This broad chronotype is characterized by a reddish yellow fabric that contains a few inclusions and is covered with a wash or thin slip.

2 finds
1 base
1 handle

38.19. Handle. PH = 0.054, PW = 0.039 (handle), Th. = 0.019 (handle). Medium-coarse, very pale brown fabric (10YR 8/3–2.5Y 7/3) with heavy encrustations and a few, medium to large dark and light inclusions. Oval handle with body join.

4.3.5.   Medium-Coarse Wares, Hellenistic

This chronotype is characterized by a reddish yellow fabric that contains only a few inclusions and can be covered with a wash or thin slip.

1 find
1 handle

1402.7. Handle. PH = 0.058, PL = 0.114, PW = 0.020 (handle), Th. = 0.012 (handle), Th. = 0.077 (body). Medium-coarse, reddish yellow fabric (7.5YR 6/6) that is heavily encrusted with a few inclusions and a very pale brown slip (10YR 8/3) on the interior and a pale yellow slip (5Y 8/2) on the exterior. Horizontal loop handle with a long, low ridge.

4.3.6.   Hellenistic Lagynoi

A lagynos is a wine jug with an ovoid body and a ridged strap handle. Lagynoi, which were manufactured in a variety of fabrics, are characterized by tall, slender necks with a single, vertical strap handle (Rotroff 1997: 226–29). These one-handled jugs first appeared in the Hellenistic period and were a popular vessel shape into the Roman period. This type of wine vessel would have been a status symbol used primarily for fine dining and entertaining. Lagynoi are common archaeological finds on Cyprus, particularly in the west near Paphos.

The one example at Koutsopetria matches Hayes' series 5 at Paphos, which dates to the late second early first century BC (Hayes 1991: 18–22).

1 find
1 handle

[501.1].39. Handle (fig. 4.26). PL = 0.063, PW = 0.022. Medium-coarse, very pale brown fabric (10YR 8/4) with gray surface (Gley 1 5/1) and a few, medium red and black inclusions. Twisted round handle. See Hayes 1991: fig. 10, no. 14.

4.3.7. Medium-Coarse Wares, Hellenistic to Early Roman

This category contains sherds that shared attributes from both the Late Hellenistic and Early Roman periods, with a pale brown to pinkish fabric, and frequent dark inclusions.

28 finds
23 body sherds
2 handles
2 rims
1 base

501.60. Base. Diam. = 0.080, PH = 0.038, PL = 0.043, Th. = 0.012 (body), Th. = 0.010. Medium-coarse fabric with a very pale brown core (10YR 7/3), a reddish yellow interior (5YR 7/6), and a pink exterior (2.5YR 8/4) with a white slip, and a few, medium to large dark inclusions. Torus base.

4.3.8. Medium-Coarse Wares, Hellenistic to Roman

This small category of sherds contains one rim that share attributes from both the Hellenistic and Roman periods, though it most likely is an early Roman piece.

1 find
1 rim

1400.64. Rim (fig. 4.16, reproduced at 1:2). Diam. = 0.120, PH = 0.057, PW = 0.058, Th. = 0.006. Coarse, light red fabric (10R 7/8) with a pale yellow slip and

a few, medium to large red and white inclusions. Downturned rim of a jar.

4.3.9. Medium-Coarse Wares, Roman

This category is characterized by a fabric that ranges in color from a light brown to a medium red, and typically has small black, white, and red inclusions.

201 finds
164 body sherds
24 rims
6 handles
5 bases
2 toes

101.9. Rim. Diam. = 0.050. Medium-grained, yellowish-red fabric (5YR 5/6) with a few, gray and lime inclusions and a very shiny coating after break with wheel-ridging below the rim. Slightly inward thickened rim.

1401.84. Rim. Diam. = 0.300, PH = 0.029, PW = 0.052, Th. (body) = 0.006, Th. (rim) = 0.014, Th. (lip) = .008. Medium-coarse, friable red fabric (2.5YR 5/6) with a few, large to very large white inclusions and fine micaceous inclusions. It is a horizontal rim that has two incised grooves on lip and the grooves are 0.002 wide and spaced 0.002 apart.

4.3.10. Medium-Coarse Wares, Late Roman

These wares are characterized by a fabric that ranges in color from red (2.5YR 5/6) to brown (7.5 YR 3/4) and that includes small red, black, and white stones. Its most frequent fabric color was either an orangish or pinkish fabric with a mottled appearance.

315 finds
250 body sherds
29 rims
22 handles
10 bases
3 toes
1 neck

12.25. Handle (fig. 4.17). PL = 0.063, PW = 0.020, Th. = 0.009. Coarse, light red fabric (2.5YR 6/8) with rounded, spherical red and white stones with some lime particles and a reddish-brown slip (2.5YR 5/4). Vertical strap handle.

17.27. Toe. PL = 0.033, PW = 0.027. Coarse pink fabric (5YR 7/4) with frequent, sub-rounded white stones. Table amphora.

502.11. Rim. Diam. = 0.140, PH = 0.033, PL = 0.047. Medium-grained pink fabric (7.5YR 7/3) with a few, medium-sized lime and mica inclusions. Outward thickened, downturned rim of a rather large pitcher.

4.4 COARSE WARES

4.4.1. Coarse Wares, Iron Age

This category includes sherds that can only be dated broadly to the Iron Age (Cypro-Archaic to Cypro-Classical periods). They are characterized by a coarse reddish or reddish yellow fabric that is often decorated with bands of black or dark gray paint.

194 finds
168 body sherds
13 handles
9 bases
4 rims

1009.36. Body sherd. PW = 0.041, PL = 0.052, Th. = 0.010. Coarse reddish yellow fabric (5YR 6/6) with a very pale brown core (10YR 7/3) and frequent, medium to large white and red inclusions. Pink wash (2.5YR 8/3) on exterior that is encrusted with frequent, fine mica inclusions. Painted dark gray bands (7.5YR 4/1) and hatched design.

4.4.2. Coarse Wares, Cypro-Classical to Hellenistic

This small ware group contains sherds that shared attributes from both the Cypro-Classical and Hellenistic periods, though they are most likely early Hellenistic pieces.

3 finds
3 handles

[501.1].74. Body sherd. PL = 0.101, PW = 0.061, Th. = 0.017. Pale yellow fabric (2.5Y 8/3) with a light red core (2.5YR 6/6) and interior. Common, medium red and white inclusions, and mica. There is a ridge (0.009 m) on the exterior with a band of lines (0.011 m) below a rouletting band (0.005 m) above.

546.22. Handle. PL = 0.106, PW = 0.040. Very coarse, very pale brown fabric (10YR 7/3) with common, medium to large dark red and white inclusions, and a few fine mica inclusions. Large round handle with an indentation on one end.

4.4.3. Coarse Wares, Hellenistic to Early Roman

This category is characterized by a fabric that ranges in color from a light brown to a medium red, and typically has small black, white, and red inclusions.

14 finds
7 handles
5 body sherds
1 base
1 rim

1010.35. Rim (fig. 4.17, reproduced at 1:3). Diam. = 0.240, PH = 0.037, PL = 0.084, Th. = 0.013 (shoulder), Th. = 0.018 (lip). Coarse, pink fabric (7.5YR 7/4) with frequent, red and dark medium to large inclusions. Red band at base of rim on light slip, and paint on top of horizontal, slightly out turned rim.

4.4.4. Coarse Wares, Early Roman

This category is characterized by a fabric that ranges in color from a brown to a reddish yellow, and typically has small black, white, and red inclusions.

4 finds
2 handles
1 base
1 body sherd

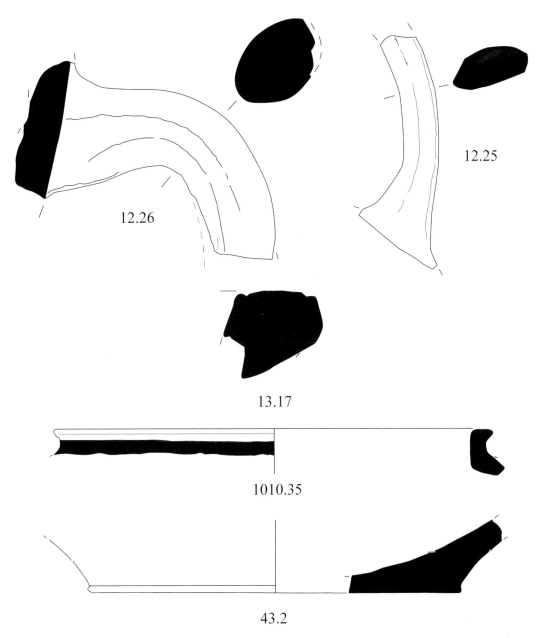

FIG. 4.17 *Late Roman Medium Coarse Wares, Hellenistic to Early Roman Coarse Wares, Roman Basins, and Late Roman Coarse Ware sherds.*

1009.62. Toe. Diam. = 0.050, PH = 0.053, Th. = 0.012. Coarse, reddish yellow fabric (5YR 7/6) with rare, medium stone inclusions and a very pale brown slip (10YR 8/4). Toe with hollow concavity.

4.4.5. *Coarse Wares, Roman*

This broad category is characterized by a fabric that ranges in color from a light brown to a medium red, and typically has small black, white, and red inclusions. The majority of the assemblage (80%) is coarse body sherds, many of which are probably amphora sherds.

136 finds
109 body sherds
16 handles
7 rims

3 bases
1 toe

509.1. Handle. PL = 0.062, PW = 0.045, Th. = 0.024. Medium-coarse pink fabric (7.5YR 7/3) with frequent, very small to medium red, black, and white inclusions as well as fine mica grains. Two raised ridges run parallel along the oval handle.

4.4.6. Roman Basins

Roman basins are large bowls with steep, vertical sides and heavy rims. The gray or grayish brown fabric is usually fairly coarse with numerous black grits. The rim can be decorated with incised lines or impressed designs (Williams 1992: 78–79). These basins can only be dated to the broad Roman period, since the basic shape of the basin changes little and the same form appears in excavation contexts spread over three or four centuries.

23 finds
20 rims
3 bases

13.17. Rim (fig. 4.17, reproduced at 1:2). Diam. = 0.30, PH = 0.008, PL = 0.072. Coarse-grained, light yellow-brown fabric (10YR 6/4) with frequent, gray and lime inclusions. Decoration consists of a single wavy line between two straight lines on top of rim. See Williams 1992: 80, no. 472.

43.2. Base (fig. 4.17, reproduced at 1:2). PL = 0.093, PW = 0.096, Th. = 0.025. Coarse, weak red fabric (10R 5/4) with frequent, white and black sub-rounded stones. Fabric also includes voids and lime up to 0.007 in size and has a light red exterior (2.5YR 6/6) and red interior (2.5YR 5/6).

48.25. Rim. Diam. = 0.380, PH = 0.020, PL = 0.134. Medium to coarse-grained, reddish-brown fabric (2.5YR 5/4) with frequent, very large red, lime, and black inclusions and a pale yellow slip (2.5Y 8/3). Rolled rim with preserved small lug handle.

61.31. Rim. Diam. = 0.250, PH = 0.057, PL = 0.086. Coarse, light red fabric (2.5 YR 6/6) with frequent, very large inclusions of lime, gray stones, and black

stones. Trapezoidal out turned flat rim with incised wavy line on rim, framed by two incised straight lines. See Williams 1992: 80, no. 472; Rautman 2003: 205, no. 207.

65.24. Rim. Diam. = 0.280, PH = 0.043, PL = 0.102. Medium to coarse-grained, light yellowish brown fabric (10YR 6/4) with lime and mica inclusions. Similar to, but less horizontal than Williams 1992: 78, no. 454.

73.30. Rim. Diam. = 0.270, PH = 0.040, PL = 0.081. Medium-grained, pale yellow fabric (2.5Y 7/4) with frequent, lime and gray inclusions. It is very hard fired with a single ridge on lip of rim and grooving on body below a slightly inturned, horizontal rim.

87.16. Rim. Diam. = indeterminate, PH = 0.026, PL = 0.024. Medium-coarse, reddish yellow fabric on exterior (7.5YR 6/6) and pale yellow on interior (2.5Y 7/4). Vessel is evenly fired, with frequent, very small to small dark and sparkling inclusions. Rim is poorly preserved at lip.

196.22. Rim. Diam. = 0.420. Medium-coarse, yellowish-red fabric (5YR 5/6) with frequent, fine mica, and common, fine to large dark grit and white inclusions, some encrustation. A thin incised line (0.003 m) on lip surface (0.010 m from interior) and crenelated on exterior surface. Piecrust decoration.

246.18. Rim. Diam. greater than 0.400, PH = 0.022, PL = 0.090. Coarse, weak red fabric (10R 5/4) with frequent lime, mica, and quartz inclusions. Square rim.

4.4.7.   Coarse Wares, Late Roman

These wares are characterized by a fabric that ranges in color from red (2.5YR 5/6) to brown (7.5 YR 3/4) that includes small red, black, and white stones. Its most frequent fabric color was either an orangish or pinkish fabric with a mottled appearance. The majority of this assemblage (80%) is coarse body sherds, many of which are probably amphora sherds.

1,327 finds
1,072 body sherds
192 handles
45 rims
17 bases
1 shoulder/neck

2.37. Handle. PL = 0.072, PW = 0.060. Coarse, light brown fabric (7.5YR 6/4) with frequent, sub-rounded white stones and a few lime inclusions. Vertical strap handle.

7.20. Rim. Diam. = 0.115, PH = 0.040, PL = 0.069. Medium-grained, smooth, reddish yellow fabric (5YR 6/6) with a few, small to medium black and red inclusions, and frequent sparkling inclusions. Vertical rim of a closed vessel with a rounded lip flattened on top.

12.26. Handle (fig. 4.17). PL = 0.075, PW = 0.046. Coarse, red fabric (2.5YR 5/6) with frequent red, black, and white sub-rounded stones, and some lime inclusions. Round vertical handle.

17.26. Handle (fig. 4.18). PL = 0.072, PW = 0.044. Coarse fabric with pinkish-gray core (5YR 6/2) and red surface (2.5YR 5/6) with common, white, black and gray sub-rounded stones, and some lime inclusions (ca. 0.002). Ridging running down vertical strap handle.

23.21. Handle (fig. 4.18). Fine pink fabric (7.5YR 8/3) with rounded and sub-rounded black and red stones. Vertical handle has two ridges.

154.15. Rim. Diam. = uncertain, PH = 0.046, PL = 0.035. Coarse, pale yellow fabric (2.5Y 8/4) that is partially encrusted with common, medium black, white, and red inclusions, a few sparkling. The sherd has a ridge demarcating the slightly out turned rim with rounded lip from the body. Closed form.

[501.1].72. Base. PH = 0.031, PL = 0.126, PW = 0.066, Th. = 0.016 (wall). Coarse, red fabric (10R 5/6) with a reddish yellow core (7.5YR 6/6) and frequent, large red and gray inclusions. The exterior has a very pale brown slip (10YR 8/3) while the interior has a reddish yellow slip (5YR 6/6). Disc foot.

[501.1].134. Rim. Diam. = 0.340, PH = 0.028, PL = 0.071, Th. = 0.008 (wall), Th. = 0.020 (rim). Coarse, light red core (2.5YR 6/6) with a light red surface (2.5YR 6/8) and with rare, large red and gray inclusions. Two grooves on upper surface of horizontal rim.

4.4.8.   *Combed Ware*

Combed ware is a term coined by Robinson to describe a style of decoration typically seen on coarse wares dated to the sixth and seventh centuries AD (Robinson 1959). It is decorated with a close set of narrow, combed lines that is often undulating in appearance. This ware is ubiquitous in Greece, but less common at sites in the eastern-most areas of the Mediterranean. Its prevalence on sites in Greece and the broader Aegean has allowed it to be used in ceramic and quantitative studies that examine urbanization and the countryside (Pettegrew 2007: 743–84; 2008: 249–66).

29 finds
29 body sherds

12.13. Body Sherd (fig. 4.18). PL = 0.060, PW = 0.041, Th. = 0.010. Coarse light red fabric (2.5YR 6/6) with silver mica and a few, black, white and red sub-rounded stones. Combing on the exterior consists of 5 grooves.

4.4.9.   *Coarse Wares, Post-Ancient*

This large ceramic class includes coarse wares from the post-Roman period to the Modern era. The centuries following the Late Roman period remain particularly problematic for ceramics since so few forms have been identified, either in excavations or by surveys. In addition, for Cyprus, the lack of datable fine wares from this period has typically hampered the dating of coarse wares. Despite this, recent work has attempted to move the discussion of coarse wares forward. For example, work by Gabrieli, Jackson, and Kaldelli at Paphos has shown that the certain compositions of complete

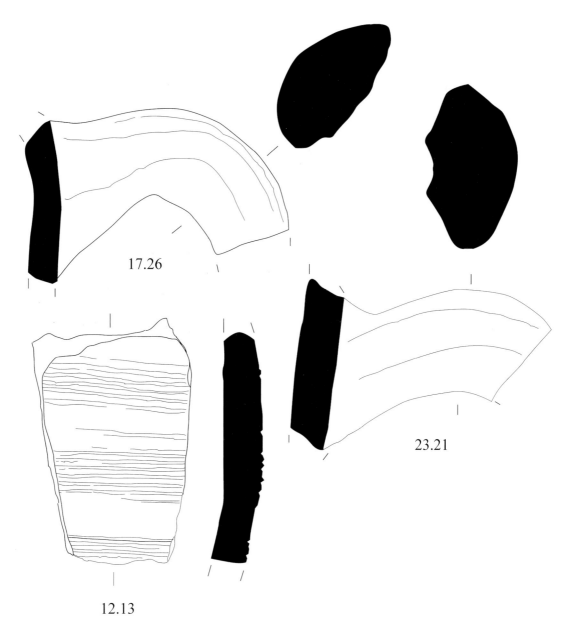

17.26

23.21

12.13

FIG. 4.18 *Late Roman Coarse Ware and Combed Ware sherds.*

assemblages of coarse and plain wares can be used to help identify seventh- and eighth-century contexts despite the lack of fine wares (Gabrieli, Jackson, and Kaldelli 2007).

Relatively little work has also been done on creating typologies for coarse wares that date to the post-Medieval period on Cyprus, due to the remarkable continuity in ware forms from the twelfth century to the present. Gabrieli has attempted to divide coarse wares from this period into three chronological divisions: the twelfth century to the end of the fourteenth century, the fifteenth and sixteenth centuries, and the sixteenth century to the present (Gabrieli 2004: 287). Another attempt at creating a typology for Cypriot coarse wares was Tim Gregory's work from the Sydney Cyprus Survey Project (Gregory 2003). He developed a tentative typology of coarse wares

(Cypriot W Series) for a large group of utilitarian wares that were characterized by a brown or red fabric that is similar in appearance to the Modern wares produced at Kornos. These wares can only be broadly dated to the period between the late Medieval and Modern period. Gregory divided these wares into seven different categories based on subtle fabric differences and, since these wares were also present at Koutsopetria, his classification system was adopted by PKAP (Moore and Gregory 2012: 211). (See Section 5.4.5 and 5.4.6 for distributional analysis).

4.4.9.1. Cypriot W1

This sub-category is characterized by a dark brown fabric with numerous black stones, and is tentatively dated to the Late Medieval to Early Modern period (Gregory 2003: 286).

4 finds
2 rims
2 body sherds

68.17. Rim (fig. 4.19, reproduced at 1:3). Diam. = 0.300, PH = 0.072, PW = 0.132. Very coarse, reddish-brown fabric (2.5YR 5/4) with very large (approx. 0.005 m) black angular and sub-rounded stones with spherical white stones. Fabric also has large voids that are approximately 0.007 in size. See Keswani et al. 2003: 203, no. 1005.1.1 and Pl. 14. Inturned rolled rim.

4.4.9.2. Cypriot W2

This second category is identical to W1 in most ways, but is characterized by a reddish fabric. It is also tentatively dated to the Late Medieval to Early Modern period.

1 find
1 rim

56.44. Rim (fig. 4.19, reproduced at 1:3). Diam. = 0.029, PH = 0.042, PW = 0.111. Coarse, reddish-brown fabric (2.5YR 5/4) with large, angular spherical black and white stones and lime particles. Rim has knobbed design.

4.4.9.3. Cypriot W3

This subcategory has a coarse reddish-brown fabric and numerous black and white stones. It dates from the Ottoman period to the Modern period (Gregory 2003: 288; Moore and Gregory 2012: 211).

41 finds
30 body sherds
10 rims
1 base

12.46. Rim (fig. 4.19, reproduced at 1:3). Diam. = 0.270, PH = 0.020, PW = 0.066. Coarse, reddish-brown fabric (2.5YR 5/4) with abundant, shiny black rounded tabular and rounded spherical white stones. Vertical rim.

13.25. Base. PL = 0.083, PW = 0.084, Th. = 0.023. Coarse, red fabric (2.5YR 5/6) with a gray core and spherical, sub-rounded white and black stones. Fabric also includes lime particles and voids. Flat base.

62.33. Rim. Diam. = 0.019, PH = 0.037, PW = 0.062. Coarse, reddish-brown fabric (2.5YR 5/4) with a thin brown slip, and a few, white and black rounded spherical and tabular stones. Outward thickened rim.

179.15. Rim. Diam. = 0.250, PH = 0.041, PW = 0.077. Coarse, reddish-brown fabric (2.5YR 5/6) with sub-rounded black and white stones, some very large (ca. 0.0025). Knobbed, square rim.

4.4.9.4. Cypriot W5

This group is characterized by coarse reddish-brown fabric that contains white and black inclusions, and a thin brown slip. It dates from the Ottoman period to the Modern period (Gregory 2003: 288; Moore and Gregory 2012: 211).

17 finds
10 rims
5 body sherds
2 handles

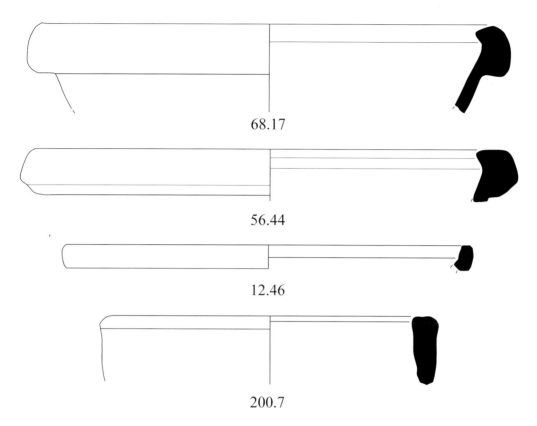

68.17

56.44

12.46

200.7

FIG. 4.19   *Cypriot W1, W3, and W5 sherds.*

2.38. Rim. Diam. = 0.020, PH = 0.061, PW = 0.068. Coarse, reddish-brown fabric (2.5 YR 5/4) with spherical, angular black stones and rounded spherical white stones. Voids and lime present. Knobbed rim.

200.7. Rim (fig. 4.19, reproduced at 1:3). Diam. = 0.170, PH = 0.053, PW = 0.073. Coarse, reddish-brown fabric (2.5YR 5/4) with a grayish core, and a few, white and black rounded spherical stones. Some quartz was also present. Rim with squared lip.

233.17. Rim (fig. 4.20). Diam. = 0.028, PH = 0.036, PW = 0.116. Coarse, reddish-brown fabric (2.5YR 5/4) with gray core. Fabric contains abundant, angular spherical and tabular sub-rounded white, black and gray stones. Fabric also includes voids and lime particles. Knobbed rim.

241.13. Rim. Diam. = 0.170, PH = 0.036, PW = 0.039. Coarse, light reddish-brown fabric (2.5 YR 6/3) with sub-rounded black and white stones, some quite large (ca. 0.003). Inturned, square lip.

4.4.9.5. Cypriot W6

This subtype is characterized by a brown fabric covered with a thin brown slip and contains black stones. It dates from the Ottoman period to the Modern period (Gregory 2003: 288; Moore and Gregory 2012: 211).

2 finds
2 rims

84.7. Rim. Diam. = 0.019, PH = 0.037, PW = 0.062. Coarse, reddish-brown fabric (2.5YR 5/4) with a thin brown slip, and a few, white and black rounded spherical and tabular stones. Outward thickened rim.

4.4.9.6. Cypriot W7

This subcategory is characterized by a bright red fabric with black and white stones. It dates to the Modern period (Gregory 2003: 289).

12 finds
7 body sherds
3 rims
2 handles

56.44. Rim (fig. 4.20, reproduced at 1:3). Diam. = 0.029, PH = 0.042, PW = 0.111. Coarse, reddish-brown fabric (2.5YR 5/4) with large, angular spherical black and white stones, and lime particles. Knobbed rim.

4.4.10. Coarse Wares, Medieval

This category of sherds is categorized by a coarse, dark fabric (red, dark gray, or black) with numerous stones, inclusions, and large voids, often and has a slightly over-fired or flaking appearance to it. It is usually decorated with incised or combed lines (Gregory 1993: 169).

6 finds
4 body sherds
2 handles

140.18. Body sherd (fig. 4.20, reproduced at 1:2). PL = 0.051, Th. = 0.012. Coarse, dark gray fabric (7.5YR 4/1–10YR 4/1) with frequent, fine to medium white and red grit, and micaceous inclusions. Sherd is decorated with a pattern of bands made of incised lines crossing other bands.

4.4.11. Coarse Wares, Medieval to Modern

This category of sherds is similar to the Medieval coarse ware category and shares many characteristics, such as a coarse, dark fabric and numerous inclusions. The fabric, however, tends to be better levigated with smaller inclusions, and typically lacks decoration or ornamentation that would allow it to be more precisely catalogued (Gregory 2003: 284–89).

19 finds
13 body sherds
4 rims
1 neck
1 base

5.31. Rim. Diam. = uncertain, PH = 0.076, PL = 0.102, Th. = 0.012 (body), Th. = 0.037 (rim). Very coarse, red fabric (2.5YR 4/6) with strong brown slip on exterior (7.5YR 5/6), and abundant, small to very large white and black micaceous inclusions. Squared rim with inward flange (0.009) of a very large vessel.

6.47. Rim. Diam. = uncertain, PH = 0.069, PL = 0.092, Th. = 0.015 (body), Th. = 0.034 (rim). Very coarse, gritty fabric with gray core (5YR 5/1) and reddish-brown exterior. Fabric has common, medium to large black red white inclusions. Outward thickened rim of a large open bowl.

8.8. Rim (fig. 4.20, reproduced at 1:2). Diam. = 0.600, PH = 0.061, PL = 0.067, PW = 0.031 (rim), Th. = 0.013 (body), Th. = 0.011 (rim). Very coarse, reddish-brown surface (5YR 4/4) with a pale yellow core (5Y 8/4), and common, medium to large dark inclusions, as well as fine mica inclusions. Slightly outturned, square rim tapers inward.

18.21. Rim. Diam. = 0.56, PH = 0.039, PL = 0.119, Th. = 0.026 (rim), Th. = 0.013. Very coarse, light gray core (2.5Y 7/2) with a weak red exterior (10YR 5/3) with medium to large, common white and dark inclusions, and some fine mica inclusions. Squared rim with a vertical strap handle beginning on rim ridge on the underside of rim.

18.24. Rim. Diam. = uncertain, PH = 0.033, PL = 0.088, Th. = 0.024. Very coarse, weak red fabric (10R 4/4) with common, small to very large white and black inclusions, and micaceous grains throughout. Squared lip is heavily eroded on surface.

38.29. Rim (fig. 4.20, reproduced at 1:2). Diam. = 0.600, PH = 0.065, PW = 0.037, Th. (body) = 0.013, Th. (rim) = 0.029. Very coarse, red fabric (2.5YR 5/6) with medium to large, common white, gray,

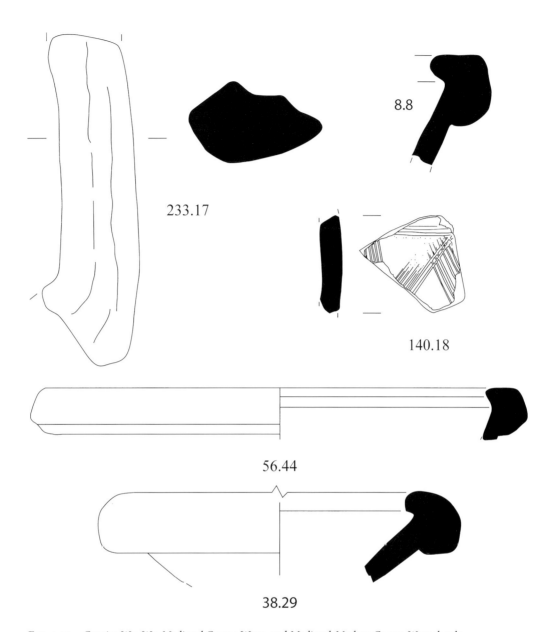

233.17

8.8

140.18

56.44

38.29

FIG. 4.20   *Cypriot W5, W7, Medieval Coarse Ware, and Medieval-Modern Coarse Ware sherds.*

and dark inclusions, as well as fine mica inclusions.   1 find
Outward, thickened rim of a large open vessel.   1 rim

4.4.12.   *Coarse Wares, Early Modern*

This category of sherds is categorized by a dark fabric (red, dark gray, or black) with numerous small stones and inclusions, and is sometimes decorated with incised lines or rouletting. The fabric is typically finer with smaller inclusions than the previous periods.

[501.1].192. Rim. Diam. = uncertain, PW = 0.039, PL = 0.028. Coarse, red fabric (2.5YR 4/6) with a dark gray core (10YR 4/1) and frequent red and white inclusions that range from small to large. Rim is not fully preserved at lip and is flat on top. Rim is thickened and outwardly tapering to a point with a narrow band of rouletting on exterior below lip. Rim of a large open vessel.

4.4.13. Coarse Wares, Modern

This category of sherds is categorized by a fabric ranging in color from a light red to dark brown and is very hard fired. The sherds are usually covered with a thick, shiny glaze that can range in color from a light brown to a dark red.

11 finds
6 rims
4 body sherds
1 base

506.7. Rim. Diam. = 0.170, PH= 0.044, PL= 0.046. Medium-grained pink fabric (5YR 7/3) with a few lime inclusions and very hard fired. Outward thickened rim See Keswani et al. 2003: 204, no. 1212.14.1.

4.5. AMPHORAE

Along with fine wares, amphorae are a class of ceramics that have typically received close attention from archaeologists over the years. Since amphorae were used for transporting goods (primarily liquids such as olive oil and wine), they can provide valuable information about trade routes, as well as local and global economies. The field received a significant boost with the development of underwater or nautical archaeology in the 1950s by George Bass. With the discovery and excavation of numerous shipwrecks, many containing thousands of amphorae, interest grew for the development of amphora typologies (Benoit 1956: 23–34; Zevi 1966: 207–47). In recent years, the development of quantification methods (Riley 1975: 25–63; Fulford and Peacock 1984) and the application of scientific analyses (Williams 1982: 99–110) have expanded the breadth of knowledge that amphora studies can provide to researchers.

The 1,672 amphorae sherds that fieldwalkers collected make up 10.3% by quantity of the total collected sherds, while the 1,348 pithos sherds make up an additional 8.3%. The overwhelming majority of the amphorae are from Cyprus, while the majority of the imports are from the eastern Mediterranean, with very few originating from the western Mediterranean. This class of ceramic vessel presents some interesting issues for classification and analysis. On one hand, the sherds that were identified as amphora were easy to place into specific chronological periods. For example, only 4% by quantity of the amphora sherds were dated to broad chronological spans. Within the chronological periods, however, only 41% by quantity were identified as specific chronotypes, such as Koan or Late Roman 1. This number is most likely inflated due to the large number of easily identifiable Late Roman 1 Amphora handles discovered in the area. It is also important to note that due to their lack of decoration or distinctive patterning, many amphora body sherds were either simply identified as generic amphora not assigned to a specific chronological period, or were not identified as amphora body sherds, but as coarse wares.

There were very few examples collected that predated the Iron Age, which is the earliest period to show significant numbers of amphora sherds (n=34), 2.0% by quantity of all amphora. The most common amphora of the period is a locally manufactured Cypriot amphora with horizontal handles that would have been transported into the area from other regions on the island. There were no foreign imports discovered in the Koutsopetria region from the Cypro-Classical period, and this combined with the low numbers of Cypriot produced amphora indicates consumption rather than production or exportation (see Section 4.3.5).

The number of amphora sherds increases in quantity in the Hellenistic and Early Roman period, 385 sherds or 13% by quantity of all amphora. Despite the increase in numbers, the majority of the amphorae from this period (290 sherds, or 75.3% by quantity) remain unclassified. The largest category of transport vessel in this period were Basket Handle amphorae, the majority of which were recovered by PKAP on the slopes of Vigla and the coastal plain of Koutsopetria. It is also during this period that the first foreign amphora imports appear at Koutsopetria, including Koan, Rhodian, and Greco-Italic amphorae, even though the number of these imports is very low: 9 sherds or 2.3% by quantity of the Hellenistic and Early Roman amphora sherds. Despite the fact that more intact Rhodian amphorae have been discovered on Cyprus than at any other location

in the Mediterranean outside of Rhodes, very few examples were discovered during the course of the survey (Barker 2013: 102).

At Koutsopetria, Late Roman amphorae accounted for 62% by quantity of all amphorae. Late Roman 1 Amphora was the most common, representing 30% by quantity of PKAP's total amphorae from the Late Roman period and 80% by quantity of the identifiable amphora types. Stella Demesticha has suggested a three generation model of classification for LR1 amphorae, and the majority of PKAP's handles, based on both handle shape and size, would be classified as LR1/C and date to the seventh century (Demesticha 2013).

A fabric analysis of the Late Roman 1 Amphora sherds at Koutsopetria shows that 25% of the LR1 amphora sherds have a fabric type that has been suggested was produced in Cilicia and Syria (Elton 2005). The largest number of Late Roman 1 Amphora by quantity (58%) has a fabric whose place of manufacture is believed to have been south-central Cyprus. This fabric, often identified as Rautman LR1(1), is also the most frequently found Late Roman 1 sherd at Panayia Ematousa and Maroni (Manning 2002: 42–43; Winther-Jacobsen 2006c: 310–11). Despite the high number of Cypriot Late Roman 1 Amphorae at Koutsopetria, there were no sherds discovered that were identified as the brick-red Late Roman 1 Amphora type produced at Kourion.

Comparing Koutsopetria's Late Roman amphorae collection with other nearby sites suggests both significant similarities and differences. In terms of similarities, Late Roman 1 Amphora sherds represent the dominant class of Late Roman amphorae at the small villages of Maroni and Kopetra, located some 50 km west of Kition. At Maroni, Late Roman 1 accounted for 21% of Late Roman amphorae by weight, while at Kopetra, Late Roman 1 Amphorae made up ⅔ of all amphora sherds. At Kopetra, however, 42% of the Late Roman 1 Amphora sherds are from Cilicia and Syria, and approximately 13% are from south-central Cyprus, which is the opposite of Koutsopetria (Rautman 2003: 170). The greater proportion of locally produced Late Roman 1 fabrics at Maroni and Koutsopetria might reflect their function as ports for exporting locally pro-

duced agricultural produce rather than as hubs for importing wine and olive oil from abroad in foreign made amphorae.

Both sites, however, produce much greater diversity of amphora types than Koutsopetria. Kopetra, for example, produced 13 identifiable amphora types compared to the 5 types identified at Koutsopetria (Manning 2002: 42–43; Rautman 2003: 168–74). In fact, Koutsopetria shows greater similarity to the village of Panayia Ematousa, another site in the immediate hinterland of Kition, some 6.5 km north and inland of the city. Panayia Ematousa, like Koutsopetria, has no Late Roman 4 amphorae, the most common imported amphora type at both Maroni and Kopetra (Winther-Jacobsen 2006c: 306). The differences in proportions between Maroni and Kopetra, on the one hand, and Koutsopetria and Panayia Ematousa on the other, reinforce the hypothesis that Koutsopetria was more heavily engaged in exporting than importing.

It is clear that Koutsopetria imported Late Roman amphorae from only a few locations in the eastern Mediterranean, primarily Cilicia and Syria, and that its importation of amphorae from other regions was limited or non-existent. Only two examples of a Palestinian bag amphora were found at Koutsopetria, and while the numbers are low for other Cypriot sites (Maroni <1% and Kopetra <3%), this is surprising considering the close proximity of the Levantine coast to the southern Cypriot coast (Manning 2002: 42; Rautman 2003: 172). A similar situation holds true for amphorae from Africa, with only one North African amphora sherd at Koutsopetria and no Egyptian amphorae discovered. Also found in fairly low numbers are Late Roman 2 amphora sherds produced in the Aegean and Black Sea region. Low numbers were reported at all nearby sites: Kopetra (1.9%), Koutsopetria, Panayia Ematousa, and Maroni < 1%. These relatively low percentages of amphora imports, especially Late Roman 4 (which is common at other sites), suggest that Koutsopetria was participating selectively in the southern Cypriot coastal trade and that factors other than availability determined Koutsopetria's participation. This is further reinforced by the variety in fabrics of the Late Roman 1 Amphora

at Koutsopetria. Such variety in Late Roman 1 Amphora fabric is not unusual on Cyprus — there were 4 main subclasses at Kopetra — but does indicate multiple production sites and suggests that trade on the island was not merely a matter of access to materials, but was selective, in fact (Rautman 2003: 168–70).

After the Arab raids began on Cyprus in the middle of the seventh century AD, the number of amphora sherds at Koutsopetria dropped dramatically. In fact, there were no Medieval or Byzantine amphorae discovered, and it is not until the pre-modern and Modern periods that a few examples of amphora sherds reappear at Koutsopetria. The lack of amphora sherds from the eighth century AD corresponds to the decline in number of fine ware sherds from the post Late Roman periods and suggests a decline in activity at Koutsopetria.

4.5.1 Amphorae, Iron Age

This category of amphora includes sherds that can only be broadly dated to the Iron Age (Cypro-Archaic to Cypro-Classical). At PKAP, this category includes examples that are from an amphora, but lack any distinguishing characteristics (decoration, specific rim, or handle shape) that would allow them to be more precisely identified. Sherds in this category are characterized by a reddish yellow or brown fabric (7.5YR 6/6) with small black, white, and red inclusions.

34 finds
14 body sherds
12 handles
5 toes
2 rims
1 base

1008.23. Body sherd (fig. 4.26). PH = 0.064, PW = 0.059, Th. = 0.012. Coarse, reddish yellow fabric (5YR 6/6) with very pale brown core (10YR 7/4), a very pale brown slip (10YR 8/3), and a few, medium inclusions of white, red, black, and micaceous inclusions. Thick, dark gray interior painted bands (10YR 4/1) and three, thin black bands enclosed by very thick black bands. All bands are horizontal.

1009.65. Base. Diam. = 0.039, PH = 0.027. Medium-coarse, reddish yellow fabric (7.5YR 6/6) with rare, small to medium black, white, and red inclusions and rare mica. Base is slightly concave and not fully preserved at bottom with eroded edges, and narrows slightly at stem with black glaze preserved above stem.

4.5.2. Amphorae, Cypro-Geometric and Cypro-Archaic

4.5.2.1. Black on Red Amphora

Two handles discovered at PKAP have cautiously been identified as Black on Red amphorae. Black on Red is characterized by a light red or pink clay with white, red, and black inclusions, a light red slip, and black paint (Sørensen 2006c: 177–78). The 2 handles discovered at Koutsopetria are fragmentary and their identification remains tentative.

2 finds
2 handles

1006.5. Handle. PH = 0.030, PL = 0.046, Th. = 0.019. Medium-coarse, light red fabric (2.5YR 7/6) with small to medium, dark and light inclusions (few 5%). Horizontal handle with slight curve.

4.5.2.2. White Painted Amphora

This amphora is characterized by a medium-coarse fabric that is covered with a pale slip and is decorated with black painted designs (Sørensen 2006b: 166–67).

1 find
1 rim

1006.3. Rim. Diam. = uncertain, PH = 0.047, PL = 0.043, Th. (rim) = 0.018, Th. (body) = 0.012. Medium-coarse, pink fabric (5YR 8/3) with few, small dark inclusions (3%). Black painted with hatched decoration beneath outturned, slightly flaring rim.

4.5.3. Amphorae, Cypro-Classical

The most common Cypro-Classical period amphora at Koutsopetria is a locally made amphora with a horizontal handle that rises above the rim and has a pale brown to pale red coarse fabric and dates to the seventh to fourth centuries BC (Winther-Jacobsen 2006b: 307). Recent work by Winther-Jacobsen has helped refine the study of classical amphorae on Cyprus (Winther-Jacobsen 1998: 319–81; 2002: 169–84).

4.5.3.1. Panayia Fabrics

The nearby site of Panayia Ematousa identified two primary fabrics: Fabric 1, which has pale brown to pale yellow fabric, and Fabric 2, which has a pale brown to reddish yellow fabric. The amphorae at Koutsopetria appear to match these two fabric descriptions quite closely. These amphorae were exported in limited numbers to eastern Mediterranean locations (Winther-Jacobsen 2006b: 303–7).

24 finds
15 handles
5 toes
2 rims
2 body sherds

Panayia Fabric 1
127.12. Handle. PL = 0.073, PW = 0.070. Coarse and sandy, light reddish-brown fabric (5YR 6/4) with abundant, sub-rounded white, red, black and brown stones. Vertical spined handle.

Panayia Fabric 2
[501.1].46. Toe. PH = 0.102, Th. (top of toe) = 0.063, Th. (join with body) = 0.060. Coarse red fabric (2.5YR 5/6) with few, small to medium white and gray inclusions and heavy encrustation. Hollow phallic toe that is eroded at base.

4.5.3.2. Unclassified Cypro-Classical Amphora

This category of amphora contains sherds that can only be dated broadly to the Cypro-Classical period due to their fabric and style of decoration. The decoration, fabric, and shape of are not distinctive enough to allow for a more precise identification. They are characterized by a medium-coarse red to reddish-brown fabric, were produced on the island, and were probably regionally manufactured.

45 finds
12 handles
6 bases/toes
2 rims
25 body sherds

[501.1].48. Toe. Diam. = 0.020, PH = 0.036, PW = 0.043. Medium-coarse, reddish yellow fabric (5YR 6/6) with rare, medium black inclusions. Toe of water jar.

4.5.4. Amphorae, Hellenistic

4.5.4.1. Basket Handle Amphora

One of the more common amphora finds was a transport amphora that was characterized by two high arching U-shaped vertical handles and a pale brown or buff fabric. These handles are similar to ones from the eastern Mediterranean that date from the Cypro-Archaic to the Late Hellenistic Age and are found at sites and shipwrecks in the eastern Mediterranean (Leonard 1995a: 141). They were used for storage and typically contained olive oil, wine, honey, or sauces (Zoroglu 2013: 43). Recent work on the Archaic and Classical Basket Handle Amphorae includes the underwater work conducted by Greene, Leidwanger, and Özdaş in their investigation of two Archaic shipwrecks at Kekova Adası and Kepçe Burnu, Turkey (Greene, Leidwanger, and Özdaş 2011: 60–68; 2013: 22–34), and the analysis of Basket Handle Amphorae from the excavation of Kelenderis in Rough Cilicia (Zoroglu 2013: 36–45). At Kelenderis they identified three basic forms of basket handles. Type 1 has a biconical body with a broad body and flat base and dates to the seventh and sixth centuries BC. Type 2 has an oval body and flat base, and dates to the sixth and fifth centuries BC. Type 3 has an oval body with a pointed toe and dates to the fifth and fourth centuries BC. (Zoroglu 2013: 43).

The vast majority of those discovered at Koutsopetria are different from the Archaic and Classical versions since they are smaller in size, with an oval handle instead of a round handle. The PKAP basket handles are similar to those in the published excavation reports of the Salamis tombs by Karageorghis and identified as olive oil containers (Karageorghis 1970; Hadjisavvas 1992: 78). They are similar in size and fabric to the Type 3 described by Zoroglu, but with a flattened cone as base instead of a pointed toe (Zoroglu 2013: 43).

While Cyprus, Rough Cilicia, and Palestine have all been suggested as possible production sites (Zoroglu 2013: 43), the large number of handles at PKAP, especially when compared to other sites on Cyprus, suggests that PKAP is very close to their place of manufacture. As our examination of fine wares has shown (in particular the wares ESA, CRS, and ARS), beginning in the Early Roman period, the area's trading connections shift eastward towards Salamis, while Rough Cilicia develops strong trading ties with northern and northwestern Cyprus. Therefore, it would not be unexpected to discover that these Basket Handle Amphorae are either manufactured somewhere between our site and Salamis, or that Salamis served as the Cypriot entry point, perhaps from Palestine. The large number of basket handles, when compared to the small number of Hellenistic fine ware sherds, could indicate that the area's focus was on exporting local agricultural products rather than importing goods.

A close examination of the handles in the PKAP collection revealed several distinct differences that allowed us to break the collection into eight different subcategories based on location and dominant visual characteristic.

64 finds
64 handles

Group 1
This type has a light buff to brownish-buff fabric (7.5YR 7/4–8/2 to 2.5Y 7/4–5Y 7/3) with frequent black stone inclusions. The handles are all oval in shape and each one contains finger imprints on the interior. These handles come from a variety of locations on the site.

4 handles

84.14. Handle. PL = 0.098, PW = 0.035, Th. = 0.025. Coarse light red core (2.5YR 7/8) with pink interior (7.5YR 7/4) and pinkish-white exterior (7.5YR 8/2) with frequent, small black inclusions and larger white and red sub-rounded inclusions. Oval, vertical handle with indented finger hole.

546.26. Handle. PL = 0.161, PW = 0.029, Th. (handle) = 0.018, Th. (join) = 0.023. Coarse pale yellow fabric (2.5Y 7/4) with common, black and red spherical rounded inclusions, and occasional white rounded spherical inclusions. Oval vertical handle with indented finger hole.

1402.2. Handle. PL = 0.148, PW = 0.071, Th. = 0.043. Coarse pale yellow (5Y 7/3) to reddish yellow fabric (7.5YR 7/6) with a few, large orange inclusions. Oval vertical handle with finger imprint.

1404.32. Handle. PL = 0.113, PW = 0.043, Th. (join) = 0.071, Th. (handle) = 0.035. Coarse pinkish-white fabric (7.5YR 8/2) with frequent, medium-sized, sub-rounded black inclusions. Oval handle with two indented finger holes.

Group 2
This type consists of handles that are characterized by their very light, buff fabric (2.5Y 7/4) and black inclusions. The handles are either round or oval and contain finger impressions at their joins. These handles come from a variety of locations on the site.

2 handles

43.10. Handle (fig. 4.21, reproduced at 1:3). PL = 0.015, PW = 0.049, Th. (handle) = 0.037, Th. (join) = 0.047. Coarse pale yellow fabric (2.5Y 7/4) with large white and black inclusions, and some voids. Oval handle with possible finger imprints.

543.5. Handle. PL = 0.092, PW = 0.045, Th. (join) = 0.083, Th. (handle) = 0.037. Coarse, pale yellow fabric (2.5Y 7/4) with frequent, rounded and sub-rounded spherical black stone inclusions. Rounded, vertical handle with a single finger imprint.

Group 3
This type has a decidedly orange fabric range (2.5YR 5/1 to 5YR 7/4) and the handles are shaped in a thinner, strap form. Black inclusions are common and several contain finger impressions on their interior. The handles in this group were discovered on the plain of Koutsopetria.

8 handles

4.40. Handle. PL = 0.079, PW = 0.048, Th. (join) = 0.056, Th. (handle) = 0.030. Coarse, light red fabric (2.5YR 6/6) with a reddish-gray core (2.5YR 5/1), frequent, rounded spherical small black inclusions, and small white inclusions (quartz and lime). Vertical handle curves up and to right with indented finger hole on interior.

8.12. Handle. PL = 0.135, PW = 0.049, Th. (join) = 0.045, Th. (handle) = 0.023. Coarse, red fabric (2.5YR 5/8) with a red (2.5YR 5/8) to pale red core (2.5YR 6/2), and a reddish yellow slip (7.5YR 6/6). Fabric has frequent, rounded and sub-rounded spherical black and red stones. Vertical strap handle.

40.9. Handle. PL = 0.110, PW = 0.064, Th. (join) = 0.071, Th. (handle) = 0.032. Coarse, pink fabric (7.5YR 7/4) with a reddish yellow core (5YR 6/6) with heavy encrusting. Fabric has frequent, small black inclusions with occasional white inclusions, possibly quartz. Vertical strap handle curves up and to the left with deep indented finger hole on interior.

64.45. Handle (fig. 4.21, reproduced at 1:3). PL = 0.084, PW = 0.049, Th. (join) = 0.056, Th. (handle) = 0.034. Coarse, pink fabric (5YR 7/4) with a light red core (2.5YR 6/6), and with rare, large black and brown rounded and sub-rounded inclusions. Vertical strap handle with two finger imprints.

65.29. Handle (fig. 4.21, reproduced at 1:3). PL = 0.171, PW = 0.042, Th. (handle) = 0.032, Th. (join) = 0.060. Coarse, pink fabric (5YR 7/4) with frequent, sub-rounded black and brown inclusions. Vertical strap handle with two finger imprints.

65.30. Handle. PL = 0.097, PW = 0.043, Th. (join) = 0.068, Th. (handle) = 0.037. Coarse, pink fabric (5YR 8/4) with common, small to medium-sized red and black inclusions. Vertical strap handle.

131.21. Handle. PL = 0.116, PW = 0.055, Th. (join) = 0.050, Th. (handle) = 0.034. Coarse, light red fabric (2.5YR 7/8 to 5/6) mottled with purple. Fabric has a few, white, black, and brown rounded spherical stones. Vertical strap handle.

[501.1].10. Handle. PL = 0.150, PW = 0.053, Th. (join) = 0.047, Th. (handle) = 0.026. Coarse, pink fabric (5YR 7/4) with a few, sub-rounded medium black inclusions. Vertical strap handle with possible finger imprint.

Group 4
This type's fabric is characterized by orange hues (2.5YR 6/6 to 7.5YR 7/6). The handles are typically strap-shaped and have a white wash (7.5YR 7/4 to 7.5YR 8/2) on their exterior. Finger impressions on the interior are common. These handles were either discovered on Vigla or to the north.

9 handles

501.14A. Handle. PH = 0.055, Th. = 0.027. Coarse, light red fabric (2.5YR 7/6) with small black and orange stones. Vertical strap handle with indented finger hold.

501.15. Handle. PL = 0.087, PW = 0.032, Th. = 0.029. Coarse, reddish yellow fabric (7.5YR 7/6) with a few, spherical rounded white and black stones. Horizontal strap handle.

[501.1].11. Handle. PL = 0.093, PW = 0.062, Th. (join) = 0.064, Th. (handle) = 0.032. Coarse, light red fabric (2.5YR 6/8) with light pink wash (7.5YR 7/4) with common, small to medium white and blue inclusions. Vertical strap handle with finger indentation.

1012.28. Handle (fig. 4.21, reproduced at 1:3). PL = 0.114, PW = 0.051, Th. (join) = 0.051, Th. (handle) = 0.030. Coarse, light red fabric (2.5YR 6/6) with pinkish-white wash (7/5YR 8/2), and with a few,

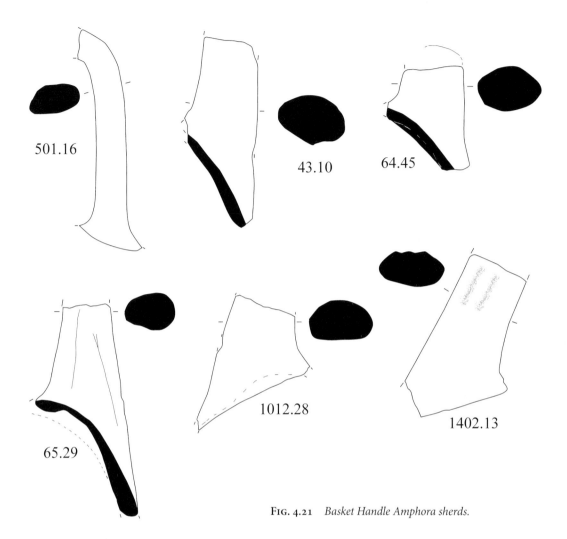

501.16

43.10

64.45

65.29

1012.28

1402.13

FIG. 4.21 *Basket Handle Amphora sherds.*

sub-rounded black inclusions. Vertical strap handle with finger imprint.

1012.29. Handle. PL = 0.088, PW = 0.051, Th. (join) = 0.055, Th. (handle) = 0.040. Coarse, reddish yellow fabric (5YR 7/6) with pink wash (7.5YR 7/4), and with a few, fine white inclusions. Oval, vertical handle with finger imprint.

1401.40. Handle. PL = 0.150, PW = 0.058, Th. (join) = 0.040, Th. (handle) = 0.029. Coarse, reddish yellow fabric (5YR 7/6) with a few orange, white and black inclusions. Vertical strap handle with finger imprint.

1402.3. Handle (fig. 4.21, reproduced at 1:3). PL = 0.138, PW = 0.051, Th. (join) = 0.048, Th. (handle) = 0.027. Coarse, light red fabric (2.5YR 6/8) with

a pink wash (7.5YR 7/4), and with a few, black and white sub-rounded inclusions. Vertical strap handle.

1402.5. Handle. PL = 0.071, PW = 0.059, Th. (join) = 0.065, Th. (handle) = 0.031. Coarse, light red fabric (2.5YR 6/8) with a pink wash (7.5YR 7/4), and with common, small to medium white and blue inclusions. Vertical strap handle with finger indentation.

1403.18. Handle. PL = 0.122, PW = 0.051, Th. (join) = 0.062, Th. (handle) = 0.027. Coarse, light red fabric (2.5YR 6/6) with a pink wash (7.5YR 7/4), and with a few, black, white, and red sub-rounded inclusions. Vertical strap handle with two finger imprints.

Group 5

Group 5 contains fabrics that are a brownish-orange color (2.5YR 6/6, 5YR 7/4–7/6, 7.5YR 7/4) with common red and black inclusions. The handles tend toward an oval shape, but can also be rounded. Several examples contain finger impressions on their interior and many well-preserved examples appear in excavated contexts. These handles were discovered on Vigla, or on the slopes of Vigla.

10 handles

501.16. Handle (fig. 4.21, reproduced at 1:3). PL = 0.170, PW = 0.047, Th. = 0.027. Coarse, very pale brown fabric (10YR 8/2) with a very pale brown slip (10YR 8/2) and frequent, medium-sized black spherical rounded stones. Vertical strap handle.

999.1 (grab). Handle (fig. 4.22, reproduced at 1:3). PL = 0.270, PW = 0.047, Max. Th. (join) = 0.056, Th. (handle) = 0.033. Coarse, pink fabric (5YR 7/4) with frequent, medium-sized, sub-rounded red and black inclusions. Oval vertical handle with finger imprint.

Group 6

This type contains a coarse, light brown fabric (5YR 7/4–7/6), with large black (and other) inclusions. The handles tend toward a thinner, oval shape and finger impressions on the interior are common. These are slightly larger than Group 6. These handles were discovered on Vigla, or on the slopes of Vigla.

4 handles

[501.1].7a. Handle (fig. 4.26). PL = 0.142, PW = 0.062, Th. (join) = 0.078, Th. (handle) = 0.031. Coarse, pink fabric (5YR 7/4) with rare, large black and red rounded inclusions. Oval vertical handle with two finger imprints.

[501.1].7b. Handle. PL = 0.085, PW = 0.059. Coarse, reddish yellow fabric (5YR 7/6) with rare, large rounded black inclusions. Only the base of the handle is preserved, at the join.

Group 7

This group of handles is characterized by a reddish-brown fabric and an oval shape. They were discovered together in a pit along the southwestern edge of Vigla where the embankment had washed out due to heavy rain during the winter of 2009, and had subsequently been looted.

4 handles

VS1. Handle. PL = 0.283, PW = 0.042, Th. (join) = 0.074, Th. (handle) = 0.028. Coarse, reddish yellow fabric (5YR 7/6) with a few, fine black inclusions. Oval vertical handle with finger imprint.

VS2. Handle. PL = 0.180, PW = 0.039, Th. (join) = 0.074, Th. (handle) = 0.033. Very coarse, reddish yellow fabric (5YR 7/6) with common, white and gray sub-rounded inclusions, rare large angular black and red inclusions, and common voids. Oval vertical handle with finger imprint.

VS3. Handle. PL = 0.115, PW = 0.047, Th. (join) = 0.061, Th. (handle) = 0.028. Coarse, reddish yellow fabric (5YR 7/6) with frequent, medium red and black sub-rounded inclusions, a few, red and black large angular inclusions, and some voids. Oval vertical handle.

VS4. Handle. PL = 0.169, PW = 0.051, Th. (join) = 0.065, Th. (handle) = 0.029. Coarse, light red fabric (2.5YR 6/6) with rare, medium-sized, sub-rounded white inclusions. Oval vertical handle.

Group 8

This type's fabric is especially coarse and can be reddish, buff, or even yellow in color (2.5YR 6/8, 10YR 7/3, 5YR 6/6–7/6, 7.5YR 6/6–7/4), and black and white inclusions are common in the fabric. All the handles are oval-shaped, with one exception, and several contain finger impressions on their interior at the join. These handles were ones that did not fit into the other seven categories and were from a variety of locations.

5 finds
5 handles

70.8. Handle (fig. 4.22, reproduced at 1:3). PL = 0.122, PW = 0.049, Th. (join) = 0.064, Th. (handle) = 0.042. Coarse, light red fabric (2.5YR 6/8) with a few, fine white and black sub-rounded inclusions. Round vertical handle with finger imprint.

120.1.35A. Handle. PL = 0.125, PW = 0.0396, Th. (join) = 0.063, Th. (handle, half of which has broken off) = 0 .025. Coarse, very pale brown fabric (10YR 7/3) with abundant, large to very large rounded and sub-rounded spherical black and white stones. Vertical round handle with finger imprint.

1023.9. Handle. PL = 0.105, PW = 0.055, Th. (join) = 0.088, Th. (handle) = 0.032. Coarse, reddish yellow fabric (5YR 6/6) with frequent, small black inclusions and few white inclusions. Oval vertical handle.

1038.17. Handle. PL = 0.138, PW = 0.053, Th. (join) = 0.072, Th. (handle) = 0.034. Coarse, reddish yellow fabric (5YR 7/6) with common, red, white, and black sub-rounded inclusions. Oval vertical handle.

1041.13. Handle. PL = 0.064, PW = 0.053, Th. = 0.035. Very coarse, porous pink fabric (7.5YR 7/4) with a reddish yellow interior (7.5YR 6/), and with common, medium-large black and red inclusions. Oval vertical handle with thumb indention on interior.

4.5.4.2. Rhodian Amphora
(Also known as Peacock and Williams 9, Ostia LXV, Camulodunum 184, and Callender 7)

This amphora has two handles that peak below its simple rounded rim. It has been found in both the western and eastern Mediterranean and primarily transported wine, though some carried figs. It was manufactured in the Aegean, primarily on the island of Rhodes and is dated ffrom the first century BC to the second century AD (Peacock and Williams 1986: 102–3, Lund 1993: 119–20; Leonard 1995a: 142).

4 finds
4 handles

189.52. Handle. PL = 0.104, PW = 0.037, Th. = 0.034. Medium-coarse, slightly porous, reddish yellow fabric (5 YR 6/6 - 4/6) with frequent, fine mica and abundant, fine to large white (lime) and dark grits. Surface has pitting and voids. Vertical handle.

208.8. Handle. PL = 0.093, PW = 0.031, Th. = 0.028. Coarse and gritty, very pale brown fabric (10YR 7/2) with frequent, fine mica and common, small to very large sub-rounded grit and rare lime. Vertical spined handle with one high central spine.

1021.5. Handle. PH = 0.036, PL = 0.077, Th. = 0.027 - 0.044. Medium-coarse, light red fabric (2.5YR 6/6) with rare, medium red, white, and black inclusions, and fine micaceous inclusions. Oval amphora handle with partially preserved rectangular stamp, perhaps figural.

4.5.4.3. Amphora, Hellenistic to Early Roman

This category of amphora contains sherds that can only be dated broadly to the Hellenistic–Early Roman period due to their fabric. The fabric and shape of these sherds are not distinctive enough to allow for a more precise identification, and the majority of the collected examples of this category are small body sherds. They are characterized by a red to reddish-brown, orange, or pink fabric.

290 finds
216 body sherds
40 handles
13 rims
21 toes.

501.21. Handle. PL = 0.133, PW = 0.041. Medium-coarse and gritty, pale yellow fabric (2.5Y 8/4) with common, medium to large dark red inclusions and small traces of fine mica. Handle is encrusted.

503.14. Toe (fig. 4.22, reproduced at 1:2). Diam. = 0.050. PH = 0.049, Th. = 0.036. Light red interior (2.5YR 6/6) with a very pale brown exterior (10YR 8/2), and very fine micaceous inclusions and some encrusting.

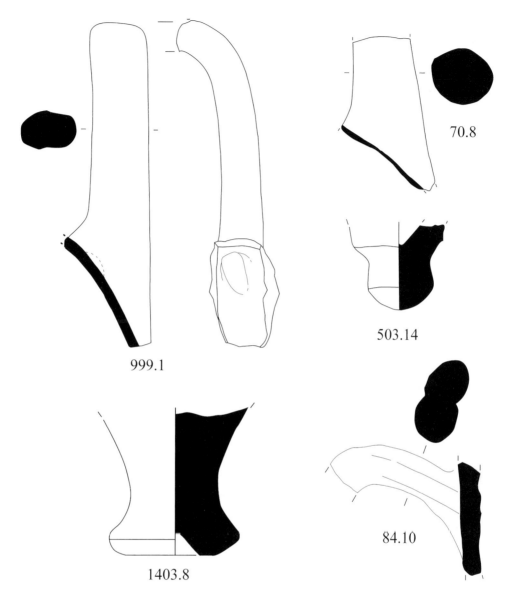

70.8

503.14

999.1

1403.8

84.10

Fig. 4.22 *Basket Handle Amphora, Hellenistic to Early Roman Amphora, and Koan and Sub-Koan Amphora sherds.*

1010.36. Toe (fig. 4.26). PH = 0.060, Th. 0.036. Medium-coarse, light brown fabric (7.5YR 6/4 - 7/4) with frequent, small to medium rounded inclusions.

1024.1. Toe. Diam. = 0.045. PH = 0.055, PW = 0.013, Th. = 0.009. Medium-coarse, light red fabric (2.5YR 6/8) with a few medium (5%) white and dark inclusions and rare, very large black and red inclusions. Toe might have paint on it.

1041.15. Toe. Diam. = 0.061. PH = 0.071, Th. 0.050. Coarse, reddish yellow fabric (7.5YR 7/6) with frequent, large to very large (5%) light and dark inclusions, and rare micaceous inclusions. Ring foot of amphora.

1400.55. Toe. PH = 0.089, Th. = 0.041 (base), Th. = 0.053 (top). Coarse, reddish yellow fabric (5YR 6/6) with gray core (7.5YR 6/1 to 6/4), and with a few, small to medium round white inclusions. Amphora toe is round at base, slightly conical with

greater thickness at top, and not fully preserved at join with body.

1403.8. Toe (fig. 4.22, reproduced at 1:2). Diam. = 0.069, PH = 0.078, Th. = 0.047. Coarse, red fabric (2.5YR 5/8) with a well-fired exterior, and rare, medium to large white and black inclusions. Toe is a hollow ring foot with mushroom shape.

1404.25. Base. PH = 0.065, PW = 0.039. Coarse, red fabric (2.5YR 5/8) with pinkish-gray core (7.5YR 6/2), and a pale yellow exterior (2.5Y 8/3) with rare, small inclusions. Base has a flattened bottom.

4.5.4.4. Koan and Sub-Koan Amphora
(Also referred to as Peacock and Williams Class 10, Greco-Roman amphora, Dressel 2–4, Ostia LI, Camulodunum 182–183, Callender 2, and Benghazi ER amphora 4)

These amphorae are characterized by round double-rolled or bifed handles formed from two rods that often split when the vessel breaks. This class of amphorae was originally manufactured on the island of Kos, but was imitated at many other sites of manufacture in both the western and eastern Mediterranean, including Italy, France, Spain, Egypt, Rhodes, and Cyprus (Hayes 1977: 100; 1991, 85–86; Lund 1993: 123; Papuci-Wladyka 2000: 737). The amphora was manufactured from the late second century BC to the mid-second century AD and principally carried wine (Peacock and Williams 1986: 106). Among ceramicists who work on these amphorae, there seems to be a lack of clarity concerning the terms Pseudo-Koan and Sub-Koan. We adopted the system suggested by Winther-Jacobsen where foreign imitations are classified as Sub-Koan and the amphorae with peaked handles as Sub-Koan (Winther-Jacobsen 2006c: 320, n. 130). Work at Panayia Ematousa has identified five distinct fabrics in their collection. The majority of the handles at Koutsopetria match their Hellenistic Sub-Koan amphorae fabric 3 (A24a4), which is reddish-yellow with white, gray, and black grits and yellow or red inclusions with a pale brown surface. It has been suggested that this fabric is a locally-manufactured Cypriot imitation

(Winther-Jacobsen 2006c: 319–21). In addition to the fabrics that have a Cypriot origin (22 finds), there are two other distinctive fabrics present at Koutsopetria: a Campanian fabric that is characterized by a pale sandy fabric and numerous small black grits (4 finds); and a Catalan fabric that has a dark red to reddish-brown fabric with large white inclusions and some gold mica (1 possible find).

27 finds
26 handles
1 rim

84.10. Handle (fig. 4.22, reproduced at 1:2). PL = 0.088, PW = 0.061. Coarse, light red fabric (2.5YR 6/6) with a very pale brown slip (10YR 8/3), and white and black sub-rounded stones, few in number, and some mica present. Vertical double rolled handle (bifed).

65.31. Handle (fig. 4.23, reproduced at 1:2). PL = 0.100, PW = 0.087. Coarse, reddish yellow fabric (7.5YR 7/6) with a few, black, red, and white sub-rounded stones and lime inclusions. Vertical double rolled handles (bifed).

1404.24. Rim (fig. 4.23, reproduced at 1:2). PW = 0.065, PL = 0.075, Th. (rim) = 0.016, Th. (handle) = 0.024. Medium-coarse, pink fabric (7.5YR 8/3) with a red core (2.5YR 5/8), with rare, medium white inclusions. Squared rim with squared lip and handle join. Vertical double round handle begins 0.017 m below lip.

4.5.4.5. Pseudo-Koan Amphora
(Also known as Benghazi ER amphora 2)

This amphora has two distinctive double rolled or bifed handles that form a sharp arch above the rim. While this amphora is found throughout the eastern Mediterranean, its place of origin is uncertain, although it appears to be modeled on the Koan amphora. It dates to the first and second centuries AD (Peacock and Williams 1986: 107–8).

2 finds
2 handles

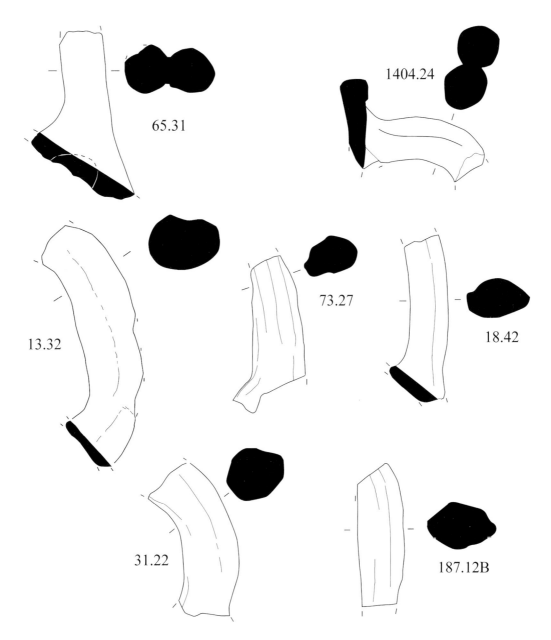

Fig. 4.23   *Koan and Sub-Koan Amphora and Late Roman 1 sherds.*

4.5.5.   Amphorae, Roman to Late Roman

Many of the common transport and utility wares of this period, such as Koan and Rhodian type amphorae, were present at the site in very small numbers, although less diagnostic body sherds certainly represented additional amphorae. Only one example of the so-called "pinched handled" amphorae common to the many Roman sites on the western part of the island emerged from our

assemblage (Leonard 1995a: 144–46; Leonard 2005: 889–905). Amphorae from all periods make up approximately 15% of our total quantity of pottery from Koutsopetria.

4.5.5.1. Middle Roman Amphora 3

This amphora, known variously as Middle Roman Amphora 3 (MRA 3), Micaceous Water Jar, or Peacock and Williams Class 45, is characterized by

a long narrow neck, rounded shoulders, and a solid toe with a deep reddish-brown fabric that is covered with ribbing and is highly micaceous. It dates from the first to sixth centuries AD, with one-handled versions dating to the first to fourth centuries AD, and its later two-handled version dating to the fourth to sixth centuries AD. It is found throughout the Mediterranean but is less common on Cyprus. Both its principal cargo and place of manufacture are unknown, but Asia Minor is its most likely site of origin (Peacock and Williams 1986: 188–90; Heath and Tekkök 2006–2009).

7 finds
7 body sherds

94.26. Body sherd (fig. 4.26). PL = 0.043, PH = 0.038, Th. = 0.011. Coarse, dark reddish-brown fabric (5YR 3/4) with lighter brown surface (7.5YR 6/3) and abundant fine mica. Sherd is decorated with a band of eight parallel grooves with a width of 0.005.

4.5.5.2. Late Roman 1 Amphora
(Also known as British Bii, Ballana 6, Kuzmanov XIII, Scorpan 8B, Carthage LR Amphora 1, Benghazi LR Amphora 1, and Keay LIII)

LR1 amphora was the largest category of Late Roman amphora at PKAP, accounting for 30% of the total amphorae from all periods. The Late Roman 1 Amphorae were among the most widely-traded amphorae of the fourth to seventh centuries AD in the Mediterranean, with examples known from the eastern Mediterranean to northern Europe, including Britain and Ireland (Williams 2005: 613). Early work on LR1 focused on determining its place of manufacture. John Hayes suggested the possibility of an Egyptian origin based on the large quantity of LR1 amphorae discovered there (Hayes 1976: 47–123), while Peacock and Williams suggested both northern Syria in the region of Antioch-on-the-Orontes and southwestern Cyprus as possible manufacturing locations (Williams 1979: 177–82; Peacock 1984: 6–28). In recent years, this hypothesis has been proven by the discovery of numerous kiln sites along the southern coast of Turkey, as well as a number of production sites along the southern coast of Cyprus (Zygi, Paphos and perhaps Amathous) (Demesticha 2003: 470; Elton 2005: 691–93). While there is still debate over the contents of LR1 amphora (Elton 2005: 691–92), they are typically associated with olive oil and wine production (Peacock and Williams 1986: 185–87, Manning 2002: 42; Rautman 2003: 168–69). Late Roman 1 Amphorae are characterized by thin walls with ridging that narrows at both the base and the shoulder. They have a thick rim and two handles, and are produced in a range of fabrics depending on their place of manufacture (Peacock and Williams 1986: 185–87, Elton 2005: 691).

Recent work on LR1 amphorae on Cyprus has been based on the research of Stella Demesticha, in particular her publication of a kiln discovered at Paphos (Demesticha 2000: 549–54; Demesticha and Michaelides 2001: 289–96). Demesticha's 2003 work divided LR1 into four categories, mainly based on differences in the neck. (Demesticha 2003: 469–76). A lack of LR1 rims prevented us from using Demesticha's 2003 typology. In 2006, when we first noticed the consistency of LR1 handle shapes, we began grouping our LR1 amphorae into categories based on fabric in order to sub-type them, if possible. In an attempt to create more specific typologies for our Late Roman 1 Amphora artifacts, 223 Late Roman 1 Amphora handles were examined and divided into the sub-categories. We have identified seven subclasses of LR1 Amphora Types based on fabric differences.

As more archaeological projects on Cyprus publish their results, a more precise classification system is slowly developing. Demesticha has recently proposed a three-generation model of classification for LR1 amphorae, which include LR1/A (fourth to fifth century AD), LR1/B (end of fifth to sixth century AD), and LR1/C (seventh century AD) (Demesticha 2013: 172–73). A reexamination of our LR1 handles, based on Demesticha's proposed three-generation model reveals that the majority of PKAP's handles, based on both shape and size, would be classified as LR1/C and date to the seventh century.

294 finds
275 handles
9 rims
10 body sherds.

Late Roman 1 Amphora Group 1
Group 1 is characterized by a buff fabric with a sandpapery texture that contains small black grits, large white stones (quartz? ca. 7.5 mm), and other small colored stones. Fabric typically ranges from 5Y 8/2 to 7.5YR 8/4.

46 finds
46 handles

13.32. Handle (fig. 4.23, reproduced at 1:2). PL = 0.128, PW = 0.038, Th. = 0.03119. Coarse, pink sandpapery fabric (7.5YR 8/4) that is damaged near top. Large, white angular stones with frequent, small black grits and three ridges curving down one side. Handle join at neck preserves interior of neck.

124.12B. Handle. PL = 0.070, PW = 0.040, Th. = 0.030. Coarse, pink fabric (7.5YR 7/3) with a few black grits and numerous white stones (0.0032) which are angular. Oval, vertical spined handle with three ridges, curving towards neck.

187.12C. Handle. PL = 0.087, PW = 0.037, Th. = 0.022. Coarse, pink fabric (5YR 7/4) with sub-rounded angular white and clack stones. Vertical spined handle.

Late Roman 1 Amphora Group 2
Group 2's fabric is characterized by numerous black stones, many very large and angular (~3 mm) and fewer stones of other colors. The fabric (10YR 8/2, 2.5YR 7/4, 5Y 7/3) can be green, pink, buff, and orange. Twin grooves create a higher ridge.

22 finds
22 handles

128.22. Handle. PL = 0.059, PW = 0.034, Th. = 0.019. Coarse, light red fabric (2.5YR 7/6) with frequent, black angular inclusions (larger ones are ca. 0.001 m). Offset, spined vertical handle.

223.19B. Handle. PL = 0.077, PW = 0.031, Th. = 0.023. Coarse, pale yellow fabric (2.5Y 8/3) with frequent, angular black inclusions (ca. 0.002). Vertical spined handle with one central ridge flanked by two smaller ridges.

Late Roman 1 Amphora Group 3A
Group 3A's fabric contains extremely numerous small black stones, with red, white, and brown stones. The red, brown, and white stones are larger than the black stones.

24 finds
24 handles

18.42. Handle (fig. 4.23, reproduced at 1:2). PL = 0.088, PW = 0.038, Th. = 0.021. Coarse, reddish yellow fabric (7.5YR 8/6) with common, red, white, brown and black rounded and sub-rounded stones - black stones are smallest. Vertical spined handle with central ridge.

31.22. Handle (fig. 4.23, reproduced at 1:2). PL = 0.085, PW = 0.033, Th. = 0.030. Coarse, reddish yellow fabric (5YR 7/6) with common, black, white, red and brown rounded and sub-rounded stones (black stones are smallest). Vertical spined handle with central ridge.

Late Roman 1 Amphora Group 3B
Group 3B is very similar in appearance to group 2B with extremely numerous small black stones covering the fabric, but more consistent in fabric. The fabric is orangish in color (5YR 7/8, 2.5YR 7/6). Some very large inclusions, 5 mm in size, some voids.

66 finds
66 handles

190.23. Handle. PL = 0.050, PW = 0.023, Th. = 0.021. Coarse, reddish yellow fabric (5YR 7/6) with vertical, offset spined handle with common, black, white, and red rounded stones.

Late Roman 1 Amphora Group 3C
Group 3C is similar to group 3A in fabric (extremely numerous small black stones), but has numerous larger, white stones, ~2 mm.

29 finds
29 handles

187.12B. Handle (fig. 4.23, reproduced at 1:2). PL = 0.074, PW = 0.039, Th. = 0.024. Coarse, pink fabric (5YR 7/4) with abundant, rounded and sub-rounded black stones, and larger, white sub-rounded and angular stones. Vertical spined handle.

189.31. Handle. PL = 0.064, PW = 0.031. Coarse, pink fabric (5 YR 7/4) with frequent, sub-rounded and abundant rounded black stones, and larger, white stones. Vertical spined handle.

Late Roman 1 Amphora Group 4
Group 4's fabric contains numerous small black stones, with larger red stones (~1.5 mm). The fabric is 5YR 7/4 core, and 2.5Y 8/2 on the surface.

7 finds
7 handles

73.27. Handle (fig. 4.23, reproduced at 1:2). PL = 0.082, PW = 0.033, Th. = 0.029. Coarse, pink core (2.5YR 8/4) with a pink interior (5YR 8/4) and a pale yellow exterior (2.5Y 8/3) exterior that has frequent, black, white, and red angular stones. Red stones are larger in size. Vertical, offset spined handle with three ridges curving down handle.

546.19A. Handle. PL = 0.055, PW = 0.034, Th. = 0.023. Coarse, light red fabric (2.5YR 7/6) with frequent, black, white and red angular stones. Red stones are larger than black stones. Vertical, offset spined handle

Late Roman 1 Amphora Group 5
Group 5 includes all other Late Roman 1 Amphorae with different fabrics that do not fit into the other 4 categories.

135 finds
109 handles
13 rims
13 body sherds

4.5.5.3. Late Roman 2 Amphora
(Also known as British Bi, Kuzmanov XIX, Scorpan 7A, Carthage LR amphora 2, Benghazi LR amphora 2, Keay LXV)

This amphora has a large rounded or globular body with a small knobbed base, deep horizontal ridging, a tall everted rim, and two small curved handles. The fabric is buff to red in color with large white inclusions and some mica. Late Roman 2 dates from the fourth century AD to the early seventh century AD. While its contents are uncertain, it was most likely manufactured in the Aegean and Black Sea region, and was widely traded throughout the Mediterranean (Peacock and Williams 1986: 182–84; Manning 2002: 42; Rautman 2003: 171).

74 finds
73 body sherds
1 handle

199.10. Handle. PL = 0.099, PW = 0.036, Th. = 0.030. Coarse and sandy, reddish yellow fabric (7.5YR 6/6) with common, large red, gray, and black grits, and fine mica. Offset handle with three spines.

1404.42. Body sherd. PH = 0.076, PW = 0.097, Th. = 0.008. Coarse, light red fabric (2.5YR 6/8) with common, medium black and red inclusions, and very large white inclusions. Small hole (0.005 m diameter), drilled through wall of sherd at lower end.

4.5.5.4. Peacock and Williams Class 35
(Also known as Late Roman North African amphora and Almago and Keay Types)

This class of amphora from North Africa was manufactured between the fourth and sixth centuries AD; it is a cylindrically shaped amphora that is broken into different classes based on its differing styles of rims and toes (Peacock and Williams 1986: 158). Keay has identified 93 different classes of this type (Keay 1984).

2 finds
1 toe

1 handle

1401.95. Handle. PL = 0.104, PW = 0.028, Th. = 0.035 (join with body), Th. = 0.018. Medium-coarse, very pale brown exterior (10YR 7/4) with a brown interior (10YR 5/3–5YR 5/4), and a few, medium grits and dark inclusions. Vertical oval handle, mostly preserved (joins body at one end), with very low spine. See Peacock and Williams 1986: 163, no. LVIIB.

4.5.5.5. Amphora, Anemurium Type "A"

This is a Late Roman amphora manufactured at the site of Anemurium in Rough Cilicia, though a Cypriot place of manufacture has been suggested by Hayes (Hayes 1977: 100). It is characterized by a medium-grained orange or dark brown fabric that contains lime particles, red grits, silver mica, and has a thin red wash. The body is cylindrical with a short neck and two small round or oval grooved handles. The identifying feature of this amphora is its tall phalliform toe that narrows towards the bottom to a thickened knob (Williams 1992: 91–92).

1 find
1 toe

65.26. Toe (fig. 4.24, reproduced at 1:2). PL = 0.09, PW = 0.075. Coarse, light reddish-brown fabric (2.5YR 6/4) with rare, sub-rounded black and red stones. Amphora toe with rounded base. See Williams 1992: 93, no. 555.

4.5.5.6. Unclassified Roman Amphora

This category of amphora contains sherds that can only be dated broadly to the Roman period due to their fabric and style of decoration. The decoration, fabric, and shape of these sherds are not distinctive enough to allow for a more precise identification. They are characterized by a range of fabric colors (pink, orange, red, and brown) that typically includes numerous small inclusions.

676 finds
487 body sherds
118 handles

34 rims
34 toes
3 necks.

1009.29. Toe. Diam. = 0.075, PH = 0.082, Th. = 0.047. Medium-coarse, red fabric (10R 5/8) with rare, medium white inclusions and a reddish yellow slip (7.5YR 7/6). Amphora toe with bell-shaped profile, and small depression in the center of the underside.

1014.29. Toe. Diam. = 0.041, PH = 0.045, PW = 0.053. Medium-coarse, reddish yellow exterior (7.5YR 7/6) and light red interior (2.5YR 6/8) with rare, medium red and black inclusions. Phallic shaped amphora toe.

1019.18. Toe (fig. 4.24, reproduced at 1:2). PH = 0.042, PW = 0.068. Medium-coarse, red fabric (2.5YR 5/6 and 7.5YR 8/4) with reddish-gray core (5YR 5/2), and a few, small dark inclusions. See Lund 1993: no. C-371; Winther-Jacobsen 2006c: 336, no. A86.163.

1037.5. Toe (fig. 4.24, reproduced at 1:2). PH = 0.033, PW = 0.064. Medium-coarse, reddish yellow fabric (5YR 6/6 to 7/6) with frequent, small white and dark inclusions, and common fine mica. Mushroom-shaped toe with a shallow indentation.

4.5.5.7. Unclassified Late Roman Amphora

This category of amphora contains sherds that can only be dated broadly to the Late Roman period due to their fabric and style of decoration. The decoration, fabric, and shape of these sherds are not distinctive enough to allow for a more precise identification. In addition, the majority of the sherds in this category are small, non-descript body sherds. They are characterized by a pink, orange, or reddish fabric, typically with numerous small, white and/or black inclusions.

753 finds
540 body sherds
139 handles
43 rims
22 toes

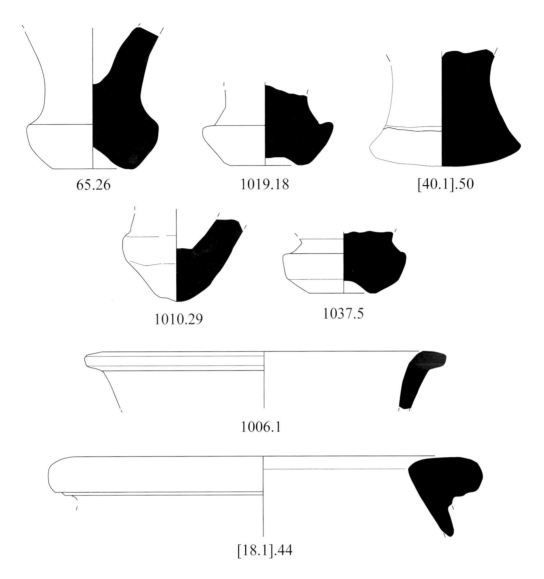

65.26

1019.18

[40.1].50

1010.29

1037.5

1006.1

[18.1].44

FIG. 4.24 *Anemurium Type "A" Amphora, Unclassified Roman and Late Roman Amphora, Cypro-Geometric Pithos, and Roman and Late Roman Pithos sherds.*

8 necks
1 base.

[40.1].50. Toe (fig. 4.24, reproduced at 1:2). Diam. = 0.054 (top), Diam. = 0.075 (base), PH = 0.600. Coarse, light red fabric (10 R 6/6) with rare, white rounded spherical stones. Flat toe that narrows as it rises before expanding.

1007.22. Toe. Th. = 0.071 (base), Th. = 0.043 (above mushroom). Medium-coarse, yellowish-red fabric

(5YR 5/6) with frequent, medium red and black rounded inclusions. Mushroom cap shape with a hollow hole (diam. = 0.030 m).

1010.29. Toe (fig. 4.24, reproduced at 1:2). PL = 0.058, PW = 0.040. Medium-coarse light red (2.5YR 6/6-5/6) fabric with small rare black inclusions and frequent fine mica. Amphora toe, rounded, not fully preserved, but preserved to start of body. Appears to taper to a point, perhaps phallic in shape.

4.6. PITHOI

The large-capacity storage vessels known as pithoi are not well-documented, particularly for Cyprus. Their large size ensured that most pithoi were locally produced and most likely required a potter who specialized in the manufacture of these vessels, perhaps a traveling specialist (Sørensen and Winther-Jacobsen 2006b: 290–91; London 1990: 69–79). They are characterized by their very coarse fabric with large, heavy rims and thick walls (Rautman 2003: 176). At Koutsopetria, 1368 pithos sherds (8% by quantity) were identified, but very few could be dated to specific chronological periods. For example, 94% of the pithos sherds by quantity date to the broad chronological period that spanned from the Late Bronze Age to the Hellenistic Age. On Cyprus, the best-documented examples of Roman pithoi are from Dhiorios (Catling 1972), Kourion (Leonard 1987: 80–116), and Maroni-Petra (Manning, 2002).

4.6.1. Pithos, Iron Age

This broad category is characterized by brown to red fabric that has red, white, and black inclusions, usually large.

14 finds
13 body sherds
1 rim

1012.17. Rim. Diam. = 0.340, PL = 0.132, Th. = 0.016 (body), Th. = 0.033 (rim). Strong brown fabric (7.5YR 5/6) with red core (2.5YR 5/6), and common, large red, white, and black angular inclusions. Everted rim with tapered lip and flattened top.

4.6.2. Pithos, Cypro-Geometric

This chronotype is characterized by a light fabric with very large black inclusions.

1 find
1 rim

1006.1. Rim (fig. 4.24, reproduced at 1:3). Diam. = 0.250, PH = 0.052, PW = 0.098, Th. = 0.015.

Medium-coarse, pink fabric (7.5YR 8/4–7/4) with frequent, medium to very large (10%) black and light inclusions.

4.6.3. Pithos, Roman and Late Roman

This category contains pithos sherds dated to the broad Roman and Late Roman period. There were only a few Roman or Late Roman pithos sherds discovered during the survey. We relied on Winther-Jacobsen's descriptions of pithoi at Panayia Ematousa for comparanda (Winther-Jacobsen 2006b: 290–300). None of the sherds collected at PKAP had any decoration and they were characterized by a coarse fabric that ranged in color from a pale yellow (2.5Y 8/2) to a reddish-brown (5YR 5/4) and typically contained numerous, large black stones.

49 finds
42 body sherds
7 rims

[18.1].44. Rim (fig. 4.24, reproduced at 1:3). Diam. = 0.130, PL = 0.144, PW = 0.059. Coarse light brownish-gray fabric (10 YR 6/2) with sub-rounded black and white stones, as well as some lime and voids. Thin light brown slip (7.5 YR 6/4). Thick, slightly up turned rim. See Winther-Jacobsen 2006b: 294, no. 242

80.17. Rim (fig. 4.25, reproduced at 1:3). Diam. = 0.120, PH = 0.063, PW = 0.075, Th. = 0.039. Coarse, reddish-brown fabric (5YR 5/4) with dark bluish-gray core (Gley 2 4/5B), and large, rounded spherical black stones. Outward thickened, squared rim. See Winther-Jacobsen 2006b: 294, no. 240.

4.7. ROOF TILES

One of the most common finds on the survey were roof tiles, which accounted for 2,188 sherds, or 13.46% of all sherds. Tile from the Late Roman period dominated the assemblage, accounting for 95.3% of all tile. Three main categories of roof tiles are known to have been present on Cyprus in the Roman period (described by Rautman for

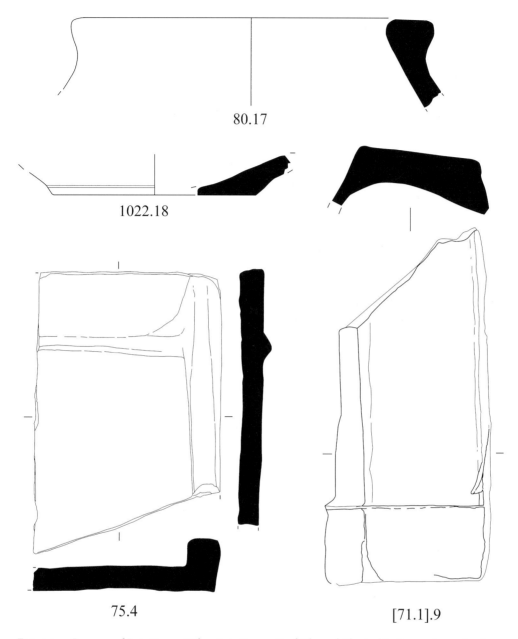

80.17

1022.18

75.4

[71.1].9

FIG. 4.25 *Roman and Late Roman Pithos, Late Roman Roof Tile, and Classical to Roman Lamp sherds.*

Kopetra), and all were found during the survey (Rautman 2003: 177–78). The similarity in form between the three different categories made it difficult to differentiate between small tile sherds, and as a result, quantification between the three categories is difficult. The first category of roof tiles is a small Corinthian style pan tile (.45 m in length) that was produced at sites near Salamis in the lower Mesaoria plain (Rautman 2003: 178; Hadjichristophi 1989: 877, type II), and which was exported to other sites in the eastern Mediterranean (Tomber 1987: 161–74; Parker 1992: 16–18; Oleson et al. 1994: 63; Rautman 2003: 178, 267–71). The second category consists of a larger Corinthian style pan tile with a border on three sides that is 15 cm longer than the first category and more than twice as heavy; this type has an unridged cover tile, and color is typically light brown to dark brown.

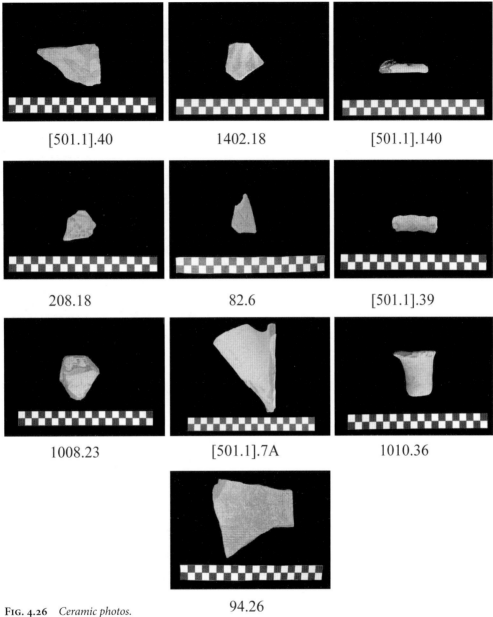

[501.1].40   1402.18   [501.1].140

208.18   82.6   [501.1].39

1008.23   [501.1].7A   1010.36

94.26

FIG. 4.26   *Ceramic photos.*

The tile may have been produced in the Vasilikos Valley, among other sites (Rautman 2003: 178), and this style of tile was the predominant type discovered at Panayia Ematousa (Rose 2006: 358–60). The third category is a Laconian pan tile that has a curved pan tile bordered on three sides by a raised ridge and a curved cover tile. This tile typically has a red fabric that is similar to the appearance of Cypriot Red Slip, and was the least common type found at PKAP (Rautman 2003: 177–78).

4.7.1. Roof Tiles, Late Roman

4.7.1.1. Kopetra Style Corinthian Roof Tile

The fabric of this type ranges in color from a pale yellow (2.5Y 8/4) to a pink (5YR 7/4), with the majority having a yellowish appearance. The pan tile has a raised, square border along two long sides and a transverse, rounded ridge near the raised border. No complete examples were dis-

covered during the survey, but we can estimate that complete tiles of this type would have been approximately 45 cm in length and nearly six kilograms in weight. The cover tile is ridged with a raised lower border. While the cover tiles were sometimes stamped with a cross, none of those were discovered during the survey (Rautman 2003: 178). (For tile illustrations see 75.4 and [71.1].9 in fig. 4.25, reproduced at 1:2.)

1,775 Finds
1,453 Pan Tile sherds
322 Cover Tile sherds

Kopetra Style Corinthian Pan
7.5. Body sherd. PL = 0.184, PW = 0.112, Body Th. = 0.018, Edge Th. = 0.037. The fabric of the interior surface is pink (2.5YR 8/3–7/3) with a light reddish-brown core (2.5Y 7/4), and a light reddish-brown exterior surface (2.5Y 7/4). The fabric is porous with rare, small to very large inclusions. Raised edges form a right angle to the body, and there are three shallow finger grooves that run parallel to edge. See Rautman 2003: 205, no. 221.

Kopetra Style Corinthian Cover Tile
7.4. Body sherd. PW = 0.105, PL = 0.134, PH = 0.058, Th. = 0.021. Medium-grained, very pale brown fabric (10YR 7/3), with rare, fine mica and small to very large grit, and encrustation on interior. Raised lower border. See Rautman 2003: 205, no. 222.

4.8. LAMPS

While lamps are a common find in excavation projects, they are a rare find in survey (Lund 1993: 117). All of the PKAP lamp fragments (n=6) are very fragmentary with few distinguishing features, except for one example that has a partially preserved male figure.

4.8.1. Lamps, Cypro-Classical to Early Roman

196.28. Rim. Diam. = 0.024. Fine-grained very pale brown fabric (10YR 8/3) with rare black inclusions. Relief figure of frontal nude male missing head, with portions of right arm and legs below

the thigh. Left arm is flexed with elbow out and hand at the breast clenching a club that rests on the shoulder. Right arm outstretched and possibly reaching down and holding an ithyphallic phallus. Waist is slightly twisted so as to see the profile of the left buttocks. See Bailey 1975: 113, no. 752.

[501.1].195. Base. PW = 0.023, Th. = 0.006. Medium-coarse red fabric (10R 5/8) with some medium voids and gray inclusions. Molded concentric circles on underside of disc base.

1022.18. Base (fig. 4.25). Diam. = 0.060, PL = 0.044, PH = 0.011. Fine-grained, light red fabric (2.5YR 7/6) with a very pale brown surface (10YR 8/4) and no visible inclusions. Flat disc base of a lamp.

4.9. CONCLUSIONS ON THE CERAMIC ASSEMBLAGE

The analysis of the sherds collected during the survey highlighted several important ceramic issues. The physical nature of the collected material from a survey project — the small, broken, and frequently nondescript sherds — affected our ability to create a traditional ceramic catalogue with numerous entries and corresponding illustrations and/or photographs. As a result, we limited our catalogue to the best representations of each ware and in some cases deliberately did not catalogue or illustrate examples since their preserved state would have nullified their usefulness to readers. In addition, since we relied on other projects' published catalogues for comparanda, such as Anemurium, Kopetra, Panayia Ematousa, and Paphos, a large portion of our sherds did not add to current ceramic knowledge with new information regarding vessel forms, unusual fabrics, or changes to established chronologies, with the exception of basket handle amphorae and LR1 amphorae. The use of these comparanda did help illustrate wares discovered during our survey that were not present at other sites or were identified at PKAP in unusual forms or different quantities (such as basket handle amphora, LR1 amphora, CRS, and ARS).

As is the case with most projects on Cyprus, the fine wares (and especially the three most common Late Roman red slips: ARS, CRS, and PHW) provided the majority of the chronological data. On one hand, this is not unexpected since the highly visible differences in fabric, decoration, and shape have facilitated the creation of numerous typologies throughout the last century. On the other hand, it is clear that there are still gaps in these typologies, and that further analysis is needed. For Cyprus, one such example is the break in datable fine wares between the Roman and Late Roman periods (Lund 1992).

The importance of fine wares can be seen most clearly in the chronological periods where few fine wares have been identified. This lack of fine wares affects the dating of other wares, such as kitchen and coarse wares, and as a result certain periods are conspicuously absent in the ceramic record, such as the Early Medieval period. In fact, the prevalence of scholarly work on fine wares only serves to reinforce the relative lack of work on kitchen wares, coarse wares, and roof tiles.

For archaeological work on Cyprus, the large volume of Cypriot Red Slip artifacts from PKAP has made this ware a crucial linchpin in the construction of many projects' timelines. Recent work examining this ware, though, has centered on two significant themes that will have a major impact on both past and future work on Cyprus in the Late Roman period. The first theme is a determination of how secure the original chronological framework proposed by Hayes is after more than four decades (Hayes 1972). Recent publications have proposed earlier production dates for certain CRS forms (Meyza 2000; 2007; Rowe 2006), while other scholars have proposed longer production periods with later dates for the cessation of certain CRS forms (Armstrong 2009). While these proposed modifications will have little impact on our interpretation of the Koutsopetria survey region, they could have a significant impact on excavation projects that are relying on CRS for important dating information.

The other theme concerning Cypriot Red Slip that has been addressed in print is the location of production centers. The recent discovery of CRS manufacturing sites in Turkey has reopened the question of how this ware should be viewed and even classified, and has important ramifications

for trade and contact in the period (Jackson et al. 2012). For Cypriot projects, this issue might beg the reconsideration of known trading routes and regional connectivity. Such issues and themes aside, an examination of the ceramic signature for the PKAP survey universe for each of the major chronological periods reveals several important points about the region and its connections. For the periods prior to the Hellenistic Age, the scarcity of ceramic evidence prevents the creation of a complete narrative for the early settlers in the area. While the locational information for the collected material allows certain conclusions to be drawn regarding the movement of the community from Kokkinokremos to Vigla to the plain (see Chapter 7), less can be garnered from the functional information provided by the sherds for certain periods.

The Cypro-Geometric, Cypro-Archaic, and Cypro-Classical periods at Koutsopetria are represented by a small but standard collection of locally manufactured ceramics. In the Hellenistic Period, the ceramic assemblage becomes larger and more diverse. Several fine wares that are common at other sites (Eastern Sigillata A and Cypriot Sigillata) are only present at Koutsopetria in small numbers, perhaps indicating changes to Koutsopetria's trading connections. A large number of basket handle amphorae is also present, perhaps indicating the nearby presence of a manufacturing site or major port of entry.

In the Roman period, as the settlement moves down on to the coastal plain, the prosperity of the region increases. While Cypriot Red Slip is the dominant fine ware at the site, African Red Slip and Phocaean Red Slip are present in appreciable numbers, indicating the presence of a growing trade component. This is supported by the fairly sizeable collection of LR1 handles at Koutsopetria dating to the seventh century. The low number of imported amphorae, however, suggests that while Koutsopetria was an active trading location, it was selective in its connections. Starting in the eighth and ninth centuries AD, though, Koutsopetria undergoes a sudden and drastic decline and the ceramic assemblage from this period provides little insight into the following periods.

Table 4.1   Concordance for ceramic illustrations.

ARTIFACT	CHRONOTYPE	FIGURE	SCALE	ILLUSTRATOR
70.5	White Painted Ware	1	1:1	MD
1006.7	White Painted Ware	1	1:1	MD
1006.9	White Painted Ware	1	1:2	MD
187.26	Archaic Fineware	1	1:1	MD
10.11	Attic and Hellenistic Black Glaze	2	1:1	MD
183.26	Attic and Hellenistic Black Glaze	2	1:1	BO
95.37	Hellenistic Colour-Coated	2	1:1	MD
1401.99	Hellenistic Colour-Coated	2	1:1	MD
71.37	Hellenistic Colour-Coated, Imported	3	1:1	MD
70.48	Eastern Sigillata A	3	1:2	BO
51.42	Cypriot Sigillata	3	1:2	MD
12.56	Italian Sigillata	3	1:1	MD
174.14	Hellenistic to Early Roman Red Ware	3	1:3	KP
68.21	African Red Slip Form 61	4	1:3	BO
62.36	African Red Slip Form 67	4	1:3	BO
23.18	African Red Slip Form 93B	4	1:2	BO
140.17	African Red Slip Form 99A	4	1:1	MD
8.49	African Red Slip Form 103B	4	1:2	KP
47.39	African Red Slip Form 104B	4	1:3	MD
47.40	African Red Slip Form 104C	4	1:2	MD
9.42	African Red Slip Form 105	4	1:3	KP
12.59	African Red Slip Form 105	4	1:3	BO
26.10	African Red Slip Form 105	5	1:3	MD
76.27	African Red Slip Form 105	5	1:3	BO
57.30	African Red Slip Form 106	5	1:1	KP
247.29	African Red Slip 104–106 Imitation	5	1:2	MD
28.25	Imitation African Red Slip Form 105	5	1:3	MD
76.35	Imitation African Red Slip Form 105	5	1:3	KP
196.26	Imitation African Red Slip Form 105	5	1:3	MD
19.10	Cypriot Red Slip Form 1	6	1:3	KP
126.23	Cypriot Red Slip Form 1	6	1:3	BO
56.53	Cypriot Red Slip Form 1	6	1:2	BO
56.55	Cypriot Red Slip Form 1	6	1:1	BO
203.32	Cypriot Red Slip Form 1	6	1:1	MD
11.45	Cypriot Red Slip Form 2	6	1:3	MD
25.33	Cypriot Red Slip Form 2	6	1:3	MD

Table 4.1 (cont.)   Concordance for ceramic illustrations.

ARTIFACT	CHRONOTYPE	FIGURE	SCALE	ILLUSTRATOR
8.43	Cypriot Red Slip Form 7	6	1:3	MD
232.31	Cypriot Red Slip Form 8	7	1:2	KP
56.54	Cypriot Red Slip Form 9	7	1:2	MD
25.31	Cypriot Red Slip Form 9A	7	1:1	KP
51.47	Cypriot Red Slip Form 9A	7	1:3	KP
61.33	Cypriot Red Slip Form 9A	7	1:2	BO
148.12	Cypriot Red Slip Form 9A	7	1:2	KP
7.48	Cypriot Red Slip Form 9B	7	1:3	KP
12.55	Cypriot Red Slip Form 9B	8	1:3	BO
4.35	Cypriot Red Slip Form 9C	8	1:3	KP
28.26	Cypriot Red Slip Form 9C	8	1:3	MD
181.21	Cypriot Red Slip Form 10	8	1:3	MD
65.35	Cypriot Red Slip Saucer	8	1:2	BO
39.33	Cypriot Red Slip Form 11	8	1:3	BO
61.32	Cypriot Red Slip Form 11	9	1:3	KP
67.31	Cypriot Red Slip Form 11	9	1:3	MD
73.33	Cypriot Red Slip Form 11	9	1:3	BO
202.17	Cypriot Red Slip Form 11	9	1:3	MD
187.24	Phocaean Red Slip Ware Form 2	9	1:2	BO
190.30	Phocaean Red Slip Ware Form 3	9	1:2	MD
9.38	Phocaean Red Slip Ware Form 3C	10	1:2	KP
12.60	Phocaean Red Slip Ware Form 3C	10	1:2	KP
94.29	Phocaean Red Slip Ware Form 3C	10	1:2	BO
203.31	Phocaean Red Slip Ware Form 3C	10	1:2	BO
126.24	Phocaean Red Slip Ware Form 3E	10	1:3	MD
188.40	Phocaean Red Slip Ware Form 3E	10	1:3	BO
188.41	Phocaean Red Slip Ware Form 3E	10	1:3	MD
[71.1].125	Phocaean Red Slip Ware Form 3E/F	11	1:3	BO
50.42	Phocaean Red Slip Ware Form 10	11	1:3	MD
62.40	Phocaean Red Slip Ware Form 10	11	1:3	BO
70.53	Phocaean Red Slip Ware Form 10	11	1:3	KP
187.25	Phocaean Red Slip Ware Form 10	11	1:2	BO
56.56	Phocaean Red Slip Ware Form 10A	11	1:2	BO
60.23	Phocaean Red Slip Ware Form 10A	11	1:3	BO
62.41	Phocaean Red Slip Ware Form 10A	12	1:3	KP
71.42	Phocaean Red Slip Ware Form 10A	12	1:3	KP

Table 4.1 (cont.)   Concordance for ceramic illustrations.

Artifact	Chronotype	Figure	Scale	Illustrator
71.45	Phocaean Red Slip Ware Form 10A	12	1:3	KP
73.32	Phocaean Red Slip Ware Form 10A	12	1:3	BO
76.33	Phocaean Red Slip Ware Form 10A	12	1:3	KP
10.13	Phocaean Red Slip Ware Form 10B	12	1:2	BO
127.20	Phocaean Red Slip Ware Form 10B	12	1:3	MD
70.51	Phocaean Red Slip Ware Form 10C	12	1:3	BO
71.41	Phocaean Red Slip Ware Form 10C	13	1:2	BO
73.34	Phocaean Red Slip Ware Form 10C	13	1:3	KP
94.30	Phocaean Red Slip Ware Form 10C	13	1:2	KP
65.21	Unclassified Roman Fine Ware	13	1:3	BO
38.32	Unclassified Late Roman Fine Ware	13	1:3	MD
191.9	Unclassified Late Roman Fine Ware	13	1:3	MD
189.46	Cypriot Sgraffito Ware	13	1:1	MD
54.4	Cypriot Green & Brown Glazed Group V	14	1:2	KP
539.13	Slip Painted Ware from Didymoteicho	14	1:2	MD
[501.1].133	Hellenistic Kitchen Ware	14	1:2	BO
501.43	Hellenistic Kitchen Ware	14	1:2	MD
1400.10	Hellenistic to Early Roman Kitchen Ware	14	1:1	BO
1400.49	Hellenistic to Early Roman Kitchen Ware	15	1:1	MD
17.31	Roman Kitchen Ware	15	1:2	MD
64.33	Roman Kitchen Ware	15	1:3	MD
[71.1].64	Roman Kitchen Ware	15	1:2	MD
186.15	Roman Kitchen Ware	15	1:2	MD
232.28	Roman Kitchen Ware	15	1:2	MD
9.43	Late Roman Frying Pan	16	1:1	BO
18.37	Dhiorios Ware	16	1:2	MD
1006.9	White Painted Coarse Ware	16	1:2	MD
1011.1	Cypro-Geometric Medium Coarse Ware	16	1:2	MD
1400.64	Hellenistic to Roman Medium Coarse Ware	16	1:2	MD
12.25	Late Roman Medium Coarse Ware	17	1:2	MD
1010.35	Hellenistic to Early Roman Coarse Ware	17	1:3	MD
13.17	Roman Basin	17	1:2	MD
43.2	Roman Basin	17	1:2	BO
12.26	Late Roman Coarse Ware	17	1:1	MD
17.26	Late Roman Coarse Ware	18	1:1	BO
23.21	Late Roman Coarse Ware	18	1:1	BO

Table 4.1 (cont.)   Concordance for ceramic illustrations.

ARTIFACT	CHRONOTYPE	FIGURE	SCALE	ILLUSTRATOR
12.13	Combed Ware	18	1:1	MD
68.17	Cypriot W1	19	1:3	BO
56.44	Cypriot W2	19	1:3	MD
12.46	Cypriot W3	19	1:3	MD
200.7	Cypriot W5	19	1:3	MD
233.17	Cypriot W5	20	1:1	BO
56.44	Cypriot W7	20	1:3	MD
140.18	Medieval Coarse Ware	20	1:2	MD
8.8	Medieval to Modern Coarse Ware	20	1:2	MD
38.29	Medieval to Modern Coarse Ware	20	1:2	BO
43.10	Basket Handle Amphora Group 2	21	1:3	BO
64.45	Basket Handle Amphora Group 3	21	1:3	MD
65.29	Basket Handle Amphora Group 3	21	1:3	BO
1012.28	Basket Handle Amphora Group 4	21	1:3	BO
1402.13	Basket Handle Amphora Group 4	21	1:3	BO
501.16	Basket Handle Amphora Group 5	21	1:3	MD
999.1	Basket Handle Amphora Group 5	22	1:3	MD
70.8	Basket Handle Amphora Group 8	22	1:3	BO
503.14	Hellenistic to Early Roman Amphora	22	1:2	MD
1403.8	Hellenistic to Early Roman Amphora	22	1:2	BO
84.10	Koan and Sub-Koan Amphora	22	1:2	MD
65.31	Koan and Sub-Koan Amphora	23	1:2	MD
1404.24	Koan and Sub-Koan Amphora	23	1:2	MD
13.32	Late Roman 1 Amphora Group 1	23	1:2	BO
18.42	Late Roman 1 Amphora Group 3A	23	1:2	MD
31.22	Late Roman 1 Amphora Group 3A	23	1:2	MD
187.12B	Late Roman 1 Amphora Group 3C	23	1:2	BO
73.27	Late Roman 1 Amphora Group 4	23	1:2	MD
65.26	Amphora, Anemurium Type "A"	24	1:2	MD
1019.18	Unclassified Roman Amphora	24	1:2	MD
1037.5	Unclassified Roman Amphora	24	1:2	MD
[40.1].50	Unclassified Late Roman Amphora	24	1:2	MD
1010.29	Unclassified Late Roman Amphora	24	1:2	MD
1006.1	Cypro-Geometric Pithos	24	1:3	MD
[18.1].44	Roman and Late Roman Pithos	24	1:3	MD
80.17	Roman and Late Roman Pithos	25	1:3	MD

Table 4.1 (cont.)   Concordance for ceramic illustrations.

ARTIFACT	CHRONOTYPE	FIGURE	SCALE	ILLUSTRATOR
75.4	Kopetra Style Corinthian Roof Tile	25	1:2	MD
[71.1].9	Kopetra Style Corinthian Roof Tile	25	1:2	MD
1022.18	Classical to Early Roman Lamp	25	1:1	MD

MD = Mat Dalton

BO = Brandon Olson

KP = Kate Pettegrew

4.10.   FIGURINES *(Maria Andrioti)*

Nine fragmentary, anthropomorphic figurines have been collected by PKAP. All are made of clay, except for two limestone pieces. As early as the mid-seventh century BC, anthropomorphic representations in terracotta became a very popular type of votive offering in Cyprus, in sizes from the miniature to the colossal (Fourrier 2007: 13), and the same phenomenon arose in limestone a bit later (late seventh century; Counts 2001: 153). The figures are commonly taken to represent worshipers, who were understood as standing in front of the deity performing the act of prayer and veneration in perpetuity (Connelly 1989), with securely identified divine figures forming a very small minority (Counts 2008: 7). Due to the overwhelming preference for either male or female figures at each sanctuary, it is believed that the votives reflect the gender of the deity (Ulbrich 2005: 199). This phenomenon persists through the Hellenistic Period and gradually dies out in the Roman period, when the local limestone was replaced by imported marble and dedications in bronze increased as the local religious practices went through significant changes (Papantoniou 2012: 323).

There are certain characteristics that are typical of Cypriot sculpture. The aspect that is most central, for both limestone and terracotta, is the detailed attention given to representing the head/ face, which is in stark contrast to the lack of attention to representing the body. (The body was very rarely shown nude. The most striking exceptions to this are the mold-made, nude, female figurines of the so-called Astarte type, which are not only special in their nudity, but also in the detail to which the human anatomy is represented; see Karageorghis 1999 for a general discussion.) The heads are worked in the round (with the exception of the mold-made, plaque-type figurines) and are often very large in proportion to the body. An effort is made to articulate the various hairstyles, hair-gear, and jewelry that, together with the different types of attire, distinguished one type of votary from the other (Counts 2001: 156–63 for an overview of the types and their interpretation).

For the limestone works, a simple, schematically shaped mass of stone stood in for the body (with paint used to render details of attire), with very little attempt at delineating the parts of the body that were understood to be under the garments (arms and feet are indicated and very schematically depicted breasts for female figures). The profiles are most commonly very thin and the back was left flat. This continued even as Cypriot carvers increasingly began to adopt the more rounded forms of Classical Greek sculpture and render more detail in the garments frontally, from the fifth century on.

The terracotta figures show the same priorities: the detailed heads are supported by bodies that are largely unarticulated, whether they are columnar (handmade), flat (mold-made) or tubular (hand- and wheel-made) (Fourrier 2007; see Caubet et al. 1998 for manufacturing techniques). This provides a glimpse into the attitudes toward votive sculptures: what was important to include was the representative information about the individual portrayed — gender and sociopolitical affiliations, which the different garments surely represented. It was evidently enough that only the salient characteristics of the above elements were depicted, which allowed for the frugality apparent in the thinness of the limestone blocks (material) and summary rendering of the forms in both media (time). The fact that these characteristics persist through to the Hellenistic Period suggests that they were not due to technical or aesthetic reasons, but rather to a lasting social and religious outlook.

This disinterest in elaborating the physical form aggravates matters of dating, as it is not conducive to a steadily progressive, internal, stylistic development in the rendering of the body, useful for establishing relative dating. The type of attire can be indicative, but only in the broadest of senses, since the same attire is shown for long periods of time. It is for the heads that a sculptural sequence can be established to a certain degree, although this is also far from straightforward. (I do not follow Vermeule 1974 here, who has recently come under criticism [Counts 2001: 151–52; Fourrier 2007: 15, n. 9] but, given the attention lavished on the heads at the expense of the bodies, focusing on them is methodologically sound.) Gradual changes in the rendering of facial features is certainly noticeable in Cypriot sculpture from the sixth century BC until the Hellenistic Period, with heavy unarticulated planes of the face giving way to more plastic forms that eventually follow Hellenistic paradigms. However, the facility with which the craftsmen abandon the developments made in their craft is remarkable and frustrating, as, for example, is seen in the rendering of eyelids, which can be omitted at any point in the sequence, especially in the smaller sculptures (Hermary 1989 is probably the most useful catalogue for tracing the development of Cypriot sculpture in general and for spotting such specific characteristics). It seems that Cypriot sculptors display a tendency toward economizing, which is probably the hallmark of Cypriot sculpture. It was absolutely necessary to have all the parts, but representing

them in their bare minimum was just as acceptable as at their most elaborate. As a result, close dating of Cypriot sculpture is notoriously difficult, with the chronological span to which a piece is assigned often covering half a century or more (Counts 2001: 141–52, for discussion of the development of the chronological schemata for Cypriot sculpture).

This is especially relevant for the PKAP material, since no heads have been recovered and the figurines are in a very fragmentary state. However, based largely on the types and styles of garments represented, the oldest piece could date to the sixth century and the youngest piece to the fourth century. Also due to the fragmentary nature of all the figurines except for one limestone piece, it is difficult to ascertain their gender, but it is likely that most of them are female, suggesting the worship of a female deity. All fragments are mold-made, and the more complete finds represent clothed standing figures, with the exception of no. 148.11, which probably portrays a nude figure.

9 finds

Z1.501. Standing female figure. Fifth century. PH = 0.054, PW = 0.070, Th. = 0.021. Creamy white, medium-grain limestone. Bottom of garments and base survive, with an irregular break on the left side and the left foot is missing. Two garments are discernible: a tunic that is made up of narrow, shallow folds that form a semi-circular bottom border and the edge of a mantle on the right side. The foot is schematically rendered, set against the base, seen from above.

72.36. Standing female figure (fig. 4.27). Late fifth to early fourth century. PH = 0.089, PW = 0.057, Th. = 0.020. Creamy white, fine-grain limestone. The head is missing and there is a diagonal break along the bottom, so that the feet are missing. The surface is very worn and there are chips and scrapes. The back is worked completely smooth and flat. The figure is clothed in a heavy garment, although the details are obscured by the state of preservation. A necklace or traces of folds hang high on the torso. The left arm is folded to the middle of the chest (probably holding a fruit or flower, but this area is too damaged to tell) and

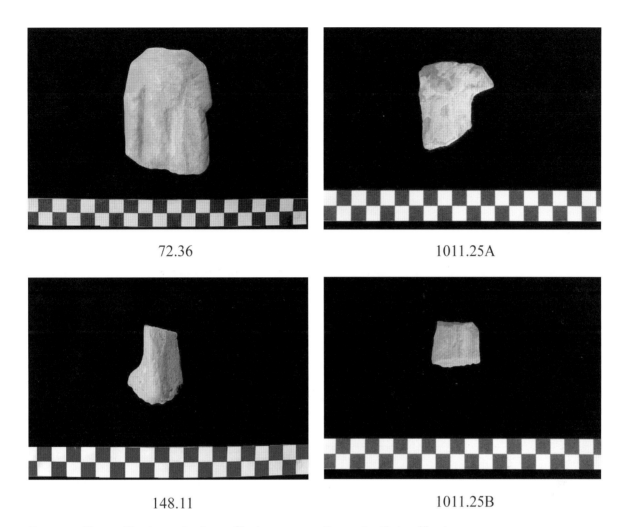

FIG. 4.27   *Photos of figurines; 148.11 is a profile view.*   FIG. 4.28   *Photos of figurines.*

the right is also bent, holding up the garments, although this is summarily rendered. The volume of the forms supports the date.

148.11. Standing female figure (fig. 4.27). Sixth century PH = 0.050, PW = 0.038, Th. = 0.032. Medium-coarse, light reddish-brown fabric (10YR 7/4), buff core with frequent (5%) black and red inclusions. Mold-made base and bottom of clay figurine. The back was smoothed flat with a tool. It probably represented a nude, female type (Astarte type).

1011.25A. Standing female figure (fig. 4.28). Fifth to fourth century. PH = 0.058, PW = 0.050, Th. = 0.020. Reddish-gray, medium-coarse fabric (10R

6/1) with rare, small to medium dark inclusions (1%). Core is a light red (10R 6/8) with a pinkish-white surface (5YR 8/2). The torso of the clay figurine survives, broken diagonally at the level of the waist, with upper part of extended, proper left arm. The torso is mold-made. The arm is a flat stump, which was made by hand and added on. The back was smoothed flat, probably with a tool. Possibly a dancer, originally part of a circle of figures.

1011.25B. Standing figure (fig. 4.28). Fifth century (?). PH = 0.030, PW = 0.033, Th. = 0.014. Coarse, reddish yellow fabric (5YR 7/6) with frequent (5%), small, light and dark red inclusions. The core is a light gray (5YR 7/1). Rectangular fragment of

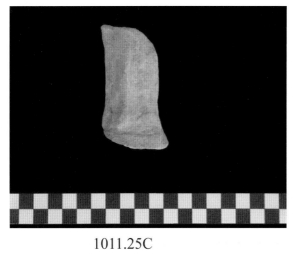

1011.25C

1011.26B

1011.26A

1011.27

FIG. 4.29   *Photos of figurines.*

FIG. 4.30   *Photos of figurines.*

mold-made figure, with one original edge. The back is concave. Only traces of what might be a leg and drapery, with faint zigzag pattern, survive.

1011.25C. Standing female figure (fig. 4.29). Fifth century (?). PH = 0.081, PW = 0.042, Th. = 0.019. Coarse light gray fabric (10R 7/1) with a light red core (10R 6/8), a pink wash (5YR 8/4), and frequent small black (5%) inclusions. The clay figurine survives from roughly the waist down, and there is a diagonal break along the bottom. It is mold-made, although the details are very faint, suggesting an old mold. The back is slightly concave. The legs of the figure are discernible outlined through a simple tunic, along with the left hand, although

this is only schematically rendered. In profile, the left leg seems to be slightly bent. It is difficult to classify this piece: at first glance it resembles the Cypro-Archaic Astarte-type figures, but on closer examination, the arrangement of the legs, placed too far apart and too low in relief, argues against this identification. It is rather a classical type, although exact parallels are lacking.

1011.26. Standing female figure (fig. 4.29). Fifth century. PH = 0.071, PW = 0.047, Th. = 0.027. A medium-coarse, light red fabric (10R 6/6) with a reddish-gray core (10R 5/1), a very pale brown wash (10YR 7/4), and rare white small inclusions (1%). The clay figurine survives from below the waist and is broken diagonally above the feet. It is badly damaged, with many cracks and chips all over the surface. Its construction suggests that its maker was not experienced with the medium. The figurine looks like it was made by fashioning by hand a rough, columnar form onto the surface of which a mold was essentially stamped, as the excess mass of clay around the molded surface suggests. The outline of the legs is visible, and there are two shallow folds indicated between them.

1011.26B. Standing female figure (fig. 4.30). Fifth century. PH = 0.072, PW = 0.073, Th. = 0.017. A medium-coarse, yellowish-red fabric (5YR 5/6) with a very pale brown wash (10YR 8/3), and rare (1%) light inclusions, some micaceous. The clay figurine survives from below the waist to the feet that are schematically rendered. Like the previous figurine (1011.26), this was also made by first fashioning a pyramidal piece of clay onto which the mold was stamped. The legs are visible in outline, and the right foot sits higher than the left, suggesting that the right leg may have been slightly bent. Folds are indicated between the legs. Shallow incisions, depicting further folds over the right leg, are probably touch-ups after molding. Figurines 1011.26 and 1011.26B are very similar, although not likely to be from the same mold.

1011.27. Standing figure (fig. 4.30). Fourth century. PH = 0.025, PW = 0.034, Th. = 0.014. Medium-coarse, very pale brown fabric (10YR 8/4) with buff core (10YR 8/2), with few (3%) black and red inclusions. Rectangular fragment of mold-made figurine, depicting plastic folds. The back was smoothed flat with a tool.

4.11. A CONTEXTUAL AND EPIGRAPHIC ANALYSIS OF THE INSCRIBED *GLANDES* (SLING BULLETS) FROM VIGLA
(Brandon R. Olson)

In 1976, 1978, and 1979, officers from the Dhekelia Sovereign Base turned over 105 *glandes*, ovoid-shaped slinging projectiles cast in lead, discovered at Vigla to the Cyprus Museum. Of the 105 bullets recovered, 32 bear inscriptions while four others depict symbols (see fig. 4.31). One of the more

interesting characteristics of *glandes* concerns the presence of inscriptions in Greek and Latin, which offer a unique window into ancient warfare and history. The problem with this material, however, is that much of it is poorly published. Archaeological reports mentioning inscribed forms rarely offer an informative interpretation, while synthetic investigations often do not go beyond providing measurements and basic translations. An epigraphic analysis of the inscribed projectiles from Vigla will help contextualize the assemblage within the greater Hellenistic world.

4.11.1. *Manufacture*

The introduction of lead *glandes* represents a significant change in light infantry technology. For the first time, uniformly-sized bullets, on average weighing 25–35 grams and measuring three to four centimeters in length and two to three centimeters in width, could easily be produced in high quantities. By offering an excellent weight-to-size ratio, leaden projectiles often carried farther than stone forms, a trait attested to by Xenophon during his great march out of Persia (Xen. *An.* 3.3.16). The ovoid shape also offered certain aerodynamic benefits, provided that the caster imparted a spin or rifling action to the projectile. The proper spin served to stabilize the *glans* during flight, which greatly increased accuracy and distance. Recently, Rihll (2007: 91–105; 2009: 160–67) suggested that *glandes* were actually catapult munitions instead of slinging projectiles. Her theory, however, has been met with skepticism by Ma (2010b). Because rifling, an action nearly impossible to achieve using a catapult, is required to take advantage of their aerodynamic shape, it remains almost certain that *glandes* were in fact developed for slings.

The production of *glandes* required specific resources and manufacturers who possessed the requisite facilities to heat and cast lead, as well as the artistic skills to design and create a variety of inscriptions and motifs. Creating inscribed bullets was an occupation left to skilled artisans well-versed in the methods of manufacture. The methods employed in the production necessitated a two-sided ceramic mold with some form of fastening device (for a modern interpretation,

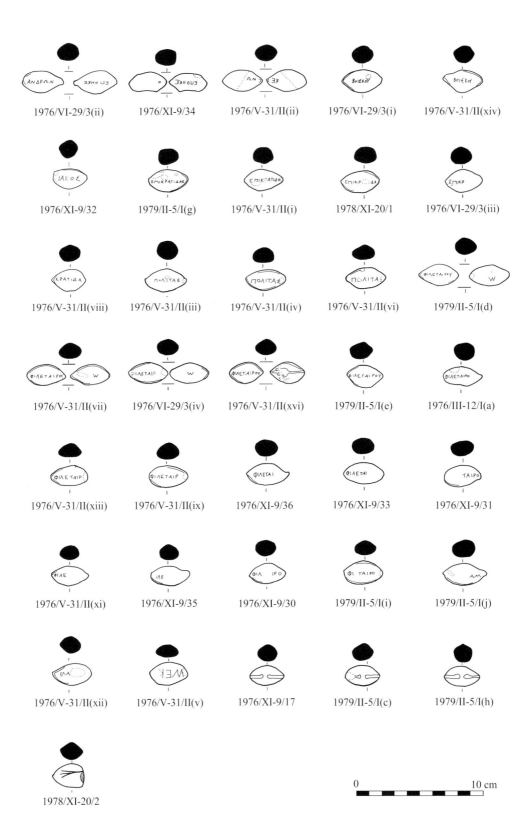

FIG. 4.31   *Illustration of cataloged inscribed sling bullets found at Vigla.*

0   5 cm

FIG. 4.32 *Two central feeder chamber fragments discovered during the 2008 season.*

see Korfmann 1973: 40). Archaeologists working at Olynthus recovered a terracotta mold capable of producing seven uninscribed *glandes* and, in another publication, Robinson notes the presence of a mold fragment found at nearby Mecyberna (Robinson 1934: n. 61; 1941: 419 and n. 148; for other sling bullet molds see also Bruneau 1968: 650 and Pritchett 1991: n. 80). Unlike the Olynthus mold, the Mecyberna form bears five Greek letters (ΧΑΛΚΙ). Manufacturers incised phrases, names, and symbols in retrograde into a mold, thus creating an inscription or symbol in low relief. A central chamber served to distribute molten lead to each bullet casing. During the 2008 field season, excavations at Vigla yielded two central feeder chamber fragments (fig. 4.32). When the lead cooled, the molds were opened and the bullets separated. Several of the *glandes* available for study bear evidence of their manufacture, such as protruding

ends from a secondary feeder chamber, creases in the bullet at the mold joins, and in one notable example from Kazaphani, some bullets are still attached to each other (Nicolaou 1977: 213).

4.11.2. *Inscription Tradition*

Several *glandes* survive that bear the names of groups of people and cities, both as full inscriptions and abbreviations. Although group and place name inscriptions were more prevalent on Latin forms, several Greek bullets survive from Olynthus and Mecyberna. Olynthus, a prosperous city in antiquity, produced nearly 500 *glandes*, of which 112 are inscribed. Of these, two group names and one city name appear in the assemblage: the Athenians, Olynthians, and Mecyberna. Robinson suggests that bullets bearing the inscription ΑΘΗΝΙΩΝ were a result of the Olynthians seizing the city from the Athenians in 421 BC (Robinson 1941: 424; Inv. 34.58a, 34.58, 38.ms127). Nine bullets recovered from Olynthus and Mecyberna possess the abbreviated inscription ΟΛΥ, which Robinson translates as "Olynthians" (Robinson 1941: 429–31; Inv. 38.ms126, 31.437, 31.467, 31.474, 31.44, 38.ms55, 38.ms144, 38.ms212, 38.ms142). Moreover, he also notes the presence of two abbreviated *glandes* inscribed MEP (obverse) and NA (reverse), which he identifies as Mecyberna (Robinson 1941: 429; Inv. 38.ms49 and 28.39. Rihll 2009: 153 doubts Robinson's translation of Mecyberna). The presence of the Olynthian and Mecybernian inscriptions are expected, since both Olynthus and Mecyberna produced clay molds, suggesting local production. The names of peoples are particularly interesting because they offer insight into ethnic identity and mobility. The Olynthian missiles sought to represent the contingent responsible for casting the bullets as Olynthian, while the Athenian bullets convey the same type of information and demonstrate an Athenian presence at the site.

Personal names, either in the nominative or genitive case, are the most prevalent inscription type. The nominative case likely represented the manufacturer, while the genitive case represented an authority figure ordering the attack or issuing the projectiles. Foss suggests that personal names in the nominative case may also represent the individual who discharged the missile, though to my knowledge a *glans* inscribed with a personal name and a verb of casting has yet to be discovered (Foss 1975: 28). As noted earlier, however, examples do survive depicting a personal name in the nominative case with ποιέω (an ancient Greek verb meaning "to make"). Returning again to the Olynthian *glandes*, Robinson most often identifies personal names in the genitive case from his assemblage (see Robinson 1931: 56; 1932: 138; 1934: 136; 1935: 23; 1941: 418–43). Two common names include those of Philip (obverse: ΦΙΛΙ, reverse: ΠΠΟΥ) and Hipponicus (obverse: ΙΠΠΟ, reverse: ΝΙΚΟΥ), both exclusively in the genitive case. Robinson, with no reservation, attributed the missiles to Philip II of Macedon, who took the city in 348 BC, and one of his high-ranking generals, Hipponicus (Robinson 1941: 418–44). The *glandes* at Olynthus were a product of Philip's siege of the city, where Hipponicus played a major role. Early in a conflict, nominal inscriptions in the genitive case served as graphic reminders of who was besieging whom (see also the *glandes* from Tel Dor: Gera 1985; Nitschke, Martin, and Shalev 2011: 142–43).

Dar.-Sag., McCaul, and Manganaro identify bullets depicting the names of certain deities (Dar.-Sag. 1877–1919; McCaul 1854; Manganaro 1982: 237–43). McCaul notes inscribed forms with the following inscriptions from Sicily: ΔΙΟΣ ΝΙΚΗ and ΝΙΚΗ ΜΗΤΕΡΩΝ (McCaul 1854: 96). Although McCaul does not offer any provenience information for the *glandes*, his publication, coupled with those of Dar.-Sag. and Manganaro, adds a religious component to the inscription tradition.

Certain bullets present more intricate designs than mere inscriptions. Although sling bullets bearing text drastically outnumber images, ornately designed missiles with motifs add another interesting component to the tradition. A pictorial relief argues for a higher level of artisanship when compared to inscriptions. The best-attested image is the scorpion (Vischer et al. 1877–1878: pls. XIII and XIV; Dar.-Sag. 1877–1919, 1610. I would like to thank Dr. Chris Hagerman for providing me with this information regarding the excavations at Stymphalos. For an introduction to the *glandes* found there, see Williams et al. 1998), while other popular motifs include eagles (Vischer et al. 1877–1878: pl. XIV; Dar.-Sag., 1610), spearheads (Vischer et al. 1877–1878: pl. XIV; Dar.-Sag., 1610), tridents (Vischer et al. 1877–1878: pl. XIV), thunderbolts (Bates 1930: 44), arrows with wings (Dar.-Sag., 1610), *phallus* (in addition to vulgar language, the Perusine assemblage contains two *glandes* depicting a *phallus* [*CIL* XI.6721.10 and *CIL* XI.6721.11]), and bundles of rods with wings (Dar.-Sag., 1610).

Inscriptions and decoration on leaden sling bullets are important pieces of historical and archaeological evidence. They not only functioned as harmful projectiles, but also conveyed a variety of messages from one group to another, which added a level of functionality to a commonly employed ancient weapon. If one considers the various intended audiences for inscribed forms, the multifarious functions of the missiles emerge. The manufacturer, thrower, or authority figure initiated a dialogue with the besieged, the bullet itself, or a deity. Manufacturers put their names on bullets to advertise their product, while casters, though not responsible for the manufacture of the missile, discharged projectiles with an explicit command. Generals made their presence known and *glandes* with humorous exclamations and commands undoubtedly harassed opponents.

4.11.3. Vigla Assemblage

Nicolaou published a majority of the inscribed forms from Vigla in his annual *Inscriptiones Cypriae Alphabeticae* (Nicolaou 1977: 209–21; 1979: 344–51; 1980: 260–66). Having consulted the acquisition records of the Cyprus Museum, inspected the *glandes* first hand, and examined Nicolaou's publications, the following discussion of the acquisition and context of the assemblage is possible. In 1976, the Cyprus Museum acquired 25 inscribed *glandes* from Alan Grace of the Dhekelia Sovereign Base and Gary Crofts (Inventory numbers 1976/III-12/1; 1976/V-31/11[i–x and xii–xiv]; 1976/VI-29/3[i–iv]; 1976/XI-9/30-36). In 1978, the Cyprus Museum acquired two more from Alan Grace (Inventory numbers 1978/XI-20/1 and 1978/XI-20/2), and the following year, M.L. Munn, also of the Dhekelia Sovereign Base, deposited another eight. Since the bullets were recovered without proper archaeological techniques, the exact spatial provenience has been lost. Given the fact that the museum acquisition records notes that the *glandes* came from the site Vigla, which has a Hellenistic occupation, and that the missiles conform to the basic size, shape, and form of known Late Cypro-Classical and Hellenistic styles from the greater Mediterranean, they most certainly date to the late fourth through third centuries BC, though continued analysis of excavation material undertaken by the Pyla-Koutsopetria Archaeological Project will likely provide a more precise chronology. Most of the bullets are damaged to some degree, and it is difficult to determine whether the damage is a result of use or several years of agricultural activity on Vigla. Of the 36 inscribed bullets, 29 possess one of seven personal names, all of which are represented in the standard lexica of Greek personal names: Ἄνδρων (nominative), Βόϊσκος (genitive), Οἴαξ (genitive), Ἐπικρατίδας (nominative), Κρατίδας (genitive), Πολίτας (nominative), and Φιλέταιρος (genitive), while four preserve one of two symbols, and three preserve fragmentary inscriptions or unidentified abbreviations (Preisigke 1967; Foraboschi 1971; Fraser and Matthews 1987).

4.11.4. *Epigraphic Commentary*

[The epigraphic conventions employed are selective and based on the systems of John Bodel (2001) and Lawrence Keppie (1991)][1]

1976/VI-29/3(ii)

Length: 3.2 cm, Width: 1.7 cm, Weight: 36.92 g
Obverse Inscription: ΑΝΔΡΩΝ
Reverse Inscription: ΕΠΟΗΣΕ
Transcription: Ἄνδρων Ἐποⁱίⁱησε
Translation: Ἄνδρων made this.
Commentary: The inscription is well-preserved and reads ΕΠΟΗΣΕ, an erroneous or abbreviated aorist form of ποιέω.

1976/XI-9/34

Length: 3.0 cm , Width: 1.6 cm, Weight: 37.12 g
Obverse Inscription: .....N
Reverse Inscription: ΕΠΟΗΣΕ
Transcription: [Ἄνδρω]ν Ἐποⁱίⁱησε
Translation: Ἄνδρων made this.

Commentary: Like the previous example, ΕΠΟΗΣΕ is an erroneous or abbreviated aorist form of ποιέω.

1976/V-31/II(ii)

Length: 3.2 cm, Width: 2.2 cm, Weight: 37.23 g
Obverse Inscription: AN..ΩN
Reverse Inscription: ....ΣΕ
Transcription: Ἄν[δρ]ων [Ἐποⁱίⁱη]σε
Translation: Ἄνδρων made this.
Commentary: Nicolaou identifies an *alpha* and *nu* on the obverse side of the *glans* (Nicolaou 1977, 211). Although the current editor could not identify these letters, it is almost certain that the obverse and reverse inscriptions are similar in form and content to 1976/VI-29/3(ii) and 1976/XI-9/34.

1976/VI-29/3(i)

Length: 3.0 cm, Width: 1.7 cm, Weight: 35.34 g
Inscription: ΒΟΙΣΚΟΥ
Transcription: Βοίσκου
Translation: of Βόϊσκος
Commentary: The *glans* is yellow (2.5Y 8/6–8/8) and differs greatly in color from the majority of the assemblage (for other color variants for *glandes* including pink and green see Rihll 2009: 148). With three exceptions, 1976/VI-29/3(i), 1976/V-31/II(i), and 1976/VI-29/3(iv), all the inscribed *glandes* from Vigla are a variation of gray. The unique yellow hue of the aforementioned missiles was likely a result of a mineral contaminate, which, through time, caused the bullets to turn yellow. Possible mineral contaminates capable of yellowing lead include Corkite [$PbFe^{3+}_3(PO_4)(SO_4)(OH)_6$], Pyromorphite [$Pb_5(PO_4)_3Cl$], Mimetite [$Pb_5(AsO_4)_3Cl$], Vanadinite [$Pb_5(VO_4)_3Cl$], Autunite [$Ca(UO_2)_2(PO_4)_2 \bullet 4(H_2O)$], and Tyuyamunite [$Ca(UO_2)_2(VO_4)_2 \bullet 6(H_2O)$]. (I would like to thank Dr. David "Duff" Gold of the Department of Geosciences at Pennsylvania State University and mineralogist Dr. Andrew Sicree for their expertise in identifying mineral contaminants capable of turning lead yellow.)

1976/V-31/II(xiv)

Length: 3.0 cm, Width: 1.8 cm, Weight: 35.44 g
Inscription: ΒΟΙΣΚΟΥ
Transcription: Βοίσκου

Translation: of Βοῖσκος
Commentary: A personal name in the genitive case.

1976/XI-9/32
Length: 2.8 cm, Width: 1.7 cm, Weight: 29.47 g
Inscription: .ΙΑΚΟΣ
Transcription: [Ο] ἴακος
Translation: of Οἴαξ
Commentary: A personal name in the genitive case.

1979/II-5/I(g)
Length: 3.1 cm, Width: 1.7 cm, Weight: 38.90 g
Obverse Inscription: ΕΠΙΚΡΑΤΙΔΑΣ
Reverse Inscription: <u>NO</u>
Transcription: Ἐπικρατίδας
Translation: Ἐπικρατίδας
Commentary: A personal name in the nominative case. Nicolaou identifies a *nu* and *omicron* with a series of unidentifiable letters on the reverse side of the *glans* (Nicolaou 1980: 262). The fragmentary nature of the reverse inscription and a lack of comparanda among *glandes* inscribed with Ἐπικρατίδας makes any interpretation of the inscription on the reverse side impossible.

1976/V-31/II(i)
Length: 3.0 cm, Width: 1.6 cm, Weight: 38.74 g
Inscription: ΕΠΙΚΡΑΤΙΔΑ.
Transcription: Ἐπικρατίδα[ς]
Translation: Ἐπικρατίδας
Commentary: A personal name in the nominative case. The *glans* is yellow (2.5Y 8/6–8/8) and differs greatly in color from the majority of the assemblage. See commentary on 1976/VI-29/3(i) above for an explanation of the hue.

1978/XI-20/1
Length: 3.0 cm, Width: 2.4 cm, Weight: 37.40 g
Inscription: ΕΠΙΚΡ...ΔΑ.
Transcription: Ἐπικρ[ατί]δα[ς]
Translation: Ἐπικρατίδας
Commentary: A personal name in the nominative case.

1976/VI-29/3(iii)
Length: 3.0 cm, Width: 1.7 cm, Weight: 37.42 g
Inscription: ΕΠΙΚΡ<u>Α</u>......
Transcription: Ἐπικρ[ατίδας]

Translation: Ἐπικρατίδας
Commentary: A personal name in the nominative case. Nicolaou notes an *alpha* after the *rho*, which the current editor could not identify (Nicolaou 1977: 212).

1976/V-31/II(viii)
Length: 2.5 cm, Width: 2.2 cm, Weight: 26.97 g
Inscription: ΚΡΑΤΙΔ<u>Α</u>.
Transcription: Κρατίδα
Translation: of Κρατίδας
Commentary: A personal name in the genitive case. The preservation of the *glans* is excellent and there were no traces of a letter after the terminal *alpha*, which demonstrates that the inscription, unlike the Ἐπικρατίδας examples, is in the genitive case.

1976/V-31/II(iii)
Length: 3.3 cm, Width: 1.7 cm, Weight: 39.55 g
Inscription: ΠΟΛΙΤΑΣ
Transcription: Πολίτας
Translation: Πολίτας
Commentary: A personal name in the nominative case.

1976/V-31/II(iv)
Length: 3.3 cm, Width: 1.7 cm, Weight: 38.51 g
Inscription: ΠΟΛΙΤΑΣ
Transcription: Πολίτας
Translation: Πολίτας
Commentary: A personal name in the nominative case.

1976/V-31/II(vi)
Length: 3.2 cm, Width: 2.2 cm, Weight: 36.97 g
Inscription: ΠΟΛΙΤΑΣ
Transcription: Πολίτας
Translation: Πολίτας
Commentary: A personal name in the nominative case.

1979/II-5/I(d)
Length: 3.2 cm, Width: 1.6 cm, Weight: 33.70 g
Obverse Inscription: ΦΙΛΕΤΑΙΡΟΥ
Reverse Inscription: <u>IM</u>
Transcription: Φιλεταίρου
Translation: of Φιλέταιρος

Commentary: A personal name in the genitive case. Nicolaou notes an *iota* and a *mu* in his transcription of the reverse side of the *glans* (Nicolaou 1980: 262). The reverse side of the *glans* is poorly preserved and the current editor could only identify a *mu,* which may symbolize a quantity; see commentary of 1976/V-31/II(vii) below.

1976/V-31/II(vii)
Length: 3.0 cm, Width: 1.6 cm, Weight: 34.03 g
Obverse Inscription: ΦΙΛΕΤΑΙΡΟ.
Reverse Inscription: Μ
Transcription: Φιλεταίρο[υ]
Translation: of Φιλέταιρος
Commentary: A personal name in the genitive case. The inscriptions on the *glans* are well-preserved, and it is clear that the reverse side contains only a *mu,* which suggests either a short abbreviation or, more likely, a sign denoting a numeric quantity. Beginning in the classical period, capitalized Greek characters often represented numbers, especially in epigraphic contexts (Smyth 348a [1920 edition]). *Glandes* were, in the context of the Vigla assemblage, locally produced and manufacturers may have inscribed a quantity sign, in this case a *mu* denoting 10,000, to keep track of their inventory.

1976/VI-29/3(iv)
Length: 3.0 cm, Width: 1.7 cm, Weight: 33.68 g
Obverse Inscription: ΦΙΛΕΤΑΙΡ.
Reverse Inscription: Μ
Transcription: Φιλεταίρ[ου]
Translation: of Φιλέταιρος
Commentary: A personal name in the genitive case. The *glans* is yellow (2.5Y 8/6–8/8) and differs greatly in color from the majority of the assemblage. The inscriptions are fairly well-preserved and, similar to 1976/V-31/II(vii), it is clear that the reverse inscriptions consists only of a *mu.* See commentary on 1976/VI-29/3(i) above for a discussion of the hue and see the commentary on 1976/V-31/II(vii) above for a discussion of quantity signs on *glandes.*

1976/V-31/II(xvi)
Length: 3.0 cm, Width: 1.7 cm, Weight: 33.71 g
Obverse Inscription: ΦΙΛΕΤΑΙΡΟΥ
Reverse: A spear motif

Transcription: Φιλεταίρου
Translation: of Φιλέταιρος
Commentary: A personal name in the genitive case. This inscription was not published by Nicolaou.

1979/II-5/I(e)
Length: 3.0 cm, Width: 1.8 cm, Weight: 36.00 g
Inscription: ΦΙΛΕΤΑΙΡΟΥ
Transcription: Φιλεταίρου
Translation: of Φιλέταιρος
Commentary: A personal name in the genitive case.

1976/III-12/I(a)
Length: 3.2 cm, Width: 1.5 cm, Weight: 37.42 g
Inscription: ΦΙΛΕΤΑΙΡΟ.
Transcription: Φιλεταίρο[υ]
Translation: of Φιλέταιρος
Commentary: A personal name in the genitive case.

1976/V-31/II(xiii)
Length: 3.0 cm, Width: 1.5 cm, Weight: 33.21 g
Inscription: ΦΙΛΕΤΑΙΡ..
Transcription: Φιλεταίρ[ου]
Translation: of Φιλέταιρος
Commentary: A personal name in the genitive case. Nicolaou notes the presence of an inscription on the reverse, which has been "worn out" (Nicolaou 1977: 212). The present editor could not find evidence of an inscription on the reverse side of this *glans.*

1976/V-31/II(ix)
Length: 3.1 cm, Width: 1.9 cm, Weight: 35.92 g
Inscription: ΦΙΛΕΤΑΙΡ..
Transcription: Φιλεταίρ[ου]
Translation: of Φιλέταιρος
Commentary: A personal name in the genitive case. Nicolaou notes the presence of an inscription on the reverse side as "completely worn" (Nicolaou 1977: 212). The present editor could not find evidence of an inscription on the reverse side of this *glans.*

1976/XI-9/36
Length: 3.3 cm, Width: 1.8 cm, Weight: 34.13 g
Obverse Inscription: ΦΙΛΕΤΑΙ…
Reverse Inscription: ΟΔ
Transcription: Φιλεταί[ρου]

Translation: of Φιλέταιρος

Commentary: A personal name in the genitive case. Nicolaou notes an *omicron, delta,* and, possibly, an *omega* on the reverse side of the *glans* and transcribes the inscription as [Λιπ]οδω[ρος] (Nicolaou 1977: 212). The current editor could not identify any letters on the reverse side of this *glans*. Although the name Λιπόδωρος is attested on other *glandes* from Cyprus, it does not appear on any of the examples from Vigla. There are five inscribed *glandes* of unknown provenience housed in the Cyprus Museum (no. M.2999/8–12) bearing the name Λιπόδωρος (see Michaelidou-Nicolaou 1972: 361). Moreover, inscribed *glandes* rarely, if ever, contain two separate personal names on one bullet.

1976/XI-9/33

Length: 3.2 cm, Width: 1.6 cm, Weight: 34.28 g
Inscription: ΦΙΛΕΤΑΙΡΟ.
Transcription: Φιλεταί[ρου]
Translation: of Φιλέταιρος
Commentary: A personal name in the genitive case. Nicolaou identifies a *rho* and an *omicron* after the *iota* (Nicolaou 1977: 212).

1976/XI-9/31

Length: 3.0 cm, Width: 1.5 cm, Weight: 34.14 g
Inscription: ….ΤΑΙΡΟ.
Transcription: [Φιλε]ταίρο[υ]
Translation: of Φιλέταιρος
Commentary: A personal name in the genitive case.

1976/V-31/II(xi)

Length: 3.0 cm, Width: 1.7 cm, Weight: 32.95 g
Inscription: ΦΙΛΕ……
Transcription: Φιλε[ταίρου]
Translation: of Φιλέταιρος
Commentary: A personal name in the genitive case. Nicolaou notes "traces" of inscriptions on both sides (Nicolaou 1977: 212). The present editor could only identify letters on the reverse side.

1976/XI-9/35

Length: 3.3 cm, Width: 1.7 cm, Weight: 33.64 g
Inscription: .ΙΛΕ……
Transcription: [Φ]ιλε[ταίρου]

Translation: of Φιλέταιρος
Commentary: A personal name in the genitive case.

1976/XI-9/30

Length: 3.0 cm, Width: 1.7 cm, Weight: 34.23 g
Inscription: ΦΙΛΕΤΑΙΡΟΥ
Transcription: Φιλεταίρου
Translation: of Φιλέταιρος
Commentary: A personal name in the genitive case. Nicolaou identifies three letters after the *lambda* (*epsilon, tau,* and *alpha*) and a terminal *upsilon* (Nicolaou 1977: 212).

1979/II-5/I(i)

Length: 3.2 cm, Width: 1.7 cm, Weight: 35.60 g
Inscription: ΦΙ..ΤΑΙΡΟ.
Transcription: Φι[λε]ταίρο[υ]
Translation: of Φιλέταιρος
Commentary: A personal name in the genitive case.

1979/II-5/I(j)

Length: 3.4 cm, Width: 1.7 cm, Weight: 37.40 g
Inscription: ΑΜ
Transcription: [----]ΑΜ
Commentary: The inscription is poorly preserved, making any transcription problematic. It is also possible that the inscription is in retrograde and could read "ΜΑ."

1976/V-31/II(xii)

Length: 3.2 cm, Width: 1.8 cm, Weight: 29.97 g
Inscription: ΕΛΑ
Transcription: ΕΛΑ[----]
Commentary: The *glans* is heavily damaged with a deep cut near the center, making an accurate transcription impossible. Given the placement of the damage, primarily in the center of the bullet where the remainder of the inscription would have been, and the lack of comparable damage within the Vigla assemblage, one must at least acknowledge the possibility, however remote, of deliberate erasure. Evidence for *damnatio memoriae,* "the damnation of memory," can be found throughout the ancient world. Although modern scholars such as Eric Varner (2004) and Harriet Flower (2006) have tended to focus on the Roman imperial realm, *damnatio memoriae* was not relegated to the upper

echelon of Roman society, but rather was a tangible concern for the entire classical world.

1976/V-31/II(v)

Length: 3.0 cm, Width: 3.3 cm, Weight: 32.66 g
Inscription: MEK
Transcription: ((MEK))
Commentary: The inscription is in retrograde and relatively well-preserved. There is no evidence of an inscription on the reverse side and the inscription is likely a nominal abbreviation similar to those found at Stymphalos (Williams et al. 1998).

1976/XI-9/17

Length: 2.7 cm, Width: 1.6 cm, Weight: 28.57 g
Image: Thunderbolt
Commentary: This particular *glans* is not published as a decorated missile by Nicolaou.

1979/II-5/I(c)

Length: 2.7 cm, Width: 1.6 cm, Weight: 27.90 g
Image: Thunderbolt
Commentary: Nicolaou notes that this *glans* was inscribed on both sides: (Obverse: I--) Reverse (O--I--O), but the current editor identified a thunderbolt motif comparable to those found on 1979/II-5/I(h) and 1976/XI-9/17 (Nicolaou 1980: 262).

1979/II-5/I(h)

Length: 2.7 cm, Width: 1.6 cm, Weight: 29.00 g
Image: Thunderbolt
Obverse Inscription: ΠΟ.ΩΡΟΣ
Commentary: Nicolaou notes "ΠΟ.ΩΡΟΣ" on the *glans* and transcribes it as [ΛΙ] ΠΟΔΩΡΟΣ. The current editor could not identify the inscription.

1978/XI-20/2

Length: 2.0 cm, Width: 1.8 cm, Weight: 31.9 g
Image: Spearhead
Commentary: Nicolaou notes that the motif present on the artifact appears to be Cypro-Minoan (Nicolaou 1979: 349). Given the relatively large size of the object and the peculiar wear pattern on one end, the artifact may not have been a *glans*, but rather a weight for a spear or javelin. The right end of the artifact has been removed and a 3–4 mm depression is present, which may have been used to attach the object to a wooden shaft. Unlike traditional lead *pila* or *hastae* weights common in the Roman period, the artifact is not hollow, which suggests that the object may have had some form of training function as a practice tip at the end of a shaft (for lead-weighted *pila* and *hastae* see Bennett 1991 and Bishop and Coulston 2006: 200–202). Whether shot mechanically or thrown by hand, properly-weighted lead practice tips would have been a low-cost alternative to bronze and iron projectiles for training purposes. Camp activities in the Roman period included soldiers training with cheap wooden swords (*clavae* and *rudes*) instead of an expensive *gladius* (see Veg. *Mil.* 1.11).

4.11.5.   *Conclusions and Discussion*

The individual names attested to on the Vigla bullets cannot accurately be attributed to known historical personages or events. Major synthetic studies of assemblages from Olynthus, Stymphalos, and Perugia go beyond offering mere dimensions and translations and approach the topic from a similar approach (for Olynthus, see Robinson 1941; for Stymphalos, see Williams et al.1998; for Perugia, see Hallett 1977 and the following examples published in the *CIL*: XI.6721.5, XI.6721.7, XI.6721.9a, XI.6721.10, XI.6721.11, XI.6721.14, and XI.6721.39). They contextualize their assemblage by coupling the known spatial provenience and archaeological context of their *glandes* with specific historical references. Unfortunately, to my knowledge, ancient authors have not mentioned the fortified promontory known today as Vigla. Furthermore, having been brought to the Cyprus museum by Dhekelia officials in the 1970s, the exact spatial provenience of the Vigla collection has been lost. Therefore, any conclusions made regarding the Vigla assemblage must be determined using a comparative model.

Unlike the assemblages from other major Mediterranean sites whose inscribed *glandes* are attributable to specific historically attested events, the diversity of epigraphic forms and content from the Vigla assemblage was a result of prolonged activity and production through time. The 2008 and 2009 Pyla-Koutsopetria Archaeological Project excavations have unearthed evidence supporting the local production of *glandes* at Vigla.

Several lead fragments, including an uninscribed *glans* fragment, sections of lead feeder chambers (fig. 4.32), and lead slag have been recovered. The artifacts preserved at the Cyprus Museum from previous work at the site consist of several lead fragments and slag, while Nicolaou, during a visit to the site, notes the presence of a considerable amount of lead slag strewn throughout the promontory (Nicolaou 1977: 214). The presence of lead by-products at Vigla, *glandes* bearing personal names in the nominative case, especially those depicting the inscription "Andron made this" (Ἄνδρων Ἐποίησε), and the presence of signs likely denoting a numeric quantity, collectively demonstrate local production. The mere presence of inscribed forms of a Hellenistic date is not too surprising, as other, larger, more established Hellenistic period sites in Cyprus and on the Levantine coast Levantine coast, such as Tel Dor (Gera 1985; Nitschke, Martin, and Sheley 2011), Ptolemais in northern Israel (Dothan 1976), and an unpublished example from Arsinoe in northern Cyprus, have produced comparable examples, but the sheer diversity of the inscriptions at Vigla is unique and conveys prolonged modes of deposition and an active military presence at Vigla during the Hellenistic period.

4.12. LITHIC ARTIFACTS (P. Nick Kardulias)

As intensive multi-period locational surveys have become common archaeological practice on Cyprus over the past 40 years, it is customary now to include a description of the lithic artifacts retrieved in the course of fieldwork. This section presents information on 104 flaked stone artifacts and eight pieces of ground stone collected during eight seasons of investigation; two flakes came from an excavated context in EU 7, but all the other artifacts were surface finds. The majority of the material in both categories was retrieved from Kokkinokremos (fig. 5.16), a not unexpected finding given the presence of a significant Bronze Age site on the cuesta that overlooks the area of the silted-in embayment at the southeastern corner of the project area. However, due to the generic nature of the artifacts, with few truly diagnostic forms, it is difficult to assign dates to the mate-

rial, especially since most of it consists of debitage produced during the reduction of cores. The retouched tools in the flaked stone assemblage could belong to almost any time period. Based on the presence of ceramics in the same units or nearby, one can argue that the majority of the lithics from Kokkinokremos are Bronze Age in date, but this identification is tentative. Despite the limitations of sample size and tentative chronology, the lithic assemblage does reveal information about economic behavior that is important for interpreting how people functioned in the survey area. In addition, the material provides another element to consider in comparing the PKAP project area with other survey zones both in the region and elsewhere on Cyprus. After a brief general discussion of the role that stone tools played in ancient Cypriot life, I present the results of the analysis and offer some suggestions about the specific things that the lithics in this assemblage reveal about activity in and around Pyla.

4.12.1. Stone Tool Use on Cyprus

The use of stone tools on Cyprus dates back to the earliest occupation of the island at Akrotiri (Simmons 1999), and lithics formed one of if not the major artifact class for the various Aceramic Neolithic phases. Flaked stone possesses several traits that make it highly useful. First, tools can be fashioned by percussion or pressure to perform many cutting and scraping functions from a variety of rocks, although those that work best as scrapers, knives, and points are flint and obsidian. While Cyprus lacks sources of obsidian, high-quality flint is available in several major formations that outcrop in various places on the island. In addition, usable nodules of material washed out from geological deposits can be found in many stream beds. Flint thus has the virtue of ubiquity. While the project zone does not contain any of the high-quality sources associated with the Lefkara Formation, flint pebbles can be found liberally scattered throughout the area. Second, while certain techniques of stone tool production require significant experience, even novices or unskilled people can manufacture serviceable tools relatively quickly. The basic elements of flintknapping were probably widely known and practiced by ancient Cypriots. People could remove sharp flakes from cores with minimal effort and use the pieces as ad hoc tools. In addition, because of the durability of stone, many tools could be curated or recycled, in some cases by people separated by centuries.

While the conventional thinking in classical archaeology for many years was that the presence of flaked and ground stone tools was an indication of prehistoric contexts, work over the past three decades throughout the eastern Mediterranean has largely debunked that notion. Careful study of lithics in the Aegean, Turkey, Cyprus and elsewhere has demonstrated that while the production of stone tools certainly has great antiquity in the region, this technology persisted not only into early historic periods, but all the way to the 20th century in the case of stone-studded threshing sledges (Pearlman 1984; Whittaker 1996, 1999, 2000). Detailed analyses have revealed that lithics remained elements in tool kits in all ancient and medieval periods after the Bronze Age (Kardulias 2009; Runnels 1982), although the quantities dropped off significantly in historic times. What has become clear from the careful study of stone tools is that these implements were almost exclusively utilitarian in nature, and in many ways were critical to daily activities from the scraping of wood, to starting fires, and grinding grain into flour.

4.12.2. Flaked Stone

Methods

The analysis reported below involved separation of the assemblage into types on the basis of morphological traits. The first step assigned each piece to one of seven possible blank types: a) core, b) core fragment, c) primary cortical flake, d) secondary cortical flake, e) secondary non-cortical flake, f) tertiary non-cortical flake, g) blade (with subdivisions for complete, proximal, medial, distal), l) debris (the characteristics of each category are described below under Findings). This sort of breakdown permits one to determine at which stage in the reduction sequence a piece was produced, and can thus potentially inform us about craft specialization and other site activities. After

the preliminary classification, each specimen was examined macroscopically with a 10× hand lens to determine the extent and nature of any retouch, which is defined as the purposeful modification of the edges in order to produce a desired shape. Minimally, retouch requires three adjacent flake scars oriented in the same direction. There is some evidence that knappers used both percussion and pressure techniques to retouch flakes and blades. Retouched specimens received labels (e.g., scraper) that, although functional in nature, carry no particular use implication; the terms are archaeological conventions that do not necessarily indicate actual past usage. The basic terminology in this typology (both for blanks and retouched pieces) derives from several standard texts on lithic analysis (Brezillon 1971; Crabtree 1972; Whittaker 1994; Andrefsky 1998). Finally, each artifact was measured and weighed to provide a metrical base of comparison (see Runnels 1985 for standard methods of measurement). The typological and metrical analyses took place in the Larnaca Museum. All information from the data sheets was transposed into a numeric code for analysis by SPSS on a personal computer.

Findings

The 104 flaked stone artifacts in the assemblage represent all stages of the reduction sequence, but with concentration in the early phases of production. Below I briefly describe each of the categories used in the analysis. The initial breakdown lists the types of blanks that make up the whole assemblage. This step in the analysis separates the pieces into categories on the basis of what stage in the production process each artifact represents. The majority of the pieces (n=81, 77.9%) in these categories received no further modification; these items form the debitage and, while unused, are critical to understanding the process followed by the flintknappers since they bear evidence of the reduction sequence. The second major group contains the retouched artifacts (n=17, 16.5%) that can be assigned to particular tool types, and the utilized flakes (n=6, 5.8%) that have edges altered by use but not systematic retouch. SPSS coding of the artifacts facilitates determination of frequencies of blank forms and tool types. After the description section, there is an assessment of the distribution of the pieces in an effort to assign them to chronological periods based on diagnostic material (primarily ceramics), followed by a discussion of tool function and what that tells us about the survey area. All pieces were measured and weighed; measurements are in centimeters, and weight is in grams.

Types of Blanks (n=104; Table 4.2)

Flake Cores, n=9
The specimens are percussion flake cores (n=4) or core fragments (n=5) with angular outlines that represent irregular, unsystematic working. Flake scars indicate several directions of removal on most specimens, and platform preparation is minimal. One complete core and three core fragments are stream pebbles.

Primary Cortical Flakes, n=23
Included in this category is any flake with cortex covering more than 50% of the dorsal surface. The cortex on chert or flint that derives from bedded outcrops is often a calcareous rind, typically white or light in color. Flakes removed from cobbles or pebbles found in streams have rounded, weathered cortexes.

Secondary Cortical Flakes, n=46
Any flake with cortex over less than 50% of the dorsal surface fits into this category. These flakes are generally smaller than primary ones, but still reflect efforts to remove the external surface that impedes the flaking process.

Secondary Non-Cortical Flakes, n=10
Flakes in this group lack cortex and have a maximum dimension of at least 1.75 cm. These flakes represent secondary trimming of a core and exhibit one or more ridges on the dorsal surface, indicative of prior flake removals before the piece in question was detached from the core.

Tertiary Non-Cortical Flake, n=1
This group is comprised of any flake lacking cortex and with a maximum dimension less than 1.75 cm.

Table 4.2   Breakdown of flaked stone by type of blank.

BLANK	FREQUENCY	PERCENT
Blade	2	1.9
Core fragment	5	4.8
Debris	13	12.5
Flake core	3	2.9
Pebble core	1	1.0
Prim cort fl	23	22.1
Sec cort fl	46	44.2
Sec n-c fl	10	9.6
Tert n-c fl	1	1.0
Total	104	100.0

Such pieces probably reflect both final core reduction and trimming of larger flakes during tool production through both percussion and pressure techniques.

Blades, n=2
A blade is defined as an elongated flake with a length at least twice its width, parallel lateral margins, and one or more dorsal ridges parallel to those margins. Blade production requires the preparation of a specialized tabular or prismatic core that yields highly symmetrical, regular blanks. Blades can be used without further modification or can be retouched to make a variety of tools. The production of blades is a consistent feature of flaked stone technology in the Bronze Age throughout the Mediterranean region and the Near East (Rosen 1997; Kardulias 2003), but is represented by only two specimens in this assemblage (see truncated blade below). The unretouched blade is a medial segment with a triangular cross-section.

Debris, n=13
The pieces that fall into this category have no recognizable platform or bulb of percussion. They tend to be very blocky and angular in shape, and were formed in the process of breaking a core. The

Table 4.3   Flaked stone tool types.

Type	Frequency	Percent
No retouch	81	77.9
Piercing/incis. tool	5	4.8
End scraper	1	1.0
Prox end scraper	2	1.9
Side scraper	2	1.9
Threshing sledge flint	1	1.0
Biface	1	1.0
Truncated blade	1	1.0
Notched piece w/ additional retouch	1	1.0
Retouched piece	3	2.9
Utilized flake	6	5.8
Total	104	100.0

abrupt, uneven edges make it difficult to use such pieces, but they represent a stage in the reduction sequence.

Modified Pieces (n=23; Table 4.3)

Utilized Flakes, n=6
These artifacts represent the expedient use of flakes detached from a core without purposeful modification. Each specimen exhibits small irregular detachments from use wear along one margin. Two pieces are primary cortical flakes, and four are secondary cortical flakes.

Retouched Lithics, n=17
Any piece that receives secondary treatment after its removal from a core in order to shape the outline is a retouched lithic. Retouch modifies the natural edge(s) and lends the piece a distinct morphology, which has traditionally been the basis for classifying tools. Even though some of the category labels imply specific functions, various studies (e.g., Keeley 1980; Yerkes 1987; Bamforth et al. 1990; Young and Bamforth 1990) demonstrate

that the suggested uses often do not stand up to rigorous micro-wear examination. Therefore, the types listed below must be viewed as categories based exclusively on morphological traits; these artifacts may or may not have been used, but they clearly differ from the unmodified blanks described above. Most of the category labels are familiar to archaeologists and as such are important as heuristic devices.

Notch, n=1
Such implements have concave indentations along one or more margins and were probably used to work rounded surfaces of wood or bone. The notch was made on a secondary cortical flake by inverse, small, irregular steep retouch at left proximal. There is additional retouch at left medial to distal, and right medial to proximal.

Pointed Pieces, n=5
Such implements, also referred to as perçoirs (see Runnels 1985), possess a pointed facet, typically at one end, but occasionally on a lateral margin. Depending on the stoutness of the tip, the tools could have been used to incise hard or soft materials. Three specimens are formed on secondary cortical flakes, one on a piece of debris, and one on a pebble core. Each piece has a distinct tip or point formed by small, marginal, converging direct and inverse retouch. The points typically exhibit some rounding, presumably from use.

Scrapers, n=5
Scrapers typically have steep working facets on a side or end. The edge is shaped by abrupt continuous retouch that forms a series of parallel to sub-parallel flake scars. The steepened edge formed by such retouch makes for a stout working facet that holds up under intense pressure. These tools can work materials with hardness varying from soft (hide) to hard (wood, bone, stone).

Side Scrapers, n=2
Both specimens are made on broken secondary cortical flakes. One has large, steep, irregular retouch from proximal to medial on both the left and right margins, forming two distinct scraper edges. The other exhibits medium, steep, irregular,

retouch that forms a convex scraper facet on the left edge.

End Scrapers, n=2

One tool is a proximal end scraper formed on a thick complete secondary cortical flake with a pebble cortex; medium, abrupt, irregular flaking forms a thick scraper edge on the proximal dorsal. The other piece has small, steep, and sub-parallel flaking from left proximal to right distal, forming a nicely rounded scraper edge on high quality material.

Truncated Blade, n=1

Deliberate shortening of one or both ends of a blank permits it to fit into a handle or haft as part of a composite tool. Truncation became a common technique of tool production in the Mesolithic, but the practice continued in the Neolithic and Bronze Age, and perhaps later. This specimen is a proximal segment with a plain platform, triangular cross-section, and a straight distal truncation formed by small, irregular, abrupt retouch.

Biface, n=1

The specimen is made on a large secondary cortical flake. Retouch along both the right and left margins is large and alternating, creating sinous convex edges. Some flakes invade the interior of both surfaces, forming a crude biface.

Threshing Sledge Flint, n=1

This complete secondary cortical flake has a point platform and limestone cortex on the dorsal surface. Retouch from left proximal to medial is alternating, medium, and irregular. This edge also exhibits some rounding, a characteristic typically seen on threshing sledge flints (Kardulias and Yerkes 1996). The banded gray chert is also similar to material used for threshing sledges in the Malloura Valley.

Retouched Pieces, n=3

These are pieces that exhibit some retouch, but which do not fit any of the other classes. All three are primary cortical flakes.

Discussion

Despite the relatively small size of the flaked stone assemblage, it is still possible to draw some significant conclusions from this analysis. One striking thing about the assemblage is its blank profile. Primary and secondary cortical flakes make up 66.3% (n=69) of the total, with non-cortical flakes constituting only 10.6% (n=11). Since core reduction generally produces more non-cortical flakes, the PKAP assemblage is somewhat anomalous. For example, in the Laconia survey material from southern Greece, non-cortical flakes make up slightly more than 30% of the assemblage (Kardulias and Ijdo 2008: 130). The PKAP distribution may in part be explained by the substantial use of pebble cherts for knapping (see below). Since the pebbles and cobbles worked by ancient flint-knappers tended to be small, one would expect a higher percentage of cortical flakes in the debitage. A significant number of the artifacts in the PKAP assemblage, if not most, seem to have been produced by percussion, a technique that prevailed in stone tool production on Cyprus throughout the prehistoric period (Karimali 2005: 192–93).

Also of interest is the use of significant numbers of cortical flakes as blanks for retouched artifacts. This distribution may have to do with the lack of chert outcrops in the survey area. Since raw material was not immediately available in large quantities, unlike other parts of Cyprus, residents made use of blanks that ordinarily would have been discarded under other circumstances. Perhaps as much as any other factor, this one indicates the pragmatic, utilitarian nature of stone tool assemblages in general.

While stone tools were important, even vital, for the completion of a number of agricultural and domestic tasks, there evidently was an attempt to minimize the effort to procure the raw material for making the tools by utilizing local sources, a practice that dates back as early as the PPNB phase (Steel 2004: 38). Forty pieces (38.5%) have a pebble cortex, indicating they were most likely picked up in the stream beds and along the shore in the project area. The lithics do provide some evidence for trade between regions as well as local procurement. Some of the flaked stone raw material is clearly exotic in origin. For example, the one piece of obsidian most likely derived from the Asian mainland, since there are no such flows on Cyprus. The threshing sledge flint is made from a banded gray chert that is similar to the material used for such purposes in the Malloura Valley to the northwest of the PKAP zone.

The retouched lithics probably served a variety of functions. Because of their ability to perform a number of tasks, scrapers not surprisingly make up almost one-third of the formal tools. Scrapers could be used to work hide by removing flesh and by softening the tough fibers to make the material more pliable. Worked hide could have been used for clothing, footwear, and containers. Scrapers could also have been used to shape wood and bone that could have served as household utensils, handles for composite tools, and shepherd staffs (see Runnels 1976). The notch was a specialized scraper for rounding wood, as in the production of arrow shafts and tool handles. The pointed pieces would have been used to incise wood and bone, and perhaps to separate plant fibers. The biface may be a preform for a projectile point, or a crude knife. The threshing sledge flint would have been inserted in a wooden plank to form a *dhoukani* for use on wheat or barley strewn on a floor (Kardulias and Yerkes 1996; Whittaker 1999, 2000). The utilized flakes indicate the use of unmodified blanks in an ad hoc manner for cutting and scraping tasks. While the precise numbers in the various categories are different, the general range of blanks and tool types found by PKAP are similar to those retrieved by the Athienou Archaeological Project in the Malloura Valley (Kardulias and Yerkes 2012b), and the Sydney Cyprus Survey Project (Coleman 2003: 57–58) in the Troodos foothills.

4.12.3. Ground Stone

Methods

The small number of ground stone implements (n=8) represent at least four types of tools. With two exceptions, the pieces are parts of complete tools. The analytical procedure differs from that for flaked stone tools in several ways. First, there is little in the way of debitage that reflects the production process. While the manufacture of these tools is reductive, similar to flaked stone implements, it involves grinding or abrading, which does not leave easily discernible residue as does flintknapping. There often is hammer dressing of nodules to form the initial stages, but the detached pieces are often not readily apparent as waste flakes, unlike with flaked stone. In addition, the significant weight and bulk of ground stone material means that initial processing often takes place at quarries (Runnels 1981), with perhaps only the final grinding operations occurring at the sites where the objects were used. Evidence of this final stage of production would be essentially invisible in the archaeological record. Second, the pieces in the ground stone assemblage represent complete objects or fragments from complete objects, whereas the majority of the flaked stone were parts of composite tools; e.g., the scrapers and other retouched pieces were almost certainly hafted. This trait leads to a different process of description, in which the whole tool is emphasized over the nature of the blank. Another difference with the flaked stone tool assemblage is the use of a wider range of raw material. In the analysis of the assemblage, I identify the tool type, raw material, and any evidence of type of working. All pieces were then measured and weighed; measurements are in centimeters, and weight is in grams.

Findings (Table 4.4)

The eight pieces in this assemblage represent four different tool types; two specimens cannot be placed in a particular tool category, although they exhibit some shaping from abrasion. At least three different types of raw material are represented in the assemblage.

Handstones, n=2
Both specimens are broken or incomplete. One is a fragment of vesicular basalt with many large voids. It is plano-convex in cross-section, and has minimal abrasion on the flat surface. The other piece is made of a dense igneous mater (perhaps andesite) with small phenocrysts in the matrix. The specimen preserves both surfaces of a handstone, or perhaps a very thin grinding slab. One surface is heavily abraded, especially along the lateral edges.

Loom weights, n=2

One piece is made of a dense igneous material with a fine granular matrix. It preserves ca. half of an ovate piece with a hole in the center. One surface is flat and somewhat abraded. The other specimen is complete, formed on a piece of very fine-grained igneous material (andesite?) with small phenocrysts. The outline is roughly circular, with one side slightly thicker. A central hole was formed by drilling from both surfaces.

Vessel, n=1

The specimen is a fragment of a stone vessel preserving a section of the wall and an up-turned spout. The material is a sandy limestone. The spout is bifurcated at the lip. There is a V-shaped opening to the hole for the spout on the exterior surface.

Celt preform/blank, n=1

This piece is a complete large, flat, ovate cobble of dense igneous material like that of one of the loom weights. On the left medial to right distal edges, a series of direct, large, irregular, partial, low flakes were removed by percussion to form a roughly rounded distal facet prior to polishing.

Unidentifiable pieces, n=2

These two pieces cannot be placed in any specific tool category, but exhibit some working. One specimen is a complete roughly cylindrical piece of whitish limestone. One end is flat and shows some abrasion. The opposite end has removals by hammer to create a roughly tapered tip. This may be a pestle, but the material is not as dense as is typically seen for such artifacts. The second specimen is a small fragment of vesicular basalt. One surface is pitted but relatively smooth. Two other edges also were smoothed. The piece is roughly broken, and has a trapezoidal shape.

Discussion

The ground stone tools represent another facet of the domestic economy of the past. These objects are larger and denser than the flaked stone artifacts, and thus required a different manner of production. While initial outlines or shapes were produced by percussive hammer dressing, the final

Table 4.4   Ground stone tools.

Tool Type	Frequency	Percent
Loom weight	2	25.0
Handstone	2	25.0
Vessel	1	12.5
Celt	1	12.5
Fragment	2	25.0
Total	8	100.0

shaping involved extensive pecking, followed by grinding or abrading of the surfaces, which would have been a time-consuming task, especially with the dense igneous rocks used as raw material for many of the implements. So, it is possible that we have evidence for two sets of distinctive skills and thus different craftsmen for the production of the two assemblages. Karimali (2005: 200) argues that "the selection of stones from local riverbeds and their subsequent manufacture was a pre-planned but non-specialized activity." While many of the flaked stone and some of the ground stone tools exhibit a haphazard level of production, a significant amount would have required skills that would not have been universal. So, while the craftsmen who fashioned the tools may not have been employed full-time in the production of lithics, they certainly had a particular aptitude for such work. Another difference with the flaked stone material is that the ground stone tools provide evidence for functions other than cutting and scraping. The loom weights suggest weaving of textiles; the handstones could have been used to crush food materials (e.g., wheat and barley) or to grind shell, bone, and other material to fashion ornaments or shape tools; the spout was part of a vessel that contained liquid; the celt would have been used for chopping or shaping wood or to dig in the soil. Seven of the eight artifacts were found on Kokkinokremos, suggesting a Bronze Age context; this distribution matches reasonably well that of the flaked stone tools, 69.2% of which were found on Kokkinokremos (fig. 5.16). While the use of stone tools continued well into historic periods, their use did drop off after the Bronze Age as metal implements became more common, so the skewed distribution is not surprising.

4.12.4. *Conclusion*

The flaked and ground stone assemblages from the PKAP investigations represent artifacts that inform us about the range of activities that took place in the project area. While the quantities of these lithics are rather small compared to the amount of pottery, the stone tools reflect a much greater range of functions than do the ceramics, including cutting, scraping, incising or piercing, grinding foodstuffs and other materials, use as vessels, and making cloth. These uses fall generally in the area of domestic economy, i.e., activities associated with the indispensable daily household tasks of subsistence, as well as preparation of clothing and tools for a wide range of mundane functions.

NOTE

1   [----] Four dashes within brackets represent missing letters, the exact number of which cannot be ascertained.

[abc] Letters within brackets represent missing letters that have been supplied by the editor.

ABC Capital letters represent letters that cannot be understood by the editor.

‹abc› Letters within angle quotation marks represent text omitted erroneously, but supplied by the editor.

… Each dot represents a missing letter in the inscription heading. The letters are then supplied in the transcription within brackets.

((abc)) Text within double parentheses represents text in retrograde.

<u>abc</u> Underlined letters represent text identified by a previous editor, namely Ino Nicolaou, but which could not be identified by the current editor.

Chapter 5

Artifact Distributions

by William Caraher and David K. Pettegrew

The goal of this chapter is to describe the evidence for settlement and land use across the entire survey region in terms of the periods and classes of material present on the surface. The chapter is divided into three parts. The first (5.1) describes the artifact assemblage documented in the course of survey. The second (5.2) describes the overall distribution of artifacts across the different zones of the survey area. The third part (5.3) analyzes the distribution of artifacts and features by period from the Bronze Age to the Modern era and makes inferences about the basic patterns of habitation and past behavior across the Pyla littoral. The reader who is interested in a basic chronological overview of the region may wish to go directly to the third section.

This chapter includes numerous maps that document the distribution of artifacts in the survey zone. In general, we have tried to simplify our maps as much as possible. Unless otherwise indicated, each dot in the distributional figures represents a single artifact. The dots represent density rather than the specific location of individual artifacts. Artifact patterning below the level of the unit is the unintentional consequence of how we are illustrating density and is unrelated to where artifacts were actually found within the unit.

5.1. THE SURVEY ASSEMBLAGE

The PKAP survey area extended over 465 units and covered an area of 99.5 ha. Our sampling strategy spaced walkers at 10 m intervals and asked them to examine the surface one meter to each side of their path through the unit (for a recent discussion of walker detection, see Banning et al. 2011). This method produced a maximum sample of 20% of the surface of each unit, which theoretically should have amounted to a physical inspection of 19.9 ha of the surveyed area. However, since the average surface visibility in the survey area was 64%, fieldwalkers actually saw only 13% of each unit on average and examined only 12.8 ha of the overall 99.5 ha survey area.

From this 13% sample of the surface, fieldwalkers collected two kinds of information:

First, walkers *counted* all artifacts visible in their path. Over the 12.8 ha of examined surface, fieldwalkers counted 37,883 total artifacts, which included 30,145 pottery sherds (80%), 6,924 tiles (18%), 109 lithic artifacts (.3%), and 705 other artifacts (1.9%), yielding an average artifact density of 2,960 artifacts/ha. Given our examination of 13% of the surface, we estimate that full coverage in perfect visibility would have generated 294,481 total artifacts across the 99.5 ha survey area: 234,330 sherds, 53,823 tiles, 847 lithic artifacts, and 5,480 other artifacts. Moreover, we estimate that scouring the entire landscape by hoovering artifacts through hands-and-knees searches (Chapter 3) would have produced an enormous surface assemblage of 1,090,671 artifacts (this figure is based on average difference of 27% between pedestrian counts and hoovering counts noted in Section 3.3): 867,890 potsherds, 199,346 tiles, 3,138 lithics, and 20,297 other artifacts.

Second, fieldwalkers *collected* representative artifacts (chronotypes) from their swaths. Walkers collected 16,784 artifacts (903 kg) from the 465 survey units, which represents 44% of the 37,883 artifacts counted through pedestrian survey, 6% of the estimated total number of artifacts (294,481) countable through 100% coverage, and 1.5% of the estimated actual surface assemblage (n=1,090,671). Such numbers indicate that although we did collect a substantial sample of the surface, this was a very small amount relative to the estimated total population of artifacts. The 16,784 artifacts collectively represented 268 different chronotypes and 1,414 batches, and the average number of chronotypes and batches per unit was 9 and 14.8, respectively.

Of the collected objects, the majority (96–97%) by count and weight were ceramic artifacts. Glass and stone artifacts comprised a very small percentage, and bone, shell, glass, metal, and other artifacts appeared in trace percentages. As discussed in Chapter 3, even experienced fieldwalkers were far more likely to miss non-ceramic artifacts during standard pedestrian survey, and higher resolution methods like hoovering would have almost certainly increased the total counts of these material categories. However, as we outlined there, our 2004 experiments in hoovering suggest that hoovering does not greatly change the relative percentages of non-ceramic material.

We complemented standard artifact sampling strategies with ten experimental units (18.1, 40.1, 45.1, 53.1, 71.1, 85.1, 120.1, 127.1, 141.1, and 154.1; cf. Chapter 3)

that produced 1,936 artifacts, 52 chronotypes, 140 batches, or, on average, 194 artifacts, 15.2 chronotypes, and 27.4 batches per unit. These units with 100% coverage produced higher percentages of pottery and lower relative percentages of other classes. Since we used alternative collection strategies to produce these experimental assemblages, we have not included that material in our aggregated totals and percentages in this chapter unless explicitly mentioned.

This section will establish the character of our artifact assemblage, including chronology (5.1.1), fabric group (5.1.2), and extant part (5.1.3), and outline how these variables influenced our subsequent interpretation of the use of the Pyla landscape over time. We will then consider how the "differential visibility" of different periods (5.1.4) and "aoristic analysis" (5.1.5) contribute to a more nuanced understanding of the survey assemblage. Section 5.2 provides a large-scale spatial context for the

Table 5.1   The assemblage of the pedestrian survey (chronotype) by material class.

MATERIAL	COUNT	%	WEIGHT (G)	%
Ceramics	16,262	96.9%	863,555	95.7%
Stone	280	1.7%	33,669	3.7%
Glass	122	0.7%	943	0.1%
Metal	22	0.1%	1,403	0.2%
Bone and Shell	24	0.1%	256	0.03%
Other	74	0.4%	3049	0.3%
	16,784	100.0%	902,875	100.0%

Table 5.2   The assemblage of the hoovering survey (total collection) of 2004 by material class.

MATERIAL	COUNT	%	WEIGHT (G)	%
Ceramics	1,898	98.0%	31,340	96.9%
Stone	19	1.0%	841	2.6%
Glass	10	0.5%	45	0.1%
Metal	6	0.3%	80	0.3%
Bone and Shell	3	0.2%	30	0.1%
Total	1,936	100.0%	32,336	100.0%

distribution of material across the survey area and Section 5.3 describes the assemblages of the narrow periods.

5.1.1. *Chronology and Chronotypes*

Chronology is among the most important properties of material culture. In material form, artifacts always stand in some relation to particular periods of production, use, and discard. The problem that all archaeologists face — most especially landscape archaeologists — is that artifact types and classes are extremely uneven in how clearly they represent time in the past. A particular coin may be dated to a generation or decade, based on the intersection of archaeological and historical evidence. In contrast, a coarse red body sherd found on the surface of the ground may contribute far less to the chronology of an artifact scatter, because it only dates to a broad period like "Antiquity" or the "Medieval Era" or, most broadly, the "Ceramic Age." The uneven diagnostic character of artifacts is problematic because each period has a different number of artifacts that a ceramicist can reliably recognize as components of the overall assemblage. Thus, the overall visibility of a period in the surface assemblage depends, in part, on how many chronologically diagnostic artifacts exist for that period.

Landscape archaeologists have typically acknowledged the variable diagnostic character of particular artifacts by collecting only those "type fossils" that can be dated most precisely, such as rims, bases, handles, and decorated body sherds. This method efficiently assigns historically significant dates to a site or artifact scatter and saves the archaeologist time in artifact processing. The cost, however, is the loss of information from less diagnostic artifact types.

One aim of the chronotype system is to reclaim some of the coarse temporal data usually lost in a typical analysis of artifacts. The chronotype system describes the entire assemblage irrespective of the broadness or narrowness of any individual object's chronological value. Each chronotype, then, represents the precision with which our analysts could locate the production and use of a particular class of artifact in time. Some chronotypes are datable only to "broad" periods that exceed 1,000 years in duration (e.g., "Cypro-Classical to Roman," "Post-Prehistoric," and "Ceramic Age"); more diagnostic chronotypes are associated with "narrow" periods lasting less than 1,000 years (e.g., "Cypro-Classical," "Late Roman"). Assigning all artifacts chronological value allows us not only to make assessments about the use of the landscape through time, but also to determine blind spots and biases in our interpretations. A unit with a large quantity of artifacts not datable to a specific narrow period, such as coarse utility vessels, roof tiles, or even flint *dhoukani* blades, could reflect the traditional and stable use of utilitarian objects for centuries or highlight marginal zones of habitation or different kinds of activities within the landscape.

Assigning chronological value to every collected object informs our analysis of artifact patterns in significant ways. Table 5.3 demonstrates what Mediterranean archaeologists have often asserted, albeit without hard numbers: much of the material visible on the surface of our region cannot be dated to periods less than 1,000 years. The most frequently occurring broad period is Ancient-Historic (note that this period coincides with Historical Antiquity in the SCSP survey project. See Given and Knapp 2003: 30), which accounts for 36% of the count of material collected from the survey area. The Late Cypriot–Hellenistic, however, closely follows with 11% of count and 30% of the overall weight of the assemblage. Collectively, broad periods that span more than 1,000 years constitute 53% of the overall count and 51% of the overall weight.

Narrow periods comprise the other half of the survey assemblage. Only two narrow periods produced relatively substantial quantities of material: the ubiquitous Late Roman period, which produced 31% of the total assemblage by count and 39% by weight, and the Roman period, which comprised 7% and 4% of the total count and weight. The other 23 narrow periods combined accounted for only 9% by count and 6% by weight of the assemblage. In fact, some 21 of the 25 narrow periods produced fewer than 200 artifacts, and 17 produced 100 objects or less. This shows that although we can say quite a bit about certain narrow periods like Late Roman or Roman, our evidence for other narrow periods is highly fragmentary.

Table 5.3   Count and weight of artifacts according to narrow and broad periods.

Period (Inclusive)	Period (Chronotype)	Dates	Duration	#	%	Weight	%
Bronze Age							
	Bronze Age	2500 BC–1000 BC	1,500	7	0.04%	37	0.00%
	Late Cypriot	1650 BC–1050 BC	600	6	0.04%	292	0.03%
	Late Cypriot II	1450 BC–1200 BC	250	19	0.1%	422	0.1%
	Late Cypriot II–III	1450 BC–1050 BC	400	173	1.0%	6,693	0.7%
Iron Age							
	Iron Age	1050 BC–312 BC	738	455	2.7%	11,119	1.2%
	Geometric	1050 BC–751 BC	299	17	0.1%	900	0.1%
	Archaic	750 BC–475 BC	275	28	0.2%	918	0.1%
	Classical	474 BC–312 BC	162	15	0.1%	585	0.1%
	Archaic–Classical	750 BC–312 BC	438	8	0.1%	186	0.02%
Iron Age–Hellenistic							
	Archaic–Hellenistic	750 BC–100 BC	650	38	0.2%	9,485	1.1%
	Classical–Hellenistic	474 BC–100 BC	374	27	0.2%	2,090	0.2%
Hellenistic							
	Hellenistic	311 BC–100 BC	211	118	0.7%	1,095	0.1%
Hellenistic–Roman							
	Hellenistic–Roman	311 BC–AD 749	1,060	3	0.0%	40	0.00%
	Hellenistic–Early Roman	311 BC–AD 299	610	209	1.3%	8,613	1.0%
Roman							
	Roman	99 BC–AD 749	848	1,238	7.4%	34,883	3.9%
	Early Roman	99 BC–AD 299	398	142	0.9%	2,889	0.3%
	Late Roman	AD 300–749	449	5,165	30.8%	350,261	38.8%
Medieval–Ottoman							
	Medieval	AD 750–1570	820	8	0.1%	268	0.03%
	Early Medieval	AD 750–1190	440	3	0.02%	33	0.00%
	Late Medieval	AD 1191–1570	379	16	0.1%	154	0.02%
	Ottoman	AD 1571–1877	306	13	0.1%	112	0.01%
	Late Medieval–Ottoman	AD 1191–1877	686	1	0.01%	6	0.00%
Medieval–Modern							
	Medieval–Modern	AD 1191–2008	817	100	0.6%	6,777	0.8%
Modern							
	Modern	AD 1878–2008	130	106	0.6%	3,120	0.4%
	Early Modern	AD 1878–1949	71	3	0.02%	66	0.01%
	Modern Present	AD 1950–2008	58	28	0.2%	1,332	0.2%
Broad (Ancient)							
	Ancient	9000 BC–AD 749	9,749	33	0.2%	2,835	0.3%
	Ancient Ceramic	3500 BC–AD 749	4,249	6	0.04%	173	0.02%
	Late Cypriot–Roman	1650 BC–AD 749	2,399	7	0.04%	1,129	0.1%
	Late Cypriot–Hellenistic	1650 BC–100 BC	1,550	1,782	10.6%	268,763	29.8%

Table 5.3 (cont.)   Count and weight of artifacts according to narrow and broad periods.

PERIOD (INCLUSIVE)	PERIOD (CHRONOTYPE)	DATES	DURATION	#	%	WEIGHT	%
Broad (Ancient) (cont.)							
	Late Cypriot–Archaic	1650 BC–475 BC	1,175	3	0.02%	31	0.00%
	Protogeometric–Hellenistic	1050 BC–100 BC	950	1	0.01%	127	0.01%
	Ancient Historic	750 BC–AD 749	1,499	6,094	36.3%	140,448	15.6%
	Classical–Roman	474 BC–AD 749	1,223	79	0.5%	1,048	0.1%
Broad (Ancient–Medieval)							
	Ancient–Medieval	3500 BC–AD 1570	5,070	372	2.2%	8,174	0.9%
	Ancient Historic–Medieval	750 BC–AD 1570	2,320	1	0.01%	52	0.01%
Broad (Ancient–Modern)							
	Unknown	9000 BC–AD 2008	11,008	299	1.8%	28,833	3.2%
	Ceramic Age	3500 BC–AD 2008	5,508	1	0.01%	41	0.01%
	Bronze Age–Modern Present	2500 BC–AD 2008	4,508	84	0.5%	2,375	0.3%
	Late Cypriot–Modern Present	1650 BC–AD 2008	3,708	7	0.04%	1,347	0.2%
	Post-Prehistoric	999 BC–AD 2008	3,007	68	0.4%	5,166	0.6%
	Hellenistic–Modern Present	311 BC–AD 2008	2,319	1	0.01%	315	0.04%
	Roman–Modern	99 BC–AD 2008	2,107	3	0.02%	231	0.03%
	Totals			16,784	100.0%	902,875	100.0%

Our chronotype data also indicates that a handful of periods dominate the overall assemblage. The majority of artifacts (78% by count, 84% by weight) were assigned to three particular periods, Ancient Historic, Late Roman, and Late Cypriot–Hellenistic. Over 95% of our artifacts were assigned to ten periods that ranged from narrow (e.g., Early and Late Roman, Late Cypriot II–Late Cypriot III) to extremely broad (Unknown, Ancient Historic). While the collected artifacts are chronologically heterogeneous, with 43 different periods, a few periods dominate the overall assemblage (Table 5.4).

Moreover, broad periods are far more homogeneous than narrow periods and contain fewer chronotypes assigned to larger batches during ceramic analysis. Artifacts dated to broad periods account for 53% of all material collected, but such broad period artifacts only represent 29% of all

chronotypes documented (n=257) and 38% of the total count of batches (n=1,384). In contrast, the smaller proportion of artifacts (47%) datable to a narrow period accounts for 71% of all chronotypes and 62% of all batches. In a similar way, the average number of chronotypes is greater for narrow periods (n=7) than for broad periods (n=4). For example, a period like Ancient–Historic, which covers a very broad span (750 BC–AD 749), has few chronotypes (n=13) relative to its 1500-year time span in comparison with very narrow periods like Cypro-Classical to Hellenistic (n=9), Late Medieval (n=9), and Modern Present (n=10). The reasons for these patterns are obvious: we could assign more diagnostic artifacts (i.e., narrow-period artifacts) to more precise typologies, and less diagnostic material into fewer, larger batches and chronotypes.

Table 5.4　The ten most common periods, arranged according to frequency.

PERIOD	DATES	COUNT	%	WEIGHT	%
Ancient Historic	750 BC–AD 749	6,094	36.3%	140,448	15.6%
Roman, Late	AD 300–749	5,165	30.8%	350,261	38.8%
Late Cypriot–Hellenistic	1650 BC–99 BC	1,782	10.6%	268,763	29.8%
Roman	99 BC–AD 749	1,238	7.4%	34,883	3.9%
Iron Age	1050 BC–312 BC	455	2.7%	11,119	1.2%
Ancient–Medieval	3500 BC–AD 1570	372	2.2%	8,174	0.9%
Unknown	9000 BC–AD 2008	299	1.8%	28,833	3.2%
Hellenistic–Early Roman	311 BC–AD 299	209	1.2%	8,613	1.0%
Late Cypriot II–Late Cypriot III	1450 BC–1050 BC	173	1.0%	6,693	0.7%
Roman, Early	99 BC–AD 299	142	0.9%	2,889	0.3%
Other Periods		855	5.1%	42,199	4.7%
Total		16,784	100.0%	902,875	100.0%

This tension between a homogeneous majority and a very diverse minority is evident also in an examination of chronotypes. The five most common chronotypes account for 59% (count) and 67% (weight) of the entire assemblage; the ten most common types account for 71% (count) and 73% (weight) of the assemblage; and the 25 most common account for 87% (count and weight) of the entire assemblage (Table 5.5). In contrast, some 90% of all chronotypes documented in PKAP (n=235 of 260) account for a meager 13% of all the artifacts collected. The picture, again, is clear: there is tremendous diversity among a proportionally small number of diagnostic artifacts.

In sum, slightly more than half of our artifacts can only be tied to a period of more than 1,000 years and most of this material is homogeneous. A smaller proportion (47%) of artifacts can be dated to narrower periods, and these artifacts are generally more diverse in terms of the number of associated chronotypes and batches. In short, the PKAP assemblage is diverse in terms of the overall number of chronotypes and batches, but the majority of these chronotypes and batches are associated with very few artifacts. The vast majority of the artifacts documented through survey belong to 1–2 dozen chronotypes. The bases for these patterns are informed by a discussion of fabric group (5.1.2), extant part (5.1.3), and differential visibility (5.1.4).

5.1.2.　Fabric Group, Chronology, and Function

As the majority of artifacts collected in PKAP represent pottery and tile fragments (97% by count, 96% by weight; see Table 5.1), we will focus in the following sections on the assemblage of ceramic artifacts and exclude from our analysis bone, shell, stone, metal, glass, other artifacts, terra cotta, and ceramic artifacts with unknown fabric. Consequently, the *totals* provided below will be different from those noted in Table 5.1, which included non-ceramic objects as well.

The Pyla-*Koutsopetria* Project assigned all ceramic artifacts to eight fabric groups that convey properties of fabric, function, and chronology. *Tiles* indicate buildings and often habitation. *Fine* and *semi-fine wares* represent dining, ritual, and display. *Kitchen wares* usually reflect food preparation. *Pithoi* mark storage of agricultural goods. *Amphorae* reflect agricultural production, storage, and commercial exchange. *Coarse* and *medium-coarse wares* have the most generic functional applications, representing "utilitarian" purposes in general. The relative proportions of these different fabric groups speak to questions of chronology (5.1.1) and to the nature of the use of the landscape (function). The intersection of fabric, chronology, and function has major implications for our his-

Table 5.5 The 25 most common chronotypes, arranged according to frequency.

Chronotype	Period	Quantity	%	Weight	%
Coarse Ware, Ancient Historic	Ancient Historic	3,252	19.4%	83,309	9.2%
Medium Coarse Ware, Ancient Historic	Ancient Historic	2,139	12.7%	20,004	2.2%
Tile, Roman Late	Roman, Late	1,883	11.2%	208,351	23.1%
Coarse Ware, Roman Late	Roman, Late	1,327	7.9%	40,680	4.5%
Pithos Ware, Late Cypriot-Hellenistic	Late Cypriot-Hellenistic	1,290	7.7%	252,471	28.0%
Amphora, Roman Late	Roman, Late	608	3.6%	34,767	3.9%
Kitchen Ware, Roman	Roman	475	2.8%	2,796	0.3%
Light-colored Utility Ware (Plain ware)	Late Cypriot-Hellenistic	346	2.1%	9,027	1.0%
Medium Coarse Ware, Ancient-Medieval	Ancient-Medieval	323	1.9%	5,690	0.6%
Medium Coarse Ware, Roman Late	Roman, Late	315	1.9%	3,829	0.4%
Amphora, Late Roman 1	Roman, Late	293	1.8%	20,740	2.3%
Kitchen Ware, Ancient Historic	Ancient Historic	286	1.7%	2,041	0.2%
Amphora, Roman	Roman	282	1.7%	22,510	2.5%
Amphora, Ancient Historic	Ancient Historic	220	1.3%	17,557	1.9%
Medium Coarse Ware, Roman	Roman	213	1.3%	3,142	0.4%
Coarseware, Iron Age	Iron Age	194	1.2%	4,502	0.5%
Tile, Kopetra Corinthian Pan Roman Late	Roman, Late	184	1.1%	25,368	2.8%
Medium Coarse Ware, Iron Age	Iron Age	176	1.0%	2,080	0.2%
Egyptian White Slip	Late Cypriot II–III	173	1.0%	6,693	0.7%
Coarse Ware, Roman	Roman	136	0.8%	3,736	0.4%
Kitchen Ware, Roman Late	Roman, Late	112	0.7%	987	0.1%
Unknown	Unknown	104	0.6%	4,881	0.5%
Cypriot Red Slip	Roman, Late	103	0.6%	1,809	0.2%
Stone, unworked	Unknown	100	0.6%	10,208	1.1%
Dark-colored Utility Ware (Plain ware)	Late Cypriot-Hellenistic	87	0.5%	2,156	0.2%
Other		2,163	12.90%	113,541	12.60%

torical reconstructions of the use of the landscape (5.3).

An analysis of relative proportions of fabric groups of pottery and tile reinforces the conclusion about homogeneity and diversity we reached in section 5.1.1. On the one hand, there is considerable diversity as most of the eight fabric groups are found throughout the survey area in significant quantities, indicating a wide array of different functions. On the other hand, two fabric groups — coarse and medium-coarse wares — dominate the assemblage in terms of total

Table 5.6   Fabric groups of ceramic artifacts by count and weight.

FABRIC GROUP	COUNT	%	WEIGHT (G)	%
Amphora	1,672	10.3%	116,500	13.5%
Coarse	5,329	32.8%	159,203	18.5%
Fine	837	5.2%	10,687	1.2%
Kitchen / Cooking	1,055	6.5%	7,416	0.9%
Medium Coarse	3,801	23.4%	62,782	7.3%
Pithos	1,348	8.3%	258,579	30.0%
Semi-fine	23	0.1%	273	0.03%
Tile	2,188	13.5%	247,470	28.7%
Totals	16,253	100.0%	862,910	100.0%

Table 5.7   Fabric groups of ceramic artifacts by broad and narrow period.

FABRIC	BROAD PERIODS		NARROW PERIODS	
	COUNT	%	COUNT	%
Amphora	295	3.5%	1,377	17.5%
Coarse	3,367	40.1%	1,962	25.0%
Fine	56	0.7%	781	9.9%
Kitchen / Cooking	351	4.2%	704	9.0%
Medium Coarse	2,907	34.6%	894	11.4%
Pithos	1,319	15.7%	29	0.4%
Semi-fine	13	0.2%	12	0.2%
Tile	91	1.1%	2,098	26.7%
	8,399	100.0%	7,857	100.0%

Table 5.8   Relative percentages of fabric groups for broad and narrow periods.

FABRIC	BROAD PERIODS		NARROW PERIODS		TOTAL
	COUNT	%	COUNT	%	
Amphora	295	17.6%	1,377	82.4%	1,672
Coarse	3,367	63.2%	1,962	36.8%	5,330
Fine	56	6.7%	781	93.3%	837
Kitchen / Cooking	351	33.3%	704	66.7%	1,055
Medium Coarse	2,907	76.5%	894	23.5%	3,802
Pithos	1,319	97.9%	29	2.2%	1,349
Semi-fine	13	52.0%	12	48.0%	26
Tile	91	4.2%	2,098	95.8%	2,189

count, comprising 33% and 23%, respectively, of ceramic objects. Fragments of pithoi, amphora, tile, kitchen ware, and fine ware individually comprise, by count, 5–14% of the ceramic assemblage. Examining weight instead of count drastically changes these relative proportions, because some ceramic objects, such as tile, pithos, and coarse, come from larger vessels with thicker walls and heavier fabrics than others (e.g., cooking and fine) (Table 5.6).

Homogeneity in fabric group is significant because it directly relates to chronological patterns (Section 5.1.1). Considering relative proportions of fabric groups for the broad periods of 1,000 years or more, coarse and medium-coarse wares dominate, comprising 40% and 35% of the total quantity of artifacts datable to broad periods. Pithoi (n=1,319; 16%), kitchen wares (n=351; 4%), and amphorae (n=295; 4%) represent smaller relative percentages of artifacts datable to broad periods, and tile (n=91; 1%), semi-fine ware (n=13; .2%), and fine ware (n=56; .7%) are relatively sparse. Unsurprisingly, the three most common broad-period fabric groups — coarse, medium-coarse, and pithoi — are the least diagnostic, and the most diagnostic groups (semi-fine and fine wares, kitchen wares, and amphorae) collectively represent less than 10% of broad-period artifacts.

In contrast, artifacts dated to narrow periods tend to come from a variety of fabric groups. The most diagnostic artifact classes, such as fine ware (10%), amphorae (18%), and kitchen wares (9%)

Table 5.9   Fabric groups ordered from most diagnostic to least diagnostic.

Fabric Group	Weighted Average
Tile	498
Fine	524
Amphora	773
Kitchen	1,013
Coarse	1,150
Pithos	1,539
Medium Coarse	1,596
Semi-Fine	1,640
Unknown	5,508

account for over a third of pottery assigned to a narrow period (Table 5.7). Semi-fine ware and pithos are rare, but coarse, medium-coarse, and tile fragments comprise major components of narrow period artifacts. The relative proportions of the fabric groups are more even for narrow periods than for broad periods.

Examining the relative chronological precision of particular fabric groups, we assigned the vast majority of tile (96%), fine wares (93%), amphora (82%), and kitchen (67%) to dates of less than 1,000 years. The more precise chronology of these artifact classes reflects more robust typologies and the relatively limited duration of circulation of artifact types. In contrast, we could only date to broad periods most pithos fragments (98%), medium-coarse wares (77%), and coarse wares (63%) (Table 5.8). The reason for this is, in part, that coarse wares, medium-coarse wares, and pithos fragments represent utility type vessels that change more slowly over time, and in part that knowledge of typologies of these vessels is less developed.

A weighted analysis of the assemblage by fabric groups supports these observations about the uneven diagnosticity of the assemblage. Table 5.9 displays the "weighted average duration" for ceramic artifacts of each fabric group. We determined the "weighted average duration" by multiplying the sum of artifacts for each fabric group by the length in years of their associated period and averaging the different values. Three fabric groups consistently date to less than 1,000 years. Tile is the most diagnostic artifact in PKAP, because Late Roman tile types — with a duration of 449 years — dominate the tile group. We were able to identify Late Roman tile types because tiles at Koutsopetria are comparable to those from the excavated site of Kopetra. The average piece of fine ware and amphora dates to 524 and 773 years, respectively; rims and feature sherds allow for much more precise identifications for these groups, but these are much less common than body sherds in fine and amphora fabrics. Fabric groups with middling diagnostic character include kitchen wares and coarse wares, which usually can be dated to about 1,000 years on average. Pithos, medium-coarse, semi-fine, and unknown artifacts are especially coarse in their dates on average.

The important point in these patterns is that the vast majority of material in the landscape cannot be assigned to temporal ranges useful for historical analysis. Most material (56% by count) discovered through survey is medium-coarse ware and coarse ware, which are not dated more precisely than 1,000 years and have an average duration of 1,100–1,600 years. More diagnostic artifacts like amphorae, fine wares, and kitchen wares represent less than a quarter of all pottery, and even these are usually less chronologically precise than 500–1,000 years. Most of our surface assemblage is blunt and coarse: diagnostic artifacts datable to a century or two are akin to needles in haystacks (Bintliff and Howard 1999).

These observations also bear important ramifications for understanding functional uses of the landscape. Fabric groups point to specific functions, but we cannot evenly assign different fabric groups to narrow periods. This is significant because most of our pottery — medium-coarse and coarse wares — were used at specific points of time, but are datable only to broad periods. That these utility wares are absent from our narrow period assemblages suggests that our analysis of the landscape in terms of function for particular narrow periods is necessarily incomplete and coarse. The uneven chronological distribution of fabric types exerts an important influence on the kinds of functional landscapes that we can construct across the micro-region.

For drawing conclusions about narrow periods, we have a wider array of fabric groups, but the most precisely diagnostic artifacts — tiles, fine wares, amphorae, and kitchen wares — still tend to have broad dates. Examining the rare feature sherds of each of these classes allows greater precision, but there are risks of relying on exceptional artifacts to reconstruct the landscape. These fabric groups encourage focusing on specific activities in the landscape, such as domestic activities, religious rituals, food preparation, and trade. Equally problematic are fine wares and amphorae that tend to reflect patterns of imports and trade, which were always variable in time. The variations of supply and demand in antiquity mean that it is risky to rely upon any single fabric group or chronotype to discuss the functional use of the landscape

through time. All fabric groups datable to narrow periods must together contribute to our picture of human activity in the area. We can partly overcome the bluntness of our data by examining the general patterns across the entire large site, and remaining wary of drawing significance from the absence of a particular artifact type.

5.1.3. Extant Part

An analysis of the extant part of the pottery reveals additional information about the way our sampling strategy intersected with the chronotype identifiers (note that this analysis examines only pottery and excludes tiles). Each batch of pottery in a unit consists of an extant part like base (b), rim (r), handle (h), neck (n), or bodysherd (s). Across the entire survey area, body sherds comprise 77% of all collected ceramic artifacts, handles 12%, rims 8%, bases 3%, and neck or other pieces less than 1% (Table 5.10).

These proportions contribute to our understandings of chronology (cf. 5.1.1). Some 50% of all pottery (n=6,966) collected were body sherds assigned to broad periods of 1,000 years or more, and some 65% of all body sherds belong to chronotypes spanning over 1,000 years. In contrast, we assigned the majority of rims, handles, and bases to chronotypes with narrower periods. Even in narrow periods, however, body sherds accounted for the majority 66% (n=3,768) of artifacts (Table 5.11). The preponderance of body sherds in the survey assemblage demonstrates that our fieldwalkers collected artifacts in accordance with the chronotype system and did not collect simply the most diagnostic parts of vessels (i.e., rims, bases, handles).

We can now turn to the differential visibility of the chronological periods to determine how our sampling strategy represents the fabric groups and extant parts actually visible in the landscape.

5.1.4. Differential Visibility

Differential visibility refers to the variation in visibility among archaeological periods; certain periods are more or less visible than others, both on the surface of the ground and in the assemblage of collected artifacts (Pettegrew 2007). Some eras

Table 5.10 Quantities and relative percentages by extant part.

EXTANT PART	SUM	%
Rim	1,056	7.6%
Base	463	3.3%
Handle	1,678	12.0%
Neck / Shoulder	34	0.2%
Body Sherd	10,735	76.8%
Other	9	0.1%
Total	13,975	100.0%

Table 5.11 Relative percentages of broad and narrow periods by extant part.

PART	BROAD	%	NARROW	%	TOTAL
Rim	441	41.8%	615	58.2%	1,056
Base	160	34.6%	302	65.4%	462
Handle	673	40.1%	1,004	59.9%	1,677
Neck	12	35.3%	22	64.7%	34
Body	6,966	64.9%	3,768	35.1%	10,734
Other	4	44.4%	5	55.6%	9

are highly visible because strong trade networks, supply patterns, or greater demand of goods resulted in the circulation of large quantities of artifacts identified by the place of production (e.g., African Red Slip or Palestinian Amphora). Other periods produced artifacts that were supplied in low volume, were hand-made, and survived poorly in the archaeological record (Bintliff et al. 1999). Periods are also differentially visible because their associated artifacts are either highly recognizable through physical attributes like surface treatment or slips, or are difficult to recognize because they appear non-distinct.

Differential visibility presents a major problem for artifact-level survey, because coarse, non-distinct utilitarian potsherds—the majority of artifacts visible—are not precisely datable from appearance. Whereas, in excavation, a ceramicist might date medium-coarse red body sherds to the Hellenistic period via association with Hellenistic

strata (dated, in turn, by highly diagnostic rims, inscriptions, or coins), surveyors have no basis for connecting poorly diagnostic coarse material to specific points in time. As some periods produce coarse material more identifiable by fabric and surface treatments than others, the differential visibility of survey assemblages poses interpretive problems. Unless surveyors understand how differential visibility has shaped the relative (in)visibility of different periods, their interpretations of continuity and change in the landscape must remain tentative.

Fortunately, it is not difficult to examine the differential visibility of the various periods present in our assemblage by patterning the fabric groups, extant parts, and particular chronotypes present. Such information allows analysts to determine what kind of artifacts in particular have made each period visible and to assess how accurately the visible (identified) sample represents the total population of artifacts on the surface that date to that period. Excavated contexts, when available, can help shed light on typical assemblages for particular contexts and periods. In the following discussion, we compare the relative proportions of fabric group, extant parts, and chronotypes for different periods. For this discussion of fabric groups and extant parts, we consider only the pottery and leave aside the tile and non-ceramic artifacts.

Examining the relative percentages of fabric groups for our narrow periods shows that very few periods display the full variety of fabric groups (Table 5.12; note that tiles and terracotta artifacts are excluded). As a whole, the pottery of narrow periods consists of a range of coarse wares (50%, n=2,851) and amphorae (24%, n=1,377), as well as fine wares (14%, n=791) and kitchen wares (12%, n=704); pithoi dated to narrow periods are rare (0.5%, n=29). In comparison, broad periods tend to comprise a much higher percentages of coarse wares (76%, n=6,274) and pithos sherds (16%, n=1,319), and much lower percentages of amphorae (4%, n=295), kitchen wares (4%, n=351), and fine wares (1%, n=66). As we showed in our discussion of hoovered units (Chapter 3; cf. Tables 3.2 and 3.10), more intensive examination of the surface of the Koutsopetria plain actually suggests the differences should be greater: the hoovered

Table 5.12   Relative percentages of fabric groups for narrow periods.

PERIOD	COARSE	%	MED COARSE	%	PITHOS	%	AMPH	%	KITCHEN	%	FINE	%
Archaic	6	22.2%	8	29.6%							13	48.1%
Archaic–Classical									3	100.0%		
Archaic–Hellenistic	38	100.0%										
Classical									1	6.7%	14	93.3%
Classical–Hellenistic	2	9.1%	2	9.1%			10	45.5%	1	4.5%	7	31.8%
Geometric	7	41.2%	1	5.9%	1	5.9%	1	5.9%			7	41.2%
Hellenistic			1	0.8%					9	7.6%	108	91.5%
Hellenistic–Early Roman	14	6.7%	28	13.5%			51	24.5%	72	34.6%	43	20.7%
Iron Age	194	42.6%	180	39.6%	14	3.1%	34	7.5%	2	0.4%	31	6.8%
Late Cypriot			1	16.7%							5	83.3%
Late Cypriot II											19	100.0%
Late Cypriot II–Late Cypriot III			173	100.0%								
Late Medieval–Ottoman											1	100.0%
Medieval	6	75.0%									2	25.0%
Medieval, Early	3	100.0%										
Medieval, Late			1	6.3%							15	93.8%
Medieval–Modern	19	19.4%	76	77.6%					1	1.0%	2	2.0%
Modern	11	30.6%	6	16.7%							19	52.8%
Modern, Early			1	50.0%					1	50.0%		
Modern, Present	1	10.0%	1	10.0%					3	30.0%	5	50.0%
Ottoman											13	100.0%
Roman	136	11.0%	221	17.9%	17	1.4%	282	22.8%	475	38.4%	105	8.5%
Roman, Early	4	2.8%					21	14.8%	23	16.2%	94	66.2%
Roman, Late	1328	43.2%	367	11.9%	11	0.4%	979	31.8%	113	3.7%	278	9.0%

assemblages consist of mainly coarse sherds (88% in 2004, 85% in 2010) and very small percentages of fine ware (5% in 2004, 12% in 2010) and kitchen ware (7% in 2004, 3% in 2010).

The analysis shown in Table 5.12 is most interesting, however, in highlighting our particular biases toward certain fabric groups for specific periods.

Our knowledge of the Late Cypriot Bronze Age, for example, derives entirely from medium-coarse sherds and fine wares. Cypro-Geometric and Iron Age pottery consists mainly of coarse potsherds and fine wares and, to a lesser extent, amphorae; medium-coarse, pithos, and kitchen wares are absent. Cypro-Archaic to Cypro-Classical material consists of fine ware and, to a lesser extent, coarse and medium-coarse ware, but kitchen ware is rare, and pithoi and amphorae absent. The broader Cypro-Archaic to Hellenistic periods and Cypro-Classical to Hellenistic periods include many more examples of coarse sherds and amphorae and a few fragments of kitchen ware. Our knowledge of the Hellenistic period derives almost entirely from fine ware and, to a lesser extent, kitchen ware. The slightly broader Hellenistic–Early Roman period, however, includes more coarse sherds, amphora fragments, and kitchen wares. In the Roman period, the assemblages show greater balance of fabric groups in general, but major imbalance remains between the fabrics present in Early Roman and Late Roman. Our knowledge of the Medieval and Ottoman periods derives entirely from fine-ware sherds and a few coarse-ware fragments. The Modern periods show a greater balance of coarse, medium-coarse, kitchen, and fine wares.

We can also summarize the same data according to the individual fabric groups. For narrow periods, sherds of coarse and medium-coarse ware together assume dominant components of the period percentages for the Late Cypriot, Iron Age, Cypro-Archaic, Cypro-Archaic to Hellenistic (broad), Late Roman, Medieval (broad), Early Medieval, and Medieval–Modern. In contrast, these fabric groups are poorly represented for the Cypro-Classical, Hellenistic, Early Roman, Roman (broad), Late Medieval, Ottoman, and Modern Present. Pithos fragments show up in small relative percentages only for the Cypro-Geometric, Roman, and Late Roman periods. Amphora percentages are substantial for the Cypro-Classical to Hellenistic, Hellenistic–Early Roman, and the various Roman periods. Kitchen wares usually appear in trace amounts, with the exception of the Cypro-Archaic to Classical, Hellenistic–Early Roman, Roman, and Modern periods, where they form a major component of the assemblages. Fine wares are the most common fabric group for the narrow periods and assume a greater share of the overall assemblage of the period than they should.

An analysis of extant parts also highlights biases toward particular classes. Experiments in hoovering in 2004 and 2010 on the Koutsopetria plain showed that rims usually assumed 3–5% of the surface assemblage, bases 1–2%, handles 4%, bodysherds 89–92%, and other parts less than 1% (Chapter 3). Generally, broad period artifacts showed percentages relatively close to the figures from the experiments: rims formed 5% of the broad period assemblage (n=441), bases 2% (n=160), handles 8%, sherds 84%, and other artifacts 0.2%. In contrast, the narrow period assemblage showed relatively greater percentages of rims (11%, n=615), bases (5%, n=302), and handles (18%, 1,004) and lower relative percentage of sherds (66%, n=3,768); other parts remained minor (0.5%). Our identification of artifacts to narrow periods, then, depended especially on feature sherds like rims, handles, and, to a lesser extent, bases.

Table 5.13 highlights how extant parts influenced the identification of particular periods from pottery classes (tiles and terracotta artifacts were excluded). Certain periods, like Cypro-Archaic to Cypro-Classical, Cypro-Archaic to Hellenistic, and Iron Age–Classical were dependent entirely on one part of the vessel, handles. While many of the other periods showed a more even distribution of extant parts, body sherds were generally underrepresented in comparison with material actually on the ground. In 10 of the 25 periods, for example, body sherds formed 50% or less of the pottery. Only in three periods (Late Cypriot, Early Medieval, and Late Medieval–Ottoman) did body sherds assume relative proportions that should reflect percentages (>85%) of body sherds actually present on the ground. In short, we were able to identify body sherds for most narrow periods, but their low relative percentages underrepresent their actual presence on the surface.

A final way of understanding the differential visibility of our identified ceramic data is to examine the specific artifact types that led to the recognition of the period during analysis. Table 5.14 shows the number of chronotypes identified to each of the narrow periods as well as the names of the chronotypes. More than half (n=14 of 26) of the narrow periods produced five or fewer unique chronotypes; nearly a third (n=8 of 26) of the narrow periods produced 6–10 chronotypes; and only four periods produced a substantial quantity of unique chronotypes (>10). Our knowledge of the Roman and Modern periods is strongest

Table 5.13   Relative percentages of extant parts for narrow periods.

Period	R	%	B	%	H	%	S	%	O	%	Total
Archaic	4	14.80%	3	11.10%	3	12.00%	17	63.00%			27
Archaic-Classical					3	100.00%					3
Archaic-Hellenistic					38	100.00%					38
Classical	2	13.30%	2	13.30%	5	33.30%	6	40.00%			15
Classical-Hellenistic	3	11.50%	5	19.20%	12	46.20%	6	23.10%			26
Geometric	2	11.80%	4	23.50%	2	11.80%	9	52.90%			17
Hellenistic	24	20.70%	22	19.00%	16	13.80%	54	46.60%			116
Hellenistic-Early Roman	19	9.10%	30	14.40%	44	21.20%	114	54.80%	1	0.50%	208
Iron Age	29	6.40%	33	7.30%	50	11.00%	343	75.40%			455
Late Cypriot					3	50.00%	3	50.00%			6
Late Cypriot II	4	21.10%					14	73.70%	1	5.30%	19
Late Cypriot II–III	3	1.70%	1	0.60%	9	5.20%	160	92.50%			173
Late Medieval-Ottoman							1	100.00%			1
Medieval	1	12.50%			2	25.00%	5	62.50%			8
Medieval, Early							3	100.00%			3
Medieval, Late	1	6.30%	6	37.50%			9	56.30%			16
Medieval-Modern	30	30.60%	3	3.10%	4	4.10%	60	61.20%	1	1.00%	98
Modern	13	36.10%	3	8.30%			20	55.60%			36
Modern, Early	1	50.00%					1	50.00%			2
Modern, Present	1	10.00%	2	20.00%			7	70.00%			10
Ottoman	7	53.80%					6	46.20%			13
Roman	116	9.40%	77	6.20%	155	12.60%	872	70.70%	13	1.10%	1,233
Roman, Early	30	21.30%	14	9.90%	32	22.70%	65	46.10%			141
Roman, Late	325	10.70%	97	3.20%	625	20.50%	1,990	65.30%	11	0.40%	3,048

in terms of diversity of chronotypes; the Late Roman assemblage is the most diverse. The Iron Age, Cypro-Geometric, Cypro-Archaic, Cypro-Classical, and Hellenistic periods are less diverse in terms of the number of chronotypes, but at least produced 5 artifact types. Our weakest narrow periods, which depend on only a few unique chronotypes, fall within the span of the Bronze Age and the Medieval period.

In sum, our knowledge of the Medieval period in PKAP is most concerning, and our knowledge of Roman period, especially Late Roman, most reliable. This trend, however, is consistent with the typologies available for the Late Roman and Medieval periods in the Mediterranean more broadly (Gabrieli, Jackson, and Kaldeli 2007: 791–92). Iron Age and Hellenistic ceramics tend to be partly visible. Some specific narrow periods (Protogeometric–Hellenistic, Cypro-Archaic to Cypro-Classical, Cypro-Archaic to Hellenistic, Iron Age–Classical, Early Medieval, Medieval, and Ottoman) are visible only via one or two artifact types. Generally, body sherds should assume higher relative percentages than they do, rims and handles lower relative percentages. Fine ware sherds should not be quite as common as they appear in these assemblages, and kitchen ware and amphorae should be more visible. This detailed

Table 5.14   List of chronotypes according to narrow periods.

PERIOD	CHRONOTYPE COUNT	CHRONOTYPES
Archaic	4	Coarse Ware, Medium Coarse Ware, Fineware, Semi-fine Ware
Archaic–Classical	2	Kitchen Ware, Figurine
Archaic–Hellenistic	1	Basket Handle Storage Jar
Classical	4	Attic Black Glazed, Fineware, Kitchen Ware, Oinochoe
Classical–Hellenistic	9	Amphora, Corinthian Black Glazed, Medium Coarse Corinthian Black Glazed, Fineware, Coarse Ware, Medium Coarse Ware, Kitchen Ware, Lamp, Pebbly Pavement
Geometric	5	Amphora, Coarse Ware, Medium Coarse Ware White Painted, Fineware, Pithos
Hellenistic	5	Black Glazed, Fineware, Colour-Coated Fineware, Kitchen Ware, Medium Coarse Ware
Hellenistic–Early Roman	6	Amphora, Coarse Ware, Medium Coarse Ware, Fineware, Kitchen Ware, Lamp
Iron Age	8	Amphora, Coarse Ware, Medium Coarse Ware, Medium Coarse Plain White Ware, White Painted Ware, Kitchen Ware, Fineware, Pithos
Late Cypriot	2	Wall Bracket, White Slip
Late Cypriot II	2	Mycenaean Fineware, White Slip II
Late Cypriot II–Late Cypriot III	1	Egyptian White Slip
Late Medieval–Ottoman	1	Slip-Painted Ware
Medieval	2	Coarse Ware, Fineware
Medieval, Early	1	Coarse Ware
Medieval, Late	9	Cypriot Glazed, Cypriot Glazed Group IV, Cypriot Glazed Group V, Cypriot Glazed Group IX, Cypriot Green Glazed, Fineware, Fineware Glazed, Incised Ware, Medium Coarse Ware
Medieval–Modern	10	Glass Vessel, Horseshoe, Coarse Ware, Cypriot W-1, W-3, W-5, W-6, W-7, Glazed Fineware, Kitchen Ware
Modern	19	Glass, Clear Glass Bottle, Green Glass Bottle, Modern Window Glass, Iron Nail, Metal, Building Materials, Bullet, Plastic, Coarse Ware, Fineware, Glazed Fineware, Ceramic Insulator, Medium Coarse Ware, Semi-fine Ware, Tile, Flat tile, Electrical Ceramic
Early Modern	3	Kitchen Ware, Medium Coarse Ware, Flat Tile
Modern, Present	10	Glass Vessel, Building Materials, Ceramic Floor/Wal Tile, Brick, Coarse Ware, Glazed Fineware, Fineware, Flowerpot, Modern Yoghurt Pot, Paving Stone
Ottoman	2	Fineware, Ottoman Drip Glaze
Protogeometric–Hellenistic	1	Terra Cotta, Architectural
Roman	11	Glass Vessel, ARS, Amphora, Pinched-Handle Amphora, Coarse Ware, Medium Coarse Ware, Fineware, Red Slip Fineware, Micaceous Water Jar, Pithos, Kitchen Ware
Roman, Early	13	Amphora, Koan-type Amphora, Pseudo-Koan Amphora, Rhodian Amphora, Fineware, Arretine Ware, Cypriot Sigillata, ESA, ESB, Red Slip, Semi-fine Ware, Coarse Ware, Kitchen Ware
Roman, Late	50	Amphora, Anemurium Type A Amphora, LR 1 Amphora, LR2 Amphora, Palestinian Amphora, Peacock and Williams 35; Basin, Basin with Piecrust Rim; Combed Ware, Narrow Combed Ware, Coarse Ware, Medium Coarse Ware; Fineware, Red Slip Fine Ware, ARS forms 61, 93, 99, 103-106, 104-106 (imitation), CRS forms 1, 2, 4, 7-12, 9 (imitation), Egyptian Red Slip, Phocaean Ware forms 2, 3, 10; Kitchen Ware, Palestinian Frying Pan Kitchen Ware; Lamp; Pithos; Tile, Kopetra Corinthian Cover Tile, Kopetra Corinthian Pan Tile; Cut Stopper, Circular Weight

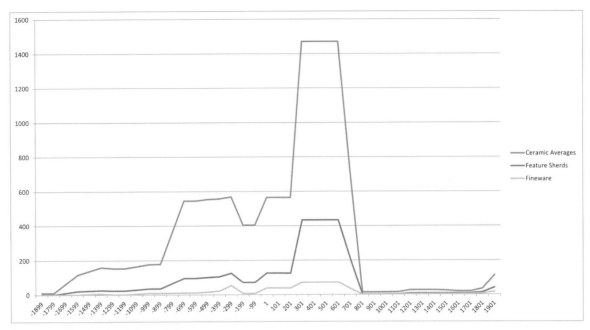

FIG. 5.1   *Results of aoristic analysis.*

analysis of the relative visibility of periods in our assemblage may appear to be a kind of archaeological navel gazing, but we will outline below (5.3) how this kind of source criticism has a specific, historical impact on understanding function and chronology within the micro-region.

5.1.5. Patterning Diversity through Aoristic Analysis

Despite the problems associated with identifying the function of large quantities of relatively non-diagnostic material, survey archaeologists have developed different ways to use broad period data to produce more nuanced analyses of chronology. Joanita Vroom and her colleagues have introduced an approach known as "horizontal stratigraphy," which aims to identify chronological associations in surface assemblages (Vroom 2003). Other scholars have recommended "aoristic analysis," which attempts to normalize through time the distribution of artifact types of varying chronological span (i.e., both broad and narrow period artifacts; Bevan et al. 2013). These more nuanced approaches to the complexity of artifact assemblages serve to counteract the problems inherent to drawing historical conclusions only from the most diagnostic artifacts.

In PKAP, we have dealt with the problem of chronology and time in artifact assemblages in two ways. As discussed above, we distinguished between broad periods and narrow periods in our analysis. Simply recognizing the incompleteness of our understanding serves as a control for the interpretive conclusions we draw. Secondly, we have conducted aoristic analysis (fig. 5.1). In this method, we weight the artifacts assigned to a particular period by the duration of the period. If an artifact has a date range of 1,000 years, for example, the artifact would have a 1/1000 (0.1%) chance to appear in any one of those specific years. We then multiply this factor by the number of artifacts present dating to that period. This allows us to group material from a single period into a series of notional depositional events that occurred at a particular point or duration over a particular time range. We can then combine all the periods (whether these are broad or narrow) that *could* date to a particular moment in time according to both the quantity of the material and the chance that the assemblage would appear in a particular duration. It is important to stress, that this is primarily a method for smoothing the various chronologies that exist simultaneously across our survey area and allowing us to aggregate these chronologies to consider the probability that a particular assemblage existed at a particular period. It allows us to read the few highly diagnostic artifacts datable to a century in conjunction with thousands of artifacts datable to 1,000 years or more.

Aoristic analysis attempts to provide a generalized assessment of time by assigning chronological weight to an artifact based on its possible date range. When applied to the entire PKAP study area, it presents a snap shot of the activity documented in the coastal zone of Pyla village. The chart (fig. 5.1) represents the limits of potential activity at the site in any given year and shows the weight of artifacts multiplied by the number of artifacts representing that period present in the entire survey assemblage.

The analysis shows interesting results. Looking at the line that displays overall "ceramic averages," we can see that gradual increase in activity beginning in the earliest years of the Cypriot Bronze Age (ca. 1,800 BC) quickens with the advent of the Late Cypriot period in ca. 1,650 BC. Our ability to identify specific Late Cypriot wares and date them precisely led to several gentle swells in the gradual increase in material datable to specific date ranges in the fifteenth century BC. However, the first large jump in the quantity of material occurred at the start of the Iron Age (900 BC). The prevalence of Ancient Historic material accounts for the steep increase in the potential quantities of pottery from 750 BC to 700 AD, as do the increasing quantities of material datable to narrower historical periods. The slight decline in the chart between 600 BC and 400 BC represents the absence of considerable quantities of material datable to the Cypro-Classical period. The single greatest leap comes around 100 AD, when the overwhelming quantity of "Roman" material from the plain of Koutsopetria caused a significant spike in the potential pottery from this date. Equally dramatic was the rapid decline in the quantity of potential pottery after AD 700. Between the fourteenth and twentieth centuries, there was a very small amount of potential material.

The lower two lines on the chart represent aoristic analysis based on feature sherds (rims, bases, handles) and fine wares, respectively. The analysis of feature sherds largely mirrors the ceramic averages trend; the quantity of material is diminished, of course, when we eliminate body sherds, but

the basic trends remain the same. On the other hand, when we base our analysis on the most common diagnostic artifacts across all periods (fine wares), the chronological trends across the micro-region appear different. The first peak in material appeared during the Hellenistic period, which is slightly later than in the overall ceramics trend. This change in the chronological position of the peak is a product of the diagnostic nature of Hellenistic fine wares, and the relatively smaller quantity of fine wares and material from the Iron Age and Cypro-Classical periods. The second peak coincides with the beginning of the Late Roman period for both lines and demonstrates that the material abundance during this period is not merely a product of highly diagnostic coarse wares (e.g. LR1 amphora handles) or tiles. Instead it should be understood both as the sign of abundance in its own right as well as the overlap of a number of less diagnostic assemblages, which may date to the Late Roman period.

5.2. THE DISTRIBUTIONAL PATTERN OF TOTAL ARTIFACT DENSITY: ZONES

In the process of survey, as well as during analysis, we divided the study area into five zones based on survey method, overall artifact density, and local topography (Section 2.2). In each zone, we employed a slightly different method for collecting data, and a zone-by-zone analysis provides a way to maintain control over our data, methodology, and the variability in the local landscape. This section, then, presents the analytical frameworks for each zone as a way to conceptualize the changing overall artifact counts and artifact densities. Designed to facilitate the diachronic analysis of activities across the entire survey area, the zones provide an archaeological short hand for describing areas of land use more extensive than the survey unit. These zones do not have absolute correlations with specific past human activities, but we maintain that there are empirical differences in the surface distributions between each zone that bear some relationship to the geographic and geological land form, as well as the past human activities in the landscape.

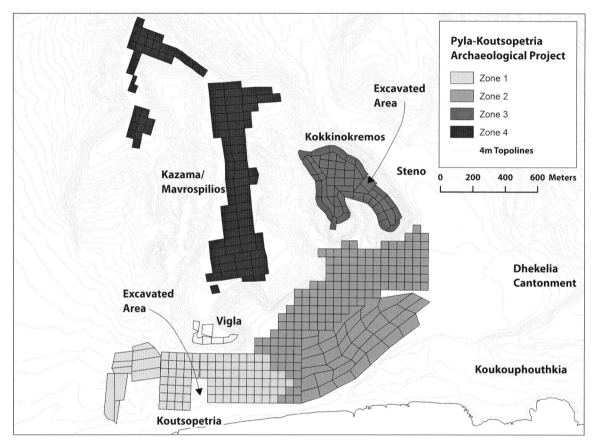

FIG. 5.2   *Map of PKAP zones.*

Table 5.15   General information related to five PKAP zones.

	ZONE 1	ZONE 2	ZONE 3	ZONE 4	VIGLA
Number of Units	100	192	58	109	6
Unit Size, in hectares (ave.)	1,976	2,218	1,804	2,344	1,984
Total Area, in hectares	20	43	10.5	25.5	1.2
Area Walked, in hectares	4	8.5	2.1	5.1	0.2
Visibility (ave.)	49%	74%	67%	60%	63%
Artifacts Counted per Unit (ave.)	157	98	119	65	596
Density per hectare (ave.)	4,773	2,726	3,417	1,215	15,606
Artifacts Collected per Unit (ave.)	58	18	46	35	179
Chronotype Count per Unit (ave.)	12	6	8	8	24
Batch Count per Unit (ave.)	27	10	14	15	76

Table 5.16 Relative distribution of broad period assemblages within zones.

Broad Periods	Zone 1	%	Zone 2	%	Zone 3	%	Zone 4	%	Vigla	%
Ancient	25	1.2%	5	0.3%	2	0.1%	1	0.1%		
Ancient Ceramic			1	0.1%	4	0.2%			1	0.2%
Ancient Historic	1,845	89.8%	1,639	90.9%	42	1.9%	2,120	96.2%	448	97.6%
Ancient Historic-Medieval			1	0.1%						
Ancient-Medieval	4	0.2%	1	0.1%	367	16.5%				
Bronze Age			4	0.2%	3	0.1%				
Bronze Age-Modern Present	47	2.3%	37	2.1%						
Ceramic Age	1	0.1%								
Classical-Roman	18	0.9%	11	0.6%			45	2.0%	5	1.1%
Hellenistic-Modern Present			1	0.1%						
Hellenistic-Roman									3	0.7%
Late Cypriot-Archaic					3	0.1%				
Late Cypriot-Hellenistic					1,782	80.2%				
Late Cypriot-Roman					7	0.3%				
Late Cypriot-Modern Present	3	0.1%	1	0.1%						
Post-Prehistoric	53	2.6%	15	0.8%						
Roman-Modern	2	0.1%	1	0.1%						
Unknown	57	2.7%	87	4.8%	12	0.5%	37	1.7%	2	0.4%
Broad Period Total	2,054	100.0%	1,804	100.0%	2,222	100.0%	2,203	100.0%	459	100.0%
Count of Broad Periods	10		13		9		4		5	

5.2.1. Zone 1

With the exception of the robust concentration of artifacts on the ridge of Vigla, the highest density area of the study area is Zone 1 (figs. 5.3–5.4). This zone consists of the units surrounding the excavated basilica and annex building on the Koutsopetria plain. We surveyed 90 of the 100 units of Zone 1 as 40 × 40 m squares, with areas of 1,600 m², while the other 10 units on the western border of Koutsopetria were larger (5,356 m²).

Of the approximately 20 ha marked out into units in Zone 1, we sampled 20% of the landscape, or 4 ha. The average visibility in these units was 49%. As a result, we actually saw a little less than 10% of the surface of the ground on average. Yet, our count of 157 artifacts per unit on average produced an average artifact density of 4,773 artifacts per ha, which is well above the density of Zones

2–4. We collected 58 artifacts from each unit on average, and our ceramicist divided this assemblage into 27 batches and 12 chronotypes per unit. Zone 1 produced the most artifacts and the most diverse assemblage per unit in the survey area.

Table 5.16 shows the relative proportions of broad periods within Zone 1, and indicates that the vast majority (90%) of material assigned to broad periods (>1000 years) dated to the Ancient Historic period. Among artifacts datable to less than 1000 years (Table 5.17), most diagnostic artifacts (96%) date to Roman times (broadly defined), and the Late Roman period, in particular, accounts for 86% of these artifacts. Apart from the Roman period, the Iron Age, Medieval, and Modern periods are all represented and represent a very small proportion (4%) of the narrow period artifacts. Most datable artifacts in Zone 1 are Late Roman or Roman.

Table 5.17   Relative distribution of narrow period assemblages within zones.

NARROW PERIODS	ZONE 1	%	ZONE 2	%	ZONE 3	%	ZONE 4	%	VIGLA	%
Archaic	2	0.1%	3	0.2%	21	5.5%	1	0.1%	1	0.2%
Archaic–Classical			3	0.2%			5	0.3%		
Archaic–Hellenistic	11	0.3%	2	0.1%			10	0.6%	15	2.4%
Classical	8	0.2%	2	0.1%			5	0.3%		
Classical–Hellenistic	6	0.2%	10	0.6%	1	0.3%	6	0.4%	4	0.7%
Geometric	2	0.1%	6	0.4%			9	0.6%		
Hellenistic	15	0.4%	23	1.5%	5	1.3%	51	3.2%	24	3.9%
Hellenistic–Early Roman	2	0.1%	6	0.4%	4	1.0%	60	3.7%	137	22.3%
Iron Age	1	0.03%	2	0.1%	2	0.5%	398	24.7%	54	8.8%
Late Cypriot					6	1.6%				
Late Cypriot II					16	4.2%			3	0.5%
Late Cypriot II–Late Cypriot III					173	45.4%				
Late Medieval–Ottoman			1	0.1%						
Medieval			3	0.2%	5	1.3%				
Medieval, Early	3	0.1%								
Medieval, Late	4	0.1%	12	0.8%						
Medieval-Modern	68	1.8%	25	1.6%	5	1.3%	2	0.1%		
Modern	26	0.7%	65	4.2%	11	2.9%	3	0.2%	1	0.2%
Modern, Early			3	0.2%						
Modern, Present	11	0.3%	13	0.8%			3	0.2%	1	0.2%
Ottoman	3	0.1%	3	0.2%			7	0.4%		
Protogeometric–Hellenistic	1	0.0%								
Roman	315	8.3%	160	10.3%	74	19.4%	545	33.8%	144	23.5%
Roman, Early	41	1.1%	32	2.1%	6	1.6%	36	2.2%	27	4.4%
Roman, Late	3,259	86.3%	1,182	76.1%	52	13.6%	470	29.2%	202	33.0%
Narrow Period Total	3,778	100.0%	1,554	100.0%	381	100.0%	1,611	100.0%	613	100.0%
Narrow Period Count	18		20		14		15		12	

5.2.2.   Zone 2

Zone 2 lies east of the first zone and marks the most extensive part of the survey area (42.6 ha) (figs. 5.5; 1.4). It includes 155 40 × 40 m grid squares (24.8 ha) with moderate to high artifact densities, and 37 larger survey units (ave. 4,805 m²; total 17.8 ha) over very low-density areas; average unit size for the zone was 2,218 m². We decided to group the higher-density units along the base of the coastal ridges and the lower density units of the infilled embayment, because these two areas are

topographically contiguous and the exact boundary between the areas is unclear. Moreover, we imagined that the entire area experienced similar formation processes related to the infilling of the low-lying lands along the coast and the subsequent smearing of artifacts through plowing of these fields.

Nonetheless, although our methods for recording artifact densities and collecting chronotype samples were the same in both kinds of units, and visibility was the best in the entire survey area (74%), these two different parts of the zone pro-

FIG. 5.3   *Photo of Zone 1, from Vigla facing southeast.*

FIG. 5.4   *Aerial photo of Zone 1, from the south. Photo taken June 11, 2007, courtesy of 84 Sqd. RAF Akrotiri.*

FIG. 5.5   *Aerial photo of Zone 1 and western end of Zone 2, from east. Photo taken June 11, 2007, courtesy of 84 Sqd. RAF Akrotiri.*

duced very different densities. In the larger units to the south, we collected only 212 total artifacts, representing on average less than 1 chronotype and batch per unit; our counts suggested densities of 866 artifacts per ha. In contrast, to the north, the total artifact counts in the grid squares suggested densities of 3,169 artifacts per ha; the artifacts collected from these units averaged 7.1 chronotypes and 12.5 batches per unit.

These differences are important to keep in mind when considering the overall figures for density and diversity (Table 5.15). At a glance, Zone 2 has the second-lowest artifact density in the survey area and the least diverse assemblage: the average number of collected artifacts, chronotypes, and batches was lower in this zone than anywhere else in the survey area. This pattern, however, is in part a result of numerous low-density units in the southern part of the zone that brought down the overall averages. In fact, in 29 units in Zone 2 — some 15% of the number of units in the zone — we collected no artifacts at all; in contrast, only two

units in Zone 1, one unit in Zone 3, and two units in Zone 4 produced no artifacts. Some units in the northern part of the zone produced assemblages as diverse as Zones 3 and 4, but across the entire zone the lower density and less diverse units to the south affected the average character of the zone. These patterns ultimately confirmed our geomorphological assessment that the southern half of the zone was an infilled embayment (Section 2.4) and the northern half perhaps marked a line of buildings, graves, or activity areas along a coastal road that ran east from the heart of the settlement of Koutsopetria.

In terms of chronology, the assemblage in Zone 2 bears a close resemblance to that in Zone 1, except there was slightly greater diversity. Most broadly dated artifacts were Ancient Historic, but there are 12 other broad periods represented among the assemblage. The assemblage of narrow period artifacts in Zone 2 is the most diverse in the survey area, with some 20 different chronotype periods represented. Some 89% of these artifacts dated

Fig. 5.6 *Detail photo of Zone 3.*

to the broad Roman period, especially the Late Roman era, but this figure is less than that in Zone 1 (96%). Of the non-Roman pottery, Medieval–Modern comprises the greatest proportion (we will discuss this at greater length in sections 5.3.6 and 5.3.7). The Hellenistic period forms 1.5% of the overall narrow period artifacts. The remaining material of narrow date consists of a very light scatter of Iron Age and Medieval material.

5.2.3. Zone 3

Zone 3 consists of the heart-shaped hill called Kokkinokremos and is the smallest zone surveyed apart from Vigla (figs. 5.6; 1.6). Three campaigns of excavation in the 1950s, the 1980s, and the last few years have uncovered the remains of a Late Bronze Age settlement. We surveyed around the excavated areas and the surrounding plateau and slopes with 58 units covering 10.5 ha of which we walked 2.1 ha (via a 20% sample). The units have an average visibility of 67% and an average density of 3,417 artifacts per ha. The units produced about

14 batches and 8 chronotypes per unit. Compared to Zone 1 and Vigla, this area produced lower artifact densities and a less diverse assemblage, but compared to Zones 2 and 4, this zone had higher densities and comparable diversity. In comparison with the survey area as a whole, the density and diversity of Zone 3 was about average.

The slightly lower than average number of chronotypes (in comparison with Zone 1) and higher than average artifact density (in comparison with Zones 2 and 4) reflect the unique chronological signature of this zone. The assemblage of broad period artifacts, for example, is dominated not by Ancient Historic periods, which comprise only 2% of the broad assemblage, but by the Late Cypriot–Hellenistic (80%) and Bronze Age (17%), especially. The more diagnostic artifacts of the narrow period assemblage suggest greater diversity of material than on the plain in Zone 2. Late Cypriot periods dominate and comprise 51% of the narrow-period artifacts, but Roman (34%), Cypro-Archaic (5.5%), Medieval–Modern (5.5%), and Hellenistic (1.3%) material exists in substantial proportions.

FIG. 5.7   *Detail photo of Zone 4.*

FIG. 5.8   *Aerial photo showing the Koutsopetria plain (bottom) and Vigla stretching into the Mavospilios Ridge to the Northeast above the water treatment plant. View from south. Photo taken June 11, 2007, courtesy of 84 Sqd. RAF Akrotiri.*

5.2.4. Zone 4

As the second largest zone, extending over 25.5 ha and 109 units, Zone 4 encompasses the fields stretching north of the height of Vigla along the top of the Mavrospilios ridgeline (figs. 5.7-5.8).

Overall, Zone 4 produced approximately 8 chronotypes and 15 batches per unit, which is directly comparable to the figures for the other ridgetop zone in our survey area (Zone 3, Kokkinokremos). In units with artifact densities over 1,000 artifacts per ha, these numbers increased, respectively, to 10 chronotypes and 20 batches per unit, suggesting that the higher density units in this zone show a greater diversity of material than units in Zones 2–4 as a whole (cf. Table 5.15).

As in Zone 2, there is some significant difference between the southern and northern parts. The highest-density units come from the area immediately north of the Vigla height and stretch along the southern edge of the coastal plateau (Units 1005–1019, 1488–1495). These units are characterized by high visibility, low vegetation, and recent plowing, and they produced a higher overall density (2,476 artifacts per ha) and average visibility (67%) than the rest of the zone (visibility was 60% for the entire zone, with 1,215 artifacts per ha). Nonetheless, despite this distinction, the average density figure for the entire zone is the lowest in the survey area, and even the high-density southern part of this zone has lower average density than Zones 1 to 3.

Units in the far northern part of the Kazama ridge (Units 1450–1487) exhibited several environmental variables that likely influenced the sampling of the surface. First, many of the fields in the northern third of the Kazama plateau were either fallow or uncultivated. Some of these units featured knee-high or even waist-high vegetation that made fieldwalking more difficult and yielded lower visibilities. There was also some evidence for scraping or bulldozing in the western units of this zone, where the top layer of bedrock had been broken up. The chipped bedrock mixed with the soil to produce fragments of similar size and color to pottery, which created a certain amount of "background disturbance" that some recent stud-

ies have suggested can make it significantly more difficult to consistently identify pottery (Schon 2002). These two factors in combination may in part contribute to the lower than average densities. Despite a high average surface visibility (76%), the units in the northwestern part of Zone 4 had a mean artifact density of only 293 artifacts per ha.

Nonetheless, the narrow and broad period data for Zone 4 show significant differences from Zones 1–3 that indicate less intensive uses of the land over time. Generally, broad period material is much more homogeneous. Some 98% of the artifacts could be dated to sometime between the start of the Cypro-Geometric and the end of the Roman era; the prehistoric, Medieval, and Modern components are virtually non-existent. Of narrower periods, 65% dates to the broad Roman era, a figure significantly lower than Zones 1 and 2 but higher than Zone 3; the greater proportion of Roman (chronotype) over Late Roman reflects the utilitarian nature of this assemblage and the dominance of coarse wares. What is quite different is that 27% of narrow period material dates to the Iron Age and 7% to the Hellenistic–Early Roman. Only the Vigla ridge has more Hellenistic material, but no area has more Iron Age.

5.2.5. Vigla

As noted in Chapter 2, the height of Vigla and its immediately surrounding slopes were not included in the four main zones of the survey territory (figs. 5.9–5.10). We held this area separate for two reasons. First, several seasons of fieldwalking at Vigla produced artifact densities between 10,000 and 16,000 artifacts per ha. This was not only exceptional compared to adjacent fields to the northeast and south, but even compared to the entire survey area in general. The assemblages of the six Vigla units were also exceedingly diverse, with an average of 76 batches and 24 chronotypes, figures two to three times greater than Zone 1. The remarkable density of this area, the diversity of the material, and the topographic isolation led us to isolate this area as a single zone. Average visibility was 63%.

Second, the six units (1.2 ha) on Vigla represent a spatially and topographically discrete area separated from both the units in Zone 4 that extend

FIG. 5.9   *Detail photo of Vigla.*

FIG. 5.10   *Aerial photo of Vigla. Photo taken June 11, 2007, courtesy of 84 Sqd. RAF Akrotiri.*

north across the plateau and the units of Zone 1 on the coastal plain below. A rock cut *taphros* or dry moat marks the barrier between Zone 4 and Vigla, and we were unable to survey the area between the dry moat and Zone 4 because of several overgrown fields and bee-hives. To the south, east, and west, the steep slopes of Vigla mark the limits of the area and separate it from the coastal plain. Moreover, a fortification wall from the Hellenistic period enclosed this ridge as a distinct acropolis. Despite this separation, there are important connections between Vigla, the Mavrospilios ridge, and the coastal plain, as we will discuss below.

Vigla most closely resembles Zone 4 in its chronological attributes. The broad period assemblage is especially homogeneous, as Ancient Historic represents 98% of the broad period assemblage. Of narrow periods, Roman artifacts dominate on Vigla and comprise 61% of the assemblage; unlike Zone 1 below, this is not mainly Late Roman material, as the Roman (chronotype) period represents half of it. Iron Age and Hellenistic–Early Roman pottery together forms the remaining 38% of the narrow period artifacts on Vigla; Bronze Age and Modern material exist in singular instances.

While there is clearly Iron Age material on Vigla, most of the periods that overlap with the Hellenistic should date to this era, since ten excavation trenches have revealed a major occupation of the late fourth to third century BC (Olson et al. 2013; Caraher et al. 2014). The dominance of the Roman period at Vigla is interesting in this respect, because excavation has revealed no definitive Roman phases on the ridge. The Roman use of Vigla, then, must have been localized.

5.3. PERIOD-BASED ANALYSIS

In the third section of this chapter, we examine the distribution and character of the material dated to narrow periods across the four zones of the study area. Each chronological section will consider 1) the assemblage of each period and the types of artifact present, including a reflective "source criticism" of the processes and methods used to produce the assemblage, 2) the distribution of material across the zone, including the presence of discrete con-

centrations, and 3) a summary interpretation of the distributions and discrete assemblages of material. Finally, whenever possible, the text is keyed to specific objects that have been read or catalogued. Catalogued objects appear in **bold**, and catalogued objects that appear in chapter four will be underlined in **bold**.

Throughout this section, we have sought to group material into interpretatively meaningful categories. Unlike projects that begin with conceptual units like sites to aid in the organization of space and time, artifact-level survey builds the site from the ground up via the building blocks of survey units containing individual chronotypes and their functional and chronological properties. This process of creating interpretable assemblages requires a flexible approach, since in some cases chronotype periods represent only single classes of artifacts and in other cases robust assemblages of material. To produce a historically meaningful landscape from the chronotypes collected from the survey units, we have grouped chronotypes and periods together to create assemblages sufficiently robust to sustain an interpretation of space in human terms.

In some cases, such as our interpretation of Cypro-Geometric to Cypro-Classical material, we combine overlapping chronotype periods within a broad period to create a more robust and easily understood assemblage of material. The reader should note that we use some chronological period designations (e.g., "Bronze Age," "Iron Age," and "Roman") to refer to both chronotype periods adopted at the time of analysis and inclusive periods created specifically for the following analysis. As one example, our ceramicist identified some pottery as "Iron Age" at the time of analysis, and other pottery as "Cypro-Geometric," "Cypro-Archaic," and "Cypro-Classical." All of these periods are technically included as part of the Iron Age, but represent narrower sub-periods. In the following discussion, we will make a distinction between *chronotype* and *inclusive* periods. When we discuss all the chronotype periods that collectively form the Iron Age period more broadly, we will use the term "Iron Age (Inclusive)." Otherwise, the reader should assume that a simple reference to "Iron Age" period refers to the chronotype period.

Table 5.18   Narrow chronotype periods in the Koutsopetria region.

Period	Unit Count	Area (hectare)	Quantity	Weight (g)	Chronotype Count	Batch Count
Bronze Age (Inclusive)	50	9.6	205	7,444	7	44
Bronze Age (Chronotype)	5	1.2	7	37	2	3
Late Cypriot	5	0.8	6	292	2	6
Late Cypriot II	11	2.4	19	422	2	8
Late Cypriot II–Late Cypriot III	41	7.6	173	6,693	1	27
Iron Age (Inclusive)	79	18	523	13,708	23	96
Iron Age (Chronotype)	42	10.4	455	11,119	8	56
Geometric	8	1.7	17	900	5	11
Archaic	17	3.6	28	918	4	18
Archaic-Classical	4	0.6	8	186	2	4
Classical	8	1.6	15	585	4	7
Overlapping (Iron Age–Hellenistic)	41	9.2	66	11,702	11	25
Archaic–Hellenistic	25	6.1	38	9,485	1	7
Classical–Hellenistic	20	4.8	27	2,090	9	17
Protogeometric–Hellenistic	1	0.2	1	127	1	1
Hellenistic	64	16.1	118	1,095	5	38
Hellenistic	64	16.1	118	1,095	5	38
Hellenistic–Early Roman	44	10.4	209	8,613	6	49
Hellenistic–Early Roman	44	10.4	209	8,613	6	49
Roman (Inclusive)	381	80.1	6,545	388,033	74	448
Roman (Chronotype)	262	55.1	1,238	34,883	11	122
Roman, Early	74	16.4	142	2,889	13	52
Roman, Late	330	70.8	5,165	350,261	50	274
Medieval–Ottoman (Inclusive)	24	4.9	41	573	15	27
Medieval (Chronotype)	4	1.1	8	268	2	5
Early Medieval	1	0.2	3	33	1	1
Late Medieval	12	1.9	16	154	9	14
Late Medieval–Ottoman	1	0.2	1	6	1	1
Ottoman	6	1.5	13	112	2	6
Medieval–Modern	61	10.8	100	6,777	10	28
Medieval–Modern	61	10.8	100	6,777	10	28
Modern (Inclusive)	79	19.5	136	4,518	31	82
Modern (Chronotype)	64	16.1	105	3,120	18	57
Early Modern	3	1.2	3	66	3	3
Modern, Present	22	6.4	28	1,332	10	22

We begin with two tables that represent in visual terms the striking differential presence of the periods in the survey and their distribution in space. The first (Table 5.18) summarizes overall quantity and diversity of material according to the different narrow periods of the survey: the number of units and total area (distribution), the quantity and weight of pottery (quantity), and count of chronotypes and batches (diversity) for each period. The highlighted periods in the table mark broader, inclusive periods that include one or more individual chronotype periods. The quantity, weight, and batch count for the highlighted inclusive period are simply summaries of the individual chronotype periods. Bronze Age (Inclusive), for example, is simply a summary of Bronze Age (chronotype), Late Cypriot, Late Cypriot II, and Late Cypriot II–Late Cypriot III. The Unit Count and Area (ha), however, is less a simple summary than a maximum amount. Because Bronze Age (chronotype) and Late Cypriot pottery may be found in the same unit covering the same space, we only count that unit and space once for the unit count and area of the inclusive period fields. The second table displays the same data as Table 5.17, but instead of foregrounding the chronological character of each zone, it highlights the relative percentages of each narrow period *between* the zones (Table 5.19). In the following sections, we will refer to this tabulated data as we discuss the history of the landscape of the Koutsopetria region from prehistory to the modern day.

5.3.1. Bronze Age

ASSEMBLAGE: The association of Kokkinokremos with Bronze Age material, and especially Late Bronze Age material, is hardly surprising. Over three campaigns, the Department of Antiquities excavated a major Late Bronze Age site on the eastern half of the coastal height (Dikaios 1971; Karageorghis and Demas 1984; Brown 2012). While the work in the 1980s also included informal and unsystematic surveys of the materials on the hill (Karageorghis and Demas 1984), our survey marked the first systematic sampling of surface material on the height. In our work, we expected to discover an impressive assemblage of both local

and imported Bronze Age pottery at least in Zone 3, the coastal height of Kokkinokremos.

Artifacts dating specifically to the Cypriot Bronze Age (Inclusive) include 205 artifacts in 44 batches (4.7 artifacts per batch). These artifacts represent 7 distinct chronotypes, of which 4 are fine wares, 1 is coarse ware, 1 is medium-coarse ware, and 1 is a medium-coarse terracotta wall bracket. This diversity in types is the result of combining different narrow and broad chronotype periods of overlapping date ranges, but it is probable, given the dates of the most diagnostic artifacts, that all of these chronotypes were deposited in the Late Cypriot II–Late Cypriot III period (Karageorghis and Demas 1984). Taken collectively, the vast majority of the Bronze Age assemblage identified consists of Egyptian White Slip (EWS) medium-coarse body sherds (78% of the total assemblage of Bronze Age [Inclusive] material), along with a small but significant assemblage of Late Cypriot II Mycenaean Fine ware body sherds (6%). If body sherds of EWS were identifiable from fabric and slip, we also documented handles (4%), rims (1.5%), and bases (.5%) in small quantities; Mycenaean Fine ware appeared only as rims and a stem.

Our knowledge of the Cypriot Bronze Age in the Pyla region, then, derives entirely from medium-coarse and fine wares, and especially Egyptian White Slip body sherds; slipped surfaces and, to a lesser extent, painted surfaces aided in the identification of sherds of the Bronze Age. While the overall amount of Bronze Age material in the region is comparable to other periods in PKAP, the diversity of chronotypes is generally poor. Moreover, we did not identify the wide range of ceramic artifacts documented in Karageorghis and Demas' excavations at the site, including pithos fragments, plain coarse ware, and storage jars and jugs (Karageorghis and Demas 1984: 50–53). In part, this may have been a result of our own inability to discern Bronze Age identifications in non-stratified utilitarian fabrics, but it is also a result of our relatively small sample of the surface, which was only a small fraction of the material on the ground (cf. Chapter 3). The numerous fine ware and medium-coarse ware body sherds, however, provide confidence that we did identify a range of Bronze Age material *actually* on the ground, since

Table 5.19   Relative distribution of narrow period assemblages between zones.

NARROW PERIODS	ZONE 1	%	ZONE 2	%	ZONE 3	%	ZONE 4	%	VIGLA	%	TOTAL
Archaic	2	7.1%	3	10.7%	21	75.0%	1	3.6%	1	3.6%	28
Archaic–Classical			3	37.5%			5	62.5%			8
Archaic–Hellenistic	11	28.9%	2	5.3%			10	26.3%	15	39.5%	38
Classical	8	53.3%	2	13.3%			5	33.3%			15
Classical–Hellenistic	6	22.2%	10	37.0%	1	3.7%	6	22.2%	4	14.8%	27
Geometric	2	11.8%	6	35.3%			9	52.9%			17
Hellenistic	15	12.7%	23	19.5%	5	4.2%	51	43.2%	24	20.3%	118
Hellenistic–Early Roman	2	1.0%	6	2.9%	4	1.9%	60	28.7%	137	65.6%	209
Iron Age	1	0.2%			2	0.4%	398	87.5%	54	11.9%	455
Late Cypriot					6	100.0%					6
Late Cypriot II					16	84.2%			3	15.8%	19
Late Cypriot II–III					173	100.0%					173
Late Medieval–Ottoman			1	100.0%							1
Medieval			3	37.5%	5	62.5%					8
Medieval, Early	3	100.0%									3
Medieval, Late	4	25.0%	12	75.0%							16
Medieval–Modern	68	68.0%	25	25.0%	5	5.0%	2	2.0%			100
Modern	26	24.5%	65	61.3%	11	10.4%	3	2.8%	1	0.9%	106
Modern, Early			3	100.0%							3
Modern, Present	11	39.3%	13	46.4%			3	10.7%	1	3.6%	28
Ottoman	3	23.1%	3	23.1%			7	53.8%			13
Protogeometric–Hellenistic	1	100.0%									1
Roman	315	25.4%	160	12.9%	74	6.0%	545	44.0%	144	11.6%	1238
Roman, Early	41	28.9%	32	22.5%	6	4.2%	36	25.4%	27	19.0%	142
Roman, Late	3259	63.1%	1182	22.9%	52	1.0%	470	9.1%	202	3.9%	5165

we were not simply reliant on feature sherds (rims, bases, and handles).

Finally, it is worth noting that the vast majority of pottery (80%) found on Kokkinokremos dated to the broad chronotype period Late Cypriot-Hellenistic. We cannot be sure whether material of this period was produced in the Late Bronze Age, Iron Age, or Hellenistic era, but some of the "missing" sherds of Late Bronze Age date certainly form a component of this assemblage.

DISTRIBUTION: The 205 Bronze Age artifacts were found in 50 units covering 9.6 ha; most of the artifacts (97% of Bronze Age [Inclusive]) concentrated, unsurprisingly, in Zone 3, the coastal height of Kokkinokremos. Only four artifacts (2%) of broad Bronze Age (chronotype) date appear in Zone 2, but two of those are at the base of Kokkinokremos and probably derived from the ridge above. Only three Late Cypriot II sherds (1.5%) come from Vigla. The rest of the material datable to the Bronze

Table 5.20   Bronze Age periods in the PKAP area.

Material	Fabric	Chronotype	Part	Quantity	%	% Bronze Age (Inclusive)
Bronze Age (Chronotype) (2,500–1,000 bc)						
Pottery	Coarse	Coarse Ware, Bronze Age	body	1	14.3%	0.5%
Pottery	Fine	Fineware, Bronze Age	body	4	57.1%	2.0%
Pottery	Fine	Fineware, Bronze Age	handle	2	28.6%	1.0%
Total				7	100.0%	3.4%
Late Cypriot (1,650–1,050 bc)						
Pottery	Fine	White Slip, Late Cypriot	body	2	33.3%	1.0%
Pottery	Fine	White Slip, Late Cypriot	handle	3	50.0%	1.5%
Pottery	Med coarse	Wall Bracket, Late Cypriot	body	1	16.7%	0.5%
Total				6	100.0%	2.9%
Late Cypriot II (1,450–1,200 bc)						
Pottery	Fine	Fineware, Mycenaean, Late Cypriot II	body	12	63.2%	5.9%
Pottery	Fine	Fineware, Mycenaean, Late Cypriot II	rim	4	21.1%	2.0%
Pottery	Fine	Fineware, Mycenaean, Late Cypriot II	stem	1	5.3%	0.5%
Pottery	Fine	Fineware, White Slip II, Late Cypriot II	body	2	10.5%	1.0%
Total				19	100.0%	9.3%
Late Cypriot II–Late Cypriot III (1,450–1,050 bc)						
Pottery	Med coarse	Egyptian White Slip	base	1	0.6%	0.5%
Pottery	Med coarse	Egyptian White Slip	body	160	92.5%	78.4%
Pottery	Med coarse	Egyptian White Slip	handle	9	5.2%	4.4%
Pottery	Med coarse	Egyptian White Slip	rim	3	1.7%	1.5%
Total				173	100.0%	84.4%

Age (Inclusive) is evenly distributed across Zone 3 without any clear concentrations (figs. 5.11–5.12).

Other than the few pieces of broad Bronze Age date, most of the material on Kokkinokremos consists of wares of Late Cypriot, Late Cypriot II, and Late Cypriot II–Late Cypriot III date. There are pocketed concentrations of LCII–LCIII Egyptian White Slip on the eastern lobe of the heart-shaped hill, in the northern half of the ridge, and in the southern part of the western lobe. Recent cultivation on the hill makes it unlikely that the material from the hill has well-defined relationships with sub-surface features in general, but these pockets

of discrete material might represent architecture disturbed in recent years by the slow expansion of plowing (fig. 5.13).

The scatter of ceramic material coincides closely with a scatter of lithics that appeared in 34 (4.6 ha) of the 58 units in Zone 3 (59%) (fig. 5.14). Lithic artifacts cannot in most cases be dated to prehistoric periods exclusively, but their frequent association with survey units with Bronze Age material is suggestive. In general, lithic objects were more common on the slopes of the Kokkinokremos hill where visibility was slightly better. It may be that the small size of lithics (ave. 15

FIG. 5.11   *Western lobe of Kokkinokremos (view from north).*

FIG. 5.12   *Eastern lobe of Kokkinokremos with area of 1980s excavation in foreground (view from north).*

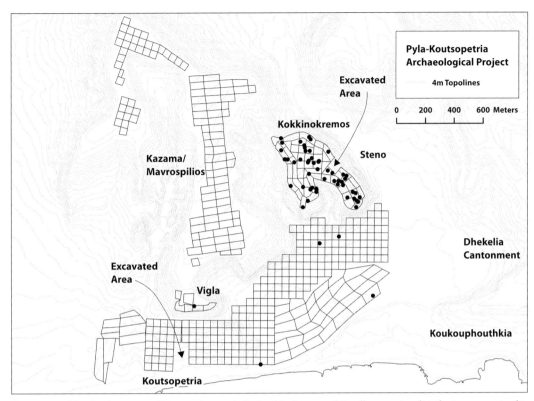

FIG. 5.13   *Distribution map of Bronze Age periods. In this figure and in all successive distribution maps in this chapter, 1 dot = 1 artifact.*

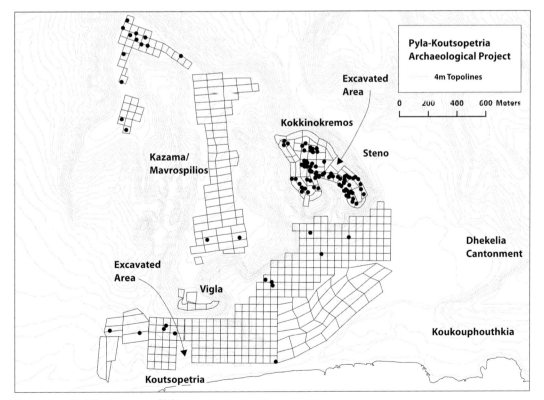

FIG. 5.14   *Distribution map of lithics.*

Table 5.21   Cypro-Geometric period in the PKAP area.

MATERIAL	FABRIC	CHRONOTYPE	PART	QUANTITY	%	% IRON AGE (INCLUSIVE)
Geometric (1,050–751 BC)						
Pottery	Amphora	Amphora, Geometric	handle	1	5.9%	0.2%
Pottery	Coarse	Coarse Ware, Geometric	base	2	11.8%	0.4%
Pottery	Coarse	Coarse Ware, Geometric	body	3	17.6%	0.6%
Pottery	Coarse	Coarse Ware, Geometric	handle	1	5.9%	0.2%
Pottery	Coarse	Coarse Ware, Geometric	rim	1	5.9%	0.2%
Pottery	Fine	Fineware, Geometric	base	1	5.9%	0.2%
Pottery	Fine	Fineware, Geometric	body	6	35.3%	1.1%
Pottery	Med coarse	Medium Coarse, White Painted	base	1	5.9%	0.2%
Pottery	Pithos	Pithos, Geometric	rim	1	5.9%	0.2%
Total				17	100.0%	3.3%

FIG. 5.15   *Southern end of Zone 4 showing area of Geometric settlement in Unit 1006 (view from east).*

g) relative to pottery (ave. 114 g) make lithics more difficult to spot in low-visibility fields (Bintliff, Howard, and Snodgrass 1999). Indeed, the distribution of lithics and Late Bronze Age material is almost exclusively concentrated on and around the imposing coastal height of Zone 3.

SUMMARY INTERPRETATION: Our identification of the Bronze Age settlement depended largely on earlier excavations, but this was confirmed by a half dozen type fossils, especially Egyptian White Slip and, to a lesser extent, Late Cypriot II Mycenaean Fine ware. The identification of body sherds for this period makes it relatively visible, despite its low diversity (chronotype count) and our inability to identify plain body sherds. Our sample indicates at least that Bronze Age material dates mainly to the Late Cypriot II–Late Cypriot III periods and is associated almost entirely with the Kokkinokremos ridge. Our survey there showed that settlement across that ridge was more extensive than previously documented.

5.3.2.   Cypriot Iron Age

Cypriot Iron Age (Inclusive) material consists of 523 sherds spread across 79 units and 18 ha (18% of the PKAP survey area). This broad period includes five chronotype periods: Iron Age (1,050–312 BC), Cypro-Geometric (1,050–751 BC), Cypro-Archaic (750–475 BC), Cypro-Archaic to Cypro-Classical (750–312 BC), and Cypro-Classical (474–312 BC). The first of these represents material dated to the Iron Age chronotype period during survey; we will refer to it simply as "Iron Age." The other periods represent narrower slices of the Iron Age. We will proceed chronologically in this section before turning to more broadly-dated Iron Age material.

5.3.2.1. Cypro-Geometric

ASSEMBLAGE: The earliest historical periods represented in the survey data are Cypro Geometric sherds. Pottery datable narrowly to the Cypro-Geometric period accounts for 17 sherds in 11 batches (1.5 artifacts per batch) and 5 chronotypes. These artifacts account for 3% of all artifacts assigned to the Iron Age period (Table 5.21).

The Cypro-Geometric sherds include five distinct fabric groups of which coarse and medium-coarse ware together form almost half (n=8 of 17). More than 50% of the Cypro-Geometric material were body sherds (n=9), 24% (n=4) were bases, and 12% rims (n=2) and handles (n=2). Such figures suggest that we identified a range of Cypro-Geometric material, but it is important to note that most of the body sherds (n=7 of 9) are decorated with paint. Our identification of pottery to the Cypro-Geometric period, then, almost entirely depended on either feature sherds (rims, bases, and handles) or decorated body sherds. This

indicates that much collected Cypro-Geometric material was identified to broader periods like "Iron Age," "Late Cypriot-Hellenistic," or "Ancient Historic." The Cypro-Geometric period in PKAP is largely an invisible period in our analysis.

DISTRIBUTION: Cypro-Geometric period artifacts were found in only 8 survey units covering an area of 1.7 ha, which are oriented mainly to the southern part of the Mavrospilios ridge (figs. 5.15–5.16). The densest concentration of material comes from nine artifacts in two units on the southern end of Zone 4 (1006 and 1011). While not adjacent, these units are relatively close, spaced only 100 m apart. Both yielded Cypro-Geometric coarse ware, and Unit 1006 produced a white painted stemmed bowl (1006.7) and several fragments of White Painted Late Geometric III storage vessels (1006.3, 1006.9). The other half of the Cypro-Geometric material is scattered along the base of the Vigla and Mavrospilios ridgeline in Zones 1 and 2, where 8 body sherds of painted fine and coarse ware were noted (**70.50**, **122.17**, 148.13, and 173.6–8).

From the presence of artifacts at the base of the ridge, one could imagine Cypro-Geometric tombs cut into the face of the coastal ridge that have subsequently eroded out, but a survey of this slope found no evidence for such. On the ridge itself, the concentration of artifacts in Unit 1006, a unit probably associated with a later sanctuary or shrine (Section 5.3.2.3), could also suggest religious function. At the least, the distribution of material on the southern part of the ridge and the coastal swath below suggest the remains of the earliest historical settlement in the area.

SUMMARY INTERPRETATION: Our reliance on feature sherds and decorated body sherds to identify the Cypro-Geometric period means that our recognition of Cypro-Geometric land use in the survey area is very incomplete. The fragmentary evidence present, however, suggests that human activity and habitation during the earliest historic periods focused on the southern part of the Mavrospilios and Vigla ridges and at the base of the ridge in Zones 1 and 2.

The Cypro-Geometric period represents only a faintly visible period in the Pyla survey region,

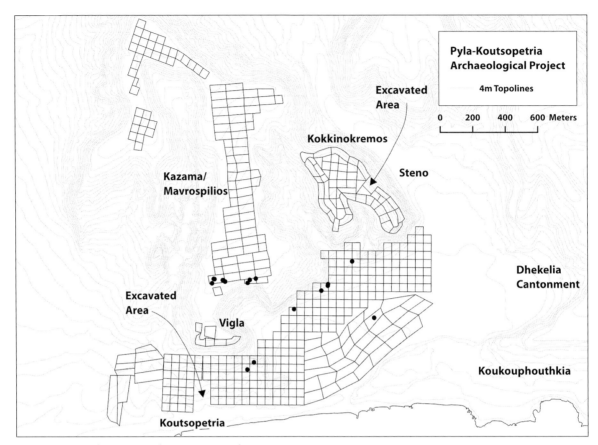

FIG. 5.16 *Distribution map of Geometric period.*

Table 5.22   Cypro-Archaic period in the PKAP area.

MATERIAL	FABRIC	CHRONOTYPE	PART	QUANTITY	%	% IRON AGE (INCLUSIVE)
Archaic (750–475 BC)						
Pottery	Coarse	Coarse Ware, Archaic	body	4	14.3%	0.8%
Pottery	Coarse	Coarse Ware, Archaic	handle	2	7.1%	0.4%
Pottery	Coarse	Coarse Ware, Archaic	rim	1	3.6%	0.2%
Pottery	Fine	Fineware, Archaic	base	1	3.6%	0.2%
Pottery	Fine	Fineware, Archaic	body	3	10.7%	0.6%
Pottery	Fine	Fineware, Archaic	rim	1	3.6%	0.2%
Pottery	Med coarse	Medium Coarse Ware, Archaic	base	1	3.6%	0.2%
Pottery	Med coarse	Medium Coarse Ware, Archaic	body	6	21.4%	1.1%
Pottery	Med coarse	Medium Coarse Ware, Archaic	rim	1	3.6%	0.2%
Pottery	Semi-fine	Semi-fine Ware, Archaic	base	1	3.6%	0.2%
Pottery	Semi-fine	Semi-fine Ware, Archaic	body	5	17.9%	1.0%
Pottery	Semi-fine	Semi-fine Ware, Archaic	handle	1	3.6%	0.2%
Pottery	Semi-fine	Semi-fine Ware, Archaic	rim	1	3.6%	0.2%
Total				28	100.0%	5.4%

but still patterns in a consistent way to indicate a marked difference in the use of the landscape from the previous period.

5.3.2.2. Cypro-Archaic

ASSEMBLAGE: For the Cypro-Archaic period, we collected 28 Cypro-Archaic artifacts representing 18 batches (1.6 artifacts per batch) and 4 chronotypes. These artifacts form a little more than 5% of Iron Age material in PKAP.

There was an even division between fine and semi-fine fabrics (n=13, 46%), and medium-coarse and coarse fabrics (n=15, 54%). The majority of Cypro-Archaic pottery was comprised of body sherds (64%, n=18 of 28), with rims (n=4, 14%), bases (n=3, 11%), and handles (n=3, 11%) accounting for smaller percentages of the pottery. The body sherds appeared in coarse and medium-coarse fabrics (n=10), and plain (n=5) or painted (n=3) fine and semi-fine ware (Table 5.22).

These patterns indicate that our knowledge of the Cypro-Archaic period derives from a range of fabric groups and extant parts, and that surface decorations did not greatly aid our identification of material to the Cypro-Archaic period. We cannot be certain that we identified every Cypro-Archaic sherd collected during survey to the Cypro-Archaic period during analysis, but artifacts identified as Cypro-Archaic suggest continued habitation during this phase of the Iron Age.

DISTRIBUTION: During the Cypro-Archaic period, artifacts extend over 17 units and 3.6 ha, only 4% of the PKAP area. Cypro-Archaic artifacts continued to be found along the base of the Vigla and Mavrospilios ridgelines in Zones 1 and 2, but are especially common on the Kokkinokremos ridge (75% of Cypro-Archaic material) (figs. 5.17–5.18; 5.43). No Cypro-Archaic artifacts extend more than 200 m south into the coastal plain. It is possible that some of the material immediately south of the eastern ridge eroded from the top, but the distance from the base of the ridge suggests that these sherds reflect past activities on the coastal plain.

In many cases, concentrations of Cypro-Archaic material are found near distributions of earlier Cypro-Geometric sherds. These include, for instance, scattered fragments of Cypro-Archaic fine ware (68.20, 184.1, and **187.26**) south of the coastal ridge in Zones 1 and 2. The overlap of these two periods indicates that areas that saw activity in the Cypro-Geometric period remained significant also in the Cypro-Archaic era. Nonetheless, there is some modest evidence for expansion in the Cypro-Archaic period into Zone 3. Cypro-Archaic medium-coarse wares appear along the southwestern edge of the heart-shaped hill (1342.6, 1343.6, and 1356.5), and semi-fine wares (1311.11–12, 1336.6, 1337.3, 1344.15–17) and coarse wares (1304.9, 1311.13–14, 1345.27) were discovered on the southern and northern ends of the Kokkinokremos ridge. The evidence is slight, but it does indicate a change from the Cypro-Geometric era.

SUMMARY INTERPRETATION: Cypro-Archaic artifacts are sparse in the Koutsopetria survey area and the Cypro-Archaic era is a poorly visible period in the landscape. Although we see an increase in overall quantity of sherds in the Cypro-Archaic era, we must keep in mind that Cypro-Archaic pottery is significantly more visible than Cypro-Geometric pottery. The presence of material in areas where Cypro-Geometric artifacts were found suggests continuity of settlement, but some true expansion seems evident in Zone 3 (Kokkinokremos). The range of identified fabrics suggests that activities in this period marked a limited investment in the landscape; there are no indicators of any kind of significant wealth or activity that would have required the displays of imported or elaborate objects.

5.3.2.3. Cypro-Classical

ASSEMBLAGE: Artifacts dating to the Cypro-Classical period include 15 artifacts in 4 chronotypes and 7 batches (2.1 artifacts per batch), representing a significant reduction in quantity from the Cypro-Archaic period. This group of artifacts represents less than 3% of Iron Age material in PKAP.

The fabric and function of this small corpus of Cypro-Classical pottery is different from other Iron Age periods in the preponderance of fine ware. Some 93% of Cypro-Classical material is fine ware (n=14), assigned to the Cypro-Classical period via

FIG. 5.17   *Base of Mavrospilios ridge showing general area of Archaic scatters (view from south).*

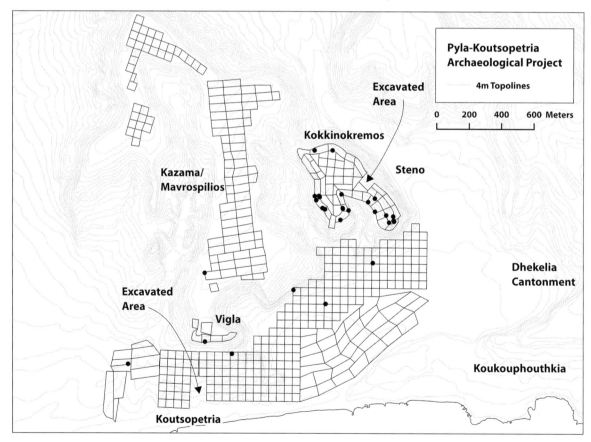

FIG. 5.18   *Distribution map of Archaic period.*

Table 5.23   Cypro-Classical period in the PKAP area.

MATERIAL	FABRIC	CHRONOTYPE	PART	QUANTITY	%	% IRON AGE (INCLUSIVE)
Classical (474–312 BC)						
Pottery	Fine	Black Glazed, Attic, Classical	body	4	26.7%	0.8%
Pottery	Fine	Black Glazed, Attic, Classical	rim	2	13.3%	0.4%
Pottery	Fine	Fineware, Classical	base	2	13.3%	0.4%
Pottery	Fine	Fineware, Classical	body	2	13.3%	0.4%
Pottery	Fine	Oinochoe, Classical	handle	4	26.7%	0.8%
Pottery	Kitchen	Kitchen Ware, Classical	handle	1	6.7%	0.2%
Total				15	100.0%	2.9%

its characteristic black-glaze surface. Black slip makes the Cypro-Classical period visible, but we were unable to identify other fabric classes besides a single piece of kitchen ware. We are confident that there were many coarse, medium-coarse, and kitchen ware sherds collected during survey that date to the Cypro-Classical period but were not identified during analysis.

The dominance of fine wares also likely explains the unusual patterns in extant parts. Compared to other narrow periods, the Cypro-Classical period assemblage has one of the lowest percentage of body sherds (n=6; 40%) in the PKAP survey; handles, rims, and bases collectively form a relatively greater portion (60%) of the assemblage than is typical of most narrow periods. The smaller proportion of body sherds may reflect the presence of highly diagnostic delicate table wares, like cups, which fragment into rims, bases, handles, and sherds in more even proportions than larger coarse-fabric utility ware vessels.

Compared with earlier and later periods, the Cypro-Classical assemblage is distinct in the relative absence of identified medium-coarse, coarse, kitchen ware, and utility ware body sherds. These artifacts must have been collected during survey and dated to broader periods, such as Cypro-Archaic to Hellenistic, Cypro-Classical to Hellenistic, Iron Age, Late Cypriot–Hellenistic, and Ancient Historic. Their absence explains why the Cypro-Classical period is so poorly visible in the PKAP region.

DISTRIBUTION: Cypro-Classical period material in PKAP appears in 8 units covering 1.6 ha, less than 2% of the total survey area. The few artifacts from this period collectively present a meager assemblage in terms of pure quantity, especially compared to material from the Cypro-Archaic and Hellenistic periods, but its distribution suggests activity in Zones 1 and 4, where 53% and 33% of Cypro-Classical pottery, respectively, was found. The complete absence of Cypro-Classical pottery from Zone 3 (Kokkinokremos) marks a change from the Cypro-Archaic age, while the paucity of material from Zone 2 (only one unit) suggests that vast areas of the survey area were undeveloped in the Cypro-Classical period.

The concentration of most of the Cypro-Classical pottery (5 of 8 units, 8 of 15 sherds) in Zone 1, in a narrow strip running half a kilometer along the southern slope of the Vigla ridge (figs. 5.19–5.20), points to a westward shift in the locus of occupation from the previous period. Other kinds of archaeological investigation have, in fact, confirmed significant activities at Vigla during the fourth–third centuries BC. The discovery of a large settling basin of Cypro-Classical or Hellenistic date dedicated by a man named Apollonios, son of Menon, to Apollo Karaiates on the plain below Vigla indicates ritual activity probably associated with olive oil processing (Hadjisavvas 1993: 75–76, 83). Our excavations on the ridge have highlighted phases of occupation and monumental wall construction toward the end of the Cypro-Classical

FIG. 5.19   *Northern strip of Zone 1 showing location of concentration of Classical period artifacts (view from Vigla, facing southeast).*

FIG. 5.20   *Area of high Classical density below Vigla ridge (view from west).*

FIG. 5.21 *Southern edge of Mavrospilios ridge (Zone 4) showing probable area of Classical sanctuary (view from southwest).*

period or the start of the Hellenistic era (Olson et al. 2013; Caraher et al. 2014). Given the frequency of our Cypro-Classical material below Vigla, and the dominance of Cypro-Classical to Early Hellenistic material on the ridge above, it seems probable that the Cypro-Classical material reflects a new phase of occupation of the area on and around Vigla in the mid to late fourth century.

Our survey did not identify Cypro-Classical pottery at Vigla itself, but we did identify significant quantities of Cypro-Classical to Hellenistic pottery there dating to the fifth-second centuries BC. If any of this material dates to the Cypro-Classical or late Cypro-Classical period, as seems certain, then the Cypro-Classical period should have a greater signature at Vigla (for further discussion of the Cypro-Classical to Hellenistic period, see Section 5.3.3). Indeed, the pottery recently excavated from the domestic contexts and a dump on the height of Vigla and currently under study should refine our understanding of the survey material (Olson et al. 2013).

One of the two units in Zone 4 with Cypro-Classical pottery may be oriented toward Vigla. Unit 1494, immediately north of Vigla on the Mavrospilios ridge, may hint at continued occupation from the Cypro-Archaic age. A small unit with a concentration of table wares about a kilometer north of Vigla on the Kazama ridge, on the other hand, points to a more isolated area of activity in the Cypro-Classical period. The sample is unfortunately too small to understand entirely the transformation of Zone 4 at the end of the Iron Age, but taking into account the significant quantity of broadly dated Iron Age material there is no reason necessarily to imagine discontinuity in this area.

Finally, we should note Unit 1011 on the southern edge of the Mavrospilios plateau northeast of Vigla (fig. 5.24) which produced a small concentration of fragmentary figurines (**1011.25, 1011.25B, 1011.25C, 1011.26, 1011.26B**). These five objects can only be dated broadly to an Iron Age period (Cypro-Archaic to Cypro-Classical), and this includes the possibility that they date to the Cypro-Classical period specifically. While the figurines could be domestic artifacts, their concentration in Unit 1011 suggest votive offerings at a shrine on the southern edge of the ridge. If these artifacts date to the Cypro-Classical era, they provide further confirmation for a small rural sanctuary on the ridge (see note on Apollo Karaiates above).

SUMMARY INTERPRETATION: That our knowledge of the Cypro-Classical period mainly depends on fine wares indicates that we did not precisely identify many collected artifacts to the Cypro-Classical period. If fine wares are taken as an index of a broader but invisible assemblage of pottery, we can read this ceramic material as evidence for a new phase of occupation that is oriented especially

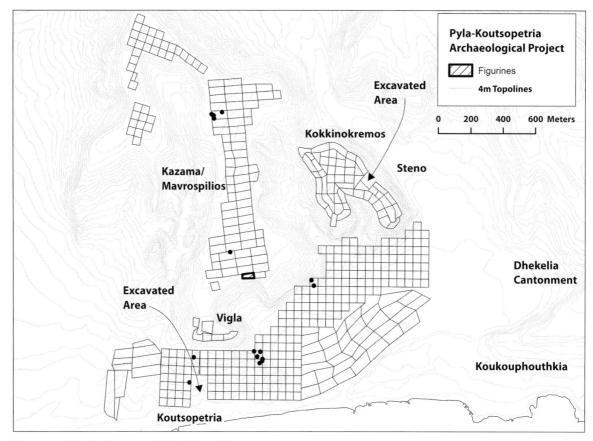

Fig. 5.22 *Distribution map of Classical period.*

around the site of Vigla. The investigations of that site through excavation suggest a date of the fourth century BC as the starting point in a new phase of occupation of the Pyla area (5.3.3 below). The concentration of fine ware in Zone 1 below Vigla indicates that the coastal plain was an important area of this new habitation. If the distribution of Cypro-Classical to Hellenistic and Hellenistic pottery is any indication (5.3.3), the occupation at Vigla included also the coastal plain below (fig. 5.22).

5.3.2.4. Iron Age (chronotype)

ASSEMBLAGE: The Iron Age chronotype period represents a span of 700 years, from 1050 to 312 BC. It extends from the beginning of the Cypro-Geometric era to the end of the Cypro-Classical period and incorporates each of the sub-periods discussed above (5.3.2.1–5.3.2.3). As with many broader categories, the identification of artifacts

to the Iron Age, rather than a narrower period like the Cypro-Classical, usually reflects the absence of diagnostic features or their poor preservation. The micro-region produced a significant quantity of Iron Age pottery, including some 455 sherds in 8 chronotypes and 56 batches (8.1 artifacts per batch) (Table 5.24). This chronotype period represents the majority (87%) of material datable generally to the Iron Age (Inclusive) in the PKAP survey area.

Body sherds (n=343) form some 75% of all Iron Age material, and handles account for 11% (n= 50), rims for 6% (n= 29) and bases for 7% (n=33). We identified multiple parts of each vessel for each chronotype except "Plain White" ware, which we only identified as body sherds. As with the Cypro-Archaic and Cypro-Geometric periods, however, surface treatments and fabric played a more important role in identification than shape.

The majority of Iron Age material (n=408, 90%) are coarse ware, medium-coarse ware, and amphora fragments. Most of these (n=275, 67%)

Table 5.24   Iron Age period in the PKAP area.

MATERIAL	FABRIC	CHRONOTYPE	PART	QUANTITY	%	% IRON AGE (INCLUSIVE)
Iron Age (Chronotype) (1,050–312 BC)						
Pottery	Amphora	Amphora, Iron Age	base	1	0.2%	0.2%
Pottery	Amphora	Amphora, Iron Age	body	14	3.1%	2.7%
Pottery	Amphora	Amphora, Iron Age	handle	12	2.6%	2.3%
Pottery	Amphora	Amphora, Iron Age	rim	2	0.4%	0.4%
Pottery	Amphora	Amphora, Iron Age	toe	5	1.1%	1.0%
Pottery	Coarse	Coarse Ware, Iron Age	base	9	2.0%	1.7%
Pottery	Coarse	Coarse Ware, Iron Age	body	168	36.9%	32.1%
Pottery	Coarse	Coarse Ware, Iron Age	handle	13	2.9%	2.5%
Pottery	Coarse	Coarse Ware, Iron Age	rim	4	0.9%	0.8%
Pottery	Fine	Fineware, Iron Age	base	4	0.9%	0.8%
Pottery	Fine	Fineware, Iron Age	body	21	4.6%	4.0%
Pottery	Fine	Fineware, Iron Age	handle	2	0.4%	0.4%
Pottery	Fine	Fineware, Iron Age	rim	4	0.9%	0.8%
Pottery	Kitchen	Kitchen Ware, Iron age	base	1	0.2%	0.2%
Pottery	Kitchen	Kitchen Ware, Iron age	rim	1	0.2%	0.2%
Pottery	Med coarse	Medium Coarse Ware, Iron Age	base	12	2.6%	2.3%
Pottery	Med coarse	Medium Coarse Ware, Iron Age	body	124	27.3%	23.7%
Pottery	Med coarse	Medium Coarse Ware, Iron Age	handle	22	4.8%	4.2%
Pottery	Med coarse	Medium Coarse Ware, Iron Age	rim	17	3.7%	3.3%
Pottery	Med coarse	Medium Coarse Ware, Iron Age	toe	1	0.2%	0.2%
Pottery	Med coarse	Medium Coarse, Plain White	body	3	0.7%	0.6%
Pottery	Med coarse	White Painted, Iron Age	handle	1	0.2%	0.2%
Pottery	Pithos	Pithos, Iron Age	body	13	2.9%	2.5%
Pottery	Pithos	Pithos, Iron Age	rim	1	0.2%	0.2%
Total				455	100.0%	87.0%

consisted of diagnostic greenware including amphorae (**501.29**, **501.59**). A small percentage (5.6%) of the sherds in amphora and coarse ware fabrics had black painted decorations (**1009.36**, **1009.65**, **1008.23**), which is not unusual for Iron Age pottery on the island. Fine ware constitutes only 7% (n=31) of all the Iron Age (chronotype) pottery for obvious reasons: table ware was tied to narrower periods. The small scatter of Iron Age fine ware — typically with black paint or black paint on white slip, and thin walled vessels with

table ware shapes — appears in the same zone as utilitarian wares: 1008, 1009, 1011, 1012, 1013, 1021, 1023, 1026, 1300, 1402, 1403, 1480, 1489, 1490, 1493, 1495 (**1402.6**, **1403.61**, **1013.30**). A small quantity of pithos fragments also appear among these units (**1012.17**) although this material only accounts for 3% (n=14) of the total assemblage. Finally, two pieces of Iron Age cooking or kitchen wares appeared in the survey area (**1402.10**, 1472.3).

This fuller range of fabric types for Iron Age material suggests a relatively complete assemblage

FIG. 5.23   *Kazama ridge (Zone 4) about 350 m north of Vigla showing area of concentration of Iron Age (chronotype) period (view from north).*

FIG. 5.24   *View of southern edge of Mavrospilios ridge, showing area of high-density Iron Age (chronotype) material in distance (view from north).*

albeit coarsely dated. Only cooking ware is obviously underrepresented, in part because we tended to date cooking vessels to broader periods like Ancient Historic, and in part because it survives poorly in surface assemblages. Generally, however, Iron Age landscapes are visible in the PKAP area.

DISTRIBUTION: Iron Age material extended over 42 units covering 10% of the survey area (10.4 ha). The distribution of Iron Age material largely complemented in extent and concentration the distribution of Cypro-Geometric and Cypro-Archaic pottery. The major differences from the more narrowly dated Cypro-Archaic and Cypro-Geometric material is that almost no Iron Age pottery derived from units on the coastal plain, and that Iron Age pottery concentrated almost entirely on the Mavrospilios–Vigla ridge.

Some 88% of Iron Age (chronotype) material comes from Zone 4. The most extensive and densest concentration occurs in an area of 25 units (9 ha) some 350 m north of the Vigla promontory (fig. 5.23). This concentration on the Kazama ridge followed closely the concentrations of Cypro-Geometric, Cypro-Archaic, Cypro-Archaic to Hellenistic, and Cypro-Classical material, suggesting that this area represented a significant locus of human activity over an extended period of time. The presence of at least one piece of a Cypro-Geometric fine ware vessel and White Painted amphora (**1006.7** and **1006.3**), as well as Cypro-Archaic figurines and coarse wares, along the southern edge of the larger Iron Age assemblage would appear to confirm the importance of this area over the broad Iron Age. The extent of material and variety of fabric classes defies a single functional categorization of this area, but the debris is consistent, as discussed above, with both settlement and cult. The concentrations of Hellenistic pottery in this area, moreover, indicate that settlement continued beyond the Iron Age (5.3.3).

In Zone 4, Iron Age material extends north along the ridge top for some 360 m before densities decline and then taper off completely. A small concentration occurs in a series of four relatively low-density units (<500 artifacts per ha) on the Kazama ridge approximately 1 km northwest of the height at Vigla (see fig. 5.7). These units rep-

resent 0.6 ha and include a low-density scatter of fine ware (1480.1), medium-coarse and coarse ware (1479.13, 1480.3, 1481.2), and cooking ware (1472.3). Considering the low density of material in these units, the presence of such a comprehensive assemblage is notable and might represent an area of particularly short-term occupation or low-intensity activity. What is important is that it represents Iron Age occupation in the northernmost part of the survey area, over a kilometer north of the coastal plain. With the exception of some Cypro-Classical pottery and a few other units with Iron Age (chronotype) material, the Iron Age is not generally extensive or significant in this area.

The only other important concentration of Iron Age material occurs on the height of Vigla, which, as we discussed above, has fortification walls, domestic architecture, and occupation phases of the fourth–third centuries BC. The material is mainly along the northern slope of the hill eroding out of a hill immediately south of the widest part of the plateau (fig. 5.24). The scatter consists of a few pieces of painted fine ware (**1402.6**, 1402.63, and 1402.64) and a range of shapes in Iron Age Greenware fabrics (1400.20, 1401.21, and 1402). It could represent either pottery produced during the Cypro-Classical period but identified only to the Iron Age, or earlier Cypro-Geometric and Cypro-Archaic period survivals of the kind that have been documented in excavation (Olson et al. 2013; Caraher et al. 2014). This material at Vigla represents some 12% of material of the Iron Age chronotype period.

Besides the Mavrospilios, Vigla, and Kazama ridges, negligible amounts of Iron Age artifacts were noted in other parts of the study area (fig. 5.25). Iron Age, Cypro-Geometric, and Cypro-Archaic fine wares on the coastal plain close to the southern slope of the Mavrospilios ridge suggest activity on or at the base of the slopes. We must always keep in mind the possibility that the later Roman remains on the plain buried a more extensive Iron Age settlement than we documented in the course of survey.

SUMMARY INTERPRETATION: Considering the Cypro-Geometric, Cypro-Archaic, and Cypro-Classical periods together with the Iron Age

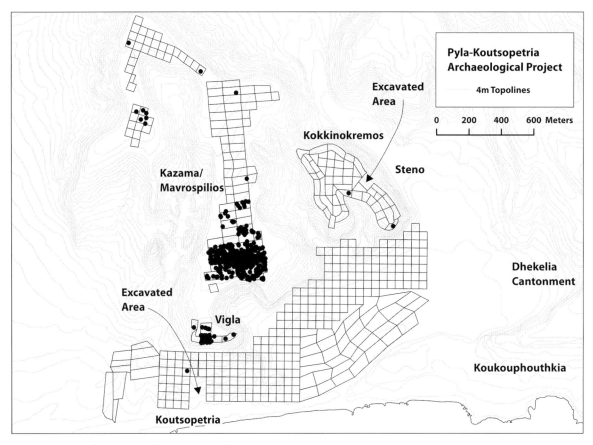

FIG. 5.25   *Distribution map of Iron Age period.*

(chronotype) pottery, we can infer from the diversity of material (fine wares, amphora, and varied coarse and medium-coarse wares) that there were extensive pockets of settlement in the area, as well as a rural sanctuary or shrine (Unit 1011), that extended from the top of the coastal ridge to the coastal plain. The densest concentration was located 350 m north of Vigla on the prominent coastal height overlooking the plain and with a clear view of most of Larnaca Bay. The presence of Iron Age material on Vigla indicates activity in the region perhaps disturbed by later Cypro-Classical occupation. The southern part of the Kokkinokremos ridge saw a significant phase of occupation in the Cypro-Archaic age, and low-density scatters of Cypro-Geometric and Cypro-Archaic to Cypro-Classical material at the bases of the ridges suggest activity across a broad swath of the upper coastal plain. Other than isolated pockets, the Iron Age (Inclusive) period does not extend to the southern half of the coastal plain,

the far western or eastern ends of the survey area, or areas more than a kilometer from the coast.

5.3.3.   Hellenistic Period

ASSEMBLAGE: Material dating to the Hellenistic Period represents a different distributional pattern from the Iron Age, albeit one with some continuities. The period is visible from 118 artifacts grouped in 5 chronotypes and 38 batches (3.1 artifacts per batch) (Table 5.25).

The fabric and function of the Hellenistic material is similar to the patterns of the preceding Cypro-Classical era, except that is more numerous and somewhat more extensive. Like the Cypro-Classical period (but unlike the Iron Age assemblage more generally), fine table wares constitute the majority (92%, n=105) of the Hellenistic assemblage, and kitchen wares largely constitute the remaining 8%. The typically ubiquitous medium-coarse and amphora sherds of Iron

Table 5.25   Hellenistic period in the PKAP area.

MATERIAL	FABRIC	CHRONOTYPE	PART	QUANTITY	%
Hellenistic (311–100 BC)					
Pottery	Fine	Black Glazed, Hellenistic	base	4	3.4%
Pottery	Fine	Black Glazed, Hellenistic	body	17	14.4%
Pottery	Fine	Black Glazed, Hellenistic	handle	3	2.5%
Pottery	Fine	Black Glazed, Hellenistic	rim	13	11.0%
Pottery	Fine	Fineware, Hellenistic	base	5	4.2%
Pottery	Fine	Fineware, Hellenistic	body	10	8.5%
Pottery	Fine	Fineware, Hellenistic	rim	2	1.7%
Pottery	Fine	Fineware, Hellenistic Colour-Coated Ware	base	11	9.3%
Pottery	Fine	Fineware, Hellenistic Colour-Coated Ware	body	28	23.7%
Pottery	Fine	Fineware, Hellenistic Colour-Coated Ware	handle	6	5.1%
Pottery	Fine	Fineware, Hellenistic Colour-Coated Ware	rim	9	7.6%
Pottery	Kitchen	Kitchen Ware, Hellenistic	base	2	1.7%
Pottery	Kitchen	Kitchen Ware, Hellenistic	body	1	0.8%
Pottery	Kitchen	Kitchen Ware, Hellenistic	handle	6	5.1%
Pottery	Med coarse	Medium Coarse Ware, Hellenistic	handle	1	0.8%
Total				118	100.0%

Age (chronotype) and Roman periods are almost entirely absent. Body sherds form only 47.5% of the overall Hellenistic assemblage, a figure similar to the 40% figure for the Cypro-Classical period, but relatively low compared to other narrow periods. Rims, bases, and handles make up 20%, 19%, and 14%, respectively, of the Hellenistic pottery.

As with the Cypro-Classical period, the paucity of kitchen ware and the near absence of coarse ware and amphora sherds indicate that during analysis we assigned artifacts of Hellenistic date to broader chronotypes like Ancient–Historic Coarse and Medium-Coarse Wares, Cypro-Classical to Roman Kitchen Ware, and Hellenistic Basket-Handle amphora. Our missed identifications are clear when we compare the Hellenistic survey assemblage with the excavated domestic assemblages of late Cypro-Classical to early Hellenistic date from the hilltop of Vigla (Olson et al. 2013; Caraher et al. 2014). Three seasons excavating ten trenches across the ridge and slope of Vigla have exposed many stratigraphic layers from a domestic site and fortification wall of late Cypro-Classical to early Hellenistic date. The results of these excavations are shown in Tables 5.26–5.27, which compare the Hellenistic assemblages produced by excavation to those produced by survey.

The comparison of fabric groups demonstrates that we identified significantly more fine ware than medium-coarse wares, amphorae, and kitchen ware in our survey assemblage. Analysis of extant part suggests that our recognition of Hellenistic body sherds in the survey assemblage was less effective (48%) than in excavation (76%), and that bases and handles formed lower proportions in excavation than in survey. In short, the quantity of feature sherds and table ware fragments identified during survey must mark but a fraction of artifacts of Hellenistic date that were collected, but dated to broader periods. Indeed, as we noted above, current studies of the ceramic artifacts recovered from excavation should help us refine the chronology of occupation and land use in the area in the Cypro-Classical to Hellenistic periods (Olson et al. 2013).

Despite our inability to identify Hellenistic plain wares, amphorae, and kitchen wares during analysis, the numerous table wares indicate major changes between the Cypro-Classical and Hellenistic periods. In comparison with the 14 fine ware sherds dating to the Cypro-Classical period, the 105 Hellenistic table ware fragments represent a veritable explosion of material in the PKAP region. If our excavated contexts are some indication, this change occurred in the later fourth and early third centuries BC. The nearly ten-fold increase in sherds dating to the Hellenistic age indicates a major expansion in occupation that is also evident in their distribution in the landscape.

DISTRIBUTION: Material from the Hellenistic period appears in 64 units covering 16 ha, an area ten times that of the Cypro-Classical period (similarly identified from table wares) and almost the same area covered by all material of Iron Age date (n=18 ha). Hellenistic wares are found in substantially smaller quantities than Roman material, but their broad distribution suggests extensive activity during these periods that marks a new medium of occupation at the coastal sites of Pyla. The Hellenistic assemblage is more evenly distributed between all five zones of the survey area, with Zone 4 showing the greatest concentration. While Iron Age material clustered in a series of units to the north of Vigla and along the base of the coastal ridges, Hellenistic material extended southward across the entire coastal plain and northward across the ridges.

Zone 4 produced the most diverse and perhaps significant assemblage of Hellenistic date (43% of HE material), especially in areas of earlier Iron Age occupation (fig. 5.26). The south edge of the coastal ridge, which also produced a diverse concentration of Iron Age material, continued to produce a robust assemblage of fine wares and kitchen wares in the late Cypro-Classical and Hellenistic periods. There are a few examples of Cypro-Classical to Hellenistic fine ware (1022.16) and at least two examples of Cypro-Classical to Hellenistic lamp fragments (**1022.17**, <u>**1022.18**</u>), which may mark the transition between the fourth and third centuries BC. The most striking feature of the assemblage in these units, however, is the massive quantity of

Table 5.26   Hellenistic assemblage from excavation vs. survey according to fabric group.

FABRIC	SURVEY	EXCAVATION
Amphora	0.0%	13.5%
Coarse	0.0%	0.8%
Medium Coarse	0.8%	16.2%
Fine	91.5%	13.4%
Semi-fine	0.0%	6.8%
Kitchen	7.6%	46.0%
Lamp	0.0%	1.9%
Pithos	0.0%	0.1%
Tile	0.0%	1.3%

Table 5.27   Hellenistic assemblage from excavation vs. survey according to extant part.

EXTANT PART	SURVEY	EXCAVATION
Rim	20.3%	15.8%
Base	18.6%	4.6%
Handle	13.6%	3.2%
Body Sherd	47.5%	76.0%
Spout	0.0%	0.2%
Toe	0.0%	0.2%
Neck	0.0%	0.1%

Early Hellenistic fine ware, including black slip and Colour-Coated wares.

There is also evidence for activity in the northern parts of Zone 4, which is evidently more extensive than Iron Age distributions, given that the Hellenistic period is so poorly visible. That the Hellenistic scatter extends to the northern edge of the Mavrospilios–Kazama plateau indicates that the plateau saw activity during this period (fig. 5.27).

That some 20% of Hellenistic pottery concentrates on the height of Vigla (figs. 5.28–5.29) is remarkable, given the small area of the ridgetop compared to the four main zones. Indeed, excavations on the ridgetop have revealed major occupation and fortification phases of Late Cypro-Classical to Early Hellenistic date (figs.

Fig. 5.26 *Southern edge of Zone 4 (view from north).*

Fig. 5.27 *The northern edge of the Mavrospilios plateau (view from south).*

FIG. 5.28   *The ridge of Vigla (view from west).*

FIG. 5.29   *The ridge of Vigla (view from east).*

5.30–5.31). Vigla seems to have been a fortified garrison from ca. 350 to 250 BC (Olson et al. 2013; Caraher et al. 2014; see Chapter 6). The Hellenistic and Cypro-Classical to Hellenistic chronotypes documented through surface survey include fine wares, lamps, kitchen wares, and utility wares, all of which indicate sustained habitation. Indeed, these artifacts are generally consistent with recent observations about the excavated ceramic assemblage: lamps, cooking pots, and utility vessels primarily produced locally, and, to a lesser degree, imported from Athens, indicate a modest community that nonetheless depended on external contacts well beyond the island (Olson et al. 2013).

Furthermore, with the presence of similar shapes, such as lamps and vessels used for consuming food (inturned-rim bowls), in both locally procured fabrics and imported Attic wares, it is clear that, although Attic imports do not dominate the assemblage, those living at Vigla had access to imported Attic vessels and their imitations.

FIG. 5.30 *Excavated trench (EU 1) on Vigla showing Early Hellenistic walls of domestic building (view from east).*

FIG. 5.31 *Excavated trench (EU 6) on Vigla showing Early Hellenistic fortification wall (view from west).*

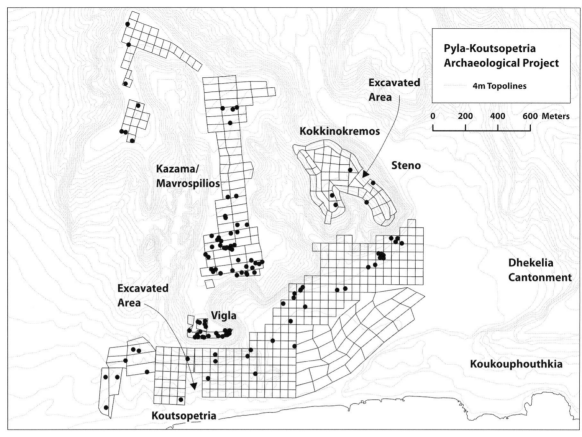

FIG. 5.32   *Distribution map of Hellenistic period.*

Significant portions of the Hellenistic assemblage (13% and 20%) come from Zones 1 and 2 on the coastal plain, where it has a close distributional association with Cypro-Classical and Cypro-Classical to Hellenistic pottery (see fig. 2.6). The material from these periods produced a crescent-shaped scatter of material that stretched for over 1.8 km along the coastal plain. The Hellenistic pottery includes fine wares and kitchen wares, and material datable to the broader Cypro-Classical to Hellenistic consists of coarse and utility wares.

Finally, the ridge of Kokkinokremos saw renewed activity in the Hellenistic era. However, since only 4% of Hellenistic pottery originated from the ridge, Zone 4 was not as significant as the other zones in the Hellenistic period (fig. 5.32).

SUMMARY INTERPRETATION: The Hellenistic period in the survey area is represented almost entirely by imported table ware fragments. Our

dependence on fine ware for identifying the Hellenistic period means that our reconstruction of Hellenistic landscapes is fundamentally incomplete. Yet, the greater number of Hellenistic fine ware sherds compared with the preceding period speaks to a remarkable expansion. Settlement continued in areas of former habitation, especially the site of Vigla and in the vicinity of the earlier Iron Age site in Zone 4. The broad distribution of material across Zone 1 and Zone 2 in the coastal plain, and the limited amount of material in Zone 3, highlight new areas of occupation. The correlation of Cypro-Classical and Hellenistic pottery in survey units, as well as the excavations on the Vigla ridge, strongly suggest that this new phase of intensive settlement was a product of the later fourth to early third centuries BC. This Hellenistic settlement marks the first narrow period appearing in substantial quantities across every zone of the survey area.

5.3.4. *The Roman Period*

The Roman period, broadly defined, produced the largest and most diverse assemblage in the study area. The distribution of Roman (Inclusive) material continues the significant shift in the local settlement pattern that began in the Hellenistic era, but also marks something new. Roman material is far more abundant than the Iron Age (12 times the amount of material) and distributed more broadly across the study area, covering 80% of the area (80.1 ha) and found in 83% of survey units (n=381). Moreover, the center of activity shifts from Zone 4 on the Mavrospilios–Kazama ridge to Zones 1 and 2 on the coastal plain.

Like the broad Iron Age period, we attempted during analysis to place Roman material into narrower groupings. The Early Roman period (99 BC–AD 299) covers the first four centuries, and the Late Roman era (300–749 AD) spans the next four centuries. We designated a generic "Roman" (chronotype) period for artifacts that could only be dated to the broad Roman period (99 BC to AD 749). In this section, we will save a summary interpretation to the end (5.3.4.4).

5.3.4.1. Early Roman

ASSEMBLAGE: The substantial and diverse assemblage of Early Roman pottery indicates an important settlement in the early Roman centuries. The 142 artifacts representing 13 chronotypes and 52 distinct batches (2.8 artifacts per batch) are more numerous and diverse than previous periods, such as the Hellenistic and the narrow periods of the Iron Age. Compared to the Late Roman period, however, the Early Roman period is relatively weak, forming a meager 2% of all material of Roman date.

The Early Roman era marks a period only partially visible in the landscape: slightly more visible than the Cypro-Classical and Hellenistic periods, but much less visible than the later Roman period. On the one hand, body sherds comprise the largest share (46%) of the assemblage and outnumber handles (23%), rims (21%), and bases (10%); thus, our identification of this period during analysis did not rely on feature sherds alone. On the other hand, most Early Roman body sherds (91%) were fine ware identified to this period because of its recognizable red slip. Because we did not identify many body sherds from utilitarian coarse, medium-coarse, and amphora vessels, the number of identified Early Roman sherds represents only a fraction of the actual number of Early Roman sherds that must have been collected and assigned to broader chronotype periods during analysis. This is a common problem in Roman landscapes in the Mediterranean (Pettegrew 2007).

Examining fabric groups highlights the same pattern. The most common types of artifacts datable to this period are fine wares that account for 66% of the overall assemblage. The most common fine ware is Eastern Sigillata A (39%; 70.48, 188.44), but Cypriot Sigillata (23%; 51.42) exists in significant quantites, as does the more generically identified Early Roman Red Slip (17%; 71.37, 174.14) and Early Roman Fine ware (19%), which do not fit into a clear typology. That Eastern Sigillata B (207.12) and Arretine (12.56) wares appear in singular instances indicates that regions west of Cyprus supplied very few of Koutsopetria's needs for table wares (in contrast to amphorae; see below). The most diagnostic and abundant Early Roman table wares (ESA and CS) suggest occupation of the area from the later second century BC to the second century AD (ESA). Significantly, there are no clear examples of artifacts from the third century AD. This gap is a known issue for Cyprus and reflects both a general economic retreat during this period and problems with the current ceramic typologies (Lund 1992; 1993: 138).

Cooking ware (16%; 204. 25) and amphorae (15%) comprise most of the remaining artifacts of Early Roman date. Amphorae were identified mainly (86%) from handles, kitchen ware from handles (56%), rims (22%), and body sherds (17%). Of the amphorae, Rhodian (208.8, 189.52), Koan-type (84.10, 1404.24, 65.31), and Pseudo-Koan type amphora handles represent the most diagnostic components of the assemblage and indicate a dependence on Aegean connections for imports (Section 4.5). Coarse wares (3%; 1009.62) are significantly less common in the Early Roman assemblage and appear in only three units; we identified no Early Roman lamps or artifacts in medium-coarse or pithos fabrics. In general, body

Table 5.28   Early Roman period in the PKAP area.

Material	Fabric	Chronotype	Part	Quantity	%	% Roman (Inclusive)
Early Roman (99 BC–AD 299)						
Pottery	Amphora	Amphora, Koan-type	body	1	0.7%	0.02%
Pottery	Amphora	Amphora, Koan-type	handle	14	9.9%	0.21%
Pottery	Amphora	Amphora, Koan-type	rim	1	0.7%	0.02%
Pottery	Amphora	Amphora, Pseudo Koan	handle	2	1.4%	0.03%
Pottery	Amphora	Amphora, Rhodian	handle	2	1.4%	0.03%
Pottery	Amphora	Amphora, Roman Early	toe	1	0.7%	0.02%
Pottery	Coarse	Coarse Ware, Early Roman	base	1	0.7%	0.02%
Pottery	Coarse	Coarse Ware, Early Roman	body	1	0.7%	0.02%
Pottery	Coarse	Coarse Ware, Early Roman	handle	2	1.4%	0.03%
Pottery	Fine	Arretine Ware	rim	1	0.7%	0.02%
Pottery	Fine	Cypriot Sigillata	base	5	3.5%	0.08%
Pottery	Fine	Cypriot Sigillata	body	15	10.6%	0.23%
Pottery	Fine	Cypriot Sigillata	rim	1	0.7%	0.02%
Pottery	Fine	Eastern Sigilatta A	rim	4	2.8%	0.06%
Pottery	Fine	Eastern Sigillata A	base	4	2.8%	0.06%
Pottery	Fine	Eastern Sigillata A	body	28	19.7%	0.43%
Pottery	Fine	Eastern Sigillata B	body	1	0.7%	0.02%
Pottery	Fine	Fineware, Roman Early	body	2	1.4%	0.03%
Pottery	Fine	Fineware, Roman Early	rim	16	11.3%	0.24%
Pottery	Fine	Red Slip, Roman Early	base	2	1.4%	0.03%
Pottery	Fine	Red Slip, Roman Early	body	12	8.5%	0.18%
Pottery	Fine	Red Slip, Roman Early	rim	2	1.4%	0.03%
Pottery	Kitchen	Kitchen Ware, Roman Early	base	1	0.7%	0.02%
Pottery	Kitchen	Kitchen Ware, Roman Early	body	4	2.8%	0.06%
Pottery	Kitchen	Kitchen Ware, Roman Early	handle	13	9.2%	0.20%
Pottery	Kitchen	Kitchen Ware, Roman Early	rim	5	3.5%	0.08%
Pottery	Semi-fine	Semi-fine Ware, Roman Early	body	1	0.7%	0.02%
Total				142	100.0%	2.2%

sherds of utility wares are difficult to assign to narrow periods, so it is not surprising that they are under-represented in this assemblage (Table 5. 28).

DISTRIBUTION: Artifacts dated narrowly to the Early Roman period appeared in 74 units in 16% of the survey area (16.4 ha), which corresponds to the same area as the Hellenistic era (63 units

covering 16 ha). Indeed, the general distribution of Early Roman pottery mirrors Hellenistic material with one major exception: the proportion of Early Roman material grows in Zone 1 (29%) at the expense of Early Roman pottery in Zone 4 (25%).

Slightly more than 50% of Early Roman material came from the coastal plain (figs. 5.33–5.35). The overlap between material datable to the Early

FIG. 5.33 *Zone 1 of the coastal plain (view from west).*

FIG. 5.34 *Zone 1 of the coastal plain (view from east).*

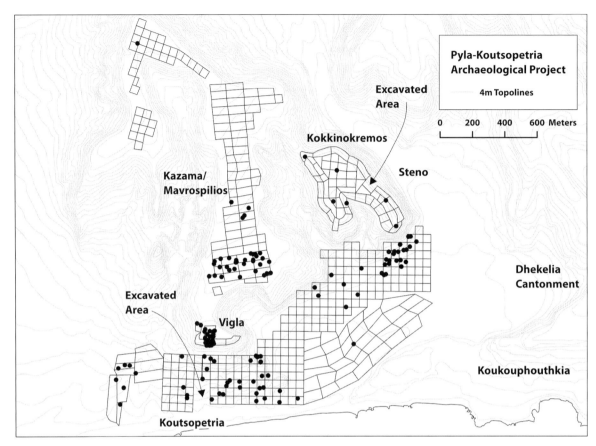

FIG. 5.35   *Distribution map of Early Roman period.*

Roman and Hellenistic eras makes it difficult to determine when this change took place, but the distribution certainly indicates a decisive shift to the coast. The Zone 1 assemblage consists primarily of Early Roman fine wares with a few amphora sherds scattered in a crescent across the Koutsopetria plain. There is a break of some 400 m before the scatter resumes in Zone 2 (see fig. 1.4). In its eastern extent, the assemblage appears more diverse with some kitchen and cooking wares present as well as fine wares. The greater density of Early Roman material on the coastal plain generally complements the distribution of Roman (chronotype) material, which may represent artifacts that date to the Early Roman era (5.3.4.3).

The ridgeline above the coast, which had been a center of activity since the Iron Age, also yielded a significant scatter of Early Roman material (25% of the assemblage). However, the scatter was more concentrated than earlier periods and did not extend in high density to the north of the main concentration. Yet, this cluster of material shows the same diverse character as assemblages from earlier periods, with an array of fine ware, amphorae, kitchen, and coarse ware.

The height of Vigla also produced important pockets of Early Roman pottery (19% of the assemblage), but the nature of this scatter is unclear. Excavation has shown extensive evidence for discontinuity in the Hellenistic settlement by 250 BC and has not revealed architecture or domestic phases associated with the Early Roman period (Olson et al. 2013; Caraher et al. 2014). The absence from the survey assemblage of highly diagnostic fine wares, such as Eastern Sigillata or Cypriot Sigillata, suggests that this area did not support habitation. The predominance of coarse ware, amphora sherds, and kitchen ware sherds may hint at a more utilitarian function to this space that was highly localized.

As in the Hellenistic era, Zone 3 produced a dispersed scatter of Early Roman finds (4% of the ER assemblage), including Eastern Sigillata

A (1332.6, 1323.10, 1311.8, 1312.15, 1338.13) and early African Red Slip (1333.15). The artifacts appear to coincide with a scatter of Roman period material that included red-slipped fine wares, amphorae, and medium-coarse and coarse wares. The material present on this height is of sufficient diversity and quantity to indicate some kind of habitation on Kokkinokremos during the Early Roman period.

5.3.4.2. Late Roman

ASSEMBLAGE: Late Roman material is the most common diagnostic period in the survey area, with 5,165 artifacts in 50 chronotypes and 274 distinct batches (19 artifacts per batch). Late Roman arti-

facts represent 79% of material that can be dated to the Roman (Inclusive) period. The abundance, diversity, and extent of the ceramic scatter point to a vibrant phase of habitation on the plain (Table 5.29).

As archaeologists have documented elsewhere in the Mediterranean, the later Roman era is a very visible ceramic period in surface survey because of the wide array of table wares and surface-treated coarse wares (Pettegrew 2007). The most common kind of pottery — storage and transport jars and jugs — were often surface-treated through combing, ridging, and grooving. As a result, ceramicists can easily assign body sherds from such common utilitarian vessels to the Late Roman period during analysis.

Table 5.29   Late Roman period in the PKAP area.

MATERIAL	FABRIC	CHRONOTYPE	PART	QUANTITY	%	% ROMAN (INCLUSIVE)
Late Roman (300–749 AD)						
Terra cotta		Cut Stopper, terra cotta	body	1	0.02%	0.02%
Terra cotta		Weight, Circular	body	1	0.02%	0.02%
Pottery	Amphora	Amphora, Anemurium Type A	toe	1	0.02%	0.02%
Pottery	Amphora	Amphora, Late Roman 1	body	10	0.19%	0.15%
Pottery	Amphora	Amphora, Late Roman 1	handle	275	5.32%	4.20%
Pottery	Amphora	Amphora, Late Roman 1	rim	9	0.17%	0.14%
Pottery	Amphora	Amphora, Late Roman 2	body	73	1.41%	1.12%
Pottery	Amphora	Amphora, Late Roman 2	handle	1	0.02%	0.02%
Pottery	Amphora	Amphora, Palestinian	body	1	0.02%	0.02%
Pottery	Amphora	Amphora, Roman Late	base	1	0.02%	0.02%
Pottery	Amphora	Amphora, Roman Late	body	417	8.07%	6.37%
Pottery	Amphora	Amphora, Roman Late	handle	125	2.42%	1.91%
Pottery	Amphora	Amphora, Roman Late	neck	1	0.02%	0.02%
Pottery	Amphora	Amphora, Roman Late	rim	38	0.74%	0.58%
Pottery	Amphora	Amphora, Roman Late	neck	7	0.14%	0.11%
Pottery	Amphora	Amphora, Roman Late	toe	19	0.37%	0.29%
Pottery	Amphora	Peacock and Williams 35	toe	1	0.02%	0.02%
Pottery	Coarse	Basin, Late Roman Piecrust Rim	rim	1	0.02%	0.02%
Pottery	Coarse	Coarse Ware, Roman Late	base	17	0.33%	0.26%
Pottery	Coarse	Coarse Ware, Roman Late	body	1072	20.76%	16.38%
Pottery	Coarse	Coarse Ware, Roman Late	handle	192	3.72%	2.93%
Pottery	Coarse	Coarse Ware, Roman Late	rim	45	0.87%	0.69%

Table 5.29 (cont.)   Late Roman period in the PKAP area.

Material	Fabric	Chronotype	Part	Quantity	%	% Roman (Inclusive)
Late Roman (300–749 AD)						
Pottery	Coarse	Coarse Ware, Roman Late	neck	1	0.02%	0.02%
Pottery	Fine	African Red Slip 103	rim	1	0.02%	0.02%
Pottery	Fine	African Red Slip 104	rim	3	0.06%	0.05%
Pottery	Fine	African Red Slip 104, Imitation	rim	1	0.02%	0.02%
Pottery	Fine	African Red Slip 104-106	rim	1	0.02%	0.02%
Pottery	Fine	African Red Slip 105	rim	15	0.29%	0.23%
Pottery	Fine	African Red Slip 105, Imitation	rim	8	0.15%	0.12%
Pottery	Fine	African Red Slip 106	rim	2	0.04%	0.03%
Pottery	Fine	African Red Slip 61	rim	1	0.02%	0.02%
Pottery	Fine	African Red Slip 93	rim	1	0.02%	0.02%
Pottery	Fine	African Red Slip 99	rim	1	0.02%	0.02%
Pottery	Fine	African Red Slip, Imitation	base	5	0.10%	0.08%
Pottery	Fine	African Red Slip, Imitation	body	2	0.04%	0.03%
Pottery	Fine	African Red Slip, Imitation	rim	4	0.08%	0.06%
Pottery	Fine	Cypriot Red Slip	base	30	0.58%	0.46%
Pottery	Fine	Cypriot Red Slip	body	60	1.16%	0.92%
Pottery	Fine	Cypriot Red Slip	handle	1	0.02%	0.02%
Pottery	Fine	Cypriot Red Slip	rim	12	0.23%	0.18%
Pottery	Fine	Cypriot Red Slip 1	base	1	0.02%	0.02%
Pottery	Fine	Cypriot Red Slip 1	rim	9	0.17%	0.14%
Pottery	Fine	Cypriot Red Slip 10	rim	1	0.02%	0.02%
Pottery	Fine	Cypriot Red Slip 11	body	1	0.02%	0.02%
Pottery	Fine	Cypriot Red Slip 11	handle	1	0.02%	0.02%
Pottery	Fine	Cypriot Red Slip 11	rim	7	0.14%	0.11%
Pottery	Fine	Cypriot Red Slip 12	rim	2	0.04%	0.03%
Pottery	Fine	Cypriot Red Slip 2	rim	4	0.08%	0.06%
Pottery	Fine	Cypriot Red Slip 4	rim	1	0.02%	0.02%
Pottery	Fine	Cypriot Red Slip 7	rim	1	0.02%	0.02%
Pottery	Fine	Cypriot Red Slip 8	rim	1	0.02%	0.02%
Pottery	Fine	Cypriot Red Slip 9	base	2	0.04%	0.03%
Pottery	Fine	Cypriot Red Slip 9	body	1	0.02%	0.02%
Pottery	Fine	Cypriot Red Slip 9	rim	30	0.58%	0.46%
Pottery	Fine	Cypriot Red Slip 9, Imitation	rim	2	0.04%	0.03%
Pottery	Fine	Egyptian Red Slip	base	1	0.02%	0.02%
Pottery	Fine	Egyptian Red Slip	body	3	0.06%	0.05%

Table 5.29 (cont.)   Late Roman period in the PKAP area.

MATERIAL	FABRIC	CHRONOTYPE	PART	QUANTITY	%	% ROMAN (INCLUSIVE)
Late Roman (300–749 AD)						
Pottery	Fine	Fineware, Roman Late	body	2	0.04%	0.03%
Pottery	Fine	Fineware, Roman Late	rim	2	0.04%	0.03%
Pottery	Fine	Phocaean Ware	rim	1	0.02%	0.02%
Pottery	Fine	Phocaean Ware 10	rim	26	0.50%	0.40%
Pottery	Fine	Phocaean Ware 2	rim	1	0.02%	0.02%
Pottery	Fine	Phocaean Ware 3	rim	16	0.31%	0.24%
Pottery	Fine	Red Slip, Roman Late	body	13	0.25%	0.20%
Pottery	Fine	Red Slip, Roman Late	rim	1	0.02%	0.02%
Pottery	Kitchen	Kitchen Ware, Frying Pan Palestinian	handle	1	0.02%	0.02%
Pottery	Kitchen	Kitchen Ware, Roman Late	base	3	0.06%	0.05%
Pottery	Kitchen	Kitchen Ware, Roman Late	body	77	1.49%	1.18%
Pottery	Kitchen	Kitchen Ware, Roman Late	handle	7	0.14%	0.11%
Pottery	Kitchen	Kitchen Ware, Roman Late	lid	1	0.02%	0.02%
Pottery	Kitchen	Kitchen Ware, Roman Late	rim	24	0.46%	0.37%
Pottery	Lamp	Lamp, Roman Late	body	2	0.04%	0.03%
Pottery	Med coarse	Basin, Late Roman	base	3	0.06%	0.05%
Pottery	Med coarse	Basin, Late Roman	rim	20	0.39%	0.31%
Pottery	Med coarse	Combed Ware	body	6	0.12%	0.09%
Pottery	Med coarse	Combed Ware, narrow	body	23	0.45%	0.35%
Pottery	Med coarse	Medium Coarse Ware, Roman Late	base	10	0.19%	0.15%
Pottery	Med coarse	Medium Coarse Ware, Roman Late	body	250	4.84%	3.82%
Pottery	Med coarse	Medium Coarse Ware, Roman Late	handle	22	0.43%	0.34%
Pottery	Med coarse	Medium Coarse Ware, Roman Late	neck	1	0.02%	0.02%
Pottery	Med coarse	Medium Coarse Ware, Roman Late	rim	29	0.56%	0.44%
Pottery	Med coarse	Medium Coarse Ware, Roman Late	toe	3	0.06%	0.05%
Pottery	Pithos	Pithos, Roman Late	body	7	0.14%	0.11%
Pottery	Pithos	Pithos, Roman Late	rim	4	0.08%	0.06%
Pottery	Tile	Tile, Kopetra Corinthian Cover Roman Late	body	6	0.12%	0.09%
Pottery	Tile	Tile, Kopetra Corinthian Cover Roman Late	edge	12	0.23%	0.18%
Pottery	Tile	Tile, Kopetra Corinthian Pan Roman Late	body	96	1.86%	1.47%
Pottery	Tile	Tile, Kopetra Corinthian Pan Roman Late	edge	88	1.70%	1.34%
Pottery	Tile	Tile, Roman Late	body	1229	23.79%	18.78%
Pottery	Tile	Tile, Roman Late	edge	641	12.41%	9.79%
Pottery	Tile	Tile, Roman Late	rim	13	0.25%	0.20%
Total				5,165	100.0%	78.9%

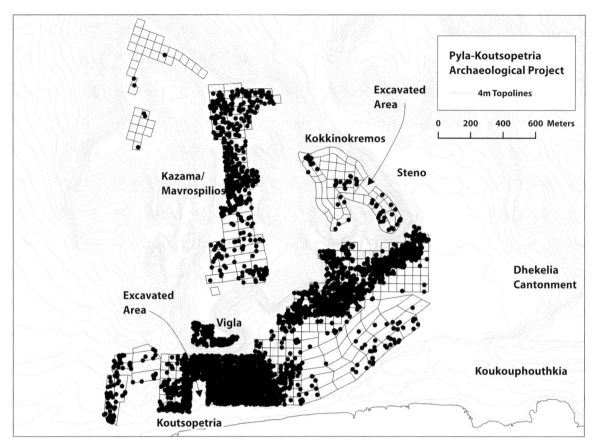

FIG. 5.36   *Distribution map of Late Roman period.*

FIG. 5.37   *The coastal plain of Zone 1 (view from northwest, above).*

In the PKAP area, the Late Roman era was especially visible for five main reasons. First, combed, spirally-grooved, and wheel-ridged body sherds made a substantial contribution to the overall assemblage of Late Roman body sherds, representing 10% of all body sherds. Although this figure is much lower than that documented elsewhere (Pettegrew 2007), it still contributed in part to our identification of the period.

Second, we were able to identify numerous Late Roman tiles by fabric group and forms because of recent work in defining typologies at the nearby Late Roman site of Kopetra (Rautman 2003). Tiles formed some 40% of all Late Roman artifacts and were especially common on the coastal plain (cf. Table 5.29 and fig. 5.41). Their presence indicates that substantial buildings concentrated in Zone 1 especially, and to a lesser extent in Zone 2.

Third, Late Roman pottery was visible because our primary survey ceramicist is a specialist in Late Roman coarse wares and amphorae and was able to identify the period from the fabric of body sherds. Some 66% of Late Roman pottery sherds consisted of body sherds, a number higher than most other narrow chronotype periods. Amphora, coarse ware, and medium-coarse ware body sherds account for 91% of Late Roman body sherds; cooking ware represents only 4% of Late Roman body sherds, fine ware less than one percent. Most Late Roman pottery consisted of body sherds, and most body sherds were coarse and medium coarse fabrics.

Fourth, Late Roman feature sherds were very identifiable during survey. Some 20% of Late Roman pottery consists of handles and 11% consists of rims. Handles come mainly from diagnostic Late Roman amphorae, especially Late Roman 1 (44% of all handles). Late Roman rims derive especially from fine table ware forms (48% of rims, n=155). Bases, which tend to be relatively non-diagnostic for the Roman period and lack diagnostic surface decorations, shapes, or decoration, drop to 3% of Late Roman material. It may be that bases tend to be assigned broader periods, but, strangely, we identified relatively few bases of broader Roman date. Other vessel parts, such as lids and necks, appear in trace amounts.

The final reason for the visibility of the Late Roman period is the considerable quantity of Late Roman fine ware at Koutsopetria. Fine ware accounted for 9% of the total assemblage of pottery of Late Roman date, and 29 different fine ware chronotypes appeared in our survey that represented 58% of the total chronotypes. The highly-diagnostic fabric and characteristic rim profiles and a well-documented typology of Late Roman fine ware made these artifacts relatively easy to identify and categorize. The most common type of fine ware present was the regional Cypriot Red Slip (60%), but Koutsopetria also produced significant quantities of African Red Slip (9%), local imitations of African Red Slip (7%), and Phocaean Ware (16%). There were a handful of Egyptian Red Slip imports (**24.24**), which are rather rare on Cyprus. In general, the quantity and variety of imported fine ware at Koutsopetria distinguished it from sites elsewhere on Cyprus and suggest a much broader network of importing than in either the Hellenistic or Early Roman periods.

The diversity of regional and imported table ware forms indicates that Koutsopetria reached its greatest extent and prosperity in the sixth–early seventh century AD. While we did identify earlier table ware forms (ARS 61 [**68.21**]), Phocaean Ware form 2 (**187.24**), and CRS 1 (**19.10**)) dating to the later fourth to the mid-fifth century AD, these were uncommon, and the majority of well-dated vessels date from later fifth to mid-seventh century contexts. Indeed, the most common local ware, CRS form 9 (**25.31**), and the most common imported forms of ARS 99 (**140.17**), 104–106 (**47.39**, **9.42**) and PHW 3 (**9.38**) and 10 (**70.53**) date from the sixth to seventh centuries (Hayes 1972). There are almost no LR fine wares before the fifth century, and most appear to be early sixth century or later.

The most common diagnostic non-fine ware pottery sherds are transport amphorae, which make up 32% of the Late Roman pottery (cf. Table 5.29 and fig. 5.42). The most common Late Roman amphora chronotype from the survey is the generic "Late Roman Amphora," which made up 62% of the total number of amphorae and represented by less-diagnostic body sherds in distinctive Late Roman fabrics. As Cyprus was a likely production center for Late Roman 1 amphorae from the fourth to seventh centuries AD, it is unsurprising

FIG. 5.38   *The excavated site of Koutsopetria (view from north).*

FIG. 5.39   *The western extension of Late Roman Koutsopetria in Zone 1 (view from east).*

that LR1 amphorae make up a large part (30%) of the assemblage of Late Roman amphorae from the survey (Demesticha 2013: 173). The diversity of fabrics present, however, indicates that not all of the amphorae collected were produced locally, although the highly-diagnostic twisted handles make them easy to identify consistently (for a more detailed discussion of this material, see the catalog). Late Roman 2 amphorae (**199.10**), which were probably produced in Greece and the Aegean, are the second most common LR amphora (8%) and date broadly from the fourth to the early seventh century AD. The Palestinian amphorae (**1404.42**), Peacock and Williams type 35 amphora (21.11), and an Anemurium Type A amphora (**65.26**) show up singularly and represent fifth to sixth centuries AD and first to fourth centuries AD, respectively. Our assemblage of transport amphorae, then, mirrors our fine wares, with primarily local and regional wares, and, to a lesser extent, some smaller percentage of imports from west of Cyprus.

The assemblage also produced some diagnostic cooking wares, including a number of examples of Dhiorios type vessels (**17.31, 71.39, 74.36**) and types common to the nearby site of Panayia Ematousa (60.22) and Anemurium (**4.37**). That cooking pots made up a paltry 3% of the total assemblage of Late Roman pottery is consistent with the figures derived from our experimental unit in 2010 (3.2.3). To judge from several diagnostic pots, these Late Roman cooking vessels reflect late sixth- or even seventh-century activity in the area.

Utilitarian medium-coarse wares and coarse wares are common across the micro-region and represent 55% of the total assemblage of Late Roman material. The vast majority of these fabric groups are body sherds that do not represent clear shapes or forms and are generally dated, on the basis of fabric, to Late Antiquity; this material provides relatively little information on specific functions across the area. Most medium-coarse and coarse ware vessels served agricultural or household storage purposes or played a role in industrial production. This group does include, however, some artifacts that fit within known typologies. Most notably, Late Roman basins of various types served a variety of industrial and household functions, such as preparing food and

temporary food storage (**13.17, 246.18**, 43.2, 48.25, **61.31, 65.24, 87.16**, and **196.22**).

In short, the Late Roman era represents the most visible period in PKAP, and we can be confident in our reconstruction of its distribution. It is important to conclude, however, that most of this "Late Roman" pottery is actually from a narrower span of two centuries. There were no finds among the later Roman material that dated exclusively to the 4th century, and there were few objects certainly produced prior to 450 AD. The most diagnostic pottery suggests a date range for the Late Roman occupation in the mid-fifth to seventh century AD, with a concentration of activity in the sixth century. Like the gap in ceramics between the Hellenistic and Early Roman, there is a break between the final Early Roman pottery and the start of the Late Antique occupation.

DISTRIBUTION: Material from the Late Roman period extends over 330 units covering 71% of the PKAP area (70.8 ha). The vast extent of material during the Roman period played a key role in the design of our survey, and the enormous quantity of Roman to Late Roman material formed a central component in the overall artifact densities. Material datable to the Late Roman period demonstrates the continued, dramatic shift of activities from the ridge to the coastal plain (Zone 1 and 2) where 86% of LR pottery was found. At the same time, Late Roman material extended to the north into Zone 4 and, to a lesser extent, into Vigla and Zone 3.

The dense scatter of Late Roman material across Zone 1 represents the most robust assemblage of material from any single period in the region (figs. 5.36–5.40). Some 3,260 Late Roman artifacts were found in Zone 1, representing 63% (total = 5,165) of all Late Roman artifacts from the survey; moreover, 86% of artifacts in Zone 1 date to the Late Roman era. Indeed, the Late Roman era marked a decisive occupational shift to the plain that influenced all subsequent periods.

The majority of Late Roman material from Zone 1 consists of roof tiles (fig. 5.41), which account for 57% of the total quantity of Late Roman artifacts (36% of the batches). Amphorae and coarse wares made up 14% and 16% of the assemblage by quantity and 20% and 19% by batch,

FIG. 5.40   *The southeastern extension of Late Roman Koutsopetria in Zone 1 (view from northwest).*

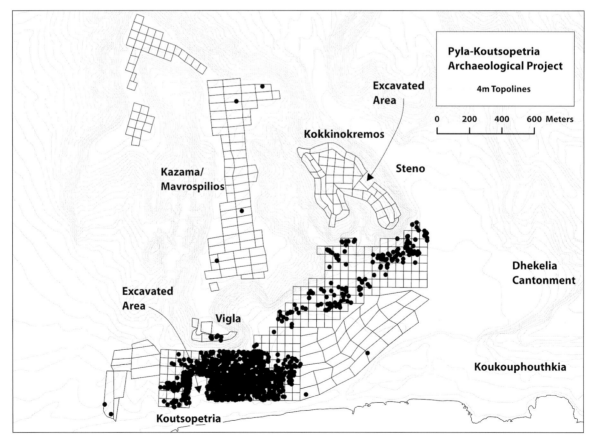

FIG. 5.41   *Distribution map of Late Roman tiles.*

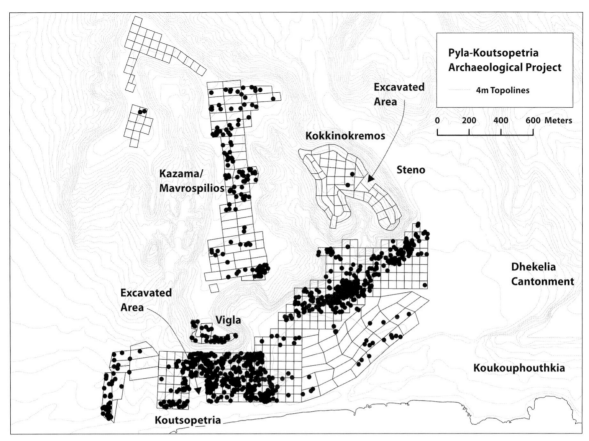

FIG. 5.42 *Distribution map of Late Roman amphorae.*

respectively (fig. 5.42). Fine wares made up 6% by quantity and 15% by batch. The significant difference between the numbers of fine wares and utilitarian wares or roof tiles is that fine ware rims are highly diagnostic and were batched separately from one another. In fact, fine wares average 1 sherd per batch, whereas tile averaged almost 4 sherds per batch, coarse wares 2.1 sherds per batch, and medium-coarse ware and amphorae 1.7 sherds per batch. Kitchen wares and medium-coarse wares in Late Roman fabrics appeared in small, yet still significant, quantities. Our relatively robust knowledge of Late Roman amphora shapes, decorations, and fabrics might account for the relative rarity of sherds identified as medium-coarse ware. The diverse assemblage, the overwhelming density of artifacts, and the significant distribution of Late Roman material throughout Zone 1 provide clear evidence for a major nucleated center of habitation.

Late Roman material extended eastward into Zone 2 as far as the border of the survey area (fig.

5.43). The similarity in the distribution of Late Roman artifacts and Hellenistic and Early Roman material suggests that little change occurred in the amount of land occupied in the eastern part of the coastal plain. The most significant change, however, is the intensity of use of this area. Zone 2 produced 1,182 artifacts of Late Roman date, which account for 23% of all Late Roman artifacts; 76% of all artifacts in Zone 2 dated to the Late Roman period. The distribution in this zone was markedly different from the material found in Zone 1. First, Late Roman tile represented only 16% of the total assemblage by quantity and batches, and most of this was concentrated near the western edge of Zone 2 bordering Zone 1. Roman coarse wares and amphorae accounted for 37% and 29% by quantity and 33% and 29% by batch, respectively. Fine wares represented 7% by quantity and 11% by batch, and medium-coarse wares 9% by quantity and batch, figures indicating their significant contribution to the overall assemblage. Altogether, this mate-

FIG. 5.43   *The eastern end of Zone 2 (view from east).*

rial suggests that Zone 2 represented habitation of some description, but not the sort of major habitation center represented in the high-density Zone 1.

The Late Roman scatter was certainly oriented to the coastal plain, but it also extended northward onto the ridges to a greater extent than in earlier periods. The dearth of tile fragments on the ridges suggests that these sherds represent either the remains of agricultural activity or smaller-scale buildings.

As in the Hellenistic and Early Roman periods, Zone 3 was the site of minor Late Roman activity. The ridge of Kokkinokremos produced 52 Late Roman artifacts, representing 1% of the LR assemblage and 14% of all artifacts dated to narrow periods on this ridge. Some 75% of these artifacts (n=39) were coarse wares in common Late Roman fabrics. A base and a rim of Cypriot Red Slip fine ware (1338.12, 1305.13), two Late Roman kitchen ware rims (1304.17, 1319.10), and a relatively well-preserved fragment of a Late Roman 1 amphora rim and handle (1328.508) present scattered evidence for Late Roman activity on the height. While the dearth of Late Roman tiles makes it unlikely

that the new occupants built monumental architecture on the plateau, the scatter may suggest a small farmstead.

Late Roman material was more significant in Zone 4, where it represented 29% of all narrow-period artifacts and 9% of Late Roman pottery. In Zone 4, LR artifacts were distributed unevenly across the area. Activity in the southern part in the area of the Mavrospilios-Kazama site declined markedly. In fact, the major concentrations of Early Roman and Roman material at the southern edge of Zone 4 appears to have seen far less intensive use by the Late Roman period. The only hint at continuity into the Late Roman period in these units is the relatively diverse assemblage of local and imported fine ware, amphorae, coarse wares, medium-coarse wares, and one kitchen ware fragment (1011.21). In the units farther to the north, the quantity and density of fine ware declines noticeably, but the quantity of medium-coarse, coarse, and amphora sherds increases. Indeed, that a low to moderate density scatter of Late Roman artifacts continues for some 800 m north of the Iron Age site above the water treatment plant indicates either extensive agricultural activity or even small-scale domestic assemblages. This material does not appear to continue in the northwest corner of the survey area, although Roman (chronotype) pottery is found there.

A meager 4% of LR artifacts were found on Vigla, which is not insignificant given the relative size of this zone. Vigla units produced one piece of fine ware (1401.93), three pieces of LR kitchen ware (1401.62 and 501), and significant quantities of coarse wares, medium-coarse wares, and amphorae; these artifacts collectively represented 33% of all narrow-period artifacts. Excavations on Vigla have confirmed the presence of small quantities of Late Roman material there, but we have not identified an occupation phase on the ridge associated with this period. Habitation on the ridge in Late Roman times was not evidently extensive.

5.3.4.3. Roman (Chronotype)

ASSEMBLAGE: The material datable to the general Roman chronotype period includes 1,238 artifacts that represent 19% of the Roman (Inclusive) period. These artifacts were assigned to 122 distinct batches (10.2 artifacts per batch) and 11 different chronotypes. Most of the assemblage derives from rather general chronotypes representing Roman kitchen and cooking pots, amphorae, medium-coarse, and coarse wares. Three types of fine ware eluded finer periodization: Roman period red slip, Roman fine ware generally, and a generic category of African Red Slip exclusively reserved for less diagnostic body sherds and bases that our ceramicist could not assign to more narrowly datable individual forms.

Most of the material datable to the Roman period consists of body sherds (71%, n=875), and a smaller percentage of handles (13%, n=155), rims (10%, n=118), and bases (4%, n=53) date to the Roman period. The most common fabric-function groups come from utilitarian vessel classes used for storage, transport, and ordinary activities: amphora (23%, n=282), medium-coarse (18%, n=221), and coarse ware (11%, n=136). The vast majority of these wares were body sherds in less diagnostic fabrics dated broadly to the Roman period. What is especially impressive is cooking

ware, which accounts for 38% of the Roman assemblage and points to the particularly diagnostic and long-lived character of Roman cooking ware fabrics, as well as the intensive use of the area as a place of habitation in the Roman period. Fine ware, which accounts for 9% (n=105) of all Roman sherds, is represented largely by body sherds (61%) and bases (28%) that derive from three chronotypes: African Red Slip, Roman Fine ware, and Roman Red Slip.

DISTRIBUTION: The Roman (chronotype) period material extends across an area of 55 ha and over 262 (56%) survey units. The highest density areas are on Vigla and in Zones 1 and 4 (fig. 5.44).

There is a significant and sustained scatter of Roman material along the coastal plain in Zone 1 (25% of LR assemblage) that declines in density as it continues into Zone 2 (13%). An interesting feature of Roman artifacts in Zone 1 is the significant concentration of fine wares and kitchen wares, which may reflect the complexity and intensity of habitation in this zone in the Late Roman period. Although theoretically Roman pottery can date any time between the first century BC and the eighth century AD, some of this material probably belongs to the Late Antique period specifically.

Roman artifacts are frequent on Vigla, where 12% of Roman artifacts were found. The assemblage shows a significant quantity of utility wares (medium-coarse, coarse, and amphora fabrics), with consistent but lower densities of fine ware. As outlined above, however, excavation has not yet revealed a major Late Roman phase on the ridge.

Some 9% of Roman pottery was found on the Mavrospilios-Kazama plateau (Zone 4), where it extends across 76% of survey units. The highest-density Roman units are in the southernmost units of Zone 4 and overlay the densest Early Roman. It seems likely that in this case Roman utilitarian wares may represent "missing" coarse ware and amphora body sherds of Early Roman date (Section 5.3.4.1).

Roman artifact scatters continue northward in Zone 4 in low to moderate density in a pattern that is very similar to the Late Roman carpet of artifacts in this area. Many of these Roman pieces presumably mark additional examples of Late

Table 5.30   Roman period in the PKAP area.

MATERIAL	FABRIC	CHRONOTYPE	PART	QUANTITY	%	% ROMAN (INCLUSIVE)
Roman (Chronotype) (99 BC–AD 749)						
Glass		Glass, Vessel, Roman	rim	2	0.2%	0.03%
Pottery	Amphora	Amphora, Roman	body	179	14.5%	2.73%
Pottery	Amphora	Amphora, Roman	handle	71	5.7%	1.08%
Pottery	Amphora	Amphora, Roman	rim	12	1.0%	0.18%
Pottery	Amphora	Amphora, Roman	toe	20	1.6%	0.31%
Pottery	Coarse	Coarse Ware, Roman	base	3	0.2%	0.05%
Pottery	Coarse	Coarse Ware, Roman	body	109	8.8%	1.67%
Pottery	Coarse	Coarse Ware, Roman	handle	16	1.3%	0.24%
Pottery	Coarse	Coarse Ware, Roman	rim	7	0.6%	0.11%
Pottery	Coarse	Coarse Ware, Roman	toe	1	0.1%	0.02%
Pottery	Fine	African Red Slip	base	16	1.3%	0.24%
Pottery	Fine	African Red Slip	body	21	1.7%	0.32%
Pottery	Fine	African Red Slip	rim	3	0.2%	0.05%
Pottery	Fine	Fineware, Roman	base	10	0.8%	0.15%
Pottery	Fine	Fineware, Roman	body	26	2.1%	0.40%
Pottery	Fine	Fineware, Roman	handle	1	0.1%	0.02%
Pottery	Fine	Fineware, Roman	rim	4	0.3%	0.06%
Pottery	Fine	Red Slip, Roman	base	3	0.2%	0.05%
Pottery	Fine	Red Slip, Roman	body	17	1.4%	0.26%
Pottery	Fine	Red Slip, Roman	handle	2	0.2%	0.03%
Pottery	Fine	Red Slip, Roman	rim	2	0.2%	0.03%
Pottery	Kitchen	Kitchen Ware, Roman	base	13	1.1%	0.20%
Pottery	Kitchen	Kitchen Ware, Roman	body	335	27.1%	5.12%
Pottery	Kitchen	Kitchen Ware, Roman	handle	58	4.7%	0.89%
Pottery	Kitchen	Kitchen Ware, Roman	lid	2	0.2%	0.03%
Pottery	Kitchen	Kitchen Ware, Roman	rim	55	4.4%	0.84%
Pottery	Kitchen	Kitchen Ware, Roman	neck	11	0.9%	0.17%
Pottery	Kitchen	Kitchen Ware, Roman	toe	1	0.1%	0.02%
Pottery	Med coarse	Amphora, Roman, Pinched Handle	handle	1	0.1%	0.02%
Pottery	Med coarse	Medium Coarse Ware, Roman	base	8	0.6%	0.12%
Pottery	Med coarse	Medium Coarse Ware, Roman	body	164	13.2%	2.51%
Pottery	Med coarse	Medium Coarse Ware, Roman	handle	6	0.5%	0.09%
Pottery	Med coarse	Medium Coarse Ware, Roman	rim	33	2.7%	0.50%
Pottery	Med coarse	Medium Coarse Ware, Roman	toe	2	0.2%	0.03%
Pottery	Med coarse	Micaceous Water Jar	body	7	0.6%	0.11%
Pottery	Pithos	Pithos, Roman	body	17	1.4%	0.26%
Total				1,238	100.0%	18.92%

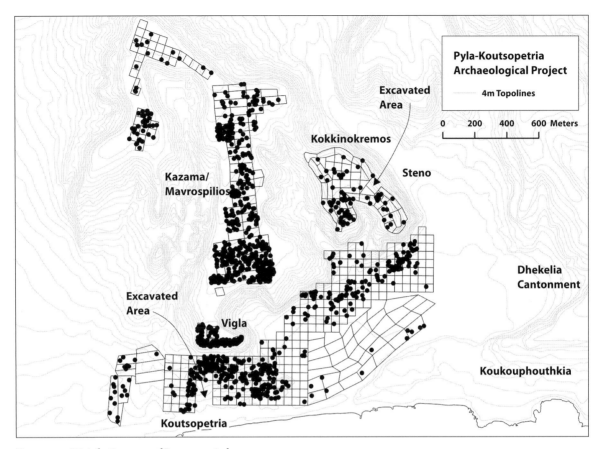

FIG. 5.44 *Distribution map of Roman period.*

Roman artifacts that were not identified precisely during analysis. Roman pottery is found in much lower density in the northwestern corner of Zone 4 on the Kazama ridge.

Finally, Roman artifacts are found in low density across the height of Kokkinokremos (Zone 3) and represent early or later Roman occupation of a small scale. About 6% of Roman pottery is found in Zone 3.

5.3.4.4. Summary Interpretation

The distribution of Roman artifacts across the study area reveals a significant shift in the main activity area from the plateau to the coastal plain. Material from the Early Roman period seems to follow more closely the pattern of artifacts from the Iron Age and Cypro-Classical to Hellenistic periods, but with a greater concentration on the coastal plain in Zone 1 and the base of the coastal ridge in Zone 2. During the Early Roman period,

then, settlement began to expand away from the ridgeline onto the coastal plain. This expansion coincides with a greater array of imported fine ware and amphorae and indicates the region's increased trade contacts with the Aegean and eastern Mediterranean.

Type fossils of amphora and table ware from the start of the third century to the later fifth century are notably absent from Koutsopetria, as they are in Cyprus and the Mediterranean generally. This could be due to issues in the creation of current ceramic typologies that might have resulted in artificial chronological gaps, and this in turn could have adversely influenced archaeological chronologies (Lund 1992; see also the discussion on CRS in 4.1.5). The nature of the Early Roman settlement in these centuries is uncertain, given the state of the evidence, but what is clear is that the Late Antique occupation begins primarily in the fifth century and reaches its greatest extent in the sixth–early seventh century. We are wary of

FIG. 5.45   *The excavated annex building south of the Early Christian basilica (view from south).*

concluding total abandonment of Koutsopetria from such a small sample of the plow zone, but the third and fourth centuries do at least suggest abatement in activity and imports.

We cannot be certain that the Roman period does not include artifacts of the middle Roman era, but the distribution of material of this period parallels the distribution of both Early and Late Roman material. At Vigla and the southern units of Zone 4, for example, we have already noted the correlation between units with Roman and Early Roman pottery. Roman pottery in Zones 1, 2, 3, and in the northern units of Zone 4 may also represent missing sherds from the Early Roman period.

By the late fifth century, the focus of activity had shifted decisively to the coastal plain where a dense scatter of fine wares, kitchen wares, and utility wares represent the remains of a wide range of activities, including habitation. The diverse and substantial assemblage of Late Roman material

documented in Zone 1 represented the core of a settlement, and the massive number of distinctive, heavy Late Roman roof tiles confirms the presence of substantial architecture beyond the partially excavated remains of the Early Christian basilica (fig. 5.45; cf. fig. 5.38). Farther west, the scatter of Late Roman material along the base of the coastal ridgeline did not preserve many roof tiles, suggesting that Late Roman activity in this area did not include large-scale architecture.

The presence of Late Roman material in Zones 3 and 4 indicates the extent of occupation in this period, but the artifacts from these zones exist in lower densities and are predominantly utilitarian in character. The scatters of artifacts in these areas indicate significantly lower thresholds of investment than on the coastal plain and may suggest short-term occupation or varied agricultural activities.

5.3.5. *Medieval and Ottoman*

ASSEMBLAGE: As elsewhere on Cyprus and across the Mediterranean, scholars have only recently begun to understand the ceramic evidence from the Medieval and Ottoman periods (Vroom 2003, 2005). In general, our knowledge of the long Medieval and Ottoman period is currently based on fine wares, which alone can be dated to the narrower Early Medieval and Late Medieval periods. Coarse and medium-coarse wares are typically only datable to very broad periods like Ancient–Medieval or Medieval–Modern. The latter will be

discussed in more detail in the next section of this chapter as evidence for the transitional Ottoman–Modern period.

Medieval (Inclusive) and Ottoman pottery consists of artifacts from five overlapping periods: Medieval (chronotype) (750–1570 AD), Early Medieval (750–1190 AD), Late Medieval (1191–1570 AD), Late Medieval–Ottoman (1191–1877 AD), and Ottoman (1571–1877 AD). These five overlapping periods mark an 800-year period, yet produced only 41 sherds, represented by 15 chronotypes in 27 batches (1.5 artifacts per batch). Most of the assemblage dates to the broad Medieval (chronotype)

Table 5.31 Medieval periods in the PKAP area.

MATERIAL	FABRIC	CHRONOTYPE	PART	QUANTITY	%	% MED–OTT (INCLUSIVE)
Medieval (Chronotype) (750–1570 AD)						
Pottery	Coarse	Coarse Ware, Medieval	body	4	50.0%	9.8%
Pottery	Coarse	Coarse Ware, Medieval	handle	2	25.0%	4.9%
Pottery	Fine	Fineware, Medieval	body	1	12.5%	2.4%
Pottery	Fine	Fineware, Medieval	rim	1	12.5%	2.4%
Total				8	100.0%	19.5%
Early Medieval (750–1190 AD)						
Pottery	Coarse	Coarse Ware, Early Medieval	body	3	100.0%	7.3%
Total				3	100.0%	7.3%
Late Medieval (1191–1570 AD)						
Pottery	Fine	Cypriot Glazed	base	1	6.3%	2.4%
Pottery	Fine	Cypriot Glazed	body	3	18.8%	7.3%
Pottery	Fine	Cypriot Glazed Group IV	base	1	6.3%	2.4%
Pottery	Fine	Cypriot Glazed Group IX	base	1	6.3%	2.4%
Pottery	Fine	Cypriot Glazed Group IX	body	2	12.5%	4.9%
Pottery	Fine	Cypriot Glazed Group V	base	1	6.3%	2.4%
Pottery	Fine	Cypriot Glazed Group V	rim	1	6.3%	2.4%
Pottery	Fine	Cypriot Green Glazed	body	1	6.3%	2.4%
Pottery	Fine	Fineware, Glazed, Medieval Late	body	1	6.3%	2.4%
Pottery	Fine	Fineware, Medieval Late	body	2	12.5%	4.9%
Pottery	Fine	Incised Ware, Medieval Late	body	1	6.3%	2.4%
Pottery	Med coarse	Medium Coarse Ware, Medieval Late	base	1	6.3%	2.4%
Total				16	100.0%	39.0%

Table 5.32   Late Medieval–Ottoman periods in the PKAP area.

MATERIAL	FABRIC	CHRONOTYPE	PART	QUANTITY	%	% MED–OTT (INCLUSIVE)
Late Medieval–Ottoman (1191–1877 AD)						
Pottery	Fine	Slip-Painted Ware, Ottoman/Venetian	body	1	100.0%	2.4%
Total				1	100.0%	2.4%
Ottoman (1571–1877 AD)						
Pottery	Fine	Fineware, Ottoman	body	1	7.7%	2.4%
Pottery	Fine	Fineware, Ottoman Drip Glazed	body	5	38.5%	12.2%
Pottery	Fine	Fineware, Ottoman Drip Glazed	rim	7	53.8%	17.1%
Total				13	100.0%	31.7%

period (20%), the Late Medieval period (39%), or the Ottoman period (32%). Early Medieval (7%) and Late Medieval-Ottoman (3%) pottery were found in only trace quantities (Tables 5.31–5.32).

While so few sherds date to the Medieval and Ottoman periods, the assemblage is still quite diverse. There are small concentrations of "Ottoman Drip Glazed ware" (n=12; **1065.15**), and locally produced Late Medieval Cypriot Glazed ware (n=4; **189.46**) and Cypriot Glazed Group IX ware (**208.18**). There are also concentrations of Early Medieval (n=3) and Medieval coarse ware (n=6; 140.18). Other chronotypes appear in singular instances.

Medieval to Ottoman pottery overwhelmingly consists of fine ware (n=31, 76%), with a smaller amount of body and coarse ware (n=9, 22%), and a single medium-coarse ware body sherd (2.3%). We identified no kitchen ware, tile, lamps, or pithos sherds to the Medieval or Ottoman periods.

The majority of sherds are body sherds (58%), with a modest number of rims (22%) and a smaller corpus of bases (12%) and handles (5%). The highly diagnostic character of glazed Medieval sherds clearly had a great impact on our identification of Medieval and Ottoman material in the survey area (Sanders 1995; Gregory 2003; Vroom 2005). Glazed sherds represent 71% (n=29) of the assemblage. Feature sherds and body sherds decorated with slip, glazing, or combing accounted for 93% of all Medieval and Ottoman pottery.

This overview of fabric groups and extant parts indicates that Medieval and Ottoman periods mark a mostly invisible landscape, represented only by the type fossils of decorated pottery and feature sherds. The 41 sherds identified to these periods mark a small fraction of the Medieval and Ottoman material actually on the ground. However, even if the identified objects represent only 10% of Ottoman and Medieval pottery collected, this still shows a remarkable contraction compared to the preceding Late Roman period. The dramatic decrease in activity at the end of antiquity persisted at a lower level into the post-antique Medieval landscape.

DISTRIBUTION: Pottery dated to the Early Medieval, Late Medieval, Medieval, Ottoman, and Medieval–Ottoman periods is distributed over a mere 24 units, covering only 5% of the survey area (5 ha). This distribution is similar to the distribution of Cypro-Archaic material, where a very small quantity of material (31 artifacts) appeared over a small area (3.3 ha), but in this case, the Medieval and Ottoman periods represent eight long centuries. Medieval and Ottoman material concentrates almost entirely on the coastal plain (71% of assemblage) with a small amount of Medieval sherds in Zone 3 (12%) and Ottoman pottery in Zone 4 (17%) (figs. 5.46–5.48).

In Zones 3 and 4, Ottoman and Medieval artifacts are found in one unit each. A small scatter

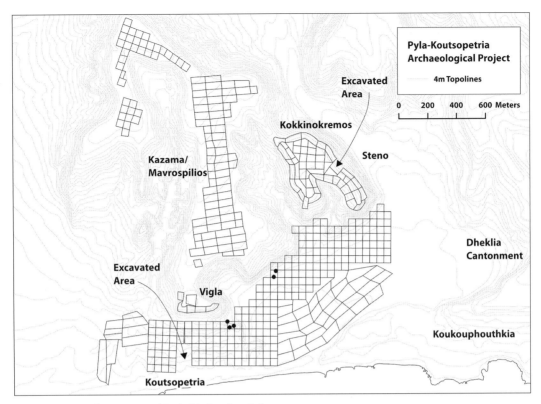

FIG. 5.46 *Distribution map of Early Medieval period.*

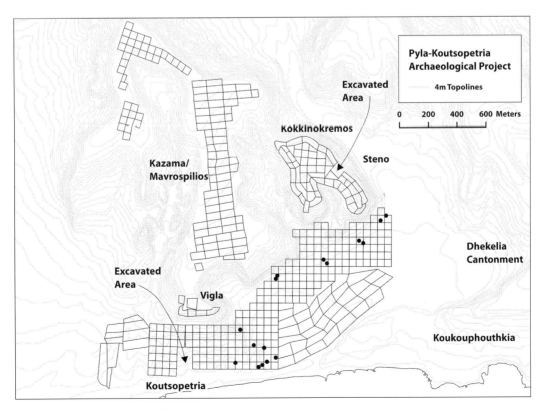

FIG. 5.47 *Distribution map of Late Medieval period.*

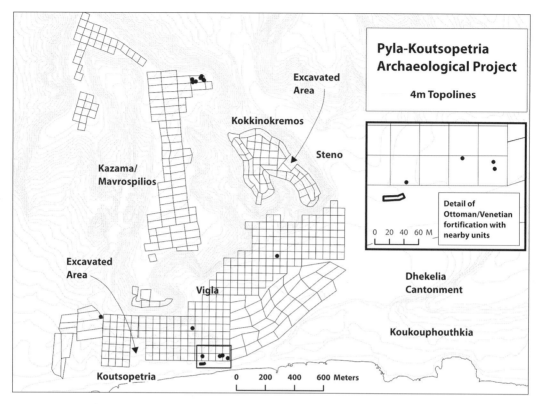

Fig. 5.48   *Distribution map of Ottoman period.*

Fig. 5.49   *Building foundation along coastal road, probably of Ottoman/Venetian date.*

of three pieces of Ottoman drip glaze appeared in Unit 1065 (1065.13, **1065.15**) along the northern edge of the Mavrospilios ridge in Zone 4. These sherds are associated with a considerable quantity of coarse and kitchen wares assigned to the Ancient–Historic period and a few fragments of Late Roman coarse ware. Since Late Roman fabrics from the area are relatively well-known, it is possible that at least some of the Ancient–Historic sherds should be associated with the Ottoman fine wares. A similar small concentration of slipped Medieval coarse wares appeared in Unit 1322 in the center of Zone 3 (1322.4, 1322.5, and 1322.6). These two concentrated scatters represent singular episodes of land use rather than systematic occupation of these two zones. They tell us relatively little about the function of these areas during the Medieval to Ottoman periods.

Zones 1 and 2, in contrast, preserve evidence for more systematic or sustained activity. The northeastern corner of Zone 1 preserved several artifacts of likely Early Medieval date, indicating activity after the end of the Late Roman period (fig. 5.46). A relatively light scatter of Late Medieval and Ottoman material exists at the eastern border between Zones 1 and 2. While there are only 12 sherds in all, the scatter consists of Late Medieval (49.35, 52.11–12, **54.4**, 159.15, and **161.8**) and Ottoman (160.17-18) glazed fine wares (figs. 5.47 and 5.48). This material appears to be associated with a wall that runs parallel to the current coastal road that may date to the Venetian period (fig. 5.49). Medieval material also appears in the units below the Mavrospilios and Kokkinokremos ridge line. The majority of this material appears to date to the Late Medieval to Ottoman period. The scatter may well be a continuation of the scatter documented in the northwestern part of Zone 2. In fact, the majority of material appears to run along the edge of the now-infilled embayment and probably indicates some continuing harbor facility in the area, before the inlet became infilled in subsequent centuries. The artifacts evidently have some association with the remains of a wall that probably belongs to a military installation along the coastal road dating to either the Venetian or Ottoman period (Section 2.4).

SUMMARY INTERPRETATION: The most striking characteristic of the Medieval and Ottoman assemblage is the dearth of diagnostic kitchen and utilitarian wares. In part, this can be attributed to the generally poor state of our knowledge of Medieval and Ottoman period coarse wares and the significant invisibility of these periods. Yet, the very limited number and distribution of fine wares and feature sherds still suggests that activity in the region declined precipitously at the end of antiquity. Unfortunately, our inability to identify the full range of possible ceramic material from these periods makes it difficult for us to determine the function of even relatively well-defined concentrations of material from this period. Since we could not identify with certainty kitchen wares or even basic utility wares, it was difficult to determine whether the material present represents any specialized activity. It is nevertheless common to associate fine ware with habitation. Despite our inability to assign a clear function, the material present hints that the coastal zone area continued to see limited activity after the end of antiquity. The concentrations along the edge of the now in-filled harbor suggest that activity in the area continued to be associated with access to the sea, the natural protection from winds and waves afforded by at least a sandy and sheltered anchorage, and buildings along the coastal road.

5.3.6. The Medieval to Modern Transition

The transition from the Medieval to the Modern period is among the more difficult to document in the archaeological record. The Medieval–Modern period is defined broadly and refers to any time in the Medieval era or Modern period, but most of the collected examples mark true transition pieces dating from the Late Medieval (or Ottoman) period and the Early Modern period. The transition from the Medieval to Early Modern period represents a complex set of political, economic, and social changes. Moreover, much locally-produced material does not represent a significant break from earlier periods, making it exceedingly difficult to understand changes in settlement or activity patterns in the surface record (Gabrieli 2004), despite the significant political changes on the island. The challenge of this ambiguity has led us to isolate material associated with these problematic periods of transition and to understand them in relation to earlier and later material.

ASSEMBLAGE: The Medieval-Modern period consists of 100 ceramic artifacts divided into 28 batches (3.6 artifacts per batch) and 10 chronotypes (Table 5.33). The vast majority of these artifacts were medium-coarse (76%) and coarse wares (19%). Such utility and storage wares are the product of long-standing technologies and practices producing shapes and fabrics that remained consistent for long periods. In comparison, fine wares and cooking wares datable to the Medieval–Modern period make up only 2% and 1% of the assemblage, respectively. Fine wares are particularly susceptible to changes in taste, technologies, and economic and political relationships.

We identified the majority of Medieval–Modern wares on the basis of fabric rather than shape, which means that feature sherds and decorated pieces played less of a role in producing the Medieval–Modern period. The majority of the sherds from this period were body sherds (60%) and most of them (95%) lacked surface treatment or decoration. Large, clunky rims in diagnostic fabrics were also relatively common (31%). The rarity

Table 5.33   Medieval–Modern period in the PKAP area.

MATERIAL	FABRIC	CHRONOTYPE	PART	QUANTITY	%
Medieval–Modern (1191–2008 AD)					
Glass		Glass Vessel, Medieval–Modern	rim	1	1%
Metal		Horseshoe		1	1%
Pottery	Coarse	Coarse Ware, Medieval–Modern	base	1	1%
Pottery	Coarse	Coarse Ware, Medieval–Modern	body	13	13%
Pottery	Coarse	Coarse Ware, Medieval–Modern	neck	1	1%
Pottery	Coarse	Coarse Ware, Medieval–Modern	rim	4	4%
Pottery	Fine	Fineware, Glazed, Medieval–Modern	base	1	1%
Pottery	Fine	Fineware, Glazed, Medieval–Modern	body	1	1%
Pottery	Kitchen	Kitchen Ware, Medieval–Modern	body	1	1%
Pottery	Med coarse	Cypriot W-1	body	2	2%
Pottery	Med coarse	Cypriot W-1	rim	2	2%
Pottery	Med coarse	Cypriot W-3	base	1	1%
Pottery	Med coarse	Cypriot W-3	body	30	30%
Pottery	Med coarse	Cypriot W-3	rim	10	10%
Pottery	Med coarse	Cypriot W-5	body	5	5%
Pottery	Med coarse	Cypriot W-5	handle	2	2%
Pottery	Med coarse	Cypriot W-5	rim	10	10%
Pottery	Med coarse	Cypriot W-6	rim	1	1%
Pottery	Med coarse	Cypriot W-6	body	1	1%
Pottery	Med coarse	Cypriot W-7	body	7	7%
Pottery	Med coarse	Cypriot W-7	handle	2	2%
Pottery	Med coarse	Cypriot W-7	rim	3	3%
Total				100	100%

of handles (4%) and bases (3%) may provide some indication of the shapes of the vessels, although handles and bases are generally less common than rims and body sherds for most periods. These patterns indicate that the Medieval–Modern period was a fairly visible period in the landscape.

The medium-coarse wares consisted of a group of Cypriot Coarse Ware types identified initially by the Sydney Cyprus Survey and designated by numbers. The assemblage of almost 70 artifacts (n=69) from our survey area produced six types of Cypriot Coarse Ware (W1, W2, W3, W5, W6, and W7), and all but the last are true transition pieces, dating between the Late Medieval–Ottoman period and the Early Modern era. Some 41% of all pottery represented fabric 3 (W3). The Sydney Cyprus Survey described the W3 (**179.15**, **12.46**, **13.25**, **62.33**), W5 (**241.13**, **2.38**, **233.17**), and W6 (138.1) wares as mostly associated with a range of utility wares, storage vessels, and coarse table wares, such as pitchers, and this holds true for Koutsopetria. These three fabrics accounted for 60 artifacts from the survey. The less common fabric termed W7 accounts for 12 sherds and most likely dates to the Early Modern period (**56.44**) (Given and Knapp 2003: 288–89).

The coarse wares appeared in only the most general category: Medieval–Modern Coarse Ware (n=25; **38.29**, **18.21**, **5.31**, **18.24**, **6.47**, **8.8**). Some of the fabrics in which these artifacts appeared may represent poorly preserved or irregular examples of the established transitional Cypriot Coarse Ware types (e.g., **5.31**, **6.47**, and **38.29**). It is also possible, however, that these artifacts represent pieces that were simply not very diagnostic. Unfortunately, little research has been done on creating typologies for Medieval and post-Medieval coarse wares on Cyprus due to the continuity in ware forms, and this limits our ability to be more precise within this category (Gabrieli 2004: 287).

The two fine ware sherds from this period were both glazed and may date to the Late Medieval or Ottoman periods (1453.6, 159.14).

DISTRIBUTION: Medieval–Modern material appears in over 61 units with an area of 10.8 ha, about twice the area as the Medieval and Ottoman periods combined. Medieval–Modern pottery occurs in Zones 1–4, but concentrates in the coastal plain (93% of total assemblage) (fig. 5.50).

Most of the Medieval–Modern pottery concentrates in Zones 1 and 2, following the distribution of the Late Medieval and Ottoman periods. The scatter of "W" wares in these areas is particularly significant because it provides a pattern that allows us to unpack the relationship between these coarse fabrics and the history of activity of the settlement. The most common type of "W" ware is W3, which is scattered throughout Zone 1 and continues to the east into Zone 2. W1, W5, and W6 wares more or less follow the same pattern, except these chronotypes tend to cluster closer to the base of Vigla in Zone 1 and only extend farther south at this zone's easternmost extent. In Zone 2, all of the so-called "W" wares appear in a scatter extending along the base of the Mavrospilios-Kazama ridgeline. In Zone 3, five examples of the "W" ware appeared in unit 1320, including a single example of W1 (1320.12), W3 (1320.13), W7 (1320.16), and two examples of W5 (1320.14, 1320.15).

The distribution of W7 ware, the latest in the W series, suggests a different pattern of activity. A distinct group of W7 sherds appears in units at the easternmost extent of Zone 1 (**56.44**, 55.9, 159.12, 160.6) and follows a pattern more in keeping with later material of a secure Modern date (cf. figs. 5.50 and 5.52). Moreover, the absence of W7 ware in units where other W-wares appear may suggest a different date for the deposition of these sherds. It is tempting to see this pattern of distribution as evidence for concentrated Modern activity in the eastern part of Zone 1, but these units also produced a scatter of clearly dated Late Medieval ceramics, and other formation processes may have influenced the distribution of material in this area.

Like W1, W3, W5, and W6 wares, Medieval–Modern coarse wares appear throughout Zone 1, but generally appear less frequently in Zone 2.

Very little Medieval–Ottoman material occurred on the ridges of Vigla, Zone 3, and Zone 4. In fact, only two artifacts of this date appear in all of Zone 4: a single sherd of coarse ware (1012.25) and a single sherd of glazed fine ware (1453.6). The latter appeared amidst a very small scatter of broad period (Ancient Historic) kitchen ware, coarse ware, and medium-coarse ware that may suggest a domestic assemblage.

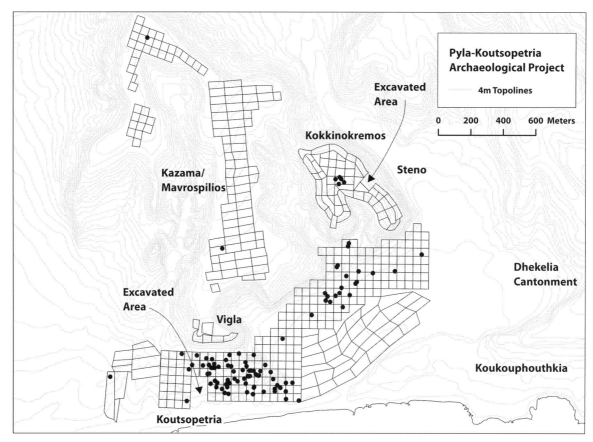

FIG. 5.50 *Distribution map of Medieval–Modern period.*

SUMMARY INTERPRETATION: The distribution of coarse and medium-coarse wares from the Medieval–Modern chronotype period may well present a moment in time in the transformation of our survey area. The continued presence of Medieval–Modern material throughout Zones 1 and 2 demonstrates that activities continued on the coastal plain from the end of the Medieval period into the early Modern era. The absence of fine ware, however, makes it difficult to assign this activity to a precise date. Since the identifiable coarse ware sherds make this a very visible period in the landscape, however, we can be sure that the 100 sherds of Medieval–Modern date truly reflect a weak period in the history of the settlement.

5.3.7. The Modern Period

ASSEMBLAGE: As a diachronic survey, PKAP documented the distribution of Modern material across the landscape, including material contem-porary with the project itself. Like earlier periods, the Modern (Inclusive) material was divided into three overlapping chronotype periods. The broadest era was the Modern (chronotype) period (1878–2008 AD), and it was complemented by the narrower periods of Early Modern (1878–1949 AD) and Modern Present (1950–2008 AD). Combined, these periods represent 136 artifacts divided into 31 chronotypes and 82 batches (1.9 artifacts per batch) (Tables 5.34–5.36).

Since artifacts from the recent past are better preserved in the archaeological record, we have a greater range of materials present than in previous periods. Indeed, over half (n=73, 54%) of the material dating to the Modern (Inclusive) period is not ceramic but metal, plastic, or glass. As projects elsewhere have noted, the quantity and character of Modern material often has caused some confusion among fieldwalkers, resulting in under-sampling of objects seen more as modern trash than archaeological artifacts (Tartaron et al.

Table 5.34   Modern Period in the PKAP area.

MATERIAL	FABRIC	CHRONOTYPE	PART	QUANTITY	%	% MODERN (INCLUSIVE)
Modern (Chronotype) (1878–2008 AD)						
Glass		Glass, Modern	body	21	20.0%	15.4%
Glass		Glass, Modern	rim	3	2.9%	2.2%
Glass		Glass, Modern	toe	1	1.0%	0.7%
Glass		Glass, Modern, Bottle Clear	base	1	1.0%	0.7%
Glass		Glass, Modern, Bottle Clear	body	4	3.8%	2.9%
Glass		Glass, Modern, Bottle Clear	rim	2	1.9%	1.5%
Glass		Glass, Modern, Bottle Green	base	2	1.9%	1.5%
Glass		Glass, Modern, Bottle Green	body	4	3.8%	2.9%
Glass		Glass, Window, Modern	body	1	1.0%	0.7%
Metal		Iron Nail, Modern		1	1.0%	0.7%
Metal		Iron Nail, Modern		1	1.0%	0.7%
Metal		Metal, Modern		3	2.9%	2.2%
Metal		Metal, Modern		6	5.7%	4.4%
Other		Building Materials, Modern	body	1	1.0%	0.7%
Other		Bullet, Modern		8	7.6%	5.9%
Other		Bullet, Modern		1	1.0%	0.7%
Other		Plastic, Modern Present	base	1	1.0%	0.7%
Other		Plastic, Modern Present	body	2	1.9%	1.5%
Other		Plastic, Modern Present	rim	1	1.0%	0.7%
Terra cotta		Ceramic, Electrical	body	1	1.0%	0.7%
Pottery	Coarse	Coarse Ware, Modern	base	1	1.0%	0.7%
Pottery	Coarse	Coarse Ware, Modern	body	4	3.8%	2.9%
Pottery	Coarse	Coarse Ware, Modern	rim	6	5.7%	4.4%
Pottery	Fine	Fineware, Glazed, Modern	rim	2	1.9%	1.5%
Pottery	Fine	Fineware, Modern	base	1	1.0%	0.7%
Pottery	Fine	Fineware, Modern	body	12	11.4%	8.8%
Pottery	Fine	Fineware, Modern	rim	3	2.9%	2.2%
Pottery	Med coarse	Insulator, ceramic, Modern	base	1	1.0%	0.7%
Pottery	Med coarse	Insulator, ceramic, Modern	body	2	1.9%	1.5%
Pottery	Med coarse	Insulator, ceramic, Modern	rim	2	1.9%	1.5%
Pottery	Med coarse	Medium Coarse Ware, Modern	body	1	1.0%	0.7%
Pottery	Semi-fine	Semi-fine Ware, Modern	body	1	1.0%	0.7%
Pottery	Tile	Tile, flat, Modern	body	2	1.9%	1.5%
Pottery	Tile	Tile, Modern	body	2	1.9%	1.5%
Total				105	100.0%	77.2%

Table 5.35   Early Modern period in the PKAP area.

MATERIAL	FABRIC	CHRONOTYPE	PART	QUANTITY	%	% MODERN (INCLUSIVE)
Early Modern (1878–1949 AD)						
Pottery	Kitchen	Kitchen Ware, Modern Early	body	1	33.3%	0.7%
Pottery	Med coarse	Medium Coarse Ware, Modern Early	rim	1	33.3%	0.7%
Pottery	Tile	Tile, flat, Modern Early	edge	1	33.3%	0.7%
Total				3	100.0%	2.2%

Table 5.36   Present Modern period in the PKAP area.

MATERIAL	FABRIC	CHRONOTYPE	PART	QUANTITY	%	% MODERN (INCLUSIVE)
Modern, Present (1950–2008 AD)						
Glass		Glass, Vessel, Modern Present		1	3.6%	0.7%
Glass		Glass, Vessel, Modern Present	base	1	3.6%	0.7%
Glass		Glass, Vessel, Modern Present	body	3	10.7%	2.2%
Other		Building Materials, Modern Present	body	4	14.3%	2.9%
Other		Ceramic Floor/Wall Tile, Modern Present	body	1	3.6%	0.7%
Other		Ceramic Floor/Wall Tile, Modern Present	edge	1	3.6%	0.7%
Stone		Stone, Paving, Modern Present		1	3.6%	0.7%
Pottery	Coarse	Coarse Ware, Modern Present	body	1	3.6%	0.7%
Pottery	Fine	Fineware, Glazed, Modern Present	body	1	3.6%	0.7%
Pottery	Fine	Fineware, Modern Present	base	1	3.6%	0.7%
Pottery	Fine	Fineware, Modern Present	body	2	7.1%	1.5%
Pottery	Fine	Fineware, Modern Present	rim	1	3.6%	0.7%
Pottery	Kitchen	Modern Yoghurt Pot	body	3	10.7%	2.2%
Pottery	Med coarse	Flowerpot, Modern Present	base	1	3.6%	0.7%
Pottery	Tile	Brick, with holes, Modern Present	body	3	10.7%	2.2%
Pottery	Tile	Brick, with holes, Modern Present	edge	3	10.7%	2.2%
Total				28	100.0%	20.6%

2006). We asked that walkers sample the unit using the chronotype system irrespective of the period, but the wide variety and substantial quantity of Modern period trash often hindered the systematic collection of material. For example, the use of an area adjacent to the survey as a military firing range produced a significant number of bullets and shell casings across the survey area, but fieldwalkers collected this material on a very selective basis owing to the potential risk of encountering an ordinance in the field, as well as the ubiquitous character of bullets.

Pottery datable to the various Modern periods (n=59) appeared in every fabric, except for amphorae, lamps, and pithoi. Fine ware was the most common type in the survey area (39%), but coarse and medium-coarse ware made up a solid 20% and 14%, respectively. Kitchen ware sherds

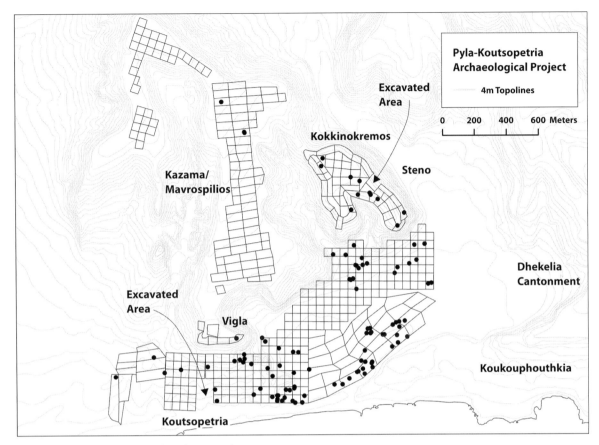

FIG. 5.51 *Distribution map of Modern periods.*

were relatively rare (7%), despite its count including the rather common Modern yoghurt pot (n=3, **55.8**). The paucity of kitchen wares in the assemblage coincides with the introduction of metal cooking pots into modern kitchens. The general absence of fine wares from the survey, as well as lack of metal cooking pots suggest that there was probably little domestic activity in the area in the Modern period. Small quantities of tile and brick (n=11, 19%) indicate either buildings or, more likely, dumping.

The majority of the pottery sherds datable in some way to the Modern period are body sherds (58%), with rims and edges (34%) following closely behind, and bases (8%) in smaller quantities. Strangely, we identified no handles dating to the Modern period, which may reflect the decline in the use of ceramic vessels for transport and table use.

The Modern (Inclusive) chronotypes include a range of building materials (tile, brick, and iron nails), electrical equipment (insulator fragments),

military artifacts (modern bullets), and garbage. The very small assemblage of pottery (n=59) does not suggest a significant domestic phase of use but points to discard practices associated with the modern coastal road and development of the area.

DISTRIBUTION: Material from the Modern (Inclusive) periods extends over 79 units over an area of 19.5 ha and appears in all five zones of the survey area. The distribution of this material is very different from material dated to earlier periods (fig. 5.51).

Only 19% of Modern artifacts occurred on the ridges above the coast. The scatter in Zone 4 is especially sparse, involving 7 artifacts in 5 units. Only two of these artifacts are ceramic: a piece of Modern (present) coarse ware in Unit 1401 and a fragment of Modern medium-coarse ware in Unit 1400. The rest of the material is metal or glass (including some vessels) and dates to the Modern or Modern (present) periods. Since this area con-

Fig. 5.52   *Southeastern corner of Zone 1 showing modern coastal road.*

tinues to be under cultivation, is cut by dirt roads, and is used by the military, it is not particularly surprising that some Modern material appears. There is no reason to conclude habitation from this light debris.

Zone 3, likewise, produced a rather modest amount of Modern material. Most of this assemblage consisted of modern bullets (8 of 11 artifacts) derived from the still-used British military firing range to the west of the height. There were two ceramic artifacts dating to the Modern period: a piece of brown glazed fine ware (1351.6) and a piece of hard-fired Modern roof tile (1318.15).

Zones 1 and 2 produced more robust assemblages of material (81% of Modern artifacts), but like the material from Zone 3, the character of these assemblages was quite different from that produced by earlier periods, reflecting the changing nature of material culture, use of the area, and the different rates of preservation. For example, the survey teams collected several fragments of ceramic insulators used on high-tension electrical wires, as well as numerous fragments of metal, window glass, and thick hard-fired bricks with their characteristic holes. Such construction debris

accounts for over half of the artifacts recovered from Zone 1 and indicates interesting new forms of connection of the site to the region.

The assemblage of vessels consisted of broken glass bottles, fine and semi-fine pottery, and medium-coarse and coarse wares. This material appears across the entire extent of Zone 1, with a particular concentration of material at the zone's southeastern corner and an area of cultivation immediately west of the excavated areas, suggesting that this assemblage relates to agricultural activities and modern traffic (fig. 5.52).

Zone 2 produced a more diverse array of material that is linked closely to the changing use of this area during the Modern period. The scatter appeared in two distinct concentrations. One extends approximately 200 m south of the modern coastal road linking Larnaca with Dhekelia, the other runs along the base of the Kokkinokremos ridge extending no more than 200 m north.

Among these units, three fragments date to the Early Modern period. Two of these come from units 506 (506.8) and 511 (511.3) and may fall along the course of a nineteenth-century coastal road through the area. These sherds appear about 200 m to the east of a scatter of Modern glazed fine wares, which seem to coincide with the so-called "Venetian" wall running parallel to the contemporary coastal road. Some 250 m farther east, there is another small scatter of Modern glazed fine ware. While this sparse and disparate scatter of material is clearly not a use assemblage, these artifacts are associated with either discard from the present road or the earlier road that passed through the low-lying section of the coastal plain.

The other Early Modern sherd appears in a unit (188) near the base of Kokkinokremos amidst an equally indistinct scatter of Modern material. Half of the material from these units is not ceramic and represents a hodgepodge of glass bottles, bullets, and modern building materials. The ceramic vessels include a light scatter of Modern tableware, yoghurt pots, and roof tiles. This material most likely derives from the military activities in these low-lying fields or the construction of dirt access roads around the base of the Kokkinokremos ridge.

SUMMARY INTERPRETATION: Very little of the Modern material appears to be associated with primary-use domestic assemblages. Most of the material, and particularly that from Zone 2, appears to relate to a road through the study area and reflects new kinds of discard associated with the movement of farm vehicles, British military trucks, and beachgoers and vacationers. As peopled moved through the area, they discarded trash along the road; indeed, the scatter of recent trash provides an analogy of this practice. Some of the material is clearly associated with the area's modern use, including the number of metal bullets found on Kokkinokremos, the construction debris associated with the erecting of electrical pylons

in the area, and the faunal material discarded as trash in the south.

5.3.8. Faunal Material

Fieldwalkers did not look specifically for faunal remains, but nevertheless collected a random sample of material from across the entire survey area. In 2010, Dr. David Reese examined the faunal remains collected during the survey. Reese's analysis showed that the vast majority of faunal remains came from goats or sheep (*ovis/capra*). Several are clearly recent and show signs of butchering. One shows clear signs of burn marks. The proximity of most of the sheep or goat bones to the road confirms our observations above about modern dumping. We also identified several bones from dogs (512.3, 112.1) from units in the southern part of Zone 2 and several examples of sheep and goat bones that do not appear as recent as those immediately adjacent to the road (520.1, 526.1). In several units, fieldwalkers recovered chicken bones. There is not enough evidence to imagine these chicken bones as anything more than discard from passing vehicles or bones brought into the survey area by local dogs.

The most sensational faunal find from the survey area was a fragment of human skull from a unit west of the road from the coast to Pyla village (537.8). Unfortunately, a solitary fragment of human bone is not adequate grounds for any substantial argument, but it is the only evidence for any human remains or burial from the survey area. The presence of a skull fragment so far west of the main cluster of building material and the highest-density units would at least be consistent with the location of a cemetery from the settlement.

Chapter 6

Features in the Landscape

by William Caraher

The intensive scrutiny of the study area as part of the pedestrian survey naturally revealed a more complex landscape than more superficial or episodic investigations of previous years. In 2005 and 2006, we conducted a separate survey of cut blocks and architectural fragments piled in snaking field clearance piles across the site of Koutsopetria. The rough outline of a Venetian fortification just north of the coastal road from Dhekelia to Larnaca came to light in conjunction with our study of textual sources documenting the history of the region. Finally, we used oblique aerial photographs, generously taken by the RAF, to observe features in the landscape, the most significant being the south wall and *taphros* of a Hellenistic fortification on the elevated plateau of Vigla. The walls on Vigla received further documentation through a series of small-scale excavations, which are currently under study (Olson et al. 2013; Caraher et al. 2014). In this chapter, we have combined the results of the feature survey, the mapping of the Venetian wall, and a preliminary study of the fortifications on Vigla as another body of material for understanding the history of the settlement.

6.1. FEATURES

In 2005 and 2006, the project documented over 500 features from across the survey area through a different method than the distributional survey procedures (Chapter 2). In the course of surveying a unit, fieldwalkers described each feature, took GPS coordinates, and measured it when fully preserved (Section 2.2.2). The most common features were cut limestone blocks, but there were also many gypsum blocks, several pieces of imported marble, and a number of pieces of agricultural implements. Most of the architectural fragments were concentrated around Vigla or in the Koutsopetria plain (Zone 1), and very few occurred in the other zones of the survey. Farmers have moved these blocks to stone piles throughout the fields, because collapsed building material, standing walls, and other compact features made it otherwise impossible to cultivate (figs. 6.1–6.2). Given the significant preservation of the Late Roman site in general, it is unlikely that this material has moved far from its place of abandonment and destruction.

6.1.1. Cut Limestone Blocks

Most of the cut stone on the surface of the Vigla ridge consists of limestone blocks that were probably quarried from bedrock outcrops around the site. None of these cut blocks adhere to a standard size, but the majority fall between 0.3 and 0.7 m in length and 0.3 and 0.5 m in width. For blocks where three dimensions were visible, their volume was between 0.03 and 0.06 m³. Given a common density figure for solid limestone (<2,700 kg / m³),

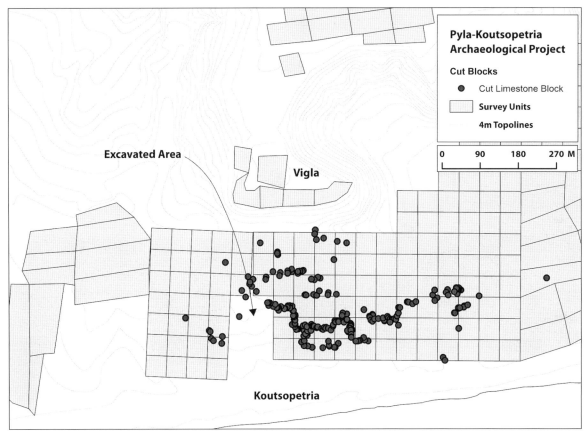

FIG. 6.1   *Map showing scatter of cut limestone blocks.*

these blocks weighed no more than 200 kg (.20 metric tons), a size relatively easily moved for construction. Some blocks, of course, could be much larger, exceeding 1 m in length and weighing close to 500 kg (.50 metric tons). With blocks of this size, there is no doubt that large scale, monumental architecture once stood in the immediate area.

Little in the way of an overall pattern arises from the distribution of limestone blocks across the Koutsopetria plain (fig. 6.1). It seems likely that many of the blocks were in secondary use, extracted from the fortification walls that encircled Vigla. Moreover, the blocks have generally been placed at the edge of plowed areas in a maze of stone piles. Several clusters of large cut blocks indicate the presence of more substantial buildings. A group of 33 blocks scattered over a 50 × 50 m area in the central part of Koutsopetria includes 18 blocks that are larger than 0.05 m³ and 8 blocks that are .1 m³ or more. These blocks are in the center of the cultivated area of Koutsopetria and

amidst units of exceptional artifact and tile density, suggesting that they should be associated with a large building.

6.1.2.   *Gypsum Blocks*

Like the cut limestone blocks, the cut gypsum blocks clustered in rock piles across the coastal plain. These blocks are generally similar in size to the cut limestone blocks, with lengths of around half a meter and widths of 0.3 m (fig. 6.3). Most blocks had a volume between 0.01 and 0.06 m³, and, like the limestone, only occasionally exceeded 0.1 m³. As gypsum has a slightly lower density (<2,300 m³) than limestone, the blocks had correspondingly lower weights, usually less than 140 kg. Many smaller fragments of gypsum were scattered across the fields and several very large blocks appeared clustered together.

Generally, the gypsum blocks occurred more frequently in the northern and eastern part of

Fig. 6.2   *Cut blocks arrayed along field boundaries.*

Koutsopetria (fig. 6.4). The significant cluster of gypsum blocks in the northern part may reflect the less intensive character of agriculture in this part of the plain and suggest that plowing destroyed some of the more delicate gypsum slabs in the south. The location of the blocks and the similar size of many of the larger and better preserved slabs could also suggest that one or several monumental buildings stood along the ridge running along the north of Koutsopetria plain or on the eastern part of Zone 1. There was an episode of destructive deep plowing in the spring of 2008 along the formerly uncultivated northern ridge of Koutsopetria where a number of gypsum blocks were found. This work produced a significant number of architectural blocks, some of which may have been *in situ* along with a dense scatter of fine ware, roof tile, and storage vessels.

Of the two large groups of well-preserved gypsum, the largest group stretches across a 120 m × 25 m wide swath across the eastern part of the Koutsopetria plain (fig. 6.4). This group contains over 30 blocks, the majority of which exceeded 0.5 m in length, and six of which were 1 m or longer. Generally, these slabs were 0.15–0.3 m wide, and the largest blocks were close to or in excess of 0.1 m³ in volume and weighed more than 200 kg. A second group of smaller blocks ran along the top of the Koutsopetria ridge. The blocks in this group were generally smaller, with most of the blocks having a maximum preserved length of 0.3 m and width slightly less than that. The thickness of the blocks was less than 0.1 m in general. These thin slabs had volumes less than 0.02 m³ and weight less than 40 kg. It seems plausible to associate these thin gypsum slabs with floor panels.

6.1.3.   Cut Marble Slabs and Revetment

Along with Cypriot gypsum and locally quarried limestone, the survey area produced a small group of cut marble slabs. Most of these came from the central area of the Koutsopetria plain (fig. 6.4) and were embedded in rock piles at the edges of cultivated tracks of land. The marble fragments are small, less than .3 m in maximum length, and

FIG. 6.3   *Large gypsum slab.*

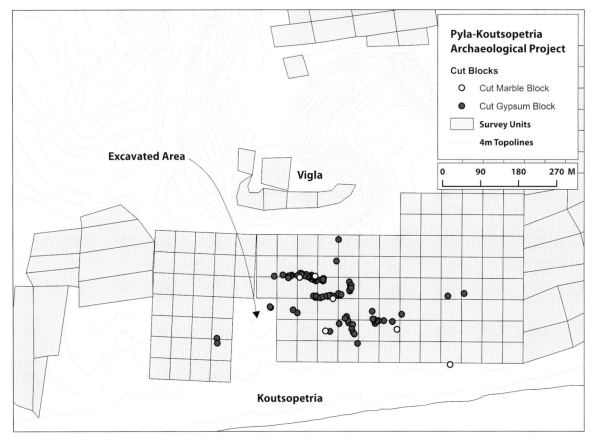

FIG. 6.4   *Map showing scatter of gypsum and marble blocks and revetment.*

relatively thin (<.04 m), suggesting that most came from wall revetment or floor slabs. The wide distribution of material perhaps indicates that there were several marble clad buildings on the plain of Koutsopetria, even though so little marble survives.

6.1.4. Smaller Fragments of Gypsum and Marble Revetment

As part of the distributional survey, fieldwalkers counted and collected numerous small fragments of gypsum (<100 g) from the survey units over the course of standard fieldwalking. These fragments of gypsum almost certainly came from larger blocks or perhaps floor tiles damaged by the plow over the centuries. The vast majority of these small fragments came from the Koutsopetria plain (Zone 1), but a number of fragments came from a light scatter of material in Zone 2 at the base of Kokkinokremos.

Fieldwalkers also collected marble fragments that were sufficiently small enough to take from the field. In general, these fragments were still significantly larger than the gypsum fragments, averaging over 100 g, with some larger fragments being over 300 g. Many of the larger fragments could be associated with revetment from a monumental building on the Koutsopetria plain (Zone 1). Smaller fragments of <100 g may derive from *opus sectile* floors common in Late Roman architecture and noted in the excavations of the basilica apse at Koutsopetria. Of course, marble originally used as revetment could have easily been reworked for tesserae in *opus sectile* floors, so the distinction between small, thin marble fragments used as revetment vs. *opus sectile* is not instructive. It is worth noting that two small fragments (<100 g) came from the eastern reaches of Zone 2, immediately below the hill of Kokkinokremos.

The presence of some small gypsum and marble fragments and a continuous scatter of Late Roman and other roof tiles (see fig. 5.41) confirms the view that large-scale architecture stood throughout the area of Zone 1. The absence of any evidence for architecture on the surface suggests that this area saw limited reoccupation and any significant structures that survive may be covered by erosional overburden.

6.1.5. Conclusions

The analysis of cut stone documented over the course of systematic study of the survey area and intensive survey suggests that monumental buildings at the site of Koutsopetria extended for half a kilometer along the coast, and the evidence of roof tiles suggests a more extensive zone of humble buildings across nearly a kilometer of Zone 2. Smaller architectural fragments were primary clustered in the area of Zone 1 on the Koutsopetria plain, but in some cases continued to the northeast along the base of Kokkinokremos and Zone 2. While it remains difficult to date the scattered architectural fragments, comparisons with building material in the excavated site on the Koutsopetria plain shows that many of the blocks now piled at the edges of the fields have been moved from their original provenience.

The frequency of gypsum need not indicate tremendous wealth in the area, but does probably indicate monumental buildings across the Koutsopetria plain. Gypsum floor slabs, for example, appear in non-liturgical spaces at the Episcopal basilica at Kourion (Megaw 2007), at the more modest church at Kalavasos-*Kopetra* (Rautman 2003), and on the first and second floors of the annex room in the basilica at Koutsopetria (Christou 1993).

The presence of marble revetment or marble *opus sectile* tesserae, on the other hand, indicates prestige architecture in the survey area. The relatively wide scatter of marble fragments indicates several well-appointed structures in the area. The continuity of marble fragments, gypsum, and roof tile suggests that the built environment of Koutsopetria continued intermittently beyond Zone 1 to the eastern border of the coastal plain. The general absence of common building material on the surfaces of Zones 3 and 4 suggests that large-scale buildings of Late Roman date did not extend onto the coastal ridges.

6.2. THE HELLENISTIC FORTIFICATION WALL AT VIGLA

The coastal height called Vigla commands the gently rolling stretch of coastal plain of Koutsopetria (fig. 6.5). This acropolis, since the late

FIG. 6.5   *View from Vigla of Larnaca Bay.*

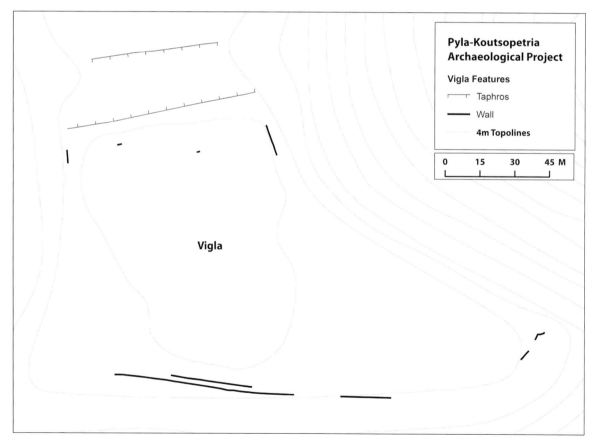

FIG. 6.6   *Map of Vigla fortification.*

nineteenth century, had been suspected as a site of substantive ancient remains (Section 1.1). Cesnola described (1877) a fortified settlement with small, square houses in this area, which could coincide with the remains at this site. The modern name, Vigla, may echo the ancient name of Dades, meaning "torches," reported by Ptolemy for a place in this area (Chapter 7) and invoking the function of this height as a "outpost" or "watchtower" on the eastern side of Larnaca Bay (Hadjicosti pers. comm.). Indeed, the discovery of a large number of lead sling bullets by illegal metal detector work had long hinted at the settlement's military past (Section 4.10). This was confirmed during the 2006 season, when we identified a substantial fortification wall at the site (fig. 6.6). Since that time, the hill has seen three campaigns of excavation in 2008, 2009, and 2012 which are currently being prepared for publication (for a preliminary report, see Caraher et al. 2014). Substantial stratified deposits recovered in 2012 date the wall to the very end of the Cypro-Classical or the start of Hellenistic period (Olson et al. 2013).

The location and topography of Vigla offered several advantages in antiquity. The height offered a valuable point of defense for the inhabitants of the region. It overlooked the ancient embayment, which would have provided a natural harbor or anchorage (fig. 6.5). The main road from Salamis to Kition and points west approached the Larnaca Bay near the embayment (Bekker-Nielsen 2004; Caraher et al. 2005: 248–50). The ridge's steep southern, eastern, and western sides made the flat top of Vigla easy to fortify. The only vulnerable approach was on the northern side of the hill, but approaching this side from the coast would have required moving in plain sight of the fortification walls. The prominent coastal height also provided clear views of almost the entire Larnaca Bay from Cape Pyla in the east to Cape Kiti in the west, adding to the strategic value of the site.

The presence of a light scatter of Bronze Age and substantial Iron Age material in the vicinity attests to the longstanding value of this area and advises against any narrow interpretation of the ridge based purely on its military or geopolitical potential. The position of Vigla near the eastern border of the *chora* of the Iron Age city of

Kition, the presence of a local cult site (cf. Sections 5.3.2.3, 7.3.1, 7.3.4, and 7.4.4), the abundant cultivatable ground in the neighborhood, and access to a natural anchorage likely drew local residents to the defensible height prior to the end of the Cypro-Classical period and the dissolution of the city-kingdoms. The topographic, geopolitical, and economic potential of the region gave Vigla a convenient and useful position on the coast of Larnaca Bay.

A complete publication of our excavations at this site and on the plain below at Koutsopetria will appear in a separate volume. For the purposes of this publication, however, we will provide a short description of the fortification at Vigla.

The wall at Vigla encompasses an area of approximately 9,900 m² (figs. 6.6–6.7). On the western, southern, and eastern sides of the plateau, the wall follows the natural contour of the slope. The longest exposed section extends along the southern slope of the hill, visible only one course above the level of the surrounding surface. Despite the poor state of preservation, we traced the wall for over 100 m, and in numerous places both faces of the wall were visible, indicating a width of 1.7–1.8 m (fig. 6.8). In this section, the wall consists of faces of locally-quarried, roughly-dressed blocks averaging generally less than 0.5 m in length with a rubble core. There is very little evidence for mortar. However, the wall that is visible on the surface today appears to be a composite of several different phases of construction and repair.

At the southeastern corner of the promontory, the wall turns to the north and appears to follow the steeply sloping eastern side of the hill. Erosion is quite significant in this area, with sections of bedrock having collapsed down-slope. It seems probable that parts of the wall along this side of the height have fallen as well. At the southeastern corner, there is a small, curved section of wall approximately 0.50 m wide and 2.3 m in length, with conspicuous quantities of white gypsum-based mortar. This wall does not clearly relate to the wall running along the southern face of Vigla, nor does the construction style fit well with walls elsewhere on the hill; it may represent a repair, modification, or reuse in the Late Roman period. Farther north from this point, the wall does not

FIG. 6.7   *Aerial photo of Vigla from west. Photo taken June 11, 2007, courtesy of 84 Sqd. RAF Akrotiri.*

appear to be visible along most of the eastern side of the hill, until a 12 m long section of wall reappears approximately 100 m north of the southeastern corner wall. Soundings conducted in 2008 along this stretch of wall showed that the wall was 1.7 m wide at this point. The wall consisted of two faces of roughly-cut, dressed blocks with rubble fill.

The northern stretch of the wall is almost completely invisible, but it appears to have followed a slight ridge along the northern part of the Vigla plateau. Excavations by looters in the early summer or spring of 2010 exposed a small section of the wall's coursed southern face (fig. 6.9) and formal excavation in 2012 exposed a wall nearly 2.5 m wide (fig. 6.10). Farther to the west, more sections of the wall are visible, but these appear to follow a different course from the section exposed by looters, suggesting that the wall changes course at some point near the northwestern corner. Farther north, there are clearly visible remains of an 18–20 m fosse or *taphros* cut into the local bedrock (fig. 6.6). This imposing feature probably combined

the practical contingency of local quarrying with the tactical advantage of providing defenders additional height from which to assault attackers approaching the fortification from the north. The fosse effectively separates the Vigla promontory from the mass of the Mavrospilos-Kazama plateau.

The western side of the wall is the least visible on Vigla, as it is most likely covered with soil eroding from the top. Soundings at the northwestern corner of Vigla exposed a 5-m-long stretch of wall that clearly underwent repair. The northwestern corner appears to be a different construction style than the other stretches of wall and could represent a later Roman phase (see above). Significant quantities of a gypsum-based mortar were used to create a substantial rubble core faced with heavily mortared blocks. It seems likely that this corner represents the remains of a tower designed to protect an entrance to the enceinte. Farther to the south, near what must have been the southwest corner of the enceinte, the wall appears once more and continues for approximately 20 m. While

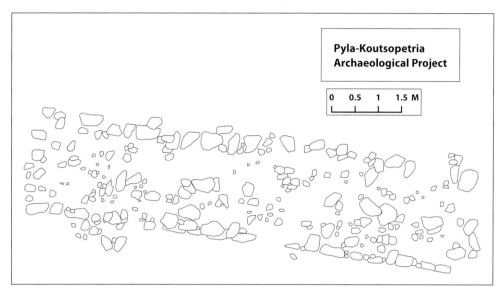

FIG. 6.8   *Plan of south wall (drawing by Mat Dalton).*

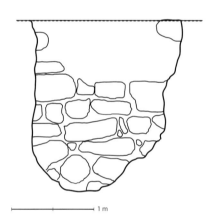

FIG. 6.9   *Profile of north wall exposed by excavators.*

only the external face of the wall is visible here, it appears similar in construction to the wall that runs along the southern face of Vigla. However, the white gypsum-based mortar could represent a later repair of an earlier wall.

Three units excavated near the perimeter fortification wall sought to establish a stratigraphic date for the wall and to determine whether the wall was the product of a single phase. The challenge to excavating the wall was that the significant slope and erosion present along the wall's well-preserved southern side made stratified deposits unlikely. As a result, we focused our soundings on areas where the wall appeared less affected by erosion and had

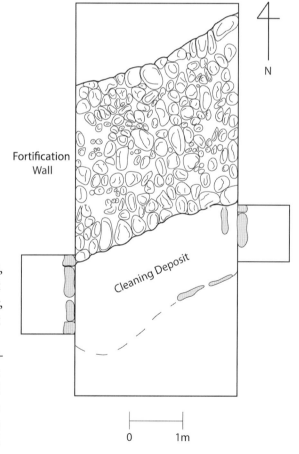

FIG. 6.10   *Plan of north wall after excavation (after Olson et al. 2013: fig. 6).*

FIG. 6.11   *Venetian/Ottoman wall.*

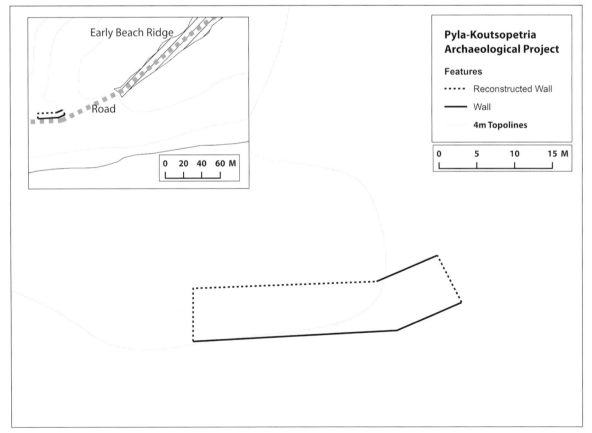

FIG. 6.12   *Plan of Venetian/Ottoman wall.*

the potential to preserve some local soil depth and stratigraphy associated with the construction of the wall. Not all of the excavations produced evidence for the date of the wall, but the major phase of construction dates to the late Cypro-Classical to Hellenistic. Thus far, we have produced no stratified evidence for Late Roman phases of the wall, although repairs are more difficult to document stratigraphically than initial construction.

The fortifications at Vigla mark the second major wave of fortifications in the coastal zone of Pyla. The first fortifications date to the Late Bronze age and appear to encircle an area that may have approached 10 ha on the coastal height of Kokkinokremos (Karageorghis and Demas 1984). The second wave involved the fortification of the smaller height of Vigla. It is notable that Kokkinokremos saw little activity during the Cypro-Classical or Hellenistic periods, and the center of activity appears to have shifted to the west as early as the Iron Age. The fortification of Vigla complemented the western center of activity in the region. Moreover, the smaller area of Vigla may have provided a more easily fortified feature than the larger Kokkinokremos. The absence of significant quantities of cut block atop Kokkinokremos may indicate that the site was quarried for cut stones during the construction of Vigla. It is also worth considering the role of memory in the decision to fortify Vigla. We have no idea how Iron Age, Cypro-Classical, or Hellenistic residents of the Pyla littoral regarded the fortifications present on Kokkinokremos, but the absence of evidence for significant activity on the hill prior to the Roman period suggests that the ruins of the Late Bronze Age settlement did not make up part of their regular activity area.

6.3. THE VENETIAN WALL AT KOUTSOPETRIA

During the first field season, we discovered a short stretch of poorly-preserved wall on the coastal plain running parallel to the main road between Dhekelia and Larnaca (see fig. 5.49). The wall itself consists of only small patches of poorly-preserved limey mortar and unworked stone most likely quarried from the earlier remains. Some 20 m north of the course of the wall, the plough had cut

through a section of gypsum-based plaster flooring revealing the ceramic packing below (fig. 6.11). Considering the proximity to the east–west wall, this floor may be associated with the same building. The ceramics in the floor packing included coarse ware of Late Roman date suggesting that the floor dated to the Late Roman period or sometime after antiquity. Unfortunately, it is impossible at present to connect the floor more definitely to the wall to the south.

The wall itself is overgrown with shrubs and largely obscured by earth. It appears to run for approximately 30 m east to west and might include a short dogleg turn to the south near its eastern end (fig. 6.12). A short stretch of wall runs approximately 5 m to the north and roughly parallel to the better-preserved wall. It appears similar in construction, and for the purpose of a conjectural reconstruction, we have identified it as the north wall of an oblong fortification following Cesnola's description quoted below. The course of the wall appears to follow an earlier, but still visible, Holocene beach ridge perhaps consolidated by a now destroyed road bed. The location of the beach ridge indicates that while most of the embayment was infilled, there remained enough for a small beachfront, and presumably the fortification stood guard over that useful stretch of coastline.

Cesnola described the fortification on his way to his summer home in Ormidhia:

Here I found the stone walls of an oblong structure, not older than the Venetian occupation of the island. It had been a small fort mounted with three guns, the embrasures of which are still standing. Along the southeast coast there are several of these guard-houses, built near the shore on elevated ground, some of which, now dismantled and roofless, are of Turkish construction, and two or three hundred years old. Most of them appear to have been erected for the protection of the neighboring villages from the Algerine pirates who not longer ago than sixty years were daring enough to land and carry off wealthy inhabitants and detain them until the required ransome should be paid."

The pirates, according to Cesnola's informants, availed themselves to the cave in the base of Kokkinokremos which we call today Mavrospilios. The small scatter of Late Medieval pottery near the fortification at the eastern edge of Zone 1 confirms Cesnola's identification of these walls as part of a small coastal battery. It is worth observing that the presence of such a coastal battery probably indicates the continued availability of the small coastal inlet.

The base maps for the mid-twentieth century cadaster maps, which date to the early twentieth century, mark the place as "Panayia (Ruin)" indicating that the cartographers interpreted the architecture as a ruined church. There is no evidence that this is a church building, and it seems unlikely that Cesnola would have understood a fortification to be a church. At the same time, it provides an interesting insight into how cartographers understood ruins in the landscape. Unless evidence existed to the contrary, they assumed substantial remains in the countryside were churches.

6.4.   THE EARLY CHRISTIAN BASILICA AT KOUTSOPETRIA

Maria Hadjicosti investigated the Early Christian basilica at Koutsopetria through two small excavations in 1993 and 1999 (Christou 1993; Christou 1994: 689–90; Hadjisavvas 2000: 692–93). These excavations revealed parts of several rooms and the apse of the church. The walls of the building included large cut blocks probably quarried from earlier buildings across the site, as well as roof tiles probably of Roman or Late Roman date. The building included paving of gypsum slabs and *opus sectile* tiles, wall paintings, and elaborate molded gypsum widow screens and decorations. The immediate vicinity of the church is littered with architectural fragments, including columns and floor slabs. As these were in an area designated for archaeological protection and subject to study as a separate phase of the project, we have not included this material here. Two seasons of small-scale excavation and documentation at the basilica will be published separately, as will studies of the architecture and the important assemblage of wall painting and molded gypsum.

6.5.   CONCLUSIONS

The remains of architecture across the study area indicate a long history of large-scale construction at the coastal settlement. Local limestone, gypsum sourced from elsewhere on Cyprus, and quarried spolia contributed to the distribution of architectural blocks and structures across the coastal plain. These features are largely associated with the highest density of artifacts across the site of Koutsopetria, especially the Roman and Late Roman material extending across the plain. It seems reasonable to imagine this architectural material as the remains of the community associated with the Early Christian basilica excavated in the 1990s. The presence of reused material in the excavated basilica reminds us that some of the ceramic artifacts might also derive from a residual context.

The density of artifacts aligns well with the concentration of features on the coastal plain, although building material is notably scant on the surface in the coastal ridges, which are associated especially with Iron Age and Hellenistic artifact concentrations. Because excavations at Vigla have consistently revealed sub-surface architectural structures associated with both fortification and residence, we must be wary about drawing conclusions from the absence of features from the heights. Continuing programs of geophysical survey should shed light on the distribution of buildings across the zones of the survey area.

Finally, it is more than a bit vexing that the coastal region did not produce much Medieval and Post-Medieval pottery, despite the presence of later fortification in the area. Our continuing work in the area will, we hope, document the less visible post-antique periods in the landscape.

Chapter 7

Historical Conclusions

by William Caraher

In this concluding chapter, we move from the diachronic patterns of archaeological material in the district of Koutsopetria to historical conclusions about the micro-region's relationship to broader economic, political, and religious patterns in Cyprus and the Mediterranean. As we have noted throughout this volume, our methods have produced an archaeological assemblage that is meaningful in light of general trends in the history and archaeology of Cyprus. In this chapter, we aim for a responsible synthesis of the material remains in terms of this broader historical scholarship.

The Pyla littoral featured a wide range of natural advantages for any settlement. The flat, narrow coastal plain and inland areas offered good agricultural land to the inhabitants of the region of Kition. The lowland east of Koutsopetria marks an embayment that is now infilled, but functioned as a natural harbor throughout antiquity and probably as late as the Medieval era. The steep, flat-topped coastal plateaus provided security for inhabitants during turbulent times and offered views of Larnaca Bay, as well as the land routes from Kition, Salamis, and the Mesaoria plain. These coastal heights were also a source of building stone as soft limestone of the Nicosia formation was easy to access and quarry. The location of this stretch of coastline, then, provided building material, fertile fields, defendable heights, and access to communication routes by land and sea (fig. 7.1).

While the site was clearly oriented toward the sea for most of its history, the Koutsopetria region was also well-connected to other inland sites of the island. The flat coastal plain to the west served as a convenient route to centers along Larnaca Bay that included, most immediately, the city of Kition 10 km away. Routes led north through the village of Pyla ("gates") to the Mesaoria plain and northwest to the foothills of the Troodos. The copper mines and forests of the Troodos fueled the Cypriot economy throughout antiquity, and scholars have generally seen copper production as one of the key considerations for understanding the settlement on the island (Given and Knapp 2003; Knapp 2008). The region's position on the eastern side of the island placed our site outside the main areas for copper production, but its position astride communication routes, access to a protected stretch of coast, and proximity to good land for agriculture tied the sites of the Pyla district to the broader island-wide economic trends and patterns fostered by the requirements and opportunities of copper production and exchange.

The following sections will bring together the foregoing analysis of the remains in the micro-region for each major period in respect to the five interrelated scholarly themes and contexts outlined in the introduction. These contexts form a point of interface between our archaeological investigations and larger historical discussions in

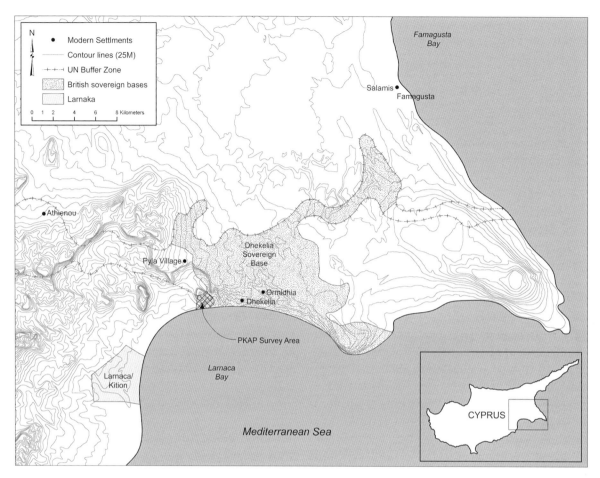

Fig. 7.1 *Map of survey area showing Pyla village and ancient sites.*

the archaeology and history of Cyprus. None of these contexts are independent analytical units, but overlap significantly with one another. They also do not provide definitive conclusions but, rather, different approaches to understanding the significance of our work at Koutsopetria.

First, we will summarize the results of our survey in terms of the assemblage and distribution of different periods at Koutsopetria. We will sketch the nature of our data, our confidence in the summary (source criticism), and an assessment of settlement in the micro-region. This theme reflects our presentation of the process and results of high-resolution survey in Chapters 2–6, and especially Chapter 5. Since it highlights the quality of the evidence, this context is foundational to the broader set of scholarly themes.

Second, we will examine the evidence for settlement and land use as it speaks to the nature of

the relationship of town and territory and the question of how administrative structures projected political and economic power in the micro-region. The littoral of Pyla stood near the eastern limits of the ancient city of Kition. With the rise of that city in the Iron Age, the micro-region fell under its direct influence, and this proximity and influence shaped its subsequent development. After the end of the independent Iron Age monarchies on the island in the early Hellenistic Era, the site continued to occupy an economically and militarily valuable stretch of coastline. Archaeological evidence demonstrates a dramatic shift in the use of the site during the politically tumultuous Hellenistic period to a sea-side harbor community in the relatively stable and peaceful Roman era. The *floruit* of the coastal settlement in the fifth and sixth centuries occurs at the moment nearby Kition undergoes dramatic change.

Third, we will examine the settlement patterns in the PKAP region in terms of the broader regional context of Cyprus. In particular, we will outline how activity in the Pyla district compares with settlement patterns on the island, especially those documented through the last generation of regional archaeological survey. The record remains lacunose, but our work at Koutsopetria offers a high-resolution contribution to the expanding body of evidence for activities in the countryside around the ancient city of Kition, the southeastern coast of the island, and the southern reaches of the Mesaoria plain. Our discussion of changes in regional settlement will highlight how the site relates to broader economic, demographic, and social patterns on the island.

Fourth, we will explore how site formation, demographic change, regional settlement trends, and political power are also manifest in the changing religious landscape of Pyla. The micro-region produced specific evidence for concentrated religious activity throughout the historical period. The remains of one or more long-lived Iron Age sanctuaries and the foundation of an Early Christian basilica marked this stretch of coastline as religiously significant. The location of religious activities at the "peripheral" site of Koutsopetria provides a useful case study for how religion and other social and economic relations intersect in the Cypriot landscape.

Finally, we will examine the Pyla littoral as a landscape formed through a dynamic range of connections extending across the island and the Mediterranean. The archaeological evidence collected and analyzed from the site functions as markers of connectivity between our region and other places. As Horden and Purcell and others have noted, the various connections that link together coastal communities in the Mediterranean basin do more than provide evidence for economic relationships: they form the building blocks of Mediterranean culture (Horden and Purcell 2000: 1–25; Knapp 2008 has sought to apply some of these same concepts to Cyprus). The distinct connections present in the Pyla littoral not only manifest a unique set of economic relationships, but also mark the site as a discrete ancient place in the Mediterranean coastline.

The history presented in this conclusion is not meant to be the final word on the history of this site and the micro-region. As the excavators at Kition, Kokkinokremos, and Pyla village bring their work to publication, and as the ceramic chronology upon which our conclusions depend becomes more resolved, these conclusions will require revision. Indeed, even as we brought our survey to publication, recent excavation work at the sites of Vigla, Kokkinokremos, and important recent publications of new material from across Cyprus (e.g., Demesticha 2013) have changed our understanding of the site. The following conclusion makes every effort to provide a comprehensive view of the area while still recognizing the ambiguities and grey areas in our understanding of the assemblage. As a result, there will be places where we offer alternate or overlapping interpretations as we attempt to resolve difficult ceramic chronology. We hope that the reader tolerates the ambiguity in the name of a more honest reading of our material.

7.1. KOUTSOPETRIA IN PREHISTORY

The prehistoric activity along the stretch of coastline near Pyla is most familiar to scholars from the excavated site of Kokkinokremos. Associated by some scholars with some of the earliest Aegean Greek settlers on the island in the Late Bronze Age (Karageorghis and Demas 1984), the site has remained politically significant and contested for arguments about ethnic identity on the island (Knapp 2008; Brown 2012). Our work initially included the study of prehistoric remains in the Pyla region through various forms of survey, but we were encouraged to exclude the study of the prehistoric period after V. Karageorghis and colleagues resumed excavation at the site in 2010. However, we think that a few general words on the broader prehistory of the region will offer some useful context for the study of the site in the historical era. The following discussion deviates somewhat from the five contexts that we will adopt to frame our discussion of the historical periods.

The sites of the Pyla region, together with Hala Sultan Tekke and Kition on Larnaca Bay, form one of the more densely settled regions in Late Bronze Age Cyprus. The most important regional center east of Kition was Kokkinokremos with its casemate style walls, facilities for large-scale storage, small-scale metallurgy, and contacts with the Levant and the Aegean basin (Karageorghis and Demas 1984). However, this site was only the largest of a series of Late Cypriot settlements in the region of Pyla (Catling 1963; Dikaios 1971; Karageorghis and Demas 1984; Brown 2012).

The site of Steno, immediately east of this site, has never been fully published, but evidently overlapped in date with Kokkinokremos and apparently featured basic harbor facilities (Catling 1963; Masson 1966, with references; for a more recent consideration, see Brown 2012). There is evidence for burials at the site of Koukoufouthkia southeast of Kokkinokremos and burial and settlement to the west at Verghies (Catling 1963; Masson 1966; Dikaios 1971). Early unsystematic work at Stavros produced evidence for Late Cypriot activity just south of the village of Pyla, some 2 km north of the Koutsopetria study area (Masson 1966, with references). Farther north of the Pyla littoral, the sites of Idalion, Ay. Sozomenos, Politiko-*Troulli*, Kalopidha, Sinda, and Enkomi demonstrate that the southeastern corner of the island saw intensive activity and settlement throughout the Late Bronze Age (for a general consideration of this region, see Knapp 2008: 237–39). If the political, economic, and chronological relationships between these sites remain difficult to assess, it is clear that the southeastern corner of Cyprus was a "busy countryside" in the Late Bronze Age (for the term, see Rautman 2000).

This regional settlement boom likely related to access to copper production areas in the southeastern Troodos range at nearby sites like Troulli (Brown 2012: 85–91 for this discussion). Control over forestry resources would have also been important for the production of charcoal necessary for smelting copper. While direct access to copper or forests probably did not account for the siting of Kokkinokremos, this settlement, as well as Stavros, likely formed part of a landscape of control in the region. These settlements may have had access to inland copper-producing areas from the coastline and via the pass near Pyla village. At the same time, the presence of a now infilled harbor highlights the site's significance within the Pyla coastline. At a convenient location for the exchange of goods with the wider Mediterranean community, the relationship between the sites of the Pyla region and the markets, policies, and control of known centers like Hala Sultan Tekke, Enkomi, or Kition remains difficult to assess. Many scholars have suggested that Kokkinokremos' distinct location allowed it to serve as a base of operation for a mercantile elite or as the port for local communities or even the entire southeastern part of the island (Knapp 2008: 239, with references). The flow of goods into Late Bronze Age Cyprus and metal from the island certainly required the existence of a number of harbor installations, and the value of the good and wealth of communities makes fortifications likely during the turbulent Late Bronze Age.

Our survey in the Pyla region produced a substantial quantity of Late Bronze Age material, centered on the heart-shaped plateau of Kokkinokremos. Compared to other periods in our survey region, the Bronze Age is a fairly visible ceramic era represented by 205 artifacts and covering nearly 10 ha. For some comparison, these figures represent 39% of the quantity of artifacts and 53% of the spatial extent of the Iron Age period, 3% of the quantity and 12% of the spatial extent of the broad Roman period, and five times the quantity and twice the spatial extent of Medieval–Ottoman date. Bronze Age artifacts date almost entirely to the Late Cypriot II–III era, and some 97% of all Bronze Age artifacts were found on the Kokkinokremos plateau, where they were spread evenly without clear concentrations. Our documentation of the distribution of material across this ridge indicates that settlement at Kokkinokremos was more extensive than previously estimated from excavation alone, although ongoing excavations should confirm our assessment. Late Bronze Age artifacts form the slight majority (51%) of the narrow-period artifacts on the ridge, but Iron Age, Hellenistic, and Roman materials form significant minor components.

It is striking that Late Bronze Age settlement seems to have been limited to Kokkinokremos. The near absence of Bronze Age material from Koutsopetria (Zones 1 and 2), Vigla, or the Kazama-Mavrospilios plateau (Zone 4) indicates that Late Bronze Age residents did not inhabit the entire plateau. As we noted above, there are other small scatters of Bronze Age material in the region that confirm that the site of Kokkinokremos was part of a network of contemporary settlements distributed around the eastern half of Larnaca Bay, but survey demonstrated that Late Bronze Age material did not extend onto the coastal plain at Koutsopetria. The absence of pottery from the coastal plain may well indicate that this area was too strategically vulnerable for sustained activities during the Late Bronze Age.

7.2. KOUTSOPETRIA IN THE EARLY IRON AGE AND CYPRO-GEOMETRIC PERIOD

The transition from the Late Bronze Age to the Iron Age represents one of the key moments in the history of the island (Knapp 2008; Smith 2009). The political organization, settlement patterns, and economic structures that emerged over the course of the Iron Age exerted a significant influence on Cypriot society for a millennium. Despite the significance of this time in the history of the island, the evidence for the transition from the Cypriot Bronze Age to the Iron Age remains problematic. There remains little consensus among scholars as to when the Iron Age polities emerged that became the major centers of ancient Cyprus and what caused their political, social, and economic consolidation.

At present, archaeologists have struggled to date precisely the assemblages of Iron Age material produced by intensive pedestrian survey and, as a result, survey finds have not contributed much to our understanding of the transitional Early Iron Age (Smith 2009). Moreover, the most significant stratified Iron Age assemblages come from the rather limited contexts of excavated urban centers, religious shrines, and burials. There are few sites and even fewer systematic publications of Iron Age material from rural settlements or landscapes (Knapp and Given 2003: 271–72). The general absence of rural sites datable to the Cypriot Iron Age makes the relatively substantial distribution of Iron Age material at the sites of the Pyla region significant. Unfortunately, the poor quality of most of our finds and the unstable character of

Iron Age chronology means that the larger archaeological context for the material and activities at Koutsopetria must remain obscure for now. As a useful indicator of our incomplete knowledge of Iron Age material, we have identified a distribution of Iron Age (inclusive) material extending over 18 ha and including a robust assemblage of 523 artifacts. However, most of these objects are utility wares of various types that we can date only to the Iron Age chronotype period, which spans more than 700 years. Artifacts identified to narrower chronotype periods (Cypro-Geometric, Cypro-Archaic, and Cypro-Classical) are uncommon in comparison, consisting of only 17, 28, and 14 sherds, respectively. As a result, we have found it particularly difficult to connect a significant and extensive array of past activities on the site to major discussions of historical development on the island during this period.

Issues of ethnicity further complicate discussions of the relationship between Iron Age settlements and their Late Bronze Age predecessors. The appearance of Greek and Phoenician communities on the island and the persistence of a recognizable indigenous community have formed a backdrop for discussions of state formation in the Cypriot Iron Age that are as informed by ancient archaeological evidence as contemporary political posturing (Knapp 2008). The persistence of Kition from the Bronze Age and its expansion during the Iron Age offers particular challenges because the city saw a Phoenician dynasty and administration for at least part of the Iron Age and an influx of Phoenician settlers by the Cypro-Archaic period (Yon 1997). Knowledge of this ethnic makeup of the population at Kition and its rulers has often informed scholarly understanding of the political and economic situation in the city and its relations with its neighbors, and has also added the complicating element of ethnicity to considerations of regional settlement.

The final issue infusing the study of the Cypriot Iron Age is the nature and extent of continuity with the earlier Late Bronze Age. The works of M. Iacovou, in particular, as well as Knapp and Smith, are central to any consideration of changes in settlement from the Late Bronze Age to the rise of Iron Age kingdoms on Cyprus (Iacovou 2008;

Knapp 2008: 281–97; Smith 2009). The nearby presence of Kokkinokremos ensured that Iron Age activity in the Pyla littoral took place in view of the material remains of a substantial earlier settlement. Moreover, the region's relationship with Kition proves challenging, as the city is among the few urban areas to preserve clear evidence for continuity between the Late Bronze and Iron Age, as well as evidence for significant cultural, political, and ethnic change (Yon 1997; Smith 2009). While the character of the Iron Age material from the site is insufficient for us to make a major contribution to any of the complex debates surrounding Iron Age settlement, the evidence from the Pyla region contributes in a small way to these considerations.

There is no evidence for continuity between the Late Cypriot site of Kokkinokremos and later settlement in the area, and our work offers no challenges to the excavators' arguments that the residents of that site thoroughly abandoned the place by the end of the Late Cypriot period (Karageorghis and Demas 1984). As in other surveys (Given and Knapp 2003: 271–73), we were not particularly successful in dating material to the early Iron Age period, which may in part explain the long gap following the end of the Bronze Age. The presence of some material from the Cypro-Geometric period, however, indicates that groups inhabited the micro-region again within 300 years of the abandonment of Kokkinokremos.

7.2.1. Artifacts and Distribution

Our distributional analysis has produced a tiny scatter of 17 Cypro-Geometric pottery sherds concentrated along the southern edge of Zone 4 and the Mavrospilios plateau. The sherds, combined with the few artifacts scattered at the base of these ridges, cover an area of only 1.7 ha. Comparatively, the extent and quantity of the Cypro-Geometric assemblage represents 16% and 8% of the area and quantity of the earlier Late Cypriot scatter, 46% and 52% of later Cypro-Archaic, and 2% and 0.3% of much later and more extensive Late Roman scatters. However, as our knowledge of this ceramic period depended on feature sherds and decorated body sherds, we must treat the Cypro-Geometric period as a largely invisible period in the landscape

and be wary about drawing conclusions from its relative absence

As our record of the distribution of Cypro-Geometric material clearly draws attention to the focus on the coastal ridges, it is curious that there is no sign of activity on the height of Kokkinokremos. On practical and economic grounds, the presence of building material from the earlier remains of that site, direct access to the harbor, and the easily defended coastal heights would have made it appealing for settlement. Yet, the complete absence of material is striking. It is enticing to speculate that the Cypro-Geometric inhabitants intentionally avoided the abandoned site of Kokkinokremos because of some historical memory of the Late Bronze Age site. Unfortunately, the general invisibility of pottery from this period brings uncertainty to such speculations. What we can say more confidently is that the inhabitants of the Cypro-Geometric age decidedly shifted the focal point of their investment to a ridge farther west of Kokkinokremos.

7.2.2. State, Settlement, and Regional Trends

The location of the early Iron Age site in the political landscape of the island may have also played a key role in its new settlement. The settlement at Kition was the only one of the major Late Bronze Age sites on Larnaca Bay to present clear and substantial signs of continuity into the early Iron Age. Iacovou has argued for Iron Age polities across the island that the persistence of Late Bronze Age political organization at Kition ensured that the Iron Age kingdom retained a highly centralized system of government (Iacovou 2008). Over the course of the Iron Age, the city continued to assert its significant influence throughout Larnaca Bay. The absence of rival centers on the littoral suggests that it was successful in both extracting resources from the larger region and projecting its political power over neighboring communities.

The relationship between developing Kition and the settlement around Larnaca Bay remains obscure, but Early Iron Age activity on the Pyla littoral must have stood at the limit of control of the developing center of Kition (Megaw 1953: 134–35; Karageorghis and Demas 1984: 5; Knapp 2008: 239).

Nonetheless, it is striking that the small Cypro-Geometric settlement at Pyla grew at a time when the regional center at Kition was itself expanding. Indeed, the political and economic authority at Kition almost certainly influenced the structure of population, resources, and trading patterns in the surrounding region. The small, but apparently vital communities in the vicinity of Pyla represented communities with sufficient access to resources and distance from Kition to develop discrete centers of population, but still remained deeply embedded within the larger sphere of Kition's political and economic influence. Whether they were politically independent or not remains outside the perspective of our current evidence.

Our documentation of material present on the Mavrospilios plateau is particularly significant because Early Iron Age settlements in regions east of Kition remain rather poorly-known. A small, but significant assemblage of material of Cypro-Geometric date appeared in the environs of the village of Ormidhia in an area set back from the modern coastline and situated to avail itself of a landlocked harbor (Hadjicosti 2001: 53–69 summarizes the mostly nineteenth-century finds dating to the Iron Age from the environs of Ormidhia). Various stray artifacts in Cypro-Geometric to early Cypro-Archaic figural style have been documented from the neighborhood of Pyla village, Dhekelia, Aradippou, and Achna (Karageorghis and de Gagniers 1974), but as of yet, none of these objects have been associated conclusively with any specifically defined concentrations of activity, much less functions in the landscape. Absent more robust contexts for this material, it is perhaps best to associate such artifacts with burials. If this is correct, we may associate these with a series of early Iron Age settlements away from the coast as an indication that peripheral coastal areas remained too vulnerable for settlement in this period.

The early Iron Age finds indicate that the micro-region was part of a broader pattern of settlement on the eastern part of Larnaca Bay that developed partly in accord with Kition. Unfortunately, our knowledge of the Cypro-Geometric period is so fragmentary that we are unable to discuss with any confidence the patterns of connectivity and religious landscapes in the early Iron Age.

7.3. KOUTSOPETRIA IN THE CYPRO-ARCHAIC PERIOD

By the Cypro-Archaic period, there is greater evidence for land use in the area. Artifacts from the micro-region indicate that activities continued in the landscape from the Cypro-Geometric period with some small evidence for expansion. The few objects displaying clear evidence for Phoenician influence in the area suggest that the population participated in larger regional networks. Considering the growth of Phoenician influence at Kition, it is probable that the appearance of Phoenician influences in the Pyla littoral represented the strengthening of political influence of Kition by the seventh century.

7.3.1.   Artifacts and Distribution

The extent of Cypro-Archaic and Iron Age material in the micro-region demonstrates that this area underwent significant expansion after the Cypro-Geometric period, but that activities were not sustained or intensive. Overall, Cypro-Archaic artifacts number only 28 sherds distributed over 3.6 discontinuous ha. While this is double the extent and quantity of the Cypro-Geometric assemblage, it represents only 38% and 14% of area and quantity of the Late Cypriot assemblage, 22% and 24% of extent and quantity of the Hellenistic assemblage, and 5% and 0.5% of the area and quantity of the Late Roman assemblage. Moreover, while fine wares still dominate the Cypro-Archaic assemblage and demonstrate that the period was not fully visible, the recognition of some utility wares indicates that the period had relatively greater ceramic visibility than the Cypro-Geometric era. This increased visibility may explain some of the increase in sherds between periods.

Generally, Cypro-Archaic material is sparse across the survey area. A low-density scatter extends across the top of the Mavrospilios plateau near a former Cypro-Geometric habitation. A small scatter of artifacts also appears on the Kokkinokremos ridge. It seems likely that the abandoned Bronze Age settlement became a useful quarry or squatting site for the growing Iron Age population of the region. Perhaps population pressures had to reach a certain level before it became appealing to quarry the ruins at Kokkinokremos for building material, or it may be that social memory about the ancient site's significance changed. The presence of Cypro-Archaic material on the coastal plain (Zone 1) suggests that the decline of maritime threats or the growth of seaborne trade encouraged a growing orientation to the sea.

While the assemblage is small, one artifact in particular suggests that the Cypro-Archaic site in the region was an important one. The best-known Cypro-Archaic object from our study area is a seventh-century statue found at the site of "Paliokastro" in the early twentieth century by Couchoud. The statue, initially published by Hermary and recently examined again by Counts, shows the head of the god Bes on a limestone cippus with an inscribed Phoenician dedication by a sculptor named Eshmounhilles to the Canaanite deity Reshef (Hermary 1984; Counts 2008). While the precise find spot of the statue is not known, the best candidate is an area that produced a scatter of Cypro-Archaic material and overlapped the earlier Cypro-Geometric material and ceramics dating to the Iron Age generally. These same units produced six terracotta figurine fragments datable to the Cypro-Archaic to Cypro-Classical period, which most likely date to the latter period (7.4.4). Combined, these features suggest the presence of a sanctuary in the area, which could have origins as early as the seventh century BC. In fact, our scatter of material parallels the Cypro-Archaic to Cypro-Classical sanctuary documented by SCSP at the site of Politiko-*Ay. Mnason* 3 (Knapp and Given 2003: 122–23, 275–76), where a scatter of figurines coincided with a range of Cypro-Archaic to Cypro-Classical table and utility wares. The absence of any evidence for monumental architecture most likely indicates that the sanctuary was open air, which would be consistent with most rural sanctuaries of Iron Age date on Cyprus (Reyes 1994: 28–32; for a recent treatment of religion in this period generally, see Papantoniou 2012).

7.3.2. State and Settlement

The combination of Phoenician, Egyptian, and Cypriot influences in the unusual statue of Bes

suggests a connection between the region and the city of Kition (Counts 2008). The presence of a Phoenician inscription on the cippus indicates that the area experienced the impact of Phoenician activities around the same time that Phoenicians began to exert significant influence over political life in the city of Kition (Yon 1997; Smith 2009). There is no reason to equate the presence of a Phoenician votive with the presence of a "Phoenician" community in the area, or to associate the growth of the sites with specifically Phoenician activities in the countryside. As Counts and others have noted, the use of material to identify specific ethnicities in the archaeological record is fraught with problems, and the presence of even the most traditionally "ethnic" features, such as objects inscribed in a particular language, does not necessarily equate to the presence of individuals or communities of a particular ethnicity (Counts 2008; cf. Hodder 1982).

The significance of the Bes statue is that it suggests that the Iron Age site on the Mavrospilios ridge developed in parallel with the expansion of the major center of Kition. In fact, the presence of a sanctuary with a dedication to Bes might hint that this site marked the eastern limit of the political authority of Kition. Counts has argued that dedications to Bes — in various forms related to "master of animals" iconography — could have particular significance at rural sanctuaries marking the boundaries of various Iron Age states in the vicinity of the Mesaoria (Counts 2004, 2010. For the borders of the various Iron Age states, see Rupp 1987, 1989). While he largely limits his argument to discoveries at sanctuaries surrounding the Mesaoria plain (Athienou-*Malloura*, Golgoi, Potamia, Idalion, Chytroi, and Lefkoniko), there is reason to suspect that the sanctuary in our survey region would fit his model as well. Most scholars accept that the eastern border of the city of Kition is somewhere near Cape Pyla (Rupp 1987: 150 and Map 6 for the classic discussion of Iron Age territorial limit). Koutsopetria may have provided a significant embayment and coastal site for travelers heading west along the coast of Larnaca Bay toward Kition. Moreover, as we have noted throughout this work, several inland routes turned north toward the Mesaoria near the site or headed northwest or east toward Ormidhia and Salamis beyond (Cesnola 1877: 178–79; Bekker-Nielsen 1993; Hadjicosti 2001). Thus, even if the site was not situated at a formal border, the steep bluffs of Vigla and Mavrospilios may have marked the stretch of coastline as an important place in the topography of Kition's *chora*.

Kition's expansion, beginning in the early eighth century, together with the city's growing administrative reach, population, and ties with the Levant, likely contributed to the expansion of the Cypro-Archaic site on the Mavrospilios ridge. In its position at the easternmost limits of Kition's territory, with a good embayment and access to agricultural land, the Pyla micro-region may have marked the expansion of Kition's political hegemony. The site would fit within Rupp's proposed tripartite system of settlement in which major political centers are key nodes in networks comprised of small secondary and tertiary settlements (Rupp 1987, 1997). For Rupp, secondary settlements served as market centers and tertiary settlements functioned as primary production sites. Even if it is unproductive to apply this typology of settlement too rigidly in any specific region, it is clear that the Cypro-Archaic site in the PKAP area represented more than a primary production site and perhaps served as a secondary settlement for the collection and trans-shipment of agricultural produce to markets elsewhere on the island and in the region. The presence of a sanctuary and its coastal location combined to produce a site of particular religious, economic, and political significance for the city of Kition.

7.3.3. *Regional Trends*

The expansion of settlement in the micro-region over the course of the Cypro-Archaic period finds parallels with the general expansion in settlement across Cyprus in the aftermath of the Late Bronze Age disruptions. While evidence for Cypro-Archaic period settlements outside the major urban centers remains sparse, the appearance of rural sanctuaries, distributed burials, and urban areas makes it clear that the period saw economic and demographic growth across the island (Reyes 1994). It is difficult to separate the growth of the

Cypro-Archaic settlement in the PKAP study area from the general expansion of settlement across the region and the emergence of Kition as an important regional center. The sites of Aradippou, Panayia-*Ematousa*, Dhekelia, and Ormidhia, for example, produced some Cypro-Archaic material suggesting settlement in those areas (Reyes 1994: 104; Hadjicosti 2001; Sørensen and Winther-Jacobsen 2006) (fig. 7.2). Farther north stand the significant sites at Pyrga, Athienou, and Golgoi. The latter two sites would have accessed the coast along the Pyla littoral. The vigorous debates concerning the relationship between such secondary sites and the major centers in the Iron Age remains plagued by chronological ambiguity and the absence of evidence for the processes of settlement development, but the sanctuary and settlement in the vicinity of Pyla indicate the ongoing expansion of activities in the larger chora of Kition during the Iron Age.

7.3.4. *Religious Landscapes*

The development of the religious landscape of the eastern part of Larnaca Bay finds parallels with the expanding settlement in the region. We have previously described the important sanctuary on the Pyla littoral, but it is useful also to point out that less than 5 km north of the site stood the wealthy Cypro-Archaic period settlement of Pyla-*Stavros*. Excavated by R. Hamilton Lang in the nineteenth century on the site of his farm, Stavros produced an impressive array of monumental Cypro-Archaic period sculpture most of which was smuggled off the island soon after its discovery (Lang 1905; Masson 1966). The quality and quantity of the statues suggest a sanctuary of some significance, perhaps dedicated to Apollo Magirios, as several inscriptions in the Cypriot syllabary and a few alphabetic inscriptions collected from the vicinity indicate. The sculptures associated with the site in various collections suggest secondary dedications to Artemis, Pan, and Herakles. The absence of any substantial architectural fragments suggests that the site was probably an open air sanctuary typical for Cyprus and a close parallel to the type of sanctuary in our survey area (Masson 1966: 2). Similarities between the sculpture associated with

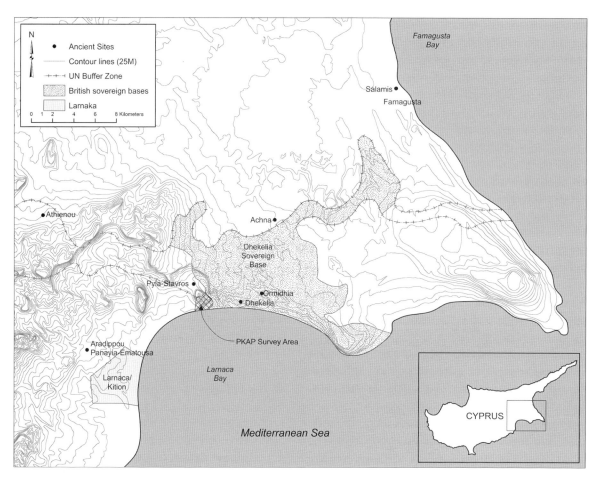

Fig. 7.2   *Pyla-Koutsopetria in regional perspective in the Cypro-Archaic period.*

Stavros and the sculpture from Idalion could testify to the presence of a regional school of artisans (Masson 1966: 14).

The sanctuaries dating to the Iron Age coincide neatly with the expansion of activities in the area and likely served the local population. Their location, however, both near a harbor and at the border of the city of Kition, makes it likely that these religious sites also regularly received visitors from beyond the micro-region. The presence of a range of cult statues devoted to Greek and Phoenician gods indicates that the sites accommodated a range of devotional traditions. Finally, the persistence of religious activity along the Pyla littoral into the Cypro-Classical period indicates that Iron Age sanctuaries formed a key component of the local landscape for many centuries.

7.3.5. Connectivity

Religious activities, settlement change, and regional political developments undoubtedly contributed to a growing body of evidence for contact and exchange along the Pyla littoral. The Koutsopetria micro-region indicates a significant level of connectivity between primary production sites, market towns, and urban areas. Moreover, there is good evidence for trade among sites on the southern coast during the Cypro-Archaic period. Reyes, for example, has located Kition as part of an exchange network that extended along the southern coast to Paphos to the west. Moreover, a well-defined group of black-on-red bichrome ware "Figure-on-the-Shoulder" jugs appeared as finds at Dhekelia, just east of Pyla, and as far west as Tala along the southern coast of the island (Reyes 1994:

107–9). While we were not able to identify any of these diagnostic fine wares and our assemblage of Iron Age material remains small, the distribution of these fine wares indicates that the Iron Age site interacted with production sites elsewhere on the island. The location of Koutsopetria would have made it a convenient stop for traders from the Levant moving west along the southern coast. The growth of Kition's ties to Phoenician settlements in the east must have contributed through greater regional traffic to the expansion of activities in the Pyla littoral.

7.4. KOUTSOPETRIA IN THE CYPRO-CLASSICAL PERIOD

In the Cypro-Classical period, Kition assumed a greater role in the political life of the Eastern Mediterranean, Aegean, and the island of Cyprus itself. The increased visibility of the city in Greek texts of the period reflects its growing prominence. The increased number of imports from the Aegean and Asia Minor testify to the position of the island relative to the Achaemenid Empire and sustained political and cultural ties to communities throughout the Persian dominion (Yon 1997). Investigations at the site of Koutsopetria show deepening economic engagement with the Aegean world in this period in conjunction with the increasingly cosmopolitan character of the island in general.

Any advantages that Cyprus enjoyed from participating within a Persian-influenced eastern Mediterranean economy, however, did not prevent the city of Kition from siding with the majority of Cypriot cities when they revolted against the Persians, despite the presence of a sizable Phoenician population (Hill 1940: 118; Nicolaou 1977: 316–17; Watkins 1987; Flourentzos 2007). Participation in the Ionian Revolt ushered in a period of regular Athenian and Persian interventions throughout the fifth century, the installation of Persian garrisons at certain key cities, and various naval actions by both Greek and Persian fleets. The continued "globalization" of Cypriot politics provided opportunities for Kition and its neighbor Salamis to play Persian and Greek interests off one another for their own benefit. The trans-regional

character of the conflicts that defined the Cypro-Classical age ensured that Cypriot cities became increasingly involved in the political, economic, and social culture of the time.

7.4.1. Artifacts and Distribution

Material narrowly dated to the Cypro-Classical period was difficult to distinguish from earlier and later ceramics. Some of the material shows close similarities to earlier Cypro-Archaic period artifacts, and other objects represent forms, fabrics, and decoration that persisted well into the Hellenistic and even Early Roman periods. As a result, of the several thousand artifacts recovered that could be datable to the Cypro-Classical period, only 15 objects are of certain date. Most of these diagnostic artifacts are fine ware and feature sherds, rendering the Cypro-Classical era one of the less visible periods in the survey region. The presence of fine ware and feature sherds of this date points to an enormous quantity of pottery collected during survey, but identified during analysis to broader chronotype periods such as Cypro-Classical to Hellenistic and Late Cypriot–Hellenistic.

All told, the 15 sherds dated to the Cypro-Classical period represented a handful of more or less discontinuous units covering 1.6 ha. In comparison, the Cypro-Classical period in the survey area is about as numerous and extensive as the Cypro-Geometric, but represents only 17% and 8% of the extent and assemblage of the Late Cypriot period, 10% and 13% of the extent and quantity of the Hellenistic era, and 2% and 0.3% of the extent and quantity of the Late Roman period. Yet, the sparse distribution of Cypro-Classical material suggests a new focus of activity in the area. While a handful of artifacts point to continued occupation of the Iron Age site on the Mavrospilios ridge, the concentration of artifacts in Zone 1 indicates the importance of the coastal plain during this period.

The fourth century BC appears to be the point of expansion in Cypro-Classical period activity across the survey area. Survey produced a larger assemblage of 27 artifacts that date to this transitional period; they are distributed widely across the coastal plain, but concentrate on the Vigla ridge. Our excavations at Vigla have demonstrated the importance of occupation there between 350 and 250 BC (Olson et al. 2013; Caraher et al. 2014). We will discuss this transition more in our examination of the Hellenistic era.

7.4.2.   State and Settlement

The Cypro-Classical period was a time of unprecedented growth for the city of Kition. The city appears to have been strong enough to offer ships to the Persian fleet in Xerxes' invasion of Greece in 480 BC, and the disappointing results of this invasion may have contributed to the installation of a new Persian-backed dynasty in Kition (Nicolaou 1976: 331). The support of Persia for this dynasty may have played a role in helping Kition extend political authority over the two closest rival cities, Idalion and Tamassos, in the fifth and fourth centuries. The city also became increasingly involved in the dynastic affairs of its neighbor and rival Salamis, but with less dramatic results (Hill 1940: 111). The adventuring of the Phoenician dynasty at Kition and their Persian allies against Salamis eventually resulted in military actions, which probably involved land forces traipsing through the Pyla littoral between Kition and Salamis (See, for example, Diod. 15.4).

If it is clear that a growing administrative bureaucracy emerged in Kition at this time, our limited evidence cannot speak to its impact on the site, which must have had, nonetheless, some formal administrative ties to the political center (Yon 1989). What is clear is that the Pyla district remained important in the Cypro-Classical period and continued occupations from the Cypro-Archaic age because the area held a significant position on the coast for inhabitants on the outskirts of Kition's periphery. Indeed, P. Dikaios excavated a substantial three-chambered built tomb on the northern slope of the Kazama-Mavrospilios plateau (Dikaios 1935). The entrance of the tomb featured a Gorgon's head and two sphinxes in low relief, which the excavator dated to the Cypro-Classical period. The existence of such a monumental tomb points to the presence of a local elite perhaps associated with the activity at sites like Stavros or Pyla village, although ties to an Iron Age coastal settlement are also possible.

As we will discuss further below (7.5), the development of the site of Vigla as a new focal point of activity at the end of the Cypro-Classical period presents strong evidence for ties to Kition. Since the ceramic evidence from excavations of the fortified settlement suggests dates from the later fourth century BC, we must postpone this discussion until the following section.

7.4.3.   Regional Trends

The continued occupation of the Koutsopetria micro-region in the Cypro-Classical period is consistent with broader regional trends across Cyprus. The sites in the vicinity of Kition, for example, showed continuity into the Cypro-Classical period. Panayia-*Ematousa* produced Iron Age pottery across the site, even if evidence for specific Cypro-Classical period architecture was quite limited (Sørensen 2006a: 51–52; 2006c). Hadjisavvas noted the presence of farmsteads of Cypro-Classical date in the vicinity of Ay. Nappa (Hadjisavvas 1997: 26–38). Northwest of Koutsopetria, Cypro-Classical settlement in the Malloura Valley was consistent in its extent with both the earlier Iron Age and the later Hellenistic period (Kardulias and Yerkes 2012a). Adovasio and colleagues reported a similar pattern in the Chrysochou Valley in far western Cyprus (Adovasio et al. 1975: 347–48; Swiny and Mavromatis 2000: 435). The Sydney Cyprus Survey Project (SCSP) saw a decline in the number of settlements during the Cypro-Classical era in the Troodos range, but the investigators suggested that this could represent a concentration of agriculture and production that featured larger, more centralized estates (Given and Knapp 2003: 277). In general, the pattern of settlement in the Cypro-Classical Age tends to follow settlement in the earlier Iron Age. There is variability across the island, of course, but the southern coast especially saw either stability in the distribution of settlements or a slight increase during the Cypro-Classical period.

7.4.4.   Religious Landscapes

The most striking assemblage of late Iron Age artifacts from the survey area was a small assemblage of terracotta figurines (Section 7.3.1). These figurines could date as early as the Cypro-Archaic era, but the types and styles suggest mainly the fifth–fourth centuries BC (Section 4.9). The figurines have parallels with the humble figurines discovered at Panayia-*Ematousa* in "Pit 2" (Sørensen 2006d: 355–57). Despite the political upheavals of the Cypro-Classical period, the religious landscape of the region remained relatively stable. The same continuity existed at the sanctuary at the site of Stavros, which likewise continued to function throughout the Cypro-Classical period and produced significant quantities of monumental sculpture (Masson 1966: 11–21). A better parallel, perhaps, for the appearance of figurines at the site of Koutsopetria is the sanctuary excavated by S. Hadjisavvas at the coastal site of Makronisos, some 22 km to the east (Hadjisavvas 1997: 161–74). The sanctuary there produced a fragment of an exquisite limestone figurine and a number of fragments of other terracotta and limestone figurines. At Makronisos, the material all appears to date to the Cypro-Classical period and is contemporary with the other ceramic material from the site. The sanctuary itself is quite modest, with its only architecture being an enclosure open at one end and some 4 m wide. Such small-scale structures would leave few traces on the surface, and it seems probable that the sanctuary identified on the coastal heights of Koutsopetria was of this type. It is notable however, that Makronisos produced very little Cypro-Archaic period material, which is typical for the southeastern corner of the island, where Cypro-Geometric and Cypro-Archaic sites are rare.

7.4.5. *Connectivity*

The development of the site of Koutsopetria continued the activities in the region during the earlier Iron Age and indicates a sustained engagement of the island with the political world of the eastern Mediterranean. In this regard, the site has close parallels with the material from Panayia-*Ematousa*, which was likely a similar-sized site situated north of Kition. Moreover, the Cypro-Classical period marks the start of a new phase of occupation of the coastal plain, which would develop in the subsequent Hellenistic and Roman periods.

The continued importance of Koutsopetria in the Cypro-Classical era clearly reflected the continued prosperity of the region in general. Despite textual evidence for military activities in the area, the site continued to thrive and expanded onto the relatively exposed coastal plain. Ceramic material specifically dating to the Cypro-Classical era was difficult to identify from either the coastal plateau or the plain, but what we did identify suggests broader engagements with the Mediterranean world. In contrast to the majority of the early Iron Age material, which was most likely produced on the island, the assemblage of late Cypro-Classical and early Hellenistic wares shows new interactions with Attica, the Aegean, and the Levant in the fifth to third centuries BC. This assemblage marked the first large-scale appearance of imported luxury objects since the Late Bronze Age, but it is still a very limited connection compared with subsequent periods.

7.5. KOUTSOPETRIA IN THE HELLENISTIC PERIOD

The Hellenistic period is among the most complex and difficult historical periods, both in the microregion and on the island in general. The period saw the complete transformation of the political organization of the island, the increased participation of Cyprus in the eastern Mediterranean economy, and the growing demand for security after the conquests of Alexander ended the Persian Empire. These shifts shaped settlement in the region and contributed to a significant development of the site's strategic importance to the Antigonid and Ptolemaic forces fighting for control over the eastern Mediterranean. Thus, the intersection of the political structure of the region and access to resources, and political and economic issues across the eastern Mediterranean, forged a landscape that mediated between the local, regional, and global. As Mitford argued (1980), the Hellenistic and Roman periods marked Cyprus' deep integration into the political and economic system of the eastern Mediterranean in contrast with the Cypro-Archaic and Classical periods when the island was more inward facing. Mitford's assessment of the Cypro-Archaic and Cypro-Classical ages is problematic, but his view of the continued outward reach of Cyprus in the Hellenistic period is hard to dispute (Mitford 1980; Gordon 2012; Keen 2012; Papantoniou 2012).

7.5.1. Artifacts and Distribution

The Hellenistic assemblage in the Pyla-*Koutsopetria* survey area marks the densest and most extensive scatter since the late Bronze Age. While Hellenistic pottery was no more visible to us than Cypro-Classical or Cypro-Geometric material, and even less visible than Late Bronze Age and Cypro-Archaic assemblages, it nevertheless appears more frequently and over a wider area in the landscape. The 118 artifacts spread over 16 ha represent 1.6 times the extent of the Late Cypriot period (but only 60% of the quantity), 9–10 times the quantity and 7–8 times the area of Cypro-Geometric and Cypro-Classical assemblages, and 4 times the quantity and extent of Cypro-Archaic material. While the Hellenistic assemblage covered less than a quarter of the area of the Late Roman, it appeared over an area that was every bit as extensive as the Early Roman period. The Hellenistic period, in short, marks an impressive new phase in the occupation of the PKAP region.

The distribution of Hellenistic artifacts overlaps in areas with the extensive distribution of artifacts from the Iron Age and Cypro-Classical to Hellenistic periods, suggesting the continued expansion of the site that began in the Iron Age. However, the Hellenistic era also marks a much more robust and extensive assemblage that prefigures the distribution of Early and Late Roman material across most of the coastal plain in Zones 1 and 2. That Hellenistic material is found in all 5 zones and in substantial quantities is indicative of a new threshold of occupation. The ridges, so important for Iron Age settlement, remained occupied in the late fourth–third centuries, but the coastal zones also evidently came under more intensive habitation, as one-third of all Hellenistic material comes from these areas.

The extent of Hellenistic material is especially impressive given the relative invisibility of the period, as noted above. Some 92% of artifacts attributed to the Hellenistic period were fine wares

and more than half of these were rims, bases, and handles. We under-identified Hellenistic body sherds, amphorae, and kitchen wares during analysis, yet the period still shows a tremendous explosion. Since the completion of our analysis, in fact, we have refined our knowledge of Basket Handle amphorae, as we outlined in Chapter 4. Our excavation work at the site of Vigla produced a number of these Basket Handle Amphora in secure contexts that date to the Hellenistic period and are clearly different from the Cypro-Archaic and Cypro-Classical versions, being smaller in size with a round handle. These are similar to those published by Karageorghis and identified as Hellenistic olive oil containers (Karageorghis 1970; Hadjisavvas 1992: 78). The large number of Basket Handles in the survey area could indicate a focus for Koutsopetria in the Late Hellenistic age on exporting, rather than importing, goods such as fine wares.

An important focus of Hellenistic occupation was the Vigla ridge, which produced 20% of all Hellenistic pottery, despite being significantly smaller in area than the other zones in our research area (Caraher et al. 2014). Excavations on the ridge have produced domestic contexts in two major phases that date from the later fourth to middle of the third centuries (Olson et al. 2013). The first phase of occupation was destroyed violently by fire, probably the result of a military attack, as weapons like spear points, arrows, sling bullets, and catapult bolts are scattered among the floors of the houses either left by the defenders or attackers. The occupants of the second phase quickly cleaned up and reoccupied the site, which then continued as late as the mid-third century BC. As we outlined in Chapter 6, the domestic structures and assemblages occurred within a fortified enceinte, suggesting that the site may have had a long term garrison. An inscribed game board featuring several ethnic names from the site may attest to the presence of mercenaries, which would be consistent with Hellenistic practices (Nikolaou 1965).

The domestic assemblages at Vigla are consistent with dates for the fortification wall that encompassed the entire promontory. These fortifications attest to the impact of the larger political world on the site, as it occupies a location that would have been strategically significant in either the waning days of the Iron Age dynasty at Kition or during the period of wars between the island's new Hellenistic overlords. The fortification certainly marked a substantial investment and complemented the overall expansion of activities in the micro-region and across the island during this dynamic period of transition.

7.5.2. State and Settlement

The Hellenistic period marked a time of significant shifts in the political organization of Cyprus — even as there were evident continuities. The successors of Alexander ended the Iron Age kingdoms and politically reorganized the island, which nonetheless retained some elements of the longstanding civic structure. After the last independent king of Kition was put to death in the late fourth century, the Ptolemaic rulers governed the island through a military *strategos* (Avraamides 1971; Bagnall 1976; Nicolaou 1976: 325–38; Papantoniou 2012), yet individual cities continued to retain some administrative functions and served as seats for local representatives of the island's military rulers, called *phrourarchs* (Bagnall 1976: 52). *Phrourarchs,* in turn, dispatched lower-level officials called *hegemones* who may have led individual military units. Epigraphic evidence from near Ormidhia confirms the presence of a *hegemon* there (*SEG* 6.823). It seems probable that these officials coordinated the construction of fortifications on the island (Bagnall 1976: 38–39; Balandier 2002: 333). Papantoniou has recently shown (2012) that many of these social and cultural transformations reflected broader processes predating Ptolemaic rule.

The political reorganization of the island could only have stimulated changes in settlement in the region. The end of the ruling dynasty and the destruction of the city's walls marked the end of Kition as an independent political power capable of military expeditions against its rival cities on the island. There is no evidence, however, for Kition's decline as an economic center. Perhaps the end of conflict between Kition and Salamis opened up economic opportunities for the southeastern corner of the island. This region may have had significant access to markets at both cities, and

seen new opportunities for investment, as citizens or subjects of the two cities developed economic relationships and cultivable land in areas that previously functioned as liminal zones between the two polities.

The most substantial signatures of the Hellenistic era in our survey area are the fortification walls and the domestic site they enclose. The walls were certainly a physical manifestation of the intersection of local resources — the harbor, agricultural resources, easily quarried stone, and strategically useful coastal views — and the new place of Kition's hinterland within a turbulent and dynamic Cyprus. The Hellenistic occupation itself, however, which extends well beyond the fortified height of Vigla across the ridges and coastal plain, attests to the changing place of the site within southeastern Cyprus and the growing importance of a community with immediate access to the sea.

7.5.3. Regional Trends

The visible expansion of Hellenistic settlement at Koutsopetria mirrors the well-documented settlement boom in the southeastern corner of the island. Hadjisavvas, for example, recorded at least six sites that showed a significant Hellenistic component, but almost no earlier material. While we know that Iron Age settlements generally existed in southeastern Cyprus (7.4.3, above), the visibility of Hellenistic and Roman settlement in the area almost certainly represents a substantial increase in investment in the area south of Salamis and near Ay. Napa (Hadjisavvas 1997: 33–36; Palio Chorko, Makronisos [cemetery], Kaounin [few sherds], Ampas [settlement and cemetery], Tornos, and Zyagin).

Other parts of the island also underwent expansion in the Hellenistic period. The Akamas peninsula on the far western side of the island appears to have experienced a similar expansion in activity (Fejfer 1995). More modest expansion of activity appears to have occurred in the adjacent Chrysochou Valley (Adovasio et al. 1975). The Palaipaphos region saw continued growth in the number and density of settlements (Sørensen et al. 1993), as did the Vasilikos Valley, which saw the number of sites almost double between the Cypro-

Classical and Hellenistic periods (Todd 2004). Finally, Catling and the Cyprus survey recorded a similar expansion of Hellenistic activity in the Yalias River Valley (Catling 1982). The ten-fold increase in the extent of occupation at Vigla and Koutsopetria, then, is consistent with the growth in settlement noted elsewhere on the island.

The presence of fortifications in both the Chrysochou Valley and along the northern coast of Cyprus suggests that some of this expansion was geared toward defending the island (Adovasio et al. 1975: 350). The Hellenistic site of Paleocastro on the northern coast of Cyprus offers an even closer parallel to the site of Vigla (Quilici and Quilici-Gigli 1972/1973). Closer at hand, the relatively unexplored site of Palio Chorko near Ay. Napa, approximately 20 km east of Koutsopetria, preserved the foundation of substantial walls suggesting possible fortification (Hadjisavvas 1997: 34). Northwest of the Pyla littoral, the site of Panayia-*Ematousa* near modern Aradippou included a settlement of the Hellenistic era as well as a structure that might have served a military purpose, such as a guard post for the route inland from Kition (Sørensen 2006a).

The patterns of expansion of settlement during the Hellenistic period, however, were not necessarily universal across the island. Most strikingly, the Sydney Cyprus Survey Project did not record an expansion of Hellenistic activity inland northwest of Kition, in the Troodos Mountains in the neighborhood of the city of Tamassos, despite the fact that this area was close to important sources of copper, and the city was seen as sufficiently valuable that the kings of Kition seized it and its territory at the end of the Iron Age (Moore 2003: 277). The Malloura Valley likewise produced little in the way of settlements for the Hellenistic period, but the ceramic assemblage concentrated near several groups of tombs of this date suggests that some settlement existed in the area (Kardulias and Yerkes 2012a: 95). It may be, then, that the development of settlement during the Hellenistic era was largely a coastal phenomenon. This would coincide well with the island's growing engagement with the wider Mediterranean world.

7.5.4.   *Religious Landscapes*

The economic and strategic value of the site complemented religious activities in the micro-region. The concentration of Hellenistic pottery at the site of the Iron Age sanctuary on the Mavrospilios plateau is suggestive, even if the assemblage gives us no precise information about a shrine. Farther north, a sanctuary with dedications to Apollo Magirios stood at the site of Stavros, which appears to have continued into the Hellenistic era (Masson 1966: 11–27). The most impressive cultic find of possibly Hellenistic date, however, is a large stone vessel, which was uncovered on the coastal plain of Koutsopetria during the installation of an electrical pylon (Hadjisavvas 1992: 76). An inscription on the vessel dedicated to Apollo Karaiates from a certain Apollonios, son of Menon, strongly suggests a sanctuary on the plain (*SEG* 20.138; Mitford 1961: 116). The basin's size, weight, and condition make it unlikely that it moved far from its original location. Hadjisavvas has identified the vessel as a separation vessel associated with the production of olive oil (Hadjisavvas 1992: 75–76). This marks the earliest evidence from the site for the production of olive oil in this area and, as Hadjisavvas noted, one of the only places on Cyprus where olive oil production is clearly associated with a religious shrine (Hadjisavvas 1992: 83). The location of an olive press on the coast in the immediate vicinity of a harbor can be read in connection to markets elsewhere in the region or on the island.

7.5.5.   *Connectivity*

In the Hellenistic age, the integration of the city and region of Kition with the wider Mediterranean world brought expanded economic opportunities and development. Inscriptions from Athens and other cities of the eastern Mediterranean commemorated citizens of Kition and demonstrate a period of expanding connections (Nicolaou 1976: 134–36). Expanded markets for natural resources, particularly timber for ships, copper, and agricultural goods from Cyprus seem to have fueled a demographic and economic expansion (Hill 1940: 174). Certainly access to a good harbor, opportunities for trade between previously rival cities, and

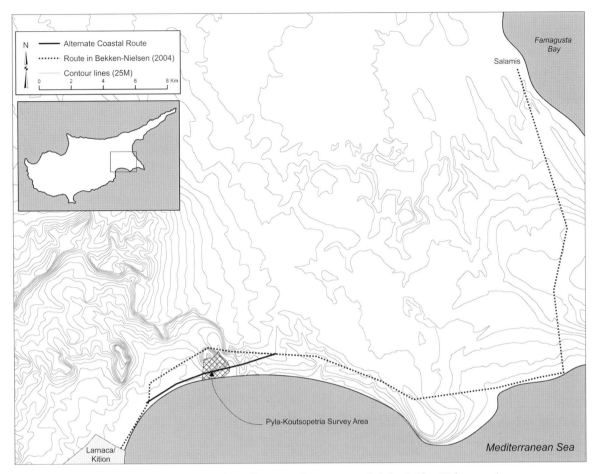

FIG. 7.3   *Major routes through the area in the Hellenistic and Roman periods (after Bekker-Nielsen 2004).*

new, nearby lands opening to more systematic exploitation would have all contributed to the growth of activities in the micro-region.

The Hellenistic period marked a redefinition of Koutsopetria's connective structures, evident firstly in some 30% of Hellenistic material originating on the coastal plain. The ridges remained occupied and Vigla received significant fortification, but the distribution and quantity of material across the plain indicates an interest in maximizing the site's maritime facility. It seems possible that more substantial maritime facilities of the harbor like the moles and warehouses developed at this time, but only more intensive archaeological investigation will determine this for certain.

The ceramic remains form a major source of evidence for a greater level of connectivity. Our evidence is best at Vigla where excavations have produced stratified deposits of occupation and

building phases associated with the late fourth and early third centuries BC. Our analysis of that material is in its initial stage and will be published as part of the excavation, but preliminary examinations indicate dependence on local supplies together with some imported artifacts from Attica (Olson et al. 2013; Caraher et al. 2014).

The construction of a fortification at this site served to protect both the harbor on the coastline and a major land route through the area leading south from the vicinity of Ormidhia (fig. 7.3. Chapter 6). Bekker-Nielsen has argued that the land route from Salamis joined the coast from Pyla village immediately south of Oroklini (Bekker-Nielsen 2004: 186–87). This road would have passed approximately 800 m to the north of the fortification at Vigla, and a garrison there would have been able to respond to a force moving along this land route. The fortification would have also protected the coastal route by preventing forces moving uncontestedly along the coastal road to Kition. An early modern road visible on the cadastral map showed a route that ran east from Larnaca through the vicinity of Koutsopetria where it turned inland toward Ormidhia before turning to the north to follow the modern routes toward Salamis. Even if this was not the main route to Salamis in the Hellenistic era, it must have been a viable one that contributed to the strategic value of the coastline. The harbor was suitable for an enemy force to land and advance on Kition or, less plausibly, march overland to attack the important city of Salamis, which, until the early second century, was the seat of Ptolemaic rule on the island. The fortification represents a response to the expanding settlement on the southern coast and the need to offer protection and project power in a rapidly growing network of places.

There was significant evidence for the quarrying of limestone around areas of exposed bedrock on the height of Vigla, which included the tactically useful extraction of bedrock to form a dry moat across the northern part of the Vigla promontory (Ch. 6). Additional evidence for quarrying exists along the western side of the infilled harbor area where stone was extracted from an exposed peninsula of bedrock. While it remains difficult to determine an independent date for the quarrying activities at the site, it finds parallels with quarrying activity at coastal sites along the southeastern littoral of the island including Potamos tou Lioupetriou and Makronisos, which Hadjisavvas connected to the expansion of settlement in the area (Hadjisavvas 1997: 33; Leonard 2005: 406-7). A similar argument could explain the quarrying at Koutsopetria. The requirements of the fortifications, the expanding activity at the site, and the potential to move extracted material elsewhere along the coast by sea spawned industrial activities in connection with a growing stretch of coastline and settlement on the island.

The Hellenistic period, in sum, marked a watershed in the connectivity of the Pyla littoral. The construction of a fortification and the expansion of activities along the coastal plain represent economic development at the junction of local ties and the larger Hellenistic Mediterranean.

The clear shift to the coastal plain meant that the Hellenistic inhabitants of Koutsopetria made substantial investments in the coastal location of the site and reoriented the center of settlement toward the maritime facilities of the harbor.

7.6.   KOUTSOPETRIA IN THE EARLY ROMAN PERIOD

The Roman period on Cyprus created a new set of conditions that encouraged the growth of the settlement, its full engagement in trans-Mediterranean trade, and participation in the network of settlement across the island. Rome formally annexed the island in 58 BC, after almost two-and-a-half centuries of control by the Ptolemaic kings of Egypt. Outside of occasional and short-lived disruptions brought about by earthquakes, plague, revolt, or invasion, the island remained largely prosperous and secure for over half a millennium under Roman rule. Scholars have documented the reputation for prosperity that Cyprus developed during the centuries of Roman rule, and it is unnecessary to rehearse these well-known statements here (Hill 1940: 226-56; Potter 2000; Leonard 2005: 200, with references). This section will focus primarily on the Early and Middle Roman periods and consider the transition from the Hellenistic to the Roman period.

7.6.1.   Artifacts and Distribution

The intensity and extent of activity in the Pyla-Koutsopetria micro-region expanded significantly during the Roman period. Material dating broadly to the Roman era appeared in 82% of the survey units and covered a largely continuous area of 80 ha. Artifacts datable to the narrower Early Roman material appear in a smaller subset (19%) of these units, but are distributed over a fairly extensive area. The Early Roman assemblage is slightly more extensive (16.4 ha) and numerous (n=142 artifacts) than the Hellenistic material, probably because it is slightly more visible. Early Roman pottery was significantly less visible than the Late Roman, as we did not identify many utilitarian or body sherds, the most common kind of Early Roman pottery present in a settlement (Pettegrew 2007).

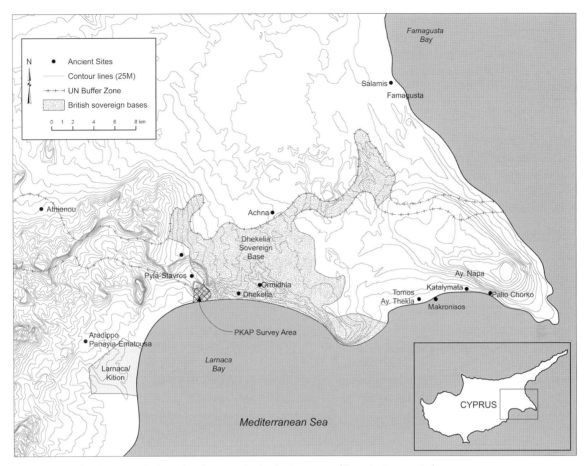

Fig. 7.4   *Pyla-Koutsopetria in regional perspective in the Roman and Late Antique periods.*

Like the earlier Hellenistic period, Roman material appeared in nearly every level area in the micro-region, including the coastal plain, the Kazama-Mavrospilios plateau, Vigla, and the height of Kokkinokremos. The greatest concentrations, however, occurred in the coastal plain where some 50% of Early Roman material was found. This shift to the plain highlights the orientation of the site to the coast, the importance of commerce, and integration into wider trading networks. The frequency of fine ware, kitchen ware, and coarse ware suggests domestic facilities in both Zones 1 and 2, but other activities are evident. On his passage through the area en route to his summer residence in Ormidhia, Cesnola excavated a series of Roman-period tombs that contained Roman lamps, glass, and "black varnished pottery of a very common kind" at a site called Paleo-Castro (Cesnola 1887: 178–79). As early modern maps of the region label Koutsopetria as "Paleo-castro" and

the coastal road as "to Ormidhia," it seems likely that Cesnola dug at an area near the densest scatters of Roman pottery.

It is important to note that the most common Early Roman table wares, Eastern Sigillata A and Cypriot Sigillata, suggest occupation phases from the mid-second century BC to the second century AD. We found little Hellenistic material of the late third to second century BC that would bridge the gap between the Early Hellenistic and Early Roman settlement. We also failed to document obvious material dating to the third and fourth centuries AD, but the scarcity of material of these centuries is well-known and points to a general gap in chronology across the island.

7.6.2.   State and Settlement

The Romans primarily adopted the Hellenistic political organization of the island when it became

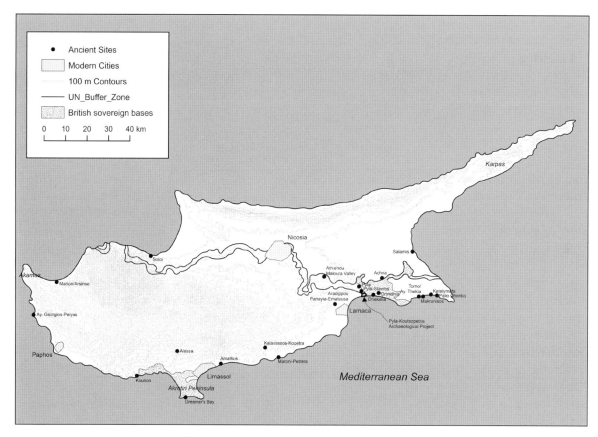

FIG. 7.5 *Cyprus in the Roman and Late Antique periods.*

a Roman province in 58 BC, although the influence of Rome as a hegemonic power in the eastern Mediterranean had existed for nearly a century (Kallet-Marx 1995), making the early stages of Roman political control difficult to identify in the material record. Over the long period of Roman rule, the expansive network of trade that emerged in the Mediterranean basin and the sometimes rapacious behavior of Roman rulers stimulated the extraction of various resources from across the island (Potter 2000).

During the Roman era, the site of Kition apparently remained the local administrative and economic center in the region, even if relatively little evidence exists for sustained Roman or imperial interest in the town. Earthquakes in the first century AD likely caused significant damage to the city, and the reconstruction and repair of the city may have attracted the imperial patronage of Nerva and later Trajan (Nicolaou 1976: 340; *IGR* 976). The seismic activities and sedimentation may

have threatened the functioning of the harbor at Kition, but it evidently remained open throughout the Early and Middle Roman periods and contributed to the prosperity of that city (Nicolaou 1976: 71–85; Morhange et al. 2000; Leonard 2005: 432–38). Despite the gap in the material culture for the third century (which is most likely due to an artificial gap in the artifact chronology), it does not appear that the seismic activities across the Mediterranean and the political and military instability of the Roman world during this period disrupted the long term economic, demographic, and settlement growth in our study area.

Koutsopetria and the sites in the surrounding region provide little evidence for these disruptions, suggesting that they were either too short-lived to appear in our ceramic chronology or that our micro-region avoided the worst of the disruptions. In fact, the extensive and flourishing settlement of the Early Roman period, which continued the general settlement pattern and the investments of the

Hellenistic era, indicates a greater economic autonomy for Koutsopetria. The continuing importance and growing prosperity of Kition contributed to the growth of smaller sites in its hinterland and the distribution of greater economic and cultural choices to the inhabitants of the region.

7.6.3. Regional Trends

Roman rule brought significant changes in the structure of settlement on the island. David Rupp has argued that Romanization saw the development of suburban zones with small and large villages standing below the level of the town (Rupp 1997). Given the range of criteria for defining settlement size and densities, it remains difficult to fit Roman Koutsopetria into typologies of Roman settlement on the island. That being said, the patterns proposed by Rupp may offer some guidance for understanding Roman settlement on the island. In the area of Paphos on the western side of the island, settlement extends 6–7 km from the major urban center of Paphos. Outside of this range stood coastal centers and sizable towns like Peyia, located approximately 10 km northwest of Paphos beyond the urban sprawl. Some of these peripheral settlements are "secondary" and others "tertiary," representing a large village or a small town and serving between major regional centers and their more remote hinterlands (Rupp 1997: 248–49). At 10 km distance from Kition, Koutsopetria parallels the location of Peyia and may represent a settlement category between the large village and the town that functioned as a local center and continued to have close administrative ties to Kition. As Mitford (1980) and others have noted, there is no evidence for administratively autonomous villages in the Roman period.

Despite the lack of political status for small and mid-sized sites, there were significant and well-known sites on the island of a rank below Roman cities. In fact, it is possible that Koutsopetria appears in the description of the Cypriot coast offered by Claudius Ptolemaios in the second century AD. He referred to a place called Dades Promontory, located east of Kition and west of the Thronoi Promontory and Town and Pedalion Promontory (Ptol. *Geog.* 5.14; Leonard 1995b: 241;

Caraher et al. 2005: 248–49). The latter is generally thought to be Cape Grecko, and the former may be the site of Tornos near Ay. Napa (Hadjisavvas 1997: 35); in that case, Dades Promontory would be Cape Pyla. While this identification of the Dades Promontory might be the simplest understanding of the text, it is nevertheless tempting to see the ancient name Dades, or "torches," as somehow related to the modern name of the site Vigla, or "outpost" or "watchtower." As torches were used to communicate between watch posts, perhaps this name preserved the memory of the earlier fortifications and their role in defending this stretch of coastline in the Hellenistic era. The identification of the site as Dades would also be consistent with Ptolemy's description of the Cypriot coast.

The Early Roman period across the island generally saw continued settlement expansion. Certainly the peace that Rome brought to the eastern Mediterranean introduced the possibility of a more integrated regional economy (Mitford 1980; Potter 2000). While the relationship between the Hellenistic and Roman periods is poorly understood, some regions show clear evidence for continuity between the two periods, and areas show evidence for significant expansion in activities. The Troodos area, surveyed by the Sydney Cyprus Survey Project, and the Vasilikos Valley, for example, saw a significant expansion of Roman-period activities, and it is clear that Roman involvement in the extraction of natural resources (timber and minerals) shaped the structure and distribution of settlement on the island (Given and Knapp 2003; Todd 2004).

John Leonard and others have argued that trade contributed significantly to the prosperity of Cyprus during the Roman period (Mitford 1980; Potter 2000; Leonard 2005: 792–965). After Pompey eradicated the last of the pirates from the eastern Mediterranean, Roman control over the Levant, the northern African coast, Asia Minor, and the Aegean basin provided both expanded markets for Cypriot goods and access to new sources of capital and patronage from the wider Roman world. Thus, peace opened the door to more systematic exploitation of natural resources across the island for commercial ends.

Leonard's thorough survey of coastal sites made clear that inlets along the southern coast showed significant activity throughout the Roman period, presumably facilitating the trans-shipment of agricultural goods to both local and foreign markets. In the vicinity of Koutsopetria along the southeastern coast, for example, there is evidence for continuity with the Hellenistic era at Palio Chorko and Makronisos, but also a developing network of new settlement at Tornos (ancient Thronoi) and the small harbors along the southeastern littoral of the island (Hadjisavvas 1997: 35). A major coastal road would have linked these new settlements east of the Pyla littoral to the city of Kition (Bekker-Nielsen 2004: 186–89). Farther west on the Cypriot coastline, the prosperity of sites like Dreamer's Bay on the Akrotiri peninsula during the Early and Late Roman periods demonstrates the security of the coast and the economic opportunities available to coastal communities (Leonard 2005: 546–58). Unfortunately, there is little published evidence for Roman activities north of the Pyla littoral in the vicinity of the village of Pyla, or even west towards Ormidhia. The absence of a significant settlement in the Malloura Valley farther north (Moore and Gregory 2012: 206–11), in an area associated with an ancient sanctuary, is a useful reminder that the expansion of activities in the Roman era did not necessarily reach every corner of the island. The coastal orientation was a primary aspect of these Roman landscapes.

7.6.4. Religious Landscapes

The Koutsopetria micro-region showed scattered evidence for religious activities from the Iron Age to the Hellenistic periods, but clear evidence for Early Roman religious activities has remained elusive. It is worth noting, however, that the area identified as early as the Iron Age as a sanctuary continued to see activity through Hellenistic and Early Roman periods. Although it is never safe to assume continuity at any religious site, it is tempting to speculate that the sanctuary located north of Vigla continued to enjoy some activity during the Early Roman period. Moreover, this might explain the abrupt and striking absence of fifth- and sixth-century-AD material in these units, perhaps as a result of the coming of Christianity and the refocusing of the community's religious energies on the basilica on the coastal plain.

7.6.5. Connectivity

Roman rule accelerated the scope of resource extraction on the island and fostered a greater degree of commercial connectivity in the Mediterranean that would persist through the Late Roman period. At Koutsopetria, the shift to the plain that began in the Hellenistic era continued in the Early Roman period, with half of Early Roman pottery coming from these zones. Excavation would clarify the developments of the harbor facilities, but the survey data show an extensive distribution of material that indicates an expansion in occupation and buildings.

On the one hand, the ceramics from both Koutsopetria and Kition show a significant engagement with centers in the Levant and less economic contact with the western part of the island. For example, the dominant fine ware at Kition, Eastern Sigillata A, originated from northern Syria, while Cypriot Sigillata, a ware common in western Cyprus, was uncommon at Kition (Marquié 2001, 2002, 2004, 2005). The overall number of Eastern Sigillata A and Cypriot Sigillata sherds was not substantial at Koutsopetria, but the former ware was more common (39% of Early Roman fine wares) than the latter (23%), confirming in some respects these noted patterns. Table wares from farther afield were more exceptional: singular instances of Eastern Sigillata B from western Asia Minor and Arretine Ware from Italy indicate that long-distance connections in the Early Roman period did not meet the demands for table wares in this period.

On the other hand, Rhodian, Koan, and Pseudo-Koan amphora types form the majority of imported Early Roman amphorae, suggesting dependence on ties to the east Aegean for wine and olive oil. Pinched-Handle amphorae, which originated either on Cyprus or southern Anatolia, are almost completely absent at Koutsopetria, as they are also unusual at other contemporary sites such as Panayia-*Ematousa* (Hayes 1991: 90–91; Williams 1992: 94; Leonard 2005: 889–905). Lund has noted that the distribution of Pinched-Handle amphorae tended to parallel the distribution of Cypriot Sigillata and has suggested, with Williams, that Rough Cilicia and Western Cyprus constituted a single zone for the trading of pottery in this period (Williams and Lund 2013: 161). The recent discovery of Cypriot Red Slip manufacturing centers near Gebiz, Turkey, certainly strengthens the argument for a long-term trading connection between this region and western Cyprus (Jackson et al. 2012) that continued into the Late Roman period. The absence of Cypriot Sigillata and Pinched-Handle amphorae, despite the relative proximity to these production centers, reveals the complexity of trade patterns for the site. Rhodian, Koan, and Pseudo-Koan amphorae indicate connections to the Aegean, but the Levantine fine wares and the absence of some wares typical of western Cyprus indicate that our region's engagement with eastern and western trade is complex.

7.7. KOUTSOPETRIA IN LATE ANTIQUITY

From the fifth to the seventh century AD, the site of Koutsopetria experienced an unprecedented period of prosperity that was consistent with the Late Roman settlement boom documented across the eastern Mediterranean (see Decker 2009). Rautman's historical assessment of a "busy" Cypriot countryside in Late Antiquity (2000, 2004), together with the relative archaeological visibility of the period in general (Pettegrew 2007), provide a context for understanding the extensive and diverse assemblage of material present at Koutsopetria during this time.

7.7.1. Artifacts and Distribution

The quantity and extent of Late Roman material on the surface alone demonstrates an entirely new threshold of intensive occupation in the micro-region that is notably different from previous phases. The assemblage of over 5,000 Late Roman potsherds, tiles, and glass covering 70% of the survey area is four times more extensive and about 40 times more numerous than Hellenistic and Early Roman assemblages, and 20–40 times more extensive and several hundred times more numerous than various narrow period assemblages dated to the pre-Hellenistic era.

In part, this apparent "explosion" from earlier periods is related to issues of relative diagnosticity. The Late Roman period was much more visible in our survey area for the different reasons outlined in Section 5.3.4.2. Late Roman coarse ware sherds and tiles were significantly visible in a way they were not in earlier periods (consider the total absence of tiles for Iron Age periods). Our ceramicist's specialization in the Late Roman period gave him confidence to identify more artifacts to that period. The diagnosticity of Late Roman feature sherds and the frequency of table wares all contributed to the recognition of this period during survey and analysis and its dramatically greater quantities.

Nonetheless, the variety of artifacts and the extent of the scatter demonstrate appreciable growth and expansion. The Late Roman scatter extended in high densities across all of Zone 1, which was clearly the center of habitation and built environment, and also continued across the northern part of Zone 2 in moderate densities. The lower frequency of tile in Zone 2, however, suggests few monumental buildings in this area and points to lower thresholds of habitation or other kinds of activities, such as graves, coastal installations, or warehouses (Section 7.7.5 below), along the ancient coastal road circumventing the embayment. Lower-density scatters of Late Roman coarse ware, amphorae, and occasionally fine and kitchen wares occur on the ridges of Kokkinokremos (Zone 3), Kazama-Mavrospilios (Zone 4), and Vigla, which probably represent small scattered farms or the residues of farming activity.

Only the far northwest of the plateau and the area identified with the Iron Age sanctuary did not produce notable Late Roman material. This indicates that some areas of the study area, which saw intensive activities in preceding periods were uninhabited or turned over to other activities, such as agriculture. This may have been a result of the continued nucleation of the main settlement on the coastal plain. The decline in material in the area of the sanctuary on the Kazama-Mavrospilios ridge could represent the changing function of this part of the study area, as the Christian church on the plain below drew attention, resources, and devotees away from areas once dedicated to poly-theistic religious functions.

The Late Roman material represented a particularly diverse range of ceramic types, both produced locally and imported from across the Mediterranean. The presence of imported fine wares and transport vessels suggests trans-shipment of luxury items as well as raw materials, which in turn indicates a thriving regional entrepôt. The assemblage of Late Roman pottery is dominated by forms dating to the late fifth through early seventh centuries, and we identified only a handful of objects dating from the fourth to the middle of the fifth centuries. The absence of a significant quantity of material datable to the first half of the Late Roman period has rendered activity in our study area obscure and the connections between this area and the rest of the Mediterranean tenuous.

By the sixth century, however, the tremendous quantity of local and imported ceramics indicates that the site of Koutsopetria bustled with activity. It seems reasonable to identify the site at this time as a significant coastal town with a built-up center of at least 40 ha and an area with considerable signs of activity extending for well over 70 ha.

7.7.2. *State and Settlement*

As with earlier periods, the relationship between the settlement on the Pyla littoral and the site of Kition remains obscure. There is little archaeological evidence for the character of Late Roman Kition and only scattered literary evidence. Despite its declining fortune, Kition retained civic status throughout the Late Roman period and became the seat of an important bishopric (Nicolaou 1976: 340). The city must have continued to perform some administrative, economic, and political functions for the region.

This continuity in function, however, is overshadowed by the coastal changes that beset the city in the later Roman era and caused infilling of the harbor. The gradual infilling seems to have begun as early as the Hellenistic period, and seismic activity during the Roman and Late Roman periods may have accelerated this process (Morhange et al. 2000; Leonard 2005: 432–38). At some point toward the end of antiquity, maritime activity may have shifted farther west from its ancient location at Bamboula toward the central area of the Medieval city near the church of Ay. Lazaros (Nicolaou 1976: 80; Leonard 2005: 442). Problems associated with the rapid silting up of Kition's port may have benefited smaller regional ports like Koutsopetria that had escaped or weathered the same geological processes. Leonard has envisioned a similar scenario for the growth of maritime activities at the harbor at Dreamer's Bay on the Akrotiri peninsula, which may have returned to prominence after an earthquake severely damaged the harbor works and civic center of Kourion in the mid-fourth century (Leonard 2005: 556–57). The displacement of trade from Kourion, Kition, and other traditional economic centers on the southern coast should have benefited smaller harbors like Koutsopetria that remained viable.

Yet, at the same time, the changing fortunes of Salamis must have also influenced the distribution of inter-regional trade on the island. Salamis appears to have experienced a renaissance in the middle years of the fourth century when the emperor Constantius II refounded the city (Leonard 2005: 164–66). The exact extent of his works at Salamis remains difficult to determine, but it seems probable that he renovated the harbor there and elevated the city's economic facilities and civic amenities. The imperial attention and the subsequent growth of Salamis as a prominent economic center almost certainly stimulated opportunities for local exchange in the area of Koutsopetria, which had both overland and maritime access to the city and its countryside, although our evidence for activity in the study area during the fourth and early fifth centuries remains problematic. Nevertheless, the presence of a market at Salamis and Kition would have provided Koutsopetria with centers of exchange for locally produced goods and a place of employment for local residents. Over time, both investment in the urban centers and changes in coastal topography may have contributed to demographic expansion in the southeastern corner of the island and brought global, regional, and local products to Koutsopetria. The expansion of Salamis and changing fortunes of Kition undoubtedly affected the development of Koutsopetria, but not in a simple binary way. Instead, these urban areas influenced local economies on a regional scale in ways that scholars have not entirely understood (Rautman 2000; 2003).

7.7.3. *Regional Trends*

In Late Antiquity, a wide range of communities developed on Cyprus that lacked formal administrative status and were smaller than major urban centers, but nonetheless flourished in a vibrant eastern Mediterranean economy. The four-fold growth of the area of occupation at Koutsopetria in the later fifth and sixth centuries, as well as the increasing complexity of the site, is consistent with changes in settlement patterns documented across Cyprus, particularly in the coastal regions. With a dense scatter of Late Roman roof tiles suggesting monumental architecture covering at least 10 ha, a significant scatter of fine, kitchen, and various coarse and utility wares covering 40 ha, and a lower-density scatter of pottery extending for over 70 ha, sites like Koutsopetria represented new significant locations of investment, commerce, and habitation. Other similar Late Antique sites that are large and complex dot the southern coast of the island and call for further study (Leonard 2005).

East of our survey area, Hadjisavvas' study of the southern coast to the west of Cape Pyla showed continued expansion of existing settlements and the appearance of significant new settlements. These include the large village or small town of Katalymata, covering an estimated 15 ha, as well as the settlement of Tornos that expanded from earlier Roman periods to cover a "huge area" (Hadjisavvas 1997: 35). The site of Panayia-*Ematousa,* north of Larnaca, shows continued activity into the Late Roman period (Sørensen 2006a: 61–62). Inland growth is less dramatic, but survey in the Malloura Valley showed some small increase in activity, and an early Christian basilica at the site of Giorkos near the ancient sanctuary at Golgoi, north of Athienou, indicates Late Roman activity and investment in that region (Bakirtzis 1976).

West of Kition, the coastal areas of the Vasilikos and Maroni valleys are dotted with Late Roman sites. The growth of these areas evidently relates to their connection to coastal and industrial landscapes. The four-hectare village at Kopetra in the Vasilikos Valley represents a settlement that emerged to support Late Roman exploitation of mineral resources in the Troodos and local trade routes along the coastal plain (Rautman 2003). In this way, it parallels the site of Alassa in the Kouris Valley excavated by P. Flourentzos, which likewise had contact with both inland production sites in the Troodos and coastal trading routes (Flourentzos 1996). Even smaller sites like the one-hectare village of Maroni-*Petrera* grew because of the importance of its coastal location in the changing landscape of the Late Roman world (Manning et al. 2002: 107).

Farther west, coastal sites like Dreamer's Bay on the Akrotiri Peninsula near Kourion, or Ay. Georgios-*Peyia* west of Paphos, appear to have been of similar size and perhaps served similar economic functions, growing in status, yet within the hinterland of major urban centers. Unfortunately, neither site is well-published at present, although both have seen some study (Bakirtzis 1995; 2000; Leonard 2005: 546–58). Even rather marginal coastal landscapes in the west, like the Akamas peninsula, saw a significant rebound in settlement after the lull that characterized the second and third centuries. Small settlements in that region, like Ay. Kononas, included churches and industrial areas like quarries. The village almost certainly drew its primary economic life from agricultural activities in marginal lands that became profitable in light of connections to the coast and broader economic changes in Late Antiquity (Leonard 1995b: 133–70).

The southeastern corner of the island was probably too far east to avail itself to the mineral or timber production in the Troodos, but the soils in this corner of the island were far better than the rocky fields of the Akamas. It seems probable that Koutsopetria gained a small part of its prosperity from quarrying, a larger part from agriculture, and a substantial part from its function as a market town and duties on exchange in the harbor, which was always a great economic resource for harbor communities (Purcell 2005).

7.7.4. Religious Landscapes

The spread of Christianity on the island significantly transformed the religious landscape of Cyprus and the region around Koutsopetria. The southern part of the Kazama-Mavrospilios plateau, where we believe a shrine or sanctuary stood from Cypro-Archaic times, appears to have been used neither intensively nor extensively. While this general area had been important throughout the Iron Age, Hellenistic, and Early Roman periods, unusually low densities are found here in the Late Roman period. It is impossible to be certain about the reason for this, but it could mark the conscious neglect of the area during Late Antiquity perhaps because of its earlier religious associations. On the other hand, there is an isolated concentration of Late Roman material at the southeastern corner of the ridge in a unit adjacent to the one that produced the Cypro-Archaic to Cypro-Classical figurines. Only excavation would determine the nature of the late phase here.

On the coastal plain, Christianization is more directly evident in a new religious center with a sixth-century Early Christian basilica, a form of architecture that is ubiquitous across the Cypriot landscape in the fifth to seventh centuries. To the west, there is evidence for Early Christian churches at Katalymata and on the coast at Ay. Thecla (Hadjisavvas 1997: 27–28, 32–33), which indicates that small communities made manifest their participation in larger social organization through the construction of monumental architecture. Manning has noted for the smaller coastal site of Maroni-*Petrera* that churches represent significant investments in surplus resources and document the growing power of the institutional church as a source of authority (Manning et al. 2002: 77–80). The relatively small village of Kopetra featured at least three churches. It is no surprise, then, that the site of Koutsopetria had at least one well-appointed Early Christian basilica, and it is quite probable that there were other churches, now undocumented, below the surface of the plain.

The presence of this church at Koutsopetria not only provided for the religious needs of the expanded local community, but also marked the site as part of the expanding administrative powers of the ecclesiastical hierarchy. The church in Cyprus battled throughout the fifth century to preserve its autonomy and independence from the See of Antioch. The island saw the construction of over 100 churches from the late fourth through the late sixth centuries, and the wealth and influence of the clergy certainly fortified their commitment to ecclesiastical independence within the Roman Empire (Maguire 2012). The rise of several powerful bishops, including the famous heretic-hunter Epiphanius of Salamis, further confirms the significant influence of the church of Cyprus on imperial ecclesiastical politics (Rapp 1993).

Finally, it is tempting to associate this church and site with a passage from John Moschos, which refers to the site of Tadai, a "market town," where a monk from Anatolia lived in a monastery (Moschos *Prat. Sp.* 30: Τάδαι ἐμπόριόν ἐστιν τῆς Κύπρου. Ἐν αὐτῷ μοναστήριόν ἐστιν πλησίον τοῦ λεγομένου Φιλοξένου). If Tadai or Tades is a corruption of Dades, which we have suggested is Vigla (Section 7.6.3), then the basilica unearthed through excavation could be part of a larger monastic complex. Such a conclusion, of course, occupies the limits of our textual and material evidence.

7.7.5. Connectivity

The expansion of Koutsopetria appears to be closely tied to its connectedness to other communities across Cyprus and the Mediterranean. The site's monumental religious architecture, enormous size, diverse assemblage of imports, and coastal orientation emphasize the impact of heightened connectivity on the development of the site. Indeed, if the coastal heights continued to see some activity, the primary settlement occurred in areas immediately accessible to the sea.

The incredibly varied Late Roman ceramic material at Koutsopetria suggests not only continued connections to production centers in Cyprus and the eastern Mediterranean, but also good connections to the western Mediterranean. The overwhelming number of Late Roman 1 type amphorae scattered across the site represent variants likely produced somewhere on the island as well as those imported from elsewhere in the eastern Mediterranean. The majority of LR1 sherds belong to a subcategory identified by Demesticha as LR1/C, which were produced at three sites along the southern Cypriot coast (Amathous, Paphos, and Zygi), on Cos, and in Cilicia in the seventh century AD. They are primarily found at sites in the Black Sea, the Aegean, Palestine, and Egypt (Demesticha 2013: 173). The limited but clear presence of Late Roman 2 amphorae, which were the second most common on the site, confirms that ties to the Aegean basin persisted into Late Antiquity. It is surprising, however, that Koutsopetria yielded very few transport vessels from Palestine, such as the highly diagnostic Gaza amphorae, which are common finds in the eastern Mediterranean. While other sites on Cyprus typically have low numbers of these types of amphora, they appeared even less frequently at Koutsopetria (Rautman 2003: 172). This may reflect either the unique patterns of cabotage and long-distance routes for the circulation of goods in the Late Antique eastern Mediterranean, or the specific demands of the community.

What is especially impressive at Koutsopetria, in comparison with sites in western Cyprus, is the relatively greater proportions of imported Late Roman Phocaean Ware and African Red Slip, and the lower relative proportions of Cypriot Red Slip. Cypriot Red Slip was the primary table ware at Koutsopetria (60% of LR fine wares), but it dominated the assemblage significantly less than at other documented sites in western Cyprus. This pattern indicates that Koutsopetria had stronger ties to production centers of table ware on the western coast of Turkey and Northern Africa than did sites on the western side of the island. The reasons for this are, again, complex, but it may be the result of the particular function that Koutsopetria played in this period, as an *emporion* or market town that redistributed goods. The concentration of Phocaean Ware in Zone 2 along a coastal road and the base of Mavrospilios and Kokkinokremos may point to the presence of warehouses beyond the settlement center, similar to the kind identified at Dreamer's Bay.

Our identification of fragments of an olive press, including a press weight and part of a crusher stone, suggests that the site was the center of agricultural production in Late Antiquity, which

must have annually attracted local producers from the district to press their fruits. The presence of a church may also hint at the role of this institution in the economy. Although the original location of the olive press remains unclear, it would not be unprecedented for it to be associated with the church. Similar arrangements appeared at Ay. Georgios-*Peyia*, the basilica of the Chrysopolitissa at Kata Paphos, and at Ay. Varvara at Amathus (Hadjisavvas 1997: 45–51). An inscribed graffito of a ship on a block excavated from the Koutsopetria basilica annex building may also hint at the tie between the church and seagoing trade (Christou 1994: 690; Leonard 2005: 428). We should not exclude the possibility that the ecclesiastical hierarchy played a role in trade (Hollerich 1982).

The distinct character of the assemblage present on Cyprus during Late Antiquity may reflect the significant administrative changes afoot in the eastern Mediterranean. In AD 536, the Emperor Justinian placed the island under the control of a new officer, the *quaestor exercitus*, along with the provinces of Moesia Secunda, the Aegean Islands, Scythia Minor, and Caria (Jones 1964). According to John Lydus, this shift in jurisdiction occurred on account of the exceptional prosperity of the island (*de Mens.* II. 28–29). The island's new administrative relationships with the Aegean placed Cyprus in the supply line for troops along the embattled Danubian frontier. The rise in the number of Late Roman 1 amphorae on the Danubian frontier in the fifth and sixth centuries may reflect a growing relationship between Cyprus and the northern Balkan provinces and Scythia (Karagiorgou 2001). At the same time, if we imagine the site being involved in exchange between the Balkans and the eastern Mediterranean, then this might account for the significant quantities of Phocaean Ware that circulated widely in the Aegean Islands, Caria, and elsewhere in the Aegean basin.

7.8.   KOUTSOPETRIA AFTER ANTIQUITY

The study of the post-antique archaeology of Cyprus remains in its infancy. The number of excavated Medieval and post-Medieval sites remains relatively small, although it grows every year. Recent excavations at Ay. Georgios-PASYDY,

Potamia-*Ay. Sozomenos*, Kouklia, and the Paphos theater have produced better stratigraphy and chronology for material from the Medieval and Ottoman periods (François and Vallauri 2001; Wartburg 2001; Lécuyer et al. 2002; Gabrieli 2006, 2007; Given and Hadjianastasis 2010, with citations). Survey projects have also embraced more diachronic attitudes and, as a result, these projects have begun to populate the urban and rural landscape of Cyprus with a growing number of sites from after the end of antiquity. Our ability to recognize Medieval ceramics remains limited and surface assemblages remain rather modest.

7.8.1. Artifacts and Distribution

The history of our study area is bracketed by two major periods of at least partial abandonment, the earliest Iron Age and the earliest Middle Ages, as well as several sub-periods (late Hellenistic, middle Roman) where artifacts are unrecognized. Material on the site dating from the Early Medieval period to the Ottoman period — a broad period lasting well over a millennium — amounts to a mere 41 sherds, distributed over 5 discontinuous ha. For some comparison, Medieval–Ottoman artifacts cover an area only half that of Late Cypriot material, less than a third of Iron Age, Hellenistic, and Early Roman, and 7% of Late Roman. The Medieval–Ottoman eras may be some of the least visible in the survey area, because our knowledge of the period is based mainly on glazed table wares (76%) and, to a lesser extent, coarse wares (24%), but there is still no question about the precipitous decline in the quantity and extent of habitation after the seventh century AD.

In general, the Medieval and Ottoman periods appear in tightly clustered assemblages that most likely represent short periods of occupation. Very little Medieval–Ottoman material derives from the ridges, and most comes from the coastal plain, especially the eastern edge of Zone 1. A possibly significant concentration of material occurs in the area where the dense Late Antique settlement meets the infilled harbor. There, in the vicinity of units with Late Medieval and Ottoman material, we observed what is evidently a small fortification, dated to either the Venetian or Ottoman occupa-

tion of the island, which Cesnola described when he visited the site in the 1880s (Section 6.3). The association of Late Medieval pottery with this coastal battery may represent the remains of a small settlement on the Koutsopetria plain. The presence of a fortification here indicates that some kind of embayment continued to exist on the Pyla littoral until at least the sixteenth or seventeenth century (Section 2.4.1).

The Medieval to Modern period transition is a particularly difficult transition to understand, because the only evidence for specifically Early Modern activities in the micro-region consists of three sherds. Given that the Late Medieval and Ottoman assemblage in our survey area is relatively more visible and robust, it is probable that most of the artifacts of the Medieval–Modern assemblage date to before the nineteenth century. Material described by Gregory as Cypriot Coarse Ware Types may help fill the gaps in our assemblage (Gregory 2003: 283–94). The frequency of these types in the survey area (W1, etc.) suggests that it saw some activity during the Late Ottoman period and the Early Modern era. Most Medieval–Modern material followed the distributional pattern of Medieval–Ottoman, frequently overlapping with these earlier concentrations on the coastal plain.

In the nineteenth and twentieth centuries, a new coastal road along the southern edge of the site left a clear scatter of trash in the fields to the north, including glass, metal, pottery, and bone. In the most recent half century, the study region became part of the Dhekelia Sovereign Base Area, after the Treaty of Establishment in 1960, which has left its own artifact signature in spent bullet casings and exploded ordinance. The installation of a water treatment plant below Vigla and the Mavrospilios plateau, and electrical pylons across the plain have left a light residue of glass insulators and metal fragments.

7.8.2. State, Settlement, and Regional Trends

The massive transformations that took place on the island at the end of antiquity remain poorly understood. The seventh century, however, clearly saw the beginning of a significant change in settlement in most littoral regions. Scholars have traditionally viewed this transformation as a product of the Arab raids or the deteriorating political and security situation, but more recent work has suggested that the decline of coastal sites had ties to larger changes in the eastern Mediterranean economy and settlement structure (Chrysos 1993). The military defeats and political disruptions during the seventh century and the resulting loss of territory in Asia Minor, the Levant, and northeast Africa isolated coastal communities on Cyprus from long-standing trading partners and led to the reorganization of settlement in Cyprus.

The site of Koutsopetria was largely abandoned by the end of the seventh century, and in this way, it follows a pattern evident from other coastal sites on the island. Maroni-*Petrera*, for example, appears to have been abandoned around the middle years of the seventh century (Manning et al. 2002), as were Kourion and Paphos (Megaw 2007). Farther inland, the sites of Kalavasos-*Kopetra* and Alassa appear to have been abandoned around the same time, and there is little evidence of activity in the Malloura Valley between the seventh century and the Frankish period (Moore and Gregory 2012: 208). Disruptions were likewise obvious in the regions examined by the Sydney Cyprus Survey Project and the Danish survey of the Akamas peninsula, although the dates are not firmly tied to the seventh century. The basilica of Ay. Kononas, for example, appears to have collapsed in the eighth century, but the settlement had drifted out of use perhaps a century before that time (Fejfer 1995: 83). Farther west, the site of Ay. Georgios-*Peyia* seems to have suffered decline earlier in the seventh century (Bakirtzis 1995, 2000). That site's excavator has suggested that this may relate to the close relationship between the site and the grain trade with Alexandria, which ended in the first part of the seventh century, after the Persian invasion of Egypt. There is little evidence for the cause of settlement decline at Koutsopetria. The city of Kition remained an episcopal seat.

The Medieval period may be poorly visible in Cyprus, but scattered archaeological evidence suggests a range of activities across the southeastern corner of the island. The presence of Late Medieval towers on Cape Pyla and near Pyla village attest to the likely presence of Frankish estates in the area. The settlement at Pyla appears to have persisted after the abandonment of the coastal areas at the end of antiquity. Set back from the sea, obscured by the coastal plateaus, and astride east–west and north–south communication routes, the siting of the village of Pyla reflected a move away from coastal settlement during the rather unstable Early Medieval period. It seems likely that the towers on Cape Pyla and Cape Kiti both served to anchor local landholdings and to monitor maritime movements in Larnaca Bay. The presence of numerous Medieval churches testifies to the continued significance of Larnaca Bay and southeastern Cyprus in general (Papacostas 1999).

The Ottoman period is an even less visible period, but Pyla village and the larger city of Kition evidently continued to prosper. The presence of a coastal battery at the site of Koutsopetria (Section 7.8.1, above) suggests that a small embayment persisted at least through Late Medieval times. The Larnaca lowlands attracted considerable investment in large-scale farming throughout the nineteenth century (Christodoulou 1959: 76–77). The bishop of Larnaca, for example, had significant landholdings in the area, and Loues has recently published the records of that estate (Loues 2004). R. Hamilton Lang leased 1,000 acres in the area of Pyla village and, with the help of irrigation, produced favorable yields in wheat, barley, beans, oats, and cotton (Lang 1878: 357–64; 1905: 635–37). Farther east, the area toward Ay. Napa saw the cultivation of pomegranates (Christodoulou 1959: 202).

In the first half of the twentieth century, grain was cultivated on the coastal plain of Koutsopetria. The light soils along the sandy dunes of the foreshore allowed for melons, market gardens, and vegetables along the coastal road (Hadjicosti pers. comm). The inclusion of the study area in the Sovereign Base Areas after 1960, however, transformed the economic structure of fields. Today, the market gardens are gone, but wheat, date palms, and alfalfa continue to grow in our study area under lease to farmers from Pyla village. The twentieth century brought the ability to bore deeper wells for irrigation, and this allowed for the introduction of the potato in the rich, red soils of the Kokkinochoria villages to the east. This has led to population growth in an area that lacked significant settlement in the nineteenth century.

7.8.3. Religious Landscapes

The wider regions of eastern Larnaca Bay preserve considerable evidence for thriving Christian communities in the Medieval period. There is evidence that the basilica at Koutsopetria underwent some late modifications, but these likely occurred prior to the abandonment of the site. The removal of floor slabs and marble revetment from the floors and walls of the excavated annex room suggests that the religious status of the building did not preclude it from being quarried. It also indicates that the building likely stood for some time after its final abandonment. The various graffiti present in the annex room may date to a period after the building's abandonment, suggesting that some religious activity persisted in the area. Moreover, the quarrying of prestigious material from the church may have served to adorn another religious structure elsewhere in the region, as occurred at the episcopal church at Kourion (Megaw 1993).

In later times, the religious landscape was closely tied to the economic landscape. The Orthodox Church and various Moslem religious institutions possessed extensive holdings in the vicinity of Pyla village. There is no evidence that the coastal lands fell under the control of either institution, but the economic requirements of these institutions almost certainly influenced local land values, labor markets, and agricultural prices. Given and Hadjianastasis have recently drawn attention to the sounds of the village, such as church bells, the *tsimandro,* or the call of the muezzin, that shaped the rhythms of agricultural life (Given and Hadjianastasis 2010: 58).

Finally, the early twentieth century base maps for the cadastral survey of Cyprus note that the ruin of Ay. Panayia stood on the route of the coastal road in our study area (Bekker-Nielsen 2004: 42–44). There is no evidence that this building was a church, and it is almost certain that this is the Venetian or Ottoman fortification described by Cesnola, which remains overgrown and visible to this day (Section 7.8.1). It is notable, however, that this building was identified at some point as

a religious structure, suggesting that in the local imagination — or perhaps merely that of the surveyor — the presence of a ruin in the countryside evoked the past religious life of the community.

7.8.4. Connectivity

Sometime in the millennium-long Medieval–Ottoman era, the connective structure of the Koutsopetria region changed dramatically. At the end of antiquity, the site could still boast one of the best natural embayments and harbors on the southeastern coast of the island (2.4). By the nineteenth century, however, the embayment at Koutsopetria had clearly ceased to function as such. When this occurred is uncertain, but the presence of a coastal fortification suggests some small inlet still was functional possibly as late as the Ottoman era (Section 2.4.1). Concentrations of Medieval–Ottoman artifacts in Zone 1 also point to maritime uses of the site, but the low quantity and quality of the pottery make it difficult to adduce the region's relationship with the rest of the island and the larger Mediterranean world.

The investments in towers at Pyla village and Cape Pyla suggest that the local agricultural lands had some value, for the towers probably indicated the presence of local estates that produced surpluses. It is difficult to know if olive trees or grains in the vicinity of Pyla did see export or were for local consumption, but the shrinking inlet must have remained the easiest way of servicing the local communities near Pyla.

The Koutsopetria area remained connected also through the land routes that ran north, east, and west of the site. The Medieval tower that today stands in the middle of Pyla village almost certainly served in some way to monitor the pass north to the Mesaoria, as well as traffic along the roads toward the coast and Larnaca in the east. The area around Pyla village and east to Ormidhia appears to have been in the economic orbit of Larnaca in the nineteenth century when documentary sources become available.

By the later nineteenth century, what was left of the embayment had completely silted up, and the micro-region's place in patterns of maritime "connectivity" had dwindled. The export of goods from the area shifted to more viable embayments like Xylotymbou-*Louma* and Ormidhia (Christodoulou 1959: 101, fig. 58; Leonard 2005: 414–18), but communication between Larnaca and Ormidhia appears to have been mainly overland (Leonard 2005: 416). The harbor at Ormidhia exported vegetables, olives, carobs, cereals, and citrus to both regional Mediterranean and European ports. Koutsopetria ceased to be a node in maritime networks.

Nonetheless, in the nineteenth and twentieth centuries Koutsopetria became an important site along the road on the southern coast of Cyprus. As the harbor eventually filled in completely, the old coastal road that once circumvented the embayment gave way to the more direct route now occupied by the modern road. Patterns of discarded glass, metal, and occasionally pottery along the southern parts of Zones 1 and 2 attest to the movements of Greeks, Turks, and British in the late nineteenth and early twentieth centuries.

In the most recent past, the PKAP survey area has witnessed a final transformation in its connectedness. The site is now protected by a military base used daily for training British military personnel, and monitored by Greek and Turkish police of the Sovereign Base Authority. Immediately west of the Defence Estates along the coastline, at the terminal point of tourist development, vacationers come from all across Europe to lounge at the hotels, swim at the beaches, and dine on fish and Cypriot *meze*. On the steamy days of summer, Cypriots from Nicosia and Larnaca drive out to the same beaches to catch a break, while international teams of college students and professors conduct archaeology in the elevated lands above.

Bibliography

Acheson, P.E.
1997   Does the 'Economic Explanation' Work?
        Settlement, Agriculture and Erosion
        in the Territory of Halieis in the Late
        Classical–Early Hellenistic Period.
        Journal of Mediterranean Archaeology 10:
        165–90.

Adovasio, J.M.; Fry, G.F.; Gunn, J.D.;
and Maslowski, R.F.
1975   Prehistoric and Historic Settlement
        Patterns in Western Cyprus. *World
        Archaeology* 6: 339–64.

Alcock, S.E.
1991   Urban Survey and the Polis of Phlius.
        Hesperia 60: 421–63.
1993   *Graecia Capta: The Landscapes of Roman
        Greece*. New York: Cambridge University.

Ammerman, A.
1995   The Dynamics of Modern Land Use
        and the Acconia Survey. *Journal of
        Mediterranean Archaeology* 8: 77–92.

Andrefsky, W.
1998   *Lithics: Macroscopic Approaches to
        Analysis*. New York: Cambridge
        University.

Armstrong, P.
2009   Trade in the East Mediterranean in the
        8th Century. Pp. 157–78 in *Byzantine
        Trade, 4th–2th Centuries. The Archaeology
        of Local, Regional and International
        Exchange*, ed. M. Mango. Farnham, UK:
        Ashgate.

Avraamides, A.
1971   Studies in Hellenistic Cyprus 323–380
        B.C. Unpublished Ph.D. dissertation,
        University of Minnesota.

Bagnall, R.
1976   *The Administration of the Ptolemaic
        Possessions outside of Egypt*. Leiden: Brill.

Bailey, D.M.
1975   *A Catalogue of the Lamps in the British
        Museum*, Vol. 1: *Greek, Hellenistic and
        Early Roman Pottery Lamps*. London:
        British Museum.

Bakirtzis, C.
1976   Παλαιοχριστιανική βασιλική στους
        Γιορκούς ΒΑ της Αθηαίνοθ. *Report of the
        Department of Antiquities, Cyprus 1976*:
        260–66.
1995   The Role of Cyprus in the Grain Supply
        of Constantinople in the Early Christian
        Period. Pp. 247–53 in *Proceedings of
        the International Symposium "Cyprus
        and the Sea,"* eds. V. Karageorghis and
        D. Michaelides. Nicosia: University of
        Cyprus.

Balandier, C.
2002   The Defensive Network of Cyprus at the
        Hellenistic Period and during the first
        Centuries of the Roman Empire (3rd c.
        BC–3rd c. AD). *Report of the Department
        of Antiquities, Cyprus 2002*: 323–37.

Bamforth, D.; Burns, G.; and Woodman, C.
1990   Ambiguous Use Traces and Blind
       Test Results: New Data. *Journal of
       Archaeological Science* 17: 413–30.

Banning, E.B.; Hawkins, A.L.; and Stewart, S.T.
2006   Detection Functions for Archaeological
       Survey. *American Antiquity* 71: 723–42.
2011   Sweep Widths and the Detection of
       Artifacts in Archaeological Survey.
       Journal of Archaeological Science 38:
       3447–58.

Barker, C.
2013   Rhodian Amphorae from Cyprus: A
       Summary of the Evidence and the Issues.
       Pp. 101–10 in *The Transport Amphorae
       and Trade of Cyprus*, eds. M. Lawall and
       John Lund. Aarhus: Aarhus University.

Bates, W.
1930   Two Inscribed Slingers' Bullets
       from Galatista. *American Journal of
       Archaeology* 34: 44–46.

Bekker-Nielsen, T.
1993   Centres and Road Networks in
       Hellenistic Cyprus. Pp. 176–91 in *Centre
       and Periphery in the Hellenistic World,*
       eds. P. Bilde, T. Engberg-Pedersen, L.
       Hannestad, J. Zahle, and K. Randsbor.
       Studies in Hellenistic Civilization 4.
       Aarhus: Aarhus University.
2004   *The Roads of Ancient Cyprus.*
       Copenhagen: Museum Tusculanum.

Bennett, J.
1991   *Plumbatae* from Pitsunda (Pityus),
       Georgia, and Some Observations on their
       Probable Use. *Journal of Roman Military
       Equipment Studies* 2: 59–63.

Benoit, F.
1956   Épaves de la Côte de Provence: Typologie
       des amphores. *Gallia* 14: 23–34.

Berlin A.; Herbert, S.; and Stone, P.
2014   Dining in State: The Tablewares from
       the Persian-Hellenistic Administrative
       Building at Kedesh. Pp. 307–22 in
       *Pottery, Peoples and Places: Study and
       Interpretation of Late Hellenistic Pottery,*
       eds. P. Guldager-Bilde, and M. Lawall.
       Black Sea Studies 16. Aarhus: Aarhus
       University.

Bevan, A., and Conolly, J.
2013   *Mediterranean Islands, Fragile
       Communities and Persistent Landscapes:
       Antikythera in Long-Term Perspective.*
       Cambridge: Cambridge University.

Bevan, A.; Conolly, J.; Hennig, C.; Johnston, A.;
Quercia, A.; Spencer, L.; and Vroom, J.
2013   Measuring Chronological Uncertainty
       in Intensive Survey Finds. A Case Study
       from Antikythera, Greece. *Archaeometry*
       54: 312–28.

Bintliff, J., and Howard, P.
1999   Studying Needles in Haystacks: Surface
       Survey and the Rural Landscape of
       Central Greece in Roman Times. *Pharos:
       Journal of the Netherlands Institute in
       Athens* 7: 51–91.

Bintliff, J.; Howard, P.; and Snodgrass, A.
1999   The Hidden Landscape of Prehistoric
       Greece. *Journal of Mediterranean
       Archaeology* 12: 139–68.
2007   *Testing the Hinterland: The Work of the
       Boeotia Survey (1989) in the Southern
       Approaches to the City of Thespiai.*
       Cambridge: Cambridge University.

Bintliff, J., and Snodgrass, A.
1985   The Boeotia Survey, a Preliminary
       Report: The First Four Years. *Journal of
       Field Archaeology* 12: 123–61.
1988   Mediterranean Survey and the City.
       Antiquity 62: 57–71.

Bishop, M.C., and Coulston, J.C.
2006 *Roman Military Equipment: From the Punic Wars to the Fall of Rome.* Oxford: Oxford University.

Blanton, R.E.
2001 Mediterranean Myopia. *Antiquity* 75: 627–29.

Bodel, J.P.
2001 *Epigraphic Evidence: Ancient History from Inscriptions. Approaching the Ancient World.* London: Routledge.

Bowersock, G.
2000 *The International Role of Late Antique Cyprus. 14th Annual Lecture on the History and Archaeology of Cyprus.* Nicosia: The Bank of Cyprus Cultural Foundation.

Brezillon, M.
1971 *La Dénomination des objets de pierre taillée: Materiaux pour un vocabulaire des préhistoriens de langue française.* Paris: Centre National de la Recherche Scientifique.

Broodbank, C.
1999 Kythera Survey: Preliminary Report on the 1998 Season. *Annual of the British School at Athens* 94: 191–214.

Brown, M.G.
2012 Landscapes of Settlement in South-East Cyprus: The Late Bronze Age Origins of a Phoenician Polity. Unpublished Ph.D. dissertation, University of Edinburgh.

Bruneau, P.
1968 Contribution à l'histoire urbaine de Délos à l'époque hellénistique et à l'époque impériale. *Bulletin de Correspondance Hellénique* 92: 633–709.

Burkhalter, F.
1987 La céramique hellénistique et romaine du sanctuaire d'Aphrodite à Amathonte. *Bulletin de Correspondance Hellénique* 111: 353–95.

Caraher, W.R., Moore, R.S.; and Pettegrew, D.K.
2008 Surveying Late Antique Cyprus. *Near Eastern Archaeology* 71.1–2: 1–8.
2010 Trade and Exchange in the Eastern Mediterranean: A Model from Cyprus. *Bollettino di Archeologia On Line*: http://www.bollettinodiarcheologiaonline.beniculturali.it/documenti/generale/2_MOORE_et%20al.pdf.
2013 Pyla-*Koutsopetria* Archaeological Project: Overview (Released 2013-11-05). Open Context: http://opencontext.org/projects/3F6DCD13-A476-488E-ED10-47D25513FCB2> DOI:10.6078/M7B56GNS.

Caraher, W.R.; Moore, R.S.; Nakassis, D.; and Pettegrew, D.K.
2014 Pyla-*Koutsopetria* Archaeological Project: Recent Work at the Site of Pyla-*Vigla*. *Report of the Department of Antiquities, Cyprus 2011–2012*: 1–12.

Caraher, W.R.; Moore, R.S.; Noller, J.S.; and Pettegrew, D.K.
2005 The Pyla-*Koutsopetria* Archaeological Project: First Preliminary Report (2003–2004 Seasons). *Report of the Department of Antiquities, Cyprus 2005*: 245–68.
2007 The Pyla-*Koutsopetria* Archaeological Project: Second Preliminary Report (2005–2006 Seasons). *Report of the Department of Antiquities, Cyprus 2007*: 293–306.

Caraher, W.R.; Nakassis, D.; and Pettegrew, D.K.
2006 Siteless Survey and Intensive Data Collection in an Artifact-Rich Environment: Case Studies from the Eastern Corinthia, Greece. *Journal of Mediterranean Archaeology* 19: 7–43.

Carandini, A.
1981 *Atlante delle forme ceramiche I: Ceramica fine romana nel bacino Mediterraneo (medio e tardo impero).* Rome: Instituto della Enciclopedia Italiana.

Catling, H.W.
1963 Patterns of Settlement in Bronze Age Cyprus. *Opuscula Atheniensia IV*: 129–69.
1972 An Early Byzantine Pottery Factory at Dhiorios in Cyprus. *Levant* 4: 1–82.
1982 The Ancient Topography of the Yalias Valley. *Report of the Department of Antiquities, Cyprus 1982*: 227–36.

Caubet, A.; Fourrier, S.; and Queyrel Bottineau, A.
1998 *L'art des modeleurs d'argile. Antiquités de Chypre, Coroplastique.* Paris: Réunion des Musées Nationaux.

Cavanagh, W.; Shipley, G; and Crouwel, J.
2002 The Laconia Survey: Background and Methodology. Pp. 1–55 in *Continuity and Change in a Greek Rural Landscape: The Laconia Survey.* Vol. 1: *Methodology and Interpretation*, eds. R. W. V. Catling, W. Cavanagh, J. Crouwel, and G. Shipley. London: British School at Athens.

Cesnola, L.P.
1877 *Cyprus. Its Ancient Cities, Tombs, and Temples.* London: John Murray.

Cherry, J.F.
1983 Frogs Round the Pond: Perspectives on Current Archaeological Survey Projects in the Mediterranean Region. Pp. 375–416 in *Archaeological Survey in the Mediterranean Area*, eds. D. R. Keller and D. W. Rupp. British Archaeological Reports International Series 155. Oxford: Archaeopress.
1994 Regional Survey in the Aegean: The 'New Wave' (and after). Pp. 91–112 in *Beyond the Site. Regional Studies in the Aegean Area*, ed. P. N. Kardulias. Lanham, MD: University Press of America.
2002 Vox Populi: Landscape Archaeology in Mediterranean Europe. *Journal of Roman Archaeology* 15: 561–73.
2003 Archaeology Beyond the Site: Regional Survey and its Future. Pp. 137–59 in *Theory and Practice in Mediterranean Archaeology: Old World and New World*

Perspectives. An Advanced Seminar in Honor of Lloyd Cotsen, eds. J. K. Papadopoulos and R.M. Leventhal. Los Angeles: Cotsen Institute of Archaeology.
2004 Cyprus, the Mediterranean, and Survey: Current Issues and Future Trends. Pp. 24–35 in *Archaeological Field Survey in Cyprus. Past History, Future Potentials. Proceedings of a Conference Held by the Archaeological Research Unit of the University of Cyprus, 1–2 December 2000*, ed. M. Iacovou,. London: British School at Athens.

Cherry, J.F.; Davis, J.L.; Demitrack, A.; Mantzourani, E.; Strasser, T. F.; and Talalay, L.E.
1988 Archaeological Survey in an Artifact-Rich Landscape: A Middle Neolithic Example from Nemea, Greece. *American Journal of Archaeology* 92: 159–76.

Christensen, A.P., and Johansen, C.F.
1971 *Hama: Fouilles et recherches, 1931–1938. III:2. Les poteries hellénistiques et les terres sigillées orientales.* Copenhagen: Nationalmuseet.

Christodoulou, D.
1959 *The Evolution of the Rural Land Use Pattern in Cyprus.* London: Geographical Publications Limited.

Christou, D.
1994 Chronique des fouilles et découvertes archéologiques à Chypre en 1993. *Bulletin de Correspondance Hellénique* 118 (1994): 647–93.

Chrysos, E.
1993 Cyprus in Early Byzantine Times. Pp. 3–14 in *'The Sweet Land of Cyprus.' Papers Given at the Twenty-Fifth Jubilee Spring Symposium of Byzantine Studies, Birmingham, March 1991*, eds. A. Breyer, and G. Georghallides. Nicosia: Cyprus Research Centre.

Clarke, J., and Todd, I.A.

1993 The Field Survey of Kalavassos-
Pampoules. *Report of the Department of
Antiquities, Cyprus 1993*: 11–28.

Coleman, D.

2003 Chipped Stone Procedures. Pp. 57–58 in
*The Sydney Cyprus Survey Project: Social
Approaches to Regional Archaeological
Survey*, eds. M. Given and A.B. Knapp.
Los Angeles: Cotsen Institute of
Archaeology.

Connelly, J.B.

1983 A Hellenistic Deposit on the Kourion
Acropolis. *Report of the Department of
Antiquities, Cyprus 1983*: 275–80.

1989 Standing Before One's God: Votive
Sculpture and the Cypriot Religious
Tradition. *Biblical Archaeologist* 52:
210–18.

2002 Excavations on Geronisos (1990–1997):
First Report. *Report of the Department of
Antiquities, Cyprus 2002*: 245–68.

2005 Excavations on Geronisos Island: Second
Report, the Central South Complex.
*Report of the Department of Antiquities,
Cyprus 2005*: 149–82.

2009 Hybridity and Identity on Late Ptolemaic
Yeronisos. *Cahiers du Centre d'Études
Chypriotes* 39: 69–88.

Coroneos, C.; Diacopoulos, L.; Gregory, T.E.;
Johnson, I.; Noller, J.; Paspalas, S.A.;
and Wilson, A.

2002 The Australian Paliochora-Kythera
Archaeological Survey: Field Season
1999–2000. *Mediterranean Archaeology*
15: 126–43.

Counts, D.B.

2001 Prolegomena to the Study of Cypriot
Sculpture. *Cahier du Centre d'Etudes
Chypriotes* 31: 129–81.

2004 Art and Religion in the Cypriote
Mesaoria: The View from Athienou-
Malloura. *Cahier du Centre d'Etudes
Chypriotes* 34: 173–90.

2008 Master of the Lion: Representation
and Hybridity in Cypriot Sanctuaries.
American Journal of Archaeology 112.1:
3–27.

2010 *The Master of Animals in Old World
Iconography*. Budapest: Archaeolingua.

Crabtree, D.E.

1972 *An Introduction to Flintworking*.
Occasional Papers of the Idaho Museum
of Natural History 28. Pocatello: Idaho
Museum of Natural History.

Davis, J.L.

2004 Are the Landscapes of Greek Prehistory
Hidden? A Comparative Approach.
Pp. 22–35 in *Side-by-Side Survey:
Comparative Regional Studies in the
Mediterranean World*, eds. S.E. Alcock
and J.F. Cherry. Oxford: Oxbow.

Davis, J.L.; Alcock, S.E.; Bennet, J.; Lolos, Y.G.;
and Shelmerdine, C.W.

1997 The Pylos Regional Archaeological
Project. Part I: Overview and the Archaeological Survey. *Hesperia* 66: 391–494.

Decker, M.

2009 *Tilling the Hateful Earth: Agricultural
Production and Trade in the Late Antique
East*. Oxford Studies in Byzantium. New
York: Oxford University.

Degest, R.

2001 *The Common Wares of Roman Sagalassos*.
Studies in Eastern Mediterranean
Archaeology 3. Turnhout: Brepols.

Demesticha, S.

2000 The Paphos Kiln: Manufacturing Techniques of LR1 Amphoras. *Rei Cretariae
Romanae Fautorum Acta* 36: 549–54.

2003 Amphora Production on Cyprus During
the Late Roman Period. Pp. 469–76 in
*Actes du VIIe Congrès International sur
la Céramique Médiévale en Méditerranée*,
ed. C. Bakirtzis. Athens : Ministère de la
Culture.

2013   Amphora Typologies, Distribution, and
        Trade Patterns: The Case of the Cypriot
        LR1 Amphorae. Pp. 169–78 in *The
        Transport Amphorae and Trade of Cyprus*,
        eds. M. Lawall and J. Lund. Aarhus:
        Aarhus University.

Demesticha, S., and Michaelides, D.
2001   The Excavation of a Late Roman 1
        Amphora Kiln in Paphos. Pp. 289–96
        in *La Céramique Byzantine et Proto-
        Islamique en Syrie-Jordanie (IVe–VIIIe
        siècles apr. J.C.). Actes du colloque
        tenu à Amman*, eds. E. Villeneuve and
        P.M. Watson. Beirut: Institut Français
        d'Archéologie du Proche-Orient.

Dikaios, P.
1935   Excavations at Erimi. *Report of the
        Department of Antiquities, Cyprus 1935*:
        6–13.
1971   *Enkomi: Excavations 1948–1958*, vol. 2.
        Darmstadt: von Zabern.

Dothan, M.
1977   Akko: Interim Excavation Report First
        Season, 1973/4. *Bulletin of the American
        Schools of Oriental Research* 224: 1–48.

Dunnel, R.
1992   The Notion Site. Pp. 21–41 in *Space, Time,
        and Archaeological Landscapes*, eds. J.
        Rossignol and L. Wandsnider. New York:
        Plenum.

Elaigne, S.
2000   Imitations locales de céramiques fines
        importées: Le cas des 'colour-coated
        ware' dans les contextes hellénistiques
        d'Alexandrie. *Cahiers de la Céramique
        Égyptienne* 6: 99–103.

Elton, H.
2005   The Economy of Southern Asia Minor
        and LR1 Amphorae. Pp. 691–95 in
        *LRCW1: Late Roman Coarse wares,
        Cooking Wares and Amphorae in the
        Mediterranean*, eds. J. Esparraguera,

        J. Garrigós, and J. Ontiveros. Oxford:
        Oxbow.

Fejfer, J.
1995   *Ancient Akamas: Settlement and Environs.*
        Aarhus: Aarhus University.

Firat, N.
2000   So-called "Cypriot Red Slip Ware" from
        the Habitation area of Perge (Pamphylia).
        Rei Cretariae Romanae Fautorum Acta
        36: 35–38.

Fish, S.K., and Kowalewski, S.
1990   *The Archaeology of Regions: A Case for
        Full-Coverage Survey.* Washington, DC:
        Smithsonian Institution.

Flourentzos, P.
1996   *The Basilica of Alassa. Excavations in the
        Kouris Valley 2.* Nicosia: Department of
        Antiquities.
2007   *From Evagoras I to the Ptolemies:
        Proceedings of the International
        Archaeological Conference: The Transition
        from the Classical to the Hellenistic Period
        in Cyprus: Nicosia 29–30 November 2002.*
        Nicosia: Department of Antiquities.

Flower, H.I.
2006   *The Art of Forgetting: Disgrace & Oblivion
        in Roman Political Culture.* Chapel Hill:
        Chapel Hill University.

Foraboschi, D.
1971   *Onomasticon Alterum Papyrologicum:
        Supplemento al Namenbuch di F.
        Preisigke.* Testi e documenti per lo studio
        dell'antichità 16. Milan: Istituto editoriale
        cisalpino.

Foss, C.
1975   A Bullet of Tissaphernes. *Journal of
        Hellenic Studies* 95: 25–30.

Fourrier, S.
2007   *La Coroplastie Chypriote Archaique:
        Identités culturelles et politiques à l'époque*

des royaumes. Lyon: Maison de l'Orient et de la Méditerranée.

François, V., and Vallauri, L.
2001 Production et consommation de céramiques à Potamia (Chypre) de l'époque franque à l'époque ottoman. *Bulletin de Correspondance Hellénique* 125: 523–46.

Fraser, P., and Matthews, E.
1987 *A Lexicon of Greek Personal Names.* Oxford: Oxford University.

Fulford, M.G., and Peacock, D.P.S.
1984 *The Avenue du Président Habib Bourguiba, Salammbô: The Pottery and Other Ceramic Objects from the Site.* Excavations at Carthage: The British Museum 1.2. Sheffield: University of Sheffield.

Gabrieli, R.S.
2004 Under the Surface: Decoration and Shape in the Coarse Ware of Medieval and Post-Medieval Cyprus. *Mediterranean Archaeology* 17: 287.
2006 Silent Witnesses: The Evidence of Domestic Wares of the 13th–19th Centuries in Paphos, Cyprus, for Local Economy and Social Organization. Unpublished Ph.D. dissertation, University of Sydney.
2007 A Region Apart: Coarse Ware of Medieval and Ottoman Cyprus. *Byzas* 7: 399–410.

Gabrieli, R.S., and Merryweather, A.
2002 A Preliminary Study of Hellenistic and Roman Kitchen Ware from Nea Paphos. Pp. 33–41 in *Céramiques hellénistiques et romaines, productions et diffusion en Méditerranée orientale,* eds. F. Blondé, P. Ballet, and J.-F. Salles. Oxford: Archaeopress.

Gabrieli, R.S.; Jackson, M.P.C.; and Kaldeli, A.
2007 Stumbling into the Darkness – Trade and Life in Post-Roman Cyprus. Pp. 791–801 in *Late Roman Coarse Wares, Cooking Wares and Amphorae in the Mediterranean: Archaeology and Archaeometry,* eds. M. Bonifay and J.-Ch. Treglia. Oxford: Archaeopress.

Galaty, M.L.
2005 European Regional Studies: A Coming of Age? *Journal of Archaeological Research* 13: 291–336.

Gallant, T.W.
1986 'Background Noise' and Site Definition: A Contribution to Survey Methodology. *Journal of Field Archaeology* 13: 403–18.

Gera, D.
1985 Tryphon's Sling Bullet from Dor. *Israel Exploration Journal* 35: 153–63.

Gerber, Y.
2005 Late Roman Coarse Ware from Petra, Jordan: Changes in Typology and Chemical Composition. Pp. 725–36 in *LRCW1: Late Roman Coarse Wares, Cooking Wares and Amphorae in the Mediterranean,* eds. J. Esparraguera, J. Garrigós, and J. Ontiveros. Oxford: Oxbow.

Gibson, E.
2001 Seeding Experiments. In: Troodos Archaeological Project Environmental Project: First Preliminary Report (June–July 2000), eds. Michael Given et al. *Report of the Department of Antiquities, Cyprus 2001*: 428–29.

Given, M., and Hadjianastasis, M.
2010 Landholding and Landscape in Ottoman Cyprus. *Byzantine and Modern Greek Studies* 34: 38–60.

Given, M., and Knapp, A.B.
2003 *The Sydney Cyprus Survey Project: Social Approaches to Regional Archaeological Survey.* Monumenta Archaeologica 21. Los Angeles: Cotsen Institute of Archaeology.

Given, M.; and Meyer, N.
2003 Mapping and Fieldwalking Procedures. Pp. 30–36 in *The Sydney Cyprus Survey Project: Social Approaches to Regional Archaeological Survey*, eds. M. Given and A.B. Knapp. Los Angeles: Cotsen Institute of Archaeology.

Given, M., Knapp, A.B.; Evans, I.; Gibson, E.; Ireland, T.; Kassianidou, V.; Noller, J.; Saunders, H.; Sollars, L.; Urwin, N.; Winther-Jacobsen, K.; and Zesimou, S.
2001 Troodos Archaeological and Environmental Survey Project: First Preliminary Report (June–July 2000). *Report of the Department of Antiquities, Cyprus 2001*: 425-39.

Given, M.; Knapp, A.B.; Meyer, N.; Gregory, T.E.; Kassianidou, V.; Noller, J; Wells, L.; Urwin, N.; and Wright, H.
1999 The Sydney Cyprus Survey Project: An Interdisciplinary Investigation of Long-Term Change in the North Central Troodos, Cyprus. *Journal of Field Archaeology* 26: 20–39.

Gjerstad, E.
1926 *Studies on Prehistoric Cyprus.* Uppsala: Universitets Årsskrift.
1948 *The Swedish Cyprus Expedition, IV.2. The Cypro-Geometric, Cypro-Archaeic and Cypro-Classical Period*s. Stockholm: Swedish Cyprus Expedition.

Goldman, H.
1950 *Excavations at Gözlü Kule, Tarsus.* I. *The Hellenistic and Roman Periods.* Princeton: Princeton University.

Gomez, B.; Neff, H.; Rautman, M.L.; Vaughan, S.J.; and Glascock, M.D.
2002 The Source Provenance of Bronze Age and Roman Pottery from Cyprus. *Archaeometry* 44: 23–36.

Gomez B.; Rautman, M.L.; Neff, H.; and Glascock, M.D.
1996 Clays Used in the Manufacture of Cypriot Red Slip Pottery and Related Ceramics, *Report of the Department of Antiquities, Cyprus 1996*: 69–82.

Gordon, J.
2012 Between Alexandria and Rome: A Postcolonial Archaeology of Cultural Identity in Hellenistic and Roman Cyprus. Unpublished Ph.D. dissertation, University of Cincinnati.

Greene, E.S.; Leidwanger, J.; and Özdaş, H.A.
2011 Two Early Archaic Shipwrecks at Kekova Adası and Kepçe Burnu, Turkey. *International Journal of Nautical Archaeology* 40: 60–68.
2013 Expanding Contacts and Collapsing Distances in Early Cypro-Archaic Trade: Three Case Studies of Shipwrecks off the Turkish Coast. Pp. 21–34 in *The Transport Amphorae and Trade of Cyprus*, eds. M. Lawall and J. Lund. Aarhus: Aarhus University.

Gregory, T.E.
1985 An Early Byzantine Complex at Akra Sophia near Corinth. *Hesperia* 54: 411–28.
1993 Byzantine and Medieval Pottery. Pp. 157–76 in *The Land of the Paphian Aphrodite*, ed. L.W. Sørensen. Göteborg: Åströms.
2003 The Byzantine Problem and Medieval to Modern Pottery. Pp. 283–94 in *The Sydney Cyprus Survey Project: Social Approaches to Regional Archaeological Survey*, eds. M. Given and A.B. Knapp. Los Angeles: Cotsen Institute of Archaeology.
2004 Less is Better: The Quality of Ceramic Evidence from Archaeological Survey

and the Practical Proposals for Low-Impact Survey in a Mediterranean Context. Pp. 15–36 in *Mediterranean Archaeological Landscapes: Current Issues*, eds. E. Athanassopoulos and L. Wandsnider. Philadelphia: University of Pennsylvania Museum of Archaeology and Anthropology.

Gunneweg, J.; Perlman, I.; and Yellin, J.
1983 *The Provenience, Typology and Chronology of Eastern Terra Sigillata.* Qedem 17. Jerusalem: Hebrew University.

Hadjichristophi, F.
1989 Rapport sur les travaux de l'École française à Amathonte de Chypre en 1988. Les tuiles de la basilique. *Bulletin de Correspondance Hellénique* 113: 875–78.

Hadjicosti, M.
2001 Ormideia: Tracing Cesnola's Footsteps. Archaeological Research and Finds. Pp. 53–69 in *Cyprus in the 19th Century AD: Fact, Fancy and Fiction*, ed. V. Tatton-Brown. Oxford: Oxbow.

Hadjisavvas, S.
1992 *Olive Oil Processing in Cyprus from the Bronze Age to the Byzantine Period.* Studies in Mediterranean Archaeology 99. Göteborg: Åströms.
1993 *Annual Report of the Department of Antiquities, Cyprus* 1993: 70–72.
1997 *Agia Napa: Excavations at Makronisos and the Archaeology of the Region.* Nicosia: Agia Napa Municipality and the Cyprus Department of Antiquities.
2000 Chronique des fouilles et découvertes archéologiques à Chypre en 1999. *Bulletin de Correspondance Hellénique* 124: 692–93.

Hallett, J.
1977 *Perusinae Glandes* and the Changing Image of Augustus. *American Journal of Ancient History* 2: 151–71.

Harris, W.V. (ed.)
2005 *Rethinking the Mediterranean.* Oxford: Oxford University.

Harrison, A.B.
1998 Focus: Bouka. Pp. 205–9 in *Sandy Pylos: An Archaeological History from Nestor to Navriano*, ed. J. Davis. Austin: University of Texas.

Hayes, J.W.
1967 Cypriot Sigillata. *Report of the Department of Antiquities, Cyprus 1967*: 65–77.
1972 *Late Roman Pottery.* London: British School at Rome.
1976 Pottery: Stratified Groups. Pp. 47–123 in *Excavations at Carthage 1975 conducted by the University of Michigan*, ed. J.H. Humphrey. Tunis: Cérès.
1977 Early Roman Wares from the House of Dionysos, Paphos. *Rei Cretariae Romanae Fautorum Acta* 17/18: 96–108.
1980a Problèmes de la céramique des VIIème–IXème siècles à Salamine et à Chypre. Pp. 375–87 in *Salamine de Chypre, histoire et archeologie: État des recherches (Lyon, 13--17 mars 1978)*, ed. M. Yon. Paris: Centre National des Recherches Scientifiques.
1980b *A Supplement to Late Roman Pottery*, London: British School at Rome.
1984 *Greek and Italian Black-Gloss Wares and Related Wares in the Royal Ontario Museum. A Catalogue.* Toronto: Royal Ontario Museum.
1991 *Paphos* III. *The Hellenistic and Roman Pottery.* Nicosia: Republic of Cyprus.
1992 *Excavations at Sarachane in Istanbul* II: *The Pottery.* Princeton: Princeton University.
2003 Hellenistic and Roman Pottery Deposits from the 'Saranda Kolones' Castle Site at Paphos. *The Annual of the British School at Athens* 98: 447–516.
2008 *Roman Pottery: Fine-Ware Imports.* Athenian Agora 32. Princeton: American School of Classical Studies at Athens.

Heath, S., and Tekkök, B.
2006–9   Greek, Roman and Byzantine Pottery
at Ilion (Troia). Retrieved (10/1/2012)
from http://classics.uc.edu/troy/
grbpottery/.

Herbert, S.C., and Berlin, A.
2003   *Excavations at Coptos (Qift) (1998–1992).*
Portsmouth, RI: Journal of Roman
Archaeology.

Hermary, A.
1984   Les fouilles de la mission française a
Amathonte (1980–1983). *Report of the
Department of Antiquities, Cyprus 1984*:
265–77.

Hill, G.
1940   *A History of Cyprus*, vol. 1. Cambridge:
Cambridge University.

Hodder, I.
1982   *Symbols in Action: Ethnoarchaeological
Studies of Material Culture.* New York:
Cambridge University.

Hollerich, M.
1982   The Alexandrian Bishops and the Grain
Trade: Ecclesiastical Commerce in Late
Roman Egypt. *Journal of the Economic
and Social History of the Orient* 25:
187–207.

Horden, P., and Purcell, N.
2000   *The Corrupting Sea: A Study of
Mediterranean History.* Oxford:
Oxford University.

Hudson, N.
2008   Three Centuries of Late Roman Pottery.
Pp. 319–45 in *Aphrodisias Papers* 4,
eds. C. Ratté and R.R.R. Smith. Journal
of Roman Archaeology Supplement
70. Portsmouth, RI: Journal of Roman
Archaeology.

Hurtado, V.
2000   Surface Analysis of the Copper Age
Settlement of La Pijotilla (Spain). Pp. 121–
31 in *Extracting Meaning from Ploughsoil
Assemblages*, eds. R. Francovich, H.
Patterson, and G. Barker. Oxford: Oxford
University.

Iacovou, M.
2008   Cultural and Political Configurations
in Iron Age Cyprus. The Sequel to a
Protohistoric Episode. *American Journal
of Archaeology* 112: 625–57.

Iacovou, M. (ed.)
2004   *Archaeological Field Survey in Cyprus:
Past History, Future Potentials.
Proceedings of a Conference Held by
the Archaeological Research Unit of the
University of Cyprus, 1–2 December 2000.*
London: British School at Athens.

Ikäheimo, J.
2005   African Cookware: A High Quality
Space Filler. Pp. 509–20 in *LRCW1: Late
Roman Coarse Wares, Cooking Wares
and Amphorae in the Mediterranean*,
eds. J. Esparraguera, J. Garrigós, and J.
Ontiveros. Oxford: Oxbow.

Jackson, M.; Zelle, M.; Vandeput, L.; and Köse, V.
2012   Evidence for Late Roman D Ware
Production in Southern Asia Minor: A
challenge to "Cypriot Red Slip Ware."
Anatolian Studies 62: 89–114.

James, P.; Atherton, M.; Harvey, A.; Firmin, A.;
and Morrow, A.
1997   The Physical Environment of Methana:
Formation, Exploitation, and Change.
Pp. 5–32 in *A Rough and Rocky Place:
The Landscape and Settlement History of
the Methana Peninsula, Greece*, eds. C.
Mee and H. Forbes. Liverpool: Liverpool
University.

Jameson, M.H.; Runnels, C.N.; and Andel, T.H.
1994   *The Greek Countryside: The Southern Argolid from Prehistory to the Present Day*. Stanford, CA: Stanford University.

Jehasse, L.
1978   *Salamine de Chypre*. VIII. *La céramique à vernis noir du Rampart Méridional*. Paris: de Boccard.
1981   La céramique attique à vernis noir de Kition de la fin du VI à la fin du IV siècle avant J.C. Pp. 75–99 in *Excavations at Kition*. IV. *The Non-Cypriot Pottery*, eds. V Karageorghis et al. Nicosia: Tmēma Archaiotētōn.

Johnson, P., and Millet, M. (eds.)
2012   *Archaeological Survey and the City*. Oxford: Oxbow.

Jones, A.H.M.
1964   *Later Roman Empire*. Norman, OK: Oklahahoma University.

Kallet-Marx, R.M.
1995   *Hegemony to Empire. The Development of the Roman Imperium in the East from 148 to 62 B.C.* Hellenistic Culture and Society 15. Berkeley: University of California.

Karageorghis, V.
1970   *Excavations in the Necropolis of Salamis.* Nicosia: Cyprus Department of Antiquities.

Karageorghis, V.; and Demas, M.
1984   *Pyla*-Kokkinokremos: *A Late 13th Century Fortified Settlement in Cyprus.* Nicosia: Cyprus Department of Antiquities.

Karageorghis, V., and Gagniers, J.
1974   *La céramique chypriote de style figure.* Rome: Consiglio nazionale delle ricerche.

Karagiorgou, O.
2001   Demetrias and Thebes: The Fortunes and Misfortunes of two Thessalian Port Cities.
Pp. 182–215 in *Recent Research in Late-Antique Urbanism*, ed. L Lavan. Journal of Roman Archaeology Supplement 42. Portsmouth, RI: Journal of Roman Archaeology.

Kardulias, P.N.
2003   Lithics: Reduction Sequence and Micro-wear Analysis. Pp. 84–93 in *Early Urban Life in the Land of Anshan: Excavations at Tal-e Malyan in the Highlands of Iran,* ed. W. Sumner. Philadelphia: University of PennsylvaniaMuseum of Archaeology and Anthropology.
2009   Flaked Stone from Isthmia. *Hesperia* 78: 307–46.

Kardulias, P.N., and Ijdo, M.
2008   The Flaked Stone from Ayios Stephanos. Pp. 128–49 in *Ayios Stephanos: Excavations at a Bronze Age and Medieval Settlement in Southern Laconia*, eds. W.D. Taylour and R. Janko. London: British School at Athens.

Kardulias, P.N., and Yerkes, R.W.
1996   Microwear and Metric Analysis of Threshing Sledge Flints from Greece and Cyprus. *Journal of Archaeological Science* 23: 657–66.
2012a   The Malloura Valley Survey. Pp. 87–105 in *Crossroads and Boundaries: The Archaeology of Past and Present in the Malloura Valley, Cyprus,* eds. M. Toumazou, P.N. Kardulias, and D.B. Counts. Boston: American Schools of Oriental Research.
2012b   Flaked Stone Artifacts from the Malloura Valley Survey and their Cypriot Context. Pp. 107–24 in *Crossroads and Boundaries: The Archaeology of Past and Present in the Malloura Valley, Cyprus,* eds. M. Toumazou, P.N. Kardulias, and D.B. Counts. Boston: American Schools of Oriental Research.

Karimali, E.
2005   Lithic Technologies and Use. Pp. 180–214 in *The Archaeology of Mediterranean Prehistory*, eds. E. Blake and A.B. Knapp. Oxford: Blackwell.

Keay, S.J.
1984   *Late Roman Amphora in the Western Mediterranean. A Typology and Economic Study: The Catalan Evidence.* Oxford: British Archaeological Reports.

Keeley, L.
1980   *Experimental Determination of Stone Tool Use: A Microwear Analysis.* Chicago: University of Chicago.

Keen P.W.
2012   Land of Experiment: The Ptolemies and the Development of Hellenistic Cyprus, 312–58 BC. Unpublished Ph.D. dissertation, University of Chicago.

Kenkel, F.
2007   The Cypriot Red Slip Ware and its Derivatives from Pednelissos in Pisidia. Pp. 131–46 in *Çanak: Late Antique and Medieval Pottery and Tiles in Mediterranean Archaeological Contexts*, eds. B. Böhlendorf-Arslan, A. Uysal, and J. Witte-Orr. Byzas 7. Istanbul: Ege Yayınları.

Kenyon, K.M.
1957   Terra Sigillata. Pp 281–88 in *Samaria-Sebaste: Reports of the Work of the Joint Expedition in 1931–1933 and of the British Expedition in 1935. III. The Objects from Samaria*, eds. J.W. Crowfoot, G.M. Crowfoot, and K.M. Kenyon. London: Palestine Exploration Fund.

Keppie, L.
1991   *Understanding Roman Inscriptions.* Baltimore: Johns Hopkins University.

Keswani, P.; Manning, S.; Ribeiro, E.; Smith, J.S.; Moore, R.S.; and Gregory, T.E.
2003   The Material Culture of the SCSP Landscape. Pp. 202–63 in *The Sydney Cyprus Survey Project: Social Approaches to Regional Archaeological Survey*, eds. M. Given and A.B. Knapp. Los Angeles: Cotsen Institute of Archaeology.

Knapp, A.B.
2008   *Prehistoric and Protohistoric Cyprus.* Oxford: Oxford University.

Korfmann, M.
1973   The Sling as a Weapon. *Scientific American* 229: 34–42.

Kowalewski, S.A.
2008   Regional Settlement Pattern Studies. *Journal of Archaeological Research* 16: 225–85.

Kramer, N.
2004   *Gindaros: Geschichte und Archäologie einer Siedlung im nordwestlichen Syrien von hellenistischer bis in frühbyzantinische Zeit.* Internationale Archäologie 41. Rahden: Leidorf.

LaBianca, Ø.S., and Scham, S. A. (eds.)
2006   *Connectivity in Antiquity: Globalization as a Long-Term Historical Process.* Oakville, CT: Equinox.

Lacau, P.
1902   Une inscription phénicienne de Chypre. *Le Bulletin de l'Institut Français d'Archéologie Orientale* 2: 207.

LaMotta, V.M., and Schiffer, M.B.
1999   Formation Processes of House Floor Assemblages. Pp. 19–29 in *The Archaeology of Household Activities: Dwelling in the Past*, ed. P.M. Allison. London: Routledge.

Lang, R.
1878 *Cyprus: Its History, its Present Resources, and Future Prospects.* London: MacMillan and Company.
1905 Reminiscences – Archaeological Research in Cyprus. *Blackwood's Edinburgh Magazine* 177: 622–39.

Lécuyer, N.; Grivaud, G.; Michaelides, D.; Nicolaides, A.; Amouric, H.; Decock, L.; Devillers, B.; François, V.; Hadjichristofi, F.; Loiseau, M.; Simon, B.; and Vallauri, L.
2002 Potamia-Agios Sozomenos (Cyprus): La constitution des paysages dans l'orient médiévale. *Bulletin de Correspondance Hellénique* 126: 598–614.

Leonard, A.
1987 A Brief Survey. Pp 80–116 in *The Sanctuary of Apollo Hylates at Kourion, Cyprus*, ed. D. Soren. Tucson: University of Arizona.

Leonard, J.
1995a The Anchorage at Kioni. Pp. 133–70 in *Ancient Akamas: Settlement and Environs*, ed. J. Fejfer. Aarhus: Aarhus University.
1995b Evidence for Roman Ports, Harbours, and Anchorages in Cyprus. Pp. 227–46 in *Proceedings of the International Symposium Cyprus and the Sea*, eds. V. Karageorghis and D. Michaelides. Nicosia: University of Cyprus.
2005 Roman Cyprus: Harbors, Hinterlands, and Hidden Powers. Unpublished Ph.D. dissertation, State University of New York at Buffalo.

Lolos, Y.A.; Gourley, B.; and Stewart, D.R.
2007 The Sikyon Survey Project: A Blueprint for Urban Survey? *Journal of Mediterranean Archaeology* 20: 267–96.

London, G.
1990 *Traditional Pottery in Cyprus.* Mainz: von Zabern.

Loues, K.D.
2004 Εκμετάλλευση του Τσιφλικίκου της Πύλας (1833–1838). *Επετρίδα του Κέντρου Επιστημονικών Ερευνών* 30: 305–45.

Lund, J.
1992 Centuries of Darkness? A Ceramic Sidelight on Cyprus and the Eastern Mediterranean between about A.D. 200 and A.D. 350. *Acta Cypria* 2: 193–213.
1993 Pottery of the Classical, Hellenistic, and Roman Periods. Pp. 79–156 in *The Land of the Paphian Aphrodite 2. The Canadian Palaipaphos Survey Project: Artifactual and Ecofactual Studies*, eds. L.W. Sørensen and D. Rupp. Göteborg: Åströms.
1996 Preliminary Report of the Danish Archaeological Excavations to Panayia Ematousa, Aradippou 1993 and 1994. *Report of the Department of Antiquities, Cyprus 1996*: 144-57.
2002a Frying Pans and Other Cooking Wares from the Akamas (Western Cyprus). Pp. 43–58 in *Céramiques hellénistiques et romaines. Productions et diffusion en Méditerranée orientale (Chypre, Égypte et côte syro-palestinienne). Actes du colloque tenu à la Maison de l'Orient méditerranéen Jean Pouilloux du 2 au 4 mars 2000*, eds. F. Blondé, P. Ballet, and J.Salles. Lyon: Maison de l'Orient Méditerranéen.
2002b The Ontogenesis of Cypriot Sigillata. Pp. 185–223 in *Pots for the Living, Pots for the Dead*, eds. A. Rathje, M. Nielsen, and B.B. Rasmussen. Danish Studies in Classical Archaeology, Acta Hyperborea 9. Copenhagen: Museum Tusculanum.
2006 Ceramic Fine Wares from the 4th Century BC to the 7th Century AD. Pp. 182–230 in *Panayia Ematousa*. I, eds. L.W. Sørensen and K.Winther-Jacobsen. Athens: Aarhus University.

Lund, J., Malfitana, D., and Poblome, J.
2008 "Rhosica vasa:" The Quest Continues. *Facta* 2: 217–19.

Ma, J.
2010 A Note on Lead Projectiles (*glandes, molybdides*) in Support of Sling Bullets: A Reply to T. Rihll. *Journal of Roman Archaeology* 23: 427–28.

Magness, J.
1992 Late Roman and Byzantine Pottery, Preliminary Report, 1990. Pp. 129–53 in *Caesarea Papers. Straton's Tower, Herod's Harbour, and Roman and Byzantine Caesarea.* ed. R.L. Vann. Ann Arbor, MI: Journal of Roman Archaeology.

Maier, F.G., and Wartburg, M.L.
1986 Excavations at Kouklia (Palaepaphos). Fourteenth Preliminary Report: Season 1985. *Report of the Department of Antiquities, Cyprus 1986*: 55–61.

Manganaro, G.
1982 Monete e ghiande degli schiavi ribelli in Sicilia. *Chiron* 12: 237–43.

Manning, S.W., Manning, A.; Tomber, R.; Sewell, D.; Monks, S.J.; Ponting, M.J.; Ribeiro, E.C.
2002 *The Late Roman Church at Maroni Petrera: Survey and Salvage Excavations 1990–1997, and Other Traces of Roman Remains in the Lower Maroni Valley, Cyprus.* Nicosia: A.G. Leventis Foundation.

Marquié, S.
2001 Les sigilleés de la côte méridionale de Chypre aux époques hellénistique et romaine. *Cahiers du Centre d'Études Chypriotes* 31: 83–93.
2002 La circulation des sigilleés d'époque impériale au sud de Chypre. Pp. 289–301 in *Céramiques Hellénistiques et Romaines: Productions et diffusion en Méditerranée Orientale*, eds. F. Blondé, P. Ballet and J.F. Salles. Lyon: Maison de l'Orient Méditerranéen.
2004 Un Dépôt de la Deuxième Moitié du Ier S. de Notre Ère à Kition-Kathari (Chypre). Pp. 251–62 in *Transport Amphorae and Trade in the Eastern Mediterranean*, eds. J. Eiring and J. Lund. Aarhus: Aarhus University.
2005 Un lot de céramiques de la première moitié du IIIe siècle de notre ère dans le secteur I. Pp. 387–403 in *Excavations at Kition, The Phoenician and Later Levels*, Vol. VI, Part 2, ed. V. Karageorghis. Nicosia: Department of Antiquities.

Masson, O.
1966 Kypriaka II: Recherches sur les antiq-uités de la région de Pyla. *Bulletin de Correspondance Hellénique* 90: 1–21.

Mayet, F., and Picon, M.
1986 Une sigillée phocéenne tardive ('Late Roman C Ware') et sa diffusion en Occident. *Figlina* 7: 129–42.

McCaul, J.
1864 On Inscribed Sling-Bullets. *The Canadian Journal of Industry, Science and Art* 9: 92–102.

Mee, C.B., and Forbes, H.A.
1997 Survey Methodology. Pp. 33–41 in *A Rough and Rocky Place: The Landscape and Settlement History of the Methana Peninsula, Greece*, eds. C.B. Mee and H.A. Forbes. Liverpool: Liverpool University.

Megaw, A.H.S.
1937 Cypriot Medieval Glazed Pottery: Notes for a Preliminary Classification. *Report of the Department of Antiquities, Cyprus 1937*: 1–13.
1953 Archaeology in Cyprus, 1952. *Journal of Hellenic Studies* 73: 133–37.
1993 The Episcopal Precinct at Kourion and the Evidence for 'Re-Location.' Pp. 53–67 in *'The Sweet Land of Cyprus.' Papers Given at the Twenty-Fifth Jubilee Spring Symposium of Byzantine Studies, Birmingham, March 1991*, eds. A. Breyer, and G. Georghallides. Nicosia: Cyprus Research Centre.

2007 *Kourion: Excavations in the Episcopal Precinct*. Washington, DC: Dumbarton Oaks.

Meyer, N.
2003 Pottery Strategy and Chronotypes. Pp. 14–16 in *The Sydney Cyprus Survey Project: Social Approaches to Regional Archaeological Survey*, eds. M. Given and A.B. Knapp. Los Angeles: Cotsen Institute of Archaeology.

Meyer, N., and Gregory, T.E.
2003 Pottery Collection, Pottery Analysis, and GIS Mapping. Pp. 48–52 in *The Sydney Cyprus Survey Project: Social Approaches to Regional Archaeological Survey*, eds. M. Given and A.B. Knapp. Los Angeles: Cotsen Institute of Archaeology.

Meyer, N., and Schon, R.
2003 Experimental Data. Pp. 52–56 in *The Sydney Cyprus Survey Project: Social Approaches to Regional Archaeological Survey*, eds. M. Given and A.B. Knapp. Los Angeles: Cotsen Institute of Archaeology.

Meyza, H.
2000 Cypriot Red Slip. Development of the Ware (An Attempt at Refinement). Pp. 23–31 in *Acts of the Third International Congress of Cypriot Studies (Nicosia, 16–20 April 1996)*, eds. I. Ioannides and G.K. Hatzistyllis. Nicosia: Society of Cypriot Studies.
2002 Cypriot Sigillata and Its Hypothetical Predecessors. Pp 23–31 in *Céramiques hellénistiques et romaines. Productions et diffusions en Méditerranee orientale (Chypre, Egypte et côte syro-palestinienne)*, eds. F. Blondé, P. Ballet, and J.-F. Salles. Lyon: Maison de l'Orient Méditerranéen.
2007 *Nea Paphos V. Cypriot Red Slip Ware: Studies on a Late Roman Levantine Fine Ware*. Warsaw: Polish Academy of Science.

Michaelidou-Nicolaou, I.
1965 Table a jeu de Dhekelia (Chypre). *Bulletin de Correspondance Hellénique* 89: 122–27.
1969–1970 Ghiande Missili di Cipro. *Annuario della Scuola Archeologica di Atene* 47/48: 359–69.

Millett, M.
1985 Field Survey Calibration: A Contribution. Pp. 31–37 in *Archaeology from the Ploughsoil: Studies in the Collection and Interpretation of Field Survey Data*, eds. C. Haselgrove, M. Millett, and I. Smith. Sheffield: University of Sheffield.
1991 Pottery: Population or Supply Patterns? The *Ager Tarraconensis* Approach. Pp. 18–26 in *Roman Landscapes: Archaeological Survey in the Mediterranean Region*, eds. G. Barker and J.A. Lloyd. Archaeological Monographs of the British School at Rome 2. London: British School at Rome.
2000a The Comparison of Surface and Stratified Artefact Assemblages. Pp. 216–22 in *Non-Destructive Techniques Applied to Landscape Archaeology*, eds. M. Pasquinucci and F. Trement. The Archaeology of Mediterranean Landscapes 4. Oxford: Oxbow.
2000b Dating, Quantifying, and Utilizing Pottery Assemblages from Surface Survey. Pp. 53–59 in *Extracting Meaning from Ploughsoil Assemblages*, eds. R. Francovich, H. Patterson, and G. Barker. The Archaeology of Mediterranean Landscapes 5. Oxford: Oxbow.

Mitford, T.B.
1961 Further Contributions to the Epigraphy of Cyprus. *American Journal of Archaeology* 65: 93–151.
1980 Roman Cyprus. *Aufstieg und Niedergang der Römischen Welt* 2.7.2: 1285–1384.

Młynarczyk, J.
1990 *Nea Paphos* III. *Nea Paphos in the Hellenistic period*. Warsaw: Éditions Géologiques.

2005   The "Pink Powdery Ware" at Yeronisos. A Local West Cypriot Ware of the Late Hellenistic Period. *Études et Travaux* 20: 138–49.

2009   Sailors and Artisans: The Egyptian Connections of Ceramic Finds from Yeronisos. Pp. 210–15 in *Proceedings of the International Conference: Egypt and Cyprus in Antiquity, Nicosia, 3-6 April 2003*, eds. D. Michaelides, V. Kassianidou, and R.S. Merrillees. Oxford: Oxbow.

2010   Sigillatae (ESA, CS) and "Pseudo-Sigillata" (PPW) at Geronisos: An Overview of Forms and Comparison of Repertoire. *Report of the Department of Antiquities, Cyprus 2010*: 349–64.

Moore, R.S.

2003   Hellenistic to Roman Landscapes. Pp. 277–82 in *The Sydney Cyprus Survey Project: Social Approaches to Regional Archaeological* Survey, eds. M. Given and A.B. Knapp. Los Angeles: Cotsen Institute of Archaeology.

2008   A Decade Later: The Chronotype System Revisited. Pp. 137–52 in *Methods and Meaning in Medieval and Post Medieval Greece: A Tribute to Timothy E. Gregory*, eds. W.R. Caraher, L. Hall, and R.S. Moore. Farnham, UK: Ashgate.

Moore, R.S., and Gregory, T.E.

2012   Athienou Archaeological Project Survey Pottery. Pp. 203–14 in *Crossroads and Boundaries: The Archaeology of Past and Present in the Malloura Valley, Cyprus*, eds. M. Toumazou, P.N. Kardulias, and D.B. Counts. Boston: American Schools of Oriental Research.

Morhange, C.; Bourcier, M.; Carbonel, P.; Goiran, J.P.; Le Campion, J.; Rouchy, J.M.; and Yon, M.

2000   Recent Holocene Paleo-Environmental Evolution and Coastline Changes of Kition, Larnaca, Cyprus, Mediterranean Sea. *Marine Geology*: 170–230.

Morris, I.

2005   Mediterraneanization. Pp. 30–55 in *Mediterranean Paradigms and Classical Antiquity*, ed. I. Malkin. London: Routledge.

Munsell

2000   *Munsell Soil Color Charts*, Revised Edition. New Windsor: Munsell Color Company.

Mušič, B.; SlapšakB.; and Perko, V.

2000   On-Site Distributions and Geophysics: The Site of Rodik-Ajdovščina. Pp. 32–46 in *Extracting Meaning from Ploughsoil Assemblages*, eds. R. Francovich, H. Patterson, and G. Barker. Oxford: Oxbow.

Nicolaou, I.

1976   *Prosopography of Ptolemaic Cyprus*. Göteborg: Åströms.

1977   Inscriptiones Cypriae Alphabeticae XVI 1976. *Report of the Department of Antiquities, Cyprus 1977*: 209–21.

1979   Inscriptiones Cypriae Alphabeticae XVIII 1978. *Report of the Department of Antiquities, Cyprus 1979*: 344–51.

1980   Inscriptiones Cypriae Alphabeticae XIX 1979. *Report of the Department of Antiquities, Cyprus 1980*: 260–66.

Nicolaou, K.

1966   The Topography of Neapaphos. Pp. 516–601 in *Mélanges offerts à Kazimierz Michałowski*, ed. M. Bernhard. Warsaw: Państwowe Wydaw.

Nitschke, J.L.; Martin, S.R.; and Shalev, Y.

2011   Between Carmel and the Sea. Tel Dor: The Late Periods. *Near Eastern Archaeology* 74: 132–54.

Noller, J.S., and Zomeni, Z.

2006   Report on the Geological Drilling of the Pyla-*Koutsopetria* Lowland. Unpublished Report.

Oleson, J.P.; Raban, A.; and Hohlfelder, R.
1994   *The Harbors of Caesarea Maritima: Results of the Caesarea Ancient Harbor Excavation Project, 1980–1985,* Vol. II: *The Finds and the Ship.* Oxford: Archaeopress.

Olson, B.R.; Caraher, W.; Pettegrew, D.K.; and Moore, R.S.
2013   The Pyla-*Koutsopetria* Archaeological Project: A Preliminary Report on Excavations at Pyla-*Vigla*, a Fortified Settlement Dating to the Hellenistic Era. *Journal of Ancient Egyptian Interconnections* 5.3: 74–82.

Olson B.R., and Killebrew, A.E.
2011   A Latin Graffito on a Recently Discovered Eastern Sigillata A Sherd from Dalbaz Höyük, Bay of İskenderun, Turkey. *Near Eastern Archaeology* 74: 116–19.

Papacostas, T.
1999   Byzantine Cyprus: The Testimony of its Churches, 650–1200. Unpublished Ph.D. dissertation, Oxford University.

Papanikola-Bakirtzis, D.
1993   Cypriot Medieval Glazed Pottery. Answers and Questions. Pp. 115–30 in *'The Sweet Land of Cyprus.' Papers Given at the 25th Jubilee Spring Symposium of Byzantine Studies,* eds. A. Breyer and G. Georghallides. Nicosia: Cyprus Research Centre.

Papantoniou, G.
2012   *Religion and Social Transformations in Cyprus: From the Cypriot Basileis to the Hellenistic Strategos.* Mnemosyne Supplements, History and Archaeology of Classical Antiquity 347. Leiden: Brill.

Papuci-Wladyka, E.
1995   *Nea Pafos. Studia nad ceramika hellenisty-czna z polskich wyko palisk (1965–1991).* Krakow: Jagiellonian University.
2000   Hellenistic Pottery from the Polish Excavations at Nea Paphos (Mouletana),

1965–1995: The Status of Research and Prospects for Future Study. Pp. 721–38 in *Acts of the Third International Congress of Cypriot Studies,* eds. G.C. Ioannides and S.A. Hadjistellis, Nicosia: Society of Cypriot Studies.

Parker, A.J.
1992   *Ancient Shipwrecks of the Mediterranean and the Roman Provinces.* Oxford: Archaeopress.

Peacock, D.P.S.
1984   Petrology and Origins. Pp. 6–28 in *The Avenue du Président Habib Bourguiba, Salammbô: The Pottery and Other Ceramic Objects from the Site,* eds. M. Fulford and D.P.S. Peacock. Sheffield: Collis.

Peacock, D.P.S., and Williams, D.F.
1986   *Amphorae and the Roman Economy: An Introductory Guide.* London: Longman.

Pearlman, D.A.
1984   Threshing Sledges in the Eastern Mediterranean: Ethnoarchaeology with Chert Knappers and Dhoukanes in Cyprus. Unpublished M.A. thesis, University of Minnesota.

Perkins, P., and L. Walker
1990   The Survey of an Etruscan City at Doganella in the Albegna Valley. *Papers of the British School at Rome* 58: 1–144.

Pettegrew, D.K.
2001   Chasing the Classical Farmstead: Assessing the Formation and Signature of Rural Settlement in Greek Landscape Archaeology. *Journal of Mediterranean Archaeology* 14: 189–209.
2007   The Busy Countryside of Late Roman Corinth: Interpreting Ceramic Data Produced by Regional Archaeological Survey. *Hesperia* 76: 743–84.
2008   The End of Ancient Corinth? Views from the Landscape. Pp. 249–66 in *Archaeology*

and History in Roman, Medieval, and Post-Medieval Greece, eds. W.R. Caraher, L. Hall, and R.S. Moore. Farnham, UK: Ashgate.

2013   Connectivity. Pp. 1708–11 in *Encyclopedia of Ancient History*, eds. R.S. Bagnall, K. Brodersen, C.B. Champion, A. Erskine, and S.R. Huebner. Malden, MA: Wiley-Blackwell.

Poblome, J., and Firat, N.
2011   A Matter of Open(ing) or Closed Horizons? Pp. 49–55 in *LRFW1. Late Roman Fine Wares: Solving Problems of Typology and Chronology*, eds. M. Cau, P. Reynolds, and M. Bonifay. Roman and Late Antique Mediterranean Pottery 1, BAR International Series. Oxford: Archaeopress.

Poblome, J.; Degryse, P.; Cottica, D.; and Firat, N.
2001   A New Early Byzantine Production Centre in Western Asia Minor. A Petrographical and Geochemical Study of Red Slip Ware from Hierapolis, Perge and Sagalassos. *Rei Cretariae Romanae Fautorum Acta* 37: 119–26.

Potter, D.
2000   Η Κύπρος επαρχία της Ρωμαϊκής αυτοκρατωρίας [Cyprus as a Province of the Roman Empire]. Pp. 763–864 in *Ιστορία της Κύπρου [History of Cyprus]*, Vol. 2, pt. 1, ed. T. Papadopoullos. Nicosia: Archbishop Makarios III Foundation.

Poulter, A.
2004   Cataclysm of the Lower Danube: The Destruction of a Complex Roman Landscape. Pp. 223–54 in *Landscapes of Change: Rural Evolutions in Late Antiquity and the Early Middle Ages*, ed. N. Christie. Aldershot: Ashgate.

Preisigke, F.
1967   Onomasticon Alterum Papyrologicum. Supplemento al Namenbuch. Amsterdam:

Milano-Varese Istituto editoriale cisalpino.

Pritchett, W. K.
1991   *The Greek State at War: Part V*. Berkeley: University of California.

Quilici, L., and Quilici-Gigli, S.
1972/73   Ricerche intorno a Melabron. *Rivista dell'Istituto Nazionale d'Archeologia e Storia dell'Arte* 19–20: 7–102.

Rautman, M.
2000   The Busy Countryside of Late Roman Cyprus. *Report of the Department of Antiquities, Cyprus 2000*: 317–31.
2003   *A Cypriot Village of Late Antiquity. Kalavasos-Kopetra in the Vasilikos Valley*. Portsmouth, RI: Journal of Roman Archaeology.
2004   Valley and Village in Late Roman Cyprus. Pp. 189–218 in *Recent Research on the Late Antique Countryside*, eds. W. Bowden, L. Lavan, and C. Machado. Leiden: Brill

Rapp, C.
2003   Epiphanius of Cyprus: The Church Father as Saint. Pp. 69–87 in *'The Sweet Land of Cyprus.' Papers Given at the Twenty-Fifth Jubilee Spring Symposium of Byzantine Studies, Birmingham, March 1991*, eds. A. Breyer and G. Georghallides. Nicosia: Cyprus Research Centre.

Redman, C.L., and Watson, P.J.
1970   Systematic, Intensive Surface Collection. *American Antiquity* 35: 279–91.

Reyes, A.T.
1994   *Archaic Cyprus: A Study of the Textual and Archaeological Evidence*. Oxford: Oxford University.

Rihll, T.
2007   *The Catapult: A History*. Yardley, PA: Westholme.
2009   Lead 'Slingshot' (*glandes*). *Journal of Roman Archaeology* 22: 146–69.

Riley, J.

1975 The Pottery from the First Session of Excavation in the Caesarea Hippodrome. *Bulletin of the American Schools of Oriental Research* 218: 25–63.

1979 The Coarse Pottery from Berenice. Pp. 91–467 in *Excavations at Sidi Khrebish, Benghazi (Berenice) II*, ed. J.A. Lloyd. Supplements to Libya Antiqua 5. Tripoli: Dept. of Antiquities, Ministry of Teaching and Education, People's Socialist Libyan Arab Jamahiriya.

Robinson, D.

1931 New Inscriptions from Olynthus and Environs. *Transactions and Proceedings of the American Philological Association* 62: 40–56.

1932 The Residential Districts and the Cemeteries at Olynthus. *American Journal of Archaeology* 36: 118–38.

1934 Inscriptions from Olynthus 1934. *Transactions and Proceedings of the American Philological Association* 65: 103–37.

1935 The Third Campaign at Olynthos. *American Journal of Archaeology* 39: 210–47.

1941 *Excavations at Olynthus* X: *Metal and Minor Miscellaneous Finds, an Original Contribution to Greek Life,* Baltimore: Johns Hopkins University.

Robinson, H.S.

1959 *Pottery of the Roman Period: Chronology.* Athenian Agora 5. Princeton: American School of Classical Studies at Athens.

Rodziewicz, M.

1976 *La céramique romaine tardive d'Alexandrie.* Warsaw: Éditions Scientifiques de Pologne.

Rose, P.

2006 Roof Tiles from the Excavation and Survey. Pp. 358–60 in *Panayia Ematousa.* I, eds. L.W. Sørensen and K.Winther-Jacobsen. Athens: Aarhus University.

Rosen, S.A.

1997 *Lithics after the Stone Age. A Handbook of Stone Tools from the Levant.* Walnut Creek, CA: AltaMira.

Rotroff, S.I.

1997 *Hellenistic Pottery: Athenian and Imported Wheelmade Table Ware and Related Material.* Athenian Agora 29. Princeton: American School of Classical Studies at Athens.

Rowe, A.

2006 Reconsidering Late Roman Cyprus: Using New Material from Nea Paphos to Review Current Artefact Typologies. Unpublished Ph.D. dissertation, University of Sydney.

Runnels, C.

1976 More on Glass Implements from Greece. *Newsletter of Lithic Technology* 5: 27–31.

1981 A Diachronic Study and Economic Analysis of Millstones from the Argolid, Greece. Unpublished Ph.D. dissertation, Indiana University, Bloomington.

1982 Flaked-Stone Artifacts in Greece during the Historical Period. *Journal of Field Archaeology* 9: 363–73.

1985 The Bronze-Age Flaked-Stone Industries from Lerna: A Preliminary Report. *Hesperia* 54: 357–91.

Rupp, D.W.

1987 Vive le Roi: The Emergence of the State in Iron Age Cyprus. Pp. 147–68 in *Western Cyprus: Connections*, ed. D. Rupp. Studies in Mediterranean Archaeology 77. Göteborg: Åströms.

1989 Puttin' on the Ritz: Manifestations of High Status in Iron Age Cyprus. Pp. 336–62 in *Early Society in Cyprus*, ed. E. Peltenburg. Edinburgh: Edinburgh University.

1997 'Metro' Nea Paphos: Suburban Sprawl in Southwestern Cyprus in the Hellenistic and Earlier Roman Periods. Pp. 236–62 in *Aspects of Urbanism in Antiquity: From*

Mesopotamia to Crete, eds. W.E. Aufrecht, N.A. Mirau, and S.W. Gauley. Sheffield: Sheffield Academic.

Rutter, J.B.
1983   Some Thoughts on the Analysis of Ceramic Data Generated by Site Surveys. Pp. 137–42 in *Archaeological Survey in the Mediterranean Area*, eds. D. R. Keller and D. W. Rupp. British Archaeological Reports, International Series 155. Oxford: BAR.

Salles, J. -F
1983   *Kition-Bamboula II. Les égouts de la ville classique*. Paris: Documentation Française.
1995   Céramiques hellénistiques de Kition-Bamboula. Pp. 397–414 in *Hellenistic and Roman Pottery in the Eastern Mediterranean – Advances in Scientific Studies. Acts of the II Nieborów Pottery Workshop. Nieborów, 18–20 December 1993*, eds. H. Meyza and J. Młynarczyk. Warsaw: Polish Academy of Sciences.

Sanders, G.D.R.
1995   Byzantine Glazed Pottery at Corinth to c. 1125. Unpublished Ph.D. dissertation, University of Birmingham.

Sanders, G.D.R.; Carter, A.; Tzonou-Herbst, I.; Herbst, J.; James, S.; Bookidis, N.; and Williams II, C.K.
2008   *Corinth Excavations: Archaeological Site Manual*. Corinth: American School of Classical Studies at Athens.

Schiffer, M.B.
1976   *Behavioral Archaeology*. New York: Academic.
1985   Is there a 'Pompeii Premise' in Archaeology? *Journal of Anthropological Research* 41: 18–41.
1986   *Formation Processes of the Archaeological Record*. Albuquerque: University of New Mexico.

Schon, R.
2000   On a Site and Out of Sight: Where Have our Data Gone? *Journal of Mediterranean Archaeology* 13: 107–11.
2002   Seeding the Landscape: Experimental Contributions to Regional Survey Methodology. Unpublished Ph.D. dissertation, Bryn Mawr College.

Shaw, B.
2001   Challenging Braudel: A New Vision of the Mediterranean. *Journal of Roman Archaeology* 14: 419–53.

Simmons, A.
1999   *Faunal Extinction in an Island Society: Pygmy Hippopotamus Hunters of Cyprus*. New York: Kluwer Academic/Plenum.

Slane, K.W.
1997   The Fine Wares. Pp. 247–393 in *Tel Anafa II:1. The Hellenistic and Roman Pottery*, ed. S.C. Herbert. Ann Arbor, MI: Kelsey Museum of the University of Michigan.

Slane, K.W.; Elam, J.M.; Glascock, M.D.; and Neff, H.
1994   Compositional Analysis of Eastern Sigillata A and Related Wares from Tel Anafa (Israel), *Journal of Archaeological Science* 21: 51–64.

Smith, J.S.
2009   *Art and Society in Cyprus from the Bronze Age into the Iron Age*. New York: Cambridge University.

Smyth, H.W.
1920   *A Greek Grammar for Colleges*. New York: American Book Co.
1956   *Greek Grammar*. Cambridge: Harvard University.

Sørensen, L.W.
1993a   General Conclusions. Pp. 185–95 in *The Land of the Paphian Aphrodite*, ed. L.W. Sørensen. Göteborg: Åströms.

1993b Cypro-Geometric and Cypro-Archaic
        Pottery. Pp. 37–77 in *The Land of the
        Paphian Aphrodite*, ed. L.W. Sørensen.
        Göteborg: Åströms.
2006a Introduction. Stratigraphy and Summary
        of the Site Analysis. Pp. 34–63 in *Panayia
        Ematousa* I, eds. L.W. Sørensen and
        K.Winther-Jacobsen. Athens: Aarhus
        University.
2006b Architectural Analysis. Pp. 64–117 in
        Panayia Ematousa I, eds. L.W. Sørensen
        and K.Winther-Jacobsen. Athens: Aarhus
        University.
2006c Painted Iron Age Pottery. Pp. 161–80 in
        Panayia Ematousa I, eds. L.W. Sørensen
        and K.Winther-Jacobsen. Athens: Aarhus
        University.
2006d Terracotta Figurines. Pp. 355–57 in
        Panayia Ematousa I, eds. L.W. Sørensen
        and K.Winther-Jacobsen. Athens: Aarhus
        University.

Sørensen, L.W., and Winther-Jacobsen, K.
2006   *Panayia Ematousa: A Rural Site in
        South-Eastern Cyprus*. Athens: Aarhus
        University.

Sørensen, L.W. (ed.)
1996   Preliminary Report of the Danish
        Archaeological Excavations at Panayia
        Ematousa, Aradippou 1993 and 1994,
        *Report of the Department of Antiquities,
        Cyprus 1996*: 135–59.

Sørensen, L.W., and Rupp, D.
1993   *The Land of the Paphian Aphrodite*, Vol.
        2. Studies in Mediterranean Archaeology.
        Göteborg: Åströms.

Sparkes B.A., and Talcott, L.
1970   *Black and Plain Pottery of the 6th, 5th,
        and 4th Centuries B.C.* The Athenian
        Agora 12. Princeton: American School of
        Classical Studies at Athens.

Stanish, C.
2003   A Brief Americanist Perspective on
        Settlement Archaeology. Pp. 161–71 in

*Theory and Practice in Mediterranean
        Archaeology: Old World and New World
        Perspectives. An Advanced Seminar
        in Honor of Lloyd Cotsen*, eds. J.K.
        Papadopoulos and R.M. Leventhal. Los
        Angeles: Cotsen Institute of Archaeology.

Steel, L.
2004   *Cyprus Before History. From the Earliest
        Settlers to the End of the Bronze Age*.
        London: Duckworth.

Stone, D., and Kampke, A.
1988   Dialiskari: A Late Roman Villa on the
        Messenian Coast. Pp. 192–98 in *Sandy
        Pylos*, ed. J. Davis. Austin: University of
        Texas.

Swiny, S., and C. Mavromatis
2000   Land Behind Kourion: Results of the 1997
        Sotira Archaeological Project Survey.
        *Report of the Department of Antiquities,
        Cyprus 2000*: 433–52.

Tartaron, T.F.
2003   The Archaeological Survey: Sampling
        Strategies and Field Methods. Pp. 23–45
        in *Landscape Archaeology in Southern
        Epirus, Greece I*, eds. J. Wiseman, and
        K. Zachos. Hesperia Supplements 32.
        Princeton: American School of Classical
        Studies at Athens.
2008   Aegean Prehistory as World Archaeology:
        Recent Trends in the Archaeology
        of Bronze Age Greece. *Journal of
        Archaeological Research* 16: 83–161.

Tartaron, T.F.; Gregory, T.E.; Pullen, D.J.;
Noller, J.; Rothaus, R.; Rife, J.L.; Tzortzopoulou-
Gregory, L.; Schon, R.; Caraher, W.R.;
Pettegrew, D.K; and Nakassis, D.
2006   The Eastern Korinthia Archaeological
        Survey: Integrated Methods for a
        Dynamic Landscape. *Hesperia* 75:
        435–505.

Taylor, J.
1933   Some Notes on Byzantine Glazed Ware
          in Cyprus. *Report of the Department of
          Antiquities, Cyprus 1933*: 24–25.

Taylor, J., and Megaw, A.H.S.
1937   Cypriot Medieval Glazed Pottery: Notes
          for a Preliminary Classification. *Report
          of the Department of Antiquities, Cyprus
          1937*: 1–13.

Todd, I.
2004   *The Field Survey of the Vasilikos Valley.*
          Studies in Mediterranean Archaeology 71
          Sävedalen: Åströms.

Toumazou, M.; Kardulias, P.N.;
and Counts, D.B. (eds.)
2012   *Crossroads and Boundaries: The
          Archaeology of Past and Present in the
          Malloura Valley, Cyprus.* Annual of the
          American Schools of Oriental Research
          65. Boston: American Schools of Oriental
          Research.

Tomber, R.
1987   Evidence for Long-Distance Commerce:
          Imported Bricks and Tiles at Carthage.
          Rei Cretariae Romanae Fautorum Acta
          25/26: 161–74.

Tringham, R.
2003   (Re)-Digging the Site at the End of
          the Twentieth Century: Large-Scale
          Archaeological Fieldwork in a New
          Millennium. Pp. 137–59 in *Theory and
          Practice in Mediterranean Archaeology:
          Old World and New World Perspectives.
          An Advanced Seminar in Honor of Lloyd
          Cotsen*, eds. J.K. Papadopoulos and R.M.
          Leventhal. Los Angeles: Cotsen Institute
          of Archaeology.

Ulbrich, A.
2005   The Worship of Anat and Astarte in
          Cypriot Iron Age Sanctuaries. Pp.
          198–206 in *Archaeological Perspectives on
          the Transmission and Transformation of*

Culture in the Eastern Mediterranean, ed.
          J. Clarke. Oxford: Oxbow.

Van de Velde, P.
2001   An Extensive Alternative to Intensive
          Survey: Point Sampling in the Riu Mannu
          Survey Project, Sardinia. *Journal of
          Mediterranean Archaeology* 14: 24–52.

Varner, E.R.
2004   *Mutilation and Transformation:
          Damnatio Memoriae and Roman Imperial
          Portraiture.* Boston: Brill.

Vermeule, C.
1974   Cypriote Sculpture, the Late Archaic and
          Early Classical Periods: Towards a More
          Precise Understanding. *American Journal
          of Archaeology* 78: 287–90.

Vischer, W.; Gelzer, H.; Burckhardt, A.;
and von Gonzenbach, A.
1877–1878   *Kleine Schriften*, Leipzig: Hirzel.

Vroom, J.
2003   *After Antiquity: Ceramics and Society in
          the Aegean from the 7th to 20th Century
          A.C.: A Case Study from Boeotia, Central
          Greece.* Leiden: Leiden University.
2005   *Byzantine to Modern Pottery in the
          Aegean.* Utrecht: Parnassus.

Waagé, F.O.
1933   The Roman and Byzantine Pottery.
          Hesperia 2: 279–328.
1948   Hellenistic and Roman Tableware of
          North Syria. Pp. 1–60 in *Antioch on-the-
          Orontes.* IV:1. *Ceramics and Islamic Coins*,
          ed. F.O. Waagé. Princeton: Princeton
          University.

Wartburg, M.-L. von
2001   Types of Imported Table Ware at Kouklia
          in the Ottoman Period. *Report of the
          Department of Antiquities, Cyprus 2001*:
          361–96.
2003   Cypriot Connections with East and
          West as Reflected in Medieval Glazed

Pottery from the Paphos Region. Pp. 153–66 in *VIIe Congrès International sur la Céramique Médiévale en Méditerranée. Thessaloniki, 11–16 Octobre 1999*, ed. Ch. Bakirtzis. Athens: Caisse des Recettes Archéologiques.

Watkins, C.
1987   *Studies in Memory of Warren Cowgill (1929–1985)*. Berlin: de Gruyter.

Webb, J., and Frankel, D.
2004   Intensive Site Survey. Implications for Estimating Settlement Size, Population and Duration in Prehistoric Bronze Age Cyprus. Pp. 125–37 in *Archaeological Field Survey in Cyprus: Past History, Future Potentials. Proceedings of a Conference Held by the Archaeological Research Unit of the University of Cyprus, 1–2 December 2000*, ed. M. Iacovou. London: British School at Athens.

Whitelaw, T.M.
1991   Investigations at the Neolithic Sites of Kephala and Paoura. Pp. 199–216 in *Landscape Archaeology as Long-Term History: Northern Keos in the Cycladic Islands*, eds. J.F. Cherry, J.L. Davis, and E. Mantzourani. Monumenta Archaeologica 16. Los Angeles: Cotsen Institute of Archaeology.
2012   Collecting Cities: Some Problems and Prospects. Pp. 70–106 in *Archaeological Survey and the City* eds. P. Johnson and M. Millett. Oxford: Oxbow.

Whittaker, J.C.
1994   *Flintknapping: Making and Understanding Stone Tools*. Austin: University of Texas.
1996   Athkiajas: A Cypriote Flintknapper and the Threshing Sledge Industry. *Lithic Technology* 21(2): 108–20.
1999   Alonia: The Ethnoarchaeology of Cypriot Threshing Floors. *Journal of Mediterranean Archaeology* 12: 7–25.
2000   Alonia and Dhoukanes: The Ethnoarchaeology of Threshing in

Cyprus. *Near Eastern Archaeology* 63(2): 62–69.

Wickham, C.
2005   *Framing the Early Middle Ages: Europe and the Mediterranean, 400–800*. Oxford: Oxford University.

Williams, C.
1992   *Anemurium. The Roman and Early Byzantine Pottery*. Subsidia Mediaevalia 16. Toronto: Pontifical Institute of Mediaeval Studies.

Williams, D.F.
1979   The Heavy Mineral Separation of Ancient Ceramics by Centrifugation: A Preliminary Report. *Archaeometry* 21: 177–82.
1982   The Petrology of Certain Byzantine Amphorae: Some Suggestions as to Origins. Pp. 91–110 in *Actes du Colloque sur la céramique antique. Carthage 23–24 June 1980*, Carthage: Centre d'Etudes et de Documentation Archéologique de la Conservation.
2005   An Integrated Archaeometric Approach to Fabric Recognition. A Case Study of Late Roman Amphora 1 from the Eastern Mediterranean. Pp. 613–24 in *LRCW1: Late Roman Coarse Wares, Cooking Wares and Amphorae in the Mediterranean*, eds. J. Esparraguera, J. Garrigós, and J. Ontiveros. Oxford: Oxbow.

Williams, D.F., and Lund, J.
2013   Petrological Analyses of "Pinched-handle" Amphorae from the Akamas Peninsula, Western Cyprus. Pp. 155–64 in *The Transport Amphorae and Trade of Cyprus*, eds. M. Lawall and J. Lund. Aarhus: Aarhus University.

Williams, H.; Schaus, G.; Price, S.-M.C.; Gourley, B.; and Hagerman, C.
1998   Excavations at Ancient Stymphalos, 1997. *Classical Views* 42: 261–319.

Winther-Jacobsen, K.

1998   Transport Amphorae Found 1993–1996.
        Pp. 349–59 in Third Preliminary Report
        of the Danish Archaeological Excavations
        at Panayia Amatousa, Aradippou,
        Cyprus, eds. L. Wriedt Sørensen et al.
        *Proceedings of the Danish Institute at
        Athens* 2: 319–81.

2002   Cypriot Transport Amphorae of the
        Archaic and Classical Period. *Acta
        Hyperborea* 9: 169–84.

2006a   Cooking Wares. Pp. 231–44 in *Panayia
        Ematousa* I, eds. L.W. Sørensen and
        K.Winther-Jacobsen. Aarhus: Aarhus
        University.

2006b   Utility Wares. Pp. 244–302 in *Panayia
        Ematousa* I, eds. L.W. Sørensen and
        K.Winther-Jacobsen. Aarhus: Aarhus
        University.

2006c   Transport Amphorae. Pp. 303–36 in
        Panayia Ematousa I, eds. L.W. Sørensen
        and K.Winther-Jacobsen. Aarhus: Aarhus
        University.

2010a   The Classical Farmstead Revisited.
        Activity Differentiation Based on a
        Ceramic Use-Typology. *The Annual of the
        British School at Athens* 105: 269–90.

2010b   *From Pots to People: A Ceramic Approach
        to the Archaeological Interpretation of
        Ploughsoil Assemblages in Late Roman
        Cyprus.* Leuven: Peeters.

Wright, J.C.; Cherry, J.F.; Davis, J.L.;
Mantzourani, E.; Sutton, S.B.; and Sutton, R.F.

1990   The Nemea Valley Archaeological
        Project: A Preliminary Report. *Hesperia*
        59: 579–659.

Yerkes, R.W.

1987   *Prehistoric Life on the Mississippi Flood
        Plain.* Chicago: University of Chicago.

Yon, M.

1989   Sur l'administration de Kition a l'époque
        classique. Pp. 363–75 in *Early Society in
        Cyprus*, ed. E. Peltenburg. Edinburgh:
        Edinburgh University.

1997   Kition in the Tenth to Fourth Centuries
        B.C. *Bulletin of the American Schools of
        Oriental Research* 308: 9–17.

Young, D., and Bamforth, D.

1990   On the Microscopic Identification of
        Used Flakes. *American Antiquity* 55:
        403–9.

Zangger, E.; Timpson, M.E.; Yazvenko, S.B.;
Kuhnke, F.; and Knauss, J.

1997   The Pylos Regional Archaeological
        Project, Part II: Landscape Evolution and
        Site Preservation. *Hesperia* 66: 549–641.

Zevi, F.

1966   Appunti sulle anfore romane.
        Archaeologia Classica 18: 207–47.

Zoroğlu, K.

2013   Cypriot Basket-handle Amphorae from
        Kelenderis and its Vicinity. Pp. 35–46
        in *The Transport Amphorae and Trade
        of Cyprus*, eds. M. Lawall and J. Lund.
        Aarhus: Aarhus University.

Contributors

MARIA ANDRIOTI is an Affiliate Research Scientist at the Science and Technology in Archaeology Research Center of the Cyprus Institute. Her current research is aimed at using votive sculpture to gain insight into religious thought and social organization during the Archaic and Classical periods in Cyprus.

WILLIAM CARAHER is Associate Professor of History at the University of North Dakota. His research interests concentrate in Late Antiquity and include survey archaeology and Early Christian architecture. He has co-directed the Pyla-*Koutsopetria* Archaeological Project since 2003.

P. NICK KARDULIAS is Professor of Anthropology and Archaeology at the College of Wooster. His research interests include lithic analysis and the use of world-systems theory in archaeological contexts. He is Associate Director of the Athienou Archaeological Project (Cyprus), and Co-PI of the Ashland/Wooster Archaeological and Geological Consortium (Ohio).

R. SCOTT MOORE is Professor of History at Indiana University of Pennsylvania. His current research focuses on trade and communication in the eastern Mediterranean from the second through the eighth centuries AD. Since 2003, he has been the co-director of the Pyla-*Koutsopetria* Archaeological Project.

DIMITRI NAKASSIS is Associate Professor of Classics at the University of Toronto. His research focuses on the archaeology and scripts of the Bronze Age, in particular the administrative practices of the Mycenaean state, with interests in archaeological survey, Greek history, and Homeric epic. He was a senior staff member in the Pyla-*Koutsopetria* Archaeological Project from 2006 to 2010 and is currently co-director of the Western Argolid Regional Project in Greece.

BRANDON R. OLSON is a Ph.D. candidate in the Department of Archaeology at Boston University. His research interests include Hellenistic and Early Roman material culture and geospatial applications in archaeology. He serves as the field director of the Pyla-*Koutsopetria* Archaeological Project and has worked extensively in Cyprus, Turkey, and Israel

DAVID K. PETTEGREW is Associate Professor of History at Messiah College. A scholar of the Roman and Late Antique Mediterranean, his interests lie in histories of landscapes. He co-directs the Pyla-*Koutsopetria* Archaeological Project and is involved in research related to the Corinthia, Greece.

Index